After Winter

After Winter

The Art and Life of Sterling A. Brown

EDITED BY

JOHN EDGAR TIDWELL

AND

STEVEN C. TRACY

UNIVERSITY PRESS

2009

OXFORD
UNIVERSITY PRESS

Oxford University Press, Inc., publishes works that further
Oxford University's objective of excellence
in research, scholarship, and education.

Oxford   New York
Auckland   Cape Town   Dar es Salaam   Hong Kong   Karachi
Kuala Lumpur   Madrid   Melbourne   Mexico City   Nairobi
New Delhi   Shanghai   Taipei   Toronto

With offices in
Argentina   Austria   Brazil   Chile   Czech Republic   France   Greece
Guatemala   Hungary   Italy   Japan   Poland   Portugal   Singapore
South Korea   Switzerland   Thailand   Turkey   Ukraine   Vietnam

Published by Oxford University Press, Inc.
198 Madison Avenue, New York, New York 10016

www.oup.com

Oxford is a registered trademark of Oxford University Press

Library of Congress Cataloging-in-Publication Data
After winter : the art and life of Sterling A. Brown /
edited by John Edgar Tidwell and Steven C. Tracy.
    p. cm.
Includes bibliographical references and index.
ISBN 978-0-19-536579-5; 978-0-19-536580-1 (pbk.)
1. Brown, Sterling Allen, 1901–: Criticism and interpretation.
2. African Americans—Intellectual life—20th century.
3. African American aesthetics. I. Tidwell, John Edgar.
II. Tracy, Steven C. (Steven Carl), 1954–
PS3503.R833Z54   2008
811'.52—dc22   2008012944

9 8 7 6 5 4 3 2 1

Printed in the United States of America
on acid-free paper

The editors respectfully dedicate this book to the memory of Sterling A. Brown and his beloved wife Daisy Turnbull Brown, his "Roseanne"

Acknowledgments

That *After Winter: The Art and Life of Sterling A. Brown* moved from conception to its final shape relatively quickly is a tribute to the scholarship, graciousness, and hard work of a number of people. First and foremost among those for whom we are grateful are the contributors who allowed us to publish for the first time or reprint their work on Brown. If this collection can be considered successful, the reason derives from an unwitting coalescing of its essays, interviews, bibliography, discographies, and reviews. These disparate pieces began speaking to each other, essentially engaging in an implicit but extended conversation. Such give and take fashioned a remarkable mode for ferreting out the nuances of Brown's life and art and for plumbing the depths of his personal and aesthetic complexity. While it is not possible to call attention to each contributor singly, we must extend special thanks to distinguished poet and scholar Michael S. Harper, whose friendship with and commitment to Sterling Brown has been and remains steadfast and heroic. His encouragement to the editors in the production of this volume has kept us excited and committed as well.

To the journals that granted us permission to reprint pieces here, we want to extend our deepest appreciation. They honored all of our requests to reprint the works and, with one exception, waived the customary fees. We feel their gesture is a tribute to Brown and reenacts the generosity for which he was so well known.

Of course, any volume such as this has a long foreground that unfolds before the volume is conceived. All scholars are helped by a number of teachers, scholarly forebears, and colleagues. We are not exceptions. Again, we are unable to acknowledge each one who has assisted us on the path we now take, but we certainly want to say thank you to Angelene Jamison, Arlene Elder,

Wayne C. Miller, Arnold Rampersad, Akiba Harper, John S. Wright, Margaret Wade-Lewis, Onwuchekwa Jemie, Thomas Clayton, and Patricia Karouma for providing us with models of scholarship and unflagging continuing support through the years. Our respective institutions have also consistently supported our scholarly work. At the University of Massachusetts, we gratefully acknowledge the expertise and support of the W.E.B. Du Bois Afro-American Studies Department and the university's library and interlibrary loan staffs. The University of Kansas has graciously lent its support through the English Department, the College of Liberal Arts and Sciences, the Office of the Chancellor, and the Kansas Collection of the Spencer Research Library.

The preparation of any large manuscript is always daunting. We were fortunate to receive the assistance of Andrea Craig Gruenbaum, a student whose value became apparent to us when she left the project to assume the more lucrative position of graduate teaching assistant. So stellar were her research and editing and so conscientious was her commitment to the project that too late we came to realize that she was, in effect, deserving of recognition as co-editor. The foundational work she performed greatly alleviated the labor we undertook. Her successors, Ryan M. Scarrow and Sanja Ludwig, brought with them an editorial acumen that aided us in completing the volume in a timely fashion. To Hobart Jackson and Tami Albin, we thank you for rescuing us when we desperately appealed for assistance with our graphics. As always, the members of KU's Digital Media Services—Paula Courtney, Pam LeRow, and Gwen Claassen—took fragments of a dream for a completed manuscript and made them whole. We cannot say enough how grateful we are for their professionalism and good humor as they patiently undertook the challenges of putting the manuscript in final form for submission.

At Oxford University Press, Shannon McLachlan and Christina "Chrissy" Gibson, our editor and her assistant, were reminders that publishing can be more than a business arrangement. Their friendship and guidance made the author-publisher relationship into a collegial journey in quest of excellence. They helped us make our way through the sometimes treacherous waters of publication approval with ease, and their dedication and assistance have been a model of professionalism and cordiality.

As we labored, we worked with our families in our minds and hearts; then the editorial tasks became much easier to perform. Steve Tracy wants his wife, Cathy Tracy, and their children, Michelle and Michael, to know that their love, support, and understanding bring him his greatest joy, undergirding and therefore making his scholarship possible. To his parents, who exemplify for him the spirit of unending perseverance portrayed so beautifully by Brown in poems like "Strange Legacies," he also offers his deepest gratitude, admiration, and love. John Edgar Tidwell thanks his mother, Verlean Tidwell, for her devout belief in the rightness of her son's work; his life partner, Carmaletta M. Williams, for her constant stream of encouragement and enlightenment, and his grandchildren—Truly, Langston, Brooklynn, Kennedy, Taylor, and Jacine—for knowing that this book is but a down payment on ensuring their futures.

Our greatest thanks go to Sterling A. Brown himself. In his work, he paid tribute to his ancestors, family, and coworkers with an intellectual and passionate insight passed through the alembic of his genius. He not only inspired the editors and contributors to this volume, but he also served his many students, colleagues, and readers as a model of commitment to humanistic value and racial advance. Even those who could not read but perhaps heard and repeated his work found something of themselves reflected in the multifaceted folklore of the tradition that both they and he loved. We hope that this volume stands as a testament to Professor Brown and as a signpost marking the direction of future work to be done. Assisting him in his life's work was Daisy Turnbull Brown, who, in their fifty years of marriage, was his steadfast source of love and equanimity. We can think of no better recognition of their life together, the love they shared, and the legacy they bequeathed us than to dedicate this book to them.

Grateful acknowledgement is made for permission to reprint the following works:

David Anderson, "Sterling Brown's Southern Strategy: Poetry as Cultural Evolution in *Southern Road*." *Callaloo* 21.4 (1998): 1023–37. © Charles H. Rowell. Reprinted with permission of The Johns Hopkins University Press.

Kimberly W. Benston, "Listen Br'er Sterling: The Critic as Liar [A Pre(r)amble to Essays on Sterling Brown]. *Callaloo* 21.4 (1998): 837–45. © Charles H. Rowell. Reprinted with permission of The Johns Hopkins University Press.

John F. Callahan, "A Brown Study: Sterling Brown's Legacy of Compassionate Connections." *Callaloo* 21.4 (1998): 896–910. © Charles H. Rowell. Reprinted with permission of The Johns Hopkins University Press.

Henry Louis Gates, Jr., "Review of *The Collected Poems of Sterling A. Brown. Black American Literature Forum* 15.1 (1981): 39–42. © Henry Louis Gates, Jr. Reprinted with permission of the author.

Michael S. Harper, "To An Old Man Twiddlin' Thumbs" and "Br'er Sterling and the Rocker." *Songlines in Michaeltree: New and Collected Poems* (Urbana: University of Illinois Press, 2000): 197 and 115. © Michael S. Harper. Reprinted with permission of the author.

Stephen Henderson, "The Heavy Blues of Sterling Brown." *Black American Literature Forum* 14.1 (Spring 1980): 32–44. Reprinted with permission of *African American Review*.

James Weldon Johnson, Introduction to *Southern Road*. Reprinted by permission of Dr. Sondra Kathryn Wilson, Executor for the Estate of Grace and James Weldon Johnson.

Alain Locke, "Sterling Brown: The New Negro Folk-Poet." *Negro: An Anthology*. Ed. Nancy Cunard. © 2002. Reprinted by permission of the Continuum International Publishing Group.

Robert G. O'Meally, "An Annotated Bibliography of the Works of Sterling A. Brown." *Callaloo* 21.4 (1998): 822–35. © Charles H. Rowell. Reprinted with permission of The Johns Hopkins University Press.

Robert G. O'Meally, "Game to the Heart: Sterling Brown and the Badman." *Callaloo* 14/15 (1982): 43–54. © Charles H. Rowell. Reprinted with permission of The Johns Hopkins University Press.

Robert G. O'Meally, "Sterling A. Brown's Literary Essays: The Black Reader in the Text." *Callaloo* 21.4 (1998): 1013–22. © Charles H. Rowell. Reprinted with permission of The Johns Hopkins University Press.

Charles H. Rowell, "'Let Me Be with Old Jazzbo': An Interview with Sterling A. Brown." *Callaloo* 21.4 (1998): 789–809. © Charles H. Rowell. Reprinted with permission of The Johns Hopkins University Press.

Mark A. Sanders, "Sterling A. Brown and the Afro-Modern Moment." *African American Review* 31.3 (1997): 393–97. © Mark A. Sanders. Reprinted with permission of the author.

Beverly L. Skinner, "Sterling A. Brown's Ethnographic Odyssey." Originally published as "Sterling A. Brown's Ethnographic Perspective." *African American Review* 13.3 (1997): 417–22. © Beverly L. Skinner. Reprinted with permission of the author.

David Smith, "A Symposium on the Life and Work of Sterling Brown with Chet Lesell, Eleanor Holmes Norton, Paula Giddings, Sterling Stuckey, Wahneema Lubiano, and Cornel West." *Callaloo* 21:4 (1998): 1038–74. © Charles H. Rowell. Reprinted with permission of The Johns Hopkins University Press.

Robert B. Stepto, "When De Saints Go Ma'chin' Home: Sterling Brown's Blueprint for a New Negro Poetry." © Robert B. Stepto. Reprinted with permission of the author.

Ekwueme Michael Thelwell, "The Professor and the Activists: A Memoir of Sterling Brown." Reprinted by permission of *The Massachusetts Review* 40.4 (Winter 1999).

Lorenzo Thomas, "Authenticity and Elevation: Sterling Brown's Theory of the Blues." *African American Review* 31.3 (1997): 409–16. © Lorenzo Thomas. Reprinted with permission of Aldon Nielsen for the Literary Estate of Lorenzo Thomas.

John Edgar Tidwell, "Slim Greer, Sterling A. Brown, and the Art of Tall Tale." Originally published as "The Art of Tall Tale in the Slim Greer Poems." *Cottonwood Magazine,* Summer/Fall 1986, 170–76. © John Edgar Tidwell. Reprinted with permission of the author.

John Edgar Tidwell, "Two Writers Sharing: Sterling A. Brown, Robert Frost, and 'In Divés' Dive.'" *African American Review* 31.3 (1997): 399–408. ©John Edgar Tidwell. Reprinted with permission of the author.

John Edgar Tidwell and Ted Genoways, "Two Lost Sonnets by Sterling A. Brown. *Callaloo* 21.4 (1998): 741–44. © Charles H. Rowell. Reprinted with permission of The Johns Hopkins University Press.

John Edgar Tidwell and John S. Wright, "'Steady and Unaccusing': An Interview with Sterling A. Brown." *Callaloo* 21:4 (1998): 811–21. © Charles H. Rowell. Reprinted with permission of The Johns Hopkins University Press.

John S. Wright, "The New Negro Poet and the Nachal Man: Sterling Brown's Folk Odyssey. *Black American Literature Forum* 23.1 (1989): 95–105. © John S. Wright. Reprinted with permission of the author.

Contents

Contributors, xvii

Sterling A. Brown Chronology, xxiii

Introduction: Sterling A. Brown's Odyssey into the Heart of Blackness, 3
John Edgar Tidwell and Steven C. Tracy

Part I: Revelations

Introduction to *Southern Road* (1932), 21
James Weldon Johnson

Sterling Brown: The New Negro Folk-Poet, 23
Alain LeRoy Locke

The Heavy Blues of Sterling Brown: A Study of Craft and Tradition, 31
Stephen E. Henderson

Review of *The Collected Poems of Sterling A. Brown*, 59
Henry Louis Gates, Jr.

Part II: "A Nachal Man": Formal and Vernacular Aesthetic Theories

"When de Saints Go Ma'chin' Home": Sterling Brown's Blueprint for a
New Negro Poetry, 69
Robert Burns Stepto

Two Writers Sharing: Sterling A. Brown, Robert Frost, and
"In Divés' Dive," 81
John Edgar Tidwell

Listen Br'er Sterling: The Critic as Liar [A Pre(r)amble to Essays on Sterling Brown], 95
Kimberly W. Benston

Two Lost Sonnets by Sterling A. Brown, 105
Edited and Introduced by
John Edgar Tidwell and Ted Genoways

Worrying the Lines: Versification in Sterling Brown's *Southern Road*, 111
Michael Tomasek Manson

Part III: Folk-Say and Living-People-Lore

"Game to the Heart": Sterling Brown and the Badman, 139
Robert G. O'Meally

Slim Greer, Sterling A. Brown, and the Art of Tall Tale, 149
John Edgar Tidwell

The New Negro Poet and the Nachal Man: Sterling Brown's Folk Odyssey, 157
John S. Wright

Authenticity and Elevation: Sterling Brown's Theory of the Blues, 167
Lorenzo Thomas

Part IV: Unhistoric History: American and African American Cultures

Sterling A. Brown and the Afro-Modern Moment, 179
Mark A. Sanders

Sterling Brown: An Ethnographic Odyssey, 185
Beverly Lanier Skinner

Sterling Brown's Southern Strategy: Poetry as Cultural Evolution in *Southern Road*, 193
David R. Anderson

In Defense of African American Culture: Sterling A. Brown, Gunnar Myrdal, and *An American Dilemma*, 209
John Edgar Tidwell

Part V: "Running Space": Legacies and Continuities

Sterling A. Brown's Literary Essays: The Black Reader in the Text, 227
Robert G. O'Meally

"A Brown Study": Sterling Brown's Legacy of Compassionate Connections, 239
John F. Callahan

The Professor and the Activists: A Memoir of Sterling Brown, 255
Ekwueme Michael Thelwell

An Integer Is a Whole Number, 273
Michael S. Harper

Part VI: "Steady and Unaccusing": Interviews

"Let Me Be with Ole Jazzbo": An Interview with Sterling A. Brown, 287
Charles H. Rowell

A Symposium on the Life and Work of Sterling Brown, 311
Edited by David L. Smith

"Steady and Unaccusing": An Interview with Sterling A. Brown, 353
John Edgar Tidwell and John S. Wright

Br'er Sterling and the Blues: An Interview with Michael S. Harper, 365
Graham Lock, with a Preface by Michael S. Harper

Clarifying Philosophy: Sterling A. Brown and the Nonviolent Action
Group, 379
John Edgar Tidwell

A Conversation with John H. Bracey, Esther Terry, and Mike Thelwell, 397
Steven C. Tracy

Part VII: "On This I Stand": A Bibliography

An Annotated Bibliography of the Works of Sterling A. Brown, 431
Robert G. O'Meally

Part VIII: "A Geography of Poetry and Song": A Discography

"Fear Did Not Catch His Tongue and Throttle His Breath": A Discography of
Recordings by and Related to Sterling A. Brown, 445
Steven C. Tracy

Vernacular Recordings Relevant to the Study of Sterling A. Brown's
Southern Road, 449
Steven C. Tracy

Index, 457

Contributors

David R. Anderson is an associate professor of English in the Department of English at the University of Louisville, as well as associate dean of Diversity and Outreach Programs for the College of Arts and Sciences. His scholarship includes publications on modernist and African American poetry. He is currently writing a book on the poet Marilyn Nelson, as well as articles on nineteenth-century African American poetry.

Kimberly W. Benston is Francis B. Gummere Professor of English and director of the Hurford Humanities Center at Haverford College, where he teaches freshman writing and courses in African American, Renaissance, performance, poetic, and critical animal studies. Among his books are *Baraka: The Renegade and the Mask; Speaking for You: The Vision of Ralph Ellison; Performing Blackness: Enactments of African-American Modernism;* and *The Autobiography of Malcolm X: A Casebook* (forthcoming). His current projects include studies of modern African American photography and the place of animals in Western philosophy and culture.

John F. Callahan is Morgan S. Odell Professor of Humanities at Lewis and Clark College. Among his several books are *The Illusion of a Nation* and *In the African-American Grain*. The literary executor of Ralph Ellison's estate, he has edited several works by Ellison, including his unfinished novel *Juneteenth*. In 2007 he published *A Man You Could Love,* a political novel spanning the tumultuous 1960s to the 2000 presidential election.

Henry Louis Gates, Jr., is the Alphonse Fletcher University Professor and the director of the W.E.B. Du Bois Institute for African and African American Research at Harvard University. One of the most influential scholars in the field of African American studies, he is most recently the author of *Finding Oprah's*

Roots, Finding Your Own (2007). His PBS documentaries on African American history have been seen by millions of viewers, and he is the recipient of forty-eight honorary degrees and numerous awards, including the MacArthur "genius" grant.

Ted Genoways is the author of two collections of poetry, most recently *Anna, Washing* (Georgia, 2008), and the editor of more than half a dozen books, including Joseph Kalar's *Papermill: Poems, 1927–1935* (2006) and *The Selected Poems of Miguel Hernández* (2001). He is the editor of the National Magazine Award–winning *Virginia Quarterly Review* at the University of Virginia and a contributing writer at *Mother Jones*. He is currently completing a book-length study of Walt Whitman and the print culture of the early Civil War.

Michael S. Harper has taught at Brown University since 1970, where he is University Professor. His new collection of poems, *Use Trouble*, will be published in fall 2008 by the University of Illinois Press. Most recently he has edited *I Do Believe In People: Remembrances of W. Warren Harper, 1915–2004*, a book about ancestors and relatives, published in limited edition. If he had any mentor-teacher-ancestors they would have been his parents, Katherine and Warren Harper, and the fearsome-foursome-inimitable: Robert Hayden, Ralph Ellison, Sterling A. Brown, and Gwendolyn Brooks—for it was Gwendolyn Brooks who stood up when most stood down. "An Integer Is a Whole Number" is a quip stolen from Sterling A. Brown. No longer a believer in "collaboration" but always committed to his students as a teacher and mentor, he remains a committee of one. At Iowa Writers Workshop, in the nadir of his writing career, he was nicknamed "The Padre," because he always wore a hat.

Stephen E. Henderson (1924–1996), late professor of African American Studies and director of the Institute for the Arts and Humanities at Howard University, was a seminal academic voice during the polemical 1960s Black Arts Movement. His *Understanding the New Black Poetry*, prefaced with the important introduction "Forms of Things Unknown," established for the first time a coherent theory for examining the history of black poetry. The basis for his critical act lay in racially specific criteria that explicitly challenged the hegemony of the New Critics, whose own aesthetic value seemingly left little room for effectively describing and evaluating poetry published by black writers. His essay "The Heavy Blues of Sterling A. Brown" (1980) was instrumental in teasing out the art of Brown's poetry and in encouraging other scholars to look more closely at Brown's achievement.

James Weldon Johnson (1871–1938) was a distinguished civil rights leader, author, and musician, a prime mentor for artists of the Harlem Renaissance through his work as an essayist, editor, poet, and novelist. He was author, with his brother J. Rosamond Johnson, of minstrel songs for the stage and "Lift Every Voice and Sing," the "Negro National Anthem," as well as coeditor of two volumes of Negro spirituals. He himself authored three volumes of poems, including *God's Trombones;* a novel, *Autobiography of an Ex-Colored Man; Black*

Manhattan, a study of Harlem; and *Along This Way*, his autobiography, among other works. His editing of *The Book of American Negro Poetry* (1922; 1931) provided a watershed moment for African American poetry publication. For over a decade he was the field/executive secretary of the NAACP.

Graham Lock is a freelance writer. He is the coeditor of two collections, *The Hearing Eye: Jazz and Blues Influences in African American Visual Art* and *Thriving on a Riff: Jazz and Blues Influences in African American Literature and Film* (both Oxford University Press). His other books include *Blutopia: Visions of the Future and Revisions of the Past in the Work of Sun Ra, Duke Ellington, and Anthony Braxton* and *Forces in Motion: Anthony Braxton and the Meta-reality of Creative Music*. From 2001 to 2004 he was a senior research fellow in the School of American and Canadian Studies at Nottingham University.

Alain LeRoy Locke (1886–1954), the first African American to win a Rhodes scholarship, described himself as "the midwife to the younger generation of Negro writers" during the Harlem Renaissance. His anthology *The New Negro*, which also contains his essayistic manifesto of the same title, has been rightly singled out for its role in defining the aesthetic and cultural pulse of African America during the 1920s. His praise of Sterling A. Brown is but one of many efforts Locke made to create an enduring literary movement by encouraging writers committed to using a folk-based metaphysic.

Michael Tomasek Manson has published on Sterling A. Brown, Jay Wright, Gary Soto, Lorine Niedecker, Emily Dickinson, Robert Hass, and Robert Frost, and he coedited *The Calvinist Roots of the Modern Era*. He is currently writing a book titled *Body Language: Modern American Poetry and the Politics of Poetic Form* and is contributing entries to the fourth edition of *The Princeton Encyclopedia of Poetry and Poetics*. He teaches at American University.

Robert G. O'Meally is Zora Neale Hurston Professor of English and Comparative Literature at Columbia University and founder and former director of the university's Center for Jazz Studies. He has written extensively on Ralph Ellison, including *The Craft of Ralph Ellison* (1980) and a collection of papers for which he served as editor, *New Essays on Invisible Man* (1989). He edited *Tales of the Congaree* (1990), and *The Jazz Cadence of American Culture* (1998), and coedited *History and Memory in African American Culture* (1994), the *Norton Anthology of African American Literature*, and *Uptown Conversation: The New Jazz Studies* (2003). O'Meally's new book is *Romare Bearden: Black Odyssey— A Search for Home*, the catalog for a show in fall 2008 at D. C. Moore Gallery on Fifth Avenue in New York. His new project is a full study of Bearden's uses of literary subjects.

Charles H. Rowell is professor of English at Texas A&M University and editor of *Callaloo*.

Mark A. Sanders, associate professor of African American Studies and English at Emory University, specializes in early twentieth-century American and African American literature, more specifically the connections between "mainstream" American modernism and the Harlem Renaissance. He is the author of *Afro-Modernist Aesthetics and the Poetry of Sterling A. Brown,* the editor of *A Son's Return: Selected Essays of Sterling A.* Brown, and the coeditor (with John Edgar Tidwell) of *Sterling A. Brown's A Negro Looks at the South.*

Beverly Lanier Skinner is associate professor of English at Millersville University, in Pennsylvania, where she has taught since 1996. As an undergraduate at Howard University, she studied African American literature with Sterling Brown during his last semester before he retired in 1969. In 1975, supervised by Arthur P. Davis, she completed a master's thesis on Brown. Brown's celebration of the folk and folklore influenced her interest in the African American oral tradition, leading to her use of ethnography in her literary scholarship. Her work on Brown has been presented at conferences at Howard University and the Library of Congress and has been published in *African American Review* and *Callaloo.*

David L. Smith is the John W. Chandler Professor of English at Williams College, the alma mater of Sterling A. Brown. His scholarly interests include Mark Twain, Southern literature, nature writing, and the Black Arts Movement. With Jack Salzman and Cornel West, he edited the five-volume *Encyclopedia of African American History and Culture,* (1996). He is currently working with Wahneema Lubiano on *The Blackwell Companion to African American Literature.* As the poet D. L. Crockett-Smith, he has published *Cowboy Amok* and *Civil Rites,* both from The Black Scholar Press. He lives in Berkshire, Massachusetts, with his wife, Vivian.

Robert Burns Stepto is a professor of English and American Studies and professor and chair of African American Studies at Yale University. His books include *Blue as the Lake: A Personal Geography* and *From Behind the Veil: A Study of Afro-American Narrative.* With Michael S. Harper, Stepto edited *Chant of Saints: A Gathering of Afro-American Literature, Art, and Scholarship,* which is dedicated to Sterling Brown. Stepto first taught at Williams College, and was instrumental in inviting Brown back to Williams fifty years after his graduation in 1922. Brown's talk on that occasion was "A Son's Return," which may be found in the Mark Sanders volume of the same title.

Ekwueme Michael Thelwell is a professor of literature and writing at the University of Massachusetts at Amherst. He was active in the nonviolent Civil Rights Movement and participated in the Student Nonviolent Coordinating Committee (SNCC) and the Mississippi Freedom Democratic Party (MFDP). As a writer of fiction as well as influential essays, his work has been published in journals and magazines including *The Black Scholar, The Massachusetts Review, Temps Moderne, Partisan Review, Presence Africaine* (Paris), and *African Commentary,* as well as in important newspapers, including the *New York Times.* He is the author of a novel, *The Harder They Come* (1980), and his political and literary essays are collected in *Duties, Pleasures and Conflicts* (1987). Thelwell prepared Stokely Carmichael's memoirs for publication under the title *Ready for Revolution: The Life and Struggles of Stokely Carmichael* (2003).

Lorenzo Thomas (1944–2005), who taught at the University of Houston–Downtown for twenty years, had a long acquaintanceship with the blues. In the 1960s, he joined Umbra, a writing workshop whose experiments with art gave rise to the Black Arts Movement. He enjoyed a varied career, and his position as writer-in-residence at Texas Southern University in 1973 caused him to adopt the Southwest as his home. Throughout his life, he maintained ties to both grassroots and intellectual communities. His participation in the Texas Commission on the Arts and Humanities and the Cultural Arts Council of Houston enabled him to serve the community and also preserve Black aesthetic traditions.

John Edgar Tidwell is a professor of English at the University of Kansas. Awards from the National Endowment for the Humanities and the American Council of Learned Societies, among many others, have enabled him to publish widely on aspects of African American literature, focusing especially on poets Sterling A. Brown, Langston Hughes, and Frank Marshall Davis, and the photographer-writer Gordon Parks. Included among his books are his editions of Davis's *Livin' the Blues: Memoirs of a Black Journalist and Poet; Black Moods: Collected Poems;* and *Writings of Frank Marshall Davis, A Voice of the Black Press,* as well as Brown's previously unpublished travelogue *A Negro Looks at the South* (with Mark A. Sanders), and the essay collection *Montage of a Dream: The Art and Life of Langston Hughes.* He continues work on *Oh, Didn't He Ramble: The Life of Sterling A. Brown.*

Steven C. Tracy is a professor of Afro-American Studies at the University of Massachusetts Amherst. Among his book publications are *Langston Hughes and the Blues* (1988); *Going to Cincinnati: A History of the Blues in the Queen City* (1993); *A Historical Guide to Ralph Ellison* (2004); and *A Historical Guide to Langston Hughes* (2003). He was also general coeditor of *The Collected Works of Langston Hughes* and editor of *The Collected Works of Langston Hughes,* vol. 12, *Works for Children and Young Adults,* as well as editor of the anthology *Write Me a Few of Your Lines: A Blues Reader* (1999). A singer and harmonica player, Tracy has recorded and served as opening act for B. B. King, Muddy Waters, Sonny Terry, and Brownie McGhee, among others.

John S. Wright is Morse-Amoco Distinguished Teaching Professor of African American and African Studies and English at the University of Minnesota. He has chaired African American and African Studies at Carleton College and the University of Minnesota and has been a research associate at Harvard University's W.E.B. Du Bois Institute and scholar-in-residence at the Schomburg Research Center. He is the senior editor of Coffeehouse Press's Black Arts Movement reprint series, and coeditor of the Givens Collection series for Simon & Schuster. His intellectual biography, *Shadowing Ralph Ellison,* was published in 2006 to critical acclaim; and his long-range book project, *The Riddle of Freedom: History, Cosmology and the TransAfrican Imagination,* is nearing completion.

Sterling A. Brown Chronology

1901	Born May 1 in Washington, D.C., to Sterling Nelson and Adelaide Allen Brown
1914–1918	Attends the prestigious Dunbar High School in Washington, D.C., and graduates class valedictorian
1918	Enters Williams College
1921	Elected to Phi Beta Kappa
1922	Wins Graves Prize for "The Comic Spirit in Shakespeare and Molière" (essay), awarded "final honors," and earns AB degree in English from Williams College
1922–1923	Earns MA in English at Harvard
1923–1926	Teaches at Virginia Seminary and College in Lynchburg, Virginia
1925	"Roland Hayes" (article) wins an *Opportunity* prize
1926–1928	Teaches at Lincoln University in Jefferson City, Missouri
1927	"When de Saints Go Ma'chin' Home" wins *Opportunity* poetry prize; selected poems appear in Countee Cullen's *Caroling Dusk;* marries Daisy Turnbull in December
1928–1929	Teaches at Fisk University
1929	Begins a more than forty-year tenure teaching at Howard University
1930	"The Blues as Folk Poetry" (essay) published in *Folk-Say*
1931–1932	Doctoral study in English at Harvard; *Outline for the Study of the Poetry of the American Negro* (to be used with the revised edition of James Weldon Johnson's *Book of American Negro Poetry*) appears; *Southern Road* (poetry) appears
1933	"Negro Character as Seen by White Authors" (essay) appears

1936–1940   Accepts part-time position as Editor for Negro Affairs by the Federal Writers Project

1937   *The Negro in American Fiction* and *Negro Poetry and Drama* both appear in the Bronze Booklet series published by the Associates in Negro Folk Education; "The Negro in Washington" appears in *Washington: City and Capital*

1937–1938   Guggenheim Fellow

1939   Master of Ceremonies, *From Spirituals to Swing* concert at Carnegie Hall on December 24

1939–1940   Researcher for the Carnegie-Myrdal Study that culminated in *An American Dilemma: The Negro Problem and American Democracy* (1944)

1940   Discussant for "A Program of Negro Folk Song with Commentary," a commemorative program at the Library of Congress featuring Josh White and the Golden Gate Quartet

1941   *The Negro Caravan* (anthology) appears, co-edited with Arthur P. Davis and Ulysses Lee

1941–1950   Member, Committee on Negro Studies of the American Council of Learned Societies (the committee met intermittently until its dissolution in 1950)

1942   Wins Julius Rosenwald Fellowship for research on *A Negro Looks at the South* (Fall semester)

1944   "Count Us In" (essay) appears in *What the Negro Wants*, edited by Rayford Logan

1945   Visiting Professor at Vassar College for the Fall semester

1946   Visiting Professor again at Vassar College for the Fall semester; records six poems for Moses Asch, released on *Sterling Brown and Langston Hughes* (Folkways LP FP 90, 1952; rpt. FL 9790, 1967); visiting professor of English and American Studies at the University of Minnesota for the summer session

1947   Visiting Professor at New School for Social Research for Spring semester

1949–1950   Visiting Professor at New York University, summers of 1949 and 1950

1956   Contributes to *The Reader's Companion to World Literature*

1967–1968   Visiting Professor, University of Illinois, Chicago Circle Campus, summers of 1967 and 1968

1969   Retires from Howard University

1971   Awarded honorary doctorate from Howard University (one of thirteen honorary degrees)

1974   *Southern Road* reissued with an introduction by Sterling Stuckey

1975   *"The Last Ride of Wild Bill" and Eleven Narrative Poems* appears

1979   Wife Daisy Turnbull Brown dies

1980   *The Collected Poems of Sterling A. Brown,* assembled by Michael S. Harper, appears in the National Poetry Series and wins the Lenore Marshall Prize for Poetry

1982   Black History Museum's *Sterling A. Brown: A UMUM Tribute* appears

1984   Named Poet Laureate of the District of Columbia

1985   Joanne V. Gabbin's *Sterling A. Brown: Building the Black Aesthetic Tradition,* the first sustained bio-critical study of Brown, appears

1989   Dies of leukemia on January 13, in Takoma Park, Maryland

1996   *A Son's Return: Selected Essays of Sterling A. Brown* appears posthumously, edited by Mark A. Sanders

2007   *A Negro Looks at the South* appears posthumously, edited by John Edgar Tidwell and Mark A. Sanders

After Winter

To an Old Man Twiddlin' Thumbs

You sit twiddlin' thumbs
"beat out," watching
your wife watch you watch her:
all this watching twiddlin' thumbs.

My children fidget while you balance
thumb controls on local news,
excerpts from a recent book on slavery,
and we finally have the scale of twiddlin' thumbs.

Old man, remember the chemistry
for your depression is alchemical.
I set out my convivial tools
measuring your need, measuring your index
finger, your thumbnails, your wife
"beat out" in her slavery of affection
for your genius at disguise.

Old man, my pestle works for your recovery;
old man, the conjure knowledge is "beat out"
with alkaline and tea,
this nightmare where you've lost your way home:
old man, the strong men must come on.

—Michael S. Harper

Introduction: Sterling A. Brown's Odyssey into the Heart of Blackness

John Edgar Tidwell and Steven C. Tracy

There are fewer than 120 poems in just over 230 pages of poems in Sterling Brown's *Collected Poems*, little more than one-third the number in Robert Frost's 500 page collected poems, and far fewer than Carl Sandburg's nearly 800-page poetic output of more than 800 poems. The sixteen volumes of Langston Hughes's *Collected Works* dwarfs the amount of Brown's work (he also wrote essays, short stories, and scholarly works), as do the collected works of Brown followers like Amiri Baraka and Michael Harper. Perhaps that explains some of the difficulty Brown has had taking his rightful place in the American canon. In a culture that lionizes the Great American Novel, not the Great American Haiku, more sprawling evidence of an author's literary work is frequently necessary for the arbiters of literary value. This holds true even for the author of that perennial candidate for the Great American Novel, *Invisible Man;* Ralph Ellison's failure to finish a second novel has proven troubling among canon-formers in some quarters. Size matters.

Certainly as an African American writer Brown has been shunted aside by some white critics, who for racist reasons have not been exposed to his work or don't have the resources to understand his employment of the folk idiom. Brown knew this, and he addressed in his work the difficulties of African American writers with their audiences and publishers—difficulties that could hamstring their attempts to gain appreciation, publication, and sales. And certainly Brown encountered the attitudes toward African American folklore and the employ-ment of that material in literature that reflected the superficial appreciation and polite dismissal of the proponents of "high art"—sometimes even among African Americans themselves.

But Sterling Brown was a strong man, a persevering man, a proud man. Like the heroes so important in his poetry, Brown was the laborer in the vineyard, the crafty man in the cabbage patch, the craftsman in the wilderness. The racy raconteur in the rarefied halls of academia. So, despite years of relative neglect spent in the spare room in the attic under the eaves of the hodgepodge house of American literature, he is still present, in the present, and a rare and well-done present to those with the good fortune to come across his work.

Brown was not a professional writer like Hughes. He had other duties as a professor who taught a range of literature, mostly not African American. And a faculty member burdened with the grading, committee, and service work that competes for time with—and sometimes provides fodder for—the gems of a literary artist burnished to a fare-thee-well must learn to make every second, and every poem, count. Of course, the work of a teacher is to teach, not to con-sider the sometimes mundane realities of classroom teaching and advising as interfering with one's work. To this end, Brown generated materials to assist with the teaching of African American literature, including coediting the im-portant volume *The Negro Caravan* (1942) and writing *Outline for the Study of the Poetry of American Negroes* (1931), *The Negro in American Fiction* (1937), and *The Negro in Poetry and Drama* (1937). As his students attest, "Prof" Brown excelled inside the classroom as well as out. He fulfilled his technical duties assiduously and with aplomb; his spiritual duties to pilot, inspire, and infuse with a sense of purpose and direction are among his lasting legacies for his students.

Like Hughes, however, Brown was also a public intellectual. He spent time writing for various journals, serving as Editor of Negro Affairs for the Federal Writers Project, working with the Carnegie-Myrdal Study of the Negro project, celebrating and analyzing folklore as a collector, writer, and emcee, and champi-oning or chastening literature by and about African Americans in proportion to its principled presentation and literary quality. He wrote seminal works, such as *A Negro Looks at the South*, that demonstrate his commitment as a prose teacher, as he was a poetic teacher, to fostering the kinds of insight and understanding that would show how unmarginal, how central, African American literature was to American history and culture. These efforts should not be seen as detracting from his output—they are of a piece with his commitment to the lives of those who generated what he called "living people lore," two trochees rushing hell-for-leather into a final, strongly accented word—the whole phrase emphasizing the three elements of Brown's aesthetic as an artist and a human being.

Size does matter. But how we measure size matters more. Judged on these terms, the size of Brown's output is enormous—in the remarkable reso-nance of his poems, both in dialect and standard English (nary a throwaway among them), the pointed wisdom of his literary pronouncements, his social commitment and work on behalf of African Americans in literature, history, folklore, and sociology, and his largesse in passing along his insights to students whom he likely knew would carry them to future generations with greater opportunities to exercise the kinds of intellectual and physical muscles that rippled in his work. Brown lives here, in the people who wrote these essays and hear the lore circulating through his work. Like Jack Johnson, John Henry, and the old nameless couple of "Strange Legacies," we are going to give it one more try, one more try, in the name of Sterling Brown.

On May 1, 1901, Sterling A. Brown was born into a world shaped by the paradoxes and contradictions of fin-de-siècle America. Its political reality, described by the eminent historian Rayford W. Logan as "the nadir" of late nineteenth-century African American life and history, culminated in the racial malaise occasioned by the North's betrayal of African Americans following Reconstruction. This loss of trust began slowly, as an erosion of constitutional protections for African Americans, and then predictably escalated into a mudslide as the very foundations of many social institutions cracked and crumbled in the wake of the 1896 legal imposition of "separate but equal." Reinvented forms of slavery emerged, under such new names as tenant farming, sharecropping, and systems of peonage, once again relegating many black people to the lowest rungs of America's social ladder. The proliferation of secret societies, such as the Knights of the Ku Klux Klan, "bulldozers," and other night riders, hell-bent on reconstituting slavery, effectively promised black life to be, at best, tenuous.

But despite the incursion on their citizenship rights, African Americans proved to be resilient and quite capable of erecting powerful stays against the forces of history. The talented writer-lyricist James Weldon Johnson looked into their hearts and souls, where he discovered hope, optimism, determination, and strength of racial character—to which he penned the homage "Lift Every Voice" (1900). New kinds of music (especially blues, ragtime, jazz, and even blackface minstrelsy) developed as strong forms of resistance to prevailing social conditions. Intellectually, the growth of black normal schools, colleges, and other kinds of educational institutions firmly established literacy as the pathway to regaining freedom and full citizenship rights. Through the American Negro Academy, the National Conference of Colored Women, the national club movement, and other groups, racial uplift became an obligation, a duty to be undertaken by the more fortunate for the benefit of their less well-heeled brethren and sisters. These efforts were complemented by such white schools as Oberlin College and Berea College, whose deep commitment to educating African Americans and women was, by this time, long-standing.

Brown, then, was born a beneficiary of the moral dilemmas prompted by this complicated social history. He inherited both the frustrated desire for full citizenship and the racial strength to defy efforts to dehumanize African

Americans. For most of his life, he confronted those who would demean the race, but he also celebrated the resiliency that enabled his people to survive and even thrive. In a literary and cultural expressivity that continues to attract the attention of appreciative scholars and admirers, Brown lives on as a principal figure in efforts to reclaim and make whole the fractured sense of African American humanity.

Brown's own elasticity undoubtedly derives from two parents who survived slavery and the broken promises of Reconstruction. From the mountains of Roane County, in eastern Tennessee, Sterling Nelson Brown (1858?–1929) followed a tortuous path from slavery, to college at Fisk University (B.A., 1885; A.M., 1890), to seminary at Oberlin College (B.D., 1888), and to an honorary doctorate from Howard University (D.D., 1900). His personal calling to the Congregationalist ministry led him to evangelize in parts of Tennessee before accepting fulltime appointments at regular churches in Cleveland and Washington. It was during his pastorates in Washington that the Reverend Brown made his mark on the world and established what he hoped would be a template for his only son. Drawing from his Oberlin training, he participated in what was then known as the "institutional church" movement, a commitment to religion that, as he implemented it, sought to uplift the race by providing a Christian Workers Training School, a first-class business college, day and night preparatory schools, Working Women's Clubs, a Household Training department, a Penny Savings Bank, a Social Settlement Center, and a reading room.[1]

His helpmate in this venture was his wife, Adelaide Allen (1860?–1948), about whom less is known. Born in Gallatin, Tennessee, she was taken at a very young age to Nashville to live with her aunt Mercy, who made a modest living as a seamstress. Living in the shadow of the state capitol, Adelaide went through primary grades at Fisk and continued on through the completion of a bachelor's degree and graduation as class valedictorian in 1891. That she read a poem at the dedication of Fisk's Livingstone Hall portends the love of literature, especially poetry, she conveyed to their son. He would later recall: "My mother had a very rich sense of humor—with punning, jokes. And was a great lover of poetry. She could read poetry very well, had a great sense of rhythm, a great sense of sound."[2]

In yet another interview, he provides greater detail about the "teachable moments" in which she imparted her love of an eclectic vision of art:

> "My mother read . . . Longfellow; she read Burns; and she read
> Dunbar—grew up on Dunbar—" 'Lias! 'Lias! Bless de Lawd!" "The
> Party" and "Lay me down beneaf de willers in de grass." . . . We lived
> on Eleventh Street then above Lincoln Temple Church, and I remem-
> ber even now her stopping her sweeping . . . now standing over that
> broom and reading poetry to me, and she was a good reader, great
> sense of rhythm."[3]

Sterling Brown's birth effectively placed him in a rarefied place, because he was the last of six children and the only boy born to this union of Sterling Nelson and Adelaide Allen Brown. As the son of a prominent minister and theology professor, he benefited from acquaintance with Washington's most powerful black political voices, including W.E.B. Du Bois, Kelly Miller, and Carter G. Woodson. His extremely fair skin color also qualified him for Washington's "colored aristocracy." Nevertheless, Brown felt divided. Despite "advantages" that would make possible a life of relative privilege, Brown never found satisfaction in the insular elitism of the black upper middle class, in a society he came to feel was disingenuous, complacent, and "dicty." He ultimately rejected its rather smug gentility and propelled himself on a trajectory that caused him to question the very privilege that was his by birth. Consequently, he found himself continually questioning his relationship to a black bourgeoisie that, despite the duties of racial uplift, often positioned itself against its less fortunate black brethren.

The intraracial liminality Brown felt eventually gave way to interracial tensions. Despite a stunning career that won him considerable academic and creative success, he nevertheless tormented himself over society's efforts to marginalize and therefore deny his place in the pantheon of American literary and cultural heroes by reducing his status as American citizen to that of three-fifths of a person. And in spite of the public perception, he struggled privately with the paradoxes, contradictions, and ironies that made him who he was and caused him to question his very self.

The quest to replace this fractionalized social status with an independent, wholly defined self began when Brown graduated as the top student in his class at Washington's renowned Dunbar High School (1918). His success enabled him to accept the token gesture of the academic scholarship Williams College annually extended to Dunbar's valedictorian. At this small but prestigious liberal arts school in western Massachusetts, Brown, from 1918 to 1922, set aside his own feelings of isolation and performed with distinction: he was elected to Phi Beta Kappa in his junior year, won the Graves Prize for his essay "The Comic Spirit in Shakespeare and Molière," and earned highest honors from the English Department his senior year. These accolades won him a scholarship to study at Harvard University, where he received a master's degree in English in 1923.

At this point, the life paths of father and son paralleled but never actually converged. Beginning in 1892, Rev. Brown served as professor of Bible mastery in Howard University's School of Religion and later established the Department of Extension Work and Correspondence Study. When a Southern black minister's wife wrote to him of her frustrations, he responded by sending her advice that provided practical assistance to her husband and other largely Southern and untutored pastors in their attempts to minister to their flock. Connecting directly to the folk in this way provided the son with precept and example.

In 1923, the son followed his father's and historian Carter G. Woodson's instructions to go South to accept a teaching position at Virginia Seminary and College, where he remained until 1926. In retrospect, there is little doubt that the subtext for this appointment was that the son would "hear the call," attend the seminary, and prepare himself to assume his father's mantle. Instead, he was lured to the folk through their lives, language, and lore, not out of their spiritual needs. This attraction became the basis for the innovative aesthetic experiments that culminated in his *Southern Road* (1932).

As valuable as this formal education was, it arguably served as preparation for the work to which he was ultimately called: that of insightful, vigorous advocate for those people Langston Hughes affectionately named "the low down folks." From them, he gained a deep and abiding informal education, one that enabled him to represent them aesthetically in remarkably cogent ways. In a series of teaching positions at Virginia Seminary and College, Lincoln University in Missouri (1926–1928), and Fisk University (1928–1929), Brown transgressed the middle class line demarcating "respectability" and sought "instruction" in the lower class world of Calvin "Big Boy" Davis, Mrs. Bibby ("illiterate and somehow very wise"), Slim Greer, and so many other members of the folk. In them, Brown located sources of racial and cultural authenticity. This immersion in and absorption of their lives, language, and lore made possible the distinctive folk-based aesthetic and poetic voice he used to celebrate a people too long burdened by misrepresentation and racial stereotype. Inspired, in part, by the New American Poetry of Carl Sandburg, Edwin Arlington Robinson, Vachel Lindsay, Robert Frost, and Edgar Lee Masters, Brown sought to bring dignity, grace, and realistic representation to black people. His was an effort to reveal the humanity denied them by social circumstance.

In three different but interrelated ways, this folk-based aesthetic figures in and shapes nearly all of Brown's writings. First, as poet, he probed the humanity that lay beneath the stereotypical representation of black people. Against the typing of black characters in white-authored works and the pigeonholing of African Americans' experiences generally, he allowed his black subjects to speak their hearts and minds. Thus language or vernacular speech played a prominent part in his poetry, the focus of which he explains in terms of his folklore interests. Brown talked about how he wanted to capture the nuances of black speech because language was a portal through which one could get at the philosophical insight or the worldview of black folk. His was not a fascination with "dis," "dat," and other orthographic representations of black dialect. He too had come to see these as stereotypic depictions. Instead, idiomatic expressions, with their pitch, point, rhythm, and wit, were, to him, the source of racial authenticity. The pursuit of language, therefore, drove him to consider the significance of culturally specific forms, such as work songs, blues, and tall tales, as well as variations on traditional ones (sonnet, ballade, hymn, villanelle, and the ballad).

Alain Locke and many other influential critics celebrated his *Southern Road* (1932) as inaugurating new directions in African American poetry. But the much anticipated second volume, *No Hiding Place,* which would signal an even newer trajectory, failed to appear later in the 1930s, as planned. In these poems, the folk metaphysic that so carefully defined *Southern Road* had shifted to a more proletarian voice. As reasons for their unwillingness to bring out this collection, publishers cited Southern antipathies toward labor causes and communist ideology and consumers' reluctance to purchase poetry collections. History, at times, is redemptive, and even corrects previous wrongs. In Brown's case, the 1970s saw a revived interest in his poetry. *The Last Ride of Wild Bill and Eleven Narrative Poems* appeared in 1975 and symbolized an older generation connecting with the younger, black insurgents of the Black Arts Movement. In 1980, poet Michael S. Harper gathered all of Brown's poetry, including *No Hiding Place,* for publication as *The Collected Poems of Sterling A. Brown.* It won the Lenore Marshall Prize for Poetry that same year.

As a literary historian, music critic, and folklorist, Brown made use of a black folk ethos in a second way. He was the first critic to define with clarity the problematic representations of blacks in American literature. His longest early foray into this literary fray occurred with his thirty-five-page essay "Negro Character as Seen by White Authors" (1933). In a careful reading of work by white American authors who used African American characters, Brown isolated and identified seven persistent but historically determined racial stereotypes: the Contented Slave, the Wretched Freeman, the Comic Negro, the Brute Negro, the Tragic Mulatto, the Local Color Negro, and the Exotic Primitive. This discussion was enlarged and set forth cogently in *Negro Poetry and Drama* (1937) and *The Negro in American Fiction* (1937). Appearing in the Bronze Booklet series, which was under the general editorship of Alain Locke, Brown's analyses provided a counternarrative to the proliferation of influential but erroneous studies by white critics, including John Herbert Nelson's *The Negro Character in American Literature* (1926). Brown systematically showed a determining relationship between social need and literary representation. The Brute Negro (or his more sexualized cousin, "the Buck Negro"), for example, evolved out of the Southern white imagination in the post-Reconstruction era. By depicting black men as uncivilized beings, the racialized body symbolically represented a not-so-subtle threat to white womanhood if social equality were to be granted to African Americans. The stereotype became its own justification for Southern white men (often through the Ku Klux Klan) to dictate the nature of interracial social contact. Or the 1920s Jazz Age's requirement for a model of primitivism and joie de vivre sent white writers scurrying to capture residual African rhythms resonating in the experiences of African Americans.

It is this same mode of analysis Brown used in his capacity as Editor of Negro Affairs for the Federal Writers' Project (FWP) in the late 1930s. There he confronted the proliferation of stereotypes written into manuscripts for the

Project's guidebook series. This meant Brown locked horns with South Carolina, Florida, Mississippi, and other states that politicized their FWP guidebooks by misrepresenting the images and place of African Americans in their state histories. To *Washington: City and Capital* (1937), the national guidebook, he contributed "The Negro in Washington," an essay so honest and revealing that the U.S. Congress caused it to be severely bowdlerized in its second edition. There were successes, though. Chief among them was the power of the Virginia Writers' Project's study titled *The Negro in Virginia* (1940). It was a singular moment in the FWP's brief history, and the research assistance Brown gave to principal editor Roscoe E. Lewis helped to make it so.

During this same period, Brown befriended and became a researcher for Gunnar Myrdal, the Swedish-born social economist imported by the Carnegie Foundation to conduct what was then the most extensive inquiry into African Americans and their relationship to the American Creed. The results of this study, the massive *An American Dilemma* (1944), were grounded in a scientific method emphasizing quantitative analysis. Despite his best efforts, Brown was unable to convince the research team of the efficacy of qualitative research. African Americans, his argument implicitly ran, were more than facts, figures, and numbers to be added up, subtracted, multiplied, or divided. They were living, breathing entities, as different as any ten or ten million personalities. Brown was perhaps most disappointed that African American cultural production, such as the blues, spirituals, jazz, folktales, and much more, was given short shrift. Even when he tried to accomplish the impossible under the rubric of "The Negro in American Culture," it was clear that the research he managed to complete was going to be contorted from its qualitative focus to one amenable to quantitative analysis. This meant for him an erasure of folk ethos.

In a broad sense, Brown's *A Negro Looks at the South* signified upon the Myrdal Study and revised some of its important conclusions. A multigenre text—part travel narrative, oral history, historical study, and ethnography—the book focuses squarely on African Americans primarily from the South and captures them in various modes of talking, doing, and being. Unpublished in his own lifetime, it nevertheless offers a third way in which Brown used black folk as an aesthetic standard. The inspiration to write *A Negro Looks at the South* no doubt came from many sources, but certainly none was greater than the need to complete the mosaic of the South created by Jonathan Daniels, a white journalist from North Carolina. Following an extended tour throughout the South, in which he gathered ideas, impressions, and observations to disabuse readers of the notion of one undifferentiated region, "the Solid South," Daniels published *A Southerner Discovers the South* (1938). In reviewing this book, Brown expressed his appreciation for the unprecedented effort Daniels made to explode this myth about the South. His only concern was that Daniels, in representing the experiences of African Americans, failed to explore them broadly enough. In his study, Brown undertook the task of extending and completing Daniels's unfulfilled mission.

Arguably the most important feature of this collage of scholarly work, personal interviews, personal narratives, and historical documents is Brown's success in astutely depicting black voices. It extended a concept first articulated by folklorist Benjamin A. Botkin as "folk-say" and later revised as "living people lore." Conceptually, this revised perspective moved folklore collecting beyond the usual documentary motives of indexing and cataloging variants of stories. It privileged the lives and lore of the folk, permitting them to be their own oral historians. From this published multigenre text, it is possible to reach this unerring conclusion: Brown's emphasis on black speech, especially vernacular language, makes *A Negro Looks at the South* a smartly conceived prose corollary of the distinctive poetry he wrote.

After the turbulent 1940s, when he performed simultaneously as FWP editor, Carnegie-Myrdal researcher, and coeditor of the massive tome *The Negro Caravan* (1942), lectured widely from Washington to Oklahoma, taught a full schedule of classes and served on committees at Howard, and still found a little time to write, Brown entered the 1950s fairly worn down by an all-consuming schedule. With the bulk of his writing behind him, Brown began feeling the shift of aesthetic vision away from the Southern folk ethos he had devoted himself to celebrating and preserving. The era of Richard Wright had captured the imaginations of writers, publishers, and readers. A more socially deterministic vision of art had become the current mode of expression. Unable to conjure up the energy and the intellectual fervor that had made him so crucial to defining the prevailing creative and scholarly of his earlier years, Brown virtually collapsed and the 1950s became for him a comparatively moribund period.

A new, reinvigorated life, though, came his way in the early 1960s, when a younger generation of students discovered that their radicality was not without precedent. The modern-day civil rights movement had gained momentum, beginning with the 1954 U.S. Supreme Court ruling that overturned the Plessey decision (1896), the 1955 murder of Emmett Till and Rosa Parks's defiance on an Alabama public bus, and the 1957 forced integration of Little Rock High School. The generational disconnect that occurred between the followers of Dr. Martin Luther King and the younger folks who became associated with SNCC and other campus groups led to different strategies for achieving civil liberties. The younger black insurgents began a radical dissociation from the goal of racial integration by embracing racial separation, a foundational principle of Black Power. At Howard, the young dissidents in the Nonviolent Action Group (NAG) began to see in Brown a radical forefather, a teacher who managed to convince them of the necessity of knowing the importance of their cultural history. Through them, he once again felt energized. Aided by such black aestheticians as Hoyt Fuller, editor of *Black World* (later to be renamed *First World*), and Stephen Henderson, director of Howard's Institute for the

Arts and Humanities, Brown enjoyed a period of protracted hagiography from the pens of appreciative scholars, colleagues, and students.

For most of the 1960s and well into the 1970s, Brown was courted by younger people who felt the need to immerse themselves in the cultural history he and earlier generations had written. The ahistorical vision they had formerly embraced proved to be shortsighted and generally flawed. Painfully they had learned an updated version of the old saw, "People ignorant of their history are bound to repeat it." Brown settled in comfortably as an elder statesman whose ability to communicate with the younger generation led some of his most zealous devotees to call for the renaming of Howard University to Sterling Brown University. More reasonable students, though, learned that militancy without studied knowledge is like rebelling without a specific cause. Under Brown's tutelage, they discovered that emotionalism had limited potential for inspiring meaningful social change. Such energy had to be harnessed, to be loosed only after they had gained a fuller understanding of the problems they sought to redress.

When asked in an interview how he would best sum up his career and outlook, Brown replied that fundamentally he was a teacher. In a career that spanned nearly fifty years, his influence on students' thought was considerable. But Brown's reply was also too modest. His poetry and prose reveal an intelligence, a sensitivity, and a compassion that were rarely found among his contemporaries. As many have testified, Brown's work was foundational in studies of identity politics, representational issues, oral history, folkloristics, and more. Fundamentally he was a teacher, but his classroom was considerably broader and more influential than his self-assessment describes.

Many scholars and artists have been drawn to the magic of Sterling Brown's work, as he was drawn to the conjuration of African American culture, especially folk culture, and they have written with insight and power on his oeuvre. The writings included in this collection—thirty-two contributions from twenty-two different authors—are what the editors feel are some of the most significant responses to the variety of materials generated by Brown during his long and varied career. Nevertheless, in order to keep the volume to a manageable length we have had to forego a number of works of great value. It seems appropriate, then, here at the outset, to refer readers to the final sections of the book, Robert G. O'Meally's updated version of his 1998 "Annotated Bibliography of the Works of Sterling A. Brown" and Steven C. Tracy's "Discography of Recordings by and Related to Sterling A. Brown." These guides will help readers range through a variety of materials related to Brown's life and work, which is, after all, exactly what we hope this volume will do—take readers, new and old, back to Brown's source materials, back to his work, and back to his commitment to a broad-ranging excellence on behalf of African American social, political, and cultural advancement. What readers will find between this beginning and those endings are essays that demonstrate that commitment as well, from generations of writers frequently inspired to that excellence by Brown himself.

One of the writers whose work has always acknowledged Brown's influence is poet Michael Harper. It seems fitting to begin with the wonderful tribute of one great poet to another in the book's epigraph, since Harper himself has latched onto the trajectory and strength of Brown's star as well, and we hope that our volume follows in kind. Part I, "Revelations," proceeds to the responses of the most prominent critics of the times when Brown's work emerged and reemerged. James Weldon Johnson recognized early on the uniqueness of Brown's poetry—he even coined a term, "Sterling-Brownian," to describe it. His introduction to Brown's first volume of poetry, *Southern Road,* marvels at Brown's great ability as a folk-poet working with what Johnson had felt was the racist, worn-out, stultifying tradition of Negro dialect to capture the visceral energy and wisdom of African American folklore. Although Johnson acknowledges the excellence of some of Brown's poems in standard English and form, he has a marked preference for the folk-influenced materials, marking, perhaps, a parallel to William Dean Howells's preference for the dialect poems of Paul Laurence Dunbar in Howells's introduction to an early Dunbar volume. There are, of course, poems that mix the two, such as "Strange Legacies" and "Virginia Portrait," demonstrating Brown's careful and nuanced knowledge and employment of the two traditions together, and other gorgeous, evocative sonnets among those works as well. But for Johnson, the dialect poems were most distinctive. Alain Locke's insightful "Sterling Brown: The New Negro Folk Poet" catalogs the difficulties African American writers faced in generating the folk poetry frequently expected of them, noting the failures of James Weldon Johnson and Langston Hughes along the way. Once again privileging the folk-influenced materials, Locke praises the "racial touch" that Brown gives his work, in subject matter, spirit, and language, praising the "local" and "genuine" elements of Brown's work that catch "the deeper idiom of feeling or the particular paradox of the racial situation." For Locke, it is these elements and Brown's "Aesopian candor"—self-reflective, self-incriminating, self-critical impulses lacking in other contemporary writers—that set Brown apart, even as he worked at uniting so-called low and high art in his work. Stephen Henderson's seminal discussion of Brown and the spirit of the blues is the earliest published post-1930s essay reprinted here, a scholarly work that deals insightfully with the ways that Brown's work manifests elements of the folk tradition. It both connects with and deepens the work of previous discussants.

Henry Louis Gates's review of Brown's *Collected Poems,* a volume that helped introduce a greater number of Brown's poems to a wider audience, builds on the discussions of Johnson and Locke. Providing the context for Brown's work in African American folklore and literature as well as the canonical Anglo-American tradition and contemporary realists and modernists such as E. A. Robinson, Carl Sandburg, Vachel Lindsay, Amy Lowell, and William Carlos Williams, Gates praises Brown's work for marking an end to the Harlem Renaissance with its distinctive contributions in portraiture and diction. He also sees Leopold Senghor, Richard Wright, Zora Neale Hurston, Ralph Ellison, and Michael Harper as beneficiaries of Brown's artistry. For Gates, one of the benefits of the volume is that it not only demonstrates Brown's clear finessing of the folk idiom and an ability to develop it from within, but also reflects Brown's "full range, his mastery of so many traditions." It is this range, not only of Brown's poetry, but of a variety of genres, that this volume seeks to explore, though the poetry remains central.

Part II, "Formal and Vernacular Aesthetic Theories," places Brown's work in a variety of appropriate settings. From Robert Stepto's consideration of New Negro Poetry to John Edgar Tidwell and Ted Genoway's considerations Brown's relation to the Anglo-American tradition to Michael Tomasek Manson's technical discussions of Brown's versification, we see Brown being turned every which way but loose with regard to poetic tradition, touching on a range of influences and strategies that inform the mastery of traditions to which Gates referred. Those traditions, of course, teem with voices, voices that, as Kimberly Benston points out in "Listen Br'er Sterling," Brown imagines and reimagines in all their transgressive ("lying") performative, culture-carrying, heterochromatic glory. Benston invokes the critical judgment of Darwin Turner's statement that "all roads lead to Sterling Brown" as an acknowledgment of Brown's work and the volcanic and Vulcanic role the teacher-critic Brown, lying in his masterly way toward the most nuanced truths, played.

The essays in Part III, "Folk-Say and Living-People-Lore," focus on the folk—us: the ways that various genres of African American folklore function in Brown's work as he holds the mirror up to black folks and sees himself. Robert O'Meally's "Game to the Heart" shows Brown the strong man, confronting racism and injustice with recourse to the "bad man" of African American folklore to herald a new day in African American literature and life. In John Edgar Tidwell's "Slim Greer, Sterling A. Brown, and the Art of the Tall Tale," Brown's deep understanding of the creative and structural nuances of the tall-tale tradition goes under the microscope as Tidwell proceeds to his conclusion that the Slim Greer poems "expose the listener to the truth of black social conditions" and provide "a liberating vision of art" through the tall tale strategy not of masking the truth, but raising the question of what the truth is. In "The New Negro Poet and the Nachal Man," John S. Wright shows Brown dealing with the prejudices of folklorists in relation to American and African American folklore, doing his bit to explore and champion black folklore by immersing himself in the materials and using his "aesthetic of reorientation" to correct the corruptions of the minstrel tradition had wrought on the folk. Lorenzo Thomas looks with a poet's and critic's eye at Brown's "Theory of the Blues," to discuss how the critic Brown "exposed vicious and persistent stereotypes" and the poet Brown "sought to counter them with a social realist portraiture based on forms indigenous to the African American community." Of course, since folk materials were so central to Brown's life and vision, other sections in this volume touch on folk materials as well, but here, careful and specific exploration of Brown's relation to the folk yields a much better understanding of the nuanced connections.

In seeking to place Brown's work in the broader context of American culture, the critics in Part IV approach Brown from a variety of perspectives. Mark A. Sanders explores Brown's relation to the broader modernism affecting American literature in the 1920s and 1930s by detailing how the Afro-Modern moment reflects a unique signifying upon the Modernist tradition, demonstrating in his discussion of "Odyssey of Big Boy" how Brown "fundamentally reconceives black modernity," not as something fragmented but as a strategic and creative synthesis of vigorous possibility. Beverly Lanier Skinner posits Brown as a "postmodern ethnographer who by the 1940s had pioneered solutions to three major problems with which today's cultural anthropologists are grappling." While not wishing to downplay the importance of the poetry, Skinner demonstrates how Brown generates a polyvocal portrait of the African American community in his work, a portrait that is contemporary and postmodern in its challenges to portrayals of African Americans in relation to hegemonic norms and cultures. That contemporary focus continues in David Anderson's "Sterling Brown's Southern Strategy: Poetry as Cultural Evolution in *Southern Road*," which examines what Brown perceived as the "cultural crisis" endemic to a mass movement of people from a rural, agrarian environment to an urban, industrial one, with the consequent loss of traditional knowledge and culture transmitted through folklore. Thus, Brown sought to "adapt the cultural production of art in black communities to an urban, capitalist society." Of course, Brown's attitude toward the commodification of African American blues by record companies as a corruption of traditional folklore caused him to reject, in some ways, the music that represents to scholars today the traditional blues because it is, along with Library of Congress recordings, one of the few ways contemporary scholars can hear music from that era. By "stressing the interdependence of art and culture" in *Southern Road*, Anderson sees Brown as providing a necessary and responsible template for African American poets to follow in their quest to preserve value elements of the culture. Finally, John Edgar Tidwell takes a cultural studies approach to Brown's involvement with the Carnegie-Myrdal Study that produced the hefty social science document *An American Dilemma* (1944). Tidwell examines the ways that Brown highlighted and heightened interest in African American vernacular culture and, through this, earned a place of honor for his "innovative use of black culture to revise the purpose, methods, and conclusions of the Myrdal project." Each essay in this section locates Brown at a wellspring of perspective or technique that had a major influence on the way African American culture is received and valued today.

Part V focuses on ways that Brown valued legacies and continuities as evidenced in his writing and teaching. Robert G. O'Meally's "Sterling A. Brown's Literary Essays: The Black Reader in the Text" takes an important look at Brown the essayist—another important hat that he wore. Placing Brown as a critical realist as well as an essayist, O'Meally established Brown's intention to bring writers and audiences closer together by championing realistic portraiture recognizable to black folks in contemporary works of art. That portraiture consisted not only of accurate transcription of the language, but an unfolding of culturally familiar scenarios that reflect the drama of African American life from the box seat to the peanut gallery. Recent scholarship on the Harlem Renaissance has taken to exploring more fully the connections that James Weldon Johnson pointed to between the Irish Revival and the Black Renaissance of the 1920s in *The Book of American Negro Poetry* (1922). John F. Callahan illuminates this nexus by discussing the ways Brown, like Synge and Yeats, sought to use culturally inherent symbols to portray the racial spirit and vivify his folk poetry. He continues by showing Brown plying those stories in the modified Eliotic Anglo-American settings of poems like "Cabaret" and seeking always for the unadulterated, unpopularized form and substance that made him and his work so pivotal. Another contribution from Michael Harper follows, making clear once again the special relationship the two of them enjoyed and Harper's gift for communicating the essence of Brown's personality and character. Novelist, scholar, and activist Ekwueme Michael Thelwell's paean to Brown is the missive of one cultural warrior to another. Brown's influence on the radical young activists on the conservative campus of Howard University, and the lessons he passed on to his young and unruly charges as a trickster and master raconteur, highlight the ways in which a distinguished professor of impeccable scholarship maintained his own horse sense in the midst of stultifying conventionality and rationalization to birth a generation of scholars and activists who were not turned away by the universities from the spiritual and creative "down home" that Brown loved so well.

Part VI brings together discussions with and about Brown that come from fellow poets, scholars, and students and disciples from 1991 to 2007. Brown's own words illuminate his roles as scholar, teacher, and craftsperson (crafty indeed), and his students delineate how his day-in-day-out activities, momentous and mundane, registered in them intellectually, aesthetically, politically, socially, and very personally. Charles Rowell's 1974 interview with Brown, conducted in two sessions, is notable for its very concrete and specific statements on Brown's understanding of the complexity of the blues and folk material, especially as he sees them being misportrayed by contemporary figures such as Amiri Baraka and Ron Karenga. Further, Brown offers a vigorous explanation of his notion of the shortcomings of the chronological and geographical limitations of contemporary discussions of the Harlem Renaissance—a term he deplored. "A Symposium on the Life and Work of Sterling Brown," in 1974, with Chet Lasell, Eleanor Holmes Norton, Paula Giddings, Sterling Stuckey, Wahneema Lubiano, and Cornel West, edited by David L. Smith, presents fond reminiscences by a number of students and acquaintances who had a variety of relationships with Brown. Some graduated from Dunbar High School or Williams College, or studied under him at Howard, or worked with him on his publications, or became very good friends with him in his later years. The range of their knowledge of Brown in a variety of settings and their responses to questions from the audience provide a broad context for understanding the teacher, writer, scholar, and man. "Steady and Unaccusing: An Interview with Sterling A. Brown," by John Edgar Tidwell and John S. Wright, is a piece that Brown had hoped to extend and revise, but it is offered here as a series of vivid snapshots of his opinions on a variety of subjects, including Alain Locke, W.E.B. Du Bois, Zora Neale Hurston, and *Negro Caravan*. It alternately gives us the scholarly and raconteur Brown, with his well-heeled sense of humor firmly in evidence before his two "prosecuting attorneys." Brown's fellow poet and colleague Michael Harper, in his interview with Graham Lock, ranges through several topics, including Brown's employment of blues and jazz in his work, his record collection, and his relation to Gunnar Myrdal and Robert Bone, presenting an insider's reflections on both the personal and professional Brown. The final two interviews, John Edgar Tidwell's "Clarifying Philosophy: Sterling A. Brown and the Nonviolent Action Group" and Steven C. Tracy's "A Conversation with John H. Bracey, Esther Terry, and Ekwueme Michael Thelwell," record the responses of students who knew Brown at Howard and speak about his educational, literary, social, and political (as well as economic, as Esther Terry points out in a very sweet anecdote) importance both at Howard and beyond, even as he was undervalued by an administration that misused him. These interviews lend further insight into Brown's mental universe, a vigorous, trickster-studded landscape where human cruelty suffered under the glaring light of exposure, pretension was sniffed out like broken wind (and speech is but broken wind, a brother wily author, yclept Geoffrey Chaucer, wrote), and the sinews of folk shit, grit, and mother wit flexed in joyful strains of life.

When the blues singer first asserted that "you don't know, you don't know my mind," at some now remote and unrecorded time, the lyric expressed the ways in which American slavery and racism dug a gulf that was sometimes the result of willful ignorance, clueless obtuseness, or treacherous self-deception on the part of the enslavers, sometimes a deliberate strategy of self-protective masking on the part of the enslaved, frequently some combination of the two. It was a time when American society didn't want to know the mind of the African American, didn't care as long as established racial roles and order were maintained and reinforced. As writers like Brown began to mine the deeper ores of group dissatisfaction on the one hand and resonating tradition on the other, that mind has come more and more to the fore. In the prison and road songs, in the whine of the blues on the proverbial National Resonator steel-bodied

guitar—both sounds harkening back to the musical traditions of West Africa—
Brown heard the mine of the mind, and sought to express it in his creative work
as well as in his teaching. To hear him speak his mind about his life and work,
and to hear others talk about him and the effects his work produced, is to hear
Brown voicing the surreptitious and inviolable voice as he heard it, and lend an
ear to the voices that grew out of Brown's, which grew out of Brown's forebears,
joining the chorus of America singing.

All of which brings us to the end and returns us to the beginning of the volume, the bibliography and discography that tell us where to go next to consult
Brown and his critics further. What the musicians call "bringing it home," back
where it started, back to the present, and back to the future. Much has been
written about Sterling A. Brown, and much remains to be written and taught
and done. Brown still buck dances "on the midnight air," "black and unceasing
as hostile waters." Having "done well what he was there to do,"

The soul of our hero
Goes marching on . . .

NOTES

1. Sterling Nelson Brown, *My Own Life Story* (Washington, D.C.: Hamilton Publishing Company, 1924), 17.
2. Carolyn Taylor, *Profiles of Black Achievement* (New York: Guidance Associates,
   1973), 32.
3. Joanne Gabbin, *Sterling Brown: Building the Black Aesthetic Tradition*. Westport, CT:
   Greenwood Press, 1985, 19.
4. Sterling A. Brown, "Virginia Portrait," *Southern Road* (New York: Harcourt Brace,
   1932), 28.

I

REVELATIONS

Introduction to *Southern Road* (1932)

James Weldon Johnson

In any inquiry regarding the important developments that have taken place in American Negro life within the past decade, I should at once cite the degree of ascendancy reached by the Negro artist, especially the Negro writer, as one of the most significant and vital.

The record of the Negro's efforts in literature goes back a long way, covering a period of more than a century and a half, but it is only within the past ten years that America as a whole has been made consciously aware of the Negro as a literary artist. It is only within that brief time that Negro writers have ceased to be regarded as isolated cases of exceptional, perhaps accidental ability, and have gained group recognition. It is only within these few years that the arbiters of American letters have begun to assay the work of these writers by the general literary standards and accord it such appraisal as it might merit.

This more sensitive awareness on the part of America as a whole to the existence and efforts of Negro writers, this wider recognition and less conditional appreciation of their work began with the rise of what is termed the "Younger Group." This group has consisted of about twenty-five writers doing acceptable work; and from them have risen some twelve who have gained more or less of national recognition. Among the writers of poetry in this smaller group the five names most outstanding are: Claude McKay, Jean Toomer, Countee Cullen, Langston Hughes and Sterling Brown. (I am naming them in the order of their emergence.) These "younger" poets are, naturally, younger in years than their predecessors, but the thing of greater consequence is that they are on the whole newer in their response to what still remains the principal motive of poetry written by Negroes—"race." In their approach to "race" they are less direct and obvious, less didactic or imploratory; and, too, they are less regardful of the approval or disapprobation of their white environment.

Sterling A. Brown is one of this group and therefore has been instrumental in bringing about the more propitious era in which the Negro artist now finds himself, and in doing that he has achieved a place in the list of young American poets. Mr. Brown's work is not only fine, it is also unique. He began writing just after the Negro poets had generally discarded conventionalized dialect, with its minstrel traditions of Negro life (traditions that had but slight relation, often no relation at all, to *actual* Negro life) with its artificial and false sentiment, its exaggerated geniality and optimism. He infused his poetry with genuine characteristic flavor by adopting as his medium the common, racy, living speech of the Negro in certain phases of *real* life. For his raw material he dug down into the deep mine of Negro folk poetry. He found the unfailing sources from which sprang the Negro folk epics and ballads such as "Stagolee," "John Henry," "Casey Jones," "Long Gone John" and others.

But, as I said in commenting on his work in *The Book of American Negro Poetry*: he has made more than mere transcriptions of folk poetry, and he has done more than bring to it mere artistry; he has deepened its meanings and multiplied its implications. He has actually absorbed the spirit of his material, made it his own; and without diluting its primitive frankness and raciness, truly re-expressed it with artistry and magnified power. In a word, he has taken this raw material and worked it into original and authentic poetry. In such poems as "Odyssey of Big Boy" and "Long Gone" he makes us feel the urge that drives the Negro wandering worker from place to place, from job to job, from woman to woman. There is that not much known characteristic, Negro stoicism, in "Memphis Blues" and there is Negro stoicism and black tragedy, too, in "Southern Road." Through the "Slim Greer" series he gives free play to a delicious ironical humor that is genuinely Negro. Many of these poems admit of no classification or brand, as, for example, the gorgeous "Sporting Beasley." True, this poem is Negro, but, intrinsically, it is Sterling-Brownian. In such poems as "Slim Greer," "Mister Samuel and Sam" and "Sporting Beasley" Mr. Brown discloses the possession of a quality that could to advantage be more common among Negro poets—the ability to laugh, to laugh at white folks as well as at black folks.

Mr. Brown has included in this volume some excellent poems written in literary English and form. I feel, however, it is in his poems whose sources are the folk life that he makes, beyond question, a distinctive contribution to American Poetry.

Sterling Brown: The New Negro Folk-Poet

Alain LeRoy Locke

Many critics, writing in praise of Sterling Brown's first volume of verse, have seen fit to hail him as a significant new Negro poet. The discriminating few go further; they hail a new era in Negro poetry, for such is the deeper significance of this volume (*Southern Road*, Sterling A. Brown, Harcourt Brace, New York, 1932). Gauging the main objective of Negro poetry as the poetic portrayal of Negro folk-life true in both letter and spirit to the idiom of the folk's own way of feeling and thinking, we may say that here for the first time is that much-desired and long-awaited acme attained or brought within actual reach.

Almost since the advent of the Negro poet public opinion has expected and demanded folk-poetry of him. And Negro poets have tried hard and voluminously to cater to this popular demand. But on the whole, for very understandable reasons, folk-poetry by Negroes, with notable flash exceptions, has been very unsatisfactory and weak, and despite the intimacy of the race poet's attachments, has been representative in only a limited, superficial sense. First of all, the demand has been too insistent. "They required of us a song in a strange land." "How could we sing of thee, O Zion?" There was the canker of theatricality and exhibitionism planted at the very heart of Negro poetry, unwittingly no doubt, but just as fatally. Other captive nations have suffered the same ordeal. But with the Negro another spiritual handicap was imposed. Robbed of his own tradition, there was no internal compensation to counter the external pressure. Consequently the Negro spirit had a triple plague on its heart and mind—morbid self-consciousness, self-pity and forced exhibition-ism. Small wonder that so much poetry by Negroes exhibits in one degree or another the blights of bombast, bathos and artificiality. Much genuine poetic talent has thus been blighted either by these spiritual faults or their equally vi-cious over-compensations. And so it is epoch-making to have developed a poet whose work, to quote a recent criticism, "has no taint of music-hall conven-tion, is neither arrogant nor servile"—and plays up to neither side of the racial dilemma. For it is as fatal to true poetry to cater to the self-pity or racial vanity of a persecuted group as to pander to the amusement complex of the overlords and masters.

I do not mean to imply that Sterling Brown's art is perfect, or even completely mature. It is all the more promising that this volume represents the work of a young man just in his early thirties. But a Negro poet with almost complete detachment, yet with a tone of persuasive sincerity, whose muse neither clowns nor shouts, is indeed a promising and a grateful phenomenon.

By some deft touch, independent of dialect, Mr. Brown is able to compose with the freshness and naturalness of folk balladry—*Maumee Ruth, Dark O' the Moon, Sam Smiley, Slim Greer, Johnny Thomas,* and *Memphis Blues* will convince the most skeptical that modern Negro life can yield real balladry and a Negro poet achieve an authentic folk-touch.

Or this from *Sam Smiley*:

> The mob was in fine fettle, yet
> The dogs were stupid-nosed, and day
> Was far spent when the men drew round
> The scrawny woods where Smiley lay.
>
> The oaken leaves drowsed prettily,
> The moon shone benignly there;
> And big Sam Smiley, King Buckdancer,
> Buckdanced on the midnight air.

This is even more dramatic and graphic than that fine but more melodramatic lyric of Langston Hughes:

> Way down South in Dixie
> (Break the heart of me!)
> They hung my black young lover
> To a cross-roads tree.

With Mr. Brown the racial touch is quite independent of dialect; it is because in his ballads and lyrics he has caught the deeper idiom of feeling or the particular paradox of the racial situation. That gives the genuine earthy folk-touch, and justifies a statement I ventured some years back: "The soul of the Negro will be discovered in a characteristic way of thinking and in a homely philosophy rather than in a jingling and juggling of broken English." As a matter of fact, Negro dialect is extremely local—it changes from place to place, as do white dialects. And what is more, the dialect of Dunbar and the other early Negro poets never was on land or sea as a living peasant speech; but it has had such wide currency, especially on the stage, as to have successfully deceived half the world, including the many Negroes who for one reason or another imitate it.

Sterling Brown's dialect is also local, and frankly an adaptation, but he has localized it carefully, after close observation and study, and varies it according to the brogue of the locality or the characteristic jargon of the *milieu* of which he is writing. But his racial effects, as I have said, are not dependent on dialect. Consider *Maumee Ruth*:

> Might as well bury her
> And bury her deep,
> Might as well put her
> Where she can sleep. . . .

> Boy that she suckled
> How should he know,
> Hiding in city holes
> Sniffing the "snow"?

> And how should the news
> Pierce Harlem's din,
> To reach her baby gal
> Sodden with gin?

> Might as well drop her
> Deep in the ground,
> Might as well pray for her,
> That she sleep sound.

That is as uniquely racial as the straight dialect of *Southern Road*:

> White man tells me—hunh—
> Damn yo' soul;
> White man tells me—hunh—
> Damn yo' soul;
> Got no need, bebby,
> To be tole.

If we stop to inquire—as unfortunately the critic must—into the magic of these effects, we find the secret, I think, in this fact more than in any other: Sterling Brown has listened long and carefully to the folk in their intimate hours, when they were talking to themselves, not, so to speak, as in Dunbar, but actually as they do when the masks of protective mimicry fall. Not only has he dared to give quiet but bold expression to this private thought and speech, but he has dared to give the Negro peasant credit for thinking. In this way he has recaptured the shrewd Aesopian quality of the Negro folk-thought, which is more profoundly characteristic than their types of metaphors or their mannerisms of speech. They are, as he himself says,

> Illiterate, and somehow very wise,

and it is this wisdom, bitter fruit of their suffering, combined with their characteristic fatalism and irony, which in this book gives a truer soul picture of the Negro than has ever yet been given poetically. The traditional Negro is a clown, a buffoon, an easy laugher, a shallow sobber and a credulous Christian; the real Negro underneath is more often an all but cynical fatalist, a shrewd pretender, and a boldly whimsical pagan; or when not, a lusty, realistic religionist who tastes its nectars here and now.

> Mammy
> With deep religion defeating the grief
> Life piled so closely about her

is the key picture to the Negro as Christian; Mr. Brown's *When the Saints Come Marching Home* [sic] is worth half a dozen essays on the Negro's religion. But to return to the question of bold exposure of the intimacies of Negro thinking—read that priceless apologia of kitchen stealing in the *Ruminations of Luke Johnson*, reflective husband of Mandy Jane, tromping early to work with a great big basket, and tromping wearily back with it at night laden with the petty spoils of the day's picking:

> Well, taint my business noway,
> An' I ain' near fo'gotten
> De lady what she wuks fo',
> An' how she got her jack;
> De money dat she live on
> Come from niggers pickin' cotton,
> Ebbery dollar dat she squander
> Nearly bust a nigger's back.
>
> So I'm glad dat in de evenins
> Mandy Jane seems extra happy,
> An' de lady at de big house
> Got no kick at all I say—
> Cause what huh "dear grandfawthaw"
> Took from Mandy Jane's grandpappy—
> Ain' no basket in de worl'
> What kin tote all dat away. . . .

Or again in that delicious epic of *Sporting Beasley* entering Heaven:

> Lord help us, give a *look* at him.
> Don't make him dress up in no nightgown, Lord.
> Don't put no fuss and feathers on his shoulders, Lord.
>   Let him know it's heaven,
> Let him keep his hat, his vest, his elkstooth, and everything.
> Let him have his spats and cane.

It is not enough to sprinkle "dis's and dat's" to be a Negro folk-poet, or to jingle rhymes and juggle popularized clichés traditional to sentimental minor poetry for generations. One must study the intimate thought of the people who can only state it in an ejaculation, or a metaphor, or at best a proverb, and translate that into an articulate attitude, or a folk philosophy or a daring fable, with Aesopian clarity and simplicity—and above all, with Aesopian candor.

The last is most important; other Negro poets in many ways have been too tender with their own, even though they have learned with the increasing boldness of new Negro thought not to be too gingerly and conciliatory to and about the white man. The Negro muse weaned itself of that in McKay, Fenton Johnson, Toomer, Countee Cullen and Langston Hughes. But in Sterling Brown it has learned to laugh at itself and to chide itself with the same broomstick. I have space for only two examples: *Children's Children*:

> When they hear
> These songs, born of the travail of their sires,
> Diamonds of song, deep buried beneath the weight
> Of dark and heavy years;
> They laugh.
>
> They have forgotten, they have never known
> Long days beneath the torrid Dixie sun,
> In miasma'd riceswamps;
> The chopping of dried grass, on the third go round
> In strangling cotton;
> Wintry nights in mud-daubed makeshift huts,
> With these songs, sole comfort.
>
> They have forgotten
> What had to be endured—
>
> That they, babbling young ones,
> With their paled faces, coppered lips,
> And sleek hair cajoled to Caucasian straightness,
> Might drown the quiet voice of beauty
> With sensuous stridency;

> And might, on hearing these memoirs of their sires,
> Giggle,
> And nudge each other's satin clad
> Sleek sides. . . .

Anent the same broomstick, it is refreshing to read *Mr. Samuel and Sam*, from which we can only quote in part:

> Mister Samuel, he belong to Rotary,
> Sam, to de Sons of Rest;
> Both wear red hats like monkey men,
> An' you cain't say which is de best. . . .
>
> Mister Samuel die, an' de folks all know,
> Sam die widout no noise;
> De worl' go by in de same ol' way,
> And dey's both of 'em po' los' boys.

There is a world of psychological distance between this and the rhetorical defiance and the plaintive, furtive sarcasms of even some of our other contemporary poets—even as theirs, it must be said in all justice, was miles better and more representative than the sycophancies and platitudes of the older writers.

In closing it might be well to trace briefly the steps by which Negro poetry has scrambled up the sides of Parnassus from the ditches of minstrelsy and the trenches of race propaganda. In complaining against the narrow compass of dialect poetry (dialect is an organ with only two stops—pathos and humor), Weldon Johnson tried to break the Dunbar mould and shake free of the traditional stereotypes. But significant as it was, this was more a threat than an accomplishment; his own dialect poetry has all of the clichés of Dunbar without Dunbar's lilting lyric charm. Later in the *Negro Sermons* Weldon Johnson discovered a way out—in a rhapsodic form free from the verse shackles of classical minor poetry, and in the attempt to substitute an idiom of racial thought and imagery for a mere dialect of peasant speech. Claude McKay then broke with all the moods conventional in his day in Negro poetry, and presented a Negro who could challenge and hate, who knew resentment, brooded intellectual sarcasm, and felt contemplative irony. In this, so to speak, he pulled the psychological cloak off the Negro and revealed, even to the Negro himself, those facts disguised till then by his shrewd protective mimicry or pressed down under the dramatic mask of living up to what was expected of him. But though McKay sensed a truer Negro, he was at times too indignant at the older sham, and, too, lacked the requisite native touch—as of West Indian birth and training—with the local color of the American Negro. Jean Toomer went deeper still—I should say higher—and saw for the first time the glaring paradoxes and the deeper ironies of the situation, as they affected not only the Negro but the white man. He realized, too, that Negro idiom was anything but trite and derivative, and also that it was in emotional substance pagan—all of which he convincingly demonstrated, alas, all too fugitively, in *Cane*. But Toomer was not enough of a realist, or patient enough as an observer, to reproduce extensively a folk idiom.

Then Langston Hughes came with his revelation of the emotional color of Negro life, and his brilliant discovery of the flow and rhythm of the modern and especially the city Negro, substituting this jazz figure and personality for the older plantation stereotype. But it was essentially a jazz version of Negro life, and that is to say as much American, or more, as Negro; and though fascinating and true to an epoch this version was surface quality after all.

Sterling Brown, more reflective, a closer student of the folk-life, and above all a bolder and more detached observer, has gone deeper still, and has found certain basic, more sober and more persistent qualities of Negro thought and feeling; and so has reached a sort of common denominator between the old and the new Negro. Underneath the particularities of one generation are hidden universalities which only deeply penetrating genius can fathom and bring to the surface. Too many of the articulate intellects of the Negro group— including sadly enough the younger poets—themselves children of opportunity, have been unaware of these deep resources of the past. But here, if anywhere, in the ancient common wisdom of the folk, is the real treasure trove of the Negro poet; and Sterling Brown's poetic divining-rod has dipped significantly over this position. It is in this sense that I believe *Southern Road* ushers in a new era in Negro folk-expression and brings a new dimension in Negro folk-portraiture.

The Heavy Blues of Sterling Brown:
A Study of Craft and Tradition

Stephen E. Henderson

Sterling Brown's poetry may profitably be studied, and his achievement precisely assessed, by implicating his work in the stylistics of the Afro-American culture in which it is saturated. There are, of course, aspects of the poetry which can properly be studied within other parameters—the formal Anglo-American tradition found in "Vestiges," for example, or the tradition of Frost and Masters, Sandburg and Robinson. But it is within the dimensions of Afro-American expressive culture that one may perceive most clearly the originality and subtlety of Brown's work.

Of the varied forms of Black expressive culture, music is indisputably the most dramatic, moving, and pervasive; and of the many forms which the music takes, the most typical, the most potently charged is the blues. At one end of the spectrum the blues are sensual ditties of lost love and hard times. At the other end they resonate on the same frequency with the spirituals, but in a somewhat different space, where the burden of salvation is equally weighty but the hope comes chiefly from self. The blues, then, are a music and a poetry of confrontation—with the self, with the family and loved ones, with the oppressive forces of society, with nature, and, on the heaviest level, with fate and the universe itself. And in the confrontation a man finds out who he is, a woman discovers her strengths, and if she is a Ma Rainey, she shares it with the community and in the process becomes immortal.[1]

The hallmark of Sterling Brown's poetry is its exploration of the bitter dimension of the blues, which he links with a view of humankind that he shares with writers like Sandburg, Frost, and Edwin Arlington Robinson. Their influence helps to catalyze the poet's work without diluting it, and he extends the literary range of the blues without losing their authenticity. When he employs other folk forms such as the ballad, the "folk epic," the "lie," and the song sermon, he does so with complete confidence, not only in his skill but in his models, both the literary and the folk. The literary models merely confirm what he already knows from the folk: that these forms embody a way of life that is valid and valuable.

Although most of the poems in *Southern Road* are not blues as such, they are suffused with the blues tradition.[2] Indeed, one can make the case that the entire volume is an extended treatment of the blues mood and spirit, that each of the sections of the book presents facets of the Black experience which evoke the world view and feel of the blues. Even the last section of the book, "Vestiges," so named because it contains poems written in the poet's earlier manner, in the formal measures of the English poets, is caught up in this spirit by virtue of its placement and its elegiac tone. Earlier in the book, however, there are a number of poems which suggest a significant range of the blues spectrum, although they are not written in blues form.

"Kentucky Blues" is an example. It is blues-like chiefly in its aphoristic imagery and its vernacular verve, as in the following stanza:

> Women as purty
> As Kingdom Come,
> Ain't got no woman
> 'Cause I'm black and dumb.

In a poem like "Riverbank Blues" the emphasis is on the blues mood rather than form. The mood is established in the first stanza:

> A man git his feet set in a sticky mudbank,
> A man git dis yellow water in his blood,
> No need for hopin', no need for doin',
> Muddy streams keep him fixed for good.

And the entire mood of seductive indolence is created through a description of the riverbank. There is an undertone of threat and danger which one associates with blues about the forces of nature:

> Towns are sinkin' deeper, deeper in de riverbank,
> Takin' on de ways of deir sulky Ole Man—
> Takin' on his creepy ways, takin' on his evil ways,
> *"Bes' git way, a long way . . . whiles you can."*

Two things stand out about this poem which justify its title: the mood created by the description, and the reaction of the persona. Blues, I observed earlier, are a music and a poetry of confrontation, and here the challenge to the persona is despair, which the poet presents in the personified river, where the persona

> Went down to the river, sot me down an' listened,
> Heard de water talkin' quiet, quiet lak an' slow:
> *"Ain' no need fo' hurry, take yo' time, take yo' time. . . ."*
> Heard it sayin'— *"Baby, hyeah's de way life go. . . ."*

The entire poem is related to traditional situations and imagery in blues poetry, as in the following:

> I'm goin' to the river
> I'm gonna buy me a rockin' chair
> If the blues overtake me,
> I'm gonna rock away from here.

But the crucial thing is the reaction—the heroic underpinning of the blues which so appeals to Brown and which merges in his poetry with the theme of the common man in the tradition of Whitman and Twain. As the man watches the slowly rolling river, something beside him

> . . . rared up an' say,
> *"Better be movin' . . . better be travelin' . . .*
> *Riverbank'll git you ef you stay. . . ."*

"Riverbank Blues" serves to remind us that the blues are not only a music, but also a complex of emotions and a certain way of looking at life; thus the poet here is justified in titling the poem as he does. There, of course, was ample precedent in the music profession itself. One might observe that Langston Hughes also followed this practice, his poem "The Weary Blues" being just one salient example.

Hughes was able to evoke the blues feeling in sharp vignettes that sometimes consist of no more than two or four lines:

> I wish the rent
> Was Heaven sent.

Brown too has this ability to capture the pithy precision of folk speech and poetry. In "Rent Day Blues," which first appeared in *Folk Say, IV*,[3] Brown's special brand of humor appears in a variation on the blues form—a sort of blues ballad. The poet omits the second line from the typical three-line blues stanza in "Rent Day Blues," making two lines, which he then breaks up into four. Langston Hughes, by comparison, often wrote the stanza as six lines. The short lines move swiftly, tersely, with snap. The opening stanza retains the effect of a couplet in the statement about the rent:

> I says to my baby,
> "Baby, but de rent is due;

> Can't noways figger
> What we ever gonna do."

The woman answers:

> My baby says, "Honey,
> Dontcha worry 'bout de rent;
> Looky here, daddy,
> At de money what de good Lord sent."

The pivoting of the voice on the word "baby" in the first stanza and the enjambment of the last two lines help establish the sense of a couplet, mentioned above. With the second stanza, however, with the words "Honey" and "daddy," the rhythms of Black speech demand a prolongation, an emphasis, which establishes the quatrain for the ear as well as the eye. The resulting ballad movement of the poem thus carries something of the flavor of a compressed blues stanza. Amplified by the typical blues situation, this handling of the poem's rhythm and movement is a further indication of Brown's skill.

"Long Track Blues," which also first appeared in *Folk Say, IV,*[4] is closer to the tradition of blues composition, in terms of its dramatic situation and mood. Note, however, that this poem too omits the second line for conciseness, although the poet sometimes supplies it when reading in public:

> Went down to the yards
> To see the signal lights come on;
> Looked down the track
> Where my lovin' babe done gone.
>
> Red light in my block,
> Green light down the line;
> Lawdy, let yo' green light
> Shine down on that babe o' mine.

For specificity of detail and evocative power this is one of Sterling Brown's finest poems. Its ease is deceptive. In order to appreciate fully his achievement here, one must acquaint oneself with the body of blues and other songs which deal with railroads and trains, with leavings and heartbreaks, particularly with the cluster of songs in which the lover rebukes the train for taking his babe away, as in "Mean Old Frisco," perhaps the most famous:

> O that mean Ol' Frisco
> And that low-down Santa Fe—
> Say, that mean Ol' Frisco
> And that low-down Santa Fe
> Come and stole my baby 'way—
> Better blow her back to me

> Lord, I wonder do she ever think of me
> Lord, I wonder do she ever think of me
> Lord, I wonder, I wonder, do my baby think of me.

And Sterling Brown consciously deepened the meanings and multiplied the implications of a Black American folk base, to paraphrase James Weldon Johnson, by his skillful selection and synthesis of the imagery which often appeared in songs of quite different types. Thus the signal lights in Brown's poem not only call up the "train with the red and green lights behind" but also a related image found in many blues: "If I could shine like the headlight on some train." Grading into this image, one finds the "gospel train" and the "little black train of death." Other related images of light and trains are found in hymns, gospels, and spirituals. These associations are not at all gratuitous, as we shall see later in the discussion of "Memphis Blues."

Let us return now to *Southern Road* and look briefly at "Tin Roof Blues," which is written in classical blues form. It is a marvelous distillation of both blues method and substance. Echoes from traditional blues appear in the very first line:

> I'm goin' where de Southern crosses top de C. & O.

One, of course, hears the undertone:

> I'm goin' where the Southern cross the Yellow Dog.

And one probably hears it in Bessie Smith's voice. The third line, too, is a distillation of hundreds of blues songs, and it is especially poignant since it stands as the second clause:

> I'm goin' down de country cause I cain't stay here no mo'.

This theme of leaving so typical of the blues appears in lines like:

> I'm going to Chicago, sorry but I can't take you.

Or:

> I'm going, I'm going, pin up black crape on your door.

And:

> I'm going down this road feelin bad, baby.

And:

> I'm going where the weather suits my clothes.

And what is the wanderer in "Tin Roof Blues" looking for? He's looking for a place where people are friendly, honest, and down-to-earth, where they take control of their own lives as best they can, where they don't wait for fate to give them a lucky hit on the numbers.

The poem closes with delightfully compressed imagery:

> I'm got de tin roof blues, got dose sidewalks on my mind,
> De tin roof blues, dose lonesome sidewalks on my mind,
> I'm goin' where de shingles covers people mo' my kind.

One might compare these lines from "Freight Train Blues," by Thomas Dorsey and Everett Murphy (© 1924 Chicago Music Publishing Co.):

> Got the freight train blues. I've got the box cars on my mind.
> Got the freight train blues. I've got the box cars on my mind.
> I'm gonna leave this town because my man is so unkind.

Notice, first of all, the subtlety of Brown's variations in the second line of his last stanza. The omission of the first two words of the first line ("I'm got") gives the second some of the shorthand quality of sung blues lyrics, in which the instrument may carry the second line, or a grunt or a deliberately muffled approximation of the words as originally sung. And one would certainly expect a skilled blues singer to take such liberties with the formally repeated lines in the "Freight Train Blues" text. The variation which Brown makes at the beginning of the line also makes it possible for him to augment the mood with the adjective "lonesome." This kind of emotional augmentation approximates the musical practice. The "I'm goin'" of the third line is a clever resolution of the syntactical ambiguity (with reference to so-called Standard English) of the expression "I'm got." It forms a visual and aural parallel to the "I'm got" of the first line, but it is more precisely a clarification which allows the imagery and the final statement to speak for themselves without obtrusion. And here, certainly, Brown achieves the kind of language which James Weldon Johnson spoke of some years before. Again, notice the compression of the lines, the economy characteristic of folk poetry. From "freight train blues" to "box cars on my mind" the jump is much shorter, less imaginative—with a tendency toward the pathetic—than the imaginative leap from "tin roof blues" to "dese sidewalks on my mind," which realistically evokes the wanderlust of Black blues living. With the last line of the "Freight Train Blues" stanza, "I'm gonna leave this town because my man is so unkind," commercial glibness, which is characteristic of so many so-called "classical blues" songs, intrudes upon the achievement of the first two lines. In contrast, the last line of Brown's stanza serves to draw the whole poem together, thematically and tonally, for here the word "shingles" is set against the tin roofs of the city—wooden, honest wooden shingles "covers people mo' my kind." So the poet accepts the challenge of suggesting the spontaneity of improvisation, although he carefully controls his effects in a manner which the commercial song writer would be unable to do, and which he would find unnecessary, since his text would be in effect a pretext for the singer to do his or her own thing in the first place.

The theme of wandering is a powerful one in folk literature and occupies a prominent place in the blues and the ballads and tales which nurtured the art of Sterling Brown. There is a well-known historical matrix of this wanderlust and leaving, which includes the migration of Blacks after the Civil War—the northward and westward migrations which peaked during the two world wars, and the movement from rural to urban areas even within the South itself. This is, to be sure, not strictly a Black phenomenon, but the effect which it had upon Black life was profound. The examples cited above are fairly self-sufficient on a literal level. On a deeper level, the theme of wandering or leaving is concomitant with the notion of the blues as a poetry/music of confrontation. The confrontation is frequently with a loved one, though often it is with one's enemies or with specific unhappy conditions in society, or with oneself. And the resolution comes through sexual triumph, or through violence, an assertion of one's manhood/womanhood, or through a bitter acceptance of the harshness, even the absurdity of life, expressed with cunning humor and with wit, or irony. The final confrontation, of course, is with death, and here the motif of the wanderlust takes on a special irony. The folk expression for it is, "You can run, but you can't hide." And the blues poet knows this. It is an ultimate knowing, but one which requires a lifetime of repetition. A man may run away after committing a murder, for example, but he can't run away from himself. ("Cain't nobody hide from God.") He may try to run away from confrontation with self, but eventually life forces him to make decisions which reveal who he is. Characteristic of Sterling Brown's figures is the heroism which the confrontation reveals, even in the case of a Joe Meek. In "Georgie Grimes," one could hardly call the character heroic, but he has his pride, and our grudging respect. He has just killed his woman. With his red suitcase in his hand he "sloshes onward through the rain. . . ." He "remembers hot words, lies, / The knife, and a pool of blood. . . ." And he remembers her sightless eyes, and he knows that fear will follow him for the rest of his life. As he stumbles through "the soggy clay," muttering to himself, "No livin' woman got de right / To do no man dat way," we realize a bitter, brutal dimension of the folk, and the blues, experience.

The three poems on Big Boy Davis which open *Southern Road*—"Long Gone," "When De Saints Go Ma'ching Home," and "Odyssey of Big Boy"—explore three stages, as it were, of the wanderlust theme. All of these poems are blues-like in tone and language, though not in overall structure. "Long Gone" depicts a typical footloose man who leaves his woman despite his mixed feelings. In "When De Saints Go Ma'ching Home," the poet's first published poem, Big Boy, the wandering songster, plays music which progresses from "the bawdy songs and blues," "the weary plaints," to his mother's favorite song, with which he ended all of the concerts for his middle-class friends. As persona, Big Boy, in effect, asserts through the shape of his concert the unity and meaningfulness of his life. Technically, the "concert" section of the poem is a microcosm of the musical tradition; and, further refined, the second section, with its series of portraits evoked by the music, is an emblem of folk society framed by the consciousness and craft of the poet.

Big Boy Davis's concert also illustrates the mingling of the religious and the secular in Black music and Black life,[5] and although that fact is now well-known, one must still realize that the means for achieving that mingling or fusion are rather more complicated than substituting "Baby" for "Jesus" in a song based on gospel tunes or chord progressions. Brown learned this quite early in his career, and expressed it with subtlety and power not only in "Odyssey of Big Boy" but in poems like "Ma Rainey" and "Memphis Blues." The wanderlust motif or feeling is an important ingredient in the Blues Universe and in the notion of Soul as the embodiment or essence of Black lifestyle.

In "Odyssey of Big Boy," one of Brown's finest and most characteristic poems, there is a classic statement of wanderlust as Soul. Big Boy envisions the final confrontation after years of wandering. He outlines his history in comic-heroic terms. He has been mule skinner, steel driver, tobacco harvester, coal miner, farmhand, roustabout, short-order cook, and dish-washer. And he has had his good times with the women, running the gamut from a "Creole gal" to a "stovepipe blond." He continues:

> Done took my livin' as it came,
>> Done grabbed my joy, done risked my life;
>> Train done caught me on de trestle,
> Man done caught me wid his wife,
>> His doggone purty wife . . .

So when his "jag is done," there is no room for complaining. He has lived his life and taken the risks, and the confrontation has produced a clear self-knowledge and a view of the moral order of the world, where he, indeed, is bone and flesh of John Henry and the archetypical Brother, the embodiment of Soul.

Although the outstanding feature of Sterling Brown's blues is their somber outlook, the poet's treatment of the blues material ranges from emphasis on mood and character, to a focus on the sociological, to an accent on the philosophical. Sometimes, as in "Odyssey of Big Boy," all three elements are present in the same poem. In "New St. Louis Blues," however, the sociological emphasis is almost clinical. The poem is a kind of blues suite, consisting of three separate but related poems entitled "Market Street Woman," "Tornado Blues," and "Low Down." All three are written in the three-line blues stanza, but there is a scientific detachment from the subjects which recalls the proletarian literature of the 1930s. One can't easily imagine these poems as songs, as in the case of "Tin Roof Blues," for example, or "Long Track Blues," which Brown recorded with piano accompaniment for Folkways Records.[6] In other words, "Market Street Woman" and "Low Down" are case studies of social oppression.

Even in "Tornado Blues" protest against oppression is the central theme, for although the "Black wind" from "de Kansas plains" has caused the initial destruction, the suffering which preceded it and which surely follows is man-made, the result of an oppressive social and economic system. It was mostly "de Jews an' us" that the tornado ruined. "Many po' boys' castle done settled to a heap o' dus'." The "Newcomers"—Destruction, Fear, Death, and Sorrow— "dodged most of the mansions, and knocked down de po' folks' do'. . . ." And this is what they found:

> Foun' de moggidge unpaid, foun' de insurance long past due,
> Moggidge unpaid, de insurance very long past due,
> All de homes we wukked so hard for goes back to de Fay and Jew.

Technically, the achievement of "New St. Louis Blues" lies in the adaptation of the strict blues form to precise sociopolitical statement, and the organiza-tion of the three separate but complementary poems into a tonal whole. But the achievement goes beyond isolated technicalities or social protest. Certainly, protest is an important part of the blues tradition, but it is an implicit protest, as Albert Murray observes. The crucial thing is that Brown goes beyond the social protest writers of his time and finds in the blues a philosophical position which is compatible with his own. It is this position, this attitude, this tone which most clearly sets him apart from others who employ the folk idiom. This "grim" perspective, to use the poet's own word, has some of its roots, at least, in the blues. There is, to be sure, a dimension of the blues which is unmistakably tragic, even fatalistic, in which human activity is pitted against the overwhelm-ing forces of nature, depicted at times as impersonal, objective, or indifferent, at other times as the embodiment of a malevolent teleology. It appeared in the "blues suite," for example, in lines like these from "Tornado Blues":

> De Black wind evil, done done its dirty work an' gone,
> Black wind evil, done done its dirty work an' gone,
> Lawd help de folks what de wind ain't had no mercy on.

In the down-home blues tradition, Furry Lewis of Memphis sings:

> Wind storm come, an' it blowed my house away,
> Wind storm come, and it blowed my house away,
> I'm a good old boy, but I ain' got nowhere to stay.

And Mississippian Son House sings of a devastating drought in "Dry Spell Blues":

> The dry spell blues have fallen, drove me from door to door.
> Dry spell blues have fallen, drove me from door to door.
> The dry spell blues have put everybody on the killing floor. . . .
>
> Oh Lord, have mercy if you please.
> Oh Lord, have mercy if you please.
> Let your rain come down, and give our poor hearts ease.

The language in the song moves from the literal to the symbolic as the singer establishes a landscape worthy of Eliot's *The Waste Land,* as it moves from references to parched cotton and corn, the price of meat against that of cotton, to a description of the world as a powderhouse where all the money men sit in their coil. With that range of language in mind, then, how lyrically right becomes the line "Let your rain come down, and give our poor hearts ease." Even the cliché of the second clause is restored to its pristine sincerity.

In a symbolic landscape, the precocious Robert Johnson sang of a veritable blues storm, through which he stumbled much like Sterling Brown's Georgie Grimes. Johnson's imagery, however, is at once biblical and hallucinatory, in the manner of the old sermons:

> I got to keep movinn', I got to keep movinnn',
> Blues fallin' down like hail, blues fallin' down like hail,
>> Mmmmmmmmmmmmmmmm-mmmm-mmm, blues
>> fallin'
>> down like hail, blues fallin' down like hail, blues
>> fallin' down like hail,
> And the days keep on worryin' me, for a hell-hound on my trail,
> Hell-hound on my trail, hell-hound on my trail.

But Johnson and other blues people lived and sang in the real world, not in a symbolic landscape, and that world was harsh and oppressive, and dangerous. There were floods and droughts and tornadoes, and a merciless social order, built on the Black man's subjugation. Even in times of natural disaster Black folks seemed singled out for special punishment. Such a time was the great flood of 1927 which left an indelible impression on blues literature. Paul Oliver, the blues historian, has a highly compressed account which warrants quotation:

> No one had anticipated the full horror of the 1927 floods. Houses were washed away with their terrified occupants still clinging to the roof-tops; the carcasses of cattle and mules floated in the swirling, deep brown water; isolated figures whom none could rescue were last seen crying for help as they hung in the gaunt branches of shattered trees. Dressers and table-tops, clothes and toys were caught in the driftwood and floating timbers, to twist madly in a sudden whirlpool, and then sweep out of sight in the surging, eddying, boiling waters which extended as far as eyes could see.

From the town of Cairo, one could accurately judge the extent of the flooding at the towns farther down river. A rise of fifty feet above minimal level indicated that a severe flood was imminent. Oliver continues, "In 1927 the water had risen to 56.4 feet—nearly two feet above the previous highest reading." And at Vicksburg, "the level had risen some sixty-five feet and with such a tremendous volume of water that the devastation was on an immense scale.

Breaches—or 'crevasses'—in the levees were recorded in fifty places and twenty-eight thousand square miles of land were under water. Whole townships were engulfed and the frightened people—largely Negroes—made for the hills at Helena and Vicksburg."

Some 600,000 people "were rendered completely destitute," and Blacks were at the mercy of white landlords who exploited a corruptly administered relief program. Total damage to the region was assessed at more than 350 million dollars.[7]

Many songs were written about the 1927 flood, but surely the best known was "Backwater Blues," which received majestic treatment by both Ma Rainey and Bessie Smith and moving treatment by others.

Sterling Brown had seen Ma Rainey in his youth, and her voice and her dignity had made a tremendous impression on him. Although he hadn't heard her sing "Backwater Blues," he had met someone who had, and he fused that account with his own impressions, his own knowledge of the people and the region and the music into one of the finest evocations of Black life that anybody has ever written, his poem "Ma Rainey." Sterling Stuckey calls it "perhaps *the* Blues poem,"[8] but to be precise, it is not a blues poem at all, in terms of structure, the way that "Tin Roof Blues" is, for example. It is, instead, a consummate dramatization of the spirit and power of the blues and their historic role as ritual in Black life.

The poem is divided into four stanzas which function in effect as movements in a musical sense. In the first, the tone is light and festive, capturing the excitement of the singer's personal fame:

> When Ma Rainey
> Comes to town,
> Folks from anyplace
> Miles aroun',
> From Cape Girardeau,
> Poplar Bluff
> Flocks in to hear
> Ma do her stuff. . . .

It's a holiday, when "Ma hits/Anywheres aroun'." Quickly the poet has established not only Ma's fame but the geography of the backwaters as well—Cape Girardeau, Poplar Bluff, all the way "fo' miles on down / To New Orleans delta / An' Mobile town." In the second stanza the pace changes as the line lengthens and the focus is closer, tighter. People come "from de little river settlements," from "blackbottom cornrows and from lumber camps." The lens zooms in, as people "stumble in de hall, jes' a-laughin' an' a-cacklin', / Cheerin' lak roarin' water, lak wind in river swamps." The high feelings and the good times and the joking keep going in the "crowded aisles." But others wait for a deeper reason. Then Ma makes her entrance, flashing her famous smile, and "Long Boy ripples minors on de black an' yellow keys." And the poet in stark dramatic terms speaks with the voice of the people. It is the communal voice, the response of the ancient ritual pattern, the answer to Ma Rainey's call to "deir aches an' miseries":

> O Ma Rainey,
> Sing yo' song;
> Now you's back
> Whah you belong,
> Git way inside us,
> Keep us strong. . . .
> O Ma Rainey,
> Li'l an' low;
> Sing us 'bout de hard luck
> Roun' our do';
> Sing us 'bout de lonesome road
> We mus' go. . . .

The expression "Sing yo' song" is still current in the Black community. People say it spontaneously when they are moved by someone who appeals to their deepest concerns, whether a gospel singer or Aretha Franklin singing about hard times in love. And they compliment her by saying, Sing your song, because the song is theirs too. She gives them back themselves and they return the love and the truth: "Now you's back" with us, "Whah you belong"—and now with this kind of singing, you're affirming our truth. And the language resonates on the mythic level, for the singer is priestess and, before that, the surrogate of the god. This was her role, in that time before time. But here it is compressed, transubstantiated into song, personal commentary transmuted into communal statement. And they know, they understand the ultimate tragic truth of human experience, and they accept it and thereby transcend it. Hard luck is irrational, but there it is. Call it fate, call it mischance, it is still there. And it will remain. So sing yo' song: "Sing us 'bout de lonesome road / We mus' go. . . ."

One would think perhaps that the possibilities of the poem had been exhausted at this point, but the poet moves into a different perspective and amplifies his effect by letting the *blues* speak for themselves. In stanza four, then, he returns to the narrative mode of stanza two. Here the point of view changes to that of a single persona:

> I talked to a fellow, an' the fellow say,
> "She jes' catch hold of us, somekindaway.
> She sang Backwater Blues one day:
>
> *'It rained fo' days an' de skies was dark as night,*
> *Trouble taken place in de lowlands at night.*
>
> *'Thundered an' lightened an' the storm begin to roll*
> *Thousan's of people ain't got no place to go.*

'Den I went an' stood upon some high ol' lonesome hill,
An' looked down on the place where I used to live.'

An' den de folks, dey natchally bowed dey heads an' cried,
Bowed dey heavy heads, shet dey moufs up tight an' cried,
An' Ma lef' de stage, an' followed some de folks outside."

Dere wasn't much more de fellow say:
She jes' gits hold of us dataway.

The communion is complete. Even song now is unnecessary, and Ma Rainey, the priestess, is spent—the spirit has left her, the spirit is loosed and surrounds and hallows them all. It is like the end of a sermon, or a baptism.

Technically, there's one final touch as the persona picks up the language of the "fellow," which had been enclosed in quotes, as an account, and repeats it, compressing and melding the account, the reminiscence, the historical flood, and the present into an acknowledgment of his oneness with the people and the experience. "Dere wasn't much more de fellow say/She jes' gits hold of us dataway." Not "somekindaway" but the way you have just experienced it—"dataway."

Just as Sterling Brown celebrates his people's health and sanity and their heroic confrontation with adversity, he attacks anything which oppresses or corrupts them. The vehemence of his attack is proportionate to his outrage and his sense of the people's loss. In "Children's Children" he directs a stream of elegant sarcasm at an unfaithful generation bent on abandoning its heritage. But in "Cabaret," one of his most important poems, the target is larger—it is nothing less than the prostituting of Black life by the large society and the capitalistic system. Here he not only dramatizes the struggle of man against nature, but the conflicts between Black and white, the powerful and the powerless, the overlords and the underlings, and the complicity of Black people in their own degradation. The enveloping event of the poem again is the great flooding of the Mississippi in 1927, but whereas "Ma Rainey" demonstrates the heroic resiliency and philosophic maturity of the people through an authentic blues ritual, "Cabaret" becomes a complex vehicle for devastating satire on all that is false and parasitical in the American way of life. It is thus a poem on the anti-blues spirit, the dialectical opposite of "Ma Rainey." Just as "Backwater Blues" provides the emotional mainspring for "Ma Rainey," the banal Tin Pan Alley song "Muddy Water Blues" provides the basis of the satire in "Cabaret." The words of the song, drifting in and out of the narrative flow, help to shape it by providing a chronological base for the action, which is amplified in the event of the poem proper, a floor show at the Black and Tan Club of Chicago, in 1927, as we learn from the poem's subtitle. The two events which govern the poem may be viewed as two concentric circles, the larger one symbolizing the outside world with the conflicts between man and nature, overlords and underlings, powerful and powerless, white and Black—the sociopolitical conditions of the Mississippi Delta, and the country itself. The smaller circle, symbolizing the event of the Club, is a microcosm of the world outside. But here there is a suspension of real time, historical time, so to speak, and substituted for it is the time of the floor show, a hollow ersatz art. The poem itself is a verbal construct which mediates between the two "events."

The reader is guided through a set of interlocking levels of perception and commentary, which may themselves be viewed as sub-events of the action in the Club. The historical event of the flood is refracted through various modalities, which we perceive as levels of feeling or meaning, as voices, or angles of perception and commentary. The first level, "A," is the narrative. The poem opens here with a scene of the rich "overlords" and their "glittering darlings" (lines 1–10). It occurs also at lines 14–16, 20–24, 26–31, 33–34, 44, 58–63, and 76–81; for a total of 35 lines. The other voices/levels are as follows:

"B"—Sardonic #1. Here are reactions to the behavior of the participants in the Club event—the band, the chorus, the waiters, and the overlords. It occurs at lines 11–13, 25, and 45–49; for a total of 9 lines.

"C"—Music/Chorus. Lyrics of "Muddy Water Blues" sung by the chorus of "Creole" beauties provide a chronological base for the action. Along with voice/level A this level provides the main structural lines of the poem. It occurs

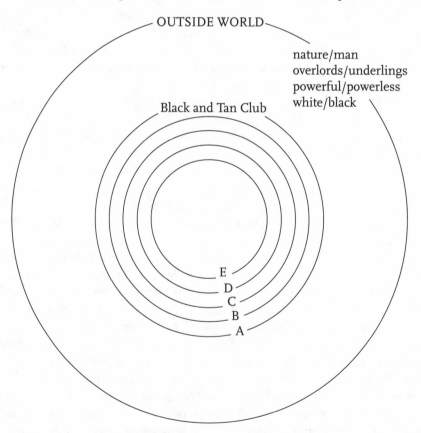

FIGURE 3.1 Mediating between Two Events.

at lines 17–19, 32, 35–36, 50–52, 57, 68–69, 74–75, and 82–83; for a total of 12 lines.

"D"—Sardonic #2. This voice/level provides reaction to the Club event by the juxtaposition of images of toil, suffering, destruction, and death resulting from the Mississippi floods. The sociological tone shades into the naturalistic and the fatalistic. It occurs at lines 37–42, 53–56, 64–67, 70–73, and 84–86; for a total of 23 lines.

"E"—Music/Instrumental. This voice/level is represented through ono-matopoeia as the music is left to speak for itself in a manner comparable to the quotation of "Backwater Blues" in "Ma Rainey." It occurs at lines 43 and 87, at the midpoint and the end of the poem.

Let us return to the poem itself. It opens with the rich "overlords" and their "glittering darlings":

> Rich, flashy, puffy-faced,
> Hebrew and Anglo-Saxon
> The overlords sprawl here with their glittering darlings.
> The smoke curls thick, in the dimmed light
> Surreptitiously, deaf-mute waiters
> Flatter the grandees,
> Going easily over the rich carpets,
> Wary lest they kick over the bottles
> Under the tables.

Then "the jazzband unleashes its frenzy." Up to this point the action of the poem is presented on level A, narrative; but suddenly we encounter a sardonic voice, printed in italics, which comments on the band, trained "doggies" per-forming for the overlords. We are on level B:

> *Now, now,*
> *To it, Roger; that's a nice doggie,*
> *Show your tricks to the gentlemen.*

When we are returned to the narrative level, A, the band is depicted in pathological images:

> The trombone belches, and the saxophone
> Wails curdlingly, the cymbals clash,
> The drummer twitches in an epileptic fit

At level C (lines 17–19), we hear the voice of the chorus singing the obscene banalities of the Tin Pan Alley song about the flood. We remember, of course, "Backwater Blues" and Ma Rainey singing *her* song. But the chorus sings:

> Muddy water
> Round my feet
> Muddy water

Back on the narrative level, A (lines 20–24), we are informed that "the chorus sways in," and in an aside, we are told that they are not really "Creole Beauties from New Orleans," as billed, but come from almost everywhere else—Atlanta, Louisville, Washington, Yonkers. And on level B (line 25), the Sardonic Voice #1 exclaims with mock preciousness:

> *O, le bal des belles quarterounes!*

The narrative voice creates a picture of mock romantic sensuality as it describes the "shapely bodies" of the chorus in their pirates' costumes, and it reflects with sarcasm upon the maudlin images of river life conjured up by the dancing, the music, and "the bottles under the tables" (lines 26–31). And it reminds us of Lafitte, the real pirate (lines 33–34), and his modern counterparts, the "overlords" themselves. There is a rich interplay of voices, tones, and perspectives at this point in the poem, as the voice of the chorus (C) surfaces—"Muddy water, river sweet" (line 32)—and the narrative voice (A) refers us to Lafitte's "doughty diggers of gold" (lines 33–34). The words of the chorus become unbearably unreal as they sing of the "peace and happiness" of the Delta (C, lines 35–36) in 1927. Sardonic Voice #2 (level D) crashes in, distinguished by parentheses, its grim tone, and its naturalistic depiction of the sociology of the flood. First, there is the virtual slavery of the Black convicts who have been pressed to work on the levees (lines 37–42):

> *(In Arkansas,*
> *Poor half-naked fools, tagged with identification numbers,*
> *Worn out upon the levees,*
> *Are carted back to the serfdom*
> *They had never left before*
> *And may never leave again)*

Amplifying these lines, in the music of the period, one finds Leadbelly singing "Red Cross Store Blues" and Big Bill Broonzy who sang:

> You'll never get to do me like you did my buddy Shine;
> You'll never get to do me like you did my buddy Shine;
> You worked him so hard on the levee till he went stone blind.

On the deepest level/voice, E, the drummer makes a break which the poet captures in terms that anticipate Langston Hughes's rendering of Be-Bop sounds in his *Montage of a Dream Deferred*. In fact, the term Be-Bop itself as a name for the music probably had its origin in onomatopoeia, and just as "Bop" singing tended toward the use of wordless "lyrics," the heart of Brown's poem demonstrates the tendency of Black musicians to employ the instrument as an extension of the voice. In certain situations, in the scat singing of Dizzy Gillespie, for example, the result is a teasing expression of the anti-rational, dadaistic impulse. And so the drummer plays (line 43):

> Bee—dap—ee—DOOP, dee—ba—dee—BOOP

As "the girls wiggle and twist" to the music (A, line 44), Sardonic Voice #1 (B) offers them at auction (lines 45–49). They, like the musicians, are ordered to go through their paces for the "gentlemen":

> *A prime filly, seh.*
> *What am I offered, gentlemen, gentlemen. . . .*

The song continues its phony sentiment (C, lines 50–52), interrupted by Sardonic Voice #2 (D), which now asks without bitterness (lines 53–56), "*What is there left the miserable folk?*" In reply, the voice of the chorus chimes in (C, line 57), "Still it's my home, sweet home," as the poet emphasizes the falseness with the "moans and deep cries for home" coming from the "lovely throats" of these displaced "Creoles." And the alcohol heightens the illusion they create (A, lines 58–63).

In the real world of the Mississippi Delta (D, lines 64–67), "*The black folk huddle, mute, uncomprehending*" the ways of "*the good Lord.*" They have no "shelter/Down in the Delta," as the song goes (C, lines 68–69). On the level of Sardonic Voice #2 (D, lines 70–73), the heavy-bellied buzzards fly low over the Yazoo, "*Glutted, but with their scrawny necks stretching, / Peering still.*" This counterpoint of images is striking, this interweaving of voices and levels, the commercial song moving in and out of the real world of the Delta, the make-believe of the cabaret, all of it held in dynamic suspension in the world of the poem. As the song, as the event for the interior scene comes to a close, the band goes mad (A, lines 76–81; C, lines 82–83; D, lines 84–86; E, line 87):

> The band goes mad, the drummer throws his sticks
> At the moon, a *papier-mâché* moon,
> The chorus leaps into weird posturings,
> The firm-fleshed arms plucking at grapes to stain
> Their coralled mouths; seductive bodies weaving
> Bending, writhing, turning
>
> My heart cries out for
> MUDDY WATER
>
> (*Down in the valleys*
> *The stench of the drying mud*
> *Is a bitter reminder of death.*)
>
> Dee da dee DAAAAH

The final notes of the trumpet, if one must seek a literary comparison, are the equivalent of Hemingway's "Nada" in "A Clean, Well-Lighted Place," in which the writer parodies the Lord's Prayer with the Spanish word for "nothing." And again one must note the anticipation of Be-Bop and the dadaist element in it, especially in the singing. However, in characteristic style, Brown has arrived at this position through essentially realistic means. On the sociological level, the political level, and the moral level, there is a powerful indictment of modern slavery, in the exploitation and prostitution of the musicians and their music. They are, in effect, no better off than the poor victims of the flood, or the convicts; and if they were aware of their condition, they too could ask "*how come the good Lord/Could treat them this a way.*" These are the heaviest blues of all, and the poet has presented them to us through an elegant indirection.[9]

To appreciate Brown's craftmanship it would be useful to study the relationship between the various voices/levels of the poem both as they fit together in a thematic scheme, as shown in figure 3.1, and as they produce a pattern left by the poem itself as its action moves through the "time" of the poem, as shown in figure 3.2. Here the "time" is indicated by the lines of the poem, perpendicular to which appear the levels/voices which I have just enumerated.

We now have a kind of grid on which we can trace the movement, the action, and, indeed, the geometry of the poem, its essence summed up in an action that flows like an arpeggio of downward turning blues. At a glance we see the movement to the various levels, the duration of the stay, and the intervals between jumps, which vary from the dramatic movement from E to A (lines 43–44), after the descending pattern begun at line 34, to jumps of a single level, as from A to B in lines 44–45. If we check the text at the movement from E to A, we discover that here at the midpoint of the poem the drummer has just played a break which makes a frivolous and ironic comment on the preceding level, D, which had just introduced the real world into the poem. In its frivolous ambiguity, the break is a dramatic introduction to the second movement of the poem at the same time that it propels the movement along as "the girls wiggle and twist." We may note also that, at the last time at this level of the poem (E, line 87), the trumpet unmistakably echoes the words "MUDDY WATER" from level C, line 83, commenting in its dadaistic way on the nothingness of life. One notes too, by way of structure, that the first instrumental appearance seems to be the drums; the second, the trumpet. Finally, level E represents an onomatopoetic extension and intensification of level C, thus faithfully following the tradition in Black music of employing the voice as an instrument.

If the poet presents the blues through indirection in "Cabaret," in "Memphis Blues" he presents them through the matrix of the oral tradition which helped to shape their growth. The poem partly draws upon the traditional notion of "preaching the blues" found in both music and oral literature, but significantly it

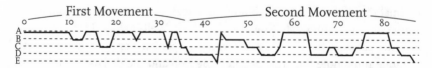

FIGURE 3.2 The Movement of the Poem's Action According to Levels in "Cabaret."

is not a parody of the sermon but a brilliant exploration of the song-sermon form in which the blues are historically and formally grounded. Its A–B–A form is a common song pattern and is shared by jazz and the sonata form. It is also the pattern which typical sermons take—text, development and application, repetition.[10] In the poem the enveloping sections are historical parallels to the present:

> Was another Memphis
> Mongst de olden days,
> Done been destroyed
> In many ways. . . .
> Dis here Memphis
> It may go. . . .

The persona cites the dangers:

> Floods may drown it;
> Tornado blow;
> Mississippi wash it
> Down to sea—
> Like de other Memphis in
> History.

That is the warning of apocalypse, the sign of the Judgment. The poem is a blues sermon on the Last Judgment. The language evokes the hymns of Blind Willie Johnson, the Texas preacher who sang and played in blues style and tonality:

> See the sign of the Judgment
> Yes, yes!
> See the sign of the Judgment
> Oh, yes, my Lord,
> Time is drawing nigh!

And the stage is set.

The long middle section of the poem consists of six stanzas, each posing the ultimate question in the life of a Christian: Where will you be on the day when God sends down Judgment? It is the *Dies Irae*—Day of Anger, Day of Judgment, and a central theme of Western literature and art. One recalls the medieval plays *Everyman* and *The Castle of Perseverance,* and the other moralities which address the theme in a form comprehensible to the common man in fourteenth-century England. One remembers, too, Marlowe's Dr. Faustus imploring the heavenly spheres to cease and bring time to a halt. And who can forget the peal of the *Dies Irae* as it strikes fear and repentance into the heart of Goethe's Gretchen?

Most of the old-time preachers were probably ignorant of Goethe and the Faust legend, but they knew the Bible fairly well, especially the Book of Revelation, and the most gifted of them knew enough history to draw lessons from it and to incorporate them into their sermons. Their knowledge was matched if not surpassed by superb rhetorical skills. The love of language was rooted in their culture. They sang as their parents had sung: "My Lord, what a mornin' / When the stars begin to fall." They sang: "Run, sinner, run and find yourself a hiding place." They admonished their congregations to work on the "building" for the Lord. They warned the gambler, the dancer, the drunkard, the "cussin' man," and the whoremonger to work on the building too, for the day was coming when "God's gonna separate the wheat from the tares." They questioned the sinner in his headlong flight: "O whar you runnin', sinner?" They asked him: "Sinner, what you goin' to do/When de devil git you?" And there would be no-where for the sinner to go, for "there's no hiding place down here."[11]

Brown builds the middle section of his poem on the pattern of these songs of the Last Judgment, a pattern which is also used in the sermon. That pattern is reinforced by a smaller rhetorical pattern of concentrated and compressed Black cultural experience, a *mascon*, and in choosing it the poet goes to the ambivalent heart of the Black man's Christian heritage. He is both Christian and Black. He is a child of God, yet not a man. There are contradictions, and conflicts, but one kind of resolution is found in the blues. However, the blues lie outside the church, are the devil's music. Still the blues came out of the church, as the singers themselves say. Thus there is no contradiction in the development of the poem. The first person to be addressed in the "Judgment Day pattern" is the Preacher Man—

> Watcha gonna do when Memphis on fire,
>   Memphis on fire, Mistah Preachin' Man?

And the Preachin' Man replies:

> Gonna pray to Jesus and nebber tire,
>   Gonna pray to Jesus, loud as I can,
>   Gonna pray to my Jesus, oh, my Lawd!

This is correct Christian behavior and the language and sentiments echo the Judg-ment Day spirituals cited above. Had the poet continued in this vein, the poem might have ended with a tonality and structure akin to the sermon-poems of James Weldon Johnson. But the poem is to be an experiment in blues tonality, as the title suggests, and we are not disappointed. Something remarkable and subtle begins to happen with the introduction of this answering refrain. For one thing, the poet has established perhaps the most characteristic pattern of Black oral/mu-sical tradition, the call-and-response, and both parts of the pattern take delightful variations of rhythm, tone, and diction as the poem proceeds. Each variation in the "call" is like a chord change, which is developed by the "response."

Although tonally and thematically the first response recalls the spirituals, the rhythm is jazzy as in gospel music. In addition, a closer examination will reveal that the call-and-response pattern is enhanced by the familiar mascon qualities of the call and the anaphora of the response. The pattern also contains an artfully concealed extension of the blues form in which the two lines of the call constitute, in effect, the first two lines of a blues stanza, while the response is a rhetorical elaboration of the third line. However, instead of the quick turn or the punch line of the blues stanza, the response stretches out into a kind of jazz melody.

Although each "change" is distinctive, we remain in the same key, as it were, as the calls are made in sequence to the Preachin' Man, the Lovin' Man, the Music Man, the Workin' Man, the Drinkin' Man, and the Gamblin' Man. Each responds in his own way, in his own rhythm and accent, but all end up with the refrain "oh, my Lawd!" first spoken by the Preachin' Man. This expression not only links the personae together, it allows for ironic variation of tone from the religious somberness of the opening section. In effect, the "Lawd" of the spirituals is subtly transformed by the "Lawd" of the blues.

The call also is a kind of blues riff which is not only found in blues songs but in other areas of the oral tradition. Thus Big Bill Broonzy sings a song called "Honey O Babe" in which these lines appear:

> Whatcha gonna do when the pond goes dry, honey, honey?
> Whatcha gonna do when the pond goes dry, babe, babe?
> Whatcha gonna do when the pond goes dry?

And the response is:

> Sit up on the bank and watch the poor things die,
> Honey, O babe o'mine.

Novelist John O. Killens recalls a chant which children of his generation sang in Americus, Georgia. The first line is the call; the second, the response:

> Watcha gonna do when the world's on fire?
> Run like hell and *holler,* "Fire!"

And Blind Lemon Jefferson sang, when John Killens was a little boy:

> Watcha gonna do when they send your man to war?
> Watcha gonna do—they send your man to war?

It is important, then, to realize that the call is a fundamental feature of blues style, and this particular call is one of the most deeply engrained in the oral tradition. This realization helps us to understand the structure of "Memphis Blues" and the reason that the title is justified. Each individual call, we may note further, is a kind of compressed blues experience, for the blues are a poetry of challenge and confrontation, and this fact is reflected in the poem's thematic concerns and its structure—its stanzas, its imagery, its rhythm, its diction, its overall shape.

In Memphis, Furry Lewis sings:

> Whatcha gonna do, your troubles get like mine?
> Whatcha gonna do, your troubles get like mine?

The wordless response comes ringing in from the guitar, but one ever-present possibility occurs in the response of another song:

> Get a handful of sugar and a mouthful of turpentine.

Again, diagrams help one to appreciate the poet's skill in the construction of "Memphis Blues."[12] Each of the six stanzas of the middle section possess the following structure. First is the *call*, which is a kind of "riff" that may be diagramed as shown in figure 3.3. Next is the *response*, which may be diagramed as shown in figure 3.4.

mascon	challenge
challenge (repeat)	persona

FIGURE 3.3 The Call.

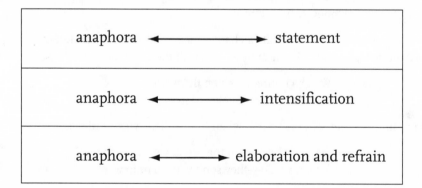

FIGURE 3.4 The Response.

As figure 3.3 dramatically demonstrates, the call is rather rigid, with a kind of singsong rhythm, characteristic of certain ritual language and of children's song. That quality is heightened by the repetition of the challenge. Variation is achieved and the poem is activated by changing the specific challenge in each call and, of course, by addressing a different persona. So we may list these elements in order:

(1) "Memphis on fire," Preachin' Man; (2) "tall flames"—a variation—Lovin' Man; (3) "Memphis falls down," Music Man; (4) "de hurricane," Workin' Man; (5) "Memphis near gone," Drinkin' Man; and (6) "de flood roll fas'," Gamblin' Man. We may note that the poet achieves coherence in the call by specific mention of Memphis in calls 1, 3, and 5, and by citing the destructive forces of nature in 2, 4, and 6.

It is the response, however, in which we best see the skillful work in the poem. The anaphora builds up a driving, jazzy pattern which the second part of the line develops into a series of brilliant explorations of the melodic variety of Afro-American speech. In the first, the preacher's voice reaches a tender intensity when he prays to "my Jesus," with the initial fillip of "oh, my Lawd!" In the second, the Lovin' Man in a sensual stammer of alliteration is "gonna love my brownskin better'n before," and the emphasis is not on his being a "do right man," but on the miracle of "my brown baby," which parallels the language of the preacher. One of the most felicitous of the responses is the third, in which the poet sets up a rocking rhythm that suggests the piano's bass line, then suddenly shifts into a lovely scattering of treble notes. Here is the entire stanza:

> Watcha gonna do when Memphis falls down,
>   Memphis falls down, Mistah Music Man?
> Gonna plunk on dat box as long as it soun',
>   Gonna plunk dat box fo' to beat de ban',
>   Gonna tickle dem ivories, oh, my Lawd!

When questioned about the hurricane, the Workin' Man in the fourth stanza makes a heroic personal response which is crucial to an appreciation of the tone and significance of the entire poem. He will not give up, and he will not be content with praying. He'll put the buildings back again, to stand, and he takes pride in his energy, his will, and above all in his style: "Gonna push a wicked wheelbarrow, oh, my Lawd!" Even the Drinkin' Man will go down in style with his "pint bottle of Mountain Corn," and the stopper in his hand. Finally, we come to the Gamblin' Man:

> Watcha gonna do when de flood roll fas',
>   Flood roll fas', Mistah Gamblin' Man?
> Gonna pick up my dice fo' one las' pass
>   Gonna fade my way to de lucky lan',
>   Gonna throw my las' seven—oh, my Lawd!

At this point we realize that the language of the poem in these six blues vignettes reflects Black life's emphasis upon style. That emphasis is at times overlooked and frequently misunderstood although it has attracted considerable attention from the media as well as the scholarly community. In effect, the style or the styling is an assertion of meaningfulness, not of frivolity or illusion, although there are, of course, assertions which may be so classified. An examination of the last response, then, is in order. The Gamblin' Man is not going to panic and fall down on his knees and beg God for mercy. That would be the coward's way. It would also be very "unhip." Death is final, but he meets it with a gambler's nerve, which is a kind of courage. He's not going to the Promised Land, but to the "lucky lan'," which he has created out of his own life, his own experience and values. He does not live in illusion and he takes responsibility for his life. The same thing applies to the Drinkin' Man, probably the most unsavory character of the group. Even he is going out in style: "Gonna get a *mean* jag on, oh, my Lawd!" These are not poor, benighted, superstitious foundlings in the hands of Fate, as Jean Wagner, for example, interprets Sterling Brown's characters,[13] but ordinary blues people heroic in their own way. As for the Drinkin' Man, we understand him better when we recall Bill Broonzy's words: "I'm gonna keep on a drinkin' / Till good liquor carry me down." Note that it's *good* liquor and "Mountain Corn," made by experts for virtuoso drinkers. And lurking behind the response are the immortal lines: "I got the world in a jug, the stopper's in my hand." So sang Bessie Smith.

These last stanzas of the group prepare us for the return to the somber theme of mutability in the final section of the poem:

> Memphis go
> By Flood or Flame;
> Nigger won't worry
> All de same—
> Memphis go
> Memphis come back
> Ain' no skin
> Off de nigger's back.
> All dese cities
> Ashes, rust. . . .
> De win' sing sperrichals
> Through deir dus'.

What warrants attention here is the loaded ambiguity of the last two lines, which one can read as an equation of the spirituals with the moaning of the wind, or as an existential projection of human value upon "objective," impersonal nature. And the songs are spirituals, not the blues, nor yet the songs of Tin Pan Alley, and the people have made them out of the substance of their lives, bleak though they might have been. An affirmation is made out of their courage, their strength, and their resilience, but equally out of their faith in themselves and their style. So when one re-examines the poem with the haunting lyricism of its enveloping sections and the artful mastery and development of folk resources in the middle, one wonders why it has not received its critical due. And one has to conclude that some of the fault, at least, can be attributed to a patronizing attitude toward the folk themselves, whom the poem celebrates.

In this brief assessment of the "blues" poetry of Sterling Brown, I have tried to demonstrate that a closer examination of the work reveals that he is, indeed, a skillful and careful craftsman, but a full appreciation of his achievement is dependent on a knowledge of and a feeling for the dynamics of the folk culture, some aspects of which have only begun to receive serious and systematic attention during the past fifteen years. Failure to appreciate these dynamics leads on one hand to the casual snobbery of a usually judicious critic like Nathan I. Huggins, who writes after a brief look at "Memphis Blues": "Such poems of Langston Hughes's and Sterling Brown's defy criticism because they lack pretension. They do not ask for academic acclaim; thus they are exempt from its contempt. In truth, Hughes was not writing to be approved as a literary poet (Brown sometimes did)." He continues, asserting that Hughes "expected his poems to be taken on the simple and unpretentious level on which they were written." By adopting folk forms, Huggins states, Hughes, and presumably Brown, obtained a freedom which while important in itself "deprived him of the control and mastery that might make each (or indeed any) of his poems really singular. Langston Hughes avoided the Scylla of formalism only to founder in the Charybdis of folk art."[14]

On the other hand, failure to respect the dynamics of the folk base also leads to distortions, and misinterpretation of the thematic aspects of Brown's art. In this regard, Jean Wagner—despite Robert Bone's citation of his "capacity for empathy" and his ability to "surmount linguistic and cultural barriers"[15]—manages to cramp the blues nuances of Brown's poetry into a rather mechanical universe of foolish faith and stoic endurance.[16] That Brown's view of life as expressed in the poems is tragic there is no doubt, but that view is expressed in terms which grow naturally out of the blues perspective, and, at times, the blues form in its many permutations. Brown's achievement, like that of the blues themselves, is a special kind of synthesis. Brown is not a folk poet, but a poet in the folk manner, who cunningly conceals his craft in the stylistics of the tradition itself. He not only mastered the academic studies and sources of his people's lore but the principles undergirding the lore itself. Thus his remarkable ability to render the sounds of speech, its nuances of rhythm and texture and meaning, was nourished not so much by his thorough knowledge of the literature written in dialect as by his immersion in the actual flow of the oral tradition, in the country homes of his students, in the barbershops and cafés of the South—Lynchburg, Atlanta, New Orleans—in all the varied places where Black folks gathered and talked and told lies, screamed at children, and sang the blues, or moaned the spirituals. He understood the contradictions in the people and in himself, and he did not sentimentalize them. He treated them roughly in his analysis, as Wagner indicates, but no rougher really than they treated themselves, not only in the dozens but in the whole range of the tradition, because survival and affirmation were their implicit objectives. If he is cynical at times and despairing, so are they. But the cynicism of the blues is ultimately cleansing. It sets limits and reinforces them—the blues allow for hope, for endurance, and, above all, for the very control that Huggins speaks of, but control of a deeper sort—moral control. Big Bill Broonzy, for example, recalls working deep in a hole under a city street. As he glanced up, he noticed another, earlier level where workers used to stand. He laughed to himself at the irony. Here he was a Black man "lookin' up at down." And he wrote a song about it. Memphis singer Furry Lewis, still alive at this writing, once sang about his misfortune: "My shoes done got thin. / I'm back on my feet again." So much for progress. And even before the Depression, long before then, some-one sang, "I been down so long it seems like up to me." And we link up the insights with Sterling Brown's poetry, in which the heavy water blues absorb the "chilling" social analysis and transmute the elegiac vestiges of his youth into a unique testament of the human will to endure.

NOTES

1. On the blues as a poetry of confrontation, see S.E. Henderson, "Blues for the Young Blackman," *Negro Digest*, August 1967, and "*Southern Road:* A Blues Perspective," *New Directions* (Howard University), July 1975; see also Albert Murray, *Stomping the Blues* (New York: McGraw-Hill, 1976), 250–52. Note, too, Murray's caption to the photos of dancers at the Savoy Ballroom (12), which reads, "Saturday Night *pas de deux* uptown any night. Confrontation . . . improvisation . . . affirmation . . . celebration."

2. Sterling A. Brown, *Southern Road* (1932; repr., with a new introduction by Sterling Stuckey, Boston: Beacon Press, 1974). All references are made to this edition.

3. B.A. Botkin, ed., *Folk-Say IV: The Land is Ours* (Norman: University of Oklahoma Press, 1932), 252ff.

4. Ibid., 251ff.

5. For further discussion, see Murray, 23–42, especially for the important distinction made between the "Saturday Night Function" and the "Sunday Morning Service." See also James H. Cone, *The Spirituals and the Blues* (New York: Seabury Press, 1972), especially chapter 6; Paul Oliver, *Conversation with the Blues* (London: Cassell, 1965); and William Ferris, Jr., *Blues from the Delta* (London: Studio Vista, 1970). Comment on the "unity" of Black music from the viewpoint of jazz musi-cians appears in the Summer 1972, issue of *The Black Scholar*. Donald Byrd, in "The Meaning of Black Music," states, "When I use the term jazz, I speak of all black music" (30). Max Roach, in "What 'Jazz' Means to Me," takes a different approach, "They are misnomers: Jazz music, rhythm and blues, rock and roll, gospel, spirituals, blues, folk music" (6).

6. *Sixteen Poems of Sterling A. Brown Read by Sterling A. Brown,* produced and edited by Frederic Ramsey, Jr. (Folkways Records FL 9794).

7. Paul Oliver, *The Meaning of the Blues* (New York: Collier Books, 1968), 268, 266, 267.

8. Stuckey, Introduction to *Southern Road*, xxvii.

9. On "elegant indirection," see the author's *Understanding the New Black Poetry: Black Speech and Black Music as Poetic References* (New York: William Morrow,

1978), 33–41. Cf. Murray: "The preeminent embodiment of the blues musician as artist was Duke Ellington, who, in the course of fulfilling the role of entertainer, not only came to address himself to the basic imperatives of music as a fine art but also achieved the most comprehensive synthesis, extension, and refinement to date of all the elements of blues musicianship" (214).

10. The repetition may be obliquely expressed or expressed through nonverbal means. In either case the completion is recognized by the congregation. In an unpublished doctoral dissertation, "The Performed African-American Sermon" (University of California, Berkeley, 1978), Gerald L. Davis develops a model of the sermon from intensive field work and a study of recordings. He provides a close critique of the scholarly literature, especially the work of Bruce A. Rosenberg and Albert B. Lord.

11. Howard W. Odum and Guy B. Johnson, *The Negro and His Songs: A Study of Typical Negro Songs in the South* (1925; repr., Hatboro, PA: Folklore Associates, Inc., 1964), 72, 77.

12. The diagrams, especially figure 3.3, are intended chiefly to show the location of structural elements, not their function.

13. *Black Poets of the United States*, trans. Kenneth Douglas (Urbana: University of Illinois Press, 1978), 488–90.

14. Nathan I. Huggins, *Harlem Renaissance* (New York: Oxford University Press, 1971), 226–27.

15. "Foreword," in *Black Poets of the United States*, by Jean Wagner, xiii.

16. See Wagner's entire discussion of Sterling Brown, especially his discussion of the poem "Southern Road" (489), and the section entitled "The Inanity of Faith." Wagner misses the nuances of Brown's position and, apparently, much of his art.

Review of *The Collected Poems of Sterling A. Brown*

Henry Louis Gates, Jr.

Nigger, your breed ain't metaphysical.
>—Robert Penn Warren, "Pondy Woods," 1928

Cracker, your kind ain't exegetical.
>—Sterling Brown, Interview, 1973

By 1932, when Sterling Brown published *Southern Road,* his first book of poems, the use of black vernacular structures in Afro-American poetry was controversial, indeed. Of all the arts, only through music had blacks invented and fully defined a tradition both widely regarded and acknowledged to be uniquely their own. Black folktales, while roundly popular, were commonly thought to be the amusing fantasies of a childlike people, whose saga and anecdotes about rabbits and bears held nothing deeper than the attention span of a child, à la Uncle Remus or even *Green Pastures.* And what was generally called "dialect," the unique form of English that Afro-Americans spoke, was thought by whites to reinforce received assumptions about the Negro's mental inferiority.

Dorothy Van Doren simply said out loud what so many other white critics thought privately: "It may be that [the Negro] can express himself only by music and rhythm," she wrote in 1931, "and not by words."

Middle-class blacks, despite the notoriety his dialect verse had garnered for Paul Laurence Dunbar and the Negro, thought that dialect was an embarrassment, the linguistic remnant of an enslavement they all longed to forget. The example of Dunbar's popular and widely reviewed "jingles in a broken tongue," coinciding with the conservatism of Booker T. Washington, was an episode best not repeated. Blacks stood in line to attack dialect poetry. William Stanley Braithwaite, Countée Cullen, and especially James Weldon Johnson argued fervently that dialect stood in the shadow of the plantation tradition of Joel Chandler Harris, James Whitcomb Riley, and Thomas Nelson Page. Dialect poetry, Johnson continued, possessed "but two full stops, humor and pathos." By 1931, Johnson, whose own "Jingles and Croons" (1917) embodied the worst in this tradition, could assert assuredly that "the passing of traditional dialect as a medium for Negro poets is complete."

As if these matters of sensibility were not barrier enough, major white critics of black writing, in a remarkably consistent line of argument that extends from David Hume in 1751 and by way of Jefferson, Kant, Hegel, Emerson, and a host of lesser lights to Dorothy Van Doren, believed, somehow, that until a black person ("full-blooded" at that) created a written masterpiece of art, black Americans would remain substandard citizens. As late as 1896, William Dean Howells, repeating almost exactly John Greenleaf Whittier's similar remarks of 1847, wrote that Paul Laurence Dunbar's dialect verse "makes a stronger claim for the negro than the negro yet has done. Here in the artistic effect at least is white thinking and white feeling in a black man . . . perhaps the proof [of human unity] is to appear in the arts, and our hostilities and prejudices are to vanish in them." Even as late as 1925, Heywood Broun could reiterate this curious idea: "A supremely great negro artist who could catch the imagination of the world, would do more than any other agency to remove the disabilities against which the negro now labors." Broun concluded that this black redeemer-with-a-pen could come at any time, and asked his audience to remain silent for ten seconds to imagine such a miracle! In short, the Black Christ would be a poet. If no one quite knew the precise form this Black Christ would assume, at least they all agreed on three things that he could not possibly be: he would not be a woman, such as the feminist Zora Neale Hurston; he would not be gay, such as Langston Hughes, Countée Cullen, or Alain Locke; and he would most definitely *not* write dialect poetry. Given all this, it is ironic that Brown used dialect at all. For a "New Negro" generation too conscious of character and class as color (and *vice versa*), Brown had all the signs of the good life: he was a mulatto with "good hair," whose father was a well-known author, a professor at Howard, pastor of the Lincoln Temple Congregational Church, and a member of the D.C. Board of Education who had numbered among his closest friends both Frederick Douglass and Paul Laurence Dunbar. Brown, moreover, had received a classically liberal education at Dunbar High School, Williams College, and Harvard, where he took the M.A. in English in 1923. Indeed, perhaps it was just this remarkably secure black aristocratic heritage that motivated Brown to turn to the folk.

Just one year after he had performed the post-mortem on dialect poetry, James Weldon Johnson, in the "Preface" to Sterling Brown's *Southern Road*, reluctantly admitted that he had been wrong about dialect. Brown's book of poetry, even more profoundly than the market crash of 1929, truly ended the "Harlem Renaissance," primarily because it contained a new and distinctly black poetic diction, and not merely the vapid and pathetic claim for one.

To the surprise of the Harlem Renaissance's New Negroes, the reviews were of the sort one imagines Heywood Broun's redeemer-poet was to have gotten. The New York *Times Book Review* said that "*Southern Road* is a book the importance of which is considerable. It not only indicates how far the Negro artist has progressed since the years when he began to find his voice, but it proves that the Negro artist is abundantly capable of making an original and genuine contribution to American literature." Brown's work was marked by a "dignity that respects itself. . . . there is everywhere art." Louis Untermeyer agreed: "He does not paint himself blacker than he is. . . ." Even Alain Locke, two years later, called it "a new era in Negro poetry." *Southern Road's* artistic achievement ended the Harlem Renaissance, for that slim book undermined all of the New Negro's assumptions about the nature of the black tradition and its relation to the individual talent. Not only were most of Brown's poems composed in dialect, but they also had as their subjects distinctively black archetypal mythic characters, as well as the black common man whose roots were rural and Southern. Brown called his poetry "portraitures," close and vivid detailings of an *action* of a carefully delineated subject to suggest a sense of place, in much the same way as Toulouse-Lautrec's works continue to do. These portraitures, drawn "in a manner constant with them," Brown renders in a style that emerged from several forms of folk discourse, a black vernacular matrix that includes the blues and ballads, the spirituals and worksongs. Indeed, Brown's ultimate referents are black music and mythology. His language, densely symbolic, ironical, and naturally indirect, draws upon the idioms, figures, and tones of both the sacred and the profane vernacular traditions, mediating between these in a manner unmatched before or since. Although Langston Hughes had attempted to do roughly the same, Hughes seemed content to transcribe the popular structures he received, rather than to transcend or elaborate upon them, as in "To Midnight Nan at Leroy's": "*Hear dat music . . . / Jungle night/Hear dat music . . . / And the moon was white.*"

But it is not merely the translation of the vernacular which makes Brown's work major, informed by these forms as his best work is; it is, rather, the deft manner in which he created his own poetic diction by fusing several black traditions with various models provided by Anglo-American poets to form a unified and complex structure of feeling, a sort of song of a racial self. Above all else, Brown is a regionalist whose poems embody William Carlos Williams' notion that the classic is the local, fully realized. Yet, Brown's "region" is not so much "the South," or Spoon River, Tilbury, or Yoknapatawpha as it is "the private Negro mind," as Alain Locke put it, "this private thought and speech," or "how it feels to be colored me," as Zora Neale Hurston put it, the very textual milieu of blackness itself. Boldly, Brown merged the Afro-American vernacular traditions of dialect and myth with the Anglo-American poetic tradition and, drawing upon the example of Jean Toomer, introduced the Afro-American modernist lyrical mode into black literature. Indeed, Brown, Toomer, and Zora Neale Hurston comprise three cardinal points on a triangle of influence out of which emerged, among others, Ralph Ellison, Toni Morrison, Alice Walker, and Leon Forrest.

Brown's poetic influences are various. From Whitman, Brown took the oracular, demotic voice of the "I" and the racial "eye," as well as his notion that "new words, new potentialities of speech" were to be had in the use of popular forms, such as the ballad. From E. A. Robinson, Brown took the use of the dramatic situation and the ballad, as well as what Brown calls the subject of "the undistinguished, the extraordinary in the ordinary." Certainly Brown's poems "Maumee Ruth," "Southern Cop," "Georgie Grimes," and "Sam Smiley" suggest the same art that created Miniver Cheevy and Richard Cory. From A. E. Housman, Brown borrowed the dramatic voice and tone, as well as key figures: Housman's blackbird in "When Smoke Stood Up From Ludlow" Brown refigures as a buzzard in "Old Man Buzzard." Both Housman's "When I Was One and Twenty" and Brown's "Telling Fortunes" use the figure of "women with dark eyes," just as the latter's "Mill Mountain" echoes Housman's "Terence, This Is Stupid Stuff." Housman, Heine, and Hardy seem to be Brown's central influence of tone. Burns' Scottish dialect and Synge's mythical dialect of the Aran Islander in part inform Brown's use of black dialect, just as Frost's realism, stoicism and sparseness, as in "Out, Out—," "Death of the Hired Man," "Birches," "Mending Wall," and "In Divés' Dive" inform "Southern Road," "Memphis Blues," and "Strange Legacies." His choice of subject matter and everyday speech are fundamentally related to the New Poetry and the work of Amy Lowell, Vachel Lindsay, Edgar Lee Masters, and Carl Sandburg, as well as to the common language emphasis of the Imagists. In lines such as "bits of cloud-filled sky . . . framed in bracken pools" and "vagrant flowers that fleck unkempt meadows," Wordsworth's *Lyrical Ballads* resound. Brown rejected the "puzzle poetry" of Pound and Eliot, and severely reviewed the Southern Agrarians' "I'll Take My Stand" as politically dishonest, saccharine nostalgia for a medieval never-never land that never was. Brown never merely borrows from any of these poets; he transforms their influence by grafting them onto black poetic roots. These transplants are splendid creations, indeed.

Michael Harper has collected nearly the whole of Brown's body of poetry, including *Southern Road, The Last Ride of Wild Bill* (1975) and the previously unpublished *No Hiding Place*, his second book of poems which was rejected for publication in the late thirties because of its political subjects, and which seems to have discouraged Brown from attempting another volume until 1975. Inexplicably, two poems of the five-part "Slim Greer" cycle, "Slim in Hell" and "Slim Hears 'The Call,'" are missing as is the major part of "Cloteel" and the final stanza of "Bitter Fruit of the Tree," oversights which a second edition should correct. Nevertheless, this splendid collection at last makes it possible to review the whole of Brown's works, after years when his work remained out-of-print or difficult to get. (Forty-two years separated the first and second editions of *Southern Road*.) Rereading Brown, I was struck by how consistently he shapes the tone of his poems by the meticulous selection of the right word to suggest succinctly complex images and feelings "stripped to form," in Frost's phrase. Unlike so many of his contemporaries, Brown never lapses into bathos or sentimentality. The oppressive relation of self to natural and (black and white) man-made environment Brown renders in the broadest terms, as does the blues. Yet, Brown's characters confront catastrophe with all of the irony and stoicism of the blues and black folklore. Brown's protagonists laugh and cry, fall in and out of love, and muse about death in ways not often explored in black literature. Finally, his great theme seems to be the relation of being to the individual will, rendered always in a sensuous diction, echoing what critic Joanne Gabbin calls "touchstones" of the blues lyric, such as "Don't your bed look lonesome / When your Babe packs up to leave," "I'm gonna leave heah dis mawnin' if I have to ride de blinds," "Did you ever wake up in de mo'nin', yo' mind rollin' two different ways— / One mind to leave your baby, and one mind to stay?" or "De quagmire don't hang out no signs." What's more, he is able to realize such splendid results in a variety of forms, including the classic and standard blues, the ballad, a new form that Stephen Henderson calls "the blues-ballad," the sonnet, and free verse. For the first time, we can appreciate Brown's full range, his mastery of so many traditions.

In the five-poem ballad cycle "Slim Greer," Brown has created the most memorable character in black literature, the trickster. In "Slim in Atlanta," segregation is so bad that blacks are allowed to laugh only in a phone booth:

> Hope to Gawd I may die
> If I ain't speakin' truth
> Make de niggers do their laughin'
> In a telefoam booth.

In "Slim Greer," the wily Greer in "Arkansaw" "passed for white, / An' he no lighter / Than a dark midnight / Found a nice white woman / At a dance, / Thought he was from Spain / Or else from France." Finally, it is Slim's uncontainable rhythm that betrays:

> An' he started a-tinklin'
> Some mo'nful blues,

> An' a-pattin' the time
> With No. Fourteen shoes.
> The cracker listened
> An' then he spat
> An' said, "No white man
> Could play like that. . . .
>
> Heard Slim's music
> An' then, hot damn!
> Shouted sharp— "Nigger!"
> An' Slim said, "Ma'am?"

Brown balances this sort of humor against a sort of "literate" blues, such as "Tornado Blues," a blues not meant to be sung:

> Destruction was a-drivin' it and close behind was Fear,
> Destruction was a-drivin' it hand in hand with Fear,
> Grinnin' Death and skinny Sorrow was a bringin' up de rear.
>
> Dey got some ofays, but dey mostly got de Jews an' us,
> Got some ofays, but mostly got de Jews an' us,
> Many po' boys castle done settled to a heap o' dus'.

Contrast with this stanza the meter of "Long Track Blues," a poem he recorded with piano accompaniment:

> Heard a train callin'
> Blowin' long ways down the track;
> Ain't no train due here,
> Baby, what can bring you back?
>
> Dog in the freight room
> Howlin' like he los' his mind;
> Might howl myself,
> If I was the howlin' kind.

In" Southern Road," Brown uses the structure of the worksong, modified by the call-and-response pattern of a traditional blues stanza:

> Doubleshackled—hunh—
> Guard behin';
> Doubleshackled—hunh—
> Guard behin';
> Ball an' chain, bebby,
> On my min'.
>
> White man tells me—hunh
> Damn yo' soul;

> White man tells me—hunh
> Damn yo' soul;
> Get no need, bebby,
> To be tole.

Brown is a versatile craftsman, capable of representing even destruction and death in impressively various ways. In "Sam Smiley," for example, he describes a lynching in the most detached manner: "The mob was in fine fettle, yet / The dogs were stupid-nosed; and day / Was far spent when the men drew round / The scrawny woods where Smiley lay. / The oaken leaves drowsed prettily, / The moon shone down benignly there; / And big Sam Smiley, King Buckdancer, / Buckdanced on the midnight air." On the other hand, there is a certain irony in "Children of the Mississippi": "De Lord tole Norah/Dat de flood was due, / Norah listened to de Lord / An' got his stock on board, / Wish dat de Lord / Had tole us too."

Brown also uses the folk-rhyme form, the sort of chant to which children skip rope: "Women as purty / As Kingdom Come / Ain't got no woman / Cause I'm black and dumb." He also combines sources as unlike as Scott's "Lady of the Lake" and the black folk ballad "Wild Negro Bill" in his most extended ballad "The Last Ride of Wild Bill." Often, he takes lines directly from the classic blues, as in "Ma Rainey," where three lines of Bessie Smith's "Backwater Blues" appear. Perhaps Brown is at his best when he writes of death, a subject he treats in a haunting lyricism, as in "Odyssey of Big Boy":

> Lemme be wid Casey Jones,
>   Lemme be wid Stagolee,
> Lemme be wid such like men
>   When Death takes hol' on me,
> When Death takes hol' on me. . . .
>
> Done took my livin' as it came,
>   Done grabbed my joy, done risked my life;
> Train done caught me on de trestle,
>   Man done caught me wid his wife,
> His doggone purty wife. . . .

He achieves a similar effect in "After Winter," with lines such as "He snuggles his fingers / In the blacker loam . . ." and "Ten acres unplanted / To raise dreams on / *Butterbeans fo' Clara / Sugar corn fo' Grace / An' fo' de little feller / Runnin' space.*"

When asked why he chose the black folk as his subject, Sterling Brown replied that "Where Sandburg said, 'The people, yes,' and Frost, The people, yes, maybe,' I said, 'The people, maybe, I hope!' I didn't want to attack a stereotype by idealizing. I wanted to deepen it. I wanted to understand my people. I wanted to understand what it meant to be a Negro, what the qualities of life were. With their imagination, they combine two great loves: the love of words and the love of life. Poetry results." Just as Brown's importance as a teacher can be measured through his students (such as LeRoi Jones, Kenneth Clarke, Ossie Davis, and many more), so too can his place as a poet be measured by his influence on other poets, such as Leopold Senghor, Aimé Césaire, Nicolas Guillen, Michael Harper, to list only a few. Out of Brown's realism, further, came Richard Wright's naturalism; out of his lyricism came Hurston's *Their Eyes Were Watching God;* his implicit notion that "de eye dat sees / Is de I dat be's" forms the underlying structure of *Invisible Man.* In his poetry, several somehow "black" structures of meaning have converged to form a unified and complex structure of feeling, a poetry as black as it is Brown's. This volume of poems, some of which are recorded on two Folkways albums, along with his collected prose (three major books of criticism, dozens of essays, and reviews, and a still unsurpassed anthology of black literature) being edited by Robert O'Meally and Robert Stepto, and a splendid literary biography by Joanne Gabbin, all guarantee Brown's place in literary history. Brown's prolific output coupled with a life that spans the Age of Washington through the era of Black Power, makes him not only the bridge between nineteenth- and twentieth-century black literature, but also the last of the great "race men," the Afro-American Men of Letters, a tradition best epitomized by W.E.B. Du Bois. Indeed, such a life demands an autobiography. A self-styled "Old Negro," Sterling Brown is not only the Afro-American Poet Laureate, he is a great poet.

II

"A NACHAL MAN": FORMAL AND VERNACULAR AESTHETIC THEORIES

"When de Saints Go Ma'chin' Home": Sterling Brown's Blueprint for a New Negro Poetry

Robert Burns Stepto

Perhaps it is fitting in celebrating Sterling Brown's eightieth birthday and career of great achievement to turn once again to his first published poem, "When de Saints Go Ma'ching Home."[1] It is a Big Boy Davis poem—"the guitar-plunkin" singer of marching saints is Big Boy—and it is the only "Big Boy" poem specifically dedicated to him.[2] The dedication reads:

> (*To Big Boy Davis, Friend.*
> *In Memories of Days Before He Was*
> *Chased Out of Town for Vagrancy.*)

Such a dedication has a way of bringing a smile to our lips; so much is afoot here in what is, for Brown, a typically mischievous way. Obviously, Big Boy was a character, a roustabout, a "terribly unemployed dude" as Toni Morrison would remark. Evidently, however, he was much more than a colorful vagrant in the eyes of some, those folks including Sterling Brown, the author *and* persona. While Brown appreciates and often reveres the "characters" in our shops and churches, neighborhoods and towns, and while he often writes about them, he rarely if ever dedicates poems to them. This poem is dedicated to Big Boy because he was not merely a character but a friend and guide, not merely an entertainer but an artist, and most particularly because he was a singer and

69

hence creator of community even though, in the eyes of the law, he was a man with no visible means of support.

Brown's dedication is therefore in some sense ironic: the town is not necessarily the community—especially as community may be constituted and defined by shared performances of expressive culture; the law is not necessarily the will of the people; the unemployed and allegedly idle are not necessarily bereft of direction and values and without employment of another kind. It is also a dedication that is sincere. Big Boy's example gave Sterling Brown a clear understanding of how to begin to create a written art which would not only portray or "call the names" of the folk but also perform the didactic functions of communal expressive culture. Quite to the point, "When de Saints" does not merely portray Big Boy—any more than Brown's "Ma Rainey" merely portrays that great singer. Instead, it offers, through its evocation of *a communal performance* of "When de Saints" inspired by Big Boy, a blueprint for a new poetry in what we inadequately call the folk manner.

Part I of the poem establishes Big Boy as a redoubtable storyteller and bard; as a figure who is something more than an entertainer. It also makes clear that his concert is a shared, communal, "folk" event. The first stanza reads as follows:

> He'd play, after the bawdy songs and blues,
> After the weary plaints
> Of "Trouble, Trouble deep down in muh soul,"
> Always one song in which he'd lose the rôle
> Of entertainer to the boys. He'd say,
> "My mother's favorite." And we knew
> That what was coming was his chant of saints,
> "When de saints go ma'chin' home. . . ."
> And that would end his concert for the day.[3]

One notices immediately that the "we" used throughout is not a gratuitous, editorial "we." It is an aggregate or shared "we" connoting terms like "neighbors," "kin," "listeners," "audience," and, more abstractly, "performance group." It refers to folk who will share in the chant, possibly by *being* "saints" to be numbered (as we observe in part II) or by telling or singing of Big Boy in future recreations of "When de Saints" such as the poem before us.

Like any other audience fully participating in the creation of a shared artistic event, Big Boy's gathering has certain expectations which he, as performance leader, must meet. The phrase ". . . we knew / That what was coming was his chant of saints" tells us that the audience expects (and apparently is about to receive) a repetition of an orchestrated performance witnessed before. They don't want something new. The repetition of the old songs, the reappearance of familiar, anchoring visions, and the reaffirmation of shared values are what they desire and, in some sense, require.

In this regard, a phrase such as "my mother's favorite" carries a special weight in that it advances poem and performance alike. As a written phrase, it suggests the generations "in their song," bound by the repetition within community of song contextualized in performance. But it is also an example of what David Buchan terms "received diction"—language which has "accrued a contextual force."[4] It is a coded message, a signal: the audience knows that it is to be quiet and respectful—this being the very way in which Big Boy wants it to join in. The glory of Brown's handling of all of this is that he is able to suggest in written art the full extent to which silence in a folk artistic event is voiced.

In short, throughout Part I the emphasis is not on whether Big Boy sings "When de Saints" well but on whether his singing re-creates the conditions in which shared performative events may fittingly close ("And that would end his concert for the day") and thus achieve artistic form. Part I initiates Brown's presentation of Big Boy's vocation—his work for and among the "kin" in attendance. Every suggestion that he does his work well and has always done so ("Alone with his masterchords, his memories . . .") refers us back to the charge with which the poem began—that Big Boy is a vagrant—and renders that charge more and more ludicrous.

As suggested before, Part II of "When de Saints" "calls the names" of some of the folk who'll be marching home. Once again, the communal aspects of Big Boy's performance are accentuated. Deacon Zachary, old Sis Joe, and Elder Peter Johnson are among those named or called, and one cannot help but imagine that Big Boy is weaving into his song—his song so set and familiar and yet so perpetually available for traditional acts of improvisation—the names of figures in the audience before him. These names may not have been in need of the call a year or two ago, but, apparently, they need calling now. We know that Deacon Zachary, Sis Joe, and Elder Peter Johnson are old. Perhaps they are sick as well and their time is nigh. Perhaps others, too, are in hurtful need of hearing their names called—of being listed in that number. The point is that Big Boy understands all of this, and knows what he's supposed to do to better their lot. This is why, when Big Boy calls for quiet, folks don't leave: though silent, they will share in the performance of "When de Saints."

As the section develops, we realize that all the "saints" listed are either elders or children, and that Brown willingly runs the risk of creating "plantation" stereotypes (Deacon Zachary's "coal black hair" is full of "hoggrease," etc.) in order to stress that Big Boy's roster of ". . . saints—his friends . . ." embraces everyday folk.[5] In this regard, Stephen Henderson is quite correct to suggest that in this section Brown fashions an "emblem of folk society."[6] But he's up to other things as well, matters which have much to do with his increasingly specific ideas on realism in Afro-American letters. The image of the children amongst the saints is, for example, far more complicated than it initially appears. It is at once an image of youth at play—"Wid deir skinny legs a-dancin"—and of youth in heaven, in death. They are, in Michael Harper's powerful words, "brown berries torn away." While we gain a certain solace from knowing that they are in heaven, we also can't help but wonder about the quality of the world they left behind. The portrait of an elder, Grampa Eli, prompts similar thoughts:

> "An' old Grampa Eli
> Wid his wrinkled old haid,
> A-puzzlin' over summut
> He ain' understood,
> Intendin' to ask Peter
> Pervidin' he ain't skyaid,
> 'Jes' what mought be de meanin'
> Of de moon in blood?' . . ."

Grampa Eli has good reason to be puzzled. He's a simple man perhaps, but he's not asking a simple question. Since we can assume that he knows something of the folk beliefs associated with the "blood-burning moon," it seems likely that what he's really asking is why is there fear, violence, hate, murder? What kind of world is this? Why are people that way? The stanza begins with a stereotype, or something close to it, and ends with that type unpacked or torn apart. Whatever it may be, Big Boy's chant is not a minstrel song.

While Part II of the poem lists those who will be in that number, Parts III and IV suggest who might be left out. Part III generally vilifies white folks— "*Whuffolks . . . will have to stay outside/Being so onery . . .*"—but justly asks what Big Boy is to do

> With that red brakeman who once let him ride
> An empty going home? Or with that kind-faced man
> Who paid his songs with board and drink and bed?
> Or with the Yankee Cap'n who left a leg
> At Vicksburg? . . .

His answer has just the right blend of reason and irony:

> . . . *Mought be a place, he said,*
> *Mought be another mansion fo' white saints,*
> *A smaller one than his'n . . . not so gran'.*

Part IV asks the even harder question of whether there are black folks who won't make the roster. There's an answer for that as well:

> Sportin' Legs would not be there—nor lucky Sam,
> Nor Smitty, nor Hambone, nor Hardrock Gene,
> An' not too many guzzlin', cuttin' shines,
> Nor bootleggers to keep his pockets clean.

To this list "Sophie wid de sof' smile on her face" is also added; apparently, "She mought stir trouble, somehow, in dat peaceful place."

These sections obviously suggest that Big Boy's heaven will be peopled with blacks and whites of a certain kind. For this reason, I think it is fair to say that they are the sections most responsible for various class analyses of the poem. However, I think it is a mistake to conclude, as Stephen Henderson has, that Big Boy's song must therefore be for "his middle-class friends."[7] Big Boy's vision of heaven—of a just world—is much more radical than that. Sis Joe and the Yankee Captain, Maumee Annie and the red Brakeman, the little children and the few guzzling cuttin' sisters and brothers who *will* be in that number constitute the *worthy*, not the bourgeoisie. In this regard, Parts III and IV initiate Brown's contribution to the proletarian art of the American 1930s. A direct line can be drawn from the idea of the People put forth here to that which can be found in Brown's *No Hidin' Place* poems. Big Boy's selection of saints is also Brown's selection of an audience and subject matter for a new poetry by the American Negro.

The closure of the poem is layered in a lovely way. Part V begins,

> *Ise got a dear ole mudder,*
> *She is in hebben I know—*

With these lines the song introduced as Big Boy's mother's favorite becomes rather fittingly a song about her and about meeting her in the "restful place":

> Mammy,
> Li'l mammy—wrinkled face,
> Her brown eyes, quick to tears—to joy—
> With such happy pride in her
> Guitar-plunkin' boy.
> *Oh kain't I be one in nummer? . . .*
> *I pray to de Lawd I'll meet her*
> *When de saints go ma'chin' home.*

Here, closure is achieved within the song itself. The mother joins the neighbors and distant kin already incorporated into the song. Embrace of all, but especially of the mother, occurs when Big Boy sings himself into the chant as well. With that, "When de Saints" is fully sung, and a certain exhilarating vision of community in both this and another world is complete.

But closure must also occur within the performance of which the song is but a part. Hence, there is yet another section to the poem, Part VI:

> He'd shuffle off from us, always, at that,—
> His face a brown study beneath his torn brimmed hat,
> His broad shoulders slouching, his old box strung
> Around his neck; —he'd go where we
> Never could follow him—to Sophie probably,
> Or to his dances in old Tinbridge Flat.

The shift from Big Boy's song to the persona's narrative, or, from his voice to that of a persona speaking for Big Boy's audience, completes the frame initiated in the poem's opening lines. One effect of our attention being returned to the audience is that the primacy of the total group performance over and above an individual's singing of a song is once more underscored. Another is that the audience's story or tale of Big Boy enters into a kind of harmony with Big Boy's song, the grand result being that song and tale join together to suggest the full dimensions of an enduring communal performance. Indirectly but clearly, the charge of vagrancy with which the poem begins is further qualified as well. One part of the town chased him away; the other, with strong feelings in their hearts, watched him go. Surely, by the end of the poem we know that Big Boy has vocation as well as visible support.

The Balladic Unit as a Written Form

Unlike many of the poets preceding him, including Paul Laurence Dunbar and Langston Hughes, Sterling Brown rarely passed up an opportunity to improvise upon traditional forms for the purposes of written art. Examples of this abound in "When de Saints," but the poem's first stanza is perhaps a special example in that it may be seen as a variation upon a traditional structural unit—the balladic unit—that is larger and yet less apparent than those to which the writer of poetry usually turns.

In most instances, especially in Afro-American letters, the "folk" poet focuses his or her attention on the traditional stanza, usually the quatrain readily found in balladry. Examples of this are easily found in the poetry of Frances E. W. Harper, Dunbar, Hughes, and Gwendolyn Brooks, to cite a few major authors. However, as Buchan has shown, the traditional balladeer frequently groups stanzas into pairs or triads which become the large structural units of a song, or, more precisely, of that song's performance.[8] The traditional poet never needs to say or otherwise indicate that a unit has been formed. The audience senses that this has occurred when a balance, antithesis, apposition, or parallelism initiated in one stanza (or "verse") is completed in another. Since these stanzaic units often function synchronically within the ballad with comparably significant units of character and narrative structure, they are far more conspicuous to the traditional poet's audience than are the individual stanzas comprising them. The audience is therefore usually more attentive to stanzaic units than to stanzas, and hence more aware of how they assume the greater role in the building of the song or poem.

Brown appears to have had all of this fully in mind while composing the first stanza of "When de Saints," which should be offered once again at this point:

He'd play, after the bawdy songs and blues,
After the weary plaints

Of "Trouble, Trouble deep down in muh soul,"
Always one song in which he'd lose the rôle
Of entertainer to the boys. He'd say,
"My mother's favorite." And we knew
That what was coming was his chant of saints,
"When de saints go ma'chin' home. . . ."
And that would end his concert for the day.

Within these lines, vestiges of two traditional balladic stanzas are easily found. The first quatrain is located within Brown's first four and a half lines. The second is found in what remains of the stanza after the caesura in the fifth line. While a precise construction of the two balladic quatrains is impossible, chiefly because there is no *ur*-text to retrieve and work from, it is safe to say that the first quatrain begins with "He'd play . . . ," and that "He'd say" initiates the second. Here, without going further, we can see how the quatrains balance one another and begin to form a large stanzaic unit. The movement from "He'd play . . ." to "He'd say" in and of itself completes a distinct pattern of repetition with variation. This pattern is further developed structurally when phrases of song are offered just before the closure of each stanza. In short, there is a basis in phrase and structure alike for the balancing, appositional construction of the vestigial balladic unit forming the core of Brown's written form.

What emerges here is a clear suggestion of written improvisation upon traditional art forms in which the writing artist has boldly decided to reproduce that art's structural logic instead of merely duplicating its meters, rime schemes, and signatures. In Brown's stanza, the vestigial balancing quatrains are best described as units of structure. They consist not so much of four strict lines as of four specific blocks of logic or meaning. Each quatrain adheres to an A, B, B, C pattern of development which can be charted as follows:

A: He'd play,
B: after the bawdy songs and blues,
B': After the weary plaints / Of "Trouble, Trouble deep down in muh soul,"
C: Always one song in which he'd lose the rôle / Of entertainer to the boys.
A: He'd say, / "My mother's favorite."
B: And we knew / That what was coming was his chant of saints,
B': "When de saints go ma'chin' home. . . ."
C: And that would end his concert for the day.

Obviously, the phrases isolated above cannot be sung or scanned as conventional balladic lines. Moreover, when assembled together in Brown's stanza, they create nine lines, not eight. For some, these points would indicate that

Brown is not working with the balladic model of paired quatrains. But that is not the case. Most certainly, the A, B, B', C pattern is a balladic pattern. Its presence as structure in Brown's stanza confirms that written poetry can be in some fundamental sense traditional or of the folk without displaying the outward trappings of traditional forms.

To write a stanza based upon the structural order of the balladic unit instead of the rime scheme of the individual ballad quatrain was obviously an extraordinary experiment for an Afro-American poet to undertake, especially in 1927. Brown assumed the challenge, and did so, I believe, for a high purpose. He wanted to create a written stanza full of folk expression (texts and textures) and direct reference to traditional performance (contexts).[9] He desired as well to write in such a way that reader response to his written art would at least approximate audience response to traditional performance. Finally, he also desired to fashion yet another reply to those who argued that traditional forms could not spawn a serious Afro-American written art. Quite astutely, he saw that he could achieve all three of his goals if he could render the balladic unit as a written form.

Principles for a Written Poetry

Throughout this discussion it has been suggested that "When de Saints" constitutes something of a blueprint for a new Negro poetry. More should be said at this point.

I think it is fair to say that when Brown came to the writing of poetry in the 1920s, most Afro-American poets, including especially those interested in creating a written folk poetry, were wrestling with two formidable and rather intimidating models. One, which we commonly associate with Paul Laurence Dunbar, asserted that a poetic line in the folk manner had to be transformed into "literary English" before it was capable of rendering what Dunbar termed ". . . the world's absorbing / beat."[10] The other model, displayed most successfully by James Weldon Johnson in *God's Trombones*, argued not so much for a literary standardization of the folk line as for its "classicization." Classicizing differed from standardizing in that while diction and often grammar were to be transformed, other "folk" stylistic features were to be retained or restrainfully simulated in new but clearly derivative rhythms, enjambments, and repetitive patterns. The following stanzas from Johnson's "Go Down Death (A Funeral Sermon)" illustrate my point:

> Weep not, weep not
> She is not dead;
> She's resting in the bosom of Jesus.
> Heart-broken husband—weep no more;

Grief-stricken son—weep no more;
She's only just gone home

"And Jesus took his own hand and wiped away her tears,
And he smoothed the furrows from her face,
And the angels sang a little song,
And Jesus rocked her in his arms,
And kept a-saying: Take your rest,
Take your rest, take your rest.
Weep not—weep not,
She is not dead;
She's resting in the bosom of Jesus.[11]

Johnson's ". . . Take your rest, / Take your rest, take your rest" means much the same thing, and is intended to have much the same effect, as Brown's ". . . take yo' time. . . . / Honey, take yo' bressed time" in "Sister Lou." But Johnson would have rejected Brown's version as the less artistic of the two or at least he would have done so in the years before he agreed to write the introduction to the first edition of Brown's *Southern Road*.

Both models seem to argue that the act of poetic closure figuratively expressing the full form *and* range of the Afro-American poetic canon cannot be achieved without radically altering the traditional features of the initiating or calling line. According to the Dunbar model, for example, a line like Brown's "Trouble, Trouble deep down in muh soul" must be standardized as "I know what the caged bird feels, / Alas!" before the Afro-American poet can venture a serious closing line such as "I know why the caged bird sings!" or, "The Master in infinite mercy / Offers the boon of Death."[12] In this example, not only is the traditional texture of Brown's line standardized (Dunbar's "Alas!" takes care of that) but the contextual posture of the persona-poet is altered as well. Indeed, one might say that the new artist of the standardized lines knows a great deal about the caged bird precisely because he has forsaken a performance-centered artistic posture for a writerly pose within the romantic prison of solitude.

Several of Brown's early poems such as "To a Certain Lady, in Her Garden" and "Virginia Portrait" clearly show his admiration for the Romantic poets. But others, including all the Big Boy poems, make clear that he for the most part rejected the role of the artist as self-garreted prisoner. This meant, in the terms used before, that Brown decided to commit himself not only to initiating a poem *and* canon with lines like "Trouble, Trouble deep down in muh soul" but to closing and shaping poem and canon alike with lines such as "When de saints go ma'chin' home." His point was nothing less than that "When de saints go ma'chin' home" is a stronger line than the standardized "The Master in infinite mercy / Offers the boon of Death" or the classicized "She's only just gone home." That was a bold claim to make in 1927.

From all of this, three major principles for a written Afro-American folk poetry seem to emerge, and all three principles are evident in "When de Saints." The first principle is that a poet need not abandon the "received diction" generated by a traditional culture's art events in order to give written poetic stature to an artistic form initiated within that culture. "When de saints go ma'chin' home. . . ." completes Big Boy's performance and Brown's poem alike precisely because it is fully capable of embodying and announcing a serious moment in each. A second principle is that while a writing poet cannot fully create a performance context in written art, he or she should not therefore assume that aspects of performance have no place in the written poem, or that the proper poetic posture for the writing artist is *ipso facto* a non-performative posture. Quite to the point, "When de Saints" presents both an artist (Big Boy) and a poet (Brown's persona) who, in accord with the enduring aesthetics of performance events, share in the creation of interrelated, multigeneric artistic forms. Within the context of a specific communal performance inspired by Big Boy, the poet has been a true listener. When the poet in turn tells his tale of Big Boy, his song, and the performance mutually created by singer, song, and audience, his act of listening in the past achieves one of its prefigured fulfillments in art. Building upon this, the third principle asserts that a serious moment in written art can be a shared moment. A poet need not sing, as does Dunbar's model artist, "From some high peak, nigh / yet remote," in order to evoke and sustain a fitting solemnity. As suggested before, Big Boy's quieting down of the boys schools us as to the great distinction between silence and solitude. His shift from "I" to "we"—apparent in the movement from "muh soul" to "de saints"—seems to confirm that the creation of silence can be an act of sharing voice. Brown's great point seems to be that the shared serious moments in communal performance events can be emotive and structural models for the shaping of comparable moments in written art. Put another way, performance aesthetics can abet the pursuit of written forms once the writing artist sees that he or she must emulate the performing artist *and* the performing audience alike.

The collection and vivid presentation of these principles in "When de Saints" renders that poem a major cultural and aesthetic document of the Afro-American 1920s. It "corrects" Du Bois's "Criteria for Negro Art," complements Hughes's "The Negro Writer and the Racial Mountain," and generally provides a point of view on Afro-American literature which was rarely offered by the chief movers-and-shakers of the Harlem Renaissance the exception being, of course, Zora Neale Hurston.

In "When de Saints Go Ma'ching Home," Sterling Brown introduces Big Boy Davis and his song, and presents an idea for a new poetry by American Negroes as well. The poem calls for social realism in a written American art which doesn't just portray communities but creates them. It urges the Afro-American poet to discover and pursue a new and more honest idea of the "serious moment" in written art. It calls for poems which Brown succeeded in giving us many times, and for performances of poetry much on the order of folk events which Brown also has given us time and again. We expect certain preachers to give us their "Dry Bones" sermon at Eastertime; we anticipate Big Boy's singing of "When de Saints"; and we eagerly await each and every portrait-in-performance Brown offers of Sister Lou, Big Boy, Old Lem, Slim Greer, Ma Rainey, and the Strong Men. In this way, envisioned some fifty years ago, Brown keeps what we share alive.

NOTES

This essay is based on a paper delivered at the Sterling Brown Festival, Brown University, May 1, 1981.

1. "When de Saints Go Ma'ching Home" first appeared in *Opportunity, Journal of Negro Life* 5 (July 1927): 48. It won the journal's award for poetry in 1928.

2. The other "Big Boy" poems are "Odyssey of Big Boy" and "Long Gone." "Odyssey" first appeared in *Caroling Dusk,* ed. Countee Cullen (New York: Harper and Brothers, 1927); "Long Gone" in *The Book of American Negro Poetry,* ed. James Weldon Johnson (New York: Harcourt, Brace, 1931). All three "Big Boy" poems were collected in Brown's *Southern Road* (New York: Harcourt, Brace, 1932).

3. The text of "When de Saints" used here and throughout this essay appears in *The Collected Poems of Sterling A. Brown* (New York: Harper and Row, 1980), 26–30.

4. David Buchan, *The Ballad and the Folk* (London: Routledge and Kegan Paul, 1972), 170.

5. I refer here to the "plantation tradition" in fin-de-siècle American popular literature, which Brown himself discusses in *The Negro in American Fiction* (Washington: Associates in Negro Folk Education, 1937) and *Negro Poetry and Drama* (Washington: Associates in Negro Folk Education, 1937).

6. Stephen Henderson, "The Heavy Blues of Sterling Brown: A Study of Craft and Tradition," *Black American Literature Forum* 14.1 (Spring 1980): 55. This essay is reprinted in this volume.

7. Ibid.

8. Buchan, *The Ballad and the Folk,* 87–104. This section of my discussion is substantially indebted to Buchan's analysis of the Scottish ballad.

9. The distinctions Alan Dundes makes between folk texts, textures, and contexts are by now familiar to all folklorists, if not all literary critics. They appear in various guises throughout this essay. See Dundes, "Texture, Text, and Context," *Southern Folklore Quarterly* 28 (1964): 251–65.

10. See Dunbar's "The Poet," *The Complete Poems of Paul Laurence Dunbar* (New York: Dodd, Mead, 1926), 191.

11. The text quoted here appears in *American Negro Poetry,* ed. Arna Bontemps (New York: Hill & Wang, 1963), 2–4.

12. See Dunbar's "Sympathy," 102, and "Compensation," 256, in *The Complete Poems.*

Two Writers Sharing:
Sterling A. Brown, Robert Frost,
and "In Divés' Dive"

John Edgar Tidwell

It is late at night and still I am losing,
But still I am steady and unaccusing.

As long as the Declaration guards
My right to be equal in number of cards,

It is nothing to me who runs the Dive.
Let's have a look at another five.

—Robert Frost, "In Divés' Dive"

In the recent proliferation of conference papers, critical articles, and books discussing the pioneering innovation and enduring significance of Sterling A. Brown's poetry, literary critics and historians have enthusiastically shown a propensity toward tracing the resonance of "influence" in his work. The persistence of this practice can hardly be faulted because, starting in the early 1960s, Brown began explicating himself to younger generations whom he felt were unacquainted with his seminal efforts to define the distinctiveness of African American literature and culture. In numerous formal and informal interviews, poetry readings, and public lectures, Brown professed an indebtedness to precursing and contemporary writers, including English poets (Ernest Dowson, Rudyard Kipling, Thomas Hardy, A. E. Housman), African American poets (Paul Laurence Dunbar, Langston Hughes, James Weldon Johnson, and nameless vernacular artists), and the New American Poets (E. A. Robinson, Edgar Lee Masters, Carl Sandburg, Vachel Lindsay, and Robert Frost).

In between professing and practice, though, lies a fundamental problem, if we elect to follow Brown's "stage directions" for understanding his poetic apprenticeship. We are challenged by the paradox engendered in his revelation: How can we effectively describe the uniqueness of his poetry and, at the same time, locate it within a tradition of poetry-making? Brown, as James Weldon Johnson discovered, always followed his supposed confessions about literary debt with denials about the extent to which anyone shaped and molded his work. Faced with the prospect that readers would interpret Johnson's use of "ultimate source," in his introduction to *Southern Road* (1932), to mean inartistic, slavish imitation, Brown stubbornly resisted Johnson's analysis with this rejoinder: "I think . . . you overstress the influence of the so-called folk epics. These have hardly been my *sources*. Folk experience has been" (Letter to Johnson). As a consequence of Brown's retreat, seekers after literary indebtedness find themselves entrapped in poetic miasmas, where the illusory substitutes for the real. I will argue that a relational strategy called "sharing" enables a more appropriate description of the category of influence informing Brown's uniqueness and his participation in a tradition of poetry-making.

My argument involves three basic concerns. I shall describe the concept of "influence" to reveal how its flexibility as a critical term enables a broader discussion of Brown's claim to poetic uniqueness than is generally found in previous studies of his work. Using arguably the most pointed example of Brown's acknowledged "indebtedness," that of Robert Frost and his poem "In Divés' Dive," I take up the question of how a feature of "influence" I call "sharing" provides both points of convergence and divergence between Frost's and Brown's vision of American poetic tradition. Finally, from my account of "sharing," I derive three general criteria I consider important to describing Brown's poetic distinctiveness and employ these criteria to advocate a relational strategy I believe most effectively applies to reading his work.

Recent study of "influence," as related especially to African American literature, has shown, among other things, that the way of reading literary interaction has generally centered on the imitation of white authors by African American writers. Essentially this relationship has been seen as a one-way street, with the motives of African American authors evolving out of a felt need to prove their "personal merit" and "racial merit" to whites. It's no small wonder, then, that, especially in the mid-eighteenth century, when "originality gained prominence and [when] influence [that is, homage to a venerated predecessor] grew suspect" (Mishkin 5), African American writers came to be viewed negatively as imitative and derivative. In his response cited above to James Weldon Johnson, Brown demonstrates a certain defensiveness about or sensitivity to such accusations.

In addition to showing us feelings of sensitivity, Brown's response to Johnson perfectly illustrates the usual way in which "influence" has been defined—poetic relationships having a generic or thematic connection, in which a younger writer adopts and subsequently modifies a precursing writer's subject matter, form, or style. Out of this pursuit, which theorist Tracy Mishkin develops more fully, came the critics' "interest in source-hunting" (5), which further crystallized "influence" as denoting a "father-son" relationship. Brown himself struggled against this familial metaphor in his denial to Johnson, but it is precisely the imposition of a precursor-imitator relational strategy that constrains many critics writing about Brown.

Joanne Gabbin, in the first book-length bio-critical study of Brown, has good intentions but is only partially correct when she argues that "the poets who most appealed to Brown during [his apprenticeship period] were those who used freedom as their banner: freedom to choose new materials; freedom from stilted, florid poetic diction; freedom to experiment with language, form, and subject matter in new, unconventional ways; and freedom from the kind of provincialism and Puritanism that Van Wyck Brooks said in *America's Coming of Age* has stymied the growth of literature and art in America" (31). This argument illustrates the tendency to see African American poets in terms of the "influence" exerted on them by white precursors, or even contemporaries. In her otherwise perceptive observation, Gabbin finds it unnecessary to interrogate the practitioners of florid language in an effort to determine where Brown agreed or disagreed with their practice. Nor does she explore the remnants of his apprenticeship work, found in the "Vestiges" section of his *Southern Road* (1932), to determine the origins of these poems in earlier poetic practice. Moreover, Gabbin's argument neglects to probe the intraracial conversation that took place among whites, whose preeminence became the standard critics used in defining "the tradition."

As critics writing about Brown, we can find ourselves caught in the same dilemma that Brown had to face: how to demonstrate his participation in a tradition of poetry-making while simultaneously showing his uniqueness. For Brown, the dilemma had personal implications: Like his integration-minded fellow poets, he sought to prove that he belonged socially to the American mainstream while maintaining his racial integrity as an individual.[1]

I would argue that one way out of the dilemma of precursor and imitator, of provider and receiver, and of group member and individual is through the complementarity of "influence" and "intertextuality." These two approaches, as Mishkin persuasively writes, are complementary, "for they can identify each other's weaknesses . . . thereby enhancing the study of literary interaction" (8). In a fuller, more serviceable explanation, Clayton and Rothstein observe:

> Strictly, influence should refer to relations built on dyads of transmission from one unity (author, work, tradition) to another. More broadly, however, influence studies often stray into portraits of

intellectual background, context. . . . The shape of intertextuality in turn depends on the shape of influence. One may see intertextuality either as the enlargement of a familiar idea or as an entirely new concept to replace the outmoded notion of influence. In the former case, intertextuality might be taken as a general term, working out from the broad definition of influence to encompass unconscious, socially prompted types of text formation (for example, by archetypes or popular culture); modes of conception (such as ideas "in the air"); styles (such as genres); and other prior constraints and opportunities for the writer. In the latter case, intertextuality might be used to oust and replace the kinds of issues that influence addresses, and in particular its central concern with the author and more or less conscious authorial intentions and skills. (3)

Although the terms "influence" and "intertextuality" are often distinguished by the question of agency, the issue of concurrent or overlapping features is of interest to the argument I wish to develop about Brown and Frost. To make the claim for two writers sharing is to argue the significance of intellectual background or aesthetic context. As "influence," the mode of literary interaction I call "sharing" is broadly concerned with questions of context, intellectual background, and tradition. However, "sharing," from a basis in "intertextuality," results not from the relationship between two writers but from literary interactions based on "the enlargement of a familiar idea." Clayton and Rothstein state this position in a different way when they write: "An expanded sense of influence allows one to shift one's attention from the transmission of motifs between authors to the transmission of historically given material. This shift does not do away with author-centered criticism so much as broaden it to take into account the multifarious relations that can exist among authors" (6). Implicit in the notion of expanding ideas is not a doctrinaire set of assumptions, to which a group of writers would pay obeisance; instead, expansion places ideas in conversation with each other, permitting us to examine points of convergence and divergence.

I have chosen as a case in point the literary interaction of Brown and Frost, using their only personal meeting—an occasion so poignant that it almost appears the archetypal example of "literary influence." In this momentous June 1, 1960, meeting, which held deep symbolic significance for Brown, these two venerable veterans of the culture wars paused briefly to reflect on the convergence and divergence of their lives and careers. Their animated conversation focused on the relative importance of Frost's poem "In Divés' Dive." In my mind, the exchange distilled dialogically the most important moment the two poets shared aesthetically.

We can perhaps distrust the authority of the few extant accounts of this fortuitous meeting because they're anecdotal; however, Frost biographer and *Negro*

Caravan publisher Stanley Burnshaw offers the most persuasive rendering of the moment. In his *Robert Frost: Himself*, Burnshaw remembers Brown's response to his question probing the nature of Brown's conversation with Frost: "Six great lines from *A Further Range*. Nobody mentions them. He says I'm the only one he knows who knows that poem" (138).

From this brief moment of reflection emerge two distinct and often overlapping views of poetry and literary history. For Brown, the "six great lines" revealed an essential commitment to a democratic vision of America, in which principle and practice coalesced in the body of governing documents that defined America. In his now familiar speech "A Son's Return: 'Oh, Didn't He Ramble,'" Brown tells us in an "autobiographical sounding off" how "In Divés' Dive" reveals "a strong statement of a man's belief *in America* and *in himself*" (22; emphasis added). To understand the significance of Brown's self-disclosure and to see how it accords with Frost's ideas, we must review some of Brown's cultural and political beliefs.

If we use Houston Baker's theory of "AMERICA," we can profitably explore Brown's self-described commitment to this nation. Baker argues that the defining signification of "AMERICA" is an inscribing and reinscribing discourse based in an "immanent idea of boundless, classless, raceless possibility in America" (65); in short, a committed belief in American democratic principles embraces egalitarianism and racial equality. That Brown was quite committed to these values is clear in his now familiar declaration, "I am an integrationist. . . . And by integration, I do not mean assimilation. I believe what the word means—an integer is a whole number" ("Son's Return" 18). In effect, Brown's quest to achieve full integration took him through the process of filling in the fractional status that existed vestigially for African Americans in the U.S. Constitution. Complete racial integration would be achieved, Brown believed, when the "three-fifths" clause placed in the Constitution for purposes of taxing Black slaves would be supplemented with the other two-fifths, thereby making a whole number and representing the achievement of complete humanity. Despite the survival of the "three-fifths compromise" in a body of de jure and de facto Jim Crow practices, Brown remained hopeful about the boundless possibility of America. The context provided by this sociocultural pursuit frames Brown's exegesis of "In Divés' Dive."

The poem focuses ingeniously on gambling, specifically playing poker, a game Brown says neither he nor Frost indulged in ("Son's Return" 20). In the representation of poker as a game, Frost creates a virtual setting to suggest larger ideas about full, participatory democratic politics. Brown found kinship with the speaker of the poem, who finds himself, late at night, losing in the game. "But still," the speaker proclaims, "I am steady and unaccusing." Brown saw himself in this line: Even at seventy-three (his age when he gave this presentation at Williams College), he was not "laying blame on anybody. If I lose I am not singing blues about anybody else causing it" (21). The source supporting his belief in the game and his right to participate in it was the Declaration of Independence. Shrouded in its protections, Brown agreed with the poem's speaker: "I'm not a good poker player, but . . . I'm going to play my hand out with the cards that come. And that to me is a strong statement of a man's belief in America and in himself" (22).

While "In Divés' Dive" no doubt reaffirmed Brown's passion for courage, belief in democratic principles, and more, Frost probably recalled these same qualities in the context of the controversy that surrounded *A Further Range* (1936), the collection in which "Divés'" was originally published. Although Frost's poetry, like that of most writers in the 1930s, was consumed with issues of social significance, he nevertheless found himself at the vortex of controversy with *A Further Range* because his conservative politics were misread or undervalued. Indeed, an argument can be made that *A Further Range* came under unusual critical scrutiny precisely because Frost's audience was divided on the question of art and its relation to social significance.

Part of the acclaim and part of the contentiousness for *A Further Range* derives from Frost's announcement of what he considered new poetic paths. He dedicated the collection "to E. F. for what it may mean to her that beyond the White Mountains were the Green; beyond both were the Rockies, the Sierras, and, in thought, the Andes and the Himalayas—range beyond range even into the realm of government and religion." As aesthetic statement, the dedication to Frost's wife Elinor tells us much about his charting new poetic territories. According to biographer Lawrance Thompson, Frost hit upon the idea of using "as metaphor the fact that his experiences had caused him to look across all the ranges of mountains in the United States, and thus to endow his poetry with a further range of themes, even social and political" (440). It is in this context that Burnshaw's observations must be viewed: Frost had a consuming concern for gambling; that is, not playing cards, but taking chances. What ranged beyond the mountains, beyond the explicitness of actual place was an implicit realm—the imagination. With this collection, Frost's approach was not so much one of imagined flight as of imagined confrontation, and as a consequence of this new direction, Frost suffered the ignominy of being accused of writing his first seriously flawed or simply bad book.

Critic George Nitchie typifies a large number of commentators when he called *A Further Range* "Frost's first bad book." He adds that his assessment is

> not based on the dubious proposition that a poet is somehow obligated to deal with certain preeminently social issues from a certain set of premises. Rather . . . it is based on the propositions, that, as poet, Frost seldom exhibits any very vital or immediate sense of collective aims, of broadly social values, and that in *A Further Range* he implies that such aims and such values are somehow undesirable in themselves, are absurd or unnecessary, wasteful or destructive. (112)

In this view, "social significance" means very little if it refers to proselytizing, propagandizing, or inspiring collective action. Frost seldom missed an opportunity to tout the virtues of New England life, as he saw them: independence, self-sufficiency, individualism, and so forth. Yet precisely these terms drew tremendous heat from reviewers and critics of *A Further Range,* who seemed to be divided on the significance of these qualities and on Frost's treatment of them.

Among the many critics, biographers, and literary historians who have written on Frost, Richard Poirier, in *Robert Frost: The Work of Knowing,* has emerged as one of the most articulate and persuasive spokespersons. By positioning Frost's popularity with a literate general public and a college audience that rejected modernism and Europeanized New York intellectuals against the poet's critical detractors, Poirier adeptly shows the mixed constituency to which Frost's poetry played (227). Frost was either soundly greeted or assailed, depending on the audience. Connected to this issue of audience is the problem of Frost's response. He felt that it was necessary to explicate himself, partly in response to the negative reviews of *A Further Range,* and also in an effort to gain acceptance from the very group that had lambasted him. To understand this issue is to accept the premise that Frost's politics and poetics became, as Poirier observed, "inseparable" (236–37). In an extended passage, Poirier discusses the implications of this claim:

> Frost takes his place in an American tradition which proposes that
> since you are most inconsequential when you are most "included" in
> any system or "stated plan" you are, paradoxically, most likely to find
> yourself, and to be saved, when you risk being excluded or periph-
> eral. This is a tradition full of political implications. The placement
> of the self in relation to the apparent organizations of things is one of
> the major concerns of Frost's later poetry, but it is a political concern
> only while it also reveals his more general contempt for a tendency
> in modern liberalism to discredit the capacity of ordinary, strug-
> gling people to survive in freedom and hope without the assistance
> of the state or any other kind of planning and despite the arrogant
> solicitude of those who think that such people would be better off if
> "provided" for. (264)

I wish briefly to consider one implication of this marvelous observation. Frost, rooted in the New England–Yankee tradition of self-help, railed against the New Deal fashioned by President Franklin Delano Roosevelt. The consensus among reviewers and critics that *A Further Range* was Frost's most polemical collection to date focused squarely upon its aphoristic, didactic quality as masking a rather thinly veiled but scathing denunciation of authority. Frost's conservative politics were fairly well known, and thus this collection revealed to critics a direct opposition to Franklin Delano Roosevelt, an attack which they characterized as ad hominem. It is true, as Burnshaw writes, that the New Deal represented for Frost an erosion of sorts. The dignity, the courage, the spirit of self-help that had made America *America* had suffered because of the Depression. To Frost, though, the New Deal not only bailed out many American people but threatened to create a class of "no-good dependents" by "infantilizing" them. The New England virtues of self-reliance, courage, and independence defined, for Frost, the quintessential American citizen, and the New Deal, according to this perspective, threatened to "take the starch out of self-reliant people" (Burnshaw interview).

Along with the question of denouncing authority, more than one critic wondered whether *A Further Range* represented a further elucidation of the human condition or a shriveling up of an enervated poetic talent capable only of a polemic masquerading as poetry. The basis for attacking this collection usually focused on its moralistic or didactic features, not Frost's poetic experimentation and ingenuity. It is precisely this kind of "telling" that many reviewers—some of whom were Leftists anyway—seized upon as evidence of a diminishing poetic talent whose political conservatism was out of step with current thought.

Brown, of course, agreed with Frost regarding the necessity of people to be free from systems or institutions that abridged individual freedoms. Like Frost, he appreciated the ruggedness of individual efforts and initiatives. The characterological qualities often found in Brown's portrait poems include stoicism, philosophical indifference, tonic shrewdness, and the like. However, Brown did not enjoy Frost's racial privilege, and, as a consequence, he parted company with Frost on the role of governmental systems. Brown's editorship for the Federal Writers' Project was made necessary by the proliferation of stereotyped representations of African Americans. The self—the *Black* self—in Brown's view declared itself against a worldview of racial stereotyping. What rescued the dignity of Blacks from warped imaginations and projections of difference was sheer will or an indomitable spirit. And it is this will that forced Brown into an imagined reckoning with the self and with the self in society.

Finally, if "In Divés' Dive" can be used as evidence, Brown departed from Frost regarding the relative use of folk traditions in advancing his views about democracy. The principal reference in the title of Frost's poem represents an important demarcation between Brown and Frost. Frost, in 1960, apparently knew nothing of the well known Negro spiritual containing the Divés reference. It is quite possible that he knew about Divés through the biblical parable (Luke 16: 19–31) and maybe Elizabeth Gaskell's novel *Mary Barton* (1848), whose theme "the rich don't get it" (45) foregrounds an idea that differs from Frost's. By turning to the formal differences in the several versions of the Divés story, we can infer more clearly the character of African American life as Brown represented it and begin to see how he enlarged an idea in ways Frost did not.

How Brown came to know the Divés-Lazarus story is not difficult to discern. The son of a renowned Congregationalist pastor and theologian, Brown admitted his thorough acquaintance with biblical readings. As a student of Harvard's legendary Shakespearian and folk song collector George Lyman Kittredge, Brown no doubt knew quite well the different folk song versions, too. And as principal editor of *The Negro Caravan,* Brown wrote with unusual sensitivity and insight about the Negro spiritual based on the Divés-Lazarus story, "I Got a Home in That Rock."

Fundamentally, as biblical parable, the Rich Man–Lazarus story anticipates a theme that resonates throughout the various forms containing this story: "the reversal of fortune" that takes place when both men die. In life, according to the Gospel of St. Luke, Divés (so named because *dives* in Latin means "rich man"), bedecked in his finest clothing, hosts a lavish banquet but fails to see (or sees but ignores!) the starving, sore-infested Lazarus (whose name means "God helps") who lies, at Divés's doorstep, begging crumbs from the bounteous table. At their death, Lazarus is borne away by angels to rest in the bosom of Abraham in heaven, while Rich Man Divés is ferried to hell, where his perpetually parched throat becomes his unending punishment and his anguish increases to the point of making him beg Abraham to send Lazarus with a cooling drop of water. Having been denied this wish, Divés pleads that Lazarus be sent to warn Divés's five brothers to repent of their selfish ways before they incur the fate he now experiences in hell. Abraham once again denies Divés's request because, "if they hear not Moses and the prophets, neither will they be persuaded, though one rose from the dead" (Luke 16: 31).

This sparse rendering hardly probes the complexities and interpretative debates about this parable: "If man chooses heaven on earth, will he sacrifice a real heaven after death?" "Was Divés intentionally cruel or did he mistakenly pass by Lazarus?" An analogy posed by one writer to demonstrate what he understands to be Divés's charitable nature reads: "Divés spoke about the colored races, but never saw the Negro who passed his gate. Divés discussed employment statistics, but never imagined himself a man out of work. *He did not see*" (*Interpreter's Bible* 291; emphasis added). Before one can be blamed for not taking an appropriate measure, one has to see the problem wholly and steadily. Although Brown never commented directly on this parable, it is possible to infer from his scholarship and poetry how "the reversal of fortunes" theme informs his vision of the folk.

As a folk song, "Divés and Lazarus" is only minimally related to the biblical parable, but Brown would hardly find this distinction or the problems posed by the song's encapsulating form compelling. In the ballad stanza, where the story is generally rendered in four iambic lines (the first and third being tetrameter and others trimeter, with the second and fourth lines rhyming), the song is characteristically condensed, dramatic, and impersonal. The narrator often begins with the climactic episode and tells the story's action tersely by means of action or dialogue. Most importantly, the narrator usually tells the story without self-reference or expressions of personal attitude or feelings. With little of the intrusiveness of the narrator, the situation is presented dramatically, often with a view that is unsentimental or ironic. Finally, because the narrative often has no connection between verses or scenes, there is no explanation of the events leading up to the climax of the narrative.

Consider these two verses from the *Traditional Ballads of Virginia*:

> There was a man in ancient times,
>> Dressed in purple and fine linen;
> He ate, he drank, but scorned to pray,
>> Spent all of his days in sinning
>
> Poor Lazarus lying at his gate,
>> All helpless in his condition,
> He asked the crumbs fell to the floor
>> That fell from his rich table. (Davis)

Brown would see the rather impersonal narrative voice as making almost no intrusion upon the text of the story and would understand that the listener is only brought into the narrative conflict through the song's lyrics. Brown's own artful use of the tall-tale tradition, which I've commented on elsewhere, effectively refutes the assumed formal qualities of the folk song.[2] Through his Slim Greer poems, for example, he establishes the necessity for a personal relationship through storytelling as a prerequisite for community.

But a significant feature of the Negro spiritual "I Got a Home in That Rock" is its capacity to represent, like most spirituals, a sense of community and an inspiration for changing the status quo. In *Black Song*, still the most comprehensive study of Negro spirituals, John Lovell poignantly observes that "the folk community of the spiritual believed in *poetry* as a maker and a reflector of change so powerful as to constitute magic" (196; emphasis added). The poetry and incipient political force of the lyrics identified by Lovell accord with Brown's scholarship on the spirituals.

In *The Negro Caravan* (1941), unarguably the most comprehensive literary anthology of its time, Brown wrote with assuredness and cogency about the "folk stuff," including the spirituals. In summarizing the major issues of this genre, using the precursing scholarship of Thomas Wentworth Higginson, James Weldon Johnson, W.E.B. Du Bois, Alain Locke, and Newman White, among many others, Brown wrote incisively about the folk origins of the spirituals (that is, whether they were composed by individuals or groups, derived from African or European music or combined, etc.) and especially its poetry. For Brown, the difference in metaphoric range functioned as an important difference between white and Negro spirituals:

> To hide yourself in the mountaintop
> To hide yourself from God. (White)

> Went down to the rocks to hide my face,
> The rocks cried out no hiding place. (*Negro Caravan* 417)

The similarity that exists between the two sets of lines lies in their "general idea, certainly not in the poetry" (*Negro Caravan* 417). In these two very different sets of lyrics rests a fundamental belief that permeates Brown's folk-based metaphysic: that the "poetry" of Negro folk language revealed wit, wisdom, and a worldview. Distilled in these two lines is an anthropomorphized vision of nature itself. The idea, once we leave the realm of the religious for the social, is that no place can provide refuge or escape from the encroachments or assaults made against African American humanity.

> Poor old Lazarus, poor as I, Don't you see? Don't you see? (repeat)
> Poor old Lazarus, poor as I, When he died had a home on high.
> He had a home in-a-that Rock, Don't you see?
> Rich man, Dives, lives so well, Don't you see? Don't you see? (repeat)
> Rich man, Dives, lived so well, When he died he found home in hell,
> Had no home in that Rock, Don't you see? (qtd. in Lovell 340)[3]

Brown and Lovell agreed that, in Lovell's words, ". . . in the Afro-American spiritual, universal justice straightens all, clarifies all, judges all, at long last" (Lovell 340).

The Negro spiritual thus emerges as a music of political as well as religious significance. Brown understood that the "I" in "I Got a Home in That Rock" signifies not just the individual but also the community. In this way, the Rich Man–Lazarus parable represents more than a reversal of fortunes in the next world; it offers profound hope to sustain aggrieved singers / listeners in this world. "The spirituals," Brown argues, "were born of suffering" (*Negro Caravan* 420). Rather than supporting a case for "You take dis worl', and give me Jesus," the spirituals derive their strength, their raison d'etre as "tragic poetry." That is, the language of the spirituals is rooted in a nearly cathartic emotional response to hardship, trial, and tribulation. In effect, the Divés-Lazarus parable teaches the listeners / singers that understanding selfishness, self-interest, and irresponsibility has consequences *in this world* and in the world that follows; therefore, the individual is connected to the community by love, care, and concern, and the community, in turn, is responsible to its individual members. By maintaining this sense of community, whatever befalls the group can be properly withstood.

Principally, then, the, points of convergence and divergence in Brown's and Frost's use of the Divés-Lazarus story focus on the two poets' respective associations of art and the social significance of art. Among the most focused critical comparisons of these two poets, Mark Jeffreys vacillates tellingly between Brown's indebtedness to and departure from Frost and other "New American Poets." Ultimately, though, Jeffreys is most serviceable and cogent when he comments that "Brown's acknowledgment of Frost is one of kindred spirit more than kindred technique" (214). Unlike Frost, who never had his identity of being an American questioned, Brown had to argue for recognition that he was "a part of," not relegated to being "apart from," America.

Even though Frost never had to argue for his identity as an American, he nevertheless attempted to define the meaning of being one. But being an American was important to Brown, too, as many of his poems suggest. In "Old Lem," for example, Brown subtly suggests a protracted history of legal and social customs in contrasting, minute gestures: "Their fists stay closed / Their eyes look straight / Our hands stay open / Our eyes must fall" (*Collected Poems* 81). Or in the raucous "Slim in Atlanta," in which Brown skillfully uses the techniques of the tall tale, the peripatetic Slim satirizes racial proscription and laughs the reader into understanding the ridiculousness of such practices: "Down in Atlanta, / De whitefolks got laws / For to keep all de niggers / From laughin' outdoors" (*Collected Poems* 81). Frost never had to write a poem like "Sam Smiley," whose last two lines elevate the poem out of the more direct social protest against lynching and into a cultural moment resonating with impressive power of human emotion: "And big Sam Smiley, King Buckdancer, / Buckdanced on the midnight air" (*Collected Poems* 46).

"In Divés' Dive" served quite different aesthetic and political purposes for these two writers. The traditional claim for "influence," as Mark Jeffreys correctly observes (see, especially, 221), has no merit if one poem or poet is set forth in hegemonic relation with the other. However, the special form of sharing that takes place between both writers rescues Brown from his own dilemma of how to acknowledge his participation in modifying a given body of ideas without accepting the burden of being "influenced."

NOTES

1. This difficulty with racial integration was only one of many dilemmas confronting Brown. See, for example, his steadfast disavowal of being included as a New Negro, only to contradict his own claims, as Robert Stepto has persuasively shown, by locating himself in the center of New Negro activity in New York during the 1920s.

2. See my essay "Slim Greer, Sterling A. Brown, and the Art of Tall Tale" in this volume (originally published in 1986 as "The Art of Tall Tale in the Slim Greer Poems").

3. It bears mentioning that either Brown misremembered or the *Chant of Saints* editors mistranscribed these lines in "A Son's Return." As published, two verses are transposed.

WORKS CITED

Baker, Houston. *Blues, Ideology, and Afro-American Literature: A Vernacular Theory.* Chicago: University of Chicago Press, 1984.

Brooks, Van Wyck. *America's Coming-of-Age.* New York: Huebsch, 1915.

Brown, Sterling A. *The Collected Poems of Sterling A. Brown*. Ed. Michael S. Harper. 1980. Evanston, IL: Tri-Quarterly Books, 1989.

———. Letter to James Weldon Johnson. 17 February 1932. Yale University Library.

———. Personal Interview. 2 December 1982.

———. "A Son's Return: 'Oh, Didn't He Ramble.'" 1974. Ed. Michael S. Harper and Robert Stepto. *Chant of Saints: A Gathering of Afro-American Literature, Art and Scholarship*. Champaign: University of Illinois Press, 1979. 3–22.

———. "Steady and Unaccusing: An Interview With Sterling A. Brown." With John S. Wright and John Edgar Tidwell. 2 August 1980 and 2 May 1981. This interview appears in this volume.

———, Arthur P. Davis, and Ulysses Lee, eds. *The Negro Caravan*. New York: Dryden Press, 1941.

Burnshaw, Stanley. *Robert Frost: Himself*. New York: Braziller, 1986.

———. Telephone Interview. 12 September 1990.

Clayton, Jay, and Eric Rothstein. "Figures in the Corpus: Theories of Influence and Intertextuality." *Influence and Intertextuality in Literary History*. Ed. Clayton and Rothstein. Madison: University of Wisconsin Press, 1991. 3–36.

Davis, Arthur Kyle, Jr., ed. "Divés and Lazarus." *Traditional Ballads of Virginia*. Cambridge: Harvard University Press, 1929. 175–76.

Frost, Robert. *A Further Range*. New York: Holt, 1936.

The Interpreter's Bible. Vol. 8. New York: Abingdon-Cokesbury Press, 1952.

Gaskell, Elizabeth. *Mary Barton*. 1848. New York: Viking Penguin, 1970.

Gabbin, Joanne V. *Sterling A. Brown: Building the Black Aesthetic Tradition*. Westport, CT: Greenwood, 1985.

Jeffreys, Mark. "Irony Without Condescension: Sterling A. Brown's Nod to Robert Frost." *Literary Influence and African American Writers*. Ed. Tracy Mishkin. New York: Garland, 1996. 211–29.

Lovell, John, Jr. *Black Song: The Forge and the Flame, The Story of How the Afro-American Spiritual Was Hammered Out*. New York: Macmillan, 1972.

Meyers, Jeffrey. *Robert Frost: A Biography*. Boston: Houghton Mifflin, 1996.

Mishkin, Tracy. "Theorizing Literary Influence and African-American Writers." Ed. Mishkin. *Literary Influence and African-American Writers: Collected Essays*. New York: Garland, 1996. 3–20.

Nitchie, George W. *Human Values in the Poetry of Robert Frost*. Durham: Duke University Press, 1960.

Poirier, Richard. *Robert Frost: The Work of Knowing*. Stanford: Stanford University Press, 1977.

Stepto, Robert B. "Sterling A. Brown: Outsider in the Harlem Renaissance?" *The Harlem Renaissance: Revaluations*. Ed. Amritjit Singh et al. New York: Garland, 1989. 73–81.

Thompson, Lawrance. *Robert Frost: The Years of Triumph, 1915–1938*. New York: Holt, 1970.

Tidwell, John Edgar. "The Art of Tall Tale in the Slim Greer Poems." *Cottonwood* 38–39 (1986): 170–76. Reprinted in this collection as "Slim Greer, Sterling A. Brown, and the Art of Tall Tale."

———. "Recasting Negro Life History: Sterling A. Brown and the Federal Writers' Project." *Langston Hughes Review* 13.2 (1995): 77–82.

Wagner, Linda W., ed. *Robert Frost: The Critical Reception*. New York: Burt Franklin, 1977.

Listen Br'er Sterling: The Critic as Liar [A Pre(r)amble to Essays on Sterling Brown]

Kimberly W. Benston

To speak of poetry is the curled line straightened;
to speak of doubletalk, the tongue
gone pure, the stoic line a trestle
whistlin', a man a train comin' on:

Listen Br'er Sterling
steel-drivin' man, folk-said, folk-sayin'. . .
                    —Michael Harper, "Br'er Sterling and the Rocker"

Can a literary and critical reputation be built on the basis not just of what someone has written but also what s/he has said, on kaleidoscopic traces of the tongue gone pure? Anyone interested in the future of African-American literary and cultural understanding must trust so, as a store of discursive and methodological wisdom remains lodged in the memories, tapes, and inscriptions of Sterling Brown's public presentations, extemporaneous tutorials, and other teacherly "rambles." From his "telephone booth" room at Williams' Berkshire Hall and his Lincoln University digs at "The Monastery" to the downstairs apartment at Fisk's Spence House and nearby Gillie's Barbershop, and finally at the Kearney St. house of the Howard years and untold lecture halls, libraries, community centers, and street corners in between, Sterling Brown created ritual spaces of vibrant African-American discourse where the boundaries of formal and vernacular expression were crossed and recrossed, the insistent rhythm of talking and listening constituting a vision of black collective consciousness not as system, essence, blueprint, or sentiment, but as dialogue.

Sterling Brown's capacity to speak in elegant, extended arcs of dazzling utterance no matter the occasion was legendary, and, everpercipient, he knew his own propensities: "Those of you who have to go to lunch may leave now," he once told a rapt Swarthmore College audience, "I will still be talking when you return." But one never had the sense with him of being suffocated by lengthy monologue. That is because Sterling's performances were acts of critical ventriloquism, populated by a plethora of voices whose varying tonal markings turned his perorations on art, cultural history, and political economy into a richly variegated commentary on the relation of meaning to style and context. This is true in a way not inconsistent with the purport of Brown's formal scholarship, for at all times he was concerned to dislodge rigid divisions between speech and thought and to regenerate expressive conventions reified by social antagonism, asking thereby how the African-American critical enterprise might aspire to the reliability and spontaneity of the living expressive culture of which it was becoming, very much through Brown's own efforts, an ever more vital element.

Etymologically, *talk* evokes guile, while *listening* entails laying before or bringing together an assemblage: they converge in the notion of the *lie*, conceived as a double-edged telling whose craft commands attention and accomplishes a gathering. The lie thus understood is designed to provoke awareness of relationship, implying an ethical concern for how fragmented members of a world can be reintegrated through therapeutic irony and critique. When Sterling ("Slim") Brown presented himself as "a great liar," he was doing more than signaling affiliation with contrasting traditions of vernacular narrative, tweaking protocols of scholarly "responsibility," and repositioning himself as an authoritative voice along the margins of official intellectual culture. He was describing a view of culture per se as always infused by strands, impulses, and significances that are at once contradictory and negotiable. He was also enunciating a political stance, the stance of the utopic ironist intent on creating alternative structures by positing the *as if* of counter-empirical or counter-intuitive images. As an act of cultural translation, the lie was the exemplary form of Brown's commitment to African-American culture as an engaged and "exegetical" enterprise (to cite the famous riposte to Robert Penn Warren, a retort that in itself enacted Brown's commitment to culture-as-interpretation, forcing as it does Warren's monologic erasure of black ontology—"Nigger, your breed ain't metaphysical"—into the call-and-response modality of ceaseless renaming and refiguration—"Cracker, your kind ain't exegetical").

For Sterling Brown, the dialogic, open nature of the lie suited his most penetrating modes of critical thinking better than the standard historical or literary essay (of which he was, nevertheless, a foundational master within the tradition of African-American literary and cultural critique). Combining the genres of preaching, porch-instruction, tall-telling, toasting, balladeering, and other registers of vernacular performance with an acute awareness of textualized conventions of knowledge, the Sterling Brown lie melded improvisation and learning into a peculiar exhibition of intellectual and creative power. It embodied something like the *sound* of thought, evoking a fresh interpretive grammar not only different from but subtly opposed to the prefabricated discursive systematizing that habitually passes for consequential thinking among our canons of critical discourse.

At the heart of the Sterling Brown lie as critical performance operates the process of analysis by imagining other voices. Not merely evocative of the precise inflections of African-American culture in its making, the lie's scenic projection of interactive soundings of Africanicity make it a mode at once of cultural preservation, ideological critique, and philosophical reflection. As archive, the lie extends Sterling Brown's signal function as cultural custodian, the "bearer" of black culture's "something precious" (to cop a phrase from Ralph Ellison) which Brown, more than anyone, perhaps, in this century, sought to envision as an intricately elaborated but integral "mosaic" (*The Negro Caravan*: cf. Deborah Barnes's discussion of Brown's development of this trope in his work as "curatorial anthologist"); as performance, the lie refracts and symbolically enacts Brown's capacity to move between and be at home within multiple worlds. Opening a heuristic space between apparently disconnected spheres of experience and influence, the lie produces a scene at once defamiliarized and freshly recognizable, thus generating meanings that both reimagine and restore the lie's cultural foundations. While memorializing what has been historically unheard or unnoted, the lie thus allows Brown to adventure into hidden or forbidden territory: it is at once mirror and mask.

Appropriately, the Sterling Brown lie entwines pitch-perfect characterization with a creative refusal to accept the world as it evidently "is," capturing the ambiguity, polysemy, and transformative potential buried within the culture's habits of being. In forging this complex instrument of interpretive repetition, Brown's lies typically nest still other lies, embedding his voice among others in a wily, double-dealing gesture of identification and reinvention. The following example, taken from an impromptu class in African-American poetics conducted at his house in the late 1970s, is illustrative of this conception of black expressive culture as, so to speak, a tissue of lies:

This was the scene: Du Bois—William *Edward Burghardt* Du Bois,
I should say—came calling on Booker T. one fine, and representatively
hot Alabama day. He stepped from his long, long black car, dressed
to the nines, you understand, and put his foot, carefully, into the dusty
Southern clay. As Du Bois liked to tell it, "Then, Sterling, as I approached Mr. Washington, he said to me, ever so kindly: 'Welcome,

Mr. Du Bois. We sure are very sorry about our oppressive Alabama heat, but you're mighty welcome all the same.' To which, Sterling, I replied: 'It's not the heat, my friend, it's the humility.'" To which I can imagine Booker T. responding, as easily as you please: "Why that's all right. And I'm sure we're not too proud to help you clean that cow-mess offa them fine patent-leathers, neither!"

Condensed in the heteroglossic play of distinct accents and postures, Brown offers here a succinct but expansive explication of a key African-American topos, the "Washington–Du Bois Debate," suggesting how black culture emerges not from deciding between such paradigmatic figures but through participation in their very encounter. Du Bois and Washington each "are" through and for the other; neither voice can be heard outside the other's reverberation, a view which Brown here renders as self-conscious mimic "sounding" by the participants themselves. That is, beyond the interplay of mutual inflection and deflection, Brown portrays Du Bois and Washington sharing a disposition for self-fashioning and artful recontextualization that affirms the anecdote's own encompassing idea(l) of dialogic cultural production. Remaining clear about differences of semantic intention, Brown's lie positions all three voices on the communal terrain of reciprocal recognition, demonstrating the view of "culture as process" that David Anderson explores in his contribution to this volume.

The Du Bois–Washington lie, characteristically, presents Sterling himself as the *figure between*, mediating rival but potentially complementary forms by moving sympathetically among their embedded psychosocial tonalities. As poet, critic, and teacher, he served to spark a simultaneity of what we'd been historically conditioned to regard as mutually exclusive: 'high' and 'low' idioms, and the folks that create them; elite institutions and the folks they have bypassed; democratic appeal and revolutionary assertion; etc. "I ain't got no principles," Brown half-jokes to John Tidwell and John Wright in the interview printed in this volume, and because of this "steady and unaccusing" stance before conflicting purposes and voices he could identify core convictions binding evidently irreconcilable agenda and the personalities that drove them. I have said that Brown's lies rather than his 'proper' scholarship best capture this alert and balanced posture, this (anti)principle of exegetical ethics; but perhaps such a divorce of lie from other discursive critical practices reasserts an antinomy nullified by the liar's very ethos. Perhaps we'd do better to attend to *all* of Brown's work, published and unpublished, written and otherwise recorded by memory and machine, listening everywhere for "the curled line" of his singular critical call.

Famous for the care with which he himself listened to others, especially those generally overlooked and not often enough overheard—beggars, blues people, students—Sterling Brown has not himself been sufficiently heeded. More than ever, we need to listen to Br'er Sterling. Having arrived at a crossroads of theoretical puzzlement and opportunity, flush with methodological profusion but uncertain of conceptual trajectory, contemporary African-American literary and cultural criticism would do well to closely regard Sterling Brown as a theoretician, artist, and teacher capable of making historical and cognitive contradiction the very condition of unified aesthetic, philosophic, and political purpose. Grappling as we are today with antinomies arising from the evolution of the Black Arts' insurgent Afrocentricity into various refigurations of black cultural identity (linguistic, anthropological, new historicist, feminist, and materialist, chief among them)—antinomies asking us to choose between subject and structure, pleasure and power, agency and critique, positionality and oppositionality, between eviscerating taxonomies and anticanonical convulsion, academic abstraction and political reductionism, and a host of derivative echoes of the (post)essentialist critical sermon on the abiding theme of "black is and black ain't"—Brown's habitually complementary vision, his embrace of all varieties of inspiriting "doubletalk" not merely as a strategy of survival but as a mode of awareness, offers vital touchstones of an African-American criticism that is both historicized and transformative, both dialectical and dialogical, both rooted and mobile.

Such, indeed, was the man himself. A scion of first-generation freedmen, Sterling Brown was born at the nexus of necessity and self-determination, and he always spoke with a blended passion of historical consciousness and idiosyncratic, one might even say idiomatic, possibility. As John Edgar Tidwell observes in his essay "Double Conscious Brother in the Veil," Brown was reared to appreciate the mutuality of intellectual exploration and cultural service, of secular vocation and spiritual calling. His father, legendary minister, teacher, and social organizer Rev. Sterling Nelson Brown, presented a model of deromanticized exploration, a pragmatic humanism impatient with doctrinal quarrels and capable of distinguishing between authentic feeling and factitious sentimentality, between rigorous analysis and recitation of established pieties. These attributes of intellectual and moral toughness in the face of historical complexity Sterling Allen Brown inflected with a self-assured, pungently irreverent voice insistent upon raising elusive questions about history, ethics, aesthetics, politics, and, most of all, their profound interrelatedness on the African-American scene.

Author of groundbreaking works in ethnology, musicology, folklore, cultural studies, media studies, urban and social history, and literary history (across several genres), as well as poetry that revolutionized relations between vernacular and 'classical' form (cf. Robert Stepto's study of "When de Saints Go Ma'ching Home" and Nicole Furlonge's reading of "Ma Rainey," which locate the junctures of structure and intention governing Brown's revisionary poetics), Brown went beyond current academic configurations of interdisciplinarity to ask, performatively, how do discrete cultural expressions interpenetrate one another, complicating their origins as regulative fictions and forging the intricate design of a continuous, if prismatic and conflictual, cultural field? Moving gracefully among diverse spheres of language, social power, and institutional identity that were, in his time, even more radically divided by caste, economics, law, and sensibility than they are today, Brown served as something of a courier between disparate fields of expressive endeavor, conveying urgent, carefully fashioned images of learning, craft, memory, and aspiration across borders separating academy and street, archive and jukejoint, city and province. As Eugenia Collier puts it in the moving reminiscence cannily titled "Sterling's Way," Sterling Brown functioned as a "link between worlds," part-trickster/part-guide (depending on audience), crossing frontiers, ranging from place to place and mode to mode, *not* in quest of some final vision ("I don't need no father," he asserts with characteristically insouciant defiance in "Steady and Unaccusing"), but as tireless agent of expressive mediation and hermeneutic exchange.

Such movement—the activity of interpretation *per se,* responsible but unfettered by scripted expectations—functions throughout Brown's work as a refractory principle of freedom within the shaping contours of an ever-evolving received tradition. Brown can speak at once as cultural nationalist (e.g., in his trickster play upon the scapegoating mechanisms of canon-formation: "I not only am not invited in, I ain't inviting them out here," as he says to Tidwell and Wright; cf. such pathbreaking essays as "The Negro in Washington" and "The American Race Problem as Reflected in American Literature") and anti-essentialist ironist (e.g., in his jocoserious parsing of the onomastics of skin color—see "Oh, Didn't He Ramble"), championing the ideal of an "integral" black expressive practice while patiently historicizing the limits of that practice (imposed and intrinsic), because for him culture was inherently both an historically marked site of struggle for power and recognition—a material matrix of intersecting intentions, motives, claims, and their embodied effects—and a discursively colored figure of collective desire. Accordingly, Brown viewed cultural meaning in a double frame, aesthetically and anthropologically: on the one hand, creation as diasporic identity forged meanings that were immanent and reflexive, the specific products of tropes and rhythms which are historically potential within the culture but awaiting activation by particular forms of black consciousness; on the other hand, creation as diasporic struggle was transitive and referential, immediately entering the culture's developing fund of symbolic resources. Brown's pursuit of cultural meaning, whether through poetry or critical history, thus conjoins visionary poetics with philosophical realism, bespeaking interwoven commitments to radical creativity and contextual function.

For Brown, whether (for example) 'chronicling' the boundary-crossing rambles of Big Boy Davis and Slim (see *Southern Road*) or charting the failure of national political consciousness in the "borderland" frontier of the nation's capitol (see "The Negro in Washington"), the crossroads of this "doubletalking" account of culture as both event and perspective was talk itself, the terrain of language that John Callahan characterizes as a landscape of "compassionate connections." Practicing a kind of applied Bakhtinian linguisitics *avant la lettre,* Brown's poetry and criticism alike critique mainstream canons of achievement for seeking to purify national expression by deciding "what counts" as properly accented utterrance (be that utterance literary or scholarly, artistic or athletic, customary or political), while showing with nuance how the seemingly silenced can redeploy reservoirs of national discourse for their own projects of survival and emancipation. One cannot therefore speak of Brown's experiments with dialect, on the one hand, and of his refinements of scholarly prose, on the other hand, without speaking as well of his abiding concern with structures of power and codes of exclusion. At the pulsating core of African-American expression for Brown lies always decision and struggle, a measured, if sometimes tragically framed, response to ideological pressure, be it a response of deflection or defiance.

Likewise, we might best speak of "voice" in Brown's work less as a particular matter of timbre or even characterization, identifying "Sterling's" interests with this or that one among his vociferous gallery of expressive heroes, than as the agency of ceaseless negotiation among possibilities and constraints, the conjoined means and medium of engaged consciousness. Fidelity to the subterranean pulse of this agency was always Brown's first imperative, guiding his experiments in vernacular composition (which was never intended to be heard as polished transcription), inflecting the texture of his critical "lies," and even surfacing in his admonition as director of African-American field projects for the WPA to interviewers confronting various dialects that "truth to idiom be paramount and exact truth to pronunciation secondary." Voice for Brown connotes the process of confrontation and mutual illumination by which historically conditioned figures stake their claims to knowledge and value. Thus conceptualizing the emergence of black subjectivity at the juncture of epistemological and ethical conflict, voice in Brown's work privileges neither the contingencies of history nor the individual's voluntaristic interventions, instead probing for a mode of black cultural identity that is both existential and genealogical, responsive at once to desire and to circumstance. Brown's "voice" thus represents and enables a robust dialogue on the nature of *freedom,* which, from Brown's earliest published essay (a remarkably bold and intricate discussion of the black singer Roland Hayes as both captive and guardian of an embattled black collective consciousness) to the final brilliant "rambles" of his last public tutorials, founds for him African-American culture's perseverance and fuels its ambition.

At the heart of this dialogue within Brownian voice is the contrast of freedom imagined as the end of domination and ultimate deliverance from strife, and freedom conceived as a ceaseless activity of revolt through which history may be perpetually transformed. Particularly in his images of blues singers before, between, or after their musical performances, and in his poetic narratives of everyday folk turning to spirituals for slyly doubled allegories of resistance or release, Brown deploys voice to ambiguate the origins of freedom in natural impulse or social prospect. In this way, his work presents the possibility, generally outlawed by the terms delimiting contemporary theoretical impasses, of developing an aesthetics of revolt that remains sensitive to the concrete workings of political authority while retaining interest in inventive possibilities of self-realization.

As Mark Sanders keenly suggests in his essay on *Southern Road,* what is at stake in grasping the transformative politics of Brownian voice is our sense of African-American culture's place within and against Euro-American modernism and its various critical offshoots. If, like much of post-Arnoldian High Modernism and its pedagogical installation in American New Criticism, Brown responded to the divisiveness of modernity by seeking to enfold the sensible within the beautiful and the true, he could not abide the Modernist/New Critical separation of ideas and action, its insistence on disinterestedness and objectification in the poet-critic's relation to aesthetic practice. Brown placed culture at the center of social experience, viewing it as encompassing imaginative and pragmatic thought, not in retreat from historical turmoil but as an instrument of resistance and self-invention in a world that for African-Americans was already ruthlessly objectified. Brownian irony, for example, which encodes the ideal of justice in the context of a disenchanted, fragmented world (see, for example, Brown's classic reading of Frost's "Divés' Dive" at the end of "Steady and Unaccusing," a reading that became a signature capstone to many rambles in the later years), might well be read as a dialectical riff upon, and refutation of, New Criticism's conscription of this trope as defensive bulwark of a hermetic poetry. For Brown, the antinomies of subject and object, freedom and determination, which Modernism/New Criticism can reconcile only under the aegis of the determined object, are themselves the hallmarks of a modernity riven by an unrealized democratic idealism, which has banished the subject from the messy contingencies of form in escape from the consequences of historical failure. As Michael Collins's probing of "the world of hurt" in Brown's poetry implies, Brownian irony reworks Modernism by re-adapting, not abandoning, that idealist search for value, relocating the subject in the quest for form. Hence the central role in his poetry of the blues singer's ethos of performance, beyond any particular content (though the poetry's persistent thematizing of affirmation amidst affliction frames performance's purchase on meaning and value). Hence his seminal examinations of the "image" of the black in mainstream culture, which took shape alongside his innovative encounter with specific modalities of contemporary vernacular expression: formal control was, Brown taught us, neither release nor alienation from politics, but was itself an interested and intentional act seeking to forge freedom for, not from, collective history.

At once embattled custodian of an endangered cultural memory and engaged participant in what Beverly Skinner in her essay aptly terms the subversive vernacular politics of a "blues and black aesthetic/ethnography," Sterling Brown envisioned history not as a monumental closure, an aprioristic erasure of change and difference, but as the very eruptive being of the present. Appropriately, imaginative vision, political critique, historical analysis, and cultural preservation were for him all equally *acts* shaped within a complex, changing social continuum. Our current debates pitting autonomous subjects against hegemonic institutions, essentialized agents against constructed enactments, dissolve in the face of this emphasis on the performative, situated, effective and therefore responsible "voice" of the interpretive "liar," whose provisional relation to any one terrain of meaning vitalizes rather than disables the quest for understanding. Whether as artist or critic, teacher or citizen, or rather, as all of these simultaneously, Brown modeled a timely alternative criticism, one that identified, within an "integral," but not spuriously unified, cultural field, forms of consciousness that in re-"voicing" inherited burdens with wit, grace, and style also constituted a living cultural archive. Such a criticism must hold fully and press simultaneously all sides of the contradictions it encounters as part of its own constitution: expressive culture as object and as intention; African-American experience as discrete domain and as continuous with spheres distinguished from it by various permeable borders; demystification of those who claim authority over this experience and fidelity to the obligation of refurbishing for the culture unrealized possibilities of meaning and presence. All that is forbidden in this mode of what Brown, signifyin' on his generation's anti-Romantic empiricism, called "critical realism" is naivety and indifference.

If, as Darwin Turner once remarked when surveying the landscape of African-American critical interests, "all trails lead to Sterling Brown," there may be no time better than the present to take the road back to Sterling again, much as Marcia Davis has "retraced" the way to Kearney Street as living legacy. In the foregoing remarks, I have tried to suggest conceptual foundations of such a return. But most resonant for me in Sterling Brown's example is the coordination of vocation and vision by which he lived his life. As he went about the scholarly work of forging for African-American cultural studies new intellectual tools across disciplinary, social, and discursive boundaries, and as he created for African-American literature a distinctive idiom of blues modernity, all the while Sterling Brown *taught* the next generations of strong exegetical black consciousness, taught with unmitigated passion, fluently connecting folks who imagined themselves posssessed of unbridgeably distinct sensibilities, histories, expectations, and desires. This he did not by speaking different languages in different places, but by opening himself and his auditors to the vibrant challenge of plural voices seeking knowledge, legitimation, and purpose in a shared, if scarred, cultural landscape. "My legacy is my students," he was fond of saying; or, as he put it in "Steady and Unaccusing," "my audience has been the classroom," the syntax cannily reconciling the spaces of professional, public, artistic, and educational instruction. Ours is a generation that needs to listen to Br'er Sterling the teacher-critic, making whole our too-often conflicting commitments to intellectual advancement and teacherly service. "I have listened understandingly," he tells us ("Steady and Unaccusing"); in listening to Br'er Sterling, we owe ourselves and our audience-classroom to do the same.

WORKS CITED

Brown, Sterling. A *Son's Return: Selected Essays of Sterling Brown*. Ed. Mark A. Sanders. Boston: Northeastern University Press, 1996.
———. *The Negro Caravan*. Eds. Sterling A. Brown, Arthur P. Davis, and Ulysses Lee. New York: Dryden, 1941.
———. "Ragtime and the Blues." *Sterling Brown: A UMUM Tribute*. Ed. Black History Museum Committee. Philadelphia: Black History Musuem UMUM Publishers, 1976. 76–88.
———. "Roland Hayes." *Opportunity* 3 (1925): 173–74.
———. *Southern Road*. New York: Harcourt Brace, 1932.
Mangione, Jerre. "Sterling A. Brown and the Federal Writers' Project." *Sterling Brown: A UMUM Tribute*. 16.
Tidwell, John Edgar. "Double Conscious Brother in the Veil: Toward an Intellectual Biography of Sterling A. Brown." *Callaloo* 21.4 (1998): 931–39.
Turner, Darwin T. "For Sterling Brown: A Remembrance." *Sterling Brown: A UMUM Tribute*. 22–24.

Two Lost Sonnets by Sterling A. Brown

*Edited and Introduced by John Edgar Tidwell
and Ted Genoways*

The emergence of Sterling A. Brown into poetic maturity resulted from a well-known dialectical engagement with the aesthetics of African American folk tradition. As Brown recounted so often, these experiential and imaginative encounters derived from a benevolent conspiracy between his theologian father, the Reverend Sterling Nelson Brown, and the eminent historian Carter G. Woodson to send the younger Brown South, to learn something about his people. Socially, this meant that at Virginia College and Seminary (1923–1926), before moving on to Lincoln University (1926–1928) and Fisk University (1928–1929), Sterling A. Brown began divesting himself of the confining black middle-class ethos of Washington, D.C., and of a New England–Ivy League sensibility instilled by formal education at Williams College (1918–1922) and Harvard University (1922–1923). Aesthetically, the move South meant an enthusiastic immersion into and embrace of the black South, especially its folk life, language, and lore—a relationship from which would come his best-known work. Lost, or at least understated, in this pursuit of a folk-based metaphysic is his point of departure.

Brown's quest for a distinctive, engaging poetic voice began, as it did for most writers, with the self. According to archival sources containing his "apprentice" work, the young Brown was thoroughly steeped in late nineteenth-century Victorian poetry. For example, many of these early experiments clearly show an effort to gain formal mastery of the ballad, villanelle, ballade, hymn, and sonnet. Conceptually, Brown located his vision in an aesthetic that critic David Perkins, in another context, calls "the nineteenth century convention of personal utterance" (*A History of Modern Poetry* 5). By developing themes of unrequited love, anger, self-recrimination, beauty, and self-doubt, he focused much of this early work on feelings, as if the very cultivation of emotion was poetry's raison d'être. These and other Brown poems self-consciously courted "racelessness," symbolic expression, and the romantic excess that places emotion on a poetic pedestal. Although Brown preserved the best of these early poems in the "Vestiges" section of *Southern Road* and the "Remembrances" section of *No Hiding Place*, other poems reveal much about Brown's developing proficiency.

Of these apprentice works, two poems—both sonnets—published by Brown during his lifetime remain uncollected: "For a Certain Youngster," published in *The Oracle* in March 1925, and "After the Storm," published in *The Crisis* in April 1927 (see Robert G. O'Meally's revised bibliography in this volume for full citations). Many other poems written by Brown during this same period of time remain tucked away in his notebooks, unpublished at Brown's own request. The two poems presented here then are merely representative and not meant as a complete record of his early work. They have been selected for publication because they are already available to any reader with the patience to search them out, because they are the only poems from these early trial pieces that contemporary editors thought worthy of publication, and because they contain elements of Brown's future genius that bear critical scrutiny. These poems above all else provide a context for the stylistic tectonic shift Brown would undergo.

The first issue that must be addressed is the question of the composition date of these poems—both relative to each other and to Brown's other work. Both sonnets appeared in the middle 1920s; however, examination of Brown's manuscript notebooks indicates they were composed years prior to their publication. And, although "After the Storm" was published two years later than "To a Certain Youngster," the notebook draft of "After the Storm" appears in an earlier entry, dated Spring 1921. (It appears in the same notebook as the later, undated "A Youngster to Young Men" that would eventually become "To a Certain Youngster.") This must be remembered, because the delay between acceptance and publication varied from magazine to magazine, often obscuring the chronology of composition. "After the Storm," for example, appeared in print roughly contemporary to much of the work later gathered in *Southern Road*, but it was composed at least six years prior to many of those poems. Indeed, both "After the Storm" and "To a Certain Youngster" must be considered products of a writer just entering his twenties, still experimenting with the limitations and freedoms of rhyme and meter.

Even without the assistance of Brown's careful manuscripts, "After the Storm" would be immediately recognizable as the work of a young poet. Written in a stilted, nearly Victorian diction, the poem is a strict Italian sonnet, employing only tight rhymes and occasionally indulging "poetic" contractions in order to adhere to iambic pentameter. The resulting poem is generally weak, and when it appeared in *The Crisis* in 1927, it was without Brown's consent or knowledge. When he received his copy, Brown wrote directly to the editor W.E.B. Du Bois. In a letter dated March 28, 1927, now in the Du Bois Papers at the University of Massachusetts, Brown wrote:

> I have at hand a copy of the April *Crisis* in which I see included
> a poem of mine, *After the Storm*. I am properly thankful that you
> thought it worth publishing, but I am in the dark as to how it got
> into your hands. I hope you will understand the spirit in which this
> is written. I did not expect to see it, and still do not quite understand
> the publishing of it. That bit of mystery I am writing you to clear up
> for me. Would you send me the source from which you got it?

He never received an adequate explanation of how Du Bois acquired his early poem, but Brown's displeasure is not hard to understand. By April 1927, he had published seven poems that would later appear in *Southern Road*. Among those, "Challenge," "Odyssey of Big Boy," "Return," "Salutamus," and "To a Certain Lady, in Her Garden" had been presented as a group in the prestigious *Caroling Dusk*, edited by Countee Cullen. Still more recent poems had been accepted elsewhere, including Brown's quintessential "When de Saints Go Ma'ching Home," which was scheduled to appear that summer in *Opportunity* as the winner of their annual poetry prize. By the time "After the Storm" appeared in *The Crisis*, the poem was long forgotten by Brown and was, by any critical estimation, the product of a much earlier stage of development.

Nevertheless, "After the Storm" does reveal one essential characteristic that runs throughout Brown's best work. The turn that begins the poem's second stanza moves from the abstract, objectified landscape to a more specified, human experience. The shift echoes the way many of his later poems turn from comedy, or occasionally nostalgia, to issues of immediate, even political, concern. In particular, race and art appear here for the first time in Brown's work. Stripped of its serpentine sentence structure, the central statement of the closing sestet is: "'Tis like that heart . . . / which . . . / has fitly learned / To stifle throes of pain, has ne'er rebelled / In angry bitterness, has merely turned / Gayness to pathos, with no beauty lost." The language is not Brown's, but the stunning juxtaposition and the conviction with which it is made are unmistakable.

Early assays like "After the Storm" also helped bolster Brown's increasing confidence as a poet, allowing him to explore further—testing both the demands of language and the strictures of form. "For a Certain Youngster" is one tangible product of such experimentation. The language is still occasionally hamstrung by poeticisms ("undue remorses") and clichés ("the blistering sun"); however, the voice has been transformed from proper and timid to forceful and sardonic.

Moreover, the strict iambic pentameter has been shed in favor of an accentual meter; each line contains five accents, but the syllable count varies from nine to twelve. The rhyme scheme is an invented hybrid of the Italian and English form, following an *ababbaba cdcdee* pattern. Equally important is the variation of the third *a*-rhyme, "upon." By loosening the rhyme slightly at that point, Brown mirrors the shift in voice in the poem. The lines become more heavily enjambed, the rhyme moves to the background, and for a span of several lines, the poet hints at the muscular combination of voice and rhythm that will be fully developed in later poems.

The poem printed here is taken from the version published in 1925 in *The Oracle,* the official publication of Brown's fraternity, Omega Psi Phi. The early notebook draft, titled "A Youngster to Young Men," differs little from the published version, with the notable exception of the final couplet. The draft version reads: "Were there no power forbidding us to quail/Haughtily ignorant of the words, we fail." The fact that this appears to be the only significant revision to the poem highlights the trouble Brown experienced with this final couplet. Powerful as the previous four lines are (especially the decidedly Brown-esque "to the hog level"), they rhetorically force him to condemn rebellion. Brown obviously struggled with ways to word his final couplet, searching for language that would be palatable both to himself and to his readers.

Appropriately, it is the very word "rebel" that these two early sonnets have in common. Brown's earliest rebellions against conventional forms, both poetic and social, are preserved vividly in these poems; we see a young man wrestling with the political issues that would define his work and his times. And as the historical record shows, the word "rebel" applies equally to Brown's personal need to define himself free not only from Victorian conventions of poetry but also from the encumbrance of "school" or "movement" that, in his view, robbed the poet of individuality, of aesthetic uniqueness. Arguably, one of the most compelling statements of this quest can be found in his application which won for him a Guggenheim Fellowship for 1937.

Brown wrote:

> I became ambitious to write while in college. My first years out of college were spent in Virginia; here I tried to learn as much as I could about folkways and folkspeech. These were the years of the so-called Negro Renaissance, and the Harlem school of writing. In contrast to the Harlem school I wanted to interpret the Negro of the South, who has been much dealt with by white authors, but only infrequently by Negroes. I therefore spent a great deal of time living with the folk and attempting to get as much of the truth as I could about them.

By 1937, then, Brown's quest in pursuit of voice was complete. The journey that had begun haltingly in the style of Victorian England successfully concluded—in the lives, the lore, and the language of the black South.

For a Certain Youngster

Never fear, my lad, the dark winter's rages;
Never the lightning, nor the blistering sun;
Fear not the hideous, side racking stages
Making the marathon that we must run.
See that you waste no whining words upon
The tiresome task of puzzling out the pages
Filling Life's textbook. We have but begun
Struggles that tortured all the elder ages.

Were there no power, stronger than the forces
Beating our weapons down, numbing the brain,
We must go then without undue remorses
To the hog level, forgetting our pain.
Oh, the proud power bidding us rebel,
Making from failure all we know of Hell!

After the Storm

There is a pathetic beauty in it all;
    O'erhead the murky, sullen rain-clouds pass,
    The sun's first darting rays have pierced the mass,
Just now so grim, so gray. Again the call
I heard of storm-hushed robins. Maples tall,
    To show the regal silver of their class,
    Rustle their thirst-slaked leaves and on the grass,
Drenched into higher color, some last drops fall.

'Tis like that heart, whose happiness excelled
    All others, which, with its gay threshold crossed
    At last by sorrow's gloom, has fitly learned
To stifle throes of pain, has ne'er rebelled
    In angry bitterness, has merely turned
    Gayness to pathos, with no beauty lost.

Worrying the Lines: Versification in Sterling Brown's *Southern Road*

Michael Tomasek Manson

In his influential essay on Zora Neale Hurston, Henry Louis Gates suggests that *Their Eyes Were Watching God* (1937) and *Southern Road* (1932) are "discursive analogues" in that they both *signify* "upon James Weldon Johnson's arguments against dialect" (*Signifying* 194), the idea that poets should abandon the vernacular because it has only "two full stops, humor and pathos" (Johnson 41). For Gates, both works mediate between "a profoundly lyrical, densely metaphorical, quasi-musical, privileged black oral tradition on the one hand, and a received but not yet fully appropriated standard English literary tradition on the other hand. The quandary for the writer was to find a third term, a bold and novel signifier, informed by these two related yet distinct literary languages" (*Signifying* 174). Gates concludes that Hurston found this "bold signifier" in free indirect discourse, which allowed her to express a "divided self" (209) in a "third language" (215). Building on this insight, I want to suggest that Brown and Hurston possessed selves that were not only divided by the opposition between the black vernacular and standard English but were also divided by other binaries, such as black and white, country and city, folk and modern, oral and written. The problem of the color line is thus accompanied by the problem of many lines.

In this essay, I will argue that Brown found his analogue to Hurston's free indirect discourse not in what Gates calls a third language, but in a variety of techniques, creating several languages over the course of *Southern Road*. These languages do not "mediate" or "resolve" the black vernacular and the standard English literary traditions, as Gates might lead us to expect; instead, they worry the line between those traditions and hence worry the line between black and white, country and city, folk and modern, oral and written.[1] Just as blues artists "worry a line" by bringing out different tones and multivalent meanings, so too does Brown find varying depths of feeling as he worries the lines between these four binaries. Instead of allowing these binaries to create alignments of black with the country, the folk, and an oral tradition and of white with the city, the modern, and a literary tradition, Brown worries all of these lines, reminding his readers that blacks have created vibrant expressive traditions in the city and as moderns, and that they are fully heirs of the standard English tradition.[2]

While the deconstruction of such binaries has become common, I will focus specifically on the rhythmic component of poetry. What is called the black vernacular tradition is really composed of four strands that may be woven in any number of ways. The first strand is diction and idiom, which writers often render through spelling ("de" instead of "the," for instance). A second strand is a common set of themes, ideas, and images such as the figures of Moses in spirituals or of the train in the blues. A third strand is characteristic expressive forms and genres, such as the sermon, the toast, the blues, call-and-response, or the ballad.[3] Much of the history of black literary expression is the expansion of the weave of each of these strands. Rural, Southern speech, for example, is no longer seen as more "black" than urban, Northern speech, and those categories themselves have grown even more nuanced as scholars and writers recognize how much sharing occurs across the color line. It has become more difficult to speak of a monolithic, black literary tradition and more accurate to speak fuzzily of a family of black literary traditions that has never stopped borrowing from white literary traditions.

Brown worried the lines between the black and white literary traditions, understanding in ways that often seem prescient today how much each tradition owed the other and how much each tradition was itself plural. But Brown was especially gifted at revealing the fourth, rhythmic strand of the black vernacular tradition, opening American poetry to a multiplicity of black voices and black expression that defies the binary logic that divides black from white, country from city, folk from modern, and oral from written.

The Rhythm of Subjectivity

Following Roman Jakobson, critics have long recognized that poetry differs from everyday speech in its emphasis on the signifier. Psycholinguistic theory has further suggested that poetry's unique emphasis on the signifier disrupts ordinary states of consciousness, releasing the unconscious to explore new patterns of association. Especially suggestive is the work of Antony Easthope, who, in *Poetry as Discourse* (1983), made two important claims about rhythm and meter. First, meter can create different kinds of subjectivity, either an *individuated subjectivity* that feels itself to be independent of social forces or a *communal intersubjectivity* that feels itself to be a product of various social forces. East-hope's argument is too complex to detail here, but its salient features emerge in the contrast of these two stanzas from Brown:

> Daniel was likely
> An' Daniel was handsome,
> Quick at his fingers,
> Promisin' lad;
> Joy of his hard-handed
> Bent-over mammy,
> Hope of his slow-drawlin'
> Upstandin' dad. (*Collected Poems* 31)

> Lady, my Lady, come out from the garden,
> Clay-fingered, dirty-smocked, and in my time
> I too shall learn the quietness of Arden,
> Knowledge so long a stranger to my rhyme. (*Collected Poems* 117)

While the first, from "Dark of the Moon," has an insistent rhythm that gathers all of its lines into a complete whole, the second, from "To a Certain Lady, in Her Garden," is rhythmically flexible. This distinction describes the relative ease with which readers can find and express the rhythm. Ask a group to read a poem together, and they will agree much more quickly and certainly on the rhythm of "Dark of the Moon" and will never get quite comfortable reading "To a Certain Lady" together. They will chant the first and stumble over the second. In this limited sense, the consciousness of the reader belongs to a group in "Dark of the Moon" and to an individuated self in "To a Certain Lady." "Dark of the Moon" creates a communal intersubjectivity as the voice produces and is produced by others, while "To a Certain Lady" creates an individuated subjectivity as the voice seeks to express the nuances of each line.

For example, in "To a Certain Lady," the enjambment of line 2 ("and in my time") allows the reader either to rush past or to savor that moment, while the rhythm of "Dark of the Moon" drives the poem from beginning to end. The beat of the lines is always there, regardless of how the reader colors the feelings or adjusts the pace. At the same time that readers submit to the insistent rhythm of "Dark of the Moon," the rhythm curiously liberates us as well. The common complaint about verse with an insistent rhythm is that it jangles, that the rhythms seem superimposed on the subject matter rather than arising from it. It is difficult to concentrate on the meaning of the words when the rhythm takes readers into a more trancelike state. And yet that state makes possible a particular kind of freedom as the reader's mind follows an associative path that may or may not follow the path laid out by the poem's semantic meaning. As Easthope explains, this associative freedom is the free play of the unconscious, and it is created by the way an insistent rhythm foregrounds the materiality of the signifier, liberating readers from the semantic meaning of the signified.

The reason for the difference between the two poems has everything to do with meter, but not meter in the conventional sense, with the traditional distinctions made between accentual and accentual-syllabic meters. The difference between the two poems is created by what prosodist Derek Attridge calls their "underlying meter." In his *The Rhythms of English Poetry* (1982), Attridge anticipates Easthope in describing verse as either rhythmically insistent (gathering lines into a complete whole) or rhythmically flexible, and he then sets about explaining which linguistic structures create insistent rhythms and which create flexible rhythms.[4] The result is a complex account of rhythm and meter, but at the foundation lies what Attridge calls the "4 × 4 formation," a rhythmic structure of sixteen beats that produces the most insistent rhythm possible in the English language, gathering several lines into a complete, rhythmic whole. This is the structure that creates the powerful rhythmic drive felt in "Dark of the Moon." While all of the more insistent rhythms rely on the 4 × 4 formation, there are two basic ways to create a flexible rhythm. One is to employ the 4 × 4 structure but to break one of its components so that the structure cannot have its full effect. A second way is to avoid the 4 × 4 formation altogether by relying on a different rhythmic structure. Since the English Renaissance, poets have relied on iambic pentameter, whose five-beat meter makes impossible the 4 × 4 formation, but in the twentieth century, poets began to rely instead on the several varieties of free verse, which avoid altogether the metrical structures that underlie the 4 × 4 formation. Although traditional prosody places metrical and non-metrical verse in separate categories and then divides metrical verse into such subcategories as accentual and accentual-syllabic meters, Attridge creates categories based on rhythmic effect. Insistent rhythms are created by meters based on the 4 × 4 formation, while flexible rhythms are created by free verse; by meters, such as iambic pentameter, that avoid altogether the 4 × 4 formation; or by meters that employ the 4 × 4 formation only to break it in some way.

Pulling together Easthope's account of subjectivity and Attridge's account of meter, we can say that one product of poetic rhythm is subjectivity and that different poetic rhythms create different subjectivities, either the communal intersubjectivity that feels its relationship to other social forces and that relies on meters created by the 4 × 4 formation or the individuated subjectivity that feels its independence from other social forces and that relies on meters or rhythms that avoid the 4 × 4 formation.

Easthope makes a second primary claim: that the spread of iambic pentameter in the Renaissance was part and parcel of the creation of modern, bourgeois consciousness. The great social and political changes of the Renaissance were accompanied and partially created by a change in subjectivity that had its poetic expression in the shift from meters based on the 4 × 4 formation to iambic pentameter. Feudal discourse, he argues, finds its rhythmic expression in the 4 × 4 formation, while bourgeois discourse finds its rhythmic expression in iambic pentameter. Attridge's analysis of the 4 × 4 formation helps us expand Easthope's argument to say that bourgeois discourse finds its expression in more than just iambic pentameter but in free verse and in broken 4 × 4 formations as well. Easthope thus significantly revises Jakobson's key insight that poetry differs from prose in its emphasis on the signifier by arguing that some poetry (namely, the 4 × 4 formation) emphasizes the signifier more than other poetry.

Turning to African American poetry, we find that much poetry in the black vernacular relies on the 4 × 4 formation, creating a black analogue to feudal discourse that I will call *vernacular discourse*. Like feudal discourse, vernacular discourse expresses a community not just in the three strands of diction, themes, and expressive forms, but in a fourth, rhythmic, strand—the communal intersubjectivity produced by the 4 × 4 formation. All four strands must be woven together to create a fully communal texture and a fully communal intersubjectivity. Brown will worry the lines between black and white, country and city, folk and modern, and oral and written, by manipulating in different combinations the four strands of the black vernacular: diction and idiom; the common set of themes, ideas, and images; the characteristic expressive forms and genres; and, finally, the communal intersubjectivity created by the 4 × 4 formation. Brown's manipulations of the 4 × 4 formation will make available not only the forms of consciousness Easthope describes but also add complexity to Easthope's otherwise simple distinction between feudal and bourgeois discourse. Unlike Claude McKay, who experienced what Michael North calls a "double dispossession" in dialect (110), Brown will use the 4 × 4 formation to elaborate on what McKay discovered only rarely, that "true creolization takes place at the level of sound itself," that to "break free of the hold of English . . . it is necessary to disorder it on the most fundamental level" (109). Before looking at particular poems, however, we need to look more closely at the structures that create insistent and flexible rhythms.

Understanding the 4 × 4 Formation

The 4 × 4 formation is a specific structure of sixteen beats. Attridge calls it the 4 × 4 because the sixteen-beat structure is often arranged on the page as four lines of four beats each. The 4 × 4 formation gains its characteristic rhythmic structure by creating a hierarchy out of the fundamental rhythmic principle of the English language—alternation. English is a stress-timed language that prefers to *alternate* strong stresses with weak stresses. The native

English speaker will likely adjust the pronunciation of "into" in the following sentences without thinking:

.   .   –   .   –   .   .
(1) They walked into the kitchen.

.   .   –   .   –   .   –
(2) They were walking into walls.

.   –   .   .   –
(3) They walked into walls.

In each sentence, the native speaker will pronounce *into* with a different stress, placing a strong stress on *-to* in the first sentence, a strong stress on *in-* in the second, and placing weak stresses on both syllables in the third sentence. Depending on the characteristics of their native languages, non-native speakers can find it difficult to master the English language's preference for alternation, and their speech will sound stilted and off-kilter to native speakers. Instead of proceeding word by word, speakers grasp language in units, even to the extent of adjusting prior units to match later ones:

/ . / .   /   .
I fix indoor plumbing.

. / . / . / . / .
I went indoors to fix the plumbing.

In the first sentence, native speakers of English will adjust the pronunciation of *I* and *indoor* to create a trochaic rhythm that matches *plumbing*, and, in the second sentence, they will adjust the pronunciation again to create an iambic rhythm that matches *to fix*. The rhythmic preference for alternation is that fundamental to the language.

Whenever poetry regularizes the alternation of strong and weak stresses, it creates *meter*, a rhythmic pattern of alternating beats and offbeats. The 4 × 4 formation creates a hierarchy by then alternating primary beats with secondary beats, creating ever-larger rhythmic units until it produces a single complete rhythmic whole of sixteen nested beats. Pairing works by alternating secondary beats with primary beats in order to create rhythmic units that have a call-and-response (or dipodic) structure:

CALL: Daniel

RESPONSE: was likely

The beat on "*Daniel*" is stronger than the beat on "*likely*," the alternation pairing the two beats into one, larger, two-beat structure. The 4 × 4 formation then pairs this two-beat structure to another, creating a larger, four-beat structure.

CALL: Daniel was likely

RESPONSE: An' Daniel was handsome,

The beat on the first "*Daniel*" is stronger than the beat on the second, the alternation pairing the two beats into one, larger, four-beat structure. The 4 × 4 formation then pairs this four-beat structure with another, creating a larger, eight-beat structure:

CALL: Daniel was likely / An' Daniel was handsome,

RESPONSE: Quick at his fingers, / Promisin' lad;

The beat on the first "*Daniel*" is stronger than the beat on "Quick," the alternation pairing the two beats into one, larger, eight-beat structure. The 4 × 4 formation then pairs this eight-beat structure with another, creating the final, fully realized structure of sixteen beats:

CALL: Daniel was likely / An' Daniel was handsome,
Quick at his fingers, / Promisin' lad;

RESPONSE: Joy of his hard-handed / Bent-over mammy,
Hope of his slow-drawlin' / Upstandin' dad.

Once again the first unit is heard as rhythmically more emphatic than the second. All together, this hierarchy of sixteen nested beats—with one rhythmic unit paired with another to create a larger rhythmic unit that is again paired—creates the largest structure that can be heard as a complete rhythmic whole.

Attridge calls the 4 × 4 formation an "underlying structure" because it can be packaged in so many ways. The classic expression is four lines of four beats, but, as seen in "Dark of the Moon," the 4 × 4 formation can be expressed in eight lines of two beats. Other variations are possible as long as the structure totals sixteen beats, but the picture is complicated by the existence of what Attridge calls "virtual beats,"[5] beats that are felt rhythmically but are not present on the page, as seen in "Mecca" (*Collected Poems* 105):

/   .   .   /   .   .   /   .   /
Maggie came up from Spartansburg,

/   .   / . /   [/]
Tom from Martinique,

.   / . . / .   /   .   /
They met at a Harlem house-rent stomp,

.   .   / . / . /   [/]
And were steadies in a week.

Although lines 2 and 4 have only three realized beats, readers feel a fourth beat at the end of each line, and linguists have measured the pause that most readers feel.[6] Thus, while this stanza has only fourteen realized beats, its two virtual beats bring the total up to sixteen, which is why this stanza is felt as a complete rhythmic whole. In fact, Attridge argues that the ballad stanza (with its beat pattern of 4.3.4.3) is more rhythmically insistent than long meter (with its fully realized beat pattern of 4.4.4.4).[7]

The rhythmically weakest of all of the common variations on the 4 × 4 formation is half meter (with its beat pattern of 3.3.3.3), as "Ruminations of Luke Johnson" demonstrates (*Collected Poems* 36):

> . / . / . / .   [/]
> But, ailus in de evenin'

> . / . / . / .   [/]
> A smell of somethin' greasy

> / . / . / .   [/]
> Sneaks fum out de cover,

> . / . / . /   [/]
> An' puhfumes up de road.

With sixteen total beats, half meter is still rhythmically insistent, but its many virtual beats make the whole sound less complete than ballad meter or long meter does. The 4 × 4 formation thus underlies many kinds of meter and stanza, but those different kinds of meter and stanza provide different shadings to the rhythmic insistence.

The creation of a great rhythmic whole is not merely a matter of the number of beats. The paired rhythmic units that comprise the 4 × 4 formation must be aligned with the syntax well enough that they can be felt as units, as seen in "Sam Smiley," which has sixteen beats but lacks an insistent rhythm:

> . / . / . / . /
> The whites had taught him how to rip

> . / . / . / . /
> A Nordic belly with a thrust

> . / . / . / . /
> Of bayonet, had taught him how

> . / . / . / . /
> To transmute Nordic flesh to dust. (*Collected Poems* 45)

Enjambment softens the dipodic (call-and-response) rhythm, making it less predictable and harder to hear. A flexible rhythm now prevails over an insistent one, muting elementary rhythmic forms and subordinating the signifier to the signified. Despite the surface similarity of having sixteen beats, "Sam Smiley" is closer to "To a Certain Lady" than it is to either "Dark of the Moon" or "Mecca."

"Sam Smiley" and "To a Certain Lady" create the individuated subjectivity of the standard English tradition because they mute their rhythms, while "Dark of the Moon" and "Mecca" create the communal intersubjectivity of the black vernacular tradition because they allow their rhythms to become insistent.

As Easthope explains, iambic pentameter provides an alternative to the 4 × 4 formation, and we can now see why:

/ .   . / . /   /   .   . /
Lady, my Lady, come out from the garden,

/ .   . / . /   . / . /
Clay-fingered, dirty-smocked, and in my time

. / . /   . /. / . /   .
I too shall learn the quietness of Arden,

/ .   . / . / . / . /
Knowledge so long a stranger to my rhyme.

Iambic pentameter has rightly gained the reputation of being the most natural and speechlike of meters, and its secret lies in the way the fifth beat in each line tends to defeat the language's gravitation toward dipodic rhythms. Some beats are more prominent than others, but they do not form consistent patterns or cluster into groups. By weakening any dipodic rhythm within the line, iambic pentameter weakens the alternation and pairing found in the 4 × 4 formation. The result is that it tends to create individual lines, each with its own character, while the 4 × 4 formation creates large rhythmic wholes that require a rigid architecture to hold them together.

Before turning to Brown, it might be worth pausing to say just three words about scansion. First, I use horizontal bars to indicate strong stresses and slashes to indicate metrical beats. A dot can indicate either a weak stress or an offbeat.[8] If a poem or line is not in meter, I mark the strong and weak stresses instead. Occasionally I employ both kinds of marking at the same time, so that the reader will see where I have promoted a weak stress to a beat or have demoted a strong stress to an offbeat. Second, those readers unfamiliar with Attridge's system of scansion will probably be using either a linguistic system derived from Halle and Keyser or the traditional system found in Paul Fussell's *Poetic Meter and Poetic Form* and in scores of poetry handbooks and textbooks. The traditional system marks the "actual scansion" while keeping the "metrical scansion" in our heads (Fussell 28). The advantage of linguistic systems such as Attridge's and Halle and Keyser's is that they are rule-bound, focusing on what makes some lines metrical and others not. Finally, readers should be aware that I offer my scansion as but one possible interpretation of the line, but they should also be aware that my scansions are also bound by linguistic rules that aim for consistency.

Perhaps the most important of these rules is what Otto Jespersen calls the principle of relative stress. Because the English language prefers to alternate between strong and weak stresses, it tends to promote one of three consecutive weak stresses into a stronger stress. Likewise, it tends to demote one of three consecutive strong stresses into a weaker stress. This principle is at work in the third line of "To a Certain Lady":

Clay-fingered, dirty-smocked, and in my time

I hear the phrase *and in my* as all weak stresses, but the principle of relative stress promotes *in* to a beat. This line also illustrates another place scansions are likely to differ. I hear strong stresses on both *clay* and *fin-* but have demoted *fin-* to an offbeat. Readers may make different choices, but I have consistently followed Attridge's definition of a meter as regulating the number of beats. A line of iambic pentameter can have no more or no less than five beats, and so either *clay* or *fin-* must be demoted. My choice is *fin-*, but others might hear something different. Disagreements over scansion thus often hinge on the use of different systems or on different choices of promotions and demotions.

Worrying Communal Intersubjectivity

With this foundation in Easthope and Attridge, we can examine how Brown worries the line between the black vernacular and the standard English tradition and hence the lines between black and white, country and city, folk and modern, and oral and written. Most critics have drawn a hard line between Brown's vernacular verse and his work in standard English literary forms, and yet his practice crosses this line in a variety of ways, for there are more than two terms in play here. The black vernacular does not always neatly line up with an insistent rhythmic structure and with communal intersubjectivity, nor does the standard English literary tradition always neatly line up with a flexible rhythmic line and with an individuated subjectivity.

Many of the poems in *Southern Road* are like "Dark of the Moon," which is written in a black vernacular and has a strong, insistent rhythmic structure, creating a communal intersubjectivity. "Odyssey of Big Boy," however, worries this line just a bit. Like "Dark of the Moon," the poem emphasizes the signifier. Although Brown has added a fifth line to the usual ballad stanza, the additional beats reinforce the 4 × 4 formation rather than breaking or muting it. Most of the poem creates the communal intersubjectivity produced by the 4 × 4 formation, but the last three stanzas worry the line between a communal intersubjectivity and an individuated subjectivity. The poem divides into four sections: an introduction (stanza 1), an account of Big Boy's travels and jobs (2–7), an account of his sexual conquests (8–10), and a summation of his life (11–13). Each stanza realizes the 4 × 4 formation, creating a rhythmically insistent poem right up until the end. It is in the summation that Brown worries the line. The penultimate stanza realizes the 4 × 4 formation but in a diminishing way. The stanza's 3.3.3.3.3 beat pattern suggests an existential emptiness:

> / .   /   . / .
> I done had my women,
>
> / .   /   . /
> I done had my fun;
>
> /   . /   .   / .
> Cain't do much complainin'
>
> /   . / . /
> When my jag is done,
>
> /   .   . / . /
> Lawd, Lawd, my jag is done.

As we saw earlier, the three-beat lines of half meter weaken the finality of the 4 × 4 formation just a bit, lending this stanza a touch of wistfulness, a touch of the speaker's real and individual pain. Finally, the last stanza breaks the 4 × 4 formation in the third line:

> . / . / . / .
> An' all that Big Boy axes
>
> .   /   .   / . /
> When time comes fo' to go,
>
> / . / . /   / . / . .   /
> Lemme be wid John Henry, steel drivin' man,
>
> /   . / . / /   .
> Lemme be wid old Jazzbo,
>
> /   . / . / /   .
> Lemme be wid ole Jazzbo. . . .

With six beats and the caesura splitting them 4/2 instead of 3/3, the third line breaks the pairing mechanism of the 4 × 4 formation. The stanza retains an insistent rhythm, but it loses the rhythmic completion characteristic of the 4 × 4 formation. To hear what the stanza could have been, we have only to drop the line's last phrase:

> . / . / . / .
> An' all that Big Boy axes
>
> .   /   .   / . /
> When time comes fo' to go,

/ · / · / / ·
Lemme be wid John Henry,

/ · / · / / ·
Lemme be wid old Jazzbo,

/ · / · / / ·
Lemme be wid ole Jazzbo. . . .

With a beat pattern of 3.3.4.4.4, this stanza now realizes the 4 × 4 formation and achieves a satisfying rhythmic completion. By breaking the 4 × 4 formation as he has, Brown shifts from the communal intersubjectivity produced by the other stanzas to creating something closer to an individuated subjectivity. While most of the poem asks the reader to perform Big Boy as a full member of his folk community, the final stanza asks the reader to perform Big Boy as a unique individual.

Worrying the lines in this way, Brown can capture in "Odyssey of Big Boy" the communal intersubjectivity of a rural Southern black culture while still creating a character who expresses himself, whose voice expands and contracts without ever giving the impression that he has transcended that community. For those who want to argue that the life of a rambler and womanizer is a life without meaning, Brown has asked readers to see that life as a journey as compelling as Odysseus's.[9] And for those who want to argue that black vernaculars either are trapped in stereotypes or represent a lower stage of evolution, Brown has revealed an individual voice within a collective one. He has called into question presumptions about the levels of individual expression available in the black vernacular tradition.

Worrying an Individuated Subjectivity

Although most of the poems in *Southern Road* are written in a black vernacular, a substantial number are written in standard English. Even here, however, Brown worries some subtle lines. "Sam Smiley," for example, tells the story of a World War I vet who returns to discover that his girlfriend is imprisoned for abortion. When she dies, Sam kills the "rich white man" who fathered the child. Although he had never before imagined killing a white person, the war taught him how to do just that, and the poem ends with his lynching. The poem is written in long meter (4.4.4.4), and thus it is ready at any moment to realize the 4 × 4 formation and achieve a fully insistent rhythmic shape. Up until its final stanza, however, "Sam Smiley" has a flexible rhythm, enjambing lines, muting any possibility of a dipodic rhythm, and focusing entirely on the signified. Readers hardly hear the rhyme of "war" and "before":

> He picked up, from the difficult
> But striking lessons of the war,
> Some truths that he could not forget,
> Though inconceivable before. (*Collected Poems* 45)

Most standard English poetry aims for an iconic relationship between signifier and signified, letting the sound, as Alexander Pope advised, seem an echo to the sense. Thus, through the narrator, readers feel they have access to Sam's consciousness, whose turnings are reflected in the verse itself: the artful enjambment that leads Sam from "difficult" to "striking" lessons, the qualification at the end of the stanza whose isolation in a single line makes the "inconceivable" ominous.

Because of these linguistic features, the poem creates an individuated subjectivity; readers are made to feel Sam's individualized presence, a presence that has been created in part by the very "education" whites have given him. There are troubling suggestions here: the implication that Sam does not become an individual until he has learned to kill whites; the idea that the acquisition of a new consciousness is best represented in standard English using conventional poetic forms. These suggestions are only heightened when "Sam Smiley" is compared to the poem that precedes it, "Frankie and Johnny." "Frankie and Johnny" also describes a lynching but does so in a black vernacular, realizing the 4 × 4 formation, and not allowing readers into the consciousness of any of the participants to the degree that "Sam Smiley" does. "Frankie and Johnny" appeals instead to a black vernacular tradition in which tragic love stories are well known. The poem is, of course, a variation on a well-known folk ballad, first told by English settlers and later adapted by African Americans.

From this perspective, "Sam Smiley" appears to harden the line between black and white, folk consciousness and modern, and yet very subtly the poem worries those distinctions, for at the end of the poem, the 4 × 4 formation reemerges:

> The oaken leaves drowsed prettily,
>   The moon shone down benignly there;
> And big Sam Smiley, King Buckdancer,
>   Buckdanced on the midnight air. (*Collected Poems* 46)

The third line breaks out into the familiar dipodic rhythm of the black vernacular poems:

$$. \quad / \quad . \quad / \quad . \quad / \quad . \quad / \quad .$$
And big Sam Smiley, King Buckdancer

In a poem thoroughly suffused with standard English diction and verse form, this line sounds almost like those black vernacular quotations that appear in so many of Brown's standard English poems, and yet the diction remains that of standard English. Only the rhythm suggests that Brown could have written a vernacular poem about the same subject.

The rhythm is enough, however, to remind readers that Sam's story is not outside the folk tradition. A King Buckdancer, lord of the jook joint, is already a trickster figure to be *signified* upon. Sam has been used, as has Johnny (who finally gives into temptation, having sex with a white woman despite his work ethic and his promise not to let any "cracker hussy . . . put his work behind" [44]), and Sam is as mistaken about the character of race relations as is Slim Greer (who in "Slim in Hell" takes inordinately long to learn that Dixie *is* Hell). The mortality of whites is not lost on the Scotty of "Scotty Has His Say," who teasingly threatens whites with "goofy dus'," "pisen ivy," and a "Blackcat's wishbone" and "ankle dus'" if they "wuk muh brown too hahd" (*Collected Poems* 35). Here in "Sam Smiley," with the suggestion of folk wisdom hovering over the scene, readers might recall the volume's epigraph, "O de ole sheep dey knows de road, / Young lambs gotta find de way."[10] That Sam has stumbled onto a way that African Americans have used many times before is suggested by the poem's nearly vernacular ending; he did not need a tour in Europe to learn what he did. The explicit purpose of "Sam Smiley" seems to be to explain and justify the rebelliousness of the black World War I veteran, a figure troubling to many whites; the hint of the vernacular in the last stanza suggests that that generation did not so much cross a line as tear at it in a slightly different way. The stately, tragic rhythms of this standard English poem, with its ironies about the lessons of war for African American servicemen, are both elevated and undercut by the vernacular reminder that African American life is rife with irony. Elevated because readers now add the image of a "buck" whose last "dance" is with death. Undercut because there is no new lesson here; no buckdancer can be "king" in a racist society.

"Sam Smiley" recalls black folk wisdom and the communal intersubjectivity of the black vernacular tradition by subtly recalling both elements in the meter of just one line, but such poems as "Bessie" bring black folk consciousness to bear on the standard English literary tradition in a more pointed way. The poem begins straightforwardly as iambic pentameter in standard English:

      · · / / · / · / · /   ·
Who will know Bessie now of those who loved her;

      / · · / · / · / · /
Who of her gawky pals could recognize

    / · · / · / · / · / ·
Bess in this woman, gaunt of flesh and painted,

      · _ / / · / · / _ /
Despair deep bitten in her soft brown eyes? (*Collected Poems* 49)

Although the first two stanzas have flexible rhythmic lines like those above, once the speaker begins to reflect on who Bessie was, he falls into the recognizably insistent rhythm of the 4 × 4 formation:

/ . / . / . / / . / . / .
Bessie with her plaited hair, Bessie in her gingham,

/ . / . / . . / . / . /
Bessie with her bird voice, and laughter like the sun,

/ . / . / . / . / . / .
Bess who left behind the stupid, stifling shanties,

. / . / . /. . / . / . /
And took her to the cities to get her share of fun. . . .

Here, Brown works with another manifestation of the 4 × 4 formation. Rewritten, the stanza reveals two underlying 4 × 4 formations:

/ . / . / . /
Bessie with her plaited hair,

/ . / . / . [/]
Bessie in her gingham,

/ . / . / . [/]
Bessie with her bird voice,

. / . / . / [/]
and laughter like the sun,

/ . / . / [/]
Bess who left behind

. / . / . / . [/]
the stupid, stifling shanties,

. / . / . /. [/]
And took her to the cities

. / . / . / [/]
to get her share of fun. . . .

The third stanza thus embodies in its rhythm the vernacular that Bessie left behind when she went to the city for "her share of fun." Even though the poem itself is in standard English and is thus by association a product of the city, it retains the vestiges of black folk communal intersubjectivity not only in its rhythm but in its wisdom: "Her mammy and her dad for whom she was a darling . . . wouldn't know her now, even if they were knowing, / And it's well for them they went just as soon as they did go." The conclusion that Bessie's parents are fortunate to have died before they could have seen her fate recalls the relief death brings at the ending of several of Brown's poems. Worrying the line between city and country, standard English and black vernacular, the poem "Bessie" provides a rhythmic model of how to thrive in the city and retain one's folk roots, a model that Bessie herself tragically could not follow.

Some of Brown's standard English poems, however, do not hint at a black vernacular at all. "Mill Mountain," for example, concludes the volume, and it describes an evening on which the speaker has climbed Mill Mountain with a young child. Here the city lights and the stars create a "Strange pastoral for poor city dwellers" (*Collected Poems* 126), replacing the "squalor" of the "brown city that we knew by day" with a "Place for communion," for "peace" and "love" (127). The poem is written in iambic pentameter. No line falls into an insistent rhythm, however; all remains conversational, emphasizing the signified and creating the illusion of an individual speaking voice. These qualities character-ize the final section of *Southern Road,* called "Vestiges," raising the question of whether anything remains at the end of the road Brown has described as lead-ing out of the South. What will happen to the vernacular music that Brown has captured for poetry in the previous three sections? The title "Vestiges" seems to suggest that Brown's folk heritage is a set of ideas and attitudes rather a "voice."[11] The speaker's quest for peace within a squalid city, his awareness of the dubious inheritance he has to pass on to his son, and his search for consola-tion are familiar themes in *Southern Road,* but one listens in vain for the sound of any folk inheritance. There is not even a folk image.

Although a black vernacular does not appear in the poem's rhythms, read-ers can hear a vernacular, though not necessarily a black one, in the diction: "The moon is but a lantern set by some / Old truant shepherd to light up a field / Where strange and brilliant stones sparkle at one / From the blue darkness" (126). To our ears today, the "Old truant shepherd" sounds quaintly poetic, however arresting Brown's description of the stars as "strange and brilliant stones," and yet Brown intends the passage as a rebuke to conven-tional poeticisms. The extended metaphor of the sheep as clouds and even his description of the scene as a "Strange pastoral" is meant to approximate the lush imagery of Keats while avoiding his difficult syntax and diction. The poem more directly alludes in scene and theme to Coleridge's "Frost at Mid-night," which, like "Mill Mountain," is what Coleridge called a "conversation poem," a genre whose intention is to create immediacy through an overheard conversation. And yet Coleridge's description of the stars is more "poetic" than Brown's:

> For I was reared
> In the great city, pent 'mid cloisters dim,
> And saw nought lovely but the sky and stars.

Brown's poem is more conversational, as it avoids contractions such as "'mid,'" inversions such as "cloisters dim," and antiquated terms such as "nought," "thou," and "shalt."

Brown instead takes his cue from the New Poets (Sandburg, Frost, Robinson, Masters) and seeks to represent an American idiom. Like those poets, he will use a plain diction and syntax. Avoiding any easy idealization, Brown will describe the world he knows realistically. He will set his pastoral in the city. Adapting the techniques of the New Poets, Brown's poems in standard English thus offer a parallel to the same phenomena he found working in folk songs. While some argued that the African American tradition in folk song corrupted the Anglo-American tradition and others argued that the African American tradition evinced a marked superiority in skill, Brown maintained that folk songs were an example of the hybridization of American culture: "Neither European nor African, but partaking of elements of both, the result is a new kind of music, certainly not mere imitation, but more creative and original than any other American music" ("Folk" 212). Thus, "Mill Mountain," which appears to draw a firm line between black vernaculars and standard English, asks that readers hear in the poem not only the themes of Brown's black vernacular poems but also the voices of Coleridge and Keats, Sandburg and Frost, reminding readers that Sandburg's voice includes the vernacular voices of Midwestern folk and that Frost's includes the vernacular voices of New Englanders. In a volume so dominated by black vernaculars, it is too easy to miss the fact that Brown's poems in standard English allude to other vernaculars, those of common white folk captured by the New Poets. Instead of seeing a hard line between black vernaculars and standard English, Brown appreciates the presence of other vernaculars within standard English and makes common cause with them.[12]

Brown connects Sandburg's Midwesterners, Frost's New Englanders, and his own Southerners most dramatically in "Sister Lou." The speaker of the poem advises another woman on the proper attitude to take toward death and the afterlife. She imagines a thoroughly familiar world in which the biblical Martha will be interested in her friend's recipe for "greengrape jellies" (*Collected Poems* 54) and the biblical Peter and Judas will require maternal chiding for their lapses just like anybody else— she tells her friend to "rub the po' head / Of mixed-up Judas" (*Collected Poems* 55). The poem's conclusion emphasizes Brown's repeated assertion that spirituals "reflect the slave's awareness of his bitter plight more than his consciousness of the oppression of sin" ("Folk" 215) when the speaker depicts heaven as a respite from the travails of black life rather than a deliverance from sin: "Jesus will find yo' bed for you / . . . / An' dat will be yours / Fo' keeps" (*Collected Poems* 55).

Strikingly, "Sister Lou" is Brown's one poem in vernacular free verse.[13] The poem's exceptionality is all the more remarkable given its pride of place in *Southern Road*. Brown places the poem at the end of "Road So Rocky," between the title poem and his signature piece, "Strong Men." As the poem that best captures the sensibilities of the spirituals, "Sister Lou" follows a work song and precedes Brown's credo. It is the middle panel of the triptych that anchors the volume:

>   — ·
>
>   Honey
>
>   · · —
>
>   When de man
>
> · — · — —
>
>   Calls out de las' train
>
> — · · —
>
>   You're gonna ride,
>
> — · — ·
>
>   Tell him howdy. (*Collected Poems* 54)

"Sister Lou" ranges between one and six strong stresses per line, with most lines having three or four, and yet no pattern emerges that would turn the stress rhythms into a meter, no regular rhythm propels the verse forward. Propelling it instead is the voice of the woman that readers imagine speaking these lines, making the principle that governs the poem's lineation the imitation of the pauses and of the rises and falls of speech. "Honey," for example, belongs on its own line because the speaker has paused before launching into the next phrase. This form of free verse is thus even more flexible than most poems in iambic pentameter. It mutes the signifier that much more and correspondingly elevates the signified.

 Thus, "Sister Lou" is a surprising poem in which an individuated subjectivity— an individual speaking voice—is more pronounced than it is in "Mill Mountain."[14] "Sister Lou," which is so thoroughly suffused with the spirit, ideas, diction, and voice of the African American spiritual, has nonetheless cut itself off from the communal intersubjectivity that informs the vast majority of Brown's black vernacular verse. While such poems as "Odyssey of Big Boy" articulates an individual voice within a collective one, "Sister Lou" is the one black vernacular poem that articulates only an individual voice.[15] This prominently placed poem thus goes even further than "Odyssey" in expanding the black vernacular. The black vernacular is capable of more than additional "stops" beyond humor and pathos. As Brown shows, it can express a great range of feeling, from a full communal intersubjectivity to a fully individuated subjectivity, with many points in between.

Worrying the Line between Subjectivity and Intersubjectivity

The most moving statement of Brown's heritage, of the folk roots that sustain him in the city, remains "Strong Men," not simply because it serves as

Brown's credo but also because it worries the line between the black vernacular and standard English in such a way that the two are almost indistinguishable, though the poem clearly belongs to the communal intersubjectivity Brown spends the volume trying to capture. The poem is written in vers libre, which, like free verse, usually creates a flexible rhythmic line, subordinating the signifier to the signified even more than iambic pentameter does. Vers libre is verse that has no regular meter, and yet occasionally, as T. S. Eliot put it, the "ghost" of a regular meter will return (34), as seen in "Cabaret":

Rich, flashy, puffy-faced,

Hebrew and Anglo-Saxon,

The overlords sprawl here with their glittering darlings.

The trombone belches, and the saxophone

Wails curdlingly, the cymbals clash,

The drummer twitches in an epileptic fit (*Collected Poems* 111)

The beginning of the poem establishes no regular rhythm and thus establishes no meter, which is why the scansion marks only strong stresses (_) and not beats (/). Even though the third line has five strong stresses, it sounds only faintly like iambic pentameter. Several lines later, however, a regular beat establishes itself for a brief passage of iambic pentameter and tetrameter before wandering off again into passages without a regular beat. The result is a verse that is more flexible and speech-like than iambic pentameter but less so than most free verse.

In "Strong Men," Brown creates a very different kind of vers libre. The "ghost of meter" that haunts Eliot and other writers in the standard English literary tradition is iambic pentameter, but haunting Brown is the 4 × 4 formation of the black vernacular tradition:

They dragged you from homeland,

They chained you in coffles,

$$. \quad / \quad . \quad . \quad / \quad . \quad . \quad . \quad / \quad . \quad / \quad .$$
They huddled you spoon-fashion in filthy hatches,

$$. \quad / \quad . \quad . \quad / \quad . \quad . \quad / \quad . \quad . \quad /$$
They sold you to give a few gentleman ease. (Collected Poems 56)[16]

The first two lines begin in a familiar dipodic rhythm, creating the insistence of the 4 × 4 formation. The next two lines mute this insistence either by break-ing into three units ("*They huddled you* || *spoon-fashion* || *in filthy hatches*") or by breaking unevenly ("*They sold you* || *to give a few gentleman ease*"). In both cases, the caesurae break the dipodic rhythm, giving the line a more speechlike feel. Although the line is worried and starting to lose its insistence, the anaphora continues to highlight the signifier. The repeated "they" keeps the rhythm prominent so that the poem pulses between an anaphoric insistence and the more familiar insistence of the 4 × 4 formation, which emerges again in the quotations of black folk songs:

$$/ \quad /$$
You sang:

$$/ \quad . \quad / \quad . \quad . \quad /$$
Keep a-inchin' along

$$/ \quad . \quad / \quad . \quad . \quad /$$
Like a po' inch worm. . . .

Brown creates a haunting melody here as each quotation marks its similarity to and difference from the speaker's voice. Each quotation moves readers from standard English to the black vernacular, from assertion to evidence, from talk to image. Each of these contrasts highlights the speaker's differences from the people he describes. The most dramatic difference is the suggestion that the speaker must explain the meaning of their songs, not merely to others, not merely to himself, but to them as well since the only voice of exposition is his own. And yet the speaker's voice remains with the folk in the communal inter-subjectivity created here.

More complexly still, the speaker and the folk are united by their common heritage as Americans as indicated by the epigraph from Sandburg: "The strong men keep coming on." Gesturing to the democratic spirit of the New Poets as he does in "Mill Mountain," Brown takes Sandburg's Midwestern vernacular and turns it into a black vernacular:

You sang:
Walk togedder, chillen,
Dontcha git weary. . . .
    The strong men keep a-comin' on
    The strong men git stronger.

Here, Brown comes as close as he will come to the way that Hurston uses free indirect discourse, for he has not only placed Sandburg's words into a black vernacular but has also placed expository rhetoric in the vernacular as well, although the voice is still clearly that of the standard English speaker of the poem. In the accents and rhythm of "The strong men keep a-comin' on," Brown brings together the voice of the standard English tradition, the voice of the New Poets, and the vernacular voice of the black folk.

While it is tempting to privilege "Strong Men" because it "mediates" be-tween the vernacular and standard English in much the same way that Gates claims Hurston's free indirect discourse does, the poem is only one among many, each poem worrying the line a little differently and thus creating its own language. Attending to the various rhythms of *Southern Road*—attending to its various poetic deployments of the signifier—readers thus become aware of the way that, in Aldon L. Nielsen's words, "Racial signifiers, like all signifiers, point away from themselves and slide over one another in their rush to an elsewhere. . . . Each speaking subject speaks a language of racial difference and amalgamation. Each child who comes to an American language is filled with a linguistic miscegenation and will never succeed in separating the imbricated genealogies of the English in his or her own mind" (7–8).

Brown's special achievement was to represent the many "voices" of his peo-ple while calling attention in the rhythms of his poems to the dynamic Nielsen describes—"each speaking subject" in Brown's poems does in fact speak "a language of racial difference and amalgamation," a language of rhythm as well as the strands of diction, themes, and expressive forms. The music of his poetry is, in this sense, the sound of rhythmic and other "racial signifiers" sliding over each other in their "rush to an elsewhere." This slide is Brown's "Southern road."

Critical Implications

An understanding of the rhythmic field in which *Southern Road* operates should bring greater nuance to interpretation. For a brief illustration of how we might bring such nuance, we can turn to Beverly Lanier Skinner's work on Brown. Skinner argues that Brown was a "postmodern ethnographer who by the 1940s had pioneered solutions to three major problems with which today's cultural anthropologists are grappling: (1) what form ethnographic writ-ing should take, (2) what methodology can result in competent ethnographies of non-hegemonic, oral-based cultures, and (3) what ways the authority of na-tive informants can be acknowledged in ethnographies" (417). In making this fine argument, Skinner attends only to the identity of the poem's speaker: "in poems like 'Strong Men,' 'Old Lem,' and 'Ma Rainey,' Brown distances the ethnographer's voice by using standard English-speaking personae who play the part of participant observer—the traditional role of ethnographers in the field. And he permits characters like Sister Lou, Slim Greer, Sporting Beasley, Scotty, and Big Boy to express vernacularly certain folk notions of life that standard English is hard pressed to express" (412).

While Skinner's point is largely true, the analysis in the pages above complicates and deepens her argument. The speaker of "Strong Men," for example, is more than a participant observer because he has absorbed into the rhythms of his language the rhythms of those he observes. He has made vers libre—which evolved from a standard English tradition committed to creating an individuated subjectivity—over into a black vernacular tradition of communal intersubjectivity. This observer, in other words, keeps the distance Skinner describes but also powerfully bridges that distance to find in the accents of his own language the consciousness of his people.

Similarly, both Sister Lou and Big Boy do more than "express vernacularly certain folk notions of life." While "Odyssey" remains in a black vernacular, "Sister Lou" crosses out of it in rhythm if not in language. In this gesture, Brown reminds us that native informants, despite all of their exotic difference as expressed in the ballads and toasts of the volume, also speak out of an individuated subjectivity. The black vernacular world may be an intersubjective one, but that is only its emphasis, not its entirety. In the quiet, loving humor of "Sister Lou," Brown gives the rhythmic strain of the voice of an often overlooked native informant. Skinner's analysis thus captures the breadth of Brown's accomplishment but not its depth. To plumb that depth, readers must attend more closely to the rhythmic dimension of the black vernacular. We must listen not only for the way that a poem's sound echoes its sense but also for the way that a poem's sound complicates its sense, a rhythm as every bit as complicated as our literature's racial history and racial heritage.

NOTES

I am grateful to Marianne Noble, Timothy A. Spurgin, Kathryn Tomasek, and Steven C. Tracy for their assistance on this chapter.

1. For similar reasons, I find Baker's terms "mastery of form" and "deformation of mastery" (*Modernism* 15) too restrictive for the variety of effects Brown's practice produces.

2. Sanders argues for "the radical contingencies at the heart of Brown's vision of black subjectivity. Rather than preserving for posterity folk idiomatic expression, in service of a romanticized vision of a mythic black past, Brown's poetic project unleashes from the blues, folk balladry, and the like their self-consciously modernist sensibilities and subjectivities" (10).

3. For the blues, see Baker (*Blues*), Tracy, and Williams; and for call-and-response, see Bowen. For essays that discuss Brown's work in these terms, see Sanders, Baker (*Modernism*), Benston, Gabbin, Gates (*Figures*), and Henderson.

4. Easthope relies on Attridge at times but ultimately parts with him (58). I find, however, that Attridge's approach to meter is better grounded than Easthope's and is more subtle.

5. In *Rhythms*, Attridge calls these "unrealised beats" (84), but in *Poetic*, he changes the terminology to "virtual beats" (58).

6. Readers will inevitably scan these lines differently than I have. Most common will be those who hear a strong stress on *rent* in the third line or a weak stress on *in* in the fourth. My scansion, however, follows Attridge in demoting some strong stresses to offbeats and in promoting some weak stresses to beats. For the full logic behind my scansions, see Attridge's chapter on "The Rules of English Metre" (*Rhythms* 158–213). For the linguistic studies Attridge cites concerning the existence of virtual beats, see *Rhythms* 84–96.

7. See Attridge's discussion of the rhythmic significance of the variations on the 4 × 4 formation (*Rhythms* 94–95).

8. In these markings, I have modified the single-line system of scansion Attridge proposes in *Poetic* (64–65). Attridge uses an "x" for offbeats, while I use dots. More significantly, Attridge marks strong stresses with slashes and beats with bars, while I do the opposite. For contrast, here is Attridge's marking of a four-beat line that has a demotion followed by my marking of the same scansion (*Poetic* 70):

$$x \ \underline{/} \ x \ \ x \ \underline{/} \ \ x \ \underline{/} \ \ \underline{/} \ \ \underline{/}$$
Then out in the mead the poor girl ran

$$\cdot \ \underline{/} \ \cdot \ \ \cdot \ \underline{/} \ \ \cdot \ \underline{/} \ \ \cdot \ \underline{/}$$
Then out in the mead the poor girl ran

While we agree on the scansion, I think my markings more quickly communicate that the four beats lie on *out, mead, poor, and ran.*

9. Many critics fail to register the scandalous nature of the poem for Brown's audience. Henderson, for example, claims that Big Boy possesses "clear self-knowledge and a view of the moral order of the world" (35). Sanders, meanwhile, sees John Henry "as a central symbol for both the poem and Big Boy" (45). While Brown would undoubtedly agree with Henderson, many of his readers would not, and Brown knew that. As for Henry's centrality, he is certainly the benchmark for black heroism, a benchmark shared by the middle class as well as the folk, but the middle class would draw the line at the dissolute Jazzbo, whose name Big Boy repeats and lingers on, marking Jazzbo as the more fitting representative of Big Boy's life. Brown identifies the poem's Jazzbo as Jazzbo Brown in his *Outline for the Study of Poetry of American Negroes* (35).

10. See Sanders's discussion of the epigraph (41–42).

11. Baker believes the section title "Vestiges" "implies self-conscious evolutionism in craftsmanship" (*Modernism* 100). Henderson asserts that the poems in "Vestiges" are "caught up in [the blues] spirit," but he interprets the title differently than most, saying the section is "so named because it contains poems written in the poet's earlier manner" (32). More persuasive are Sanders's account of the meaning of "Vestiges" (81–82), and even more so Smethurst's (84–85). See also Kutzinski's discussion of the meaning of the road in *Southern Road* (21), as well as Sanders's (38–41).

12. Hutchinson describes both the importance of the New Poets and the debates about the meaning of folk-song for Brown and the men and women with whom he worked (170–208). As Gabbin explains, Louis Untermeyer's anthology *Modern American Poetry* "struck Brown as a bold manifesto" (24). Brown believed his poetry would complement experiments by other American vernacular writers. For a more detailed discussion of Brown's work in the standard English literary tradition, see my article on "Vestiges," in which I explore four ways of seeing the blues in the sonnet "Challenge."

13. The meaning of the term "free verse" is still contested. In this context, I am using it to describe any verse that does not count beats and/or syllables.

14. When Easthope suggests that free verse is like four-beat verse in its emphasis on the signifier (74), he is thinking of his later analysis of Pound's *Cantos* (134–59). Most free verse, particularly contemporary free verse, is like "Sister Lou" in its attempt to capture the flexible quality of speech. Language poets and others in the Pound-Eliot tradition have found ways of emphasizing the signifier without relying on the 4 × 4 formation that Brown uses so effectively.

15. The poem's exceptionality raises some interesting questions about how gender and particularly maternity are represented in Brown's work. There are more prostitutes and fallen women than there are mothers in *Southern Road*, and "Sister Lou" is the only poem whose speaker is a woman. As the lone mother and as the lone speaker of an individualized vernacular, "Sister Lou" becomes the center of what Doyle might call a "racial matrix" for the volume.

16. My scansion of the third line should follow relative stress and promote *-shion* to a beat, but the underlying structure is pushing my ear to hear the end of a rhythmic unit after *fashion* and the beginning of another with *in*. I would not insist on this scansion.

WORKS CITED

Attridge, Derek. *Poetic Rhythm: An Introduction.* New York: Cambridge University Press, 1995.
———. *The Rhythms of English Poetry.* English Language ser. 14. London: Longman, 1982.
Baker, Houston A., Jr. *Blues, Ideology, and Afro-American Literature: A Vernacular Theory.* Chicago: University of Chicago Press, 1984.
———. *Modernism and the Harlem Renaissance.* Chicago: University of Chicago Press, 1987.
Benston, Kimberly W. "Sterling Brown's After-Song: 'When de Saints go Ma'ching Home' and the Performances of Afro-American Voice." *Callaloo* 5.1–2 (1982): 33–42.
Bowen, Barbara E. "Untroubled Voice: Call and Response in *Cane.*" In Gates, *Black Literature and Literary Theory*, 187–203.
Brown, Sterling A. *The Collected Poems of Sterling A. Brown.* Ed. Michael S. Harper. Chicago: TriQuarterly, 1989.
———. "Folk Literature." *A Son's Return: Selected Essays of Sterling A. Brown.* Ed. Mark A. Sanders. Boston: Northeastern University Press, 1996. 207–31.

————. *Outline for the Study of the Poetry of American Negroes*. New York: Harcourt Brace, 1931.

Doyle, Laura. *Bordering on the Body: The Racial Matrix of Modern Fiction and Culture*. Race and American Culture. New York: Oxford University Press, 1994.

Easthope, Antony. *Poetry as Discourse*. New Accents. London: Methuen, 1983.

Eliot, T. S. "Reflections on Vers Libre." *Selected Prose of T. S. Eliot*. Ed. Frank Kermode. New York: Harcourt Brace Jovanovich, 1975. 31–36.

Fussell, Paul. *Poetic Meter and Poetic Form*. 1965. Rev. ed. New York: Random House, 1979.

Gabbin, Joanne V. *Sterling A. Brown: Building the Black Aesthetic Tradition*. Westport, CT: Greenwood, 1985.

Gates, Henry Louis, Jr., ed. *Black Literature and Literary Theory*. New York: Methuen, 1984.

————. *The Signifying Monkey: A Theory of African-American Literary Criticism*. New York: Oxford University Press, 1988.

Halle, Morris, and Samuel Jay Keyser. *English Stress: Its Form, Its Growth, and Its Role in Verse*. New York: Harper, 1971.

Henderson, Stephen E. "The Heavy Blues of Sterling Brown: A Study of Craft and Tradition." *Black American Literature Forum* 14 (1980): 32–44. (Reprinted in this volume.)

Hutchinson, George. *The Harlem Renaissance in Black and White*. Cambridge: Harvard University Press, 1995.

Jakobson, Roman. "Concluding Statement: Linguistics and Poetics." *Style in Language*. Ed. T. A. Sebeok. Cambridge: MIT Press, 1960.

Jespersen, Otto. "Notes on Metre." 1900. *The Structure of Verse: Modern Essays on Prosody*. Ed. Harvey Gross. Greenwich, CT: Fawcett, 1966.

Johnson, James Weldon. Preface to the First Edition. *The Book of American Negro Poetry*. 2nd ed. Ed. James Weldon Johnson. New York: Harcourt Brace, 1931. 9–48.

Kutzinski, Vera M. "The Distant Closeness of Dancing Doubles: Sterling Brown and William Carlos Williams." *Black American Literature Forum* 22 (Spring 1982): 19–25.

Manson, Michael Tomasek. "Sterling Brown and the 'Vestiges' of the Blues: The Role of Race in English Verse Structure." *MELUS* 21.1 (1996): 21–40.

Nielsen, Aldon L. *Writing between the Lines: Race and Intertextuality*. Athens: University of Georgia Press, 1994.

North, Michael. *The Dialect of Modernism: Race, Language, and Twentieth-Century Literature*. Race and American Culture. New York: Oxford University Press, 1994.

Sanders, Mark A. *Afro-Modernist Aesthetics and the Poetry of Sterling A. Brown*. Athens: University of Georgia Press, 1999.

Skinner, Beverly Lanier. "Sterling Brown: An Ethnographic Perspective." *African American Review* 31 (1997): 417–22. (The essay is reprinted in this volume as "Sterling Brown: An Ethnographic Odyssey.")

Smethurst, James E. "The Strong Men Gittin' Stronger: Sterling Brown's *Southern Road* and the Representation and Re-Creation of the Southern Folk Voice." *Race and the Modern Artist*. Ed. Heather Hathaway, Josef Jarab, and Jeffrey Melnick. New York: Oxford University Press, 2003. 69–91.

Tracy, Steven C. *Langston Hughes and the Blues*. Urbana: University of Illinois Press, 1988.

Williams, Sherley Anne. "The Blues Roots of Contemporary Afro-American Poetry." *Afro-American Literature: The Reconstruction of Instruction*. Ed. Dexter Fisher and Robert B. Stepto. New York: MLA, 1979. 72–87.

III

FOLK-SAY AND
LIVING-PEOPLE-LORE

"Game to the Heart": Sterling Brown and the Badman

Robert G. O'Meally

Forget about your Jesse James,
And Billy the Kid;
I'll tell you instead what
A black boy did.

> —Sterling A. Brown, "A Bad, Bad Man"

You had what we need now, John Henry.
Help us get it.

> —Sterling A. Brown, "Strange Legacies"

Janie in Zora Neale Hurston's *Their Eyes Were Watching God* agrees with Tea Cake that blacks are subject to quick and easy classification by whites: "De ones de white man know is nice colored folks. De ones he don't know is bad niggers."[1] Nor has this subtle classification strategy been limited to the late 1920s South Florida of that novel's setting. Instead it seems to have been an enduring American system, documented in the literature of the slave trade and in the execution narratives, as early as the eighteenth century. In these latter, a disproportionate number of the gallows narrators were black, and their grueling stories were popular among whites, perhaps because of what Ralph Ellison has described as a willingness, on the part of many whites, to project onto blacks those barely suppressed fears and cravings that haunt the white psyche.[2] Little wonder that the image of the "bad nigger"—the stereotypical "brute Negro" in Sterling Brown's masterful cavalcade in his "Negro Character as Seen by White Authors"[3]—has persevered in Anglo-American literature, popular and serious. In the "bad nigger" they could examine, at the distance provided by racial antipathy and sometimes by humor, the unsuppressed will in human likeness; they could see crime personified.

But whites alone did not construct this figure of the audacious black man, the "bad nigger." He is the one, Ellison points out, who responds to the "free-floating hostility" of Harlem by becoming "enraged at the world."[4] And if we count Gabriel Prosser, Nat Turner, and Jack Johnson as magnificent badmen in Afro-American history, and Stagolee, Casey Jones, and John Henry as bad-men in Afro-American folklore, the difference in white and black perspectives is clear. For blacks, black badmen represent not so much fearful as exemplary figures. These badmen and "nachul men" were so bad and so "nachul" that they threatened to live forever in the eternal arch of myth: to kick ass (as the vernacular would have it) for one lifetime and to take names for the next. Like his counterpart and sometimes his adversary, the trickster, the badman violates social conventions and spaces, virtually at will, and thereby represents not just black disdain for American oppression (and, by extension, trouble of all sorts), but the ability to face hardship and to win. The improvising trickster fakes and shifts to freedom; the rawhide-skinned badman blasts and socks to freedom. When he does not win, the badman nonetheless goes down swinging or shooting, not sorry for his deeds, requesting no mercy at all; if anything, just "a cool drink of water before I die."[5]

In the case of black badmen like Stagolee or Railroad Bill, virtually no law or custom but their own was binding. And the ballads and tales suggest—as they do in the case of the trickster—that blacks told badmen tales in part to warn each other of the badman's impredictable violence. Stagolee and Rail-road Bill respect neither whites nor blacks, nor family structures. Even their own mothers and wives are not safe from them. Blacks seemed to spin these badman yarns with much the same didactic purpose that the trickster tales often had: to prepare one another for a topsy-turvy world of much cynicism and much trouble, a world where—who knew?—your own brother might nick-name himself Stagolee and shoot you for touching his Stetson; a fallen world where one had to remain ever at the ready. Nevertheless, what Bruce Jackson has written about the badman in Texas prisons is true for America in general: as long as there is a Stagolee with "a tombstone disposition and a graveyard mind . . . a bad motherfucker who didn't mind dying" in the place, it cannot be-come absolutely totalitarian.[6] Probably since they got here, blacks have admired black badmen, real life and folkloric, for their brash unwillingness to accept any mistreatment, and to enforce their own codes, down to whether or not you can touch their hats, with quick fists or a big gauge gun.

Not that all black badmen were created equal. At least two clear divisions are to be made in this fast company: the *bad badman,* and *moral badman.* Although one verse says that "he'd fit all the trains so the rounders could ride,"[7] otherwise black folklore's Railroad Bill was *a bad badman* "from a bad bad land," a man without limits. He "shot the lights out o' de brakeman's hand,"[8] imperiling the entire train he rides. No law governs him: he rolls his cigars inside ten-dollar-bills, and even his gun is unorthodox: "I got a .38 special on a .44 frame," he trumpets. "How in the world can I miss when I got dead aim?"[9] He was "so mean and bad," he "whipped his mammy" and "shot a round at his dad."[10]

John Henry and Joe Louis, on the other hand, are *moral badmen.* Working within American social structures, for the most part, they achieve their victories by annihilating stereotyped conceptions about black strength and aggression under pressure; by coolly beating the white man at his own game.[11] John Henry and Joe Louis recognize *certain* limits: they are loyal family men and hard workers who pursue their tasks with superhuman force and style. And they are epic heroes, whose deeds of old are too magnificent to die. Professor Guy Johnson, who tracked down the John Henry tales in the 1920s, found that all over the South black people could tell three times as much about John Henry's life as they could about Booker T. Washington's.[12]

A realist in the tradition of W. B. Yeats and Carl Sandburg, Sterling Brown stared down whatever temptations there were to counter the tinsel white images of razor-toting badmen of minstrelsy—truer to white folklore and fakelore than to black life and lore—with mere monsters of virtue: black stereotypes in reverse. Instead, Brown drew upon the rich and ironic and badman-patrolled lore of the people themselves. Indeed, his first poem of *Southern Road* (and, in turn, of the *Collected Poems*), which is "Odyssey of Big Boy,"[13] couples the name of the ancient Greek culture hero, Odysseus the shape-changer, reveler, and dragon slayer, with that of the bluesman and badman Big Boy, the sometimes gentle but tough-if-you-crossed-him singer who helped initiate Sterling Brown in his first-hand study of the black lore in and around Virginia Seminary.[14] This "Odyssey" invokes, in its first lines, the names of both bad badmen and moral badmen:

> Lemme be wid Casey Jones [*moral madman*]
> Lemme be wid Stagolee [*bad badman*]
> Lemme be wide such like men
>   When Death takes hol' on me,
>   When Death takes hol' on me . . .

Like many badmen, Big Boy is what Brown calls a "womanizer." In a few stanzas, he has a "sweet mommer on [his] knee," a "stovepipe blonde in Macon" (where such company required some badness), a "yeller gal," a "choklit brown," "two fair browns in Arkansas/And three in Tennessee," and a "Creole gal in New Orleans, / Sho Gawd did two time me— / Lawd, two time, fo' time me—."

Proving that he's more the moral badman than say, Railroad Bill (who seems to disdain all women), Big Boy sings of *a favorite* woman:

> But best gal what I evah had
>   Done put it over dem,
> A gal in Southwest Washington
>   At Four'n half and M—
>   Four'n half and M. . . .

But lest sentimentality outflank badness, the essence of which is anti-sentimentality, the poet sings these stanzas:

> Done took my livin' as it came,
>   Done grabbed my joy, done risked my life;
> Train done caught me on de trestle,
>   Man done caught me wid his wife,
>   His doggone purty wife . . .
>
> I done had my women,
>   I done had my fun;
> Cain't do much complainin'
>   When my jag is done,
>   Lawd, Lawd, my jag is done.

This poem, framed as a boast about work and women and travel—three an- tidotes to the bluesy fact that "the jag" eventually will be done—is in fact set up as an up-tempo blues, invoking the spirits of figures Big Boy needs "when Death takes hol' on me": with Casey Jones, Stagolee, and Big Boy in his band of tough angels, Death will have his hands full. Bringing the song of the spirits full circle, Big Boy speaks of himself in the third person, and calls on two more badmen to help him to confront the blue devils' "ultimate test" of death:

> An' all dat Big Boy axes
>   When time comes fo' to go,
> Lemme be wid John Henry, steel drivin' man,
>   Lemme be wid old Jazzbo
>   Lemme be wid old Jazzbo.

What Albert Murray has written about the blues hero—that he is a figure not of lamentation but of confrontation[15]—is true of the hard-hitting badman, a veteran stomper and shotgunner of the blue devils of trouble and defeat. Bad- men and near-badmen confront trouble in many Brown poems. Several are just bad and mean, like Stagolee, and are, like Stack, very aware of personal style and very willing to fight about it. Scrappy, in "Puttin' on Dog,"[16] drives and dresses for square-business:

> With a brandnew silk shirt pink as a sunset,
> With a pair suspenders blue as the sky,

> With bulldog brogans red as a clay road—
> Pull up, mule wagons, let the mail train by.

In the poolroom, Buck is angry at the sight of the stylish traveler and badman, and says something smart to our hero, Scrappy, who wastes no time in his reply. Scrappy "winds up like Babe Ruth aimin' for a homer / And bends his cuestick around Buck's head." Badman Scrappy shares the disdain of Stagolee or Railroad Bill for laws and lawmen:

> He laughed with his lawyers, and he winked at the judge,
> Stuck his fingers up his nose at the jury in the dock. . . .

The rogue returns to his role as man of style and ladies' man as he

> Waved good-by to the gals when they sent him to the workgang,
> And even had his own way of bustin' up rock.

It's badman versus badman once Scrappy is released. He calls "for the bad man Buck":

> Buck saw him comin', pulled his thirty-two forty,
> Got him once in the arm, and twice in the side;
> Scrappy switched his gat, like they do it in the Western,
> And let the daylight into Buck's black hide.

Scrappy goes down, but again, true to the badman yarns, his toughness in life lets him live on in legend. As if still alive, Scrappy's body was "waitin' for the undertaker's wagon." And at his funeral, stylish dress, "puttin' on the dog," is stronger than sorrow:

> In his box-back coat and his mutt-leg britches,
> And a collar high enough for to choke a ox;
> And the girls stopped crying when they saw how Scrappy
> Was a-putting on dog in a pinewood box.

In his ballad, with its reeling dance-like rhythms—dance being another way to rock and rattle loose the blues—the narrator lauds the badman's badness:

> O you rascal, puttin' on dog,
> Puttin' on dog, puttin' on dog,
> O you rascal, puttin' on dog,
> Great Gawd, but you was a man!

Wild Bill, of "The Last Ride of Wild Bill,"[17] is also a cool and stylish badman. Like Railroad Bill, who stole canned goods not to give them to the poor but to sell to blacks who lived along the rails (threatening their lives if they refused),[18] Sterling Brown's Wild Bill is an outlaw businessman. He's a numbers runner. As such, he is a kingpin in the underworld economy, and, for his customers, a dealer in more than numbers: he is the local dream-merchant, the exemplar of rakish dressing modes and derring-do. Like Railroad, Wild Bill is a fast traveler whose trade is threatened by the local sheriff, but who has no more fear of the new sheriff than does Railroad Bill. If Railroad was known to have "successfully robbed a train which he knew carried a posse sent to hunt him down,"[19] Wild Bill heard of the sheriff's threats, and taunted him with a phone call and with a telegram, sent C.O.D., reading, "Guess it will have / To be you and me." In the worlds of their ballads, both lawless figures were widely popular, Railroad becoming a hero in both black and white balladry, and Wild Bill—who runs numbers for bankers and preachers, *hoi-polloi* and bigwigs alike, white and black—is cheered by well-wishers along the numbers route. One of several trickster Negroes who help Bill in his getaway flags down the lawmen, interrupting their hot chase after Wild Bill:

> They pulled up murderous
> But they pulled up quick.
> The fellow talked slow,
> Meek and low:
> "You see it's like dis,
> My wife is sick
> And when I heard de siren blow
> I thought dat dis was de ambulance.
> I wants to beg yo' pardon
> In advance."

Both Bills are tricksters in their own right, too. Railroad Bill was known to turn himself into a sheep, a dog, or a fox, if lawmen approached him too narrowly.[20] Wild Bill is called a fox, stalked by hunter and hounds. But like Railroad, Wild Bill is doomed to be out-tricked by his pursuers. For the $2150 reward for Railroad, "Dead or Alive," two men ambush him and nearly blow his head off.[21] Wild Bill's foe plants a bomb in the car. Though both characters preyed upon their people, their bodacious recklessness and disdain for legal structure let them pass on into legend. And in the legends themselves, these outlaws achieve a certain immortality. As Carl Carmer reports, "there are people in the little shacks far back in the woods who do not believe that Railroad Bill is dead. 'Not *him*,' they say, and laugh and tell of the time he changed into a sheep to watch the posse go by."[22] Wild Bill drives his battered car into hell and sees "the worst looking mob / He had ever seen." The devils rushed him, shouting his name until

> Their shouting roared
> And rang through all the streets of Hell:
>
> "Give us the number
> Wild Bill

Tell us
What fell!"

Bill does not turn to dust. His rambling spirit goes around to a tar-black hell where Bill will still, as he says, run the numbers down.

Most of Brown's hard heroes have more socially redeeming qualities than do Railroad or Stagolee; most are not quite as wild as Wild Bill. Nat Turner's tragic battle may have been forgotten by local folk, who split the sign marking his last stand to make a kitchen fire; but still he was an unremorseful fighter for his people's freedom.[23] And less famous warriors play the fearless badman's role in Brown's poems:

> But Jess fired on the Alabama Central
> Man in full, babe, man in full. . .
>
> Crackers craved the job what Jess was holding,
> Times right tough, babe, times right tough,
> Warned Jess to quit his job for a white man,
> Jess he laughed, baby, he just laughed.[24]

Like John Henry and Joe Louis, Big Jess did a job that whites wanted for themselves, and he did it with zest, talking on the train whistle to his woman, "sweet hipted Mame": "So long sugar baby, so long babe." Typically, this moral badman is brought down by a mob: the whites ganged Jess, shot him, and left him on Black Bear Mountain—"Break of day, baby, break of day."

The tragic hero of "Ole Lem"[25] is another such moral badman: hard, but not without conscience or cause to be hard. He is one of Brown's "nachul men":

> "Six foot of man
> Muscled up perfect
> Game to the heart. . .
> Outworked or outfought
> Any man or two men. . . ."

A black sharecropper, and thus the lowest man down in the realms of Kings Cotton and Corn, terrorized by racial codes and legal lynching, this badman

> ". . . spoke out of turn
> At the commissary
> They gave him a day
> To git out the county
> He didn't take it.
> He said 'Come and get me.'
> They came and got him
> And they came by tens.

He stayed in the county—
He lays there dead."

The refrain of this ballad is perhaps Brown's most haunting of all. The bad-man's protest is quickly muffled by the march of the terrible facts, as reported by shrewd Old Lem:

". . . They don't come by ones
They don't come by twos
But they come by tens."

Other moral badmen started out very quiet and even jocular, but they witness their people's humiliation and oppression once too often, and something snaps: they come up fighting or they go get a gun. Joe Meek is the classic example:

. . . Strolling down Claibourne
In the wrong end of town
Joe saw two policemen
Knock a po' gal down.

He didn't know her at all
Never saw her befo'
But that didn't make no difference
To my ole boy Joe.

Walks up to the cops
And, very polite
Ast them ef they thought
They had done *just* right.[26]

As in many Brown poems, no politeness excuses an infraction of the Jim Crow "ethics." So the cops respond as if Joe Meek were Wild Bill:

One cracked him with his billy
Above the left eye,
One thugged him with his pistol
And let him lie . . .

When Joe comes to, he's a changed man: Badman Joe now, he gets a gun, goes on a rampage that makes the cops call out the national guard. But even that does not faze him. Athletically, he pitches back grenades thrown at him.

. . . with an outshoot drop
An' evvytime he threw
They was one less cop.

Lured out of hiding by a promise of armistice, Joe is shot twice by a cop hiding behind a post. Joe returns the favor "and the cop fell dead."

At the ballad's end, Joe joins forever the tragic badman's ranks by speaking the final words of Po' Lazarus and John Henry:

> "Won't be here much longer
>> To bother you so
> Would you bring me a drink of water
>> Fo' I go?"

And the metamorphosis is complete when the "very last words / He was heard to say, / Showed a different Joe talking / In a different way." He goes down not meek but bragging:

> "Ef my bullets weren't gone
>> An' my strength all spent—
> I'd send the chief something
>> With a compliment

> "And we'd race to hell,
>> And I'd best him there,
> Like I would of done here
>> Ef he'd played me fair."

In two of Brown's finest poems, "Strange Legacies"[27] and "Strong Men,"[28] direct references are made to badmen and the lore surrounding their deeds. In these poems, the allusions to the form itself evoke this tradition of cool, tough resistance to abridgements of the badman's freedom to be himself. Jack Johnson and John Henry, in "Strange Legacies," help inspire the "old nameless couple in Red River Bottom" to *give it one mo' try . . . give it one more try.* Perhaps from them they get a sense of what their real names are. And in the chorus of encouraging voices in "Strong Man," amidst the singers of spirituals, blues, work songs, and ballads—all calling for the march of the strong men—is the bass voice of giant John Henry:

> You sang:

>> Ain't no hammah
>> In dis lan',
>> Strikes lak mine, bebby,
>> Strikes lak mine.

Smashing the stereotype with these songs of the unsinkability of the human spirit, Brown drew upon the badman lore as created by the people he knew best. It was a new day for black Americans, when Brown's poetic voice was first raised in the 1920s. It was still a time when trickster tales were told and craft was necessary for black survival. But the New Negro, emerging from the ashes of World War I and the riots after the war, intended to face his enemy more directly, more like John Henry had done. Brown knew that with a hammer like

John Henry's, or the ability of Shine to "peep through muddy water and spy dry land" or of Wild Bill to play to work his beat no matter what hounds hounded him, the strong medicine poetry of the new day, and the strong and stronger men themselves, and the women, would relentlessly keep coming on.

NOTES

1. Zora Neale Hurston, *Their Eyes Were Watching God* (Urbana: University of Illinois Press, 1937, 1978), 255.
2. Ralph Ellison, *Shadow and Act* (New York: Random House, 1964), 100.
3. Sterling A. Brown, "Negro Character as Seen by White Authors," *Journal of Negro Education*, 2 (April 1933): 179–203.
4. Ellison 301.
5. Many versions of "Po Laz 'us," "John Henry," and even Stagolee include this final request. See Sterling A. Brown, Arthur P. Davis, and Ulysses Lee, *The Negro Caravan* (New York: Dryden, 1941).
6. Bruce Jackson, *"Get Your Ass in the Water and Swim Like Me"* (Cambridge: Harvard University Press, 1974), 31.
7. Dorothy Scarborough, *On the Trail of Negro Folk-Songs* (Cambridge: Harvard University Press, 1925): 252.
8. Scarborough, 251; see also Alan Lomax, *Folksongs of North America* (Garden City: Doubleday, 1960), 569.
9. John Cohen and Mike Seeger, eds., *The New Lost City Ramblers Song Book* (New York: OAK, 1964), 164.
10. Ibid.
11. Lawrence W. Levine, *Black Culture and Black Consciousness* (New York: Oxford University Press, 1977), 407–20.
12. Levine 421.
13. Sterling A. Brown, *The Collected Poems of Sterling A. Brown* (New York: Harper and Row, 1980), 20–21.
14. See Robert G. O'Meally, "Reconsideration: Sterling A. Brown," *The New Republic*, February 11, 1978, 33–36.
15. Albert Murray, *Stomping the Blues* (New York: McGraw-Hill, 1975).
16. Brown, "Puttin' on Dog," *Collected Poems*, 227–28.
17. Brown, "The Last Ride of Wild Bill," *Collected Poems*, 121–35.
18. Carl Carmer, *Stars Fell on Alabama* (New York: Farrar and Rinehart, 1934), 122–213.
19. Levine 411.
20. Ibid.
21. Carmer 125.
22. Ibid.
23. Brown, "Remembering Nat Turner," *Collected Poems*, 199–200.
24. Brown, "Break of Day," *Collected Poems*, 146.
25. Brown, "Old Lem," *Collected Poems*, 170–71.
26. Brown, "The Ballad of Joe Meek," *Collected Poems*, 149.
27. Brown, "Strange Legacies," *Collected Poems*, 86–87.
28. Brown, "Strong Men," *Collected Poems*, 56–58.

Slim Greer, Sterling A. Brown, and the Art of Tall Tale

John Edgar Tidwell

A well-known story goes something like this: "One time a fellow was walking across the river road when he seen a hat laying in the road, so he gave it a kick and it was on a man's head. He asked him if he needed help and he said, 'I guess not; I'm on horseback.' "[1] While the story's brevity and hyperbole deliberately understate the horseman's predicament, they heighten his bravado, self-reliance, and courage to endure hardship. Such qualities place this improbable story at the heart of the tall tale tradition.

Among folklorists, collectors of tales, and even literary critics, some agreement exists that the "lie" is an exacting art form, which means that it has its own structural integrity and coherence. While some writers determine the quality of the achievement by the size of the tale's exaggeration, others, including Sterling A. Brown, lament that the size of the exaggeration supplants the more important "fixin's," much to the detriment of the tradition.[2] The truer artistic expression, in other words, is found in the many stylistic devices employed by the speaker, including understatement, the occasional truthful element, its logic and structure (that is, its development from plausibility to climax), and the crucial pause at the point of highest suspense (intended to induce a listener to ask a question, therefore, revealing his gullibility).[3]

By a rather shrewd adaptation of these characteristics, Brown exploits the literary potential of an essentially oral art form. In his Slim Greer poems, where the most obvious examples of this interpolation occur, Brown experiments with the "lie" shared casually at the barbershop, at the "jook-joint," or on the street corner, where superb storytellers transform prosaic experience into performances celebrating their uncommon valor and heroic exploits. The vernacular speech and sense of "style" of these raconteurs, however, contain a potential for something greater than entertainment: the "lie," as an exacting art form, communicates a way of life and a way by which people make philosophic sense of an often hostile world. Although the poetry of Paul Laurence Dunbar, Langston Hughes, and James Weldon Johnson is suffused with the extraordinary experiences and language of Black folk, none equals Brown's studied integration of traditional Euro-American and Black American folk forms. The success Brown enjoyed results from his recognition of what lies between inchoate experience and finished art—in other words, *technique*. By examining Brown's use of techniques from American tall tale, we can discover the distinctive manner in which his poetry celebrates the heroic character of Black folk life and sets forth a Black vernacular vision.

The aesthetic view Brown brings to the Slim Greer poems is shaped by different but complementary academic and actual experiences. The New England–Yankee–Puritan traditions of Williams College (1918–1922, Phi Beta Kappa, BA) and Harvard University (1922–1923, MA) coalesce in Brown to become a form of intellectual equipment enabling him to develop a critical appreciation for literatures as diverse as *The Song of Roland* and the New American Poetry. In several interviews, Brown has pointed specifically to the importance of his study under distinguished faculty, such as Harvard's George Lyman Kittredge, and of his discovery of seminal studies, including Louis Untermeyer's anthologies of American and British literature. While it is clear these sources are quite significant, calculating their influence is, in Ellison's metaphor, a little like commanding a smoky genie to retreat orderly back into its traditional bottle. Inasmuch as academic training is only capable of providing theory, we must turn to the many raconteurs from whom he gained actual experience as well as informal instruction into the art of Black folk storytelling.

One such instance occurred in 1926–1928 when, as professor of English at Lincoln University (Missouri) and teacher of French in its high school, Brown frequented a "socially-undesirable" section near campus called "The Foot." It is here, according to a retrospective view given by Nathaniel Sweets, a student of Brown's at the time, that Brown's association with popular characters like "Preacher," Duke Diggs, and Slim Greer actually took place.[4] Although little is known of the actual Greer, a sometimes hotel waiter and railroad porter, Brown has clearly stated Slim's importance as raconteur. In one anecdote, Brown acknowledges playfully something of this indebtedness: "[Slim] says I owe him some money because I shouldn't have taken his name."[5]

Although anecdotal and even a bit facetious, Brown's reminiscence is hardly an invitation to confuse the poem's Slim Greer for a transcription of the actual one. For the achievement of Brown rests not on duplicating but adapting the qualities of actual persons he met and places he'd seen. At best, Brown's characterization of Slim is a composite of many superb storytellers he encountered from Virginia to Missouri to Tennessee. What each of these master liars imparted was a profound revelation into the nature of narrative art and social satire; therefore, an examination of the poems' artifice, not their specific biographic references, is in order.

When the poem "Slim Greer" opens with "Listen to the tale / Of Ole Slim Greer . . . Talkinges' guy / An' biggest liar, / With always a new lie / On the fire," the reader is invited to share in a "lie."[6] But the "lie" is hardly credible with such exploits as "passing" for white ("An' he no lighter / than a dark midnight"), falling in love with an Arkansas white woman, and escaping the territory just ahead of the lynch mob that discovered in his mournful playing of the blues his actual racial identity. One of the immediate questions posed by the poem concerns the form and function of the "lie." Is the purpose of the lie to deceive, as in something dishonest or lacking in truth? Is it supposed to entertain? Or is the lie a form of deception in which listeners or audience are tricked into understanding, awareness, or even self-knowledge?

At some level, perhaps all these functions can be demonstrated in the poem, although dishonesty and entertainment are the two least desirable readings. When S. P. Fullinwider observes that Slim is an incipient "con man," brought to maturity by the 1960s Black Aestheticians,[7] his argument, in effect, centers on Slim's supposed basic dishonesty. But the image of Slim as a 1960s urban hustler, for whom "money talks and bullshit walks" and for whom jive talk and the ability to "rap" define the self, is hardly consistent with the Southern and essentially rural folk storytellers Brown knew. Instead of rapid fire rap, Slim tells his story "in a long-drawled / Careless tone, / As solemn as a Baptist / Parson's moan" (77). It is the familiar tall tale technique of the deadpan manner.

The success of a humorous story, Mark Twain writes in "How to Tell a Story," depends on the speaker's bland, innocent face and the restraint he exercises in not laughing at his own story.[8] The reason, of course, lies in the self-conscious, purposeful way in which the listener/reader is deceived into awareness of the story's humor. In the oral tradition, the extent to which the storyteller conceals his knowledge of anything remotely funny becomes a litmus test of his artistry.

In "Slim Greer," part of the remarkable achievement of the poem owes to the successful adaptation of Twain's principle. The purposeful use of tall tale techniques begins the process of artfully deceiving the reader by first creating a performative environment, such as a barbershop or a "jook joint," and by making the customers become a hypostatized audience. In the interplay between speaker and audience, then, the act of narration becomes a performance much like the ones given by the actual Slim Greer and other master yarnspinners.

Slim's mode of narration, then, as "long-drawled, careless tone" not only "conceals" his knowledge of something funny, but builds dramatically, rhythmically towards climax. At the snapper ending, the audience no doubt would question the veracity of the tale, as is the custom. It is here that Brown employs the familiar technique of feigning hurt surprise at any question of the tale's truth: Slim sells out "With lightnin' speed," and proclaims to his listeners: "Hope I may die, sir— / Yes, indeed. . . ." Even though he "swears" to the truth of his story, his "listeners" would perhaps see the tale as sheer entertainment, and might be moved to question its truth as a ploy to egg the speaker on. But because we know that Slim is darker "Than a dark midnight," the narrator's and therefore Brown's point is not entertainment. For the story's purpose lies in its "deception," which is intended to laugh us into an awareness of the ludicrousness of racial segregation.

The other poems in the series—"Slim Hears 'The Call,'" "Slim in Atlanta," "Slim in Hell," and "Slim Lands a Job?"—contain many of these same features. For example, "Slim Lands a Job?" reenacts a form of exaggeration called "the impossibility that is the actuality of the poem." The unemployed Slim wanders down to Arkansas into Big Pete's Cafe seeking a job waiting tables. Big Pete is described in Herculean terms as "a six foot / Hard-boiled man / Wid a forty-four dungeon / In his han'." In a deliberate play on the "slowness" of Pete's current waiter, the employee is described this way: "A noise rung out / In rush a man / Wid a tray on his head / An' one on each han / Wid de silver in his mouf / An' de soup plates in his vest / Puffin' / A red wagon / Wid all de rest." The self-consciously contrived play on "slowness," in one regard, induces pure, gut-bucket laughter. But part of the contrivance accomplished by using tall tale techniques makes the story a poignant discussion of labor conditions. How slow the "slow coon" and "wuthless lazy waiter" is is not the point of the poem. But the actual conditions of his employment are. The poem thus creates a dramatic situation which uses humor as a way of leveling a scathing social commentary.

"Slim in Atlanta," which develops a similar theme, begins on the note of exaggeration by introducing a Georgia law forbidding "all de niggers / From laughin' outdoors." Using the technique of appealing to the audience, the speaker states: "Hope to Gawd I may die / If I ain't speakin' truth / Make de niggers do deir laughin' / In a telefoam booth." The poem is then developed in terms of the overpowering comedic impact this scene has on the peripatetic Slim. His sight of all these Black folk in misery because they're forced to hold in their laughter sends him into convulsions of laughter, requiring him to break through the suffering crowd of Blacks waiting their turn in line at the telephone booth.

Although the stupidity of segregation is the point of the poem, it is not conveyed in such obvious terms. Similarly, "Slim Hears 'The Call,'" the least funny poem in the series, does not warrant the criticism that it surrenders to bald social statement. Critics have largely seen "Slim Hears 'The Call'" as sardonic because it is nearly Swiftian in its descent from a wry amusement at the folly of racism to a more vocal expression of outrage at religious hypocrisy.

Understandably, the rather blatant warning that concludes the poem has incited many of these views: "An' I says to all de Bishops, / What is hearin' my song— / Ef de cap fits yo, brother, / Put it on" (88). Jean Wagner was moved to observe in this poem a "greater bitterness and more chilling cynicism" that could only have been generated by the Marxist ideology that had an appeal for Black intellectuals after the Crash of 1929.[9] But although the harsher tone of this poem differs from that of the others, the use of tall tale techniques rescues it from the pessimistic mire to which Wagner condemns it. The ultimate effect of "Slim Hears 'The Call'" derives largely from its performance milieu and rhetorical embellishment. "Down at the barbershop / Slim had the floor" announces place and performative environment. As in the other poems, much of the subsequent exaggeration must be seen in the context of verbal jousting with an hypostatized audience. The nearly down and out Slim is "So ragged, I make a jaybird / About to moult, / Look like he got on gloves / An' a overcoat." Weakened physically and financially, Slim hears the Lord's "call" to come save lost souls, an idea nurtured by seeing a former card-playing buddy whose similar conversion has netted "a house / Like de State Capitol" and a "wife / As purty as sin, / An' his secketary, twict / As purty again' (85). Clearly, the poem is scathing in its criticism of religious hypocrisy. But rhetorical embellishment, not Slim's "conversion," is the center of the poem. "An' I swear, as sure / As my name's Slim Greer, / He repohted to de school / Sixteen dollars clear" is another example of the familiar technique of appealing to the audience to believe in the veracity of the tale. Its use tones down the abusive criticism implied in the poem.

Like "Slim Hears 'The Call,'" "Slim in Hell" raises a question about the bitterness of its tone. In this poem, which seems to adapt the "Colored Man in Heaven" folktale and the myth of Orpheus and Eurydice, the peripatetic Slim is sent by Saint Peter on one last journey before he's admitted to heaven's pearly gates. His mission is to fly to Hell to observe and report on the devil's latest tricks. Slim's use of the silvery wings to cavort like Lindy "in the Spirit/ Of St. Louis Blues" is an object lesson in itself. But the incredible sights and sounds of Hell set forth the satirical point. Bawdy houses and cabarets remind Slim of New Orleans; roulette wheels and fighting people remind him of Rampart Street and Beale Street; and white devils using pitch forks to throw Black ones into the furnace remind him of Vicksburg, Little Rock, Jackson, Waco, and Rome, coaxing him to say, "Dis makes / Me think of home." At this climactic moment, the devil changes into a "cracker" with a sheriff's star. Slim hauls out with unprecedented speed to report back to St. Peter: "De place was Dixie / Dat I took for Hell." Such naiveté is not accorded ample preparation to enter the pearly gates and Slim is sent packing away.

In each of these poems, tall tale techniques point up a kind of absurdity. In its focus and kind, this absurdity differs from the existentialist philosophy wherein man is seen as isolated, cast out in an alien world and destined to return to the nothingness from which he started. For Brown's view of humankind affirms a belief in a potentially orderly social structure in which individual dignity and heroism are recognized and even rewarded. His is a world acknowledging not only self-worth and rugged individualism but the foibles and defeats of humankind too. The absurdity exposed in the poems is defined in terms of the whole cast of Jim Crow laws, which impinge upon the assertion of individual rights.

In his review of Gunnar Myrdal's *An American Dilemma,* Ralph Ellison wrote: "Myrdal sees Negro culture and personality simply as the product of a 'social pathology.'"[10] The thrust of Brown's use of techniques from American tall tale is to disprove what Myrdal and so many other social scientists regarded as "the Negro problem." Instead of social aberration, a healthy Black humanity grew and took shape despite the efforts of Jim Crow laws to subjugate or depress Blacks. Blacks were not beaten down by segregation, in other words; they grew in spite of and perhaps because of it. In either case, Blacks grew. By borrowing from the storehouse of tall tale techniques, Brown, unlike his Black contemporaries, understood one of the basic assumptions of American tall tale: its impulse toward democracy and egalitarianism.

Contained in the "lie" is a belief that one man is as good as the next and perhaps a whole lot better. In the oral tradition, one's ability to spin yarns held the potential for attracting respect from others, thereby creating a leveling effect in society. Brown recreates the illusion of leveling by transposing democratic ideals of the Old West to meet the needs of Black folk and their purpose for storytelling. The *process* Brown uses can be explained in terms of Levine's observation that "marginal" groups often tell jokes containing racial stereotypes about themselves as means for diffusing hurt and anger by stripping it naked and exposing it to scrutiny.[11] These motives in Brown's Slim Greer poems function as a need to get at truth, which means exposing the debilitating Jim Crow practices and holding them up as ridiculous. When the devil in "Slim in Hell" is changed into a "cracker" sheriff, the burden of this poem is not on some cynicism caused by racial oppression, but on its satire. Although diffusing the hurt and turning it into laughter do very little to alter actual social conditions, something even more remarkable is actually accomplished. Inverting the horrific into the comic becomes a celebration of the heroic character that sustains Black man- and womanhood and prevents degeneration into self-hate and other sociopathic forms.

What separates Brown's social consciousness from others is his manner of expression and how technique promotes function. In these poems, the essential function of the tall tale form approximates what James Cox has observed of *Roughing It.* That is to say, Twain "pursues the possibilities of the tall tale, evoking humorous skepticism in relation to event. The skepticism is the essential act of form in *Roughing It.*"[12] The form and function of the lie ultimately lead the reader to see not a lie that deceives but one that reveals instead the truth.

Exposure as a motive of Brown's humor should not lead to the conclusion he's merely a debunker of racial stereotype. Although not inappropriate, this view is only narrowly applicable. An iconoclastic bent certainly runs throughout Brown's poetry, pointing up the racial myopia through which Black people have been viewed. But undue attention given to the exposure of social problems sacrifices the more compelling concern of the art of the poem. For the singular achievement of the Slim Greer poems is the manner in which social protest is turned into an act of art.

The techniques of tall tale at once dramatize and define the motives of the form in the Slim Greer poems. The lie in this "lie" is not intended to deceive or trick the listener but to expose the listener to the truth about Black social conditions. As James Cox explains, "In a world of lies, the tall tale is the only true lie because it does not mask as the truth but moves the listener to ask what the truth is."[13] The question of truth ultimately turns on exposing the absurd notions of those who would obscure or prevent the attainment of the demo-cratic and egalitarian promise implied in the Constitution. When individual rights are assaulted, some form of response is required. And often it means rising above an ensnaring mire. In this regard, the religious hypocrisy in "Slim Hears 'The Call'" and the Jim Crow laws of "Slim in Atlanta" are equally "ab-surd" because each denies the completion of selfhood. It is not cynicism but exposure of those things preventing attainment of selfhood and individual worth that motivates these poems.

The use of vernacular language, casually inserted details that build up to the frantic impossibility, the bland self-righteous veracity that yielded to hurt surprise at any expression of doubt, the snapper climax or exposure at the end—these reveal for Brown character, a way of speech, and a way of life.[14] Because these qualities rendered by Brown as an act of art ran counter to the usual claptrap of stereotypes, a different view of Blacks emerged, one that was subversive. By astute adaptation, the techniques of tall tale transformed this experience into a liberating vision of art.

NOTES

1. In Roger Welsch, *Shingling the Fog and Other Plains Lies* (Lincoln: University of Nebraska Press, 1972), 50. A variation of this "lie," as an example of bravado and bravery in folk tales, is quoted by Sterling A. Brown, "In the American Grain," *Vassar Alumnae Magazine* 36.3 (1951): 6.

2. Brown, "In the American Grain," 6.

3. In addition to Brown and Welsch, see Gerald Thomas, *The Tall Tale and Philippe D'Alcripe* (St. John's: Memorial University of Newfoundland, 1977); and Richard Dorson, *Jonathan Draws the Long Bow* (Cambridge: Harvard University Press, 1946).

4. Nathaniel A. Sweets, "Prof. Brown at Lincoln Univ. The Roaring Twenties," *Sterling A. Brown: A UMUM Tribute*, ed. Black History Museum Committee

(Philadelphia: Black History Museum UMUM Publishers, 1982), 47 and 48. See also W. Sherman Savage, *The History of Lincoln University* (Jefferson City, MO: Lincoln University, 1939), 179–228; and Raymond Wolters, *The New Negro on Campus* (Princeton: Princeton University Press, 1975), 192–229.

5. Quoted by Joanne Gabbin, *Sterling A. Brown: Building a Black Aesthetic Tradition* (Westport, CT: Greenwood Press, 1985), 136.

6. The source for "Slim Greer" and the other poems in the series is Sterling A. Brown, *The Collected Poems of Sterling A. Brown* (New York: Harper/Colophon Books, 1983), 77–92. The original 1980 edition contains textual errors and omissions.

7. *The Mind and Mood of Black America* (Homewood, IL.: The Dorsey Press, 1969), 215–16.

8. *The Complete Essays of Mark Twain,* ed. Charles Neider (Garden City, NY: Doubleday, 1963), 156.

9. Jean Wagner, *Black Poets of the United States* (Urbana: University of Illinois Press, 1973), 493.

10. Ralph Ellison, *Shadow and Act* (New York: Random House, 1964), 316.

11. Lawrence W. Levine, *Black Culture and Black Consciousness* (Oxford: Oxford University Press, 1977), 336.

12. James Cox, *Mark Twain: The Fate of Humor* (Princeton, NJ: Princeton University Press, 1966), 96.

13. Cox, *Mark Twain,* 103.

14. Brown, "In the American Grain," 6.

The New Negro Poet and the Nachal Man: Sterling Brown's Folk Odyssey

John S. Wright

In 1936, the year Sterling Brown and John Lomax joined forces supervising the collection of oral slave narratives for the Federal Writers' Project (see Mangione 257–63), Lomax and his son Alan published the first extended study of an American folksinger. That singer, one Walter Boyd, alias Huddie Ledbetter, alias "Leadbelly," had been the self-proclaimed "King of the Twelve String Guitar Players of the World," as well as the number one man in the number one gang on the number one convict farm in Texas. He had fought his way into prison and had sung his way to freedom, to fleeting fame, and to what would be a pauper's death in Bellevue in 1949. A man of prodigious physical strength, emotional volatility, unpredictable violence, and indisputable creativity, unschooled if not unassuming, he was shaped by record, film, and the printed page into the prototypic national image of the "folk Negro." For the recording industry, his songs were a golden hedge against hard times. For the generation of newly professional folklorists that the Lomaxes represented, he was a "find" that helped buttress the assault of the Depression era folklore radical democrats against the old aristocratic folklore scholarship. For the thinkers and artists of the black world-within-a-world from which he came, however, Leadbelly made concrete an old enigma alternately energizing and embarrassing—and one left largely unplumbed by the outspokenly "folk conscious" New Negro movement of the twenties. Lawbreaker, illiterate, brawler, boozer, womanizer, cottonpicker, and vagrant; singer of prison dirges, work songs, cowboy ballads, children's songs, spirituals, lullabies, and barrel-house blues, Leadbelly was a grinning, gold-toothed incongruity. Vernacular tradition's "nachal man" incarnate, he was in one rough frame the bruised and imbruted "man farthest down" for whom Booker T. Washington and the organizations of racial uplift had lowered their proverbial buckets, *and* he was the voice of that transcendent "Negro genius" which W.E.B. Du Bois and the Talented Tenth had exalted as creator of "the most beautiful expressions of human experience born this side of the seas" (265). In the preceding decade Jean Toomer, Claude McKay, Zora Neale Hurston, and Langston Hughes had all directed their imaginative energies to penetrating the layers of abstraction that created incongruity from the folklife Leadbelly nonetheless had to live. But perhaps nowhere had so clear a perspective emerged for seeing such a man whole as in the work of Sterling Brown.

In 1932 Brown had published *Southern Road;* and with a social realism honed to poetic precision, he had struck through the masks with which minstrelsy, local color, the plantation tradition, and Jazz Age primitivism had defaced the folk. Alain Locke, self-professed "literary midwife" of the New Negro movement, in reviewing *Southern Road,* hailed Sterling Brown as "The New Negro Folk Poet" and described him as an artist who had revealed better than any of his contemporaries the "racial touch," independent of dialect, which enabled him to catch the deeper "idiom of feeling" (89). Locke had predicted some years earlier that "the soul of the Negro will be discovered in a characteristic way of thinking and in a homely philosophy rather than in a jingling and juggling of broken English" (89). The secret of Sterling Brown's poetic effects was that he had "listened long and carefully to the folk in their intimate hours," talking to themselves, their protective masks dropped. A "more reflective, a closer student of the folk-life, . . . a bolder and more detached observer" than his fellow poets, Sterling Brown had recaptured what was "more profoundly characteristic" than types of metaphors or mannerisms of speech—he had recaptured the philosophic attitudes, material and metaphysical, that lay beneath the surface of folksongs, fables, proverbs, and argot (90). And in giving the folk credit for thinking he had discovered the "poetic divining-rod" for rendering, with Aesopian clarity and Aesopian candor, that ancient common wisdom of the group which promised to bridge the then highly publicized gap between the Old Negro and the New.

Rejecting the Old Negro and the traditional poetry of folk caricature, James Weldon Johnson had advocated a symbolic rather than a phonetic literary mimesis, and had forecast the doom of dialect poetry. But Sterling Brown perceived that the problem of defining a poetic language for folk portraiture was a problem not so much of materials as of perspective. "Dialect, or the speech of the people," he maintained, "is capable of expressing whatever the people are. And the folk Negro is a great deal more than a buffoon or a plaintive minstrel. Poets more intent upon learning the ways of the folk, their speech, and their character, that is to say, better poets, could have smashed the mold. But first they would have to believe in what they were doing. And this was difficult in a period of conciliation and middle class striving for recognition and respectability" (qtd. in Redmond 227–28). Brown's less conventional strivings provided critical as well as poetic demonstrations of his own unshakable belief in "the validity, the power, and the beauty of folk culture." His was an aesthetic of reorientation, and its achievement rested no less surely on his poems than on the critical paths he cut through the jungle of theory and interpretation, censorship and commercialization, romanticism and mysticism, that engulfed the study of Afro-American folklore between the 1920s and the 1950s.

The twenties, besides hosting the New Negro movement, fostered another phenomenon not unconnected to the black cultural ferment of the time with its artistic focus on, in Locke's terms, "the revaluation of the Negro": After a war decade remarkable for the *accumulation* of major folklore collections in America, the twenties became a decade remarkable for the *publication* of folklore collections. Several decades earlier, in 1888, the American Folklore Society had been founded as a kind of rescue operation to record what were thought to be the "fast vanishing relics" of rural folk groups before their projected disappearance from an urbanizing, industrializing modern culture (Brunvand 9). Though the academic study of folklore would not be established in the United States until the 1940s, an interim throng of avid amateurs and bootlegging scholars trained in other fields—English literature, anthropology, sociology, musicology, history, and languages—began consolidating in the twenties a vast repository of folklore and folksong which by the forties had tapped extensively the traditions of such occupational, regional, ethnic, and racial groups as Western cowboys, Nova Scotian sailors, Midwestern lumberjacks, Pennsylvania Germans, Southwest Mexican-Americans, Utah Mormons, and Ozark mountaineers (Brunvand 9, 19).

In this surge of folklore collecting, studies of Afro-American lore and song loomed large. Such collecting was not new, of course: The first serious collection, *Slave Songs of the United States,* had been made in 1867. Between the end of Reconstruction and the turn of the century, a series of literary figures, beginning with William Wells Brown (*My Southern Home,* 1880) and including Joel Chandler Harris, with his Uncle Remus collections, and Charles Chesnutt (*The Conjure Woman,* 1899), made literary capital from black folktales and anecdotes. White collectors like C. C. Jones, Jr., and Virginia Boyle transcribed folk myths and devil tales in the Sea Islands Gullah dialect. And during the 1880s and '90s a black folklore group met regularly at Hampton Institute in Virginia and published summaries of papers and the texts of oral lore in the *Southern Workman* (Dorson 110). Interest in the folk, though, had waned enough by the opening years of the new century to lead Booker T. Washington to complain, in his 1904 introduction to Samuel Coleridge-Taylor's *Twenty-Four Negro Melodies,* that the plantation songs were dying out with the generation that had given them birth (Lovell 494).

When the resurgence of Afro-American folklore collecting appeared early in the twenties, it was with the force of a revitalized national interest in native traditions behind it. John Lomax's publication of *Cowboy Songs and Other Frontier Ballads* in 1910 and Cecil Sharp's *English Folksongs from the Southern Appalachians* in 1917 had pioneered a turnabout in American folklore research by revealing living folksong traditions that were not vanishing but instead surviving and in fact being continually reborn. In 1915, amidst a flurry of regional collecting, music critic Henry Krehbiel had directed attention away from the ongoing "ballad wars" and toward the Afro-American folksongs he sought "to bring into the field of scientific observation" (v). Krehbiel had centered his study around the questions of "whether or not the songs were original creations of these native blacks, whether or not they were entitled to be called American, and whether or not they were worthy of consideration as foundation elements for a school of American composition" (vi). Krehbiel had answered all these in the affirmative; and his formulation then of the problems of origins, of methods of composition, and of provenience did much to set the terms of discourse for the new black folklore studies that flowed out into the public arena in the twenties and early thirties.

Those studies revealed a body of Afro-American oral tradition that was massive, vital, and portentous. The published collections included Thomas Talley's *Negro Folk Rhymes* (secular songs and linguistic lore) and Ambrose Gonzales's *With Aesop Along the Black Border* (coastal fables in Gullah dialect) in 1922; Elsie Parson's *Folklore of the Sea Islands* in 1923; Dorothy Scarborough's *On the Trail of Negro Folk-Songs* in 1925; Howard Odum and Guy Johnson's *The Negro and His Songs* and *Negro Workaday Songs* in 1925 and 1926, respectively; James Weldon Johnson's *Book of American Negro Spirituals* and *Second Book of American Negro Spirituals* in 1925 and 1926; Newbell Niles Puckett's *Folk Beliefs of the Southern Negro* in 1926; Newman White's *American Negro Folk Songs* in 1928; E. C. L. Adams's *Congaree Sketches* and *Nigger to Nigger* (coastal jokes and tales) in 1927 and 1928. Howard Odum's novelistic trilogy about travelin' man Left Wing Gordon—*Rainbow Round My Shoulder, Wings on My Feet,* and *Cold Blue Moon*—appeared in 1928, 1929, and 1930; Guy Johnson's *Folk Culture on St. Helena Island* in 1930; J. Mason Brewer's slave-tale collection *Juneteenth* in 1932; Zora Neale Hurston's *Mules and Men* in 1935; and John and Alan Lomax's *Negro Folk Songs as Sung by Leadbelly* in 1936.

In the face of this expanding repository of traditional art and customs, the prevailing notion that no distinctive Afro-American culture existed, or that such culture as did exist was one of either fossilized African survivals or debased imitations of white models, began to give ground. And the folk ideology so central to the New Negro creed formulated by Alain Locke received a concrete foundation of folk myths, legends, symbols, and character types upon which many of the major black literary achievements of the next two decades would build. Prospects for employing the new folklore studies either for aesthetic purposes or in support of the sociopolitical "literature of racial vindication," however, were vitiated by a trio of conceptual problems and controversies that implicated the whole of folklore research and interpretation at the time.

First, American folklorists, who, as Richard Dorson has noted, were rarely trained in folklore and rarely Americanists, subscribed heavily to Eurocentric theories that (a) predicated the existence of folklore on the presence of a traditional peasantry that did not exist in America, (b) treated folklore genres hierarchically, with the Anglo-Saxon ballad first and foremost, and (c) approached American folk forms generally as corrupted, inherently inferior imitations of Old World originals (Dorson 4–7). Under the disabling influence of these theories, Fisk professor Thomas Talley, for example, in his pioneering study of Afro-American folk rhymes, labored tortuously to force his materials into an elaborate system of ballad classification based on his defensively mystical proposition that "all [Negro] Folk Rhymes are Nature Ballads" with call-and-response structures that somehow "hover ghostlike" over them (250, 285).

Second, nineteenth-century racist ethnology, though under attack in the anthropological work of Franz Boas and his students, remained a potent force in the new folklore research—reinforced by lingering Social Darwinism and the currents of popular nativism and racism. The mystique of racial "gifts," "temperaments," and "geniuses" helped contort the endless debate over the origins of folk forms waged between diffusionists, who believed in a single origin of folk themes with their subsequent spread, and polygeneticists, who argued for the repeated reinvention of similar materials because of similar psychological or historical conditions (Brunvand 11). Their romantic racialism made studies like Odum and Johnson's *The Negro and His Songs,* which presented the earliest extended analysis of the blues, read, as contemporary folklorists have acknowledged, "like a Music of the Darkies with a bit of enlightened sociological body English" (Jackson 7).

Third, the new folklore studies were hampered by the absence of any scientific or humanistic theory of American culture and national character capable of comprehending, as a cultural matrix for folklife, this country's modernity, its radical heterogeneity, and its peculiar blend of social fixedness and fluidity. Moreover, the folkloric enterprise was subject to pressures from popularization, commercialization, and the emerging mass media that were plagued with distortions and fabrications of folk culture that produced the "bankrupt treasuries" Stanley Edgar Hyman lambasted in the mid-forties and that led Richard Dorson eventually to coin the distinction between folklore and the rising tide of "fakelore" (Dorson 5–7).

Into this fray Sterling Brown brought a keen critical intelligence, his convictions about the cultural integrity and aesthetic significance of folklife, and his instincts as a creative writer. Afro-American folklorists were scarce to say the least, and in the quarter-century of folkloric fervor that spanned the Jazz Age, the Great Depression, and the Second World War, Sterling Brown's essays in *Opportunity* and *Phylon*, and his editorial and scholarly work with the Federal Writers' Project Negro Affairs division, filled the void with a wide-ranging folk-lore critique fully cognizant of the shifting grounds of folklore scholarship yet fixed unerringly on the perspectives of the folk themselves. Brown had spent the years after the publication of *Southern Road* absorbed in Afro-American lit-erary history and the iconography of racial stereotypy—preoccupations fleshed out in his *The Negro in American Fiction* and *Negro Poetry and Drama*. With his appointment to the Federal Writers' Project in the spring of 1936, he turned toward the sociohistorical study of the black folk and urban experience, im-mersing himself first in the gathering of ex-slave narratives which was then underway and which would be perhaps the Writers' Project's greatest contribu-tion to the study of Afro-American life.

The collection of slave narratives had been begun in 1934 by the Federal Emergency Relief Administration, at the instigation of black historian Law-rence Reddick, who had voiced the growing historical consensus that the story of slavery and Reconstruction could not be complete "until we get the view as presented through the slave himself" (Mangione 257). The Writers' Proj-ect had inherited the undertaking; and in 1936, when John Lomax became the Project's first folklore editor, Sterling Brown began guiding the interview-ing efforts that would lead finally to the publication of seventeen volumes of manuscripts containing over two thousand slave narratives (Mangione 263). Under Lomax's supervision, and after 1938 under the leadership of Benjamin Botkin, the Project proceeded to collect folk materials on a scale larger than ever previously attempted.

Under Botkin's influence especially, the Writers' Project countered the antiquarian orientation of academic folklorists with an emphasis on oral his-tory and "living lore." Sterling Brown, who had contributed poems and critical reviews to Botkin's four-volume regional miscellany *Folk-Say* between 1929 and 1932, found Botkin's proletarian emphasis congenial to his own. "The folk movement must come from below upward rather than from above downward," Botkin contended; "otherwise it may be dismissed as a patronizing gesture, a nostalgic wish, an elegiac complaint, a sporadic and abortive review—on the part of paternalistic aristocrats going slumming, dilettantish provincials going native, defeated sectionalists going back to the soil, and anybody and every-body who cares to going collecting" (Mangione 270). Folk imagination more than folk knowledge became the Project's aim, and the outlook and skills of writers such as Sterling Brown became crucial to capturing it.

For Sterling Brown the aim also was, in his words, to "produce an accurate picture of the Negro in American social history," to reveal him as an integral part of American life and to do so in a way that mediated between the compet-ing chauvinisms of both white and black historians (Mangione 259). The device of correlating folklore with social and ethnic history was the tactic Brown em-phasized in his editorial role and in his efforts to have Afro-American materials included in the Project's state guidebooks then being compiled around the country. The publication of *The Negro in Virginia* in 1940 demonstrated the value of this approach. It was produced under the local supervision of black historian Roscoe Lewis, but Brown's role in this field project was considerable. Built upon years of carefully collected oral histories and interviews and on painstaking re-search that traced neglected materials back to the arrival in Virginia of the first Africans in 1619, *The Negro in Virginia* became a model of documentary research and narrative drama (Mangione 260–61).

In a talk before the Conference on the Character and State of Studies in Folklore on April 11, 1942, Brown looked back at his years with the Writers' Project: "I became interested in folklore," he recalled, "because of my desire to write poetry and prose fiction. I was first attracted by certain qualities I thought the speech of the people had, and I wanted to get for my own writing a flavor, a color, a pungency of speech. Then later I came to something more important— I wanted to get an understanding of people" ("Approach" 506). Respectful of the scientific approaches to folklore but untroubled by any definitional or proce-dural obstacles that might block his access to the "living-people-lore" of, for in-stance, so fascinating a tribe as urban jazzmen, Sterling Brown had developed a flexible, functionalist approach to folklore. It was an approach that, as Alan Lomax advocated in the same session, rejected views of the folk "as ignorant receptacles for traditions and ideas which they do not themselves understand, and which make very little sense until they are pieced together and explained in historical terms by the comparative scholar." Such an approach instead saw folklore as "equipment for living," saw the folklorist as performing not only an archaeological role but one of recording a vigorous human tradition, and it recognized that "the best interpretations of folklore may be obtained in the end from the folk themselves" (Lomax, "Functional Aspects" 507).

In the early forties, the conviction that the folk may be their own best inter-preters became one of the trademarks of Sterling Brown's series of articles on black folk expression. His synoptic essay in *The Negro Caravan* in 1941, on the sources and genres of black oral literature, stands even today as the single best introduction to the subject because, in threading its way through all the schol-arship and interpretative quandaries of the previous decades, it maintains its balance by never falling victim to the disorienting proposition that, as Newman White had myopically insisted, "the Negro never contemplated his low estate."

"Nigger, your breed ain't metaphysical," one of the voices in Robert Penn Warren's poeticized fable "Pondy Woods" had proclaimed, confronting New Negroes with the old stereotype of the crusading New South. "Cracker, *your* kind ain't exegetical," Sterling Brown responded dialectically, as he outlined a critique that treated black forms as distillations of communal *mind* and *ethos* (Brown interview). In his essays on the blues in particular, Brown treated the products of folk imagination as *self-conscious* wisdom—tragic, comic, ironic, shrewd, emotionally elastic and attitudinally complex, capable of supporting a variety of stances toward life, and resistant, as such, to ideological straitjacketing or implications of naïveté. Worldly and self-aware, the spirit of the blues, he submitted, is defined by the songs themselves, in lines which assert that "the blues ain't nothin' but a poor man's heart disease" or "the blues ain't nothin' but a good man way, way down" or, more obliquely, "Woke up this morning, blues walking round my bed / Went in to eat my breakfast, blues was all in my bread." The blues fused stoicism in a concrete, *metaphoric metaphysic:* It was a frank Chaucerian *attitude* toward sex and love that kept even the bawdiest authentic blues from being prurient and pornographic. It was "elemental *honesty*," "depth of *insight*," and *sophistication* about human relations that lay behind their appeal across caste lines. It was *imagination* making the love of life and the love of words memorably articulate which turned the best blues into potent lyric poetry.[1]

Brown's reading of the blues tradition did not go uncontested. In a lengthy, two-part essay on the spirit and meaning of black folk expression published in *Phylon* in the early fifties, he acknowledged that "the field of folklore in general is known to be a battle area, and the Negro front is one of the hottest sectors" (Autumn 1950: 319). But he needed no new battlepieces, no defensive ethnic chauvinism. Incorporating the insights of Stith Thompson's then definitive study of the folktale, he found, in the newly revealed patterns of interchange and diffusion characteristic of even Old World African folklore, support for his vision of the underlying unity of the world's and the nation's many cultural traditions. After all, he noted, in the cosmology of black folk traditions themselves, "tales about the origin of the races leave little room for chauvinism about a chosen people. The slaves knew at first hand that the black man had a hard road to travel, and they tell of the mistakes of creation with sardonic fatalism" (Autumn 1950: 325). Looking then at the prospects for the future of folklife, he knew that hard road was all too literal. Black folk culture was breaking up, he thought. In migrating to the city "the folk become a submerged proletariat. Leisurely yarn-spinning, slow paced aphoristic conversation become lost arts; jazzed-up gospel hymns provide a different sort of release from the old spirituals; the blues reflect the distortions of the new way of life. Folk arts are no longer by the folk for the folk; smart businessmen now put them up for sale. Gospel songs often become showpieces for radio-slummers, and the blues become the double talk of the dives." And yet, he interjected, "the vigor of the creative impulse has not been snapped, even in the slums," and the folk roots "show a stubborn vitality" (Winter 1953: 60–61).

Leadbelly was a few years dead then, his pauperized last seasons spent as a resident "living legend" in Greenwich Village coffeehouses. The "blues boom," the "rediscovery" of New Orleans jazz, and the folk revivals of the fifties were taking hold. *Southern Road,* though, was out of print and Sterling Brown's poetry largely unremarked since the thirties by the canonizers of American verse. In his various roles as teacher, scholar, poet, husband, mentor, and self-confessed

"Teller of Lies," Brown weathered those years, and the years after, sustained by the same lyric loves he found in the blues—the love of words, the love of life, and the love of all things musical, as he was wont to say, "from Beethoven to the boogie-woogie." And perhaps concluding with this one of Brown's own pointed incongruities makes sense if, blues-like, we "worry" it a bit. Beethoven, save for the tarbrushings that allege him to be quite literally a "soul brother," is a relatively unambiguous reference for defining one aesthetic pole and one kind of hero on the spectrum of "strange legacies" Sterling Brown's work embraces. The boogie-woogie, though, evokes almost as unruly an image as Leadbelly, for the phrase masks onomatopoetically a complex legacy of juxtaposed folk meanings: The boogie-woogie was simultaneously a fast-stepping, Kansas City Jazz-influenced piano blues in which the bass figure comes in double time; it was the knee-flexing jitterbug one danced in accompaniment; it was a racial epithet; it was a wartime moniker for enemy aircraft; it was an intransitive vernacular verb connoting the uninhibited pursuit of pleasure; it was a reference to the devil and all the troubles associated with him; and it was, less openly but no less significantly, a Southern euphemism for a case of secondary syphilis. There was a multilayered joke proffered, in other words, in Brown's wry conflation of Beethoven with the boogie-woogie, an irreverent populist riff that counterpointed democratically the classical with the vernacular, the academy with the Southern road, white icons with black reprobates; and that now, in remembrance, binds Brown the scholar/poet with the many-monikered chaingang songster as nachally as a professing Teller of Lies might be to the legend with the gold-toothed grin.

NOTE

1. Sterling Brown, "The Blues as Folk Poetry"; "Blues, Ballads and Social Songs"; and "The Blues."

WORKS CITED

Brown, Sterling. "The Approach of the Creative Artist." *Journal of American Folklore* 59 (October 1946): 506–7.
———. "The Blues." *Phylon* 13 (Autumn 1952): 286–92.
———. "The Blues as Folk Poetry." *Folk-Say.* Ed. Benjamin Botkin. Norman: University of Oklahoma Press, 1930. 324–39.
———. "Blues, Ballads and Social Songs." *Seventy-five Years of Freedom.* Washington: Library of Congress, 1940. 17–25.
———. "Folk Literature." *The Negro Caravan.* Eds. Sterling Brown, Arthur Davis, and Ulysses Lee. 1941. New York: Arno and *The New York Times,* 1970. 412–34.
———. Interview with Sterling Brown. With John Edgar Tidwell and John S. Wright. Washington, 13 July 1980. (Reprinted in this volume as "Steady and Unaccusing.")
———. "Negro Folk Expression." *Phylon* 11 (Autumn 1950): 318–27.

————. "Negro Folk Expression: Spirituals, Seculars, Ballads and Work Songs." *Phylon* 14 (Winter 1953): 45–61.

Brunvand, Jan Harold. *Folklore: A Study and Research Guide.* New York: St. Martin's, 1976.

Dorson, Richard. *American Folklore and the Historian.* Chicago: University of Chicago Press, 1971.

Du Bois, W.E.B. *The Souls of Black Folk.* 1903. *Three Negro Classics.* Ed. John Hope Franklin. New York: New American Library, 1969. 207–389.

Jackson, Bruce. Foreword. American *Negro Folksongs.* By Newman White. 1928. Hatboro, PA: Folklore Associates, 1965.

Krehbiel, Henry. *Afro-American Folksongs: A Study in Racial and National Music.* New York: Schirmer, 1914.

Locke, Alain. "Sterling Brown: The New Negro Folk Poet." *Negro Anthology.* Ed. Nancy Cunard. 1934. New York: Ungar, 1970. 88–92. (Reprinted in this volume.)

Lomax, Alan. "The Functional Aspects of Folklore." *Journal of American Folklore* 59 (October 1946): 507–10.

Lomax, John, and Alan Lomax. *Negro Folk Songs as Sung by Leadbelly.* New York: Macmillan, 1936.

Lovell, John. *Black Song: The Forge and the Flame.* New York: Macmillan, 1972.

Mangione, Jerre. *The Dream and the Deal: The Federal Writers' Project, 1935–1943.* New York: Avon, 1972.

Redmond, Eugene. *Drumvoices: The Mission of Afro-American Poetry.* Garden City, NY: Anchor, 1976.

Talley, Thomas. *Negro Folk Rhymes.* 1922. Port Washington, NY: Kennikat Press, 1968.

Authenticity and Elevation: Sterling Brown's Theory of the Blues

Lorenzo Thomas

Every poet must confront a serious problem: how to reconcile one's private preoccupations with the need to make poetry that is both accessible and useful to others. A failure in this area does not, of course, prevent the production of poems. Indeed, some poems—like many of T. S. Eliot's—may be records of this struggle, while others have the disturbingly eloquent beauty of Church testifying or 12-step program witness. One manner of reconciliation is an embrace of what may be called *tradition,* but even this is problematic.

The idea of tradition made Eliot uneasy; at best he saw it as a living artist's colloquy and competition with the dead (48–50). In his essay "Tradition and the Individual Talent" (1920), Eliot points out that acquiring the "consciousness of the past" is both necessary and perilous for a poet; and eventually, in his description of it, tradition begins to assume the proportions of a face that "sticks that way" (52–53).

As a poet somewhat younger than Eliot, Sterling A. Brown delighted in experimentation yet also valued his role as a contributor to a tradition. In the poems he composed in the 1920s, Brown "sought to combine the musical forms of the blues, work songs, ballads, and spirituals with poetic expression in such a way as to preserve the originality of the former and achieve the complexity of the latter" (Gabbin 42). Brown's relationship to tradition was, in other words, something like a mirror-image of Eliot's. Where Eliot cringed before a weighty past, Brown—focusing on the African American vernacular tradition—perceived an originality and creativity to be mastered and then practiced in an even more original manner. In fact, Brown's poetics document an attitude toward tradition that is not very different than the one held by the blues singers themselves.[1] It is worth noting, also, that Brown did not necessarily see his valorization of African American folk tradition as inconsistent with his practice of contemporary poetic experiment. Just as Hart Crane and others fled the stultifying worldview of their parents, Brown could warn against "an arising snobbishness; a delayed Victorianism" among educated African Americans ("Our Literary Audience" 42). And when he analyzed the blues, Brown discerned a poetic approach that paralleled the Imagists and other Modernists "in substituting the thing seen for the bookish dressing up and sentimentalizing" that characterized nineteenth-century literary verse ("The Blues as Folk Poetry" 378).

In addition to addressing the dilemma of privacy and access, of the proper value of tradition, Sterling Brown's work also shows how one writer negotiated the relationship of the creative arts—both "highbrow" and "folk"—to the political agenda of the African American struggle for self-determination as it developed in the period between the two world wars. In choosing to study the blues, Brown found himself engaged with a genre of poetry that offers its own clever solution to these problems. The blues, Brown discovered, "has a bitter honesty. This is the way the blues singers and their poets have found life to be. And their audiences agree" ("The Blues" 288). Indeed, it is this agreement between poet and audience that is the reality and the purpose of the blues.

Houston A. Baker, Jr., has rightly noted the unusual circumstance of the awesomely intellectual young Sterling Brown embracing a form devised by the unlettered (92–95), and perhaps an important clue is found in Brown's poem "Ma Rainey." Rainey's art and its powerful effect on her audience, her ability to "'jes catch hold of us, somekindaway'" (*Poems* 63) through song, is precisely the ambition of every poet, and may explain one source of Brown's attraction to the blues. There are some other possibilities as well. Whether or not one sees Brown's poetry as part of the Modernist direction—or of the Regionalism that seemed to make a number of largely regional "splashes" during the 1930s—Brown's poems also clearly embody and represent two decidedly pre-Modern projects. One of these is the "corrective" gesture of African American scholarship, and the other is the desire of both poets and critics to create a "national literature" for black Americans.

In 1930, Brown declared "a deep concern with the development of a literature worthy of our past, and of our destiny; without which literature we can never come to much." He added, "I have deep concern with the development of an audience worthy of such literature" ("Our Literary Audience" 42). In a sense this aim balances Brown's Modernist tendencies and leads him toward the compilation of "antiquities" found in the folk tradition. As Charles H. Rowell has noted, Brown belonged to a group of writers who "realized that to express the souls of black folk, the artist has to divest himself of preconceived and false notions about black people, and create an art whose foundation is the ethos from which spring black life, history, culture, and traditions" (131). This effort is also consistent with the "Correctionist" mission first assumed by David Walker in his 1829 rebuttal of Thomas Jefferson's racial slurs in *Notes on the State of Virginia* (1785) and continued by Carter G. Woodson, J. A. Rogers, Lerone Bennett, Jr., Ivan van Sertima, and others.

Sterling Brown's contribution to this effort was to identify and analyze the stereotypes—derogatory in varying degrees but *never* "just clean fun"—that proliferate in literature and the media. This he did in both scholarly and popular arenas—as both critic and poet. The urgency of Brown's efforts derive from his understanding, as stated in *The Negro Caravan* (1941), that "white authors dealing with the American Negro have interpreted him in a way to justify his exploitation. Creative literature has often been a handmaiden to social policy" (3). As critic Brown exposed these vicious and persistent stereotypes; as a creative artist, he sought to counter them with a social realist portraiture based on forms indigenous to the African American community.

The need for this type of work should not be underestimated. Although minstrelsy began in the 1830s, it was—incredibly—still going strong a century later. In 1922, for example, George Gershwin and Buddy DeSylva wrote *Blue Monday Blues,* a one-act "jazz opera," for a Broadway musical production. As a run-up to Gershwin's classic *Porgy and Bess* (1935) this was more like a stumble. The review in the New York *World* called it "the most dismal, stupid and incredible blackface sketch that has probably ever been perpetrated. In it a dusky soprano finally killed her gambling man. She should have shot all her associates the moment they appeared and then turned the pistol on herself" (qtd. in Goldberg 122). As late as 1932, *George White's Scandals* filled seats on Broadway with songs such as "That's Why Darkies Were Born." Writing in *Opportunity,* Brown acknowledged the popular and degradingly inaccurate depictions of the Negro from Stephen Foster to Al Jolson as an "epidemic" which spread its contagion anywhere money was to be made: "Tin Pan Alley, most of whose dwellers had been no further south than Perth Amboy, frantically sought rhymes for the southern states, cheered over the startling rediscovery of Alabammy and Miami for their key word Mammy . . ." ("Weep" 87). It is against this tide of doggerel that Brown built a levee of authentic African American folksong.

As poet also, notes Stephen E. Henderson, Brown's subtle and insightful understanding of the folk forms "extends the literary range of the blues without losing their authenticity." In fact, Brown approaches the African American folk forms of spiritual, shout, work song, and blues exactly as he had used "the formal measures of the English poets" in his earliest attempts at writing poetry (Henderson 32). It is clear that, for Brown, these stanzas had achieved an equal dignity and utility as literary models.

Among the formal qualities of the blues, Brown's study also focused on language and dialect. Brown's important essay "The Blues as Folk Poetry" (1930) is not so theoretically elaborate or ambitious as the archetype of "Ebonics" offered in Zora Neale Hurston's "Characteristics of Negro Expression" (1934). While the dialect recorded in folklore is integral for Brown, it is *not* of mystical import: "There is nothing 'degraded' about dialect. Dialectical peculiarities are universal. There is something about Negro dialect, in the idiom, the turn of phrase, the music of the vowels and consonants that is worth treasuring" ("Our Literary Audience" 45).

In "The Blues as Folk Poetry," Brown finds that the images presented in this dialect form are "highly compressed, concrete, imaginative, original" (383). He cites beautifully conceived lines such as

> My gal's got teeth lak a lighthouse on de sea.
> Every time she smiles she throws a light on me.

But Brown was not primarily interested in collecting poetic, or the more numerous quaint, expressions. As he noted in 1946, his interest in folk materials "was first attracted by certain qualities that I thought the speech of the people had, and I wanted to get for my own writing a flavor, a color, a pungency of speech. Then later I came to something more important—I wanted to get an understanding of people, to acquire an accuracy in the portrayal of their lives" ("Approach" 506).

Brown's work also participates in the creation of an African American "national literature" by endorsing and contributing to a project carefully outlined by Alain Locke in the 1920s. This is not a Modernist program but a modernized replication of the model first articulated in Europe by those who saw a national literature as the refinement of indigenous folk expression. Locke and James Weldon Johnson applied this nineteenth-century model quite specifically to music, seeing in the spirituals the material that—in the hands of gifted black composers—would escape "the lapsing conditions and fragile vehicle of folk art and come firmly into the context of formal music" (Locke, "Negro" 199). The Fisk Jubilee Singers, performing concert settings composed by R. Nathaniel Dett and others, represent the first movement of Locke's envisioned symphony.

Folklorist Arthur Huff Fauset applied the same principle to literature. Writing in Locke's *The New Negro* (1925), Fauset decried the derogatory misrepresentations of authentic African folklore in its American survivals, called for a more professional ethnographic study of it, and predicted that "Negro writers themselves will shortly, no doubt[,] be developing [the folktales and oral traditions of the South] as arduously as [Joel] Chandler Harris, and we hope as successfully, or even more so" (243–44).

While Locke foresaw a great classical music born of the folk forms shaped by slavery, James Weldon Johnson surveyed Broadway's stages and declared a victory for Negro genius, citing the rhythmic impulse of African American music as "the genesis and foundation of our national popular medium for musical expression" (*American Negro Spirituals* 31). Johnson's political interpretation of this development was not hidden. In the preface to his 1926 collection of Negro spirituals, he noted that "America would not be precisely the America it is except for the silent power the Negro has exerted upon it, both positive and negative" (19). Johnson also asserted that authentic folk art posed a serious challenge for any academically trained artist who aspired to transcend, or even match, its distinctive qualities of honesty and emotionally overwhelming beauty.

That the type of reclamation effort Arthur Huff Fauset prescribed for African American folktales should also be required for the blues—a form that only emerged in the first decade of the century—should not surprise those who consider the carefully built and well-maintained mechanism of racism that was running at full throttle before World War II.

Texas A&M College professor Will H. Thomas's *Some Current Folk-Songs of the Negro* was the very first publication of the Texas Folklore Society. While this essay provides evidence that the blues was a widespread and authentic form in Texas in 1912—two years before W. C. Handy published "The St. Louis Blues" and launched its commercial development—the paper also offers disturbing documentation of white academics sitting around enjoying their own genteel version of "darkie" jokes. Sympathetic song collectors were also somewhat tainted by the general paternalism of the region and era. Folklorist John A. Lomax, one of the earliest commentators on the blues, characterized them as "Negro songs of self-pity" in an article published in *The Nation* in 1917. Even when employed by a liberal, such terminology supported the negative social construction of the African American image that James Weldon Johnson succinctly summarized as the view that black people were, at best, "wards" of American society.

Benjamin A. Botkin, writing in 1927, accepted the Texas folklorists' idea that self-pity was "a trait of the Negro, bred in him by centuries of oppression" (231); but Botkin was perceptive enough to understand that out of this "sense of self-pity develops an inevitable conviction of social injustice and an indictment of the existing order" (233). Botkin and Sterling Brown would become allies. They were the same age and shared similar interests in folklore, the experiments of the New Poetry movement, and a high regard for proletarian self-expression as encouraged by intellectuals connected with *The New Masses* and similar journals (Hutchinson 271–73); thus Botkin's annual anthology *Folk-Say: A Regional Miscellany* provided a venue for Brown's essays and the blues-influenced poems collected in *Southern Road* (1932).[2]

"The blues," wrote Brown in *Negro Poetry and Drama* (1937), "tell a great deal about folk-life. The genteel turn away from them in distaste, but blues persist with their terse and tonic shrewdness about human nature" (27). It is also true that the blues differ from the spirituals because the secular form highlights vicarious and ventriloquial qualities. "Nobody heah can a-walk it for you / You gotta walk it by yo'self" is, as Brown puts it, the "sour truth" of the ancient spiritual "Lonesome Valley" (*Poems* 98–99). The message of any blues, of course, is just the opposite. The blues singer bids his listener to learn from his or her example before, as Roosevelt Sykes put it, you "make a mistake in life." The poems Brown originally published as a sort of suite titled "Lonesome Valley" in Botkin's 1931 *Folk-Say* seem designed to explore this aspect of blues songs.[3]

Brown's three-part "The New St. Louis Blues" is deeply and pugnaciously political. In the first poem, even the natural disasters that are so often the topic of blues songs are politicized. After a tornado brings destruction and a flood of refugees, Brown sings:

> Newcomers dodge de mansions, and knocked on de po' folks' do',
> Dodged most uh de mansions, and knocked down de po' folks' do,
> Never knew us po' folks so popular befo'. ("Lonesome Valley" 119)

When he turns his attention to the way things go in the man-made world, the picture is bleaker still:

> Woman done quit me, my boy lies fast in jail,
> Woman done quit me, pardner lies fast in jail,
> Kin bum tobacco but I cain't bum de jack fo' bail.
>
> Church don't help me, 'cause I ain't got no Sunday clothes,
> Church don't help me, got no show-off Sunday clothes,
> Preachers and deacons, don't look to get no help from those.
>
> Dice are loaded an' de deck's all marked to hell,
> Dice are loaded an' de deck's all marked to hell,
> Whoever runs dis gamble sholy runs it well. ("Lonesome Valley" 121)

Another poem, "Convict"—not written in the blues stanza form—comments on the Southern penal system. Jim, serving ninety days on the chain gang, passes his own home each day as he shuttles between "handcuffs / And a dingy cell, / Daytime on the highways, / Nights in hell" (115).[4]

In the poems grouped as "Lonesome Valley," Brown is quite deliberately revising both the folklorists' and the Broadway song-pluggers' misinterpretations of the blues. In his prose writings on the blues from the late 1930s to the early 1950s, Brown would explicitly restate the principles that informed his blues poems. "As well as self-pity there is stoicism in the blues," Brown wrote in 1937. He also directed attention to the collector Lawrence Gellert's discovery of songs that contained searing evidence of "otherwise inarticulate resentment against injustice." The arch language used here is, of course, intended to mock the Southern (and, perhaps also, academic) etiquette of oppression. Brown characterizes the songs Gellert collected as ironic, coded, but defiant protest, representing not self-pity but "a very adept self-portraiture" (*Negro Poetry and*

Drama 27–29). The kinds of songs Gellert collected can be judged by the following verses, recorded in Southern Pines, North Carolina:

> Ah wants no ruckus, but ah ain' dat kin'
> What lets you all shoe-shine on mah behin'. ("Negro Songs" 233)

Gellert, a contributor to *The New Masses*, met Brown in Boston while traveling with Nancy Cunard in 1932. The three impressed each other greatly (Gellert, "Remembering" 142–43). For his part, Brown cites Gellert's work in almost every article on the blues he subsequently published.

The development of the blues simultaneously as a folk music, vulnerable to scholarly misinterpretation, and as an offering of the commercial music industry, on phonograph records and on the vaudeville stage, is intriguing. For those interested in the study of "pure forms" this dual development offered problems from the start. Nevertheless, unlike Alain Locke, Sterling Brown seemed unworried about the possible fading away of authentic folk expression or its commercial exploitation. What remained important to him was that "the vigor of the creative impulse has not been snapped, even in the slums" of big cities, as far from the source of Southern tradition as anyone might imagine ("Negro Folk Expression" 61). Brown also clearly articulated his understanding of what the living blues form represented, and what the true purpose of the "creative impulse" embodied in the blues really is. "Socially considered," Brown wrote in 1952, "the blues tell a great deal about one segment of Negro life. It is inaccurate, however, to consider them completely revelatory of the Negro folk, or of the folk transplanted in the cities, or of the lower class in general. The blues represent the secular, the profane, where the spirituals and gospel songs represent the religious" ("The Blues" 291). As he had pointed out in 1930, "There are so many Blues that any preconception might be proved about Negro folk life, as well as its opposite. As documentary proof of dogma about the Negro peasant, then, the Blues are satisfactory and unsatisfactory. As documents about humanity they are invaluable" ("The Blues as Folk Poetry" 372). What becomes apparent to anyone who dips into the considerable musicological and sociological literature about African American music published in recent years is that Sterling Brown's early efforts to properly complicate our interpretations have, indeed, achieved a great measure of success.

The same cannot be said of Brown's interest in building a literary edifice on the unique blues form. Though Langston Hughes created masterpieces with that form, and though W. H. Auden, Raymond Patterson, James Emanuel, and Sterling Plumpp have—like Brown himself—also created notable blues works, the attempt to elevate the blues stanza to literary rank has not been so successful as the campaign for the sonnet. It may be fair to consider, however, that the partisans of the sonnet began to promote it 300 years before Sterling Brown discovered the blues.

What Brown certainly did accomplish, however, was to identify the authentic poetic voice of black America, making it heard above the din of racist parody and well-intentioned, sympathetic misinterpretation. In 1953, during the height of the McCarthyist assault on creative expression, Brown saw fit to foreground the political power inherent in the blues songs composed by his friend Waring Cuney and by the popular Josh White. These songs "on poverty, hardship, poor housing and jim crow military service, come from conscious propagandists, not truly folk," Brown wrote. "They make use of the folk idiom in both text and music, however, and the folk listen and applaud. They know very well what Josh White is talking about" ("Negro Folk Expression" 60).[5] It is interesting—and a subtle index of Sterling A. Brown's character—to note that, while in "Ma Rainey," written in 1930, he was content to quote an audience member's appreciation that "'she jes catch hold of us, somekindaway,'" in the 1950s—at a time when it mattered—he was brave enough to explain exactly *why.*

NOTES

1. An intriguing discussion of how the New Negro movement attempted to re-site the idea of tradition is offered by Charles H. Rowell's view of the poet as a sort of adept: "In a word, when Brown taught and traveled in the South, he became an insider to the multifarious traditions and verbal art forms indigenous to black folk, and through his adaptations of their verbal art forms and spirit he, as poet, became an instrument for their myriad voices. Hence *Southern Road*" (134). How this approach to reclaiming tradition in the service of literary innovation also served Alain Locke's program for the arts as an instrument of race "redemption" via political and social progress is indicated by a comment from Langston Hughes and Arna Bontemps in their introduction to *The Book of Negro Folklore* (1959): "The blues provided a tap-root of tremendous vitality for season after season, vogue after vogue of popular music, and became an American idiom in a broad sense" (vii).
2. Typically placing important but accessible essays by scholars such as Henry Nash Smith in the company of poems by John Gould Fletcher and others, *Folk-Say* was more literary anthology than academic journal. An excellent discussion of Botkin's project is found in Hirsch (12–14).
3. Sterling Brown actually uses the blues stanza form in three ways in his own poems. The earliest approach is found in "Ma Rainey," first published in *Folk-Say* in 1930. Here, as in Langston Hughes's poem "The Weary Blues" (1927), the actual blues verses are set within a more elaborate structure of different free-verse stanzas. The 1931 edition of *Folk-Say* contains Brown's "Tin Roof Blues" and "New St. Louis Blues," both of which are entirely composed in the standard three-line blues stanza form. In 1932 Brown published "Long Track Blues" and "Rent Day Blues"—and here the blues stanzas are disguised as quatrains.
    It is important to distinguish between the poems in which Brown uses the actual blues stanza form and those poems which appear to have a "blues feeling" or depict a socioeconomic milieu that might be typical or evocative of the blues. The poem "Southern Road," for example, is not a blues song but a work

song—quite specifically of the type used to accompany or "choreograph" the rhythms of sledgehammer or pickaxe work. Similarly, the poem "Memphis Blues" is not a blues; it is an elaborate structure similar to "Ma Rainey" which provides Brown with a setting for an apocalyptically parodistic spiritual.

4. The system of local prison farms and the practice of leasing convict labor were major concerns to African Americans in the South in the early years of the century. As Lawrence Gellert noted regarding his travels in South Carolina and Georgia in the 1920s: "These roads are kept in repair by chain-gangs. Work on them, of course, is in proportion to the number of convicts available. Hence no crime goes long unpunished. Not if there can be found a stray Negro within a hundred-mile radius" (229). This system was in place as early as 1906, as Ray Stannard Baker reported in *Following the Color Line* (95–99). John L. Spivak's contribution to Nancy Cunard's *Negro: An Anthology* includes photographs of prisoners in Georgia being tortured by fastening in stocks or being stretched between posts, situations even more brutally repressive than those recorded by Baker a quarter-century earlier. "No pretext had been necessary to kidnap Africans and bring them to America as slaves. But pretexts would be necessary to kidnap Black Americans and reenslave them," observes H. Bruce Franklin. The answer was, of course, that "the victims would have to be perceived as criminals" (102).

    Many of the songs Lawrence Gellert collected were recorded on the prison sites. Gellert's articles appeared originally in *The New Masses;* the field recordings he made have been released by Rounder Records as *Negro Songs of Protest* (see Bastin 64–67).

5. Testifying before the House Committee on Un-American Activities, White explained his performing for Communist-organized benefits and rallies in the following statement: "Dozens of artists of all races and colors . . . have also given their names and talent and time under the innocent impression that they were on the side of charity and equality. Let me make it clear, if I can, that I am still on that side. The fact that Communists are exploiting grievances for their own purpose does not make those grievances any less real" (*Josh White Songbook* 33).

WORKS CITED

Baker, Houston A., Jr. *Modernism and the Harlem Renaissance*. Chicago: University of Chicago Press, 1987.

Baker, Ray Stannard. *Following the Color Line: An Account of Negro Citizenship in the American Democracy*. 1908. Williamstown, MA: Corner House, 1973.

Bastin, Bruce. *Red River Blues: The Blues Tradition in the Southeast*. Urbana: University of Illinois Press, 1986.

Botkin, B. A. "Self-Portraiture and Social Criticism in Negro Folk-Song." 1927. *The Politics and Aesthetics of "New Negro" Literature*. Ed. Cary D. Wintz. New York: Garland, 1996. 230–34.

Brown, Sterling A. "The Approach of the Creative Artist." *Journal of American Folklore* 59 (Oct.–Dec. 1946): 506–7.

———. "The Blues." *Phylon* 13 (1952): 286–92.

———. "The Blues as Folk Poetry." *Folk-Say: A Regional Miscellany*. Ed. B. A. Botkin. Norman: University of Oklahoma Press, 1930. 324–39. Rpt. in Hughes and Bontemps, *The Book of Negro Folklore* 371–86.

————. *Collected Poems*. Ed. Michael S. Harper. 1980. Chicago: Tri-Quarterly Press, 1989.

————. "Lonesome Valley" [9 poems]. *Folk-Say: A Regional Miscellany*. Ed. B. A. Botkin. Norman: University of Oklahoma Press, 1931. 113–23.

————. "Negro Folk Expression: Spirituals, Seculars, Ballads and Work Songs." *Phylon* 14 (1953): 45–61.

————. *Negro Poetry and Drama*. 1937. New York: Arno Press, 1969.

————. "Our Literary Audience." *Opportunity* 8 (February 1930): 42–46, 61.

————. "Weep Some More My Lady." *Opportunity* 10 (March 1932): 87.

————, Arthur P. Davis, and Ulysses Lee, eds. *The Negro Caravan*. 1941. Salem, NH: Ayer, 1987.

Cunard, Nancy, ed. *Negro: An Anthology*. 1934. New York: Ungar, 1970.

Eliot, T. S. "Tradition and the Individual Talent." *The Sacred Wood: Essays on Poetry and Criticism*. 1920. New York: Barnes and Noble, 1960. 47–59.

Fauset, Arthur Huff. "American Negro Folk Literature." Locke, *New Negro*, 238–44.

Franklin, H. Bruce. *Prison Literature in America: The Victim as Criminal and Artist*. New York: Oxford University Press, 1989.

Gabbin, Joanne V. *Sterling A. Brown: Building the Black Aesthetic Tradition*. 1985. Charlottesville: University Press of Virginia, 1994.

Gellert, Lawrence. "Negro Songs of Protest." Cunard, *Negro*, 226–37.

————. "Remembering Nancy Cunard." *Nancy Cunard: Brave Poet, Indomitable Rebel, 1896–1965*. Ed. Hugh Ford. Philadelphia: Chilton, 1968. 141–44.

Goldberg, Isaac. *George Gershwin: A Study in American Music*. 1931. New York: Ungar, 1958.

Henderson, Stephen E. "The Heavy Blues of Sterling Brown: A Study of Craft and Tradition." *Black American Literature Forum* 14 (Spring 1980): 32–44. (Reprinted in this volume.)

Hirsch, Jerrold. "Folklore in the Making: B. A. Botkin." *Journal of American Folklore* 100 (January–March 1987): 3–38.

Hughes, Langston, and Arna Bontemps, eds. *The Book of Negro Folklore*. New York: Dodd, Mead, 1959.

Hurston, Zora Neale. "Characteristics of Negro Expression." 1934. *The Sanctified Church*. Berkeley: Turtle Island, 1981. 49–68.

Hutchinson, George. *The Harlem Renaissance in Black and White*. Cambridge: Harvard University Press, 1995.

Johnson, James Weldon, and J. Rosamond Johnson. *The Book of American Negro Spirituals*. 1926. New York: Da Capo Press, 1981.

Locke, Alain. "The Negro Spirituals." Locke, *New Negro* 199–210.

————, ed. *The New Negro*. 1925. New York: Atheneum, 1992.

Lomax, John A. "Self-Pity in Negro Folk-Songs." *Nation*, 9 August 1917: 141–45.

Rowell, Charles H. "Sterling A. Brown and the Afro-American Folk Tradition." *Studies in the Literary Imagination* 7 (Fall 1974): 131–52.

Spivak, John L. "Flashes from Georgia Chain Gangs." Cunard, *Negro*, 124–30.

Thomas, Will H. *Some Current Folk-Songs of the Negro*. 1912. Austin: Texas Folklore Society, 1936.

White, Josh, with Robert Shelton and Walter Raim. *The Josh White Songbook*. Chicago: Quadrangle, 1963.

IV

UNHISTORIC HISTORY: AMERICAN AND AFRICAN AMERICAN CULTURES

Sterling A. Brown and the Afro-Modern Moment

Mark A. Sanders

When Robert Penn Warren wrote his highly ironic line "Nigger, your breed ain't metaphysical" (321), he compressed into five deceptively economic feet nearly a half-millennium of white hegemonic philosophy, both its rhetorical strategies and underlying presuppositions. Buzzard, "the carrier of the ostracizing power of white discourse, the trope which declares the otherness of the black" (Nielsen 117), does not simply assert black inferiority but reconstructs and reaffirms the mutually exclusive mythic realms "white" and "black" must inhabit in order to sustain five hundred years of radical inequity. As ametaphysical, "the black" (or, better yet, blackness) must exist beyond the aesthetic, beyond the redemptive possibilities central to the humanistic tradition of arts and letters. As "fictive signifier of the nonwhite" (Nielsen 10), blackness serves as a repository of reifying antitheses: anti-intellectual, illiterate, subhuman, and ahistorical. All in all, Warren constructs a blackness thoroughly banished to the margins of the human community, a blackness of radical absence proclaiming the final and ultimate abstraction of damning eternal sameness. Indeed Warren (and by extension what I will call hegemonic or conventional modernism) achieves much of his coherence through the assertion of objectified blackness, through a tropic vocabulary of necessarily reductive poses impervious to change over time (see Nielsen, North).

Yet it is precisely the cultural force of these poses and the pervasive nature of the objectifying language which would drive James Weldon Johnson, William Pickens, Carter G. Woodson, and even W.E.B. Du Bois (in "A Conservation of Races") to advance a countering but often equally reductive discourse. Johnson's ragtime piano players, for example, are "guided by their natural musical instinct" and their "extraordinary sense of rhythm"; thus Johnson effectively reinscribes essentializing tropes in an attempt to assert a "Negro exceptionalism" worthy of notice and, ultimately, of citizenship (20).

The profound condensation of Warren's single line was not lost on Sterling A. Brown, whose famous retort some years later undermined entirely the conception of ahistorical blackness. His reply in a 1974 interview with Steven Jones, "Cracker, your kind ain't exegetical," appropriates Warren's five-foot economy in order to parody both the sound and sense of his poetry. Through such "signifying" Brown points to a crucial blindness which makes possible an assertion of black ametaphysicality. Signaling much more than a lack of specific exposition, Brown alludes to a profound illiteracy, a lack of attention to a broad corpus of texts and cultural idioms which assert African American complexity and change. So, too, Brown remained skeptical of these countering tropes on the part of New Negroes, tropes which could not account for the burgeoning complexities he found in Southern black life. Positioning himself outside (or perhaps beyond) the two competing discourses, Brown questions the fundamental assumption (or acceptance) of ontological blackness, and so begins to formulate an Afro-modernism (both a poetic vocabulary and a theory of folk culture) capable of exploring a more dynamic range in African American being. In short, Brown embarks upon an artistic and aesthetic project which fundamentally reconceives black modernity. Appropriating contemporary notions concerning subjectivity and process, and applying them to a range of black idiomatic expressions and rituals, Brown reworks the language and tropes he inherited in order to explore the inventive ways in which African Americans articulate their modernity; that is, express a presence, a historicity, an ongoing engagement with the contemporary moment.

A reading of "Odyssey of Big Boy," both within and beyond Southern Road, helps to illustrate Brown's larger concerns. Brown introduces Southern Road with an allusion to travel and experience, to independence, self-discovery, and the romantic possibilities of immortality. "Odyssey of Big Boy," in its gesture toward the mythic, initiates the road as witness, odyssey, and highly ambivalent duality, and thus presents the major motifs and metaphors which will develop through the course of the collection. "Odyssey," for Calvin "Big Boy" Davis, resonates with Homeric implications—extended travel resulting in catholic experiences and the possibility of heroic stature—but Davis's odyssey embarks upon an innovative variation on the standard theme and approach.

Significantly, Big Boy Davis's proclamation is not a third-person narrative rehearsing the past deeds and mythic status of cultural heroes; it is not the ballads of John Henry, Casey Jones, or Stagolee. Instead, as he confronts his imminent death, Davis embarks upon a personal odyssey toward self-realization, an incomplete journey into the future. This fundamental dynamic depends heavily upon the intricate play between past and future, a play which propels the poem out of the static sphere of traditional balladry into the dynamics of highly personalized subjectivity. Davis begins and ends not with a statement about the past, but with a vision of the future:

> Lemme be wid Casey Jones,
>> Lemme be wid Stagolee,
> Lemme be wid such like men
>> When Death takes hol' on me,
>>> When Death takes hol' on me . . .
>
> An' all dat Big Boy axes
>> When time comes fo' to go,
> Lemme be wid John Henry, steel drivin' man,
>> Lemme be wid old Jazzbo,
>> Lemme be wid ole Jazzbo . . . (20–21)

With such a framing, Davis delivers a history which plays upon the creative tension between past and future, and thus transforms his odyssey into one of present voice. His "future link with the past" depends entirely upon the oral re-shaping of his history; therefore the vocal act of proclamation and assertion becomes the odyssey toward apotheosis—hence the voice as passage and "mode of knowing" (Benston 33).

Driven by this central tension, Davis's chronicle takes on a particularly personal urgency, while continuing to embrace the collective cultural potential for recreation. His history, a review of jobs, travel, and romantic conquests, invokes a masculinist tradition defining personhood in terms of physical and psychological autonomy, in terms of mobility and abundant vitality. And thus the road alludes to those larger cultural icons of superlative success. Having "seen what dey is to see" (20), his life should find fulfillment once assigned the same symbolic stature as that of his heroes.

But just as Davis's odyssey toward myth and immortality depends upon the statement of his life, it also depends upon the form that statement takes, essentially the formal poetic constructions which aid in his search for voice. In short, Davis rhetorically reconstructs himself in the form of John Henry as he is received and preserved through balladry. In terms of stanza form—specifically the number of lines, rhyme scheme, and repetition—Davis directly mimics "John Henry," the ballad Brown uses in Negro Caravan. The only major formal difference is the length of the line. Thus, the process of shaping Davis's own history through the invocation of an historical form reveals the vital acts of reclaiming and refashioning; Davis's gesture is historical, reaching into the past to claim a form and voice that will allow him to envision his future. So this process intertwines the personal and the collective.

This formal appropriation also effects a kind of "double voicing," where his "semantic orientation" colors the established cultural articulation—to use Henry Louis Gates Jr.'s application of Bakhtin (50). But distinct from Bakhtin's sense of parody, Davis's double voicing "evaluates" the John Henry ballad as the superlative sign of mythic heroism and masculinity. Thus, Davis's sense of enduring meaning depends entirely upon an absolute identification with John Henry's transcendent signification. Here Davis grafts his biography onto a cultural continuum; his blues-inflected lyric odyssey signifies his own progression as well as the larger cultural modality.

Playing on this dramatic tension between past and future, "Odyssey of Big Boy" concerns itself, then, with the present moment of vocalization, with the ongoing dynamic of self-articulation and self-recreation, and the ability of voice to project and reconstruct. For Davis the past looms as power and evidence; the future serves as hope and possibility dependent upon the present voice and its ability to shape the past and thus the future. For Big Boy Davis, his performing voice, enacting a ritual of mythic invocation, works as a visionary tool, allowing him to access the broader meaning which leads beyond his immediate circumstances. In short, "Odyssey" dramatizes the perpetually temporal, the entirely subjective moment which is at once excruciatingly private yet self-consciously public and representative, both in process and aspiration. In this sense, "Odyssey of Big Boy" addresses the dynamics of individual and collective history; it exults the challenge to rationalize, reshape, and rediscover the past and, by extension, the challenge to discover expansive possibilities for the future. As Davis reshapes himself in the form of John Henry, and thus shapes his life-song in reference to the culture's superlatives, his vocal odyssey also constructs Davis as artist, both musician and poet able to squeeze from his experience "a near-tragic, near comic lyricism" (Ellison 129). His successful vocalization projects Davis as a metaphor for the artist and his/her ability to shape and recreate reality, to access alternative and liberating psychic spaces. And of course implicit in this reading is Brown himself, the poet able to envision and provoke profound transformation.

These larger concerns force "Odyssey of Big Boy" beyond an insulated ritual of self-proclamation to an eloquent introduction to the entire collection, and perhaps Brown's larger poetic project, which stresses dynamics and movement. Brown reconceives the past and history as active agents in the ongoing present. Kimberly Benston comments: "Brown's poems inscribe the past not as a nostalgic after-thought but as a process engendering unlimited visions, not as a feeble gesture toward an unrealizable ideal but as a dynamic proposition, an *after-song* that is both petition and re-petition" (Benston 35).

Thus, as "Odyssey of Big Boy" works as perpetual vocal epic, Big Boy Davis—improvisationalist, student of tradition, and blues hero—serves as the sign of the modernity of folk culture, and as the possibility of artistic expression born of eclectic antecedents. Davis synthesizes idioms, voices, traditions, and forms, and thus exacts the essentially eclectic process at the heart of Brown's aesthetic project. Davis establishes the metaphoric perimeters for *Southern Road*'s master trope, the road, and thus anticipates "When the Saints Go Ma'ching Home," "Strong Men," "Ma Rainey," and "Southern Road." Each of these poems and the collection as a whole explore the triumphs and vicissitudes of contemporary Southern black life, and thus they stress the ongoing agency of folk forms in confronting contemporary dilemmas.

Finally, recognizing the critical interdependence of New Negroism and American modernity, Brown pursues an ultimately synthetic poetic project, exposing and dramatizing the dynamic hybridity fundamental to African American being. But in order to forge a project re-envisioning modernist and New Negro formulations, he must confront and subvert the exclusionary nature of the racial discourse in which both hegemonic modernism and bourgeois New Negroism participate. If the dichotomy dividing hegemonic modernism and New Negroism is in fact false—a point which Brown's poetry ultimately suggests—then Brown must demonstrate the ways in which modernist aesthetics and techniques may actually aid in the deepening and widening of African American artistic representation. But Brown does not draw upon an homogenized Anglo/Eliot-styled modernism, one marked by fragmentation, malaise, and cultural exhaustion; Big Boy Davis's moment is not one of Prufrock-like retreat and psychic paralysis. Rather, Brown invokes a modernism of possibility, animated by new combinations, synthesis, or "superintegration" (McFarlane 92) and marked by formal experimentation, modal progression, and perpetual process. Employing a notion of "strategic essentialism," Brown posits the political and cultural category "black," yet suspends indeed perpetually troubles—any sense of conceptual fixity which may serve the rival discourses of primitivism and exceptionalism.

As the proposition of ontological blackness dissolves into a constellation of historicized contingencies, into subjectivity, fluidity, and modality, all play key roles in a poetics invested in the radical temporality of the present moment. Brown's sense of modernity leads him to a vision of the past as a "process engendering unlimited visions," a "dynamic proposition" which must be perpetually reconfigured, reconstructed (Benston 35). Brown's poetics hold up both past and future as ultimately malleable resources; it is the present moment of consciousness itself, the perpetual moment of manipulation—through voice, ritual, performance, and so forth—which constitutes the thoroughly historicized black subject, the historical actor continually reconstructing the self, and thus the political and cultural landscape. In distinct yet complementary ways, Anne Spencer, Jean Toomer, and the later James Weldon Johnson (of *God's Trombones*) participate in a similarly hybrid, Afro-modernist poetic project. That "strong men keep on a-comin' on" is not simply a statement of political agency or black heroism, but an assertion of historicity, of modality which keeps in play those dimensions of being and personhood which lie beyond (or perhaps beneath) the limitations of crude categorization. From Big Boy Davis's expansive orality to Joe Meek's highly textured sense of irony, Brown's "profoundly Modernist consciousness of poetry's radical historicity, its desire to be both original and related to what precedes it" (Benston 34) leads him to a fundamental reformulation of modernism, one demanding exegesis and giving full voice to a burgeoning Afro-modernism.

WORKS CITED

Benston, Kimberly W. "Sterling Brown's After-Song: 'When de Saints Go Ma'ching Home' and the Performance of Afro-American Voice." *Callaloo* 14–15 (1982): 33–42.

Brown, Sterling A. "Odyssey of Big Boy." *The Collected Poems of Sterling A. Brown.* 1980. Chicago: TriQuarterly Press, 1989. 20–21.

Ellison, Ralph. "Richard Wright's Blues." *The Collected Essays of Ralph Ellison.* Ed. John Callahan. New York: Modern Library, 1995. 128–44.

Gates, Henry Louis, Jr. *The Signifying Monkey: A Theory of African-American Literary Criticism.* New York: Oxford University Press, 1988.

Johnson, James Weldon. "Preface." *The Book of American Negro Poetry.* New York: Harcourt, Brace, 1922. 9–48.

Jones, Steven. Interview with Sterling A. Brown. 4 May 1974.

McFarlane, James. "The Mind of Modernism." *Modernism, 1890–1930.* Ed. Malcolm Bradbury and McFarlane. New York: Humanities Press, 1976. 71–93.

Nielsen, Aldon Lynn. *Reading Race: White American Poets and the Racial Discourse in the Twentieth Century.* Athens: University of Georgia Press, 1988.

North, Michael. *The Dialect of Modernism: Race, Language, and Twentieth-Century Literature.* New York: Oxford University Press, 1994.

Warren, Robert Penn. "Pondy Woods." *A Robert Penn Warren Reader.* New York: Random House, 1987. 320–22.

Sterling Brown: An Ethnographic Odyssey

Beverly Lanier Skinner

I would like to propose a method for reading the poetry of Sterling A. Brown in light of Brown's complete oeuvre. My proposed method is informed by interdisciplinary inquiry, including recent ethnographic theory and qualitative research methodology and an emerging cultural studies discourse that I and others term *black cultural critique*. This approach is not intended to overlook any aspect of the aesthetic values or artistic achievement of Brown's poetic output. Rather, this approach intends to offer an additional, interdisciplinary, theoretical context in which to appreciate Brown's poetic achievement. My thesis is that Sterling Brown was a postmodern ethnographer who by the 1940s had pioneered solutions to three major problems with which today's cultural anthropologists are grappling: (1) what form ethnographic writing should take, (2) what methodology can result in competent ethnographies of non-hegemonic, oral-based cultures, and (3) how the authority of native informants can be acknowledged in ethnographies.

James Clifford and George Marcus offer an eloquent explanation of why I feel it is important to look at Sterling Brown's poetic output from an ethnographic perspective. They see ethnography as an "emergent interdisciplinary phenomenon [whose] authority and rhetoric have spread to many fields where 'culture is a newly problematic object of description and critique'" (*Writing Culture* 3). I suggest that, if we consider Brown's entire oeuvre— poetry, literary criticism, oral history, and cultural critique—from an ethnographic perspective, we can emerge with the understanding that the sum of his writings constitutes an ethnographic methodology that reflects postmodernist sensibilities. However, it was not until the 1970s and '80s that ethnographers like Clifford Geertz, Mary Douglas, Claude Lévi-Strauss, and the late Victor Turner advocated the pursuit of what Sterling Brown already had accomplished—namely, "blurr[ing] the old distinction between art and science and challeng[ing] the very basis of the claim to exacting rigor, unblinking truth telling, and unbiased reporting that marked the boundary separating" art from science (Vidich and Lyman 41). Brown's methodology answers the call of numerous ethnographers and anthropologists who seek honest, nontraditional, competent ways of writing the ethnos of non-hegemonic and non-Western cultures.

Before I proceed with my argument, let me offer some definitions. The *Encyclopedia of Cultural Anthropology* defines *ethnography* as "writing about customs or, more generally, the description of cultures based on firsthand observation and participation in fieldwork. Fieldwork is the process of observing and participating in life ways of people. Anthropologists report the results as ethnography" (416). Postmodern ethnographers, in the words of Vidich and Lyman, "tak[e] seriously the aim of such deconstructionists as Derrida . . . , Lyotard . . . , and Baudrillard." The postmodern ethnographer is one who eschews such traditional pursuits as "the quest for valid generalizations and substantive conclusions" and replaces them with "thick descriptions," in the language of Geertz, so that postmodern ethnography encompasses the "lived experience," "dispriveleg[ing] all received texts and established discourses on behalf of an all-encompassing critical skepticism about knowledge . . . [instead] giv[ing] contingency . . . [to] language, . . . selfhood, . . . and . . . community" (Vidich and Lyman 41).

The ethnographic approach that Sterling Brown pioneered answers the call made by several of today's cutting-edge social scientists for a radical, multivocal, culturally astute approach to cultural studies. In fact, the brand of ethnography that Brown developed is one that can be appreciated by the most radical of cultural scholars. African-American sociologist John H. Stanfield II explains the problem cultural anthropologists have long faced in their attempts to describe and learn from non-hegemonic cultures. He implies in the following quotation that radical approaches to cultural study simply are not in the mission of universities that currently train ethnographers: "The oral basis of most African cultures and among aboriginal peoples around the world offers a major challenge, because adequate study of such cultures requires a different portfolio of skills from what researchers reared in written word-based cultures acquire easily. In oral-based cultures, . . . records . . . come in the form of poems, songs, testimonies, stories, performing arts, and proverbs, rather than diaries, newspapers, census reports, and surveys" (184–85). Contemporary literary studies like Gayl Jones's *Liberating Voices*, Henry Louis Gates's *The Signifying Monkey*, Houston Baker's *Blues, Ideology, and Afro-American Literature*, and

Stephen Henderson's "The Form of Things Unknown" have helped establish African-American culture as an oral-based one. But even earlier, before the New Negro Renaissance that spawned Brown's literary endeavors, W.E.B. Du Bois had established the oral basis of African-American culture in his 1903 essay collection *The Souls of Black Folk*.[1]

The methodology that Stanfield outlines for studying oral-based cultures is one that Sterling Brown had already employed before, during, and after his tenure as administrator of the WPA Writers' Project and researcher in the Gunnar Myrdal–Carnegie study that resulted in the celebrated treatise *An American Dilemma*. (Joanne Gabbin chronicles Brown's professional and artistic accomplishments in her groundbreaking work *Sterling A. Brown: Building the Black Aesthetic Tradition*.) In fact, Brown anticipated Stanfield and Afrocentric cultural scholars like Asante, Ladner, Hamnett, and Merton by writing poetry and collecting oral histories in addition to publishing academic-style treatises to enlighten the world about African-American culture. In other words, rather than using a strictly empirical methodology for treating the unquantifiable and unprovable, and rather than generalizing from the particulars he culled from his travels among black folk in the South, Brown found a culturally functional alternative to the established but inadequate academic form of ethnographic reportage. He created a multi-voiced, polyphonic, self-reflexive, diversely genred oeuvre. He self-consciously and, I might add, defiantly represented an *emic* ethnography, one that reflects the values of the culture being described, rather than the traditional *etic* ethnography, which reflects the values of the newcomer to a culture (Vidich and Lyman 26). I call such an emic approach an *autoethnography*, since one writes of one's own culture from the position of cultural insider.

The autoethnographer is more than the sum of native informant and participant observer, the former being the so-called native guide for the ethnographic researcher and the latter being the outsider ethnographer engaged in fieldwork. The autoethnographer is more than what James Clifford terms the "fieldworker-theorist," whose "cultural description [as of the 1920s was] based on participant observation" (*Predicament* 30). The autoethnographer is nothing like the cultural anthropologist, whom Vidich and Lyman describe as a self-defined newcomer to the habitat and life world of his or her subjects (41). Rather, the autoethnographer has cultural roots in, and an insider's grasp of, the group being described and therefore needs no native informant to assist in the translation of language and culture. Of cultural necessity, the autoethnographer renders the description of his or her own culture on levels that exceed the narrow boundaries of the academic report from the field.

During the time that Brown wrote and studied his own culture, Margaret Mead and Ruth Benedict were ascending to the anthropological throne of intellectual and scholarly authority and were influential in discrediting native informants on the grounds that natives of a culture lack impartiality and objectivity. According to Clifford, "It was tacitly agreed that the new-style ethnographer, whose sojourn in the field seldom exceeded two years, and more frequently was much shorter, could efficiently 'use' native languages without 'mastering' them." Mead and others, in spite of objections from followers of Franz Boas, "established that valid research could be accomplished on the basis of one or two years' familiarity with a foreign vernacular. A distinct primacy was accorded to the visual: interpretation was tied to description. After Bronislaw Malinowski, a general suspicion of 'privileged informants' reflected this systematic preference for the (methodical) observations of the ethnographer over the (interested) interpretations of indigenous authorities" (*Predicament* 31).

Brown, however, questioned the importance and validity of objectivity and impartiality in cultural study and hotly questioned the usefulness of outsider reports of culture. He interrogated the intellectual establishment that presumed it was possible, interesting, and profitable to study the culture of a group whose differences rendered it fair game for examination, interpretation, and explanation. In Brown's famous and frequently anthologized essay "Negro Character as Seen by White Authors," he invalidates the ethnographic claims of literary artists who exploited the so-called Negro as literary subject, and in so doing he discredits the entire ethnographic enterprise widely embraced by the academy and the literati of his era. Ostensibly, the essay chides literary artists for making ethnographic claims best left to what Brown terms professional ethnographers; but, reenacting the trickster aspect of the African-American folk ethos, Brown is actually critiquing the field of ethnography for perpetuating the fiction that a university-trained ethnographer can master a culture in six months or two years, or even in ten years.[2] Brown consciously set standards for ethnography that were impossible for the establishment ethnographers of his day to satisfy. In "Negro Character," he writes:

> The exploration of Negro life and character rather than its exploitation must come from Negro authors themselves. This, of course, runs counter to the American conviction that the Southern white man knows the Negro best, and can best interpret him. . . . But whether Negro life and character are to be best interpreted from without or within is an interesting by-path that we had better not enter here. One manifest truth, however, is this: the sincere, sensitive artist, willing to go beneath the clichés of popular belief to get at an underlying reality, will be wary of confining a race's entire character to a half-dozen narrow grooves. He will hardly have the temerity to say that his necessarily limited observation of a few Negroes in a restricted environment can be taken as the last word about some mythical *the* Negro. He will hesitate to do this, even though he had a Negro mammy, or spent a night in Harlem, or has been a Negro all his life. The writer submits that such an artist is the only one worth listening to, although the rest are legion. (639)

In reference to the form ethnography should take—Vidich and Lyman, among others, assert that "an ethnography is now to be regarded as a piece of writing—as such, it cannot be said to . . . represent . . . an accurate portrait of the culture of the 'other.'" They discredit traditional ethnography's claim of creating an "unmodified and unfiltered record of immediate experience" (41). But these cutting-edge scholars of the dominant hegemonic culture do not go far enough in discrediting traditional ethnography's modus operandi. They do not understand that their proclamation—that ethnography is a piece of writing— ignores the experiential quality a successful ethnographic study should impart. To reduce ethnography to writing ignores the irony, the subversiveness, the double consciousness of the non-hegemonic cultural experience. Such pigeon-holing does not acknowledge the musical, artistic, and performative aspects of non-hegemonic cultures.

Brown's references to music in poems like "Cabaret" and to physical posturing in poems like "Sporting Beasley" and to gesticulation in poems like "Wild Bill" acknowledge the possibility that ethnography is more than writing—that it encompasses performance, oral history, oral story-telling, and other non-written forms of expressivity. Stanfield argues that, since "many non-Westerners view the social, the emotional, and the spiritual as integral parts of a whole person linked to a physical environment, it [is] crucial for a qualitative [research] method's epistemology to be grounded in holistic rather than fragmented and dichotomized notions of human beings" (185). Brown acquiesces to the problematics of recording immediate experience by creating the fictional character of Slim Greer, who through humor and insider knowledge critiques the hegemonic structure that had led to apartheid and modern-day slavery in the land of Dixie.

"Slim in Atlanta" is a case in point. In this poem, the rascal Greer dominates the one "telefoam booth" blacks are allowed to use when they feel the need to laugh. Within this poetic tall tale is a vitriolic critique of the so-called "separate-but-equal" accommodations blacks had to put up with during the days of apartheid in the pre–Civil Rights Act South. But within even this poem, Brown radically interrogates and discredits the monologism of traditional ethnography by wearing two hats in his poetic study of the Southern black folk community. Brown writes as a native observer, along the lines of autoethnography, but at the same time acknowledges his limitations as a city dweller, identifying some of his experience as tangential to some aspects of folk culture. He does this in "Slim in Atlanta" through the device of Slim Greer's disbelieving laughter, but in other poems he uses the device of distanced language. This is to say that, in poems like "Strong Men," "Old Lem," and "Ma Rainey," Brown distances the ethnographer's voice by using standard English-speaking personae who play the part of participant observer—the traditional role of ethnographers in the field. And he permits characters like Sister Lou, Slim Greer, Sporting Beasley, Scotty, and Big Boy to express vernacularly certain folk notions of life that standard English is hard pressed to express.

James Clifford, a widely celebrated ethnographer of the postmodern era, focused his attention in 1988 on academia's recently acknowledged problems representing the authority of native informants in ethnographic field research: "Current ethnographic writing is seeking new ways to represent adequately the authority of informants . . . ethnographic exposition routinely folds into itself a diversity of descriptions, transcriptions, and interpretations by a variety of indigenous 'authors.' How should these authorial presences be made manifest?" (45–46). Brown didn't seem to have a problem manifesting indigenous authorial presences. In "Slim in Hell," for example, Saint Peter turns Slim back from the pearly gates when Slim explains that, instead of surveying hell as Saint Peter had requested, he had mistakenly gone to Dixie:

> St. Peter said, "Well,
>   You got back quick.
> How's de devil? An' what's
>   His latest trick?
>
> An' Slim say, "Peter,
>   I really cain't tell,
> The place was Dixie
>   That I took for hell."
>
> Then Peter say, "You must
>   Be crazy, I vow,
> Where'n hell dja think Hell *was*,
>   Anyhow?" (*Poems* 92)

Certainly the indigenous authorial voice is present here, as it is in poems like "A Bad, Bad Man" (*Last Ride* 46) and "Sister Lou," whose poetic autobiographer understands that this black woman Lou's vision of eternal life is different from the dominant culture's, that Lou's concern for the biblical Judas Iscariot involves a deep cultural concern for the scapegoat:

> Give a good talkin' to
> To yo' favorite 'postle Peter,
> An' rub the po' head
> Of mixed-up Judas,
> An' joke awhile wid Jonah. (*Southern Road* 49)

In "Traveling Cultures" Clifford critiques establishment ethnography and sets up the ideal goal of ethnographic research. He asserts that, "in much traditional ethnography, . . . the ethnographer has localized what is actually a regional/national/global nexus, relegating to the margins a 'culture's' external relations and displacements" (100). He calls for analyses of "constructed and disputed *historicities*" (101). Sterling Brown's sensitivity to depicting "disputed historicities" is perhaps best exemplified in his poem "Remembering

Nat Turner." There, a cackling old Caucasian woman, herself on the margins of the dominant culture, is depicted as the repository of an eventful moment in African-American and American history, the rebellion of Nat Turner. But this hag-like person (as depicted in Brown's poem) is inadequate to the task of preserving and conveying even a single momentous event of African-American history. Her confused and distorted rendition of the events surrounding the Nat Turner rebellion, trial, and execution is reminiscent of many official lies and cover-ups that eventually become local truths, marring the scattered remains of African-American material culture:

> "Ain't no slavery no more, things is going all right. . . .
> We had a sign post here with printing on it,
> But it rotted in the hole, and thar it lays,
> And the nigger tenants split the marker for kindling.
> Things is all right now, ain't no trouble with the niggers
> Why they make this big to-do over Nat?". . .
> We remembered the poster rotted through and falling,
> The marker split for kindling a kitchen fire. (*Poems* 209–10)

In another example of the ideal mission of ethnography, the poem "Strong Men" reveals what Clifford calls "sites of displacement, interference, and interaction" ("Traveling Cultures" 101). Clifford uses this phrase to describe unfairly weighted clashes between hegemonic and nonhegemonic cultures. He argues that ethnographers should provide deep contextualization for cultural beliefs and behaviors contaminated by these clashes rather than provide mere description of cultural differences from the hegemonic norm. In "Strong Men," Brown graphically illustrates the culture of dissent that historically has developed among African Americans in response to the discriminatory practices of the dominant culture:

> *They heard the laugh and wondered;*
> *Uncomfortable;*
> *Unadmitting a deeper terror.* . . .
> The strong men keep a-comin' on
> Gittin' stronger. . . . (*Southern Road* 53)

Thus, Clifford and Marcus's call for ethnographic analyses that are "situated *between* power systems of meaning" (2) was already in place in Brown's oeuvre, particularly in such poetic answers to hegemonic bias in depictions of African Americans. In fact, the bulk of Brown's poems, oral histories, and essays show the connection between African-American culture and oppressive hegemonic societal influences.

Sterling Brown wrote ethnography by offering a diverse oeuvre of material from which to glean an understanding and appreciation of the richness and diversity of black folk culture. This is not to diminish his poetry as poetry, but the fact remains that one cannot escape the rich portrait of African-American life and culture that Brown's poetry renders. Brown never tried to offer a univocal or unified description of the culture he chose to examine. Rather, by using diverse forms of expressivity, he pioneered a postmodern ethnographic methodology that turns the tables on a discipline, the depths of whose elitism, arrogance, and chauvinism have barely been tapped.

NOTES

1. For a cogent argument concerning Du Bois's ethnography of African-American culture and epistemology, see Schrager.
2. For an excellent retrospective of the development of the field of ethnography, see Clifford, "On Ethnographic Authority" (*Predicament* 21–53).

WORKS CITED

Brown, Sterling A. *The Collected Poems of Sterling A. Brown.* New York: Harper, 1980.
——. *The Last Ride of Wild Bill and Eleven Narrative Poems.* Detroit: Broadside, 1975.
——. "Negro Character as Seen by White Authors." *Journal of Negro Education* 2.2 (1933): 179–203. Rpt. *The New Cavalcade: African American Writing from 1760 to the Present.* Ed. Arthur P. Davis et al. 2 vols. Washington: Howard University Press, 1991. 1: 607–39.
——. *Southern Road.* New York: Harcourt Brace, 1932.
Clifford, James. *The Predicament of Culture: Twentieth-Century Ethnography, Literature, and Art.* Cambridge: Harvard University Press, 1988.
——. "Traveling Cultures." *Cultural Studies.* New York: Routledge, 1992. 96–116.
——, and George E. Marcus, eds. *Writing Culture: The Poetics and Politics of Ethnography.* Berkeley: University of California Press, 1986.
Denzin, Norman K., and Yvonna S. Lincoln, eds. *Handbook of Qualitative Research.* Thousand Oaks, CA: Sage, 1994.
"Ethnography." *Encyclopedia of Cultural Anthropology.* Ed. David Levinson and Melvin Ember. New York: Holt, 1996. 416–22.
Gabbin, Joanne V. *Sterling A. Brown: Building the Black Aesthetic Tradition.* 1985. Charlottesville: University Press of Virginia, 1994.
Schrager, Cynthia D. "Both Sides of the Veil: Race, Science, and Mysticism in W.E.B. Du Bois." *American Quarterly* 48 (1996): 551–86.
Stanfield, John H., II. "Ethnic Modeling in Qualitative Research." In Denzin and Lincoln 175–88.
Vidich, Arthur J., and Stanford M. Lyman. "Qualitative Methods: Their History in Sociology and Anthropology." In Denzin and Lincoln 23–59.

Sterling Brown's Southern Strategy: Poetry as Cultural Evolution in *Southern Road*

David R. Anderson

With the publication of *Southern Road* in 1932, Sterling Brown portrayed, and sought to address, what he perceived to be a profound cultural crisis facing African Americans: the gradual disappearance of their rural cultures as they entered the urban, industrialized economies of the North and South, and their consequent loss of autonomous art. Brown especially feared the loss of folklore, which he believed helped African American culture renew itself, not only by preserving and strengthening traditions and social practices, but also by serving as a conduit through which individuals devised and communicated new strategies for surviving racial oppression. Once African Americans moved to urban areas, Brown believed that they would no longer produce songs and stories reflecting their communities' needs and interests and, accordingly, would no longer devise and communicate new strategies for survival. Instead, he feared they would passively consume a bigoted popular culture, or worse yet, be co-opted into producing art that pandered to the economic demands and stereotypes of the dominant culture.

In response, *Southern Road* was not merely an attempt to preserve oral traditions on the printed page, but to adapt the cultural production of art in black communities to an urban, capitalist society. In a close reading of "Strong Men," I examine Brown's portrayal of folklore as an evolving cultural process that adapts and preserves traditions despite external changes and threats.

In addition, with readings of "Children's Children" and "Cabaret," I discuss Brown's portrayal of mass culture and commercialism as threats both to folk traditions and to artistic creation. Finally, I examine Brown's attempt to write poetry that, despite the distance between writer and audience, could perform many of the social functions traditionally performed by folklore.

Although numerous scholars praise Brown's poetry for its realism, cultural authenticity, and portrayal of folklore's social usefulness, they do not analyze Brown's ideas concerning folklore's role in cultural evolution—specifically, art's role in adapting cultural practices to social or environmental changes or threats. For instance, such scholars as Stephen Henderson, Charles Rowell, and Joanne Gabbin have written extensively on Brown's reliance on vernacular traditions, and both John Wright and Gabbin discuss Brown's portrayal of folklore's functions within the black community, such as maintaining group values, identities, tradi-tions, and loyalties. Nevertheless, these studies do not emphasize Brown's con-ception of culture as a process and folklore's important role within that process, so that black culture and consciousness in these works often seems unitary and static, even trans-historical, that is, exempt, to quote Ronald Radano, from "the circumstances of political, cultural, and social change" (73). Even when Hous-ton Baker notes the "self-conscious evolutionism" of the final "Vestiges" section of *Southern Road*, in which Brown cordons off his early Romantic poetry as an aesthetic dead end, Baker reads the section only as Brown's comment about his artistic development, not as a broader comment about the relationship between African American art and culture (Baker 100; see Brown, *Collected Poems* 115).[1]

Nevertheless, Brown's criticism and poetry overtly link artistic production to cultural evolution and group survival. For instance, in arguing for realistic portrayals of all elements of black life, not merely of the educated and middle class, Brown wrote: "We are cowed. We have become typically bourgeois. Natu-ral though such an evolution is, if we are *all* content with evasion of life, with personal complacency, we as a group are doomed ("Our Literary Audience" 46). Brown presented this threat in "Tin Roof Blues," the penultimate section in *Southern Road* which documents the social problems wrought by the Great Mi-gration. Some recent migrants suffer from social alienation:

> Gang of dicties here, an' de rest wants to git dat way,
> Dudes an' dicties, others strive to git dat way,
> Put pennies on de numbers from now unto de jedgement day.
>   (102.10–12)

Others experience personal and sexual insecurity ("Effie"), cultural alienation ("Children's Children"), conspicuous consumption ("Mecca" and "Sporting Beasley"), sexual exploitation ("Chillen Get Shoes" and "Harlem Street Walk-ers"), and cultural co-optation ("Cabaret").

The ten "Vestiges" poems which follow "Tin Roof Blues" in *Southern Road* are an evolutionary dead end because they ignore social problems for the sake of literariness—ostentatious titles ("Nous n'irons plus au bois . . . "), apostrophe, hyphenated adjectives, inverted word order, and literary allusions:

> . . . gone
> Is all your arrant nimble grace,
> And worms preposterous feed upon
> The sweet flesh of your lovely face . . . (125.5–8)

As Maureen Honey has noted, most African American poets in the 1920s and early 1930s used British Romantic poetry as models for their own writings and favored such forms or elements as "the sonnet, the ode, the elegy, and classical allusion" (6). Accordingly, these "Vestiges" poems reflect the forms, themes, and diction common among such well-published New Negro poets as Claude McKay, Countee Cullen, and Georgia Douglas Johnson, including six sonnets, an ode to the poet Anne Spencer ("To a Certain Lady, in Her Garden"), a blank verse meditation ("Mill Mountain"), and even imagistic free verse ("Thoughts of Death"). Their themes are well worn, ranging from the racial protest sonnet ("Salutamus"), to pastoral ("Return," "Nous n'irons plus au bois . . ."), to death and the fleetingness of beauty and love ("Thoughts of Death," "Challenge," "Telling Fortunes," "Against That Day"). Absent from these poems are any attempts to portray everyday rural life, dialect, and expressive conventions that characterize much of his mature work—for instance, the earthy humor of a tall-tale teller in "Slim in Atlanta":

> Down in Atlanta,
> > De whitefolks got laws
> For to keep all de niggers
> > From laughin' outdoors.
>
> Hope to Gawd I may die
> > If I ain't speakin' truth
> Make de niggers do deir laughin'
> > In a telefoam booth. (81.1–8)

Indeed, these "Vestiges" poems exemplify the aesthetic equivalent of the social alienation, breakdown, and vulnerability cataloged in "Tin Roof Blues," particularly since they illustrate a gulf separating poetic creation from community interest, to the detriment of both. By contrast, Brown desired that literature, similar to folklore, participate in the cultural process of constructing, communicating, negotiating, and re-constructing social practices and beliefs—notions of heroism, appropriate behaviors, worldviews, the meanings and values of rituals, and so on.

For instance, Brown portrays folklore's dynamic role in cultural evolution in his poem "Strong Men." Charles Rowell has aptly described this poem as a portrayal of "black people's strength to survive in the face of racism and economic exploitation" (326). Yet the poem portrays not only a static "stoicism" (326), but also African American folk culture as a kind of Darwinian juggernaut—a process that selects adaptive responses to an oppressive environment and leads to a stronger people and culture. As the speaker says at the end of the poem, "*One thing they* [whites] *cannot prohibit*— / The strong men . . . coming on / The strong men gittin' stronger" (57–58.62–64).

The poem enacts this process of cultural development through its rhetorical structure, presenting catalogues of racial oppression followed by excerpts from folk songs, culminating in the refrain "The strong men git stronger" (Rowell 326):

> *They broke you in like oxen,*
> *They scourged you,*
> *They branded you,*
> *They made your women breeders,*
> *They swelled your numbers with bastards. . . .*
> *They taught you the religion they disgraced.*
>
> *You sang:*
> > *Keep a-inchin' along*
> > *Lak a po' inch worm. . . .*
>
> *You sang:*
> > *Bye and bye*
> > *I'm gonna lay down dis heaby load. . . .*
>
> *You sang:*
> > *Walk togedder, chillen,*
> > *Dontcha git weary. . . .*
> > > The strong men keep a-comin' on
> > > The strong men git stronger. (56.5–21)

As the poem unfolds as a pattern of abuse and cultural response, we witness the folk devising and communicating strategies for action ("*Keep a-inchin' along,*" "*Walk togedder, chillen, / Dontcha git weary*") and constructing a worldview ("*Bye and bye / I'm gonna lay down dis heaby load*") (56.12, 18–19, 15–16). Additionally, we witness a folk tradition taking form, and with it the reinforcement of group identity and solidarity (with the constant juxtaposition of "they" and "you") and the growth of political sophistication and power as the community moves from stoicism ("*Keep a-inchin' along / Lak a po' inch worm . . .*") to group effort ("*Walk togedder, chillen, / Dontcha git weary*") to pride ("*Ain't no hammah / In dis lan', / Strikes lak mine, bebby, / Strikes lak mine*") to political reflection ("*They bought off some of your leaders / . . . / You followed a way. / Then laughed as usual*") and ultimately to the point of contemporary revolutionary action (56–57.12–13, 18–19, 27–30, 41, 43–45).

Yet Brown did not usually portray African American life as inevitable evolutionary progress, but rather as a series of necessary adaptations in the grim,

Malthusian struggle for subsistence.[2] For instance, farmers and sharecroppers in the section entitled "On Restless River" often fight against storms, floods, and other natural disasters that threaten to annihilate them and their ways of life. In "Old King Cotton," the economic precariousness of sharecroppers renders them all the more vulnerable to the vicissitudes of nature:

> Buy one rusty mule
> To git ahead
> We stays in debt
> Until we'se dead;
>
> Ef flood don't git us
> It's de damn bo' weevil
> Crap grass in de drought,
> Or somp'n else evil;
>
> Ef we gits de bales
> When de hard luck's gone,
> Bill at de commissary
> Goes right on. (64.17–28)

Similarly, the flooding Missouri River in "Foreclosure" is described as a senile "treacherous skinflint" (70.19) who "gratuitously" loans out rich farmland (70.3), then seizes it and whatever prized possessions the farmers place upon it. Even in the "Tornado Blues" portion of the triptych "New St. Louis Blues," natural and economic calamity occur hand in hand:

> Dey got some ofays, but dey mostly got de Jews an' us,
> Got some ofays, but mostly got de Jews an' us,
> Many po' boys castle done settled to a heap o' dus'.
> . . . .
> Foun' de moggidge unpaid, foun' de insurance long past due,
> Moggidge unpaid, de insurance very long past due,
> All de homes we wukked so hard for goes back to de Fay and Jew.
>   (68–69.22–24, 28–30)

Despite adverse natural and social conditions, African Americans in Brown's poems are determined to survive and embody that determination in their folk culture and folklore. For instance, the first section of the poem "Memphis Blues" stresses African Americans' ability to outlast power and oppression, comparing Memphis, Tennessee, to fallen ancient empires and thus hinting at the natural or divine destruction that awaits the segregated American South:

> Nineveh, Tyre,
> Babylon,

Not much lef'
Of either one.
All dese cities
Ashes and rust,
De win' sing sperrichals
Through deir dus' . . .

. . . .

Dis here Memphis
It may go;
Floods may drown it;
Tornado blow;
Mississippi wash it
Down to sea—
Like de other Memphis in
History. (60.1–8, 13–20)

It does not matter whether Providence or nature destroys these cities—
more fundamental than causation is the conviction that African Americans must and will survive, a point stressed in the second section of the
poem. Far from being upset about the end of the United States, the disparate members of the black community share a comic lack of concern, as
well as a mode of expression (call and response) to relate their plans for
survival:

Watcha gonna do when Memphis on fire,
    Memphis on fire, Mistah Preachin' Man?
Gonna pray to Jesus and nebber tire,
    Gonna pray to Jesus, loud as I can,
        Gonna pray to my Jesus, oh, my Lawd!

Watcha gonna do when de tall flames roar,
    Tall flames roar, Mistah Lovin' Man?
Gonna love my brownskin better'n before—
    Gonna love my baby lak a do right man,
        Gonna love my brown baby, oh, my Lawd!

Watcha gonna do when Memphis falls down,
    Memphis falls down, Mistah Music Man?
Gonna plunk on dat box as long as it soun',
    Gonna plunk dat box fo' to beat de ban',
        Gonna tickle dem ivories, oh, my Lawd! (60–61.21–35)

With his poem "Ma Rainey," Brown illustrates how folk culture sustains
such resolve—indeed, how Rainey's concerts are not merely a single person's
performance but a communal event during which people share experiences,

reaffirm values, and renew bonds of loyalty and support. First, Ma Rainey's presence draws black audiences together from all over the South:

> When Ma Rainey
> Comes to town,
> Folks from anyplace
> Miles aroun',
> From Cape Girardeau,
> Poplar Bluff,
> Flocks in to hear
> Ma do her stuff. . . . (62.1–8)

Each concert brings together working-class people from different areas and livelihoods, enabling them to become acquainted or reacquainted, to talk, joke, and commiserate:

> Dey comes to hear Ma Rainey from de little river settlements,
> From blackbottom cornrows and from lumber camps;
> Dey stumble in de hall, jes a-laughin' an' a-cacklin',
> Cheerin' lak roarin' water, lak wind in river swamps.
>
> An' some jokers keeps deir laughs a-goin' in de crowded aisles,
> An' some folks sits dere waitin' wid deir aches an' miseries,
> Till Ma comes out before dem, a-smilin' gold-toofed smiles
> An' Long Boy ripples minors on de black an' yellow keys. (62.19–26)

Besides strengthening a sense of community, the blues, as Sherley Anne Williams notes, also gives audiences an opportunity to reflect upon their experiences. Williams argues that "the blues singer strives to create an atmosphere in which analysis can take place," helping audiences put "analytic distance" between themselves and traumatic experiences (125). Ma Rainey's rendition of "Backwater Blues" in part four of the poem exemplifies the blues' capacity to help listeners comprehend chaotic experiences. "Backwater Blues" was composed by Bessie Smith from folk materials after the disastrous Mississippi River floods of 1927 and is peculiarly apt, since the towns and cities listed in the poem are on or near floodplains:

> It rained fo' days an' de skies was dark as night,
> Trouble taken place in de lowlands at night.
>
> Thundered an' lightened an' the storm begin to roll
> Thousan's of people ain't got no place to go.
>
> Den I went an' stood upon some high ol' lonesome hill,
> An' looked down on the place where I used to live. (63.42–47)

The crowd experiences an emotional catharsis ("An' den de folks, dey natchally bowed dey heads an' cried" [63.48]), partly because the song brings a broad

tragedy and blur of events into a tight, personal focus that people can comprehend. The song shifts from the havoc wreaked upon an entire community by
the river to individual experience (from *"Thousan's of people"* to "I"), and from
the midst of chaos to a detached perspective, high on a hill, to assay the personal damage from the flood (*"looked down on the place where I used to live"*).
As the speaker notes, the power of this music on the audience is profound,
almost ineffable: "Dere wasn't much more de fellow say: / She jes' gits hold of
us dataway" (63.51–52). By portraying the social impact of Rainey's performance,
Brown was insisting upon the ability of folklore to sustain old values while
creating opportunities for communication of new ideas and strategies, thus
contributing to cultural evolution.

Not surprisingly, Brown's linking of folklore and cultural evolution mirrors the work of recent folklorists, who describe folklore as a social process for
creating and selecting new, adaptive strategies for survival. For instance, John
Roberts notes in his book *From Trickster to Badman: The Black Folk Hero in Slavery and Freedom* that cultures endure through individuals "endlessly devising
solutions to both old and new problems of how to live under ever-changing social, political, and economic conditions" (11). Individuals, not groups as a whole,
develop these adaptive strategies and communicate them to others: "Just as a
species does not 'struggle to survive' as a collective entity, but survives or not as
a consequence of the adaptive changes of individual organisms, so too do sociocultural systems survive or not as a consequence of the adaptive changes in
the thought and activities of individual men and women who respond opportu-
nistically to cost-benefit options" (Harris 61). Folklorists have long insisted that
folklore is a social process for creating and communicating such new adaptive
strategies. Simon Bronner has written that "folklore changes as people adapt
it to different situations and needs. [It] becomes manipulated knowledge" (2).
Similarly, W .F. H. Nicolaisen notes that folk performers often consciously select, rearrange, and modify traditional materials for new performances, and
that such variation sustains tradition: "Far from being at odds with each other,
creativity and tradition, individual and community, together produce vital vari-
ability thus keeping alive the very items that their integrated forces help to
shape" (Bronner 11).

Similarly, Brown wrote about the continued evolution and utility of African
American traditions, examining folklore as a creative process and a source for
useful social strategies. For instance, he tried to understand the process by
which individual performers selected or adapted inherited materials, as with
the composition of spirituals:

> It is unlikely that any group of worshipers and singers, as a group,
> composed spirituals. Single individuals with poetic ingenuity, a
> rhyming gift, or a good memory "composed" or "remembered"
> lines, couplets, or even quatrains out of a common storehouse. The

group would join in with the refrain or the longer chorus. When one leader's ingenuity or memory was exhausted, another might take up the "composition." ("Folk Literature" 414)

Additionally, Brown described how tales and songs were orally transmitted and often extemporaneously composed, with narrators or singers freely drawing upon a common stockpile of rhymes, images, themes, and expressions (413–14). Yet audiences and succeeding generations of performers selected those variations that helped people address environmental and social needs, as well as satisfy individual preferences. Folklore remained functional, performing a wide variety of needed tasks in rural communities, such as socializing children, spreading news, voicing protest, pacing and timing work, defining individual identity, and reaffirming group loyalty. For instance, African American parents used animal folktales before and after slavery to instruct children to overcome their social powerlessness. These stories presented seemingly weak heroes who learned to trick stronger opponents: "Outsmarting was one of the few devices left [slaves]. So they made heroes out of the physically powerless [creatures such as Brer Rabbit or Brer Squirrel] who by good sense and quick wit overcame animals of brute strength who were not right bright. 'You ain't got no cause to be bigger in de body, but you sho' is got cause to be bigger in de brain'" ("Negro Folk Expression" 323).[3] Spirituals, as another example, could profess faith, protest treatment, even spread important news ("Negro Folk Expression: Spirituals, Seculars, Ballads and Work Songs" 46–48).

Besides describing folklore as a process of *cultural* selection, Brown also described folklore as a process of *artistic* selection, in which the interaction between artists and audiences ensures songs' or stories' social usefulness, realism, concreteness of imagery, and emotional impact. Brown noted that some blues singers "must still sing for the jealous creators of the Blues," so that audiences influenced performance, subject matter, and group portrayal ("The Blues as Folk Poetry" 324). Rural audiences expected a blues performer to have first-hand knowledge of rural hardships: "As Negro musicians put it: 'You can't play the blues until you have paid your dues'" (Brown, "The Blues" 291). Consequently, "The true blues were sung by people close to the folk such as Ma Rainey, Mamie, Bessie, and Clara Smith, Victoria Spivey . . . " (286). Repeated performances within such tightly knit communities reaffirmed cultural identities and values, and reinforced artistic conventions. For instance, Brown was arguing that audiences were touched by Ma Rainey's performance of "Backwater Blues" partly because they influenced the song's creation and performance.

Accordingly, folklore for Brown was an exemplary poetics because it united literary and cultural evolution. Folk artists shaped their performances in response to environmental and social pressures, which in turn honed folklore's aesthetic quality and social usefulness. African American audiences demanded and received art that was concrete, representative, and useful—more so than art over which they had little social or economic influence, such as commercial imitations of the blues. Brown demonstrated this artistic difference by contrasting "Backwater Blues" to "Mississippi Flood Song," a commercial ballad also composed after the 1927 floods:

> I am dreaming to-night in the moonlight
> Of the friends it has taken from me.
>
> All the world seemed so happy and gay.
> The waters rose quickly above us
> And it swept my beloved ones away-ay-ay-ay ("The Blues as Folk
>   Poetry" 330)

By insisting upon "bitter honesty" and "frankness of revelation and language," rural audiences encouraged a style which, to Brown's mind, was more concrete, realistic, and sympathetic ("The Blues" 288). "The gain in vividness [in "Backwater Blues" over "Mississippi Flood Song"], in feeling, in substituting the thing seen for the bookish dressing up and sentimentalizing," Brown argues, "is an obvious one" ("The Blues as Folk Poetry" 331).

Brown's comments about "Mississippi Flood Song" reflect his concerns that economic pressures from the Great Migration would sever the symbiotic relationship between African American artists and audiences. He specifically feared that African American culture would cease to be determined by the needs and interests of the community, but would be dictated increasingly by the marketplace, especially by the demand and interests of any economically dominant group. Linking economic and cultural autonomy, Brown warned: "One of the by-products of exploitation is the development in literature of a stereotyped character of the exploited, which guards the equanimity of the 'superiors' and influences even the 'inferiors' when they are unwary ("A Literary Parallel" 152).

For instance, he argued that Tin Pan Alley and minstrel show performers were not interested in rendering the complexity of human behavior from within a tight focus, but in selling ready-made sentiment. Racism for Brown was a cultural industry, and falsified history a commodity: "America, since [Stephen] Foster, has been set clamoring for idyllic content beneath Carolina skies, in the sleepy hills of Tennessee, where one may tuck oneself to sleep in his old Tucky home while the Mississippi—that lazy river—rolls on and Dandy Jim strums chords to Lucinda in the canebrake ("Weep Some More My Lady" 87). Brown regularly denounced the "imbecilities of the lyrics ground out in Tin Pan Alley," such as those for the song "That's Why Darkies Were Born":

> *Someone had to pick the cotton*
> *Someone had to hoe the corn*
> *Someone had to slave and be able to sing*
> *That's why Darkies were born.*
> *Someone had to laugh at trouble,*

Someone had to be contented with any old thing,
So sing! sing! . . .
That why Darkies were born. (87)

By demanding and paying for such perspectives on black life, audiences reinforced extant prejudices and stereotypes: "What does the mob-mind care that it is bald-faced lying? The mob-mind wishes it, will have it so" (87). Yet black audiences, who had wielded tremendous social power during folkloric performances, wielded little economic power in the mass market, and accordingly could not exert enough economic pressure to shape their own portrayal, or to influence the artistic agenda. Worse yet, African American artists were often co-opted by market forces into producing stereotypes themselves: "One can do no more than register a horse-laugh at the obvious Americanism of setting up sham in place of unpleasant truth, and at the Negro's easy complaisance in accepting a stereotype, and reaping his own shekels by perpetuating it" (87).

Brown illustrated such artistic exploitation in "Cabaret," in which black performers are no longer offering criticism and models to the black community, but are perpetuating stereotypes of black rural life to a segregated white audience. The poem constantly cuts between images of black peonage in the Deep South in 1927 and images of black chorines, waiters, and musicians performing for an all-white audience at a Chicago speakeasy. While we are presented with images of forced labor on the levees of Arkansas (111–13.37–42), and communities in Mississippi destroyed by some of the worst flooding in the century (112.53–56, 64–67, 70–73, 84–86), scantily clad chorines wearing bandannas sing a tribute to the river and the plantation South that bears little resemblance to the living conditions of African Americans in that region:

> There's peace and happiness there
> I declare
>
> . . . .
> I've got my toes turned Dixie ways
> Round that Delta let me laze
>
> . . . .
> My heart cries out for
> MUDDY WATER (112-113.35–36, 74–75, 82–83)

While "Cabaret" portrays the market's influence on African American artistic production, "Children's Children" portrays a new generation of urban dwellers who have ceased producing their own culture, and who instead passively consume the products of the dominant culture. The effects of this change from producer to consumer are threefold. First, these African Americans are portrayed as alienated from their history and culture, not only failing to understand spirituals, but greeting them with derision: "They laugh," "They sigh / And look goggle-eyed / At one another," "They have forgotten / What had to be endured"

(104.5, 10–12, 20–21). Secondly, because they do not create for themselves the meaning of their heritage and experiences, they become frozen in an intellectual and sexual adolescence, "babbling young ones" who can only "Giggle / And nudge each other's satin clad / Sleek sides" in a preening, sneering immaturity (104.22, 28–30). Worse still, they define themselves using the dominant culture's shallow standards of beauty, applying bleaching cream to have "paled faces" (104.23), and "cajol[ing]" their hair to "Caucasian straightness" (104.24).

Given the threat that commercialism poses to African American artistic production and cultural evolution, Brown proposed that black writers seek some way to *internalize* the kinds of environmental influences that folk artists experienced in their lives and during their performances. Accordingly, Brown valued literary regionalism, because he wanted "to relate the American artist to his environment, which is founded upon a direct return to the folk."[4] Brown hoped that cultural knowledge can act as both a creative source and constraint, encouraging African American writers to shape their portrayals in accordance with black people's material conditions and social concerns. As he argued in his essay "Local Color or Interpretation," the statement that an artist "knows 'the Negro' is of course a patent absurdity. 'The Negro' does not exist; and he never did" (223). Instead, "It would be more accurate to say that she has carefully studied a certain section of Negro life, restricted in scope and in character, and that she has revealed skillfully and beautifully and from a single point of view the results of her study" (223). Brown believed that dialect poetry from the previous generation of black poets was often rife with stereotypes precisely because these writers lacked the cultural knowledge needed to exercise artistic self-constraint: "Dialect, or the speech of the people, is capable of expressing whatever the people are. . . . Poets more intent upon learning the ways of the folk, their speech, and their character, that is to say better poets, could have smashed the mold [of stereotyping]" (*Negro Poetry and Drama* 43).

Additionally, Brown called upon poetry to perform the same kinds of social roles performed by folklore in rural areas. For instance, "Children's Children" is a didactic poem aimed at a young, urban black audience, providing the socio-historical contexts needed to appreciate the romantic ideals expressed in slave songs, but also warning readers about the price paid by those who ignore or reject their cultural heritage. In the first two stanzas, the speaker challenges readers to drop their negative preconceptions of the songs by contrasting their elevated diction to the blunt, immature derision of young, urban African Americans:

> When they hear
> These songs, born of the travail of their sires,
> Diamonds of song, deep buried beneath the weight
> Of dark and heavy years;
> They laugh.

When they hear
Saccharine melodies of loving and its fevers,
Soft-flowing lies of love everlasting;
Conjuring divinity out of gross flesh itch;
They sigh
And look goggle-eyed
At one another. (104.1–12)

By associating self-consciously inflated diction ("Diamonds of song," "travails of their sires," "Conjuring divinity") with the "Saccharine melodies" and lyrics of the slave songs, the speaker seemingly invites ridicule, but the utter vicious-ness with which the young people deride the songs ("They laugh," "They sigh / And look goggle-eyed / At one another") is quickly characterized as ignorant and inappropriate. The speaker explains that such derision results from a lack of knowledge and experience:

They have forgotten, they have never known,
Long days beneath the torrid Dixie sun
In miasma'd riceswamps;
The chopping of dried grass, on the third go round
In strangling cotton;
Wintry nights in mud-daubed makeshift huts,
With these songs, sole comfort.

They have forgotten
What had to be endured— (104.13–21)

Within its proper historical context, the romantic idealizing of love and sex ceases to be old-fashioned prudery, but becomes acts of self-empowerment and transcendence amidst the quotidian squalor of slavery—that is, group insis-tence on the *humanity* rather than the animality of their sexual drives, and con-sequently the dignity of their existence and aspirations. Readers are cautioned, even shamed about reacting too hastily or negatively to these folksongs, and encouraged to bring the same knowledge and maturity to listening that the original singers and listeners brought to their construction.

By placing such didactic poems as "Children's Children" throughout *Southern Road,* and by allowing his "Vestiges" poems to trail portraits of urban alienation and degradation, Brown was stressing the interdependence of art and culture, and the need for African American poets to sustain this symbiotic relationship in ways similar to folklore. He calls attention to his own attempt at cultural sustenance with an epigraph for "Vestiges" from A. E. Housman: "When I was one-and-twenty / I heard a wise man say—" (115). The wise man, by contrast, is the voice from a spiritual quoted on the frontispiece of *Southern Road:* "O de ole sheep dey knows de road, / Young lambs gotta find de way."

NOTES

1. Subsequent references to Brown's *Collected Poems* will be cited in the text by page and line numbers separated by a period.
2. I wish to thank Robert O'Meally for suggesting that I complicate Brown's ideas about cultural evolution, particularly by noting that Brown does not stress progress so much as adaptation and survival in most of his poems—hence the many poems portraying storms and natural disasters.
3. For a fuller discussion about the relationship between hero formation in folktales and building cultures, see Roberts' *From Trickster to Badman*, 1–64.
4. Brown quotes this phrase from an unknown writer in his January 1931 essay, "The Literary Scene: Chronicle and Comment" (20).

WORKS CITED

Baker, Houston A., Jr. *Modernism and the Harlem Renaissance*. Chicago: University of Chicago Press, 1987.

Bronner, Simon J. "Introduction." *Creativity and Tradition in Folklore: New Directions*. Ed. Simon J. Bronner. Logan, UT: Utah State University Press, 1992. 1–38.

Brown, Sterling A. "The Blues." *Phylon* 13 (1952): 286–92.

———. "The Blues as Folk Poetry." *Folk Say: A Regional Miscellany, 1930*. Ed. B. A. Botkin. Vol. 2. Norman: University of Oklahoma Press, 1930. 324–39.

———. *The Collected Poems of Sterling A. Brown*. The National Poetry Series. New York: Harper, 1980.

———. "Folk Literature." *The Negro Caravan* (1941). Eds. Sterling A. Brown, Arthur P. Davis, and Ulysses Lee. New York: Arno Press and the *New York Times*, 1969. 413–34.

———. "A Literary Parallel." *Opportunity* (May 1932): 152–53.

———. "The Literary Scene: Chronicle and Comment." *Opportunity* (January 1931): 20.

———. "Local Color or Interpretation." *Opportunity* (July 1932): 223.

———. "Negro Folk Expression." *Phylon* 11 (1950): 318–27.

———. "Negro Folk Expression: Spirituals, Seculars, Ballads and Work Songs." *Phylon* 14 (1953): 45–61.

———. *Negro Poetry and Drama* (1937). *The Negro in American Fiction* and *Negro Poetry and Drama*. Afro-American Culture Series. New York: Arno Press, 1969.

———. "Our Literary Audience." *Opportunity* (February 1930): 42–46, 61.

———. *Southern Road*. New York: Harcourt, 1932.

———. "Weep Some More My Lady." *Opportunity* (March 1932): 87.

Gabbin, Joanne V. *Sterling A. Brown: Building the Black Aesthetic Tradition*. Contributions in Afro-American and African Studies 86. Westport, CT: Greenwood Press, 1985.

Harris, Marvin. *Cultural Materialism: The Struggle for a Science of Culture*. New York: Vintage, 1979.

Henderson, Stephen. *Understanding the New Black Poetry: Black Speech and Black Music as Poetic References*. New York: Morrow, 1973.

Honey, Maureen, ed. "Introduction." *Shadowed Dreams: Women's Poetry of the Harlem Renaissance*. New Brunswick: Rutgers University Press, 1989. 1–41.

Radano, Ronald. "Soul Texts and the Blackness of Folk." *Modernism/Modernity* 2 (1995): 71–95.

Roberts, John W. *From Trickster to Badman: The Black Folk Hero in Slavery and Freedom.* Philadelphia: University of Pennsylvania Press, 1989.

Rowell, Charles H. "Sterling A. Brown and the Afro-American Folk Tradition." *Studies in the Literary Imagination* 7 (1974): 131–52. Rpt. in *The Harlem Renaissance Reexamined.* Ed. Victor Kramer. Georgia State Literary Studies 2. New York: AMS Press, 1987. 315–37.

Williams, Sherley A. "The Blues Roots of Contemporary Afro-American Poetry." *Chant of Saints: A Gathering of Afro-American Literature, Art, and Scholarship.* Eds. Michael S. Harper and Robert B. Stepto. Urbana: University of Illinois Press, 1979. 123–35.

Wright, John S. "The New Negro Poet and the Nachal Man: Sterling Brown's Folk Odyssey." *Black American Literature Forum* 23 (1989): 95–105. Reprinted as an essay in this collection.

In Defense of African American Culture: Sterling A. Brown, Gunnar Myrdal, and *An American Dilemma*

John Edgar Tidwell

Two years after the appearance of *Invisible Man* (1952), novelist Ralph Ellison, in a moment of candor not intended for publication, wrote his good friend Albert Murray about the visit he had just made to Howard University. To Murray, Ellison expressed shock and disappointment because the hosts at a party honoring him had asked "the most provincial questions put to me anywhere." At this gathering were some of the best-known scholars of African American culture, including E. Franklin Frazier, Arthur P. Davis, John Lovell, and Sterling A. Brown. He continued: "Can you imagine me standing before a group of so-called leading Negro so-called scholars and saying that they had failed to define 'Negro' except in blood terms, and not have one open his mouth? *Maybe it's because they're afraid*" (Murray 75, emphasis added).

The accusation of scholarly timidity leveled at these eminent intellectuals probably speaks more accurately to Ellison's own efforts, through the success of his novel, to initiate a paradigmatic shift in ways of considering race and culture. His critique continues one that he had begun in his then-unpublished review of Gunnar Myrdal's *An American Dilemma: The Negro Problem and Modern Democracy* (1944). In it, Ellison minced few words in denouncing the black sociologists whose research contributed to a dubious conclusion: "American Negro culture is not something independent of general American culture. It is a distorted development, or a pathological condition, of the general American culture" (*American Dilemma* 928). While the list of social scientists who entertained Ellison that fateful night had already proven themselves to be worthy custodians and defenders of "Negro culture," no one mounted a stronger effort than Brown in the work he conducted for the Myrdal Study. Brown, as will be seen, not only opened up a personal relationship with Myrdal but sought to redefine the mode of social science Myrdal's staff used to reach this demeaning conclusion. As a researcher, a friend, and a writer, Brown tried to educate Myrdal about the most effective manner of determining the nature of black life and the significance of its expressive culture.

In the mid-1930s, the Carnegie Corporation had begun rethinking the manner in which it had committed itself to black racial advance. Its usual policy of appropriating the bulk of its racial funds to Negro schools in the South began to seem less effective in bettering interracial relations. What was needed, the philanthropic organization concluded, was a comprehensive study of the nature of those relations. The organization further determined that a reasonable expectation for success demanded a researcher who "could approach his task with a fresh mind, uninfluenced by traditional attitudes or by earlier conclusions" (Southern 2–3). After thoughtful deliberation, the organization's choice was Gunnar Myrdal, the eminent social economist, professor at the University of Stockholm, economic advisor to the Swedish government, and member of the Swedish Senate.

The supposedly dispassionate, objective approach that Myrdal brought with him, however, concealed a deep paradox. His own methodological penchant for determining the value premises of social groups made him, at the same time, vulnerable to charges of purposive social science or social engineering (Odum 96). Simply put, Myrdal was hired to determine the facts of black-white interracial relations but arguably wound up constructing a practical plan for improving those conflicted relationships, a violation of "objective" social science.

As it relates more specifically to Brown, Myrdal's so-called objective methodology also brought about a conflict between two ways of knowing in scientific study, scholarly investigation and personal experience. These radically different approaches have generally been viewed as antagonists in determining "the known" in scientific inquiries. The former is usually characterized as dispassionate, "objective," and unbiased; the latter as subjective, intimate, and humanistic. The decision of the Carnegie Corporation to choose Myrdal meant that scholarly "objectivity" won out over personal experience, since the subjective, intimate, and humanistic were supposedly "unscientific" and therefore unhelpful in making generalizations about values, beliefs, and attitudes. In Brown's view, the decision to discount a more personal approach profoundly subverted the most effective means of ascertaining the nature of "the Negro problem" in American culture.

While historians have acknowledged Brown's work for the Myrdal Study, his participation has not, for a number of reasons, been the subject of careful scrutiny. Indeed, most of the published material merely documents Brown's employment as a researcher for Myrdal. But as other historians have reconsidered and interrogated the study's significance, much of their literary criticism and historical commentary presents a critique of Brown that is both uncharitable and misplaced. For instance, David W. Southern, writing about the use and abuse of *An American Dilemma,* implies that Brown's acceptance of a generous research stipend was disingenuous or opportunistic and therefore disreputable, almost dishonest, since Brown's assignment to write a large, summarizing memoranda was completed too late to be applied usefully in determining the project's final outcome (Southern 67). Walter Jackson's claim that Myrdal was uninterested in music and imaginative literature further suggests that Brown's effort to introduce Myrdal to black folk life and culture was ineffective, unproductive, and wasteful (Jackson 132). Against this narrative of trivialized, panned, or outright rejected involvement, I propose an alternative reading of Brown's participation in the Myrdal Study. Brown's thinking revises Myrdal's premise that black culture and institutions are "primarily reactions to the dominant white civilization" (Southern 44). In its place, Brown foregrounds a radically different representational mode of preserving black cultural expression, one rooted in the shared values of black folk.

For literary theorists and historians, cultural preservation functions in much the same way as textual recovery. Recovering the literary past, Cary Nelson reminds us, is never free from our contemporary ways of studying culture (Nelson 11). We are inescapably forced to view earlier experience through the determining lens of new modes of analysis unavailable to previous cultural investigators. Instead of revisiting Brown's involvement in the project for the sake of preserving an historical record—in other words, documenting his presence on the project—a more productive pursuit might be to interrogate Brown's thinking about culture during the Myrdal Study for what it might tell us about ourselves today.

When Gunnar Myrdal arrived in the United States in September 1938, with his family and Swedish associate Richard Sterner in tow, he was prepared to learn about African American life by reviewing the myriad of sociological studies that had already been done. Carnegie's president, Frederick Keppel, countermanded Myrdal's initial plan of conducting exhaustive library research and ordered him instead out into the field to gain experience up close. Beginning in early October 1938, Myrdal embarked on an extensive two-month fact-finding tour of the South, during which, as he later reported to Keppel:

> [I] established contact with a great number of white and Negro leaders
> in various activities; visited universities, colleges, schools, churches

and various state and community agencies as well as factories and plantations; talked to police officers, teachers, preachers, politicians, journalists, agriculturists, workers, sharecroppers, and in fact, all sorts of people, colored and white. Our contacts, and particularly those with the common people, were very free and without difficulties. Being foreigners seemed, in most instances, to work out as an advantage rather than the contrary, even in our contacts with various southern leaders (Myrdal to Keppel 1).

It was during this whirlwind tour that Myrdal first met Sterling Brown. This fortuitous meeting positioned Brown's effort to influence the project's research method in two ways. First, he augmented Myrdal's meager personal understanding of black life by introducing him to a variety of black social experiences and cultural forms. Then Brown accepted a paid position as project researcher, charged with writing a set of summarizing memoranda under the extraordinarily ambitious title of "The Negro in American Culture."

Myrdal, as Brown later recalled, proved an eager pupil in the effort to move him beyond what cultural critic Beverly Lanier Skinner calls the limiting "etic ethnographic" or newcomer's understanding to the more informed position of cultural insider or "emic ethnographer" (Skinner 418). He proved to be an even better friend: a genuinely warm personal relationship began to grow as Brown introduced Myrdal to black music and escorted him to cultural events where whites were generally unwelcome. As Brown said in an interview, "I took Gunnar up to the Elk's Rendezvous, where the Caucasoids were not welcome and got [him] in there. And I took him to the Howard Theater. I let him hear records. . . . So, I was one of his influences and he has said that I was his best friend on the project" (Interview by author).[1] It is safe to say that the "tourist" perspective Myrdal gained from these junkets would never develop into a "cultural insider" position. Nevertheless, it is through Myrdal's relationship with Brown—as well as with others, especially Ralph Bunche, who later worked much more closely with Myrdal than Brown did—that Myrdal came to understand what he, as a certain kind of social scientist, was unprepared to see: that an important aspect of blacks' experiences was about to go unexplored in the Negro Study.

Myrdal's own commitment to a rather detached form of social science forced him to interpret the significance of what he saw in terms that differed from Brown's experiential focus. Reviewers of *An American Dilemma*, Ralph Ellison wrote, "have made much of Dr. Myrdal's being a foreigner, imported to do the study as one who had no emotional stake in the *American Dilemma*. And while this had undoubtedly aided his objectivity, the extent of it is apt to be overplayed" (Ellison 313). Ellison brings into dramatic relief the personal and intellectual investment Myrdal made in the project. Myrdal could never free himself from scholarly bias, or develop an emotional commitment to the black life he intended to study. His "objectivity" therefore translated into the outsider perspective of a newcomer to black American culture, precisely what Skinner describes as "etic ethnography."

In theory, Brown challenges the efficacy of "detached" social science to be "objective," thus exposing a conceptual weakness in Myrdal's approach. Skinner comments: "Brown . . . questioned the importance and validity of objectivity and impartiality in cultural study and hotly questioned the usefulness of outsider reports of culture. He interrogated the intellectual establishment that presumed it was possible, interesting, and profitable to study the culture of a group whose differences rendered it fair game for examination, interpretation, and explanation" (Skinner 419). For Brown, cultural studies meant more than privileging writing. It meant studying, as Skinner says, the "musical, artistic, and performative aspects of nonhegemonic culture" as markers of a vibrant expressivity that developed in spite of—and perhaps because of—the hegemonic culture's refusal to acknowledge the legitimacy of its less influential and powerful cousin. The focus on performance, oral history, oral storytelling, and other forms of expressivity separated Brown's approach from Myrdal's.

In brief, the Southern trip expanded Myrdal's vision by giving him, first of all, a rather vivid portrait of the disparity between the ideals of the American creed and the realities of black life. As a result, the insight he gained enabled him to focus on the study's inquiry as a dilemma. Nevertheless, it is possible that Myrdal found himself trapped in a dilemma of his own, between his research methods, on the one hand, and his personal relationships on the other. As nearly all historians writing about the project point out, the study presented its goals and objectives as outside the province of "culture." The official definition of the project within a particular social-science ideology refused to acknowledge any place for culture—loosely defined as art, music, literature, and so forth. Despite Brown's tutelage, as Jackson tells us, "Myrdal . . . never had much of an ear for music and was much more interested in politics than literature" (Jackson 132). Given this observation, Brown's recollection seems curious. "There was so much missing," Brown reminisced, "[so] he set up, in order to understand this better, a program which he called 'The Negro in American Culture.' Which to him covered everything" (Interview by author). In effect, Myrdal's and Brown's cultural views coalesced around a compromise between culture as oral and written expressivity and as a reformulated Arnoldian idea of culture as the best that has been thought and known, stressing the achievements of individuals. Since Myrdal was ultimately interested in documenting the consequences of racial disparity and racial difference, he found the category "cultural achievements" suitable to his research needs.[2]

The accommodation of culture to Myrdal's purpose in the form of "cultural achievements" required a project that would interrogate the nature and consequence of racial difference in order to quantify the data that might support or refute the Carnegie Corporation's belief that black racial accomplishments were few. Thus when Brown proposed to write his summarizing memoranda, he was attempting, with Myrdal's encouragement, to research comprehensively an impossible list of cultural areas: "The Negro in American Literature," "The Negro in the Movies," "The Negro on the American Stage," "The Negro in American Art," "The Negro in Music," "The Negro in the American Dance," "The Negro on the Radio," "The Negro in American Humor," "Contributions of the Negro to American Speech," "The Negro in Sports," "The Negro in Science," and "The Negro Audience." Brown had virtually no research assistance, and yet the expectation was that the project would still be completed in *five months*. Both Brown and Myrdal apparently clung to their hope that the focus of this study could be narrowly construed and therefore doable. They would eventually see disappointment displace hope as it became apparent that finishing such an enormous project was unrealistic.

Brown, of course, wanted to provide insight and understanding into the expressive nature of art and culture. Ultimately he was betrayed, not only by the overly ambitious scope of the project but also by a method that could not reveal the information he sought. He tried valiantly, but in vain, to elicit humanistic or qualitative findings from subjects set up for quantitative research. As he wrote in an undated reader's report about "The Negro on Stage": "The author rejects, in this as in his other studies, all explanations that are based on the assumption of a difference in the innate endowments of the two races. He favors interpretations that place the emphasis on cultural and environmental factors" (Brown, Research Summary, 2).

In denying outright racial essence as an explanatory model for racial difference, Brown felt he had found surer footing in a focus on attitudes and attitudinal change. What he discovered, though, was a methodological nightmare: a confusing synthesis of quantitative and qualitative approaches. For example, in order to understand the Negro artist's social background, he proposed to explore the size of the reading public, racial sensitivities, and the double standard of aesthetic criticism. To analyze the situation of Negro actors, he planned to determine their names and achievements, their opportunities to act, their financial compensation, and the (un)written codes of Hollywood that prescribed what parts they could play.

How this data was to be collected is as curious as the variety of questions Brown pursued. In the case of Negro actors, for example, his plan was to seek out career stories, conduct some interviews, use his personal experience as director of plays, send out questionnaires, elicit from his students the number of plays they saw and their access to theaters in their hometowns, and create a newspaper clipping file. To gather information about the Negro in art, he proposed interviewing art critics and teachers and corresponding with artists.

This partial list of research objectives and the methods for accomplishing them make it clear why futility set in. Of the various subjects Brown researched, only three—"The Negro in Sports" (142 pages), "The Negro on the Stage" (185 pages), and "The Negro in American Music" (236 pages)—were written up when the study was published in 1944. And these were only partially completed. A number of distractions exacerbated Brown's difficulties: his wife, Daisy, underwent emergency surgery, he joined with Arthur P. Davis and Ulysses Lee to edit *The Negro Caravan,* and later he won a Rosenwald Fellowship to work on *A Negro Looks at the South.* These situations, on top of what he confessed was his own naïveté about so monumental an undertaking, added up to a personal embarrassment for Brown. As he wrote Samuel Stouffer, who served as interim project director during 1940 and 1941, when Myrdal returned to Sweden because of the outbreak of the war: "Frankly I did not know what a memorandum was. I started doing serious study for a useful book, not a mere summary of the existing literature, but as serious a scholarly job as I was able to do. I had to start from scratch in many of the fields, in some cases because of my unfamiliarity and lack of training in the fields (music, art); in others because of the paucity of material. I got swamped" (Brown to Stouffer 2). The task was even more complicated because Brown aspired to write a monograph for the Carnegie Series on the Negro, like Melville J. Herskovits's *The Myth of the Negro Past,* Charles S. Johnson's *Patterns of Negro Segregation,* and Otto Klineberg's *Characteristics of the American Negro.*

Nevertheless, in the "Negro Achievements" section of *An American Dilemma,* the fruits of Brown's research subtly resonate as Myrdal, using especially "The Negro in Music" and "The Negro on Stage," sought to document, from his own particular social-science perspective, the main fields in which blacks had made notable accomplishments, and even some of the exemplary figures.[3] Although Brown's inability to complete the entire assignment of "The Negro in American Culture" certainly contributed to the marginal use Myrdal made of it overall, it remains questionable whether a successful completion would have made a difference in the project's outcome, given Myrdal's editorial approval of the claim his associate Arnold Rose made for African American culture as an arrested development in American culture. It seems likely that the study would still have lost an excellent opportunity to refashion its views about African American cultural significance and its meaning for the study's undertaking. It seems unlikely, in other words, that the Myrdal Study was willing to revise its ultimate conclusions about the importance and centrality of culture as an evolving set of humanistic assumptions.

Instead of conceding to the study's stubborn obeisance to its methodological path, Brown implicitly asserted himself and his approach to culture. Taken together, several essays Brown wrote during and following the study reveal the extent to which he departed from Myrdal's imperatives. As a group, "The Negro Author and His Publisher" (1941), "Count Us In" (1944), "Contributions of the American Negro" (1945), and "Athletics and the Arts" (1951) document differential racial treatment. But they escape what Brown would consider a narrow social-science vision. They fairly sparkle with the strivings of African Americans for self-definition and a sense of individual and racial pride. This focus places Brown on the side of Ralph Ellison's critique that the black sociologists working for the Myrdal Study assisted the project in reaching its conclusions about the supposed distortion of black culture because their commitment to the assimilationist philosophy of sociologist Robert Park engendered a kind of "timidity" that discouraged them from reaching any other conclusions (Ellison, "Review" 307). Unlike the other black researchers on the project, Brown refused to accede to its imperative to document victimization and racial inferiority.

"Count Us In" (1944), his longest essay, appeared in the collection *What the Negro Wants*, edited by Rayford W. Logan. It presents a rather compelling example of Brown's unwillingness to play a racial "blame game," because rhetorically it revises the conclusion about black pathology.[4] On this subject, Mark A. Sanders is most persuasive: "As Brown plays on the highly ironic tension between African American cultural presence and political invisibility—that is, the peculiar ways in which African Americans do and do not 'count'—he critiques the larger American paradox: the reality of economic and political servitude at radical variance with the highest ideals of the republic" (Sanders xvli).

This radical essay reveals Brown's determination to be free of the limitations imposed by traditional social-science perspectives.[5] In his own way, he sets forth the virtues of an experiential perspective. Methodologically, this means using an ethnography not dependent on the familiar social-science research pursuit of quantifiable evidence. Instead, Brown privileged, as Skinner said, "performance, oral history, oral storytelling, and other nonwritten forms of expressivity" (Skinner 420). In "Count Us In," Brown masterfully appropriates a social-science form and, in a bold tropological display, asserts the value of a qualitative representation of black life. Although *What the Negro Wants* was not conceived as a direct response to Myrdal's *An American Dilemma*, Brown's "Count Us In" can be read as foregrounding a missed research opportunity. It rhetorically addresses Myrdal, the study's method, and its conclusions in what emerges as a daring revisionist act.

"Count Us In" is no less polemical than the thirteen other essays in *What the Negro Wants*, including Logan's "The Negro Wants First-Class Citizenship," Roy Wilkins's "The Negro Wants Full Equality," and Langston Hughes's "My America." In tone and tenor, it expresses an equivalent urgency, insistence, and assertiveness. Although this essay participates in an avowedly polemical forum, Brown simultaneously manages to address, with remarkable cogency, two reading audiences. First, he poses the question "What does the Negro want?" to the larger, predominantly white readership to whom the collection was actually directed. Second—and this is my focus—he addresses Myrdal rhetorically and, in so doing, extends beyond the period of researching and writing *An American Dilemma* the process of educating Myrdal about African Americans.

In setting forth the terms of his argument, Brown locates a workable strategy in a modernist multivocal narrative in which he presents multiple forms of corroborative evidence. The essay begins:

> A young European scholar, back from a swift trip through the South, picked up from my desk a copy of Hal Steed's *Georgia: Unfinished State.* A passage on the last page confused him. It read: "I would not say that the Anglo-Saxon is superior to other races, but that this race makes up nearly one hundred per cent of the population of the South augurs well for unity—unity in political beliefs, in religion, in social problems." The European was amazed at the figure—nearly one hundred per cent Anglo-Saxon. "But I saw so many Negroes there," he said. (308)

In this representation of the "European scholar," Brown refashions the actual Myrdal into a fictive character beset by incredulity, amazement, and naïveté. The focal point for this characterization rests on the disjuncture between what the European actually saw on his Southern tour and what published testaments claim.

The narrative voice, of course, reflects Brown's aesthetic vision, formed in the crucible of black vernacular culture. Here, in the matrix of a folk-based aesthetic and in the object lessons of the lives of the Mrs. Bibbys, "Big Boy" Davises, Slim Greers, and other nameless vernacular characters from his poetry, Brown found responses to questions of cultural authenticity or accurate racial representation. It was under their astute tutelage—during which, as Brown said, "the teacher by day became the student at night"—that he came to develop the heightened aesthetic vision that informed not only his oeuvre of original poetic expression but his searching critique of African American representation in white American literature. Through this process, Brown escaped his own middle-class upbringing and developed an ethnographic position as cultural insider. This vantage point enabled him to trust what he saw with his own eyes and to distrust what many whites depicted in fiction as "the Negro" and other reductive images. From this perspective, the essay's narrative voice replies to the European's observation: "I assured him that the evidence of his eyes could be trusted" (308). Thus Hal Steed's assertion that the South is unified or "solid" is shown to be fallacious. The misguided view of "unity" is therefore exposed for what it actually is: just another way that African Americans have been counted out.

Following the premise that equates "seeing clearly" with "truly knowing," the remainder of the essay narrativizes evidence to convince the confused fictive Myrdal of the desirability and necessity of "counting us in." In a perfectly balanced orchestration of proof, the story unfolds in six parts: (1) the Negro as counted out or the white refusal to count Negroes in, (2) Negroes sensing that they did not or could not belong, (3) rare instances of genuine respect between

African and European Americans, (4) the national scope of the racial problem, (5) the "no trespassing" signs as indications of maintenance of the status quo, and (6) finally, the meaning of being counted in or the quest for democracy. The argument advanced in these several sections effectively mounts to a climactic declaration: "Negroes must join . . . in a truly interracial program, or better, a democratic program. . . . But [first] we must be counted in" (344).

En route to delivering this emphatic assertion, the narrative voice reveals itself as that of an astute ethnographer, whose authority and cogency emerge from the persuasive emic ethnography it details. Brown, as narrative voice, locates cultural authenticity in the many anecdotes, personal testimonies, and reportage he gathered from a wide range of Southern black informants when, in 1942, he embarked under a Rosenwald Fellowship on a six-month tour of the South to collect material for a response to Jonathan Daniels's *A Southerner Discovers the South* (1938)—a project Brown announced as *A Negro Looks at the South*.[6] It is this emphasis on people talking and describing themselves that the narrative voice captures and shares with the reconstituted Myrdal.

By representing black people in various modes of self-description, the narrative voice provides a kind of evidence that clearly questions conclusions that might be reached by an outsider. Anecdotal evidence, for example, could help the European understand the dynamics of Southern white–African American social relations "from the bottom up," as in the parable of the rich white man and the poor white man Brown quotes from the writer and social critic Lillian Smith: "There's two big jobs down here that need doing: Somebody's got to tend to the living and somebody's got to tend to the nigger. Now, I've learned a few things about making a living you're too no-count to learn. . . . But one thing you can learn easy, any white man can, is how to handle the black man. Suppose now you take over the thing you can do and let me take over the thing I can do. What I mean is, you boss the nigger, and I'll boss the money" (310).

This instance of "counting Negroes out" is complemented by efforts to force African Americans to accept ostracism. In the midst of World War II, which purported to be a fight to preserve democracy for all American citizens, residents of Charleston, South Carolina, were urged to commit to the following social norm as a way of expressing their patriotism: "If the peoples of this country's races do not pull together, Victory is lost. We, therefore, respectfully direct your attention to the laws and customs of the state in regard to segregation. Your cooperation in carrying them out will make the war shorter and Victory sooner. Avoid friction. Be patriotic. White passengers will be seated from front to rear; colored passengers from rear to front" (318). The specific examples abound, but together they can be characterized as multiple responses to a very complicated set of social circumstances. The logic of "dividing and ruling," that is, playing poor whites against African Americans, proved not just an impediment to African Americans but to everyone who sought the attainment of the highest ideals of a democratic nation. And the effort to make the acceptance of segregation into a patriotic act merely exacerbated an obvious exclusionary process.

At the time that it appeared, *An American Dilemma* seemed to present fresh perspectives on the old problem of race, culture, and African Americans' relationship to American democracy. Its large research team and voluminous size, however, only belied what seemed to be a sui generis investigation. The question Myrdal probed had been asked well before W.E.B. Du Bois's eloquent query in *The Souls of Black Folk* (1903): "How does it feel to be a problem?" (Du Bois 37). Twenty years later, Alain Locke would signify upon Du Bois's query by declaring the emergence of a New Negro, one who was no longer "more of a formula than a human being—something to be 'kept down,' or 'in his place,' or 'helped up,' to be worried with or worried over, harassed or patronized, a social bogey or a social burden" (Locke 3). A vibrant new group psychology, he proclaimed, now permeated the spirit of the younger writers coming of age in 1925 (Locke 3). Brown, as poet, folklorist, and humanist, would venture into the social-science world when, prior to publication, he used portions of Charles S. Johnson's *The Negro in American Civilization* (1930) in his class at Fisk University (1928–1929). Despite his intellectual eclecticism, Brown wrote with the soul of a poet, even though his weaving of anecdotes, personal testimony, and other language forms became powerful evidence of an ethnographic narrative. It is the coalescing of poetry, folk sensibility, and social science that enables an appreciative portrait of Brown in "Count Us In," later included in his posthumously published *A Negro Looks at the South* (2007). His is an aesthetic that is at once contemporary and, at the same time, precursory.

Without invoking his name, Sissela Bok, the daughter of Gunnar Myrdal, unwittingly validated Brown's importance to the Myrdal Project, even though his influence was not directly felt. Fifty years after *An American Dilemma* appeared, she wrote a smart but largely hagiographic essay that traced her own intellectual debt to her father's philosophical vision. Myrdal used to tell her, she said, "that some people were better than their books, whereas others were not as good as their books" (Bok 1). She then writes that "no matter what the personal sacrifice, he would rather leave behind him at least one great book than the memory of a life that, however worthy in other respects, had produced only mediocre writings. This was the passionate scholarly commitment that he brought to the writing of *An American Dilemma*" (Bok 1). Brown was no less passionate and certainly much better than his uncompleted work. Whereas Myrdal needed a scientific, supposedly "objective" approach to define the nature of his work, Brown, as humanist, needed only to turn to the people themselves to divine the interior of their lives. His work was anchored experientially, in a way of seeing clearly as a way of knowing.

Writing about Ralph Ellison, Arnold Rampersad cogently explores the meaning of humanistic inquiry of African Americans. When Ellison and

Myrdal came together to receive honorary doctorates from the University of Michigan, Ellison "warned [Myrdal] against accepting too readily the findings of sociologists." The problem, Rampersad quotes Ellison as saying, was that in "treating people as abstractions rather than individuals . . . sociology has ignored the complexity of human life [and worse has] created young Negroes who believe the sociological definitions of themselves" (Rampersad 438). Ellison is here returning to his earlier critique of *An American Dilemma*, effectively demonstrating his own distrust of sociological method as a heuristic to examine African American life and, more important, as an approach to creative writing.

Myrdal, according to Rampersad, did not go away quietly. While admitting that sociology had its limitations, Myrdal also acknowledged the reality of social evil and retorted, "We must have radical reforms and rational information to cement them to" (Rampersad 438). This perspective inspired Gene Roberts and Hank Klibanoff with the idea for their Pulitzer Prize–winning study *The Race Beat: The Press, the Civil Rights Struggle, and the Awakening of a Nation* (2006). Especially inspiring was the premise Myrdal wrote in *American Dilemma*, "that if the mainstream press told the southern racial story, the rest of the nation would be 'shocked and shaken' and demand sweeping changes" (*American Dilemma* 48). While Myrdal was, for these two writers, prophetic in his view of the role the press could play in igniting social change, their impressive history paid scant attention to Myrdal's conclusion about the material plight of African Americans as "pathological." Thus Brown's view of culture becomes even more necessary. It is rooted most decidedly in what we now call oral history, and it provides a heuristic more capable of probing the interiority of everyday African Americans.

The set of descriptors Kim Lacy Rogers offers in her impressive *Life and Death in the Delta: African American Narratives of Violence, Resilience, and Social Change* (2006) frames the disciplinary boundaries erected by many oral historians writing today. In this study of African American narratives, she writes about "patterns of stability and change that often structure life stories," "oppositions and dualities that marked narrators' accounts of [their] lives," "significant markers of status and difference within . . . communities," the meaning narrators made of their journeys, "their own process of education, growth, and self-discovery," "concrete memories of ordinary daily life and experience," "historical events and processes of national and regional importance," and much more (Lacy 10–11). These issues are imbued with a complexity that Brown, as poet, folklorist, and humanist, never directly broached in theoretical terms, but his astute insight into answers to these issues, artfully encased in his body of poetry and, in prose, in *A Negro Looks at the South,* dramatize a mind and soul capable of capturing the spirit of these same narrators. Brown presaged the many oral historians writing today, and he bequeathed a legacy capable of eliciting information about how people work, what they do, and what they reveal about themselves. From the axis of oral historians, these are the questions that most fully document a people's culture.

NOTES

1. The eminent poet Michael S. Harper confirms the depths of this friendship. Harper, on a State Department tour of Sweden in 1980, requested an audience with Gunnar Myrdal. By this time, Myrdal was so busy that he saw very few people unless it was urgent. Harper sent this message: "I bring you greetings from Sterling Brown." It not only got him admission but also Myrdal's declaration that "without Sterling Brown, there would have been no *An American Dilemma!*" (Harper and Tidwell, phone conversation, 30 July 2003).

2. See "Negro Achievements" in *An American Dilemma* (chapter 44, section 5) for a detailed discussion of this issue.

3. See the footnotes to "Negro Achievements," *An American Dilemma*, 436–37. In this brief, eight-page section, Myrdal quotes five times from two of Brown's memoranda. Just as important are the indirect quotes. Myrdal follows rather schematically the list of questions Brown proposed to research. Ostensibly within the contexts of art and culture, Myrdal's descriptions of the social relations of African- and Euro-Americans forego questions of aesthetic excellence and emphasize instead their boundaries, tensions, and interactions.

4. "Count Us In" has since been reprinted as the epilogue to Brown's *A Negro Looks at the South*, published posthumously in 2007. Further references to this essay will be to the Logan edition and cited parenthetically by page number in the text.

5. Evidence of the startling radicalism achieved by *What the Negro Wants* is the response of University of North Carolina Press director Terry Couch. In a nearly unprecedented gesture, he wrote a Publisher's Introduction in which he attempted to disclaim the conclusions reached by Logan and the other essayists. Couch had proceeded under the assumption that all contributors to the book would agree with his belief that gradualism was the best remedy to "the Negro problem." He was shocked when the writers declared in one voice: "We want racial integration and we want it now!" Casting about for a rejoinder, Couch, in a fit of desperation, attributed the failings of the book to what he perceived as the undue influence exerted by *An American Dilemma*.

6. Brown wrote a largely appreciative review of the Daniels book for *Opportunity* in December 1938. Although he felt Daniels's chats with blacks were too few, Brown still applauded the book's candid photographs, since he felt they helped to defuse the notion of an undifferentiated or "solid" South. Brown found that the "symbolic incidents and speeches, bits of excellent description, humorous anecdotes, glimpses of tragic allusions to well known books and places" contributed to a realistic portrait of the South.

WORKS CITED

Bok, Sissela. "Introduction to *An American Dilemma Revisited*." *Daedalus* 124.1 (1995): 1–13.

Brown, Sterling A. "Athletics and the Arts." *The Integration of the Negro into American Society*. Ed. E. Franklin Frazier. Washington, DC: Howard University Press, 1951. 117–47.

———. "The Contributions of the American Negro." *One America*. Eds. Frances Brown and Joseph Roucek. New York: Prentice-Hall, 1945. 588–615.

———. "Count Us In." *What the Negro Wants*. Ed. Rayford W. Logan. Chapel Hill: University of North Carolina Press, 1944. 308–44.

———. Interview. Institute for the Arts and Humanities. 14 May 1973.

———. Letter to Samuel Stouffer. 5 November 1941. "Negro Study General Correspondence: Brown, Sterling A., 1939–1943." Carnegie-Myrdal Study Papers. New York: Schomburg Center for Research in Black Culture.

———. "The Negro Author and His Publisher." *The Quarterly Review of Higher Education among Negroes*. 9 (July 1941): 140–46.

———. *A Negro Looks at the South*. New York: Oxford University Press, 2007.

———.Interview by author. 24 June 1983.

———. Research Summary on "The Negro in American Culture." Undated. "Negro Study General Correspondence: Brown, Sterling A., 1939–1943." Carnegie-Myrdal Study Papers. New York: Schomburg Center for Research in Black Culture.

Du Bois, W.E.B. *The Souls of Black Folks*. 1903. Eds. David W. Blight and Robert Gooding-Williams. Boston: Bedford Books, 1997.

Ellison, Ralph. "*An American Dilemma:* A Review." *Shadow and Act*. New York: Random House, 1964. 303–17.

Gabbin, Joanne. *Sterling A. Brown: Building the Black Aesthetic Tradition*. 1985. Charlottesville: University Press of Virginia, 1994.

Harper, Michael S. Telephone conversation. 30 July 2003.

Jackson, Walter. *Gunnar Myrdal and America's Conscience*. Chapel Hill: University of North Carolina Press, 1990.

Johnson, Charles S. *The Negro in American Civilization*. New York: H. Holt and Company, 1930.

Keppel, Frederick. Foreword. Myrdal, *An American Dilemma*. xlv–xlviii.

Locke, Alain. "The New Negro." *The New Negro*. 1925. New York: Atheneum, 1992. 3–16.

Murray, Albert, and John Callahan, eds. *Trading Twelves: The Selected Letters of Ralph Ellison and Albert Murray*. New York: Vintage Books, 2000.

Myrdal, Gunnar. *An American Dilemma: The Negro Problem and Modern Democracy*. New York: Harper and Row, 1944.

———. Letter to Frederick Keppel. 28 January 1939. "Negro Study General Correspondence: Brown, Sterling A., 1939–1943." Carnegie-Myrdal Study Papers. New York: Schomburg Center for Research in Black Culture.

Nelson, Cary. *Repression and Recovery: Modern Poetry and the Politics of Cultural Memory, 1910–1945*. Madison: University of Wisconsin Press, 1989.

Odum, Howard. "Problems and Methodology in *An American Dilemma*." *Social Forces*. 23 (1944–1945): 94–98.

Rampersad, Arnold. *Ralph Ellison: A Biography*. New York: Alfred A. Knopf, 2007.

Roberts, Gene, and Hank Klibanoff. *The Race Beat: The Press, The Civil Rights Struggle, and the Awakening of a Nation*. New York: Alfred A. Knopf, 2007.

Rogers, Kim Lacy. *Life and Death in the Delta: African American Narratives of Violence, Resilience, and Social Change*. New York: Palgrave Macmillan, 2006.

Sanders, Mark A. Foreword. *A Son's Return: Selected Essays of Sterling A. Brown*. Boston: Northeastern University Press, 1996.

Skinner, Beverly Lanier. "Sterling Brown: An Ethnographic Perspective." *African American Review.* 31.3 (1997): 417–22. (Reprinted in this collection as "Sterling Brown: An Ethnographic Odyssey.")

Southern, David W. *Gunnar Myrdal and Black-White Relations: The Use and Abuse of "An American Dilemma," 1944–1969.* Baton Rouge: Louisiana State University Press, 1987.

Wright, John S. *Shadowing Ralph Ellison.* Jackson: University Press of Mississippi, 2006.

V

"RUNNING SPACE": LEGACIES AND CONTINUITIES

Sterling A. Brown's Literary Essays:
The Black Reader in the Text

Robert G. O'Meally

All poetry is the reproduction of the sounds of actual speech.
—Robert Frost

Whenever I feel uneasy about my writing, I think: what would be the response of the people in the book if they read the book? That's my way of staying on track.
—Toni Morrison

You can read my letter, baby, But you sure can't read my mind.
—Blues lyric

A realist not only by artistic and critical persuasion, but by temperament, Sterling A. Brown has shown concern throughout his career with poetry as an art of communication—not just among airy Muses and free spirits, but among real people in this world, actual writers and their readers. Publishers, editors, reviewers, and "blurbists" shape this communication process, as do those persons whose lives are depicted in literature. Brown's critical writings deal mainly with the literary portrayal of Afro-Americans. The question sounding through virtually every critical piece he writes is this one: How true is this work to the lives of the people portrayed, as their real-life counterparts themselves see it?

Here literary virtuosity is just *one* test for value: Granted a given work about black life is well-made and "interesting" (to use Henry James's key term); but would the blacks put in the book recognize their own speech and actions, their own sense of life? Or are these more stick and stock "Negro Character[s] as Seen by White Authors"?[1]

Complicating these questions is the issue that Sterling A. Brown laments in several critical pieces of the 1930s and 1940s: Afro-Americans, for the most part, "are not yet a reading people."[2] When blacks did read works about themselves, too many reacted with insecurity or "bourgeois" diffidence. Why was this true of a group for whom, as many authors of slave narratives made clear, writing and reading were deemed near magic gifts, ones for which nineteenth-century blacks prayed, stole, tricked, studied in secret, and sometimes paid with lashings and other dire punishments? And what are the literary implications of the black audience's neglect and misperception? What are the costs for black writers who, observes Brown, are the only ones really called upon and able to give a comprehensive "insider's" look at Afro-American life?[3] Finally how, considering the tastes and distastes of black readers and potential readers, might the black writer reach them?

In many of his early essays and reviews, Brown turns his attention to the vagaries of the Afro-American audience. One reason blacks did not read was that to do so seemed frivolous for a group beset by the crushing economic pressures of the Depression. "What help in books for an increasing breadline?" they asked.[4] "Why should poor people needing their money for necessities such as bread and shoes, rent and coal, pay from two dollars to five dollars for a book?"[5] But even those not under the threat of economic collapse usually did not read: "Our practical man, often self made, and often admirably so, distrusts mere book learning as a useless appendage." When the black college graduate picked up a book, he tended, Brown says, to shun books by or about blacks:

> Some of this is based upon an understandable desire to escape the
> perplexities and pressures of the race situation in America. Some
> of it is based upon the ineptitude of immature authors dealing with
> difficult subject matter. Quite as much is based upon a caste-ridden
> disdain of Negro life and character, and anguish at being identified
> with an ignorant and exploited people to whom many "upper class"
> Negroes are completely unsympathetic.[6]

In a key essay, "Our Literary Audience," Brown declares that "there is a great harm that we can do our incipient literature. With a few noteworthy exceptions, we are doing that harm, most effectively."[7] The short answer to the essay's topic question—Why aren't black readers good readers?—is quoted from Brown's "young friend" whose survey reported: "Too much bridge."

Charging that many blacks who read are put off by realistic literature about Afro-American life, Brown cites four fallacies that distract black readers:

... We look upon Negro books, regardless of the author's intention,
as representative of all Negroes, i.e. as sociological documents.
... We insist that Negro books must be idealistic, optimistic tracts for
race advertisement.
... We are afraid of truth telling, of satire.
... We criticize from the point of view of bourgeois America, of racial
apologists.[8]

Each of these categories is rife with complexities. As for the fallacy of "repre-
sentativeness," it is suffered by the reader who sees any realistic black character in literature as "a blanket charge against the race." For this super-sensitive
reader "the syllogism follows: Mr. A. shows a Negro who steals; he means
by this that all Negroes steal; all Negroes do not steal; Q.E.D. Mr. A. is a
liar and his book is another libel on the race."[9] Made defensive by attacks by
propagandists like Thomas Dixon and Thomas Nelson Page, this part of the
black audience "cannot enjoy 'Green Pastures' for fear that the play will be
considered typical of all Negroes."[10] Nor can they really approve of Cane, Their
Eyes Were Watching God, or the fiction of Richard Wright. We are not all like
the characters in these books, they complain. Here of course the problem involves over-concern among the black audience with what the white audience
is thinking.

These "best-foot-forward" readers want books as "race advertisements,"
with pictures not of Hurston's fresh Janie or Wright's bumptious Big Boy, but
of the "best" Negroes. And "by the 'best' Negroes these idealists mean generally the upper reaches of society, i.e. those with money." By this standard, says
Brown, "a book about a Negro with a mule would be, because of the mule, a better
book than one about a muleless Negro; about a Negro with a horse and buggy
a better book than about the mule owner; about a Negro and a Ford, better than
about the buggy rider; and a book about a Negro and a Rolls Royce better than
the one about a Negro and a Ford. All that it seems our writers need to do,
to guarantee a perfect book and deathless reputation is to write about a Negro
and an aeroplane." This Negro with an "aeroplane" would be too refined to in-
dulge in satire. Nor would he speak dialect, because "Negroes of my class don't
use dialect anyway," quoth our highbrow reader. "Which mought be so," taunts
Brown, "and then again it moughtn't."[11]

This yearning for self glorification in art, says Brown, typifies the "racial"
audience member who, "after the fashion of minorities, is on a strict defensive
when any aspects of its life are presented." The same "minority" reaction beset
Lady Gregory, Synge, and Yeats, pioneers in modern Irish theatre whose work
challenged the British stereotype of the "simple" Irishman, "smiling through
his tears," with true-to-life portraits. To their dismay these writers found their
works "misunderstood by the people whose true character they wanted to
show, and whose latent geniuses they wished to arouse and sustain. Riots were

frequent when in contradistinction to the stereotype of the vaudeville stage they refused to set up plaster-of-paris saints."[12]

Typical, too, of other oppressed minorities, blacks generally misunderstood the new drama of the 1930s—by O'Neill, Paul Green, and Langston Hughes—because of sheer *inexperience*. Rather than sad and shocking plays set on the wrong side of the tracks, such audiences desired either "complete escape" or what they called "worth-while" books and "elevating" shows. In Brown's words, "They are pleading, one has reason to suspect, for musical comedy which may have scenes in cabarets, and wouldn't be confined to Catfish Row. With beautiful girls in gorgeous 'costumes'; rather than Negroes in . . . tattered clothing."[13] Elsewhere, Brown writes that "the typical audience of our small towns has a confused idea of drama as compounded of a church pageant, a fashion show, and an object lesson in etiquette, and that of our larger towns is sold to Hollywood. Neither furnishes much sustaining interest for our aspirant Ibsen."[14]

Well-cropped black youngsters, "with some Little Theatre Movements the honorable exceptions, want to be English dukes and duchesses, and wear tuxedoes and evening gowns. Our 'best' society leaders want to be mannequins."[15] And too often black colleges failed to modernize and broaden students' literary tastes by failing to offer them good courses in writing. "Within the not too distant past," wrote Brown in 1932, "the chronicler has known educators whose idea of literature was a concoction of Emily Post, the Boy Scouts handbook, and somebody's cyclopedia of quotations, and who knew that the only authors were dead authors and since his students were alive, authorship (for them) was out of the question."[16]

Like other critical realists Brown not only analyzes the mind-set and class adhesions of the audience, he makes moral assessments of them, too. His most cutting charge against the black audience is that they are worse than "typically bourgeois": too many lack the "mental bravery" and family loyalty to face the unvarnished truth about themselves and their ethnic brethren. These are the Negro Babbitts whose "deities are pocketbooks and fine cars and what they misname 'Kultchoor'": those who cannot respond to lowly Porgy or Teacake or Big Boy because of class prejudice, those guilty of "a cowardly denial of our own." In Brown's words: "It seems to acute observers that many of us, who have leisure for reading, are ashamed of being Negroes. This shame makes us harsher to the shortcomings of some perhaps not so fortunate economically. There seems to be among us a . . . fundamental lack of sympathy with the Negro farthest down."[17] This shallow grasper after "Kultchoor" "preferred Spanish folksongs to Negro"; he called "the song of the Volga boatman a classic whereas 'Water-Boy' was beneath contempt. He was so far removed from the Water-Boy, he said."[18]

Miseducated, riddled with class prejudices, conservative, escapist—"our literary audience" is depicted by Sterling A. Brown in his early criticism. He quotes Whitman's cryptic complaint and warning: "To have great literature, there must be great audiences, too."[19] But in these essays Brown goes far beyond mere scoring against inept black audiences. He not only pointed out their failings, but he put these failings into perspective, analyzed them (E. Franklin Frazier called Brown "my favorite literary sociologist"),[20] and persuaded against them with great force. In so doing he presented a rigorous defense of literature as more than a social phenomenon but as "equipment for living." "There is more to lowliness than 'lowness,'" he wrote. "If we have eyes to see, and willingness to see, we might be able to find in Mamba, an astute heroism, in Hagar a heartbreaking courage, in Porgy, a nobility, and in E. C. L. Adams' Scip and Tad, a shrewd philosophical irony. And all of these qualities we need, just now, to see in our own group."[21] "A vigorous literary movement," wrote Brown, "is part and parcel of social change."[22]

Brown also presented in his early essays an excellent course in how to read a modern book. He dealt with questions like these: When does tragedy give way to mere sentimentality? When does comedy yield to farce? What is the significance of "point of view"? What is the relation of realism and melodrama? How might the use of folklore in art provide more than "local color"? In his companion booklet to James Weldon Johnson's *Book of American Negro Poetry*, Brown defined literary realism with succinctness. He termed it:

> . . . the attempt to create the illusion of life, generally by the use of contemporary material. It deals with the familiar and the usual. The so-called "new poetry," dating from 1912, is in the main realistic in tendency. It was a reaction to sentimentality, to didacticism, to Pollyanna optimism, to exotic escapes from modern conditions by dreaming. It aimed instead at reflecting contemporary life . . . Social protest took the place of optimistic complacence; and unflinching acceptance of the realities of life as subject matter, a greater objectivity instead of an all-consuming subjectivity, these are a few of the changes that came in with the new poetry. The influence . . . is to be seen in what James Weldon Johnson calls the "younger group" of Negro poets.[23]

Beyond offering to readers that rarest of commodities, intelligent criticism, Brown also addressed black *writers,* and called on them to add their voices to the "new poetry." He even suggests ways in which black authors might reach through the briar patch of their audience's flaws and command their attention. Despite everything the potential audience was there, witness the success of Atlanta University's Summer Theatre and, on a national scale, Richard Wright's fiction. Of the Atlanta Players' 1934 season, which included not only stage items like "Lady Windemere's Fan" but Shaw and some contemporary American works, Brown wrote: "In a city known for a full round of social activities, the intruding summer theatre was nevertheless received with hospitality."[24] And though many white and black readers spurned Wright's *Uncle Tom's Children* as "propaganda"—for certain readers labeled as such all fiction about blacks refusing to show "Harlem to be a round of cabarets and parties or the South to be a sunny pastoral"—Wright's success nonetheless proved that "social protest fiction, even about Negro experience, can sell widely . . . Wright is a craftsman who can tell a story with the best of them today; he can reach out and hold an audience. He is a publisher's find."[25] *Native Son*, Brown reported with enthusiasm, was "a literary phenomenon . . . discussed by literary critics, scholars, social workers, journalists, writers to the editor, preachers, students, and the man in the street." The book inspired debates "in grills and 'juke joints' as well as at 'literary' parties, in the deep South as well as in Chicago, among people who have not bothered much to read novels since *Ivanhoe* was assigned in high school English."[26]

In calling for realistic literature about Negro life, Brown invited not special pleas or exaggerations; quite the contrary: he called for books containing the unprettied truth of Negro life, just the facts well rendered. The point here is not that dubious whites could read the real truth of life among the black lowly and, at last, Give a Damn. Though interested in all readers, whatever their background, Brown most urgently desired the creation of a community of *black* readers who received from literature images expressing the meanings of their lives, and strategies for coping with them. Brown seemed to have had in mind something like what Robert Stepto has termed a call-and-response[27] (or call-and-recall) pattern between black writers and their readers, an enriched exchange between "implied writers" and "implied readers" (both, according to one terminology, "embedded in the text")[28] and *actual* readers recognizing their experiences transformed in literature. For this literary "conversation" or "group creation" (to maintain the black church or blues metaphor, for call-and-recall sermons and songs are *communally* created) to be fully realized—for a book to be a success—the reader must read well. And, to be sure, the writer must create image and action well enough to invoke in the reader a déjà vu so irresistibly vivid that in his heart (if not out loud) he says, "Amen."

In his criticism Brown taught several ways for black writers to win black readers' attention. Crucial here, of course, is the matter of *form*. "Form," writes Kenneth Burke, may be defined as "the psychology of the audience" and "the creation of an appetite in the mind of the audience, and adequate satisfying of that appetite."[29] Effective literary form involves meeting the audience—as the vernacular has it—"part way down the road." The black audience was sold on the sudden turns of plot and the coincidences of melodrama, so black writers could capture their attention using some of these same techniques. "Melodrama," wrote Brown, "can be expert and inexpert in its cogency."[30] Moreover, "a critic would have to be blind," he wrote in 1938, "to deny that . . . melodrama and tragedy abound [in] southern Negro life."[31] The trick here, as critics from Aristotle to Booth have written, involves preserving verisimilitude while keeping the audience interested.

Controlling the point of view was another key aspect of Brown's poetics of effective communication in literature. Seen from the peanut gallery, a razor-toting badman laying to cut his women can be a tiresome minstrel cliché, a hackneyed stage joke. But told from the viewpoint of the women whose terror, in Faulkner's "That Evening Sun," is real, the old story comes frighteningly to life.[32] Likewise the comic Negro is a stock stage figure; but shift the point of view, and the reader laughs not just at the figure of fun but *with* him: even the "rough and ribald" humor of Caldwell's *Kneel to the Rising Sun* does not descend to mere burlesque.[33] Hurston's characters are often comic, but they are not cartoons.[34] And as Brown points out, blacks laugh not *only* "to keep from crying," they sometimes laugh because they are *tickled.*[35]

Brown's main point here is that of the realist: To reach the reader, the writer presents the reader with "the familiar and the usual" aspects of a world he already knows. Thus middle- and upper-class black life should not be treated with the worn conventions of "copybook gentility" comedy, but with modern techniques revealing first-hand, lived experience.[36] Like most realists, Brown wrote with greatest force about the portraits of poor blacks—not, in Brown's case, because they are "simpler" and thus easier to get on paper;[37] this pastoral and prejudiced stance is challenged in virtually everything Brown writes. He considered the "dominance of the lowly as subject matter" in modern literature to be "a natural concomitant to the progress of democracy."[38] And anyway most blacks *were* poor, especially during the depression. Brown felt that if black middle and upper classes became comfortable in their evasiveness about the terrors and trials of being poor, they themselves would be dragged down, both morally and economically, or their children would be.[39] If literary realism could shock the reader out of his dreaminess and blindness, that, too, was one of its saving features. Brown's realism reflected the artistic movement in Europe and America which claimed as proper subjects for serious treatment the forgotten men and women at the bottom of the social hierarchy: migrants, workers, roustabouts, dwellers on the outskirts of town. In one essay Brown quotes Thomas Hardy's words, which might be taken as a credo of Brown's realism:

> That if way to the Better there be,
> it exacts a full look at the worst.[40]

To view the world from the standpoint of the black masses themselves, several writers of the 1930s and 1940s tapped the rich source of black folklore: that other crucial element informing the tastes of Afro-American audiences, highborn and lowly. This use of black lore was natural enough, for, as Brown says, through the nineteenth century there was no written black poetry to compare with the spirituals or with the "sly and sardonic" couplets of secular folk verse. In the folktales and the blues, the worksongs and the ballads, lay a goldmine of material: here were figures of speech, characters, themes, and narrative and lyric shapes created by black Americans themselves—obviously from their own point of view—and tempered with centuries of New World living. Nor was folklore merely a localizing ingredient: Melville, Mark Twain, Faulkner—creators of American masterpieces—had taken a page from "the *fabliaux*, Boccaccio, Chaucer, Rabelais, and Münchausen and like them had drawn artistic strength from the speech and the folkways of people around them, and from their tales and songs."[41] These writers had found the passage to the universal "through the narrow door of the particular." In America, wrote Brown, quoting Constance Rourke, "this (vernacular) tradition is 'subtle, sinewy, scant at times, but not poor'; it "is the new thing prophetically seen by Emerson over a century ago . . . a new literature that sought the meaning of 'the milk in the firkin, the meal in the pan, the ballad in the street,'" and explored "the familiar and the low."[42] Chesnutt, Johnson, Hughes, Hurston, and, of course, Brown himself, had continued, often with magnificence, to work this folk vein as it ran through black America.

Like black folk, black lore had been much abused, to be sure. Roark Bradford's *John Henry* "presents certain features of the lives of roustabouts and migrant workers along the Mississippi, the 'back' of such towns as New Orleans and Memphis, gris gris, coonjining, and folk-songs."[43] Thus his writing had many of the elements of realism. But even so the book is "more of a study in local color . . . than the showing of a folk hero . . . John Henry just isn't there." Here again the issue involves point of view:

> *John Henry* poses the interesting problem of how many liberties an artist may take with folk material. That is, between mere recording and alteration that leaves the folkstuff unrecognizable, where is the place of genuine artistry, of the Burns or of the Hardy? . . .
> *Certain it is that the artist must look at the material in as nearly as possible the manner of the ultimate creators of it.* One has the feeling that Mr. Bradford's attitude is still one of sophisticated condescension.[44]
> (Italics mine)

Julia Peterkin, on the other hand, uses black folklore more realistically, and thereby sets an example for black writers: "One thing might be suggested to our writers by this woman. She has shown in our day the truth of Wordsworth's belief in rural as significant, suggestive of truth. She is with Hamsun, Anderson, Powys, Hardy. From her we might get a hint of the need of going back to the soil; of digging our roots deeply therein. —There is strength there, and coolness for draught."[45]

Sad to say, some of "our writers" were afflicted by the same disease that plagued "our literary audience": Brown termed it "an aristocratic disdain of our masses." Straightshooting Brown brings this high-falutin writer down from his perch: "Though it may be *lese majeste* to say so, our elite is only one remove—even our 'ritziest' only one and a half removes—from our masses. . . . Our folklore and songs are being assiduously collected by white editors. . . . Material in abundance exists; do our artists believe it to be so far beneath their notice? Has it been so easy, then, for school and society to fix in us a savage contempt for the rock whence we were born?"[46] There are significant exceptions: Bontemps's novel *God Sends Sunday* has some of the quick turns and refrains one hears in Negro ballads; Hurston's *Their Eyes Were Watching God* has characters with some of the "unabashed shrewdness of the Blues."[47] At a conference on folklore, Brown said: "I became interested in folklore because of my desire to write poetry and prose fiction. I was first attracted by certain qualities that I thought the speech of the people had, and I wanted to get for my own writing a flavor, a color, a pungency of speech. Then later I came to something more important— I wanted to get an understanding of people, to acquire an accuracy in the portrayal of their lives."[48]

The lasting power of Brown's poetry derives not only from its technically accurate capturing of folk speech—at times Roark Bradford could manage that—it derives too from his deceptively straightforward ability to portray, in vigorous American language—sometimes country, sometimes city, sometimes in folk language, sometimes not—the complex drama and richness of what it meant to be Sister Lou, Sporting Beasley, or Old Lem. The durability of Brown's poetry comes too from his perspective as a realist in a world with no hiding place. Certainly his poems show that Brown is not the "outsider" or the blind escapist he wrote about in this passage from *The Negro in Washington* (1937):

> . . . When the outsider stands upon U Street in the early hours of the evening and watches the crowds go by, togged out in finery, with jests upon their lips—this one rushing to the pool-room, this one seeking escape with Hoot Gibson, another to lose herself to Hollywood glamour, another in one of the many dance halls—he is likely to be unaware, as these people momentarily are, of aspects of life in Washington of graver import to the darker one-fourth. This vivacity, this gayety, may mask for a while, but the more drastic realities are omnipresent. Around the corner there may be a squalid slum with people jobless and desperate; the alert youngster, capable and well trained, may find on the morrow all employment closed to him. The Negro of Washington has no voice in government, is economically proscribed, and segregated nearly as rigidly as in the southern cities he contemns. He may blind himself with pleasure seeking, with a specious self-sufficiency, he may point with pride to the record of achievement over grave odds. But just as the past is not without its honor, so the present is not without bitterness.[49]

As a critic, too, Brown is a realist. Part of what is so durable in Brown's criticism is the compelling drive to see the complete picture of literature, its makers, their sources, the effects on readers. As we have seen, he is particularly concerned with bringing together black readers and black writers (not only them, but especially them). The way to do it, aside from somehow getting both writers and readers to give up the false gods of Babbittry, was for the writers to put the readers and potential readers right between the covers of books: to capture on the page real people, full of anguish and beauty, frailty and roguishness, and the love to lie. The trick was to do so as Sterling Brown had done in his poetry: to portray black characters with so much vividness that not only will a conference of writers and teachers say of the poem, "How realistic!" "How mythic in reference!" "How well structured!" "How well deconstructed!" But in the backrow, or in the Amen Corner, even Wild Bill or Joe Meek or Ma Rainey or Big Boy Davis or Jack Johnson or Sporting Beasley Daniels might hear Sterling Brown's poetry and say, "*Ouch,* I do believe this man Brown, he is talking about me!"

NOTES

1. Sterling A. Brown, "Negro Character as Seen by White Authors," *The Journal of Negro Education* 2 (April 1933): 179–203.
2. Brown, "The Literary Scene," *Opportunity* 9 (February 1931): 53–54.
3. Brown, "More Odds," *Opportunity* 10 (June 1932): 188.
4. Brown, "The Literary Scene," 53.
5. Brown, "The Negro Writer and His Publisher," *The Quarterly Review of Higher Education among Negroes* 9 (July 1941): 143.
6. Brown, "The Negro Writer and His Publisher," 143.
7. Brown, "Our Literary Audience," *Opportunity* 8 (February 1930): 42.
8. Brown, "Our Literary Audience," 42.
9. Brown, "Our Literary Audience," 42.
10. Brown, "Poor Whites," *Opportunity* 9 (October 1931): 320.
11. Brown, "Our Literary Audience," 42.
12. Brown, "A Literary Parallel," *Opportunity* 10 (May 1932): 153.
13. Brown, "Our Literary Audience," 43.
14. Brown, "Concerning Negro Drama," *Opportunity* 9 (September 1931): 284.
15. Brown, "Our Literary Audience," 43.
16. Brown. "Signs of Promise," *Opportunity* 10 (September 1932): 287.
17. Brown, "Our Literary Audience," 46.
18. Brown, "More Odds," 188.
19. See Walt Whitman, "Ventures on an Old Theme," *Prose Works* (Philadelphia: David McKay, 1924), 324: quoted by Sterling A. Brown in "Our Literary Audience" (42) and in "The Negro Author and His Publisher" (146).
20. Inscribed in Sterling A. Brown's personal copy of E. Franklin Frazier's *The Negro Family in the United States* (Chicago: University of Chicago Press, 1939).
21. Brown, "Our Literary Audience," 46.
22. Brown, "More Odds," 188.
23. Brown, *Outline for the Study of the Poetry of American Negroes* (New York: Harcourt, Brace, 1931), 49–50.
24. Brown, "The Atlanta Summer Theatre," *Opportunity* 12 (October 1934): 309.
25. Brown, "The Negro Author and His Publisher," 144.

26. Brown, "Insight, Courage, and Craftsmanship," *Opportunity* 18 (June 1940): 185.
27. See Robert B. Stepto, *From Behind the Veil* (Urbana: University of Illinois Press, 1979).
28. See Susan R. Suleiman, "Introduction: Varieties of Audience-Oriented Criticism," *The Reader in the Text,* ed. Susan R. Suleiman and Inge Crosman (Princeton: Princeton University Press,1980), 3–45; see also Jane P. Thompkins, *Reader-Response Criticism* (Baltimore: John Hopkins, 1980).
29. Burke's definition is quoted by Stanley Edgar Hyman in *The Armed Vision,* revised edition (New York: Vintage, 1955), 375.
30. Brown, "Six Plays for a Negro Theatre," *Opportunity* 12 (September 1934): 280.
31. Brown, "From the Inside," *The Nation* 166 (April 16, 1938): 448.
32. Brown, "The Point of View," *Opportunity* 9 (November 1931): 347.
33. Brown, "Realism in the South," *Opportunity* 12 (October 1935): 311.
34. Brown, "'Luck is a Fortune,'" *The Nation* 166 (April 16, 1938): 448.
35. Quoted from a conversation with Brown, November 22, 1977.
36. See Brown, "Biography," *Opportunity* 15 (September 1937): 216; also see Brown, "Not Without Laughter," *Opportunity* 8 (September 1930): 311–12.
37. See George Becker, *Documents of Modern Literary Realism* (Princeton: Princeton University Press, 1963), 24.
38. Brown, "Our Literary Audience," 44.
39. Brown, "Our Literary Audience," 44.
40. Brown, "Never No More," *Opportunity* 10 (February 1932): 56.
41. Brown, "In the American Grain," *Vassar Alumnae Magazine* 36 (February 1951): 8.
42. Brown, "In the American Grain," 8.
43. Brown, "Never No Steel Driving Man," *Opportunity* 9 (December 1931): 382.
44. Brown, "Never No Steel Driving Man," 382.
45. Brown, "The New Secession—a Review," *Opportunity* 5 (May 1927): 148.
46. Brown, "More Odds," 189.
47. Brown, "'Luck is a Fortune,'" 410.
48. Brown, "Remarks at a Conference on the Character and State of Studies in Folklore," *Journal of American Folklore* 59 (October 1946): 506.
49. Brown, "The Negro in Washington," *Washington: City and Capital* (Washington, D.C.: Government Printing Office, 1937), 89.

"A Brown Study": Sterling Brown's Legacy of Compassionate Connections

John F. Callahan

1

Struggling to write about Sterling Brown, his poetry and criticism, at first I could utter only half-remembered, half-invented fragments from the many conversations we had during the fifteen years I knew him and was his friend. Hearing Sterling's voice so tinged with sorrow songs and trainwhistle blues, I thought of William Butler Yeats, whom Sterling loved for his music and his discovery and twentieth-century redirection of Irish folklore, and whose shivering, sinewy voice Sterling had heard on a recording from the 1930s. Some lines came into my head, and like the folks who drop in unexpectedly in Sterling's poems, they lingered on the front porch of my mind:

> I sought a theme and sought for it in vain.
> I sought it daily for six weeks or so.

So Yeats wrote of his writer's travail of old age in "The Circus Animals' Desertion" before he realized that his theme was the heart. And not the heart of sentimental Valentine's Day metaphors but the funky "foul rag-and-bone shop of the heart."

Ah, I thought, Sterling Brown's true journey, like Yeats's, was to the interior of his people and their tradition. There he found himself, and there he rooted his modernist poetry of the folk.

Many times man lives and dies
Between his two eternities,
That of race and that of soul,
And ancient Ireland knew it all.

These lines are from Yeats's epitaph, "Under Ben Bulben." And as epitaph to Sterling Brown in the tenth year since his passing, I decided to write up the talk I gave on his eightieth birthday at a festival put together by Michael Harper—the "Providence conductor" Fanny Ellison was fond of calling this poetic son of Sterling—at Brown University on May 1st, 1981. "Sterling Brown and the Irish Connection" was the name I gave it. And I wasn't talking about Irish Americans, for like several African-American writers the connection Sterling made was back to Ireland. (Not to the black Irish either, though he knew the phrase did not refer only to the black-haired, dark-eyed Irish, or to the melancholy, bitter brooding associated with a certain Irish temperament, but also to the fact that from the time of the Spanish Armada stretching back before the Danish invasions, Moors had sailed to and been shipwrecked along the coasts of Ireland, especially off County Kerry in the Southwest where the Gulf Stream blows a warm plume of air past incongruous, thriving palm trees. Some of these Moors stayed behind and intermarried with Irish women.) Like Frederick Douglass before him, Sterling Brown found affinity with the soulful, stoical quality of Irish expression. When Douglass sought a point of contact with African-American slave songs, he found it in Irish music. "Nowhere," he wrote in his old age, "outside of dear old Ireland, in the days of want and famine, have I heard sounds so mournful."

And surely Brown's stubborn refusal over the years to accept the Harlem Renaissance as a name for the burst of energy in African-American letters during the 1920s and early 1930s had strong reference to the Irish tradition. Who would have thought to call the Irish Revival the Dublin Renaissance? Who but Joyce perhaps, and he was off enjoying his self-generated exile in Paris and Zurich. No, the roots Yeats, Lady Gregory, and John Synge put down after sojourns in London and Paris, were in the folk country of the west, from the desolate moonscape County Clare, to the sudden wild, green, fog-and-wind-obscured, sea-roaring Cliffs of Moher, up to Galway with its bleak, off-shore Aran Islands and their curraghs, north past Sligo to Ben Bulben, as much a mythical creature of Irish folklore as it is a mere mountain, finally to Donegal in the North and the likes of Bloody Head frothing away at the edge of the sea. One of Yeats's most moving observations appears on the wall leading up the winding stair to his tower, Thoor Ballylee. There, on a plaque are words of Yeats, words wishing he'd brought Jimmy Joyce to the west of Ireland where that brilliant, copious, sometimes parsimonious soul could have witnessed the richness of peasant speech and imagination, experienced the lush green and the wild, rocky coast of the West of Ireland, and heard the Gaelic spoken there.

Like Yeats, Sterling Brown learned his people's spiritual geography in the country—rural Virginia, Tennessee and Missouri—more than in the city, though like his soulmate Yeats who could turn a mean line about life in Dublin, Sterling Brown wrote with bite about Washington, D.C., and Chicago. Like Brown on his forebears, Yeats wrote of his attraction to the lineage of Irish poets before him. Yes, Yeats knew their verse was mannered. "But they had one quality I admired and admire; they were not separated individual men; they spoke or tried to speak out of a people to a people; behind them stretched the generations." Yeats's words bear an uncanny resemblance to the literary conclusions Sterling Brown drew from his journey to the interior of his people. Like Yeats, Brown never forgot "what had to be endured" by the ancestors. He never neglected the spirituals as a musical legacy of blues-toned *thought* as well as lyric poetry. Little wonder one of his most trenchant lines came in response to a line uttered by a buzzard in Robert Penn Warren's "Pondy Woods":

"Nigger, your breed ain't metaphysical."

Brown's retort impaled more than one dozing New Critic on his yeoman's bayonet in a whiplash rhetorical thrust reminiscent of Irish rebels speaking from the dock of British justice before their execution:

"Cracker, your kind ain't exegetical."

As the foregoing suggests, Sterling Brown favored the particular and loved to give the bite and flavor of drama to an argument. I have found one such quotation first in the pages of *The Negro in American Fiction* (1937), then repeated in "The Negro in American Literature," a talk he delivered at Fisk several years later in tribute to James Weldon Johnson. It also turned up in his indispensable essay, "A Century of Negro Portraiture," published in 1966 in the *Massachusetts Review*. And I was lucky enough to hear him recite the passage with brightening eyes and slow, revealing voice without a hint of a brogue (though Sterling could do a brogue that damn near rivaled my Irish-born grandfather's) in a talk he gave on stereotypes in American literature in the 1970s. "I swear," he began, "their nature is beyond my comprehension. A strange people!—merry 'mid their misery—laughing through their tears, like the sun shining through the rain. Yet what simple philosophers they! They tread life's path as if 'twere strewn with roses devoid of thorns, and make the most of life with natures of sunshine and song!"

Surely, I thought on first hearing the words in 1974, this is the stereotype of the contented slave. Of course it isn't, as Sterling Brown hastened to point out *after* he'd hooked his audience. "This passage," he explained, "is dealing with the Irish, in a play written by an Englishman in one of the most tragic periods of Ireland's long history of persecution." And as I discovered while reading Brown's 1931–32 course thesis for English 85 at Harvard, the play is called *The Shamrock and the Rose*. Incidentally, that thesis, *Plays of the Irish*

Character: A Study in Reinterpretation, stands up today. Like so much of Brown's literary criticism, it is disciplined, particular, cogent work, characteristic of Brown's ability to plow rough untilled soil into hospitable ground for others to plant, raise and harvest crops illuminating neglected facets of American literature. Brown's criticism is consistently the work of a critic more concerned with restoring and extending the canon than with his own place in it.

After his "careful study of American poetry" at Harvard in the early 1920s, Brown put Irish historical and literary connections to use in his own African-American vernacular ballads and blues. First of all, he acknowledged the conscious literary parallel between Irish and African-American literature as spelled out by James Weldon Johnson. "What the colored poet in the United States needs to do," Johnson wrote in his 1922 preface to the *Book of American Negro Poetry,* "is something like what Synge did for the Irish; he needs to find a form that will express the racial spirit by symbols from within rather than symbols from without, such as the mere mutilation of English spelling and pronunciation." And this is precisely what Sterling Brown did in his folk poetry.

Listen.

Hear Big Boy Davis stake out a place in the pantheon of stoical folk heroes:

> An' all dat Big Boy axes
>> When time comes fo' to go,
> Lemme be wid John Henry, steel drivin' man,
> Lemme be wid old Jazzbo,
>> Lemme be wid ole Jazzbo . . .

Overhear a lifer on the chain gang hold his own by holding it in, honing his fury to the low growl of a last irrevocable word, his hammer in his hand all the while:

> White man tells me—hunh—
> Damn yo' soul;
> White man tells me—hunh—
> Damn yo' soul;
> Got no need, bebby,
> To be tole.

Catch the religious and historical changes (and change) aspired to in the advice the poet gives old Sister Lou in an idiom tender, strong, and soulfully hers:

> Honey
> Don't be feared of them pearly gates,
> Don't go 'round to de back,
> No mo' dataway
> Not evah no mo'.

Tap your foot to the subtle, simple beat of an epic blues about the ebb and flow of cities and civilizations, and pick up the bluesman's onomatopoetic insinuations of tradition in the sighing of the elemental, everlasting wind:

> Memphis go Memphis come back,
> Ain' no skin
> Off de nigger's back.
> All dese cities
> Ashes, rust . . .
> De win' sing sperrichals
> Through deir dus'.

In his adaptations of the African-American oral tradition in *Southern Road*, Brown so well expressed "the racial spirit by symbols from within" that James Weldon Johnson changed his mind about the literary possibilities of dialect. Like John Synge, Sterling Brown made folk idiom both symbol and enactment of the inner life of his people. Like Synge, Sterling Brown could also speak in the devil's own tongue. In "Remembering Nat Turner," he counterpoints black idiom with an old white woman's self-deluding version of the racial situation in the early 1930s. Because he hones her speech and lets her speak for herself, Brown drives home his point about the corrupt, surviving scheme of things under Jim Crow:

> Ain't no slavery no more, things is going all right,
> Pervided thar's a good goober market this year. . . .
> Things is all right, now, ain't no trouble with the niggers.
> Why they make this big to do over Nat?

Who knows but that these words twang on some hybrid Scotch-Irish frequency?

Again, taking his cue from Ireland on the matter of portraiture, Brown worried lest black audiences emulate those Irish who had railed at Synge because of his realism. It may be he wrote, that "the Negro audience frequently wants flattery instead of representation, plaster saints instead of human beings, drawing rooms instead of the homes of the people." But what did Sterling Brown want? Like Yeats, and building on those American writers who, like Twain, Robinson, Sandburg, and Frost, observed the extraordinary in ordinary lives, Brown sought to "make possible a literature that, finding its subject matter all ready in men's minds, would be not as ours is (Yeats is speaking of Irish literature before the Renaissance of the early twentieth century), an interest for the scholars, but the possession of a people." In these days when literary criticism tends to graze more and more exclusively on the parched lands of theory, Brown's pursuit of a wide democratic audience is both a strange and needful legacy.

"I want to be in the best American tradition," Brown said in "A Son's Return: 'Oh Didn't He Ramble,'" the extended solo he played on his life and times and traditions upon his return to Williams College in 1973. His wish "to be accepted as a whole man" echoes the creed of Yeats's *Essays and Introductions*.

"I wanted," the Irish poet wrote, "to cry as all men cried, to laugh as all men laughed, and the young Ireland poets when not writing mere politics had the same want, but they did not know that the common and its befitting language is the research of a lifetime, and when found may lack popular recognition." Sterling Brown knew these things and made the effort his life's work.

Along the way he forswore the ivory tower for the world and set a worldly example, as Yeats and Synge had, for those who followed his vocation of teaching. He warned the professorial breed against their own worst enemy in a 1937 poem called "Uncle Joe," written in Creole idiom:

> Yo sho' dat you a teacher?
> You doan ack much like a teacher to me.
> You ain't got, nohow, de teacher's talk.
> Mos' times, I can make out tings wat you say.

That's the challenge Sterling Brown laid down in the spirit and idiom of Mark Twain and John Synge, of the blues and spirituals, and his glory was that the exacting ghost of language and right speech never left his side.

2

After I'd given that talk about Sterling Brown and the Irish connection, I realized I had not yet made a true or complete connection with the complex sensibility at the heart of the man and his work. Just as the middle passage was not the end of the line during slave trading days, so there's a journey beyond Yeats and Synge to Sterling Brown's connection with the Anglo-American modernist tradition of T. S. Eliot. After all, it was Eliot's fate to come of Northern Abolitionist stock and grow up in St. Louis with ambivalent feelings about many things, not least himself. "A small boy with a nigger drawl" was Eliot's characterization of an old identity before he booked passage north by northeast to Harvard and east by northeast to London. I suspect that Eliot's reaction against the "turning loose of emotion," against the fires of passion and chaos, derived somewhat from the danger and violence so palpable in turn-of-the-century St. Louis. At that time St. Louis was a border city that possessed many habits of the old brawling, frontier rivertown that beckoned to Eliot's imagination from life, from the blues, and, not least, from the pages of Mark Twain.

That Eliot remained fascinated and repelled by the violent, riverbound Mississippi spirit of St. Louis is conjecture. Less so is that Sterling Brown knew *The Waste Land* and, like Ralph Ellison decades later in *Invisible Man*, bent some of Eliot's techniques to his different purposes in "Cabaret," the last poem in the *Tin Roof Blues* section of *Southern Road* (1932). Unlike "When de Saints Go Ma'ching Home," which Robert Stepto in a brilliant essay (included in this volume) calls a performance poem of beginnings—perhaps the first modern (and modernist) African-American poem—"Cabaret" is a poem of endings. Indeed, it is an anti-performance poem of performance, a poem of chronicle and satire, of almost Swiftian savage indignation. Inside the cabaret "(1927, Black & Tan Chicago)," landscape and sensibility are antithetical to those that define the folk experience during the devastating 1927 flood. (Of that flood, Sterling Brown remembered before he read "Cabaret" in 1974: "I was in Missouri teaching then. And I saw the Missouri in flood. I saw the Mississippi; I saw Arkansas at that time. And then I go into the cabaret and hear the popular muddy water business and the contrast struck me.") Like Eliot, Brown absorbed but did not accept the conventions of popular culture; in "Cabaret" the AfricanAmerican entertainers are degraded as part of the act. Here Brown's technique is no longer the portraiture he learned from Edwin Arlington Robinson, from Robert Frost, from Paul Laurence Dunbar, and possibly from his contemporary, Langston Hughes. Like *The Waste Land,* "Cabaret's" technique undermines ideas of coherence and continuity. Yet Brown departs from Eliot. He invokes no substrata of literary allusion to shore up and transcend his satire on commercial, popular distortions of African-American culture.

Unlike Eliot, Brown insists his poetry be accessible to everyone, particularly his own people, of whom he would write in 1930: "We are not a reading folk." Not yet, he adds, and works to further what in the nineteenth century Walt Whitman saw as the imperative of democratic art: "Without great audiences we cannot have great poets." Nonetheless, the cabaret Brown writes of is a wasteland destructive to AfricanAmerican personality and culture. And Brown does not claim redemption by the folk as he did in "Children's Children." Only through stark discontinuities does Brown pursue the theme of connection in "Cabaret." Even more than T.S. Eliot's readers, Brown's audience must arrange the poem's fragments keeping in mind the spuriousness of the musical arrangement enacted in the poem.

"These fragments I have shored against my ruin": Eliot's annunciation near the end of *The Waste Land* prepares for concluding lines that allude to the potential renewing power of literature. In "Cabaret" Brown's fragments are decidedly less affirming and redemptive; rather, the snatches of language that emerge from the poem's closing situation appear unrelievedly bleak. "The band goes mad," and the last look at the chorus girls is of "seductive bodies weaving / Bending, writhing, turning." From there "Cabaret," like *The Waste Land,* tails off in several voices:

> My heart cries out for MUDDY WATER
>
> (Down in the valleys
> The stench of the drying mud
> Is a bitter reminder of death.)
>
> Dee da dee D A A A A H

The "muddy water" allusion to "home, sweet home" is a monstrous illusion. Down in the Delta black folks are dead; some drowned, some exposed and exhausted, others beaten on the chain gang or murdered trying to escape. What's happening in the Black and Tan Cabaret in Chicago is a social, cultural, and economic variation on the natural devastation taking place all along the Mississippi River. What's more, the entertainers know it, and in the inarticulate desolation of their cry, they testify to the painful and empty illusions behind the song they sing, the public lives they lead. Here Sterling Brown is almost harshly scrupulous. He offers no consolation, no genuine blues voice. Could that be lost, he seems to ask? And what would happen if the blues were lost?

Instead the final "jazz" notes, in their expiring, orgiastic, soul-dying sigh, return to the original sexual meaning of *jass*. The chorus girls and musicians mime sexual climax to this audience of "overlords" who perhaps are about to seek similar satisfaction from "their glittering darlings." What makes the poem's ending so terrible is that African American musical and sexual styles are twisted into the service of vicious and prurient ends. It is hard to miss the chord of sweeping pain beneath the orgiastic cries of Dee da dee D A A A A H, for these are not Dada artists and artistes blasting away at bourgeois conventions of art and society from Paris and Berlin cabarets in the broken world after World War I. In the voices and instruments of these black performers there is no release, no letting go, no passage to life's intensity but instead a desolate yielding up of soul at the point of bodily climax. And Brown's last reverberation is that there is a "more bitter reminder of death" in this grotesque, orgiastic racial ritual of the cabaret than in all the buzzards circling over the Delta's devastated flood plain.

To experience "Cabaret" you need that "slightly different sense of time" Ellison's Invisible Man associates with invisibility. He means "you're never quite on the beat. Sometimes you're ahead and sometimes behind. Instead of the swift and imperceptible flowing of time you are aware of its nodes, those points where time stands still or from which it leaps ahead." You need, to steal once more from Ellison, "to slip into the breaks and look around." Once there, you see that in "Cabaret" Sterling Brown indeed uses discontinuous, modernist techniques to break up this music and this dance. He intends to jar his audience out of complacency and away from complicity with the uncritical assumptions of the Jazz Age. And there is yet another variation on time in "Cabaret." Alongside the discontinuous fragments there does exist a chronology, a line of passage from slave women on the auction block to the chorus girls in the 1920s floor show "creole beauties" as far removed from Creole blood or background—or the "overlords" fantasies of same—as the Muddy Water tune is from the blues.

In the synchronic effect of the ending of "Cabaret" Brown achieves a modality akin to what Ellison had in mind when he referred to the capacity of improvised jazz to fuse performance with creation "in a single complex act." Although his subject is the degradation by which performance becomes prurient entertainment, Brown himself renders a virtuoso jazz performance in "Cabaret." Unlike Eliot in *The Waste Land,* he does not invoke *Shantih, shantih, shantih* or any other transcendent, affirming fragment. His fragments—Dee da dee D A A A A H—do not translate. They are anti-cathartic. They are sounds, not words, and in their reverberation they provoke reconsideration of Eliot's idea that in the 1920s you could effectively shore aesthetic fragments against your ruin. On the contrary, the sound and sense of Brown's last notes cast doubt on whatever expectations linger of modernism's ability to affirm convincing new beginnings either for self or for community without the low, painful fires of critical intelligence and historical consciousness.

3

There is indeed "no hiding place," as Brown asserted years after "Cabaret" in the title of his next volume of poems. There are his connections to African-American, American, Irish, even Anglo-American traditions. And because of his ability to connect folk and modern traditions, his work stands not as fragments but as a coherent body of expression. Toward his work Sterling Brown kept that flat, understated, ironical, open stance embodied in lines he gave an anonymous Virginia black man in "Remembering Nat Turner" (1932):

> "Pears lak I heard that name somewheres or other.
> So he fought to be free. Well. You doan say."

In his storyteller's guise Sterling Brown kept that same stance toward himself. I know. I met him in his seventy-fourth year when he was a septuagenarian nowhere near his anecdotage. On the contrary, as raconteur he was trenchant, alert, and sensitive as a seismograph, and in his moods he could be as volatile and dangerous as one of the fault lines watched over by that intricate machine. In this connection I should say that lowering my nets to catch a theme for this essay, I suppressed my instinct to tell of Brown the character and storyteller as well as the poet and critic. I was loathe to embrace his stories—why I don't know. But by now I am convinced that my original impulse was perfectly natural, not the easy way out at all. On the contrary, to note and celebrate Sterling Brown's storytelling is consistent with the whole man he aspired to be. Hell, his stories had the same range, the same command of the different stops of language, experience and sensibility as his poems and literary essays.

For Sterling Brown was a character able to put himself aside even as he put his vitality and sharp eye and ear to work bringing to life the many characters he wrote about. He was proud that the wellsprings for many of his poems were characters he'd met, like the comic yet dignified Sporting Daniels of "Sporting

Beasley," a figure from his Washington, D.C., youth, or those he met in his travels South and West during stints at Negro colleges during the 1920s: Calvin "Big Boy" Davis, Mrs. Bibby, Gillie the Nashville barber, and so many others whose portraits he drew in poems like "Odyssey of Big Boy," "Sister Lou," "Ma Rainey," "Sporting Beasley," and "Old Lem." By no means least, in "After Winter" Brown rendered the tender side of his father, the Reverend Sterling Nelson Brown, remembering that usually austere man's song for Sterling's sisters and for Sterling as he tended the small family farm in Maryland:

> "Butterbeans fo' Clara
> Sugar corn fo' Grace
> An' fo' de little feller
> Runnin' space. . . ."

In truth, Sterling Brown possessed a storyteller's gift for portraiture reminiscent of Kenneth Burke's idea of the "representative anecdote." His improvised, oral portraits are snapshots suggesting the style, form and flow of lives lived and spoken by the people. I learned these things first hand back in 1974 when I asked Sterling Brown to be keynote speaker in a two-day program at Lewis and Clark College called "The Souls of Black Folk" featuring Sterling along with Ernest Gaines, Michael Harper, and the late bluesman, Robert "Pete" Williams. The occasion I speak of took place after hours on the first night. Sterling had delivered his lecture, taken questions for almost another hour, then lingered in front of the lectern telling more "lies" to students and some of the others who'd turned up at Lewis and Clark, before he retired to my apartment overlooking the West Hills of Portland. It was bourbon time, and though he should have been three hours ahead on eastern time, Sterling was only beginning to jam.

"Michael, Ernest," (he insisted on calling Ernie Gaines Ernest, and, ever courtly, Gaines appreciated the good-humored gesture of ceremony and respect; neither would Brown call Michael Harper Mike as many did in those days), he asked the other two writers, "does Brother Callahan know about Sam Jones?" Of course, Sterling knew he could bet the family homestead that I didn't know the story, but only his flashing eyes cast suspicion on the deadpan cast of his face.

"Shall I tell him?" he pressed his fellow writers for an answer.

Gaines was quiet. He didn't know quite what Sterling was up to, so Sterling turned to Harper. "Michael, are you sure the Chairman of the Department won't take offense? There's some color and some off-color in the story."

Harper grinned. It amused him that Sterling was so tickled by the fact that the vernacular, irreverent likes of me was department chair in my early thirties. Never mind that there were only ten people in the Lewis and Clark English Department, that the Chair rotated, and had more in common with the manager of a minor high school sport—you washed the socks and towels—than with the stern, often inquisitorial headship Sterling had chafed under for decades at Howard.

Never mind all that, there was a story to be told, and Sterling Brown was using me as a whetstone against which to sharpen the blade of his voice and wit. And this is how he told the ballad of Sam Jones that memorable evening within spitting distance of the Oregon Trail. . . .

"Someone the likes of whom we used to call an evil Negro in those days went down to the train station," he began. "His name was Sam Jones, and he had a ticket to take him from New York to Philadelphia. So Sam walks into Grand Central, looks around for an open information booth and sees that every last one is closed. And I don't mean temporarily. They were boarded up.

"'Damn,' Sam said. 'Been gone from here too long.' It was a Sunday night and the great waiting room was nearly deserted. Finally, Sam spotted a large machine in the middle of the room with a sign across the top reading Automatic Timetables and a little slot for coins belt-high on the ten foot contraption.

"'Damn,' Sam said, to no one. 'Got to pay a goddam machine to find out about you train.'

"Well, Sam hemmed and hawed. Eventually he fished a dime out of his pocket and, as if he were allergic to metal, put it into the slot.

"'Whrrrrrrr,' the machine spun, whined and carried on before it wound down long and slow, and a voice drawled from deep inside, like Jonah from the whale's belly.

"'Yo name is Sam Jones. You six-foot-two, weigh a hundred eighty-five pounds, on yo way from New York to Philadelphia. And yo train leaves at eight-thirteen.'

"'Damn,' said Sam. 'Damn god-damn big robot son-of-a-bitch taking my money and talkin to me that way.'

"Now Sam wandered off all upset," Sterling told us.

At this point with a storyteller's privilege, he got up, glass of Jack—for Jack Daniels—in hand and imitated Sam Jones walking in anger and befuddlement across the train station. As Sterling walked and talked, my living room and that old fashioned train station waiting room seemed to grow wide as a prairie.

"Sam," Sterling continued, "was damned if he wouldn't outwit that machine, so he snuck over to a corner of the room behind a pillar—one of those imitation Greek columns they put into turn-of-the-century train stations. Once Sam figures he's out of sight, he yanks an old cap out of his back pocket, pulls it down over his eyes, and sashays sideways up to the machine. He takes another dime out of his pocket, drops it in the slot like it's on fire, tiptoes back a step or two, and waits.

"'Grrrrrrrr Whrrrrr, the machine grumbles, and comes to a sudden stop, like a truck slamming on air brakes or a freight shrieking to a halt before a sleek silver passenger train crosses its track without warning at the last possible minute.

"'Grr. Yo name Sam Jones. You still six-foot-two, hundred eighty-five pounds, slow-talkin, ornery Negro on yo way from New York to Philadelphia. And like I tole you, yo train leaves at eight-thirteen.'"

At that, Sterling paused to enjoy his mimicry. But not for long. Soon done slapping his hand against his leg, he climbed back inside Sam Jones's skin.

"'Damn god-damn,' Sam growled, now mad as hell. 'I don't believe that machine. It's not a real thing. No sir. Somebody messin with Sam. I'll show 'em. Goddamn, I'll show 'em, whuffolks or black.'

"Sam," Sterling continued, "goes muttering to himself all the way out of the waiting room into a little anteroom. All of a sudden he sees an Indian standing there in full regalia. That stops him. But only for a minute until he gets an idea.

"'Howdy, Chief,' he says. He gets the Indian in cahoots with him against the machine. Even slips him a twenty and borrows his headdress, robe, moccasins, tomahawk, and a daub or two of war paint.

"Now Sam, dressed up like old Sitting Bull for the government photographers, approaches the machine with an exaggerated, slow-time walk.

"'How; he says with a deep bow. He puts some wampum in the machine's mouth. Then he waits, lighting a peace pipe the Chief threw in after Sam gave him the twenty.

"Grrrrrrrrrrrrrrrrrrrrrr!, the machine winds up in a growl as fierce and long as old Jack-the-Bear when he saw the first hunters stalking him in the Mississippi woods or Satch Paige throwing sidearm strikes past Ty Cobb in one of those exhibition games he played with the Negro All Stars against the big leagues' best.

"Sam waits, a Cheshire cat smile showing beneath the war paint on his brown face. He don't have long to wait. That machine starts in like a car radio turned full blast when the static from a thunderstorm breaks in over every frequency.

"'Yo name Sam Jones,' the machine's voice blares in righteous anger. 'You *still* six-foot-two, weigh hundred eighty-five pounds, . . . big black buck nigger on yo way from New York to Philadelphia. And while you was fucking with that Indian, yo train done gone.'"

After his words ceased and laughter highballed past the book shelves in my living room, Sterling slipped back into his chair. Like a master storyteller, he knew to be silent and let his story's aftereffects accentuate the good feeling he had created among the company twenty-two stories above the streets of Portland.

I know now that the tale of Sam Jones and the timetable machine is an old story told in many guises as a take-off on the John Henry folk tale of man testing his strength and wits against the machine. As Sterling told it, it's a story of hubris expressed not as tragedy but farce. At the time it was hilarious, all the more so because of Sterling Brown's masterly performance—his mimicry and timing and the joy with which he threw in a new detail here and there that had occurred to him on the spot, like the wampum and the peace pipe. As a storyteller, Sterling Brown combined the gestures of silent movies with the liberating sound of the talkies. Not least, I was surprised and pleased—honored is not too strong—to be allowed into the charmed circle where African American idiom is tasted and savored, straight-no-chaser as the musicians say, without euphemism, apology or fear of betrayal.

4

Not all of Sterling Brown's stories cleared the palette as clearly and cleanly as did his tale of Sam Jones. That same visit to Oregon in 1974 he was so charmed by my six-month-old daughter's persistent cooing sounds that he asked to hold her. When he did and began swaying back and forth, the baby smiled and gurgled louder. The scene reminded me of my urge to make up little sayings for Eve in the weeks after she was born because I was so convinced she heard and understood me. "You're a little girl and your name is Eve—that much we can say," I crooned over and over leaning above her cradle, delighted by the sounds she never failed to make in response.

"I don't have a swan-song for you, little goose," Sterling told her, feeling her call, "but it's never too early to know about Sister Goose, and I better not leave it to your father to tell you the story."

Sterling rocked the baby back and forth in his arms and started to hum "Sometimes I Feel Like a Motherless Child." Soon he caught himself. "Don't mind me, little one," he said. "You have a mama, and very pretty, too. So I'll let that spiritual go and just tell you the story of old Sister Goose. We're all her children, you know, even a little snow goose like you."

The baby was quiet now looking up at Sterling through deep, liquid eyes.

"Sister Goose was swimmin on the lake," he began in a voice tuned for a lullaby. "She was swimmin on de lake enjoying every minute 'cause de lake was so wide and deep and blue like the sky and like your eyes, little one. Pretty soon she see de fox come creepin along at the edge of de lake. Dat fox all red and him waving his bushy tail back and forth like he was callin her. But Sister Goose, she not fooled. She look in at de willow trees beyond de fox and keep on swimmin.

"And de fox he say: 'Hey, you no account goose you, what you do dere? What you mean swimmin on my lake?'

Sterling stopped and looked at Eve; her eyes had opened wider at the approach of the fox. So he smiled at her as he gave his voice back to Sister Goose.

"Sister Goose, she answer dat fox: 'This not you lake, Mister Fox. An I will too swim in dis lake. This not just you lake. Dis everybody lake. My lake too, Suh.'

"De fox, he look out at Sister Goose like she crazy swimmin away in the middle of the lake. He know he can't reach her, so he say, 'Awright den, goose, you won't get off my lake, I'm takin you to court—cause this lake indeed my lake.'

"Sis Goose, she look toward shore and say to the fox. 'Dat's fine, Mister Fox. I go to court wid you. Den you'll see that dis lake belong to everybody. To me and my folks just like you and you people,' Sis Goose, she say."

Sterling Brown looked down at Eve; she'd grown completely quiet and her eyes were indeed as lush and bright as the lake in the story he was telling.

"Well, Eve, Sister Goose she go to de courthouse. And she see de guard at the door. He a fox. Inside de courtroom, de bailiff a fox. Judge come in, he look lak fox. Prosecutor: fox. Defense attorney he a fox. Jurymen foxes every one. People stopped in to see the goings on, dey foxes, too.

"Judge Fox he hold de gavel in his right front paw, I mean hand," Sterling corrected his extravagance, "then de judge he bang on de table and say, 'Dis court will come to order in de case of plaintiff, Mister Fox and defendant, dis goose over heah.'

"Judge motion de fox to speak.

"Yo honor, Judge, Suh, I brings de following complaint. Dis goose here was swimmin in de lake out neah de county line. I tells her stop, tells her she caint swim in de lake, dat de lake my lake and property. And she just keep on, insolent like. Say she not afraid of no court, no judge or jury neither.'

"Sis Goose, her feathers rustle and her long neck start rise up.

"De judge, he look at her stern-like, motion her come forward.

"Well, little sister goose of an Eve, Sis Goose stand up in front of the court real straight and serious. The judge, he say, 'Awright den, Sister Goose, what you have to say in you defense to de charges brought by Mister Fox heah?'

"Sis Goose, she bow a little, just a little, mind you, being polite, rememberin her raisin', and she say. 'Mister Judge, I wants equal justice under de law—dat's all. Mister Fox ovuh dere, wid all due respect, he wrong. Dis lake not his lake. Everybody have de right to swim in de lake. I pleads not guilty, yo honor.'

"Well, little Eve, soon as she say this, de judge he bang his gavel down and tell de jury retire. They do, walkin real slow so you almost cain't tell theys foxes. And they come back real soon lookin right at. Sis Goose.

"'Does you have a verdict for de court?' de judge ask.

"Forefox—I mean foreman," Sterling corrected himself, "of de jury stand up.

"'Yes, your honor,' he bark a little, 'we does. We find defendant guilty as charged.'

"Judge tuck his tail under his robe. His teeth look white and sharp as he stare down at Sis Goose. Den he bang down his gavel on de tree stump he using for a podium. 'You goose dere, you entitled to strict justice under de law—nothin less, nothin mo'. So de sentence I pass on you, dis here lowly goose, is sentence of death.' Den widout no more ado, de foxes execute Sister Goose—dey do. And pick her bones clean."

As Sterling patted her head, little Eve seemed to pick up a snatch or two of the lullaby tune—mmmmmm-ahmmmmm—Sterling had been humming as accompaniment to his story of Sister Goose. Now he paused, aware again of the whole company sitting beyond the inmost circle—the close-up tableau of Eve and himself. He looked at the rest of us, at the bourbons in our hands, handed me back the baby, and took up the drink I'd freshened for him.

"I hope," he said, "this little girl won't have cause to mistake any of you all for foxes." Now he looked down again at Eve, the lush green of her eyes shuttering closed, and whispered to her.

"So, little Eve, that's the story of Sister Goose and the fox."

With that, reminiscent of Sterling's portrait of Big Boy Davis in "When de Saints Go Ma'ching Home," there appeared "a far / And soft light in his strange brown eyes." Though he was surrounded by company, like Big Boy, Sterling Brown was suddenly "[a]lone with his masterchords, his memories. . . ." His face, too, like Big Boy's after his performance of "When de Saints . . ." became a "brown study." He did not leave the room, but he was somewhere else—"where we / Never could follow him."

And we did not try.

5

Eight years after Sterling Brown's passing, I write down his stories of Sam Jones and Sister Goose because, as he told them, they were full of the stops he associated with the African-American oral tradition and, *always,* the ever-fluid range of his own emotions and mind. For Brown tenderness and irony were mutually nourishing rhetorical kinfolk. A wonderful raconteur and an original *character* himself, Brown's gift was the power to evoke in images and in the tricks and rhythms of speech the particularity of character and experience. In his stories and poems his subject was the vicissitudes of personality and, as Michael Harper's little known poem, "To an Old Man Twiddlin' Thumbs," testifies, Brown forged his style in the annealing fires of the African-American condition—first slavery, then segregation and discrimination with their legalities and the not-so-last resort of official *and* vigilante violence—and the stoical affirmation that in his view marked the best of both African-American and American experience. "Guess we'll give it one mo' try" runs the refrain spoken by "an old nameless, couple" in "Strange Legacies." Brown's line is an African-American variation on Robert Frost's poker player's signature in "In Divés' Dive," a poem Brown loved and loved to quote:

> "What's it to me who runs the dive?
> Let's have a look at another five."

In front of me as I write is a pencil drawing of Sporting Beasley that Sterling drew in 1980, not more than a year after the death of his beloved wife, Daisy Turnbull Brown, as he struggled to master his seizures of grief by entertaining my young daughters, Eve and Sasha. Like Sterling's work in words, the drawing is a portrait. The figure is wearing an outfit Brown remembered from a man-about-town of his youth named Sporting Daniels whom he brought to life in the portrait poem, "Sporting Beasley":

> Prince Albert coat
> Form-fitting, corsetlike; vest snugly filled,
> Gray morning trousers, spotless and full-flowing,
> White spats and a cane.

Like the true artists of any time or place, Sterling Brown sought a form and venue for his compassion. In the drawing, old Sporting Beasley is standing in a half-strut, maybe about to tap his left foot, maybe about to stride. His left arm is extended, holding what looks like a cigar or cigarette holder. He's just blown a puff of smoke out of his mouth, and maybe he's answering a taunt or a jibe from some person or persons outside the frame of the drawing. He's in his element. His pose, by turns formal and informal in a style all his own, calls up Sterling Brown's valedictory line about another unforgettable character—old Scrappy in "Puttin' on Dog":

> "Great Gawd, but you was a man!"

In death, his voice stilled and yet unstilled, like the archetypal African Americans of his signature poem, "Strong Men," Sterling Brown, through his work and in the memories of those who knew him, remains out there, exposed, on the line: a strong man, gittin' stronger, in keeping with the standard he set for his nation and its literature.

The Professor and the Activists:
A Memoir of Sterling Brown

Ekwueme Michael Thelwell

A couple of years ago I attended a conference on Sterling Brown, organized by the English Department at Howard University. The event was part of the ongoing campaign being conducted by the estimable Eleanor Traylor, the department's relentlessly resourceful chair and intellectual leader, to amass the wherewithal to endow a chair in literature in the poet's name.

For a graduate of that department like myself, the conclave was something of a homecoming even if the upper campus had undergone some considerable physical change since my undergraduate years. The Armour J. Blackburn Campus Center is new, big, imposing. Its massive brick and glass facade seems crammed into a space where—in my student days—three lesser buildings had stood quite comfortably. One of those time-banished ghosts had been the long, undistinguished, paint-peeling wooden barracks housing the *Hilltop*, the student newspaper. In the early Sixties, we had labored there mightily and with some success to convert that organ into an instrument of political agitation and student activism—much to the consternation of the venerable Dean whose name adorns the splendid new edifice now occupying the space and dominating the upper quadrangle. Further evidence of the remorseless march of time, change and . . . progress?

Inside the Blackburn, the conference staff is cheerful, polite, helpful, in a word, very welcoming. They conduct us to a hall already full and where a movie is in progress. Suddenly, magically, time is rolled back. The voice: that rich, soft, quintessentially southern baritone capable of ranging in mid-sentence from the courtly to the folksy, the poetic to the gruff. You catch it in mid-sentence, definitely in the gruff mode. ". . . *While the literati was up in New York drinking Carl Van Vechten's cheap wine, I was in Virginia teaching. . . . My students were real people, soldiers, veterans from the war, farmers. . . ."* Then you see the screen, the familiar rumpled figure. The craggy face a little seamier now, somewhat fuller, hair grayer, a little thinner, but the voice and the spirit are the same—combative, irreverent—and you remember instantly what about him was so valuable and so lovable, so rare and important to your education.

Though you caught him in mid-answer, the question—obviously something to do with that ambiguous eruption of literary clientelism and bourgeois patronage celebrated as the Harlem Renaissance—was not hard to infer.

And even the timing seemed fortuitous beyond mere coincidence since you were fresh from a frustrating session of a graduate seminar on that, or at least a related subject: McKay's *Home to Harlem.* Your best efforts notwithstanding, the students did not appear to see exactly how alien and alienating the language; how reductive and parodic the portraiture; how superficial, condescending and barren of understanding; how ultimately derivative, external, imposed, literary and consequently false the perspective and vision as a representation of black American life, that famous bestseller really was.

"That's it right there," I thought, "in a nutshell."

The gruff economy of that single throwaway sentence fragment caught exactly what was so discomfiting about the so-called Renaissance. So damn close to the New York literary *poseurati,* so damn far from the people.

I'll let the students read Prof's essay on the exotic primitive then look again at the novel, I thought.

The conference itself is rather good, almost as good as the idea. That it is indeed fitting and appropriate that this department in this university should be the convenor of such a gathering.

One early speaker is Prof. Bernard Bell of Penn State. A graduate student under Prof. Brown and our contemporary at Howard, Bernie's brief remarks were thoughtful, gracefully reminiscent and informed by a sense of the man and the times. They establish a useful tone for what is to follow.

The presenters who follow are black, young, scholarly, seem "well trained" and have obviously done considerable research and some thinking. They are solemn, serious, and very earnest. There are a great many Howard students in the audience.

But as the day unfolds I keep being unable to dismiss a growing feeling that there is a dimension of Prof. Brown—of the "Sterling Brown phenomenon"—that continues to elude the young scholars. That there are elements—important elements—of the Brown persona which are not easily or satisfactorily encompassed by the categories of thought or the idiom and analytic structures into which contemporary discourse in the humanities is constrained. For example, the kind of conceptual distancing implicit in approaching the subject as "a culturally removed ethnographic investigator," or words very much to that effect.

Now that is not the actual formulation used, because either I neglected to write it down or, if I did, the note has long since been lost. But I distinctly remember my reaction to the phrase, whatever it was.

"Whooie, Child. You sho is lucky that Prof ain't sitting here hearing you call him no damn 'ethnographic investigator.'"

Because while his kindness was legendary, so was a wicked instinct for the absurd and pompous as well as a formidable talent for mimicry and parody. He had no patience at all for pretentiousness of manner or of language. Prof did not suffer cant gladly.

But the dissonance of that phrase underscored what, for me, was inevitably missing in the conference. The presence. The torrential, life-affirming, life-changing cultural force of Prof. Brown's humanity, sensibility, and commitments. And this absence was in no way the fault of those earnest young scholars. For no amount of digging into archives, interrogation of correspondences, or even the most careful reading of his groundbreaking literary and cultural commentaries could possibly have yielded that. For that you had to have been there.

Some weeks after that conference I was with Kwame Ture, a friend from Howard days, and happened to casually mention that I was thinking of doing this piece on Prof. Brown. We'd been driving along, lightly joking, arguing and teasing each other. But on hearing the name his mood and demeanor changed. The brother came upright and all levity left his voice.

"I shall always be eternally grateful to that man," he declared solemnly, "for first showing me how to really appreciate and love our people's culture."

To an observer the sudden mood shift, the ringing solemnity in the tone of the declaration almost certainly would have seemed a little odd, even portentous. But having been there I understood perfectly.

"If I write the piece, I'm gonna quote you," was all I said.

"I wish you would," he said.

And now I have.

The Moment

As a consequence of a series of remarkable historical, geographic and demographic consequences, the opening years of the 1960s were a particularly exciting time to be on the Howard campus. In retrospect, it could clearly have been one of the most exciting times in the history of the institution, and indeed of the race.

Consider: when I arrived on campus in 1959 the famous "winds of change" were ruffling up the political landscape of the black world. Previously colonized peoples in Africa and the Caribbean were moving confidently and expectantly into political independence. Where reactionary resistance to these currents manifested itself, armed liberation movements arose to militantly engage it. Across black America the nonviolent direct action phase of the civil rights movement was beginning to summon entire communities into massive, popular, public confrontation with legalized racism. And, the student component of that movement was aborning.

The Student Community

The Howard student community was—in geographic and cultural terms— perhaps the single most representative collection of the youth of the black diaspora to be found in any one place. The Americans, some 65 percent, were a disparate group coming from the cities of the North: D.C., Philly, New York, Boston, Detroit, Chicago, or from the cities, small towns and farms of the old Confederacy: Mississippi, Louisiana, Georgia, Alabama, the Carolinas and Virginia, places where Jim Crow still held sway and which to me then were only exotic names out of literature and history.

We foreigners (some 35 percent) were mostly from the Continent and the Caribbean. From every island and territory of the English-speaking Caribbean, the Howard contingent—largest in any American university—was a vibrant and vocal presence, some 20 percent of the studentry.

Next in numbers was the delegation from the Continent (perhaps 15 percent), mostly from English-speaking Africa. So that in the new men's residence hall, apart from guys I'd gone to high school with in Kingston and roommates from Guyana and Trinidad, my freshman circle of friends included casually and naturally Luoa and Kikuyu men from Kenyatta's Kenya; Igbo and Yoruba brothers from independent Nigeria; and Fanti, Ashanti, and Ewe folk from Nkrumah's Ghana. Not to mention a stocky, serious, bespectacled brother from Harlem called Claude Brown (later of *Manchild* fame) or Laverne, a cheerful, diminutive Air Force veteran from Birmingham who first told me about his home town police chief, a super-mean, one-eyed cracker cop named "Bool" Connor. Who purely hated blacks because according to the oral tradition he had lost the eye trying to arrest a "baad nigger." It was Laverne in his generosity that gave me my first practical demonstration of the absurdity of racism. He was probably the most affluent guy on a floor mostly of foreigners. As a veteran he regularly got "money from Uncle Sam," as he put it. He also had another source of income from a (to me) rather surprising source, "Mr. Charlie."

One day brandishing a handful of mail he said, "You hongry, mah man, come I'll buy you a steak."

I was hungry and quite grateful. In the Kenyon Bar and Grill he become expansive when the steaks appeared. "Eat hearty, my man, compliments of the great and sovereign state of Alabama." Then a pained expression crossed his face and his tone became very bitter.

"They don't want our black asses in their lily white colleges, man, so they pay us money to go to college out of state."

The transcendent value and desirability of cultural diversity had yet to be discovered and proclaimed by the American academy. But our student body, though unquestionably black, was nothing if not diverse. Indeed with students coming from every conceivable situation afforded by the black world—ancient cultures and modern societies where the foment of momentous political change quivered electric in the air—it was possible, if one were alert, curious, and engaged, to achieve a superior education merely by hanging around campus and the dormitories, listening carefully.

The Location

Given the composition of the student body and the charged political atmosphere of the time, the school's location in the nation's capital became significant in two ways. As more black countries became independent new embassies were opened with much fanfare and celebration. The diplomats reached out to their nationals at Howard and one went with one's friends to various annual celebrations of national independence at black embassies. There was a tangible heady aura of Pan-African internationalism to the time and place.

Then, as the southern student movement gathered steam, the challenging proximity of the White House and Capitol Hill presented Howard activists with a clear duty: to carry the southern student uprising to the very seats of national government. Besides, we merely had to leave the District to meet of Jim Crow himself, face to face, in Virginia and Maryland. It was almost inevitable, therefore, that a vigorous student civil rights activism would develop at Howard. And that I would not be able to resist its pull.

The Faculty

We students were, ironically enough, beneficiaries of the last vestiges of open and vulgar racism in the American academy. Before the full force of the civil rights movement made itself felt, most white universities simply did not, as a general and unquestioned rule, hire black scholars no matter how distinguished the work nor aristocratic the academic pedigree. So the Howard faculty was adorned with a number of pioneering scholarly presences whose work gravitated naturally, and as a matter of duty into the then wide-open, uncluttered field: that of the meaning, effect and consequences of our black presence in the world.

Some of the luminaries had recently departed—Ralph Bunche to the United Nations and Nobel Peace Prize, the "Little Doctor" Eric Williams to the prime ministry of Trinidad and a knighthood—but they were lingering presences that lived on in the library and the oral tradition.

But others were still very much present and available to us. The historians Rayford Logan and Harold Lewis, for example, as were the sociologists, E. Franklin Frazier (excoriator of *The Black Bourgeoisie*) and G. Franklin Edwards. There were the pioneering Africanists—Leo Hansberry, with Chancellor Williams following closely in that groundbreaking tradition. There was the classicist Frank Snowden, the irrepressible poet/dramatist Owen Dodson, master of the Howard Players and the Ira Aldridge Theatre; the irascible Eugene Holmes, materialist philosopher and friend of Bertrand ("Oh, I got a letter from Bertie today") Russell, who, so went the folklore, when summoned before the HUAC at the height of McCarthyism, gave his occupation thus: "I am, Sir, by profession a Thinker." The student radicals loved that story.

From the English Department I remember the critic/anthologist Arthur P. Davis and of course Sterling Brown himself. There are, of course, others I've failed to name like Lois Mailou Jones the artist and Mrs. Dorothy Porter, archivist in the Moorland-Spingarn collection. Almost as important as studying with these people—i.e., actually enrolling in their courses—was the fact of what they represented, that they were there and their work existed. That one could, if one wanted and were assertive enough, seek them out to talk with them.

But presence and proximity aside, it was the example that was important. The example of conscious black intellectuals whose professional lives were devoted—very naturally—to the study of our people at a time when it was neither professionally fashionable nor advantageous to do so. (Who could have dared to imagine, much less predict, that the enterprise would ever become the primrose path of scholarly fashion, professional preferment, and careerist success in the academic establishment that it now has?) As important as any facts, concepts or processes one might learn from them in the classroom was the reality of what they represented: stubborn commitment and a sense of duty and purpose. As scholars of black people they were keepers of the tradition.

The Institution

Their mere presence was all the more important because the institution was not all of a piece. We were fond of saying that the institution represented at the same time both the highest values and the worst failures of the black tradition. As Junebug Jabbo Jones observed famously, "effen you ain't understand the principle of eternal contradiction you ain't goin' understand diddly 'bout black folks' life in these United States."

On one hand a tradition of struggle, yet the highest administration had regularly to walk a crooked line drawn by the whim and caprice of Congressional committees dominated by southern Dixiecrats, the political products and institutional protectors of *de jure* of white supremacy in the country.

On the campus, stunted elements of the administration, faculty, and large numbers of the students seemed to have internalized the most vulgar aspects of white American culture: gross materialism, conspicuous consumption, status anxiety, social climbing, class snobbery, and, most aggravating, the handkerchief-headed nineteenth-century notion that the mission of "Negro Education" was to *"civilize"* us young Negroes, thus rendering us "responsible and acceptable" to white American sensibilities, thereby to uplift the race. Academically and culturally, therefore, the emphasis should be to recapitulate uncritically the curricula and attitudes of American higher education. (There was for example the Dean of Fine Arts who famously declared that jazz would never profane the precincts of Crampton Auditorium so long as he was the Dean.)

By my third year, the terms of my own engagement with the place had pretty much been established. I was an English major, an editor of the student newspaper and a member of NAG, the Nonviolent Action Group, which was the SNCC affiliate in D.C. By then we regularly staged demonstrations at Capitol Hill, the White House, and the South African embassy (after the Sharpeville Massacre), and conducted campaigns against segregation in Maryland and Virginia.

Some of us—Bill Mahoney, Stokely Carmichael, Dion Diamond, and Hank Thomas—had serious battlefield credentials, having done sixty days in Parchman Penitentiary, Mississippi's notorious Delta prison farm. Most of the other members had already undergone their baptisms of fire in obligatory civil disobedience misdemeanor arrests closer to home.

Though a numerically insignificant organization, we were highly visible in the press and on campus where we proselytized furiously. We had deliberately infiltrated the student government and pretty much controlled the student newspaper. We had also brought to campus activist speakers like Malcolm X, James Baldwin, Herbert Aptheker, and Bayard Rustin to increase "awareness" and cut through student apathy. Our membership, about equally divided between northerners and southerners, participated in general campus life, but the central, defining element of our Howard experience was Movement activism. A close-knit, fiercely loyal little community, we hung out, partied, shared apartments, dropped in and out of school to follow the Movement south, established couples and even a few marriages, and battlefield friendships that endure to this day.

One day Ed Brown came into the *Hilltop* office with a message.

"Yo, Rasta," he growled in his deep blues voice, "Cuz Brown say he want to see us tonight, Bro."

Ed, a refugee from Louisiana, actually spoke that way. He had been a freshman at Southern University, had been one of a large group of activist students purged by President Fenton Clark for sit-ins in Baton Rouge and had transferred to Howard seeking refuge. He was followed shortly by H. Rap, his younger brother.

"Prof wants to see us? Why?"

"Yea, Bro, he say come to the office after five. . . . He say 'usses goin' drink some liquor and tell some lies.' "

Ed, a veritable virtuoso of southern black culture, delighted in singing the raunchy blues, prison work songs, preaching song sermons, and exhibiting a truly impressive repertoire of folk aphorisms. Which almost certainly is why upon arrival he gravitated naturally towards Sterling Brown. Prof. Brown, perceiving the refugee's financially straitened circumstances and, no doubt, intrigued by his southern sensibility, offered Ed informal work-study by hiring him for various tasks around his house and office. Both professor and student addressed each other as "Cuz" Brown.

So the messenger was no surprise though the message was unusual and intriguing. Invitations to "drink some likker" with a professor were, in my experience at Howard anyway, quite unprecedented. We all greatly respected Prof. Brown's work, and I knew him slightly. He had been gracious enough to read my first piece of fiction and encouraging enough to give me serious, detailed, and helpful criticism. We all liked him a lot: his unpretentiousness, his accessibility, and of course we all knew and admired his poetry. Our admiration for him personally had skyrocketed when someone discovered that the Leadbelly song "It's a Bourgeois Town" referred to the black Washington "elite," and found the line *It's a bourgeois town an' the only decent man is Sterling Brown*. We figured the Prof and ol' Leadbelly must have "drunk some likker and told some lies" in their time.

Some semesters earlier, in fact soon upon arrival, I had hastened to sign into the only undergraduate course offered by the celebrated professor, an internationally known expert on black culture. This turned out to be (though it took me quite some time to admit and recognize this, and even longer to figure out why) a somewhat anticlimactic, vaguely disappointing intellectual experience.

The course was the department's standard survey of "literature," hence cast completely within the conventional meaning of that term in that time and place. The departmentally prescribed text was a large part of the problem. It was one of those generic fifties anthologies comprised entirely of the usual canonical suspects from both shores of the Atlantic, represented by their standard, i.e., most frequently recycled offerings.

"Literature" in its European aspect would appear to be a mostly French and Russian phenomenon with a couple of Irishman, a German, a Czech, and a

Pole (Mann, Kafka, and Conrad) thrown in for, one suspects, balance and good measure. The American literary tree was white pine or white oak whose trunk was Hawthorne and its topmost branch Faulkner.

Our professor was, if not enthusiastic, at least correct and conscientious, painstakingly conducting the forty-five or so students on a tour of the genres, conventions and techniques of the short story, instructing us, as it were, how to (closely) read "great literature." By no means a complete waste of our time, even if nineteenth-century European sensibilities, situations, characters, issues, and prose styles seemed desiccated and remote by several removes from our experience and concerns. We took the course to be another evidence of Howard's "civilizing mission" and understood the literature to be "great," hence by definition "universal." Therefore it did not *really* matter that no writer(s) from our peoples or specific cultures were to be encountered at the rarefied altitudes of literary achievement represented by that anthology. As part—however peripheral—of the human family, our experience was covered, if only by implication, in the universality of human experience held to be represented there. In fact, our presence only by implication was almost a blessing in disguise, because in those rare instances when our presence was literal rather than implied (Messrs. Kipling, Conrad, Faulkner, or as a game-beater or gunbearer for Bwana Hemingway, for example) did not fill our hearts with joy.

This was, of course, the kind of course that could have been—and was— offered by any number of barely competent professors or conventionally trained graduate students in thousands of English departments across the land. But what did its presence here say about the Howard department's sense of its mission? What, especially, did it say about their appreciation and deployment of a uniquely valuable intellectual resource, to have this kind of course offered by Sterling Brown?

Of course Prof. Brown would have considered it unseemly and unprofessional to have suggested anything of the kind to the class. So he never did. (But then he didn't really have to.) He merely soldiered on through the anthology, giving the material careful often brilliant explication without extraneous comment. Somehow and for some reason *Maltese Falcon* sticks in my mind.

Well, perhaps not entirely. He did come to our last meeting accompanied by a friend. This diminutive, dapper, older Negro gentleman in a vested suit, red homburg and red bow tie, he introduced as Willie "The Lion" Smith, jazz pianist and virtuoso of the stride technique. Either a baby grand had been brought into the classroom or we relocated for the occasion, but that last meeting was a master class: concert cum lecture with learned and appreciative commentary courtesy of Sterling Brown. It was the only time that semester that the entire class and the professor seemed truly engaged.

The office (in Ed's invitation) proved to be a tiny white, wooden-frame house standing somewhat incongruously on a sloping lawn to the east of Founder's Library. It housed the History of Howard, a project on which two faculty luminaries—Rayford Logan, the historian, and Sterling Brown—had been enlisted in preparation for Howard's centennial in 1966. The association might arguably have been the original pairing, indeed the very platonic ideal, from which the model of the Odd Couple had devolved. The two collaborators could not have been more different in their disposition and affect. Prof. Logan was a short, proper, reserved, formally attired, inordinately dignified brown gentleman with all the stiffness of manner and deportment of a Victorian headmaster. While Prof. Brown was a large, rumpled, easy-smiling man of democratic instincts whose twinkling eyes carried an unmistakable air of mischief and irreverence. My impression was that the two men respected, even *truly* liked each other, but that the sternly respectable Prof. Logan might not entirely approve of his colleague's insouciant unpredictability, an impression which had taken root upon my arrival and introduction to Prof. Logan.

"Mike, this is Prof. Rayford Logan. We're doing the 'History of Howard.' Prof. Logan's responsible for the official history, the respectable part. Me? Hah! I'm doing the nitty gritty, down and dirty part—the 'real' history."

Prof. Logan had not cracked a smile.

On arrival, I'd been admitted by a large, muscular, totally bald, slightly older fellow in a suit who seemed somewhat puzzled by my appearance. Prof. Brown confirmed that I was expected but the besuited young man—who was introduced as Prof. Brown's graduate student—did not seem entirely reassured. Nor did the arrival, one after the other, of Ed Brown, Courtland Cox, Cleve Sellers, Stokely Carmichael, Tom Kahn, and Butch Conn—well known radicals all—do much to allay his evident puzzlement which was visibly moving towards alarm and outright disapproval. Clearly Bernie was reluctant to abandon his beloved professor to such dubious company. But inevitably every little task he could conjure up to delay his departure was completed.

"Anything else you need, Prof?" he asked hopefully.

"I'm fine, Bernie, thank you very much."

"You're sure? You going be OK, Prof?"

"Bernie's a good man," Prof explained as soon as we were alone. "Very loyal. But he's an ex-sergeant of the Marines and so he feels he has to protect me."

The door was closed. A bottle of Austin Nichols Wild Turkey was produced from his briefcase with a ceremonial flourish and placed on the desk. Cups were found. We were invited to help ourselves and the bottle disappeared into a bottom drawer. We looked at him, basking in a vague glow of conspiratorial expectancy.

He took an appreciative gulp, leaned back in his chair, loosened his tie, regarded us with a grin and said something like:

"Good to see you. Mighty good to see y'awl. So . . . where do you want to start? The real history of Howard? Well . . . you sho' in the right place . . . 'cause you looking at the only man in the history of the place who's been hired, fired, re-hired, re-fired, retired, rehired, retired, hired, retired again and soon to be re-re-retired."

With this version of the folkloric boast began the first of our series of remarkable evenings with Sterling Brown.

These evenings were many things, part seminar, part lecture, part performance, part role-playing, part conversation. One thing they patently were *not* was a group of students sitting around getting drunk with a renegade professor. The Wild Turkey was largely ceremonial, its presence and availability required by tradition and male southern practice. It signified initiation, confidence, resistance, and escape: that this space and company was liberated for that moment from the restrictive protocols of institutional respectability, rigid bourgeois propriety, and academic class stratification. Yet it was in these evenings that he was most profoundly our professor and we most truly his students.

On the most obvious level it was an evening of flat-out fun and what would today doubtless be called something distressing like "intergenerational male bonding." Prof. Brown's celebrated skill as raconteur in the grand black tradition was no exaggeration. He was great company and we were treated to the full repertoire: word play, wicked mimicry, tale-telling, signifying, folk poetry. But it was also instruction of a very high order. An inordinately wise and worldly elder, scholar par excellence, and celebrator of his people handing down the information and insight of a rich life experience to the youth of the nation.

But it was not merely performance or lecture on his part, it was conversation. For he talked to and with us, clearly as interested in us, our backgrounds and interests, our adventures in the movement, and especially our ongoing struggle with administration and the institution's rigidity, as we were fascinated by the stream of stories and anecdotes which seemed to flow so spontaneously and artfully.

That first evening, for example, Prof stayed close to home, a kind of living institutional memory. He recounted: the organized and protracted struggle of a previous generation of faculty, administration and students to win the appointment of the first black President; Dean Charles Hamilton Houston's transforming the law school to a training ground and launching pad for the judicial strategy; Mordecai Johnson's courage and principle in organizing a dinner in honor of a beleaguered Dr. Du Bois then under attack and cravenly abandoned by the black leadership and so on. Elders, ancestors, formerly mere names—Dean Kelly Miller, Alain Locke—were humanized and brought to life, warts and all.

An evening of high comedy, laughter, and instruction. So much the former that we never stopped to realize how much we had actually been learning, nor the extent to which our perceptions of the institution with which we considered ourselves "locked in struggle" had been ever so subtly enriched, deepened and nuanced.

Towards ten o'clock, Prof signaled impending closure by glancing at his watch, beginning to pack up his briefcase and put on his coat.

"'Bout that time," he announced, "get much later Mrs. Daisy begins to worry. We can't let that happen, can we?"

Someone requested a poem. Would the Professor? Yes, he would. What would we hear? That too became a tradition. Thereafter our evenings always ended with Prof reading "*Old Lem*."

> They don't come by ones
> they don't come by twos . . .

Whereupon he would pick up his briefcase, adjust his tie and we would walk out to find a yellow and black capitol cab pulling up in front of the building. That too became a ritual, same cab, same driver. Like clockwork. A little brother who always said something like "Mrs. Daisy she count on me to bring Prof home safe."

That first time evolved into the remarkable series of extracurricular meetings which had galvanized Ture's memory some thirty odd years later. "I shall always be eternally grateful. . . ."

As well we all should be. We surmised that these occasions became Prof's regular "night out with the boys." That semester, on what in memory seems close to a weekly basis, we would make our way to the little office at the end of the day. Occasionally on a Sunday afternoon we would be invited home to be fed and pampered by Mrs. Daisy. It was clear from the first time that she had already heard about us. "Oh, you must be Courtland (or Mike or Tom). I've heard so much about you. I would have known you anywhere."

The "at homes" with the Browns were even better because there the full resources of his formidable library and collections—rare books, classic records, field tapes, pictures, etc.—could be brought to bear to illustrate a literary point, demonstrate a blues style, a special Leadbelly lick on the twelve string, or an innovation by his childhood pal and lifelong friend, Edward Kennedy Ellington.

The sessions went, so it seemed to us, where the "spirit say go." Some took a literary turn, insightful analysis illustrated by readings and personal anecdotes and sharp thumbnail character sketches of literary ancestors or elders like Langston Hughes, Countee Cullen, Ralph Ellison, Richard Wright, and the like. Some were musical; capsule road maps of the character and evolution of black popular culture, peopled with old friends like Ma Rainey, Billie Holiday, Leadbelly, Fats Waller, Satchmo, the "Duke," Paul Robeson, all leavened by Sterling Brown's remarkable capacious mind and analytic intelligence. And naturally—inevitably—to lead us down those long southern roads, almost as though prophetically, he was arming us culturally and psychologically for the people most of us would be working with in the Mississippi Delta.

The rural South was indeed Sterling Brown country, and folks like Fannie Lou Hamer, Hartman Turnbow, E. W. Steptoe, Miz Susie Ruffin were Sterling Brown characters. Because of him we later met them with the recognition of family members you'd never seen but had grown up hearing about.

Would that time and space permitted a full account of a few hilarious adventures into which we, his all too willing foot soldiers, eagerly followed "Prof." The time, for example, he wrote and produced the "Faculty Follies." My impression was that this was his revival of a long dormant Howard tradition. This one was a cabaret-style parody of a then-popular TV series, *Gunsmoke*. Friends and admirers of Sterling Brown from the upper reaches of the faculty were pressed into theatrical service. Harold Lewis, booted, bejeaned and cowboy-hatted, looked uncannily like Marshall Dillon. The very charming Prof. Eaton, chair of Classics, appeared as the Marshall's enamorata, the saloon keeper Miss Kitty. An amazingly tall, dark, and lanky professor of Education, Elias Blake (who Prof called Watutsi) was Chester the deputy, and so on. On campus it was a smashing success, ironic, witty, free-wheeling, presenting our teachers in a warmer, gentler light. They displayed good humor, high spirits and in some cases, unsuspected comedic talents. The proverbial good time was had by all. In the warm afterglow immediately following Prof had another inspiration.

"This is good stuff, you know. We ought to take it downtown."

Not surprisingly, there were demurrers and defections.

"Now look, fellas, I love Sterling too. We all do. Which is why I was quite prepared to make a fool of myself once, cavorting about the stage up here for the amusement of my students. But I'm sure as hell not going to make a similar spectacle of myself on some stage in downtown Washington."

Which was quite understandable then, and which has become all the more so with every year that passes. Even more amazing, though, was that enough folk hung in so that with some revision and considerable reservations, the show could be moved. To fill in Prof wrote himself into the script where, adorned with string tie and Stetson, he would look and sound like Big Daddy in *Cat on a Hot Tin Roof*. A small downtown theater was duly found. A certain student-activist cohort was enlisted as technical crew. The show must go on, and it did indeed with delightfully mixed results. It felt, as we told each other gleefully, exactly as though we had wandered into the middle of one of Prof's more outrageous tall tales.

As technical crew we were accomplished social agitators. Our hearts were willing but our collective stagecraft was slight to nonexistent. I, for example, had never before in my life seen or contemplated a theatrical lighting board. A quick run through by Prof and I was sent aloft with the reassuring "any fool can do this, Mike, you'll be fine."

It was undoubtedly a function of this inexperience that caused the prop man (Ed—"ain't nobody told me about no damn tea"—Brown) to stock the stage bar with at least one huge bottle of real, red bomber whiskey.

This bit of theatrical realism would prove crucial to the success of the venture since all the action was set in Miss Kitty's saloon and a great many of the punch lines were to be punctuated by the dramatic tossing back of brimming shot glasses, cowboy style.

The salutary effects of Ed's literalness manifested itself very early when poor Chester—Bro Blake was a committed teetotaler—tossed back the first one with a dramatic flourish. Show stopper, big time.

His eyes bugged out. His ears stood out from his head. His Stetson seemed to levitate straight up as he clutched his throat, mewled piteously, and strove manfully to keep the whiskey in. But a fine spray of whiskey mist spewed from his nostrils and arced gracefully across the stage as his fellow troupers looked on in consternation and amazement. Big Daddy growled something about "real rotgut whiskey." The audience roared their approval of what must have seemed some unusually inspired, realistic, and sustained comic acting on Chester's part. Thereafter the look of naked terror that crossed his face whenever he was in the vicinity of that bottle always brought a laugh.

Big Daddy, a natural crowd favorite, prowled the stage improvising lines and growling out directions. As the level in the bottle visibly declined, the improvisation became freer and more inspired, the quality of the acting more robust. Snatches of dialogue, muttered threats and imprecations, entire scenes nowhere to be found in the script and with a spontaneous manic quality that could not possibly have been imagined by a writer entirely sober, miraculously appeared. It was something.

The audience—mercifully small—and having no idea of what was scripted, what inspired improv, and what desperate damage control, appeared to love it all. For example, at the end of one scene, the light operator helpless with laughter did not hear his cue, if indeed it had ever been said.

"Lights." Prof prompted softly. "Lights." Then shaking his fist at the heavens like Lear on the heath, he bellowed.

"Goddammit, Mike, you moron, bring the lights down."

The audience roared and applauded mightily. So it went. And of course, it all became even funnier in Prof's telling second time round. After the final curtain, cast and crew sat on stage finishing what little whiskey remained, revisiting the night's events unable to meet each other's eyes without dissolving into laughter. "Damn Watutsi, I sure thought you was dead."

Not long thereafter an ANTA production of a theater piece, *Brecht on Brecht*, came to town. It was a most excellent production and unusual in one important respect for those times: half the cast was black. And, our representation was not token. In the company was the irrepressible Roscoe Lee Browne, the admirable Ms. Dolores Sutton in the earth-motherish parts, with a Miki Grant doing the ingenue bits. Prof took some of us to a performance and the cast party which followed. The piece was powerful. The black presence adding an American dimension and resonances to Brecht's grittily ironic class politics. The combination captured the political mood of the time nicely. For instance, one dramatic highlight was Ms. Tyson's chilling rendering of Pirate Jenny's song from "Three Penny Opera." I still remember that young black woman facing an essentially white audience, singing

> And the ship,
> the black freighter
> Turns around in the harbor,
> Turns around shooting guns.
> Asking me,
> "Kill them now . . . or later?"

The blacks stole the show and Prof was enthusiastic the way he always was in the presence of black excellence. (I pray I shall be able to summon even a small fraction of his capacity for enthusiasm when I enter my sixties.)

"Fine show. Very fine. Howard University should see this. I want Howard to see it," he declared. But, he was told, the company was moving on in a matter of days.

"No, no. I want Howard to see this," he persisted. Did I tell you Prof could be exceeding stubborn?

"Howard must see this. There must be a way. Look, what would it take to hold it over for a week?"

There were hurried consultations. A quick phone call or two, some hasty calculations. Then the tour manager and the theatre director came over and said something in Prof's ear. Prof. nodded and reached purposefully for his checkbook.

"Yes, Howard must see this." The play would be held over.

It wasn't entirely clear to us exactly what had been consummated. Had Prof merely guaranteed a minimum gate for five performances or had he, in fact, bought out the house for a week? And, whichever the case, how was his real purpose—that of "Howard" seeing the play—to be guaranteed?

As soon as was polite we rushed back to campus for a late-night strategy session. We agreed that at all costs two things had to be accomplished. The first being to find a way to insulate our Prof from the fiscal consequences of his impulsive generosity and overly loyal spirit, and then to ensure that "Howard" bottoms would indeed fill those seats.

Fortunately NAG was a strategic presence on campus that year. Tom Kahn—very shrewdly—had captured the position of Treasurer of the Liberal Arts Student Council and the infinitely charismatic and popular Carmichael as floor whip was good at lining up the votes. Before they knew it the Student

Council had become a patron of the arts, having voted to buy out the remaining performances. It was a classic win/win. Members of the Council got patronage packets for distribution to friends and constituents and we met both our objectives.

I will always remember the cloud of utter benevolence I felt swirling about me as I strolled the campus like a ward politician, roll of tickets in hand accosting every courting couple I saw.

"What a charming couple. You like the theater? Great. How'd you like to treat this lovely lady to an evening of theater downtown, courtesy of the Liberal Arts Student Council, the Nonviolent Action Group, and Professor Sterling Allen Brown?"

"Free? No, my sister, these are your student government taxes at work. But if you take the tickets you gotta go."

I knew that whether or not the brother was interested in theater, he was interested in the sister and she would do the rest. I believe Prof had every reason to be pleased at the full houses and enthusiastic student audiences during that extra week.

I know that we were neither the first nor the last group of Howard students to have benefited from Prof's outgoing generosity of spirit, clarity of vision, encyclopedic knowledge and unmeasured love of our people during his forty years (hired-fired-retired) service at Howard.

Indeed, his children are legion, recognizable, and widely dispersed. Through them one can detect his influence across the academy and in the world of politics and literature. From the life of Kwame Ture (peace be unto him) to the focus and commitment of Toni Morrison's distinguished oeuvre.

But, in that politically engaged moment for us a most formative time, when without necessarily realizing it we were forging the terms of our own engagement with a racist world—we were the ones fortunate enough to be chosen for Prof's special attention and guidance. Why were we so fortunate? What recommended us to his attention in the first place?

We never paused to give that a moment's thought then. Now, I try to see us as he must have: articulate, smart enough and with a certain radical-activist swagger, attitude if you wish, which we always backed up by action. Later, he must have realized how deeply interested we were in those things he knew so well and valued so highly. How desperately we needed his knowledge and perspective on our people. Which may be why he invested as much time as he did in us. Whatever his reasons we certainly were the beneficiaries.

Of that little group of activists there is not one whose subsequent life choices and commitments does not—for much the better—reflect Prof's influence and example. Carmichael/Ture's clarion call, for example, for "undying love for our people" was no mere slogan. It was for Carmichael a life principle, first articulated for him not in words, but in the observable example of Sterling Brown's entire life. The full measure of that life, his way of being in the world. The way in which without rhetoric or bluster, Prof simply embodied that principle.

As teacher, nurturer of youth, poet, folklorist, literary critic, cultural historian, blues scholar, jazz enthusiast, comic wit, fierce polemicist, tireless defender of his people, custodian of our culture, natural man,[1] he taught us much. But for all the marvelous things he *taught* us, he *showed us* even more.

He showed us—up close—how a supremely engaged and responsible black intellectual could be in this world and deeply rooted in his people. He did not merely study black culture; he reveled in it. His was a spontaneous, unapologetic, unsentimental joy in our people and our shared heritage, an enthusiasm that was infectious, inspiring, and instructive.

He showed us how one could do infinitely serious work yet not take oneself too "seriously"; that one could do very important things without making oneself an "important" Negro; that pomp, pretension, and status were snares and delusions of the weak and the small. He showed us that where respect was earned it would be freely given; that where it was not merited it could not be commanded. That irony was a shield and humor a sword and one could go into battle with a grin on your face. That, most of all, it was our people's humanity that was our greatest legacy and protection. And that we, in turn, must cherish it and pass it on.

Like the great poet he was, he never told us these things; he showed them to us, teaching by example. And I, for one, have never forgotten them. Like Kwame, I too am eternally grateful. . . .

NOTE

1. Mike Winston's elegant formulation.

An Integer Is a Whole Number

Michael S. Harper

Br'er Sterling and the Rocker

Any fool knows a Br'er in a rocker
is a boomerang incarnate; look at the blade
of the rocker, that wondrous crescent
rockin' in harness as poem.

To speak of poetry is the curled line straightened;
to speak of doubletalk, the tongue
gone pure, the stoic line a trestle
whistlin', a man a train comin' on:

Listen Br'er Sterling
steel-drivin' man, folk-said, folk-sayin',
that chair's a blues-harnessed star
turnin' on its earthly axis;

Miss Daisy, latch on that star's arc,
hold on sweet mama; Br'er Sterling's rocker glows.

Daisy Turnbull Brown, the Poet's Muse: Rose Anne

When Daisy died in June 1979 I was at Yaddo, the artists' retreat, in Saratoga Springs, N.Y. I was called to the phone by Eloise Spicer and returned to the

FIGURE 21.1 Michael S. Harper and Sterling A. Brown, 1974.

dinner table without comment; the poet June Jordan approached and said: "Across your face is the sign of death. Who died?" I left that evening for Washington, D.C. Sterling, of course, was inconsolable. I was already working on his *Collected Poems*, which I'd selected for the National Poetry Series, and we were beyond deadline. The book was to be a surprise to "Rose Anne" (Daisy) after Sterling's 78th birthday celebration, planned to be at the Museum of African Art in the District. I thought we would have all summer to work on this book— all Sterling's poetry collected in one volume. Now I would have to read his "Thoughts on Death" at Daisy's funeral.

I met Daisy at the Brown residence in Brookland, 1222 Kearny St. NE, Washington, D.C., on a cold day in January 1973. Sterling answered the door, though Daisy had answered the phone earlier. I was with Ernest J. Gaines, and we were paying a visit, a "debt" from the Black Academy of Arts & Letters banquet, which had been in NYC the previous October. All three of us, Ernie, Sterling, and I, as well as a host of others, had been celebrated—"c.p." time. Sterling was celebrated as Dean of African American Letters—"the invisible Mr. Brown" was how he put it at the table. Sterling was always in good form with guests; an autodidact at home and everywhere else, now he would be full of questions for Gaines and myself about the Creative Writing Seminars held at the Library of Congress in his hometown. In the house, Gaines was respectful and quiet, admiring the Brown library, the books, the tidy home. As always, Daisy deferred to Sterling, though when she was nearby she had the habit of touching the back of his head, an act of affection one could not miss.

(Later, when Sterling read my portrait of him, "To an Old Man Twiddlin' Thumbs," he would say, "You Did What You Did!" while he maintained a code of silence between us. "Out back" in the garden, Daisy translated his mood in a millisecond.)

Now, I started our conversation with a mention of the "Vestiges" section of *Southern Road;* I'd studied the Rockefeller Library copy before our first visit:

"Who, pray tell, was 'Rose Anne?'"

"Sterling recited Housman on our honeymoon," Daisy began. "He told me I was his costliest flower, and my own conceit—"

Sterling broke in, changing the subject:

"Mr. Gaines, I think you've written a fine novel about Miss Jane Pittman, maybe better than Dick Wright, who was no master of local color, or his neighborhood, which in the end was probably Paris, not Natchez. Do you think his work suffered because he left the country?"

Gaines, always the diplomat, and polite, called Sterling "Professor Brown," said he didn't know much French, but liked Wright's short stories. Gaines had written his first novel, *Catherine Carmier,* about a Creole character in Louisiana, seven times over. His collection of short stories, *Bloodline,* was out on the table in front of us.

I told Sterling about N. Scott Momaday's reading of the poem "Plainview 2," about a horse being inculcated into his Kiowa tribal pantheon. I also talked about Ralph Ellison's comments (he gave no formal presentation), and his avoidance of Paul Engle at cocktail hour. I mentioned my short time at the Iowa Writers Workshop right after the JFK inauguration, and the physical I took in Des Moines, Iowa. I described how, upon paying money for a passport, I had received a draft notice, how quickly I got into graduate school at the State University of Iowa, with Christopher Isherwood, Henri Coulette, and Wirt Williams as my undergraduate recommenders and how I went to Iowa with no money, no car; it had broken down in Needles, California, loaded with books and records. I also told Sterling how everyone loved Elliot Coleman from Johns Hopkins.

But Ernie's reading from *The Autobiography of Miss Jane Pittman* was the highlight of my narrative. I mentioned how many critics had taken Ernie's novel for a real "autobiography," how money had been withdrawn because it was "only" a novel. Then, on this evening of our meeting with the Browns, Ernie read "Just Like a Tree," his short story from *Bloodline.* His reading was dedicated to Sterling and his lovely wife, Daisy—Rose Anne. I recorded the event, which began:

> *Just Like a Tree*
>
> I shall not,
>> I shall not be moved.
> I shall not,

I shall not be moved.
Just like a tree that's planted 'side the water.
    Oh, I shall not be moved.
I made my home in glory,
    I shall not be moved.
Made my home in glory,
    I shall not be moved.
Just like a tree that's planted 'side the water.
    Oh, I shall not be moved. (from an old Negro spiritual)

(Later, in the cab going to National Airport for our flight to Providence, Ernie already knew he would read it again at Brown University, and within a week I invited Sterling to the campus to lecture and read his poetry. Daisy said he could travel, by train if he wanted, but she wasn't coming along.)

Daisy had the strongest, clearest handwriting I can remember, always legible. She was a student of William Faulkner's fiction and poetry, and she graduated from Virginia Seminary and College in Lynchburg, Virginia. Her parents never married. Her father was a white Virginian; her mother, colored, died early. It was illegal for them to marry. Daisy was raised by her grandmother, an ex-slave, in Rocky Mount, Virginia. When Sterling saw her in a white dress one Sunday, Daisy had two children in tow, Connie and Jack, the offspring of her sister, who had died of tuberculosis. Daisy and Sterling adopted one of these children.

"When I first saw Daisy she was a rose without thorns dressed up in a white dress. I was playing tennis; it was Sunday afternoon. It was match point. She had two little kids in tow, "Connie" and "Jack;" then the train whistle blew four times: Wheep, wheep, wheep-wheep. She was the most beautiful woman I'd ever seen. Then I finished my service; I double-faulted." (Sterling, on first seeing Daisy)

The Education of the Poet

Sterling Allen Brown called himself a 4 H Man: Homer, Heine, Hardy, Housman. Sterling was also a red-ink English teacher. (One of his favorite comments when he did crossword, or taught poetry, was "No 'nice,' no 'cute,' no 'amazing.'" These words were anathema to him.) Sterling was always aware of the Founding Fathers—Jefferson, Franklin, Madison, Washington—always concerned with "who could conceive of whom." The slave masters could conceive of the slaves only as brutes. The slaves could conceive of the whites as masters and more: they could have children by them. Jefferson's agrarian freeholder-landowner status was for white men only, despite miscegenation. How does one get around an ancient taboo when one demonizes the slaves while copulating with them?

Sterling recognized that it was the black community that had always included both cultures. He became a master teacher with the training of both his families—the one he was born into, with five sisters, Clara, Grace, Edna, Elsie, and Helen, all schoolteachers, all older than he, and the one he encompassed as a pioneer in the academy. (In high school, at Paul Laurence Dunbar, Sterling worked on *The Crimson & Black*, the school literary magazine, from which he was fired after one issue because it was censored. He was also captain of the debate team, but when he went on to Williams College, he was not allowed to compete, or try out for the varsity tennis team.) At Williams, George Dutton taught him "critical realism." At Harvard, "Kitty," George Lyman Kittredge, taught him Shakespeare, line by line. This was his primary source. He would say, "I learned the arts and sciences at Williams and Harvard. I learned the humanities in Lynchburg, Virginia." (Lynchburg was where he met "Big Boy," and his wife, Daisy.) Sterling was always aware of both elements. When I asked him why he did not include all five sisters in the poem written for his father, "After Winter," Sterling, thinking of Frost, quipped: "it would mess up the meter."

> He thinks with the winter
> His troubles are gone;
> Ten acres unplanted
> To raise dreams on.
>
> The lean months are done with,
> The fat to come.
> His hopes, winter wanderers,
> Hasten home.
>
> *"Butterbeans fo' Clara*
> *Sugar corn fo' Grace*
> *An' fo' de little feller*
> *Runnin' space."* (excerpt from "After Winter")

Sterling's first book, *Southern Road*, pioneers the combination of folk speech and formal poetry. The title poem, "Southern Road," is the first ever in which a work song is given a narrative, a storyline fully cadenced as a ballad: a communal epic. It is about how blacks were used as forced labor, a natural resource "without any speech, as though they were brutes and nothing more."

> White man tells me—hunh—
> Damn yo' soul;
> White man tells me—hunh—
> Damn yo' soul;
> Got no need, bebby,
> To be tole.

> Chain gang never—hunh—
> Let me go;
> Chain gang never—hunh—
> Let me go;
> Po' los' boy, bebby,
> Evahmo'. . . .

"Odyssey of Big Boy," the first poem in the book, is about the *Odyssey*, the efforts and exploits of an entire people, hidden in the voice of Big Boy Davis, an illiterate guitar player, kicked out of town for vagrancy. Race and class are vital to all those caught up between a "rock and a hard place," or "between the dog and the tree," in rural black artifice, short, pungent, full of what Sterling said in close company, "my people's double-talk." The ears of the Sirens, the rocks of Gibraltar, Scylla and Charybdis—all of these are rites of passage through which Odysseus had to pass, in order to get home. The ballad form is sonorous and soulful because this journey motif was Sterling's chordal inheritance and mastery.

No poem like "Strong Men" existed when, in 1929 at Fisk University, Charles S. Johnson heard it recited. It begins:

> They dragged you from homeland,
> They chained you in coffles,
> They huddled you spoon-fashion in filthy hatches,
> They sold you to give a few gentlemen ease.
>
> They broke you in like oxen,
> They scourged you,
> They branded you,
> They made your women breeders,
> They swelled your numbers with bastards. . . .
> They taught you the religion they disgraced.

At the time, Johnson's response was: "Sterling, don't you think that poem is too . . ." The sentence was never completed. In "Strong Men," white supremacy acts with orchestral composition and is answered with a minimal, terse "folk response" in the folk idiom. More than "militant," "Strong Men" is a clear enunciation of the way white supremacy is bested by folk art, art couched and framed in what Sterling always called "the folk idiom."

At the time of Johnson's comment, Sterling was teaching at Fisk, the alma mater of his parents. Sterling's mother had been the valedictorian of her class; his father, a slave from Eastern Tennessee, took twelve years to complete the requirements. He went on to Oberlin and became a student of theology, and a minister. It was Sterling Nelson Brown, the poet's father, who wrote *Bible Mastery* so that illiterate preachers, taken by evangelicalism, could learn the order and literacy of the Bible, where no one was present to teach them. Not all of them went to school, nor were they in tutelage to what Du Bois called "the steady march of New England schoolmarms." It was Du Bois who captured the steadfast poignancy of the spirituals, in his chapter "The Sorrow Songs" from *The Souls of Black Folk* (1903). Sterling Nelson Brown, Congregational minister and Professor of Religion at Howard University, taught with Kelly Miller and often welcomed visitors like Du Bois and James Weldon Johnson, for lectures, sometimes even teaching Sunday School lessons. Du Bois also studied at Fisk and was a classmate of Sterling's parents. Du Bois later transferred to Harvard and became the first black Ph.D. to graduate from there.

Through this connection to Du Bois, Sterling mastered both classical and folk patterns, and in 1935, it was Sterling who educated Dr. Du Bois, while proof-reading *Black Reconstruction in America*. As a thank-you, Du Bois gave Sterling a bottle of crème de menthe. (Sterling had been weaned on "white lightning" hidden under the culvert near Coolwell, Virginia, where he honeymooned with Daisy at the Bibby farm.)

The Manuscript: Collected

Sterling and I built his manuscript—from three handwritten notebooks—on an Olivetti typewriter that I had brought in baggage on a commuter flight from Providence to National Airport. Sterling would constantly delay, debating whether to include "Call Boy" for Ralph Bunche or "Uncle Joe" from Frilot Cove or "Remembering Nat Turner" for Roscoe E. Lewis. (In Sterling's edition of Lewis's *The Negro in Virginia* is the inscription "To Dutch— from Lewis.")

One section of this manuscript was the Slim Greer cycle. Sterling always said the "I" in many of his poems, was a dramatic "I" and seldom autobiographical, but rhetorical. Slim Greer was a composite character, part Gilly from the Jefferson City hotel, but all Sterling Brownian. There was also "Ma Rainey," composed after John Work and Sterling collected folk-say at a country concert. Though unstated, it is about black workers chained to the levees in the Great Mississippi Flood of 1927. This teacher knew that the art of the poem was to make the reader cry.

Yet Sterling had a sense that his *Collected Poems* would never see the light of day. Even after I selected his book, the project had no publisher. When Sterling eventually traveled by train to New York to meet with the editor I had found, Fran McCullough of Harper & Row, there was a torrential rainstorm. When, at last, we mailed the copyedited manuscript from National Airport to New York after a weekend, among weekends, of editorial conjuring, the book was lost in the mail with no paper trail, and no insurance. I kept this news from him while I tried to rebuild the book with the help of Darryl Pinckney, McCullough's assistant at Harper & Row, a distant relative of Sterling. Then there was no time for proofreading, no galley proofs before publication. It seemed even my name made Sterling suspicious: "Do you own any stock in Harper & Row? Your name is Harper, after all."

Throughout the process, Sterling grieved for Rose Anne. It was she who had kept him in harness, though seldom on deadline. One of Sterling's great regrets was that he had not maintained a proper correspondence with his contemporaries, including Jean Toomer, author of *Cane* (1923) and fellow Washingtonian, more comfortable in Greenwich Village than in Harlem, but never in doubt about his race, his class. As Sterling said about him, "it was beneath him to 'pass for white,'" though he didn't live in Brookland, Sterling's favorite enclave in "his" section of Washington. I have a copy of only one letter from Sterling, written in 1977, in pencil, with the request that it be returned. The telephone, as communication device, had paralyzed him.

The Teacher

When the book was finally published, I took a copy to Gunnar Myrdal's residence in the old section of Stockholm, Sweden. The meeting transpired in this way: at the airport I told the consulate diplomat that I had one request: would he contact Gunnar Myrdal with this message: "I bring greetings from Sterling Brown." I was cautioned by my host that everyone wanted to see Gunnar Myrdal. At 11 a.m. I got a call at the Hotel Diplomat that Mr. Myrdal would see me at his residence at 2 p.m. It was Sterling's birthday, 1980.

At the end of Myrdal's *An American Dilemma* is the hope for universal enlightenment, something Sterling had not seen in his own survey of the country: literacy, democracy, "an integer is a whole number." Documentation of American slavery and its aftermath, artful commentary from the man lowest down, was fragmentary and unheeded. Sterling's comment "Cracker, your kind ain't exegetical," was published in the defunct *Washington Star* in an interview about race relations and race rituals in America. Sterling had been appointed poet laureate of Washington D.C., his hometown, by the mayor, who had been a student of his. Later came an invitation to the Library of Congress, which he accepted "in the name of his students."

In a country dominated by tribalism from its inception, Sterling always had a quip. Here are a few:

"Prof, you run them verbs; I'll drive the thought."
"They're always burying the hatchet and it's always in my head."
"My favorite poem? Every damned one of them."
"FFOV? First Families of Virginia: all literate Virginians, black and white are related, one generation removed."

I spent many an evening debating the impact of modernism on American poetry: how modernists who taught in universities "hid their thought line by line." Sterling always answered with Frost's riff on unrhymed poetry: "like playing tennis without a net." Then he would recite his "modernist poem: "I / have / a / bad / belly- / ache." He believed in tradition and voice; he always ended his readings with "Strong Men"; when lecturing he would say, parenthetically, "now what about my own people?" For him integration was not assimilation: an integer is a whole number. One did not apologize for slavery, or being Negro, or black; one reveled in it; hence: "Black Cryptogram." This poem is something Sterling said; I just wrote it down:

> When God
> created
> the black child
> He was showing
> off.

Sterling once gave a talk at the Guggenheim Museum in NYC. The building was closed but the auditorium was open. He came up on the train with a bustle of books and his three notebooks full of original poems, and the talk was recorded by Elizabeth Kray of the Academy of American Poets. Sterling's topic was "The Education of the Poet." He spent most of the evening reading from the published texts of his nemeses, the Agrarians: Donald Davidson, Robert Penn Warren, Allen Tate. He read only a handful of his own poems. That day also happened to be Allen Tate's birthday, and he was being honored in Washington, D.C., for lifetime achievement, a coincidence, but still an indicator of how deeply Sterling Brown resented the New Critics, Agrarian, white-supremacist theoreticians on race and class. The talk went long, with no reception. When we were leaving the building, Ms. Kray handed me the recorded cassette tape with the comment: "This is libelous. I don't think we need to get sued." Sterling lost his notebooks the same evening, to be recovered the next day, by me; I xeroxed them before returning. We needed those villanelles and sestinas, those sonnets to Rose Anne.

The poem "Sister Lou" is his tour de force in a poet's vernacular, along with "Virginia Portrait" in standard English. It recalls Sterling's immersion with the Bibby family, in Coolwell, Virginia, three miles from Amherst, twelve miles from Lynchburg. The Bibbys' son would fall asleep in Sterling's class. Sterling soon found out that this young man was not only a student in mathematics but also worked on a farm. One weekend, he invited Sterling out to Coolwell. From then on Sterling was welcome to visit and the Bibby son seldom slept in class. One evening the neighbors were in to visit the Bibby family and Sterling told the story of "Brother Moore." Brother Moore was trifling, though often well-intentioned; he borrowed tools without returning them, failed to tether animals; he was willing, but inane. Around the Bibby stove, glowing red, some neighbors were smoking the local tobacco, "Life Everlasting," and some were spitting into the hot stove. Sterling had his pipe, and Mrs. Bibby had hers, and when she spat, she aimed perfectly into the glowing stove. Out of nowhere, and directly to Brother Moore's face, while talking back to Sterling, "Sister Lou" (Mrs. Bibby) said: "He may mean good, but he DO so doggone po'." This was Sterling's story against rural sentimentality. Now, several generations later, Jim Bibby, ex-pitcher and alumnus of the Pittsburgh Pirates, lives on the same piece of property. When Zora Neale Hurston, in her famous *Their Eyes Were Watching God*, wrote "black women are the mules of the world, always doing the world's work," she could have been describing the Bibby family, in particular, old Mrs. Bibby. Sterling would say of himself, when working with Mr. Bibby cutting wood for the stove, that he was a young enthusiast. Mr. Bibby would caution him: "Take your time, take your time, and don't try to raise no hell." Daisy's grandmother had the same quiet strength and fortitude.

> Honey
> Go Straight on to de Big House,
> An' speak to yo' God
> Widout no fear an' tremblin'.
>
> Then sit down
> An' pass de time of day awhile.
> Give a good talkin' to
> To yo' favorite 'postle Peter,
> An' rub the po' head
> Of mixed-up Judas,
> An' joke awhile wid Jonah.
>
> Then, when you gits de chance,
> Always rememberin' yo' raisin',
> Let 'em know youse tired
> Jest a mite tired
>
> Jesus will find yo' bed fo' you
> Won't no servant evah bother wid yo' room.
> Jesus will lead you
> To a room wid windows
> Openin' on cherry trees an' plum trees
> Bloomin' everlastin'.
>
> An' dat will be yours
> Fo' keeps.
>
> Den take yo' time . . . .
> Honey, take yo' bressed time (excerpt from "Sister Lou")

(I once returned to Coolwell to read at the local schools. In the downtown section were two barbershops, one black and one white, two doors apart. The black barber had only a clipper but no scissors. The white barber and the black barber had little business but wouldn't share space. The students I read to, mostly white, with a scattering of blacks, did not rave over those poems "that jumped the gap" of the generations.)

When I was asked by the Library of Congress to select poems from their archives for a poetry album comprised of black Americans, five consultants, Robert Hayden, Gwendolyn Brooks, Rita Dove, Stanley Kunitz, and William Meredith, had their opinions. None could agree about "an integer is a whole number"—how to manipulate around the white poets. As always the ambivalence of inclusion was at the center of American discourse. Sterling and Frost debated this predicament—the stack of the deck—in the context of "In Divés' Dive," Frost maintaining, in accordance with his rhetoric, that the game is *not* crooked. But his belief in the Declaration of Independence was not Sterling's belief in the same Declaration, though he postured that it was 'fair' in poems

FIGURE 21.2 Daisy Turnbull Brown, late 1970s.

like "The Ballad of Joe Meek." But the real problem was failure of whites, out of ignorance, *to conceive of equity*. The result: benign/malign neglect: an enhanced capacity to ignore.

Sterling respected Ernie Gaines because Gaines, the artist, had mastered his own neighborhood. Though he had learned his craft from one of his teachers, Walter Van Tilburg Clark, author of *The Ox-Bow Incident*, Gaines was no show-piece in Harlem, but a Louisianan whose short story " Just Like a Tree" was told from "the multiple point of view," a story told in eight voices, one of them a child's. Gaines moved the parish schoolhouse/plantation church of his childhood to his residence in Oscar, Louisiana, as a memorial to his kin who were buried in the graveyard near the slaves' quarters. Sterling also had a lifelong commitment to "the children." As he said in "All Are Gay," "Say of them then: Like Topsy, they just grew." Sterling, the teacher, always called me Telemachus, though he had many sons and daughters. Yet he often said that the worst thing that could happen to Negroes was a Harvard education. From this American Dilemma—multiple cultures, inclusion/exclusion—comes enlightenment. What should we study, then? By Sterling's example, both/and would be the answer: the Classics and the Folk.

> "She done put huh little hands
> On the back uh my head;
> I cain't git away from her
> Twill I'm dead.
>
> "She done laid her little body
> Beneaf my breast,
> And I won't never
> Git no rest.
>
> "She done been in my arms
> Twill the break of day
> Won't never
> Git away. . . .
>
> "She done put her little shoes
> Underneaf my bed
>
> Never git away from her
> Twill I'm dead.
>
> "Won't want to leave her
> Then," he said.
> "Oh, baby, gotta lay
> So long
> Alone. . . ." ("Conjured," by Sterling A. Brown)

VI

"STEADY AND UNACCUSING": INTERVIEWS

"Let Me Be with Ole Jazzbo": An Interview with Sterling A. Brown

Charles H. Rowell

An' all dat Big Boy axes
When time comes fo' to go,
Lemme be wid John Henry, steel drivin' man,
Lemme be wid old Jazzbo,
Lemme be wid ole Jazzbo. . . .
                    —Sterling A. Brown, "Odyssey of Big Boy"

This interview was taped in two sessions at Professor Brown's home in Washington, D.C., during April 1974.

CHARLES H. ROWELL: In an essay on the blues, you say that Irving Berlin's "Schoolhouse Blues" and Jerome Kern's "Left All Alone Blues" are not the form or feeling of true blues as sung by the people.

STERLING A. BROWN: That is true. That is true. I think they're not blues at all. It's just that they used "blues" in their titles because it was popular to do so. A Tin Pan Alley title. It entered the language of popular music, but they are not blues. They are not blues feeling. Actually they are the opposite of blues. Berlin's "Schoolhouse Blues": when you think of schools for Negroes in the South (and you're thinking of this as a writer), you can see that Berlin was just a Tin Pan Alley writer. Critics talk about him as a poet of ragtime, but "Alexander's Ragtime Band" became a popular number at the conclusion of the ragtime period.

The blues and ragtime still belong to the Negro. I call the kind of thing Berlin and Kern were doing "bluing" instead of "blues." What they were doing is very much diluted, and some of them don't even have much blue in them. We have the same thing in many of our bands; many of the good jazz bands play music that is not blues—unless you're going to just say blues means anything that has a slightly sad tint. I think that blues should be kept authentic. And then again the qualities of the blues are so strong and distinctive that it's easy to recognize the fake blues. Now, when I started to write poetry, I used the word "blues" sometimes for forms that weren't blues in structure, but I thought the feeling was the important thing. For instance, "Memphis Blues": in that poem I was trying to give the picture of Memphis life that I thought was soaked in tradition, and so I used the word "blues." But the poem is not true blues form. I've also written poems in blues forms.

ROWELL: What is your reaction to the recent rage, beginning a few years ago, over Janis Joplin as a blues singer?

BROWN: I think her songs are adaptations of the blues, and I think they appeal largely to a white audience rather than our audience. There is an excellent essay that [Julius] Lester has written in which he denies that the blues are dead. And he denies the inference that at concerts you have a large number of whites and not many blacks. He says that you can't infer from that that the blues are dead. He says that if you go back to the source you'll find that people are still playing blues and listening to them, and a lot of people have a longing for them. Lester has written a very good essay. . . . Then you get an Englishman like Tom Jones coming over (and Elvis Presley farther back). There's something about Tom Jones that appeals . . . appeals to a free-er generation. There's something about the artistry of true blues. There's something about the beauty of the word that separates it from that time to this, and I think the blues have established themselves as an important thing in the music world. But I wouldn't speak of Joplin and the others as blues singers. I don't know too much about them; I know that they don't appeal to me too much. And Tom Jones—I've got too many blues artists to hear; I don't have the time or place to listen to him. Much of his appeal is his being some sort of sex symbol.

ROWELL: When you say the "blues feeling," what do you mean?

BROWN: Well, the blues feeling is a very complex thing. There's no single blues feeling. Some of the best scholarship on the blues has come from Englishmen, and I think Paul Oliver has done good work. Paul got Richard Wright to write an introduction to his book on the blues. I don't think Richard Wright felt the blues very deeply, and I don't think too much about him. He speaks about the blues as being orgiastic. That is so untrue of so many blues. "I woke up this morning with blues all around my bed," or "Been down so long that down don't bother me"—there's nothing orgiastic about that. The second and last thing I'm going to say about Dick Wright is that he was a very talented novelist, but Dick was not an authority on certain aspects of folk culture. I don't think he felt jazz, and I don't think he felt the blues. Dick was an intellectual who became a spokesman, and Paul Oliver wanted a big name to introduce his book. But the essay that Dick wrote was not a good essay on the blues. This is not a heated attack on Wright; it is a defense of the blues. He says that the blues are "shorn of all hyperbole." It seems to me that the blues are full of hyperboles, some of the greatest hyperboles there are. "All you men and children make me tired" and "You got a handful of gimme and a mouth full of much oblige" are good examples of hyperbole. And lines like "My gal's got teeth like a lighthouse on de sea, / Everytime she smile, she throw a light on me" or things like "klondike cold, every time she smiles, she sends me some soul," this is hyperbole. It seems to me that Dick was making a protest point instead of getting at the source of the blues. I don't find an understanding of folk culture in his admirable *Uncle Tom's Children* or *Black Boy* or *Native Son*. I don't think he had to have it; I can't see why you can't have other things which he had. But he wasn't an authority on folk culture. Why not go to Ralph Ellison or Langston Hughes for an introduction to a book about the blues?

ROWELL: What do you think of LeRoi Jones (Amiri Baraka) on the blues?

BROWN: I think that LeRoi Jones proved to have known very little about the blues but much more about avant-garde music, which is not about blues or about blues people. Jones leaves out the old blues singers, and there's no mention of the later crop of blues singers. He starts talking about Ornette Coleman; he starts talking about avant-garde musicians. They appeal to a very small number of people. If he's talking about the masses of people . . . the masses of people, of course, are not blues people. The masses would be gospel song people, and you can't leave out religion if you're going to talk about the people. That's what I missed in Jones's book, and I think it's a kind of declaratory book in which he's making a statement for a certain kind of freedom for the Negro artist. I think Jones's instincts are sound in much of the book, but I did not learn anything about the blues from it. He dismisses people like Ma Rainey and Bessie Smith . . . there's no mention of them; and people like Lonnie Johnson and Jelly Roll Morton are the blues. All of these people are missing. He doesn't even say much about W. C. Handy. So I don't think it's a good book on the blues.

ROWELL: What is your reaction to Ron Karenga's comments on the blues?

BROWN: I disagree with him. The blues are full of consciousness of the ugly situation. They talk about it with irony; they talk about it with fortitude; they talk about it in good humor at times—they're not being fooled. You see, blues songs, and feeling blue and despondent and despairing are different things. The blues are not despairing, but the blues are not surrendering. What happens is this: a man has a beef, and the blues helps him to solve that beef. But very often you get "amen," and very often you get what used to be the equivalent of "right-on." And so they're singing about a beef, but they're in the artistic sense really changing music as they are changing styles of music. To me the spirit of the blues is the blues but not despondency. I listen to the blues for a lift, and I get a lift from the quality of the singing and the poetry they've created. . . . I don't agree, for instance, with Countee Cullen's expression: "To make a poet black and bid him sing"—he feels as if this is a "curious thing," "To make a poet black and bid him sing." Hardship is what great music has emerged from. I know Beethoven came out of great suffering. So what you have is great poetry. Tragic poetry has come out of suffering, and I look on the blues in those terms. I don't think that it's a handicap for a man to be black as far as being a poet is concerned. I think he has been given great poetic material. I don't want to seem negative to all of these; I just want to be honest. Countee Cullen was a very talented and gifted person, but I don't think it is terrible to be a Negro. They say, "Isn't it hard to be a Negro?" "Isn't it hard to be a nigger?" I don't agree with that. I think I have been blessed, as far as my poetry is concerned, by being a Negro.

Now you see, I used the word "Negro," because I do not believe that the word "Negro" meant what people said it meant. It did not mean bourgeois; it did not mean forgetting one's roots. You could find that in any middle class. I do not think bourgeois is an accurate picture of the black middle class. I've heard a person like Ossie Davis say that the first man he knew was Malcolm X. The first man he knew was probably his grandfather, because if he hadn't had a wonderful grandfather Ossie wouldn't be the important person he is today.

We very often adjust to claiming new desires. The spirit of the blues to me is strength; it's stoicism; it's fortitude; it's humor; it's directness; it's frankness. That's the reason these kids like the blues. It's being honest about the facts of life. Some of those facts are sexual, and they're asking about sex; it's being honest about sexual relationships, about men and women. If you put the blues up against Tin Pan Alley's slick love songs . . . when you play some of that slush, which was popular . . . you get all of that business about love everlasting and all that business about the idealistic side of love. I think the kids now recognize that the blues are telling a whole lot of truth about human nature, and it's not only black human nature; it's about all human nature. I think that is the approach to take to the blues—not Karenga's approach that we've been singing the blues too long; now let's get up and do something. The blues never told people not to get up and do something—not that I know of. When the blues says, "Been down so long, down don't bother me," the blues is not saying, "I'm satisfied with being down and I think I should've been down." This is a fact of life that the blues recognized. A very realistic fact. It is rough; it was tough and they said it.

ROWELL: What do you think of Ron Karenga?

BROWN: His argument on the blues is based on, let's say, literature as propaganda. I think that is the context in which he made his statements. I don't think that all literature must be direct propaganda. Some literature may be propaganda to aid in "a revolution," for example. But a poet, I think, has a right to talk about the beauty of a sunset if he or she wants to. Contrary to what Karenga says, blues lyrics (or blues itself) are not counter-revolutionary.

There's a recording of the problems, for example, and that keeps alive the sense of them. Ultimately the person might want to do something about the problems upon hearing them in the music.

ROWELL: In one essay you said that both Uncle Remus and Leadbelly portray sides of the Negro folk, but to round out the portraiture, we need Bessie Smith, Georgia White, and others . . .

BROWN: That's right! Well, I think that would be obvious enough. Uncle Remus was.

ROWELL: That's the person I wanted to concentrate on, the whole thing of . . .

BROWN: Uncle Remus is a very complex person. Uncle Remus tells the tales, and these were folktales that Joel Chandler Harris gathered and put in Uncle Remus's mouth. Harris caught them with a good local colorist's ear. The idiom and the phrases.

So Uncle Remus talks well. When the tales stay as talks, when the tales stay with the animals who, of course, are human . . . when Harris does that, he's in a very rich tradition, and this is valuable because they would have been lost without him. I think that our own second generation respectability wouldn't have kept them because of our ignorance of how good folk stuff is. The folk don't know how good they really are. They just say this is something my grandmother told me, which means one woman's old stories and that sort of thing. You know that from your own collecting. So here comes a man [Joel Chandler Harris] who was to a degree an outsider and to a degree an insider. . . . He was an insider in that he, as a lonesome kid, was thrown in contact with black people. The people who taught him were black—these "old uncles" and kids and the rest. They had something that he learned. So he learned the superficial local color idiom and other superficial things. But he collected the tales. Now, when you've got Uncle Remus becoming the teacher for the little white boy, that is Joel Chandler Harris creating a framework, and he had to do that because his audience was going to be chiefly white and chiefly plantation tradition-minded; but the stories themselves are not plantation tradition. But then you've got Uncle Remus becoming the crackerbox philosopher. Uncle Remus becomes a spokesman for what Joel Chandler Harris would put into his mouth . . . in Harris's editorials . . . you get the kinds of things I pointed out . . . how he attacks education and how he attacks Negroes leaving the South, and how he attacks. . . . He used him. Therefore you've got several Uncle Remuses, and I don't know whether he's so much a complex as compound thing. The idea is he's made up of many, but the stories themselves are very rich and very valuable. I dislike dismissing them merely because of Joel Chandler Harris. He was not a liberal; he was a reactionary, but he was more decent than [Thomas Nelson] Page. Harris was still a reactionary, but I think you ought to distinguish between them. I've been anxious to do that.

Leadbelly gives you another kind of thing, too. Leadbelly gives you the very wild, free improvising singer of songs, many of which he changes around and forgets. But he's a valuable singer: this fine guitar player and this wonderful personality. But that is not "folk" completely either. And Bessie Smith's blues and Ma Rainey's blues and Lonnie Johnson's blues—you need the four, and you need Mahalia Jackson's gospel; you just can't say you need Negro folk. Negro folk are too complex and too various. There are all kinds. You got Bible folk and you got blues folk and you got some religious folk and you got people who combine all of them like Big Bill. Big Bill gives a wonderful thought on not confusing the religious and the secular. He can do it himself, but he sings the religious songs with dignity and with feeling. He doesn't like them jazzed up . . .

Folklorists and historians make too many generalizations about what people were singing in the quarters. I think that is oversimplification. In the first place, all the divisions between the house Negro and the field Negro dismiss too many social facts about history. In the first place, most white farmers weren't planters; they weren't landlords; they just had four or five servants. What the hell is going to keep a man from working in the house after the breakfast cleaning up, and gettin the hell out in a field to pick the hell out of cotton in the afternoon? I mean, he could be both fieldhand and a house Negro. What in the world would there be to do in those houses for all the people you call "house Negroes"? There wasn't that much house. I mean, housekeeping ain't that rough, you see. So what you get is simplification, and this is the kind of thing that I think LeRoi Jones and all the rest are guilty of. I think Adam Clayton Powell fell for it. It's political, and what he wants to do is set up a certain division. I mean Adam Clayton Powell has an unbelievable section where he insists that he's a black man, a descendant of field Negroes, and that he's a field Negro. Well, Adam Clayton Powell ought to stop lying, because he tried to pass for white when he went to Colgate University. His wives have never been "black" women. For a long time he wouldn't have taken the word "black."

I'm very happy that the word "black" has now come to mean what it has come to mean. And I'm very happy that *Blackness* is no longer a term of shame. I'm very happy. I'm very glad; I have no objections. People call me a black poet. If you write an article on *Blackness* or *Brownness,* it's perfectly all right with me. I just do not yield to the belief that Paul Robeson and W.E.B. Du Bois and James Weldon Johnson and Roland Hayes and Countee Cullen and Langston Hughes and Richard Wright—name them, just name a whole list of people up to seven or eight years ago—were not proud to be called "Negro." We've got something in *The Negro Caravan* in which Marcus Garvey started the sentence with "I am a Negro," and he speaks of how proud he was to be a Negro. I refuse to believe that they would sell us out, that they were nothing but hustlers, that they denied their people. All this folk stuff we're learning came from those who people called "Negroes." You've got Du Bois. . . . I've got a book that I've been using for my class, and the three titles are 1) *Up From Slavery,* 2) *The Autobiography of an Ex-Colored Man,* and 3) *The Souls of Black Folk.* Now you've got the word "Negroes"; you've got all of them on one title page, you see, and it's called *Three Negro Classics,* edited by John Hope Franklin. I think that we are self-destructive in that we are multiplying distinctions of names and things of that sort. The heart and core of the thing is being destroyed. The core is a very long tradition. Now I think that is happily changing—I mean for a young scholar like you to be interested in this is a sign of it. In a recent article, I said, I've been a Negro for seventy-five years and I'm going to die a Negro and I defy anybody to say that I turned my back on tradition. And all this other nonsense about somebody saying that he was "so and so" years old before he discovered he was a Negro . . . I ask him this question, "Didn't your house have any mirrors in it?" I mean no damage to the culture but my color is against me. When I use "Negro," they think I don't want to say "Black" because of color, but that's not it at all. When I was a kid if you called a man, you never said "black." As a matter of fact, when we were kids, we didn't use any terms of color because they were fighting words. If I called somebody "black" who was darker than I, I got my head knocked off; if he called me "yellow" because I was lighter than he, he got his head knocked off—if I could knock it off, you know. So we would never say "black." It was a term of reproach. There's no question about it. It was a bad word. Now it's no longer a bad word, and I'm happy about that but I still use "Negro" out of habit, and I accept "black" very easily. It's not difficult at all, and if someone says "black poet," then good, good! But I called Countee [Cullen] Negro in our talks; I called Dick Wright a Negro—these were all my friends. And Ralph Ellison. I know them; I know them well; I admire them. Langston [Hughes] . . . and Langston had some of the best poems in the world; you're talking about "I am a Negro," "Black Experience."

Daisy, come and meet Dr. Rowell. [*Sterling Brown calls his wife, who speaks later in the interview.*] There was a great deal of material written that people don't know about. A lot of them haven't done their homework. For instance, the back issues of *Phylon,* which reveal so much; *Opportunity* and *Crisis;* I think it's an inferior book. I did an article on the blues, "Folk Poetry of the Blues," in 1930, and it's not mentioned in bibliographies. Now, it might not have been a good article, but I don't see that they've added too much to it. The book that Samuel Charters wrote on the poetry of the blues . . . I wrote the blues was poetry in the 1930s. A whole lot of my work came out in obscure periodicals: one, because they didn't want the kind of thing I was saying in big periodicals; and two, because I just didn't send any to them. It could have been my fault, but they weren't interested in my approach. Now you've got a whole lot of books in which things are discovered, but really aren't discovered; they're just being handled. There are books on music, books on the blues. And I would say even a book like *Blues People* got a big press when there wasn't a whole lot in it that hadn't been said by others. It's only from the European scholars that you get appreciation of the great things in blues history, from Muddy Waters and Howling Wolf and John Lee Hooker and the rest who are deserving. I'm so happy to see them making good livings. Still they did not start a tradition and are not worth that much more knowledge than the pioneers of the blues. The pioneers are just dismissed, and I think LeRoi just dismisses them in *Blues People*. I was looking for things in not just the major singers but secondary people who were so influential in records sold, something like Victoria Spivey and Alberta Hunter. A whole group of men singers. . . . Let's see, Big Bill has come to attention. I'll tell you an organization that's doing something quite good: that's Folkways, and Moe Asch has brought out a lot of these blues singers and deserves a lot of credit for it. Moe Asch just brought out a record of mine called "Sixteen Poems of Sterling A. Brown." You ought to get a copy of that when you go to New York. Go by and give my name, and tell them what you're doing. What was your next question?

ROWELL: In one of your essays, you define the "folk" as rural people living in a kind of isolation without easy contact with the outside world. Would you describe the folk as . . .

BROWN: I would keep to that in most discussions of folk stuff. I think that's about as serviceable as I could be. But today you've got the people in the city, and I'm not going to leave them out of consideration. For the purposes of that essay I needed some kind of delimiting definition. I didn't want to make everything into folk.

ROWELL: Certain slaves looked at slavery ironically . . .

BROWN: They did. The first good collector of them really was Thomas Talley, a Fisk professor of chemistry. A Fisk professor . . . but he came up out of a rural background and he knew the stuff and he loved it. His *Negro Folk Rhymes* was the first full look I had at the secular. And then old [Guy B.] Johnson came along; I saw this irony; yes, I think it was irony. There's irony all through the folk tales. I had some students do masters theses on folk tales.

ROWELL: You also said—and I think it's the same essay—that Negro culture is breaking up.

BROWN: Yes, well, Negro folk culture, not Negro culture. I mean the folk culture; after all, we're becoming more and more an urbanized people. I think the barbershop is declining. The barbershop was once a beautiful source of tall tales—wonderful irony and satire and I think that's breaking up.

ROWELL: Is there anything replacing it?

BROWN: I don't know. I haven't made a good study of variable culture, but I think that urbanization does break up folk culture whether it be the Appalachian Mountains or . . .

ROWELL: Perhaps television, also . . .

BROWN: And television and radio. You see it, for instance, in Leadbelly. Of course, the way he would change it would be marvelous, but Leadbelly for many years packed houses. I think that soul music has come in now, and there's not been any sharp cutting through fog; there's just been a change, a change that changes—I imagine—the singing style. The gospel songs have kept it, but notice how they've been commercialized and glittered and put on television.

I think television and radio do that, but folk culture is still strong. It's very strong in our writers. I'm very glad to see it strong. I think it's coming into its own scholarship. I just hope it won't be too late.

ROWELL: In the South now, the rural South at least, some of the folk tales are still alive. Very recently I recorded some in my hometown, Auburn, Alabama.

BROWN: I taught a lesson last semester on the folk tale and the aphorism of blues and spirituals. The semester ended too soon. I was going to do a contrast between the phony conception of the Negro joke and what I call the authentic Negro joke. As you can see, it was going to be on Negro humor.

ROWELL: You've written a lot about the image of black characters or black figures in literature. What is your reaction to recent white writers' treatment of black characters—for example, William Styron's Nat Turner?

BROWN: I don't think that's a good book. No, I think he tells us more about Styron, and he shows that he's not the converted liberal that we thought he was. He goes back to the stereotypes. I think he has distorted the picture. He did it consciously; he did it consciously and unconsciously. You just cannot take a figure like Nat Turner without giving him certain qualities. I haven't read it recently, but I didn't like it. There have been books by Negroes recently on Nat Turner that nobody paid attention to. I think the ten writers who answered that book did a good job, and in responding they revealed a great deal about Nat Turner. I did a poem called "Remembering Nat Turner." In it I was very disheartened by the loss of his memory.

ROWELL: In other words, then, you agree with Jean Wagner's treatment of your poem in his study?

BROWN: I don't remember just what he said.

ROWELL: His position is that you in the poem showed that black people have forgotten, but that the white woman in the poem remembers, but not necessarily out of admiration.

BROWN: If he said that, that wasn't exactly accurate for her. She misremembers. That is, she just confuses folklore about people who fought for freedom. She confuses John Brown with Nat Turner, and so has given a lot of phony legends about Nat Turner. I tried to set in contrast what she would say and what the actual facts were. She said that he was riddled with bullets; of course, he was not—he was hanged. I showed that she had misinformation, and my folks had no information. I closed the poem with "The marker split for kindling a kitchen fire." That's survival and just the bare necessities of life which made it so that they'd forget it; they were surprised that a person fought for his freedom—not that they didn't want freedom but that he fought for it. It was a disheartening thing. Forgetting has been a way, but that's changing. That's another good thing about the Black Movement; the heroes are coming back into their own.

ROWELL: In his preface to the 1968 combined edition of your *Negro Poetry in Drama* and *The Negro in American Fiction*, Robert Bone describes your studies as "comprehensive surveys in the field of iconography, tracing through American fiction, poetry, and drama the changing image of the Negro. Their real focus," he says, "is a sociology of literature, the politics of culture. They are concerned with the uses and abuses of the image-making function in society." It seems to me that your studies are more than a sociology of literature.

BROWN: I think Bone is straining there to stay in with the New Critics. It was an ungenerous introduction. He speaks, for instance, of its not being great criticism, but who in the world is writing great criticism today? You keep the phrase "great criticism" for Matthew Arnold. . . . Bone knew that the book was written for a very definite purpose, and he knew that the book had to be confined. You see, I could not write at full in the book. This was part of a series and it had to be a certain length and so I was kept down. But I have just as much literary criticism of many of those novels as he did in his work that was devoted only to Negro novelists. He worked under me. I was his advisor on his thesis, you see. He knew that. I never meant the book as great criticism. I stated what the book was. I had two jobs to do: I had to evaluate the books, and I also had to discuss certain stereotypes. I think I did in the book as a whole. I think I did it better in *The Negro in American Fiction* than in *Negro Poetry and Drama,* because the confined space was just too much to handle poetry and drama. I got in trouble with Alain Locke who edited the series because I ran *The Negro in American Fiction* a little longer than I was supposed to; I was to keep it to 125 pages, but I just couldn't do it. A lot of stuff I wanted to say I . . . but my criticism of single works is running through *Opportunity,* a magazine. . . . Anybody who ever took a course from me knows that I always paid attention to the craft of fiction. I pay attention to craft, but in this book there was a whole lot to do, to cover the range of American fiction with all of its stupidity and all of its ignorance and to prove it. Most people just dismiss books and say that the white man is stereotyping. Of course, I didn't do that. Most of the white books were stereotyping blacks, but some were not.

ROWELL: You mentioned Alain Locke. Recently, in Beinecke Library at Yale, I read a letter from Zora Neale Hurston to James Weldon Johnson attacking Alain Locke. She had submitted an essay to *Opportunity* that was never published. The essay, which attacked Locke, was entitled "A Chick with One Hen."

BROWN: Yeah, I think that's what she said to me. Somebody said it. I heard it somewhere. I don't know where I have heard it. No, I was not his chick at all. We were friends, and I learned from him. We were colleagues, but we differed on many things. And we differed on those books. He would change many things that I said, and I would change them right back. That made the printing bill go up. He insisted that I pay the printing bill. I refused to pay it, so he refused to pay me my money. I never got paid for my second book, *The Negro in American Fiction.* He was riding on the analytic kick back then and I wasn't. He would find a whole lot of Africanisms that I wouldn't find. And he was taking *God's Trombones,* and he was getting a relationship to Africa. It would have been a relationship to Africa, but the first relationship [for Locke] certainly wasn't to the old Negro preacher in the South. I think that this sort of jumping over that tradition to get back to Africa is not as sound as first finding our own tradition here and getting that true tradition and then finding out how African it is.

ROWELL: I think Zora Neale Hurston also accused Locke of not having a real knowledge of black folk tradition. She said he sat and listened to what other people said and then wrote about the tradition.

BROWN: That is not fair. She was angry. She fell out with most men. She was an early women's liberator. She was kicked around. She had much right on her side. She fought with Langston Hughes. She fought with Dick Wright, and she wrote a bad attack on Dick Wright. She fought with me, because of what I said about her novel called *Their Eyes Were Watching God,* which I think is a good novel. It is the best thing she ever did. *Mules and Men* is second. On that novel I stressed the hard lives the people on the farm lived. I stressed this from a viewpoint of social realism. She said I wasn't going to make a communist out of her, and she turned away. But now, see, she was all involved with Fannie Hurst with whom I had a big quarrel. Zora Neale [Hurston] was involved with literary patrons in New York City. I never had any dealings with those people. I don't even know what's in the Van Vechten business at Yale because of my distaste for the man. I have tremendous distaste for Carl Van Vechten. I don't ever say "Harlem Renaissance," because it wasn't Harlem. It was the "Negro Renaissance." What I disliked was black writers' reliance on Van Vechten and their acceptance of his leadership. I felt that he set up an exotic primitive. His heart was not really with us in that he was a voyeur. I'm doing an essay in this book for the Howard University Press called "Carl Van Vechten Voyeur and Robert Penn Warren Informer." Both of them are very false friends. Zora Neale was very friendly to us. She came here, sat on the sofa there [*pointing*] and told us some stories. She was a beautiful storyteller; she was a wonderful actress. She knew a lot of stuff, and I think she's been underestimated. She battled, and she battled men. She had some grouch. I didn't know this little thing you told me about Locke. I didn't know about the *Opportunity* essay. She couldn't get along with people.

As far as Locke is concerned, it is not true that he just read whatever other people wrote. Locke, intellectually and intuitively, knew the importance of the spirituals, and when he wrote about them he was good. Now Locke did not know jazz, and he did not know the blues, but intellectually he knew their importance. He was at first trying to stress them. His book on the Negro in music was not a good one. It's full of errors. He just doesn't dig blues. For Locke, if Stravinsky liked it, it had to be good. And that's bad. Locke did know the importance of jazz on the world scene, but he could not hear jazz and he did not see jazz in its own terms. He had a couple of blues records. One of them was "Ticket Agent, Let Your Window Down," something of that sort. Locke would play those records as examples; he had about two of them. Behind him out in the alley, the people would really be singing the blues. He would pull his window down to keep from hearing them. That was too rough for him. Now you've got to understand that here is a very sheltered gentleman of the most delicate sensibilities. So you've got to distinguish between a personality and a mind; the mind of the man knew that these were important. When I wrote an article on the blues as folk poetry, it appeared in a magazine in which Locke and I collaborated on, an article on *Hallelujah* and *Hearts of Dixie*. We pointed out the good points and the stereotypes of both of them; he and I sided. He knew my essay on the folk poetry. When he wrote an essay on me called "The New Negro Folk Poet," he showed a knowledge of folk stuff. I would say that I cannot agree with Zora Neale Hurston on his ignorance of it. I could agree with anybody on Locke's failure to be absorbed in it and really soak it up. He was not like James Weldon Johnson; he was not like Langston Hughes; he was not like Ralph Ellison; and he was not like me.

I've already said that many Negro intellectuals are not like that. Ron Karenga is not like that, and LeRoi Jones is not like that really. LeRoi is still with Ornette Coleman and way out there with Cecil Taylor. By the way, Cecil Taylor dedicated one of his programs to me, which I think is marvelous because I don't dig his music; he's too advanced for me. But I'm appreciative. Miles Davis knows me, too. I think they know one or two of my poems. I think they know "Strong Men," and that hits them. They know what I've stood for. I'm not alone, but I've been alone. I've never run with any crowd, and I certainly didn't run with that damn Van Vechten kind of foolishness. I've had no patrons. I think Cecil Taylor and Miles Davis respect that. Miles Davis wanted to get out of the sick bed to hear me read poetry. I read at the American Academy of Poets last Tuesday, Tuesday a week ago in New York. It was a wonderful experience. I haven't heard of them for God's sake, and they hadn't heard of me. But Michael Harper pushed me. Michael Harper believes in my work. Well, Miles Davis of all people wanted to come. He's got a bad leg, and the doctor wouldn't let him do it. Well, I appreciate that a great deal. My wife swears that as soon as I put a Miles Davis record on I go out back. I tell her I'm just going to wait for the next note because he takes so long between notes. I do like Miles, I've always liked him, and I know him personally. He remembered that. I would say that LeRoi [Jones] has a deep feeling for music, but I think LeRoi is so avant-garde. I think that Ralph [Ellison] is a very close student of jazz and the blues. I think Langston [Hughes] was very definitely. Now Countee [Cullen] did not have it. James Weldon Johnson had it. Most of the elder statesmen—and Charles Johnson probably—had more of it, but [W.E.B.] Du Bois never had it. Du Bois did one of the greatest essays in the world on sorrow songs. Zora [Neale Hurston] has an essay in which she denies that the spiritual is a sorrow song. You've got to listen to her, too. But for a core, for a central kind of theme, Du Bois' essay is great. That needs to be understood. Du Bois recognized intellectually the importance of these, and I think Locke recognized intellectually these. Locke's essay on the spirituals in *The New Negro* is good, but his book *The Negro in Music* is not good. He makes errors; he just slams things together and he calls Scott Joplin a white man. Margaret Butcher just took Locke's things and kind of put them together again. Margaret Butcher repeats the same; she didn't even check on them. She repeats the same tale.

I was with Locke when Zelma Watson Duke—she's married to a big political figure in the Midwest now, but she was doing her doctoral dissertation on songs written by American Negro composers—turned up a fantastic list of songs. She and Locke didn't get along. Now, just as Zora [Neale Hurston] couldn't get along with men, Locke couldn't get along with women, particularly a great big, aggressive woman like Zelma Duke. He caught Zelma Duke at something and she says, "Well Dr. Locke, everybody makes a mistake." She said, "You said in your book that Scott Joplin was a white man," and Locke turned to me and said, "Well you know," he says, "you can't always tell what these creoles are. Isn't that so, Sterling?" And I said, "Dr. Locke, Scott Joplin was a black man. Scott Joplin was as black as the ace of spades." He tried to turn it off, but she had caught him, and he could get caught. He could be very inaccurate, but I do not agree with what Zora said about him. His contribution in establishing a respect for Negro folk culture is strong, is true, is genuine. It did not come, however, from an absorption or deep love. It came intellectually. The spirituals had a dignity and a beauty and a richness that he could respond to. He was still a bronze Beethoven. That was his upbringing. You see, Locke learned and Locke blossomed when he came to Howard. There were all these young men around there who were in there pitching: Ralph Bunche, E. Franklin Frazier, Abe Harris, Emmett Dorsey, and myself. Then later Rayford Logan. Locke had to get up and do something, and he did *The New Negro* in 1925. Then we started jumping and Locke got back into it. Then he got a Carnegie grant and he did work on the Negro in art and the Negro in music. He had me do *Negro Poetry and Drama* and *The Negro in American Fiction*. He had Ralph [Bunche] do one called *The World View of Race;* he had Arnold Hill do something on economics; he had Ira Reid do something on adult education; and he had Eric Williams do something on the Caribbean. That series should be better known. You see, it was a series published at the end of the 1930s, and it's not well known. A lot of stuff is taken from it without credit, and then a lot of stuff is being done that's already been done.

ROWELL: You mentioned the 1930s. Will you talk about the WPA Federal Writers Project?

BROWN: Well, one of the ridiculous things in [Nathan Irvin] Huggins's book and in a whole lot of this nonsense about the so-called Harlem Renaissance is that it ended with the Panic of 1929. It's ridiculous because many of the best things came out in 1930 and 1931. Arna's [Bontemps] best novel, *Black Thunder,* came out in 1936. Actually, there weren't any Negroes jumping out of windows because of the Panic in 1929. The publishers might have tightened up on publishing, but writing by Negroes did not stop. There was not any sudden change, because Negro writers actually made more money during the Depression than they had made before. Because they got on WPA, they got a regular check. Almost all of the writers were on WPA. Dick Wright was on it, Arna was on it . . . almost all of them except Langston. These were young writers, and they were getting a regular check. Henry Lee Moon, Ted Poston (a newspaper man), Roi Ottley, Margaret Walker (very young, right out of school), Ralph Ellison, and Claude McKay. The checks cushioned Claude McKay's last years. Claude didn't have too much work to do. There were very few recognized writers when these projects started. There were very few recognized Negro writers. As you know, there are very few still, but there are so many more today than then. A man was a writer even if he was a newspaper reporter or had a book out. In the Southern states, you had a hard time finding people who were qualified as writers. For instance, in a town like Auburn, Alabama, do you see, you'd get a reporter. So by and large, the prejudice of the South and a kind of a proof that there weren't too many kept them from having Negro writers. Then those Negro writers were segregated, were set apart.

I was the editor here. I worked full time for Howard University and part time for WPA. They wanted somebody here in that position. My job was really overwhelming. I had to edit the stuff that came in the state guides. . . . There was a young man on the Oklahoma project; I think his name was Harmon. I think he was a newspaper man or something. He was a token, maybe the only one. At any rate, he would send over the wire that they would not let him use the drinking fountain. They had to have a Colored drinking fountain in this place, and so I would have to straighten that out. So they said "Hell, stop this foolishness. A drinking fountain is a drinking fountain is a drinking fountain. Everybody drinks out of the drinking fountain." In the meanwhile, I'm going to get somebody on down to Georgia. I'm trying to straighten out a mess in New York, because up in New York you had the battle between the communists, the socialists, Trotskyites, the conservatives, the whites, the blacks. You had all this fighting in New York. Some cities wouldn't pay any attention to us. For instance, Chicago got out a book called *The Cavalcade of the Negro,* which was not a good book. We wouldn't have let it out, but they just slid it on through. We had to insist upon proper representation of the Negro in these books. Now, this was in the 1930s when there was racial segregation. There's no question about it. In order to get Negroes in, we had to have an essay on Negroes. For example, Tennessee would send in something about Nashville and not even mention Fisk University. You wouldn't believe this, but at the start they didn't even count Negroes in the population. They'd give the white population. That is why we insisted that there be an essay on Negroes. All references on Negroes came from our office. I was editing there all day. Then a long distance call would come. Somebody would run into some kind of prejudicial treatment, and I'd have to take it up. My job was very comprehensive and very complex. Meanwhile, we were editing.

I did an essay, which was going to be in my book of essays, called *The Negro in Washington*. There's a reference to that essay in *The Dream and the Deal*. I did a good essay; it got us in great trouble. I was accused of being a communist, because I had spoken about the slum conditions right in the shadows of the Capitol and about the segregated school system and about the inequalities and so forth in Washington life. It was a strong essay, the strongest essay that the government had ever sponsored on the American Negro. And that's not saying much, because they haven't sponsored much of anything. They got in trouble with it, and the Senator from North Carolina read me into the record as a communist. The Congressman from Wisconsin, named O'Keefe, read me into the record as a communist. See, they just copied each other because of my article. Now, what they didn't like was my attack on the real estate interest, but what they got me for was saying that George Washington Parke Custis had a colored daughter, and he did have one. This caused a whole lot of stink, and one white woman from the South, writing from Wisconsin, said it would take a Yankee congressman not to know what really went on down there; and if I needed any help, call on her. Kelly Miller also said, "Sterling, you ought to be ashamed of yourself for listening to backstairs gossip." He said, "But if you need any help, call on me." We had fights with the South Carolina people. They said all I was doing was relying on abolitionists and Yankee sociologists. I wrote back that I got the material from [Howard] Odum of the University of North Carolina and Guy Johnson. This is an interesting thing to me that North Carolina was considered a Yankee state. And it is. You know, it's the vale of humility between two mountains of conceit. So I had fascinating experiences on that, but I had a hard time getting people employed. I had a hard time, because it was hard for people to prove that they were writers, you know, and there weren't many. You go to a small Southern town, and you don't even have a newspaper there.

We set up a Negro project in Virginia which got out a book called *The Negro in Virginia*, one of the best publications of the project. That book was edited by Roscoe Lewis, whose brother Harold Lewis is a professor of history at Howard. Roscoe Lewis used to chat with me on "Remembering Nat Turner." The poem is dedicated to Roscoe. In his book, he did a brilliant job, and he made use of ex-slaves. He made use of their narratives. He handled one full collection of material that people at the University of Virginia are now trying to put into some kind of shape. But he did not deposit his ex-slaves narratives with the main body which went down to the Library of Congress. Therefore, down at the Library of Congress you have a very uneven collection. You have most of the white interviewers. Very frequently when you had a black interviewer and a white interviewer different stories come out. Then you'd have a battle. I've had correspondence in which the white supervisors would say "You see, you can't trust a black interviewer. Look at the lies that are put here; my point of view is really what the truth is." But the white interviewer was the one that wasn't getting the truth. You had that kind of battle. *The Negro in Virginia* was a combination of straight history with the slaves' memories as background. It's a fascinating book, and I recommend it to you. Roscoe Lewis is responsible for it. I had Ulysses Lee working with me. He later became one of the editors of *The Negro Caravan* and a professor at Lincoln in Pennsylvania. He died very recently. Eugene Holmes, a professor of philosophy at Howard, was working with me. We had quite a staff.

ROWELL: But did the WPA have any aesthetic effects on the writing?

BROWN: I think it taught a lot of them that writing was worthwhile and that writing was a craft. You had to know something to write. It gave them a social background, and it gave them a great sense of regionalism. It might have given them a sense of accuracy. I think it taught them to be writers. I think that all of them learned from it. I think that Ralph Ellison and Margaret Walker learned from it. Now a person like Dick Wright was a favorite. Dick Wright wrote these brilliant short stories which the story magazines published. He didn't have much to do on the guides. Claude McKay was petted. Claude McKay was ego-centered. He was a famous writer. Claude McKay didn't want to do this kind of thing, so we let him write poetry. I think Roi Ottley became a good social journalist because of the experience from the project. Yes, I think it had a great aesthetic effect. It was one of the best things that ever happened to our writers. It would be good if we had something like that right now . . . because a lot of our writers really need discipline.

ROWELL: You seem more positive toward the WPA Project than what was called "the New Negro Movement."

BROWN: Charles! Charles! Charles! No! No! I'm positive toward the Writers Project, and I'm positive toward the New Negro Movement. I'm opposed to what they call a renaissance from 1925–29; you can't have any renaissance in that kind of period. I'm opposed to the glorification of Harlem, because the writers didn't come from Harlem. The only Harlemite writing was Countee Cullen, and he disliked Harlem. Countee Cullen was a very talented man, but he was no man for the sidewalks of Harlem. Now Langston [Hughes] becomes the laureate of Harlem later on. Simple [Jesse B. Simple] is a wonderful creation, but that's not part of any Harlem Renaissance; that's much later. Langston grew with years. *Weary Blues* is a good book of poetry, and Langston kept producing good poetry in the 1930s. It's ridiculous to say 1929 or 1930 is the end of the movement. If you're going to start with Claude McKay and come down to Dick Wright, to *Uncle Tom's Children* or *Native Son,* I think you have a wonderful thing. I'm not negative toward the New Negro Renaissance. I am negative toward the misnamed Harlem Renaissance. In New York the influence of Carl Van Vechten was a bad thing. Most of what was done was partying. I think they just wanted to be shown off to these white folks. You had a whole lot of writers you never heard of, and some of the best writers are not mentioned in Huggins's book [*Harlem Renaissance*]. One of the writers mentioned is [William] Waring Cuney. Now Waring Cuney was no Harlemite.

Waring Cuney went to Lincoln. He was writing out of Washington. I'm not in the Harlem Renaissance. Frank Horne was in New York; well, if you tell a Brooklyn guy he's from Harlem, he's going to fight you. Anne Spencer is not mentioned in Huggins's book. Anne Spencer was writing down in Lynchburg, Virginia. You had bright young Negroes all over the country who were waking up and writing. Now, the magazines, *Crisis* and *Opportunity*, were published in New York City, though not in Harlem, by the way. The Harlem people knew very little about this; the Harlem man in the street knew very little about this. The publishing houses were there in New York City, but the publishing houses were not as welcome as people say they were. Knopf was, Harcourt Brace was, and what became Viking Press was. They had publishers like that who would take one or two books by Negro authors. Now Langston [Hughes] has written that they would say they've got their one Negro book; they had that kind of a situation. Knopf had Van Vechten as their advisor. Mencken and Van Vechten kind of set the tone. In his book, Huggins talks about the intellectuals and then limits them to a few poets and novelists. The intellectuals were Phillip Randolph and Chandler Owen. The intellectuals were Charles Johnson and James Weldon Johnson. Du Bois did not care much for the Harlem writers. Du Bois cared a great deal more for the very genteel, NAACP programmatic writers. The whole business of Harlem has been blown out of focus. The New Negro Renaissance was an excellent thing. I just want it named "New Negro Renaissance," and I don't want it limited to those years.

ROWELL: During that period, who in your opinion is the most important fiction writer to emerge and why do you consider him/her to be so?

BROWN: I don't like to say "most"; I don't like to arrange them. I would say that Rudolph Fisher has some first rate short stories and a light, ironic, but not to be underestimated, touch in his novel *The Walls of Jericho*. Rudolph Fisher was talented. Claude McKay was a better poet than a novelist. You see Claude wasn't having anything to do with the movement. He has attacked it, you know. He said these writers were lazy and would hang around white folks all the time. I think that *Banjo* and *Home to Harlem* and *Gingertown* and *Banana Bottom* deserve to be carefully considered. I have a student working on McKay's fiction about Jamaica. I think that Walter White was a courageous race fighter but not a novelist. I think his novels are kind of cliché, but they said some important things. You've got the anti-lynching novel in *The Fire and the Flint*. He showed some aspects of life that should have been shown. Jessie Fauset was conventional, the women's magazine kind of writer; that's what she knew best, and that's what she could do. I don't think it's too important as fiction. Nella Larsen had a little more insight in *Quicksand*. I think *Passing* was slight. Jean Toomer's *Cane* is a great book; it is an important book. Toomer had very little relationship to this Harlem business. *Not Without Laughter* by Langston [Hughes] is a good novel. I wish he had followed it up. It never received the attention. I think Arna Bontemps' *God Sends Sunday* is engagingly written, but it is not important.

I think his *Black Thunder* is a very important novel. I've said that in the essay I did on Bontemps. I may have left out some important people.

ROWELL: You didn't refer to Eric Walrond.

BROWN: Eric Walrond was tremendous. He wasn't a novelist, but his *Tropic Death* was really quite a book. *Tropic Death* and *Cane* were the brilliant high marks in fiction. Wallace Thurman was an interesting guy; he was interested in creating a spoof. So was George Schuyler's *Black No More*. Most of what I would say would be repetitious of what's in the *Negro in American Fiction*. All those books said something that needed to be read, even the ones I said I didn't think much of. People should still know about them.

ROWELL: In his introduction to your *Southern Road*, James Weldon Johnson says that you took raw material from Afro-American folk poetry, and deepened its meaning and multiplied its implications. Was that one of your objectives in writing the poems?

BROWN: I wouldn't have phrased it in that way, but I'm glad he said I did that. I certainly believe a poet should do that. I didn't want to give any raw material. I wanted to use it. Take a poem like "Southern Road." I'm using the chain gang swing of the hammer, but I tell a story in there that no chain gang song tells. A chain gang song is inconsecutive. You've got a couple of stanzas together, and then another one will *go somewhere else.* "Take this hammer, carry it to the captain and tell them I'm gone. If they ask you any more questions, tell them you don't know. Lordy, Lordy! Yes, I'll make my home in Jacksonville." You got a split right there in the poem. But in my poem I build it up; and the same thing with "The Odyssey of Big Boy" and "Long Gone." I wanted the speech of Big Boy Davis, but I wanted to build Sterling Brown's creation in those poems.

ROWELL: Will you comment on the organization of *Southern Road?* It is divided into four sections. One section deals with urban folk life. Another section, "Vestiges," is written in standard English. Will you comment on the organization of your collection of poems?

BROWN: In the introduction he's going to do, Sterling Stuckey is going to write about the organization. The organization was divisional. The first poems were about Virginia and the earlier experiences. I think the second ones were Lincoln and Fisk, when I was there in those neighborhoods. The ones in part three, "Tin Roof Blues," are the city. The fourth part, "Vestiges," contains personal poems. I don't think it was too organic. I feel that each one belongs where it is. It's not as rigid as Toomer's *Cane:* folk life in the South; middle-class life in the border cities in the second part; and the third part is a combination. It's not that organic. Because I was in a rush to get *Southern Road* off. "Long Gone" came out with one stanza missing. That stanza is corrected in *The Negro Caravan*, and it's also to be corrected in the new edition of the poems.

ROWELL: Based on what you said, I realize that "Big Boy" is a real person. Will you talk about him as a real person and how you transformed him in the poem?

BROWN: I hope that he's alive, but I fear he's not. Well, Big Boy was a head taller than I, had broad shoulders. A great big wandering guitar picker, he'd been a coal miner. The students at Seminary knew my interest in folk stuff. Now I've always been interested in language and did my first years of graduate work at Harvard. I went over to Boston one day and bought a copy of Untermeyer's *Modern American Poetry*. I was studying Shakespeare line by line, word by word, with [George Lyman] Kittredge. I was studying Milton. I was in a straight traditional English curriculum. I was brought up on [Paul Laurence] Dunbar. My mother recited poetry beautifully. I came from a house of books. I loved poetry. I was interested in writing. I'd written a few conventional sonnets at Williams [College]. I hadn't intended to major in English, but I met at Williams a teacher who inspired me. His name is George Dutton. He taught me to see the importance of English. This is a long way to Big Boy. I read Edwin Arlington Robinson, particularly the poems about Tilbury Town, where he takes the poor, the undistinguished, and the ordinary; he gets at the extraordinary in their lives. Of course, I knew Burns; I knew Wordsworth; I knew Thomas Hardy; and I knew Mansfield. In American literature, I had Robinson and [Robert] Frost. Frost was a great influence—and Sandburg. I always loved language, I loved slang, and I loved the folk stuff I knew. I lived here in Washington; I was brought up here. I heard some folk stuff. As a kid, I heard a good "John Henry" here in Washington. But it was the railroad John Henry; I mean it was the hammering John Henry. It was not the ballad John Henry. It was one about the hammer: "This old hammer killed John Henry; this old hammer killed John Henry. Won't kill me, baby. Won't kill me. Take this hammer." That was all. I didn't know about the contest at all, but I'd heard of John Henry. As kids then in the high school, we had semi-folk; we had the traveling man; we had minstrels that come down to us in semi-folk song. So I always had an ear for the spoken word. I always had an ear for the ballad. I go to college, and I get this book. I read Frost and I read Sandburg and I read Edgar Lee Masters. I saw what could happen with the American idiom. But I hadn't seen it done with the Negro folk idiom much. Langston [Hughes] was writing about the same time. It's not true that I'm a disciple of Langston. We are contemporaries. My book came out later than his, but I was doing the same thing in *Opportunity*. For instance, I was writing blues when Langston was writing. Langston wrote blues in which he would split the line. I would write blues in the long line, the three lines. There's no question that Langston's success influenced me. *The Weary Blues* was an important book to me—but not as important as *Cane*. The kids at Seminary knew my interest. I was writing these poems, and they brought ["Big Boy"] to my room one night . . . my room was a gathering place for bull sessions, because these students were about my age. They were old to be in school, and I was young to be out of school. They were coal miners, farmers, hard workers, waiters down at the hotel. This was called Virginia Seminary and College. Many of them were studying to be ministers, but they had to work like hell in order to make enough money to come for those school months. So these kids knew my interest, and they brought Big Boy to the room. Big Boy came there with his guitar. He was an education for me. He knew a full John Henry. Though the second night he'd sing a different John Henry. It wouldn't be the same one at all. I'm inaccurate by saying "at all." It would be the same one seven-eighths or another eighth. Or he'd forget it. He'd say, "Oh, Mr. Brown, you remember that. I forgot that one." Then he'd change it, you see. But I heard a wonderful John Henry. Then he'd tell me lies about John Henry. He'd tell me tales in addition to the song. Then he told me about Railroad Bill. He told me about Stagolee. But he did not know Railroad Bill as you know Railroad Bill. He didn't know that much; he just knew a little. Then he had a beautiful song that later Louis [Armstrong] sang. This was "The Hobo Song." Big Boy was riding a train; with his guitar, he would have the rumble of the wheels and he would have the whistle. He said when the train comes to a crossing, it never blows its whistle. It blows this way . . . two longs and two shorts. . . . He used a bottle and he'd break a bottle and put the glass top over his thumb and he'd run out. Then he'd use a knife. He would say that when a freight train goes through the yards it doesn't blow its whistle; it rings its bell. And he'd ring his bell on his guitar, and he was talking all the time about this hobo. He sees this brakeman, and the brakeman wants to throw him off. He looks at the brakeman, and he sees the brakeman is a blues man. Then he plays the blues: "If you ever been down, you know just how I feel, like a broken down engine, got no driving wheel." He would knife this. Then he'd run into the conductor. The conductor wanted to throw him off, and he saw the conductor was a religious man. So he would play for him "Nero my God to thee." And he always made it N-E-R-O "my God to thee." He was playing that, and you could hear the rumbling in the wheels. It was a little fascinating performance. When he finished, he played the blues, low down blues. When that was over, he would always sing his mother's favorite; he'd play "When the Saints Go Marching Home." Then he'd leave. His picture is in three poems of mine. His picture is in "Odyssey of Big Boy," "Long Gone," and "When de Saints Go Ma'ching Home." I used to write his letters for him; he couldn't read and write. I'll try to get you a copy of that. Big Boy came to the house here. (*Daisy,* [calling] *I'm getting kind of run-out of voice for a moment. Could you tell him, just a moment, about Big Boy's visiting here . . . ? Could you tell him about the ticket I bought for Big Boy?*)

DAISY BROWN: Big Boy would turn up at the most unexpected moments. One day we were sitting in the back eating and the bell rang. I said, "It's Big Boy." Of course, we went to the door, and there was Big Boy with his guitar over his shoulder. He stayed several days at that time, and he came back later. Sterling took him around Washington and had him play in groups at different places. They would always take up a collection for him, which he hated. One time he stayed quite a while and got away from us and went down in an area and met some people that weren't good for him.

So he turned to us, and he told Sterling what had come over him. Sterling said *okay;* he gave Big Boy the money for his ticket. And Sterling gave him some money that he had collected for him; Sterling was holding it for him. Sterling called a cab and sent him to the station to get on the train. We thought Big Boy had gone home. A few days later, Big Boy calls up crying. He had gone back into that area with his ticket and his money and his guitar. Somebody had taken everything from him and he was ashamed to call up. So Sterling said, "Get a cab and come out," and he did. Then I think Sterling gave him some clothes and a bag. Sterling called a cab and went with him to the station and bought the ticket and put him on the train. . . .

BROWN: He was a kind-hearted guy. . . . And he thought he could take care of himself. He had been a coal miner, and a load of slate did curve around his head. That's my phrase; he just said a load of slate fell, fell on him, you know. He had a beautiful voice, but he had dust on his lungs—silicosis or something. At any rate, his voice was husky and foggy. I had him record at the Department of Interior; I had him make a "John Henry." I let him meet my students. This was in the 1930s. Left-wing movements would have these get-togethers and invite cultural workers. There would be, I guess, three-quarters white workers. One white gal come in and cussed us out for calling him "Big Boy." But that was all he'd ever heard. He wanted to take his guitar and hit her over the head with it. She said, "How would you like it if one of them called you 'Big Boy'?" I said to myself, well, I've never been called Big Boy. I don't want to be called Big Boy. I couldn't quite explain it, but I had never thought of it in those terms, you see. I know damn well how much I would have resented it if one of them had called me "boy," but "Big Boy" was his name. That's all he knew. He wanted to hit the woman. She was one of the ultraliberals. He was a heavy drinker.

My guide in all of this stuff was Poodle, Poodle Williams. I dedicated one of the sections in the book to Poodle. He was a student of mine. Poodle was from North Carolina. He was a wonderful tale-teller and a wonderful student, one of my best students, very bright, very thoughtful, and a very nice guy. He told me Big Boy was in town. So we went over to see Big Boy at this place. It was a dump, of course. . . . After I knocked on the door, Poodle grabbed me and pulled me away from the door. And I asked, "What's the matter?" He said, "Don't ever stand at that door when you're knocking on it. You don't know what the hell is coming out of there." So we stood on the side. A woman opened the door and she said Big Boy was stretched out on a bed. He wasn't drunk, but he wasn't sober either. And he was very ashamed that I found him that way. I think he told me that day that he'd found his guitar again. At any rate, he got himself another guitar. Then he came and he dug out front of us, for Daisy. He was a wonderful guy but had little control. . . .

I used to write his letters. One time he was scared to death because some woman was coming to Lynchburg. He had this other woman in Lynchburg, and he was wondering what to do about the other woman. I had to write his letters. I was his boy—no question about it. He would have done anything for me and he knew I would have done anything for him; I sent him some money sometimes down to South Carolina. He came from Greenville. So many singers came from Greenville. Big Boy never made any records. Loved to hear records and was a good guitarist. I'm afraid he's dead now. I haven't been in touch for years and years, not since way back in the 1920s and 1930s. "Long Gone" is not Big Boy. "Long Gone" is a picture of a picture of a man who likes to wander. He's gentler than Big Boy; I tried to get that there. The jobs Big Boy had in "The Odyssey of Big Boy" he never had: I just got a bunch of jobs together, all different kinds of work. Some of them I see he wouldn't have done. He wouldn't have "busted suds," for instance. I wanted to get a picture of the itinerant Negro worker in all these various jobs. It is possible that one man could have had all these jobs. But the business about the "slate curved around his head" is my phrase. Big Boy said he wouldn't work in any more mines. He didn't have to work in the mines, you see. He would go to the mining camp and his guitar got him through. So he became an artist. He became the wandering artist. He made money from his guitar. He wasn't doing much work, and I tried to get that in the "Odyssey of Big Boy," which is as much my personal statement as it is his story. Now, "When de Saints Go Ma'ching Home" is more Big Boy's portrait. I made up stuff about his attitude toward heaven. The truth in the poetry is that it was his last song; that's the truth. After that what he dreams about is me; I put that in his mind. I do know he was very much attached to his mother; and I do know she was a little woman. I never really thought of it—except today—in terms of what is Big Boy and what is me.

ROWELL: In the first and final stanzas of "The Odyssey of Big Boy," there are lines that run something like this: "Lemme be wid Stagolee" and "Lemme be wid John Henry. . . ." Do these lines mean "Count me among these heroes"?

BROWN: No! No! No! That's what many people read it as. I'm glad they do, but those are the people he wants to be with. He's wondering whether it's heaven or hell or whatnot. Those are his boys; he doesn't want anybody's thanks. He wants strictly important people. These are folk heroes. "I got to go. When I go, whom do I want to be with? Who are my companions; who are my boys? Whom do I want to be with? I don't want no parks. I don't want no angels. I want to be with Jazzbo. I want to be with Stagolee. I want to be with John Henry, steel driving man." Those were his heroes. Daisy, tell him about Michael and his little boy.

DAISY BROWN: Michael Harper's son was just five. Michael was leaving, and the child followed him to the door. He said, "Dad, where are you going?" Michael said, "I'm going down to Washington to visit Sterling Brown." He said, "You remember Sterling Brown, don't you? He was here at our home and spent several days with us. He gave you chewing gum. He gave you candy." As Michael went out the door, the child snapped his fingers and said, "Let me be with ole Jazzbo!"

BROWN: I dedicated "The Odyssey of Big Boy" to Michael's son when I read in New York. Michael introduced me, and he gave the anecdote. Then I dedicated the poem to his son. You tell him the rest.

DAISY BROWN: That's all. I was going to say that Michael introduced you. The last part of the introduction was about Michael's son. Michael could snap his fingers so loud. The people loved it—and the reading.

A Symposium on the Life and Work of Sterling Brown: With Chet Lasell, Eleanor Holmes Norton, Paula Giddings, Sterling Stuckey, Wahneema Lubiano, and Cornel West

Edited by David L. Smith

CHET LASELL: Good morning ladies and gentlemen. My name is Chet Lasell, and I'm Director of Alumni Relations for Williams College. On behalf of the College, it's my pleasure to welcome you to this symposium on the life and work of Sterling Brown. The connections between Williams and Dunbar High go back to the era of the 1920s, when there was an influx of Dunbar graduates, including Sterling Brown, to Williams. Thus began a close and fruitful relationship that continues today. We greatly appreciate the valuable assistance that Dunbar's representatives have provided for this program today. This weekend's events, which honor Sterling Brown and celebrate the visiting professorship established at Williams in his name, would not have been possible without the generosity and dedication of the members of our Williams black alumni network and several of our graduated classes. I also want to acknowledge the hard work and involvement of the members of our Washington Alumni Association and the twenty-one Williams alumni who are members of the highly effective Sterling Brown Events Committee. We sincerely appreciate all of your efforts.

We're very fortunate to have one of the leading alumna of Dunbar High School and Yale University with us this morning. She is the Honorable Eleanor Holmes Norton, who represents the District of Columbia in Congress. Formerly the Chair of the Equal Employment Opportunity Commission, she's the ranking minority member on the House Government Reform and Oversight Committees, and she also serves on the Transportation and Infrastructure Committees. Congresswoman Norton is an attorney and a professor of law. She's a member of the Congressional Black Caucus, Vice Chair for the Congressional Caucus for Women's Issues and Secretary to the Democratic Congressional Campaign Committee. For many years she's been a leader in championing the cause of civil rights. It's a privilege for me to introduce Congresswoman Eleanor Holmes Norton.

ELEANOR HOLMES NORTON: Thank you very much. Thank you very much. Thank *you* very, very much. Friends and alumni of Williams College and ladies and gentlemen: I can't tell you what a pleasure it is for me to extend my greetings to you this morning. I can only express my regrets that I will not be here to hear the content of the symposium. I would really like to be able to do that. I apologize that Saturday is the day when members of Congress make their rounds. That is to say, you get scheduled into many events in your community. This is the first event of the day and it is one that I would certainly not have missed under any circumstances, for I am so pleased and proud that Williams College has essentially made this Sterling Brown weekend in Washington, D.C., with this wonderful symposium inaugurating the establishment of the Sterling Brown Visiting Professorship.

Like you I am of course proud of the achievements of Sterling Brown, Class of '22, but I come in special tribute to Sterling Brown, Class of 1918, because that is when he graduated from Dunbar High School, where I was also educated. And that is what Dunbar High School did for us. We did not attend Dunbar High School. We were educated at Dunbar High School. So I come not so much as Congresswoman Eleanor Holmes Norton, but as Eleanor Holmes Norton, Class of '55, proud to pay tribute to Sterling Brown, Class of 1918.

Brown as an intellectual and a poet surely was influenced not only by legendary Dunbar High School, but by the great poet for whom Dunbar was named. If Paul Laurence Dunbar was the father of the poetry of the Negro idiom, Sterling Brown was the son. Brown studied the idiom and he spoke it and he wrote it. And he wrote it and spoke it with such great wonder, I am sure, in no small part because he was from the city and was educated at Dunbar. Actually, Brown spoke two languages. Listen to Brown, the intellectual, the student of American literature, the American poet; these few lines from "Mill Mountain"

> The moon is but a lantern set by some
> Old truant shepherd to light up a field
> Where strange and brilliant stones sparkle at one
> From the blue darkness. . . .

And now hear part of what he had to say in a very different voice, using the idiom brilliantly to capture a part of the black psyche, as nothing else possibly could. It's from a poem called "Sister Lou," and the poem is about how to accept death.

> Let Michael tote yo' burden
> An' yo' pocketbook an' evahthing
> 'Cept yo' Bible,
> While Gabriel blows somp'n
> Solemn but loudsome
> On dat horn of his'n.
>
> Honey
> Go straight on to de Big House,
> An' speak to yo' God
> Widout no fear an' tremblin'.
>
> Then sit down
> An' pass de time of day awhile.
>
> Give a good talkin' to
> To yo' favorite 'postle Peter,
> An' rub the po' head
> Of mixed-up Judas,
> An' joke awhile wid Jonah.

The Brown of the first poem, "Mill Mountain," and the Brown of the second poem, "Sister Lou," both bear the strong influence of Dunbar High School and Paul Laurence Dunbar. For most of its history, Dunbar was the only college preparatory high school for Negroes. Dunbar took its role very seriously. Dunbar was very self-conscious about its role. I graduated from Dunbar the year after the Brown decision. For decades Dunbar students had been besieged by talent scouts from all the best colleges. That's how Sterling Brown got to Williams.

This school passed on its tradition, which Sterling Brown passed on to me and to today's students. Although the Dunbar of today faces very different challenges, because young people today and the city today, face very different challenges. And, of course, because of what time has done to all the old cities. Nevertheless Dunbar still takes seriously its role in the tradition of Sterling Brown. I thank Williams for the honor it is paying a great alumnus and for the honor you pay Dunbar by deciding to come to his hometown in order to celebrate his life and his achievements here where he began them. Thank you very much.

DAVID L. SMITH: I'd like to thank you all for coming out this morning. Thanks to Chet for that nice introduction. And thanks to Representative Norton for coming to welcome us to Washington. My impulse was to come in this morning and read one of Sterling Brown's blues poems, but I restrained myself. I thought I'd just bring the book and let him watch us as we proceed. And we will be hearing bits of his poetry from various voices throughout the day.

The work of a college extends beyond its locality, just as the work of professors extends beyond their classrooms, so it's very fitting for us to have a Williams occasion here in Washington. It's part of a college's mission to be an actor on the world stage, and it's so fitting for us to be honoring Sterling Brown, who was both a very distinguished alumnus of the college and a unique figure in African-American cultural and intellectual history. It's a special event for us to be honoring him and it's good for us to be here in Washington to do it.

I want to say a little bit about what makes Sterling Brown special and then to go on and attempt to introduce today's panelists. Before I go on, I'd like to ask the speakers to come up and join us: Paula Giddings, Sterling Stuckey and Wahneema Lubiano. [*Applause*] Thank you.

Sterling Brown was special for many reasons: because of his great intellectual power, because of the scope and depth of his scholarship and because of his poetic talent, but also because of his sensibility and the commitment that he brought to his work—his unique ability to combine "the high and the low" as Langston Hughes put it. To escape from that dilemma of self-defeating double consciousness and to say that to be a black person does not mean that you must reject one part of your heritage for the pursuit of some other part of it; that you can be two different things at the same time, so that you can be a high-toned Howard professor and you can still embrace the blues. That was a message that nobody in the academy had delivered on the national stage before and too few of us have managed that since. So he's very important to us as intellectuals because of what he represented in his ability to unite those two essential aspects of our work: that is, the roots in the black common culture and the training in the best institutions of the land (Williams and Harvard in his case). The speakers that we have asked to join us today embody those qualities. There are a lot of people who would love to be here to participate, to talk about Sterling Brown, who were his students and protégés and I think you've done very well this morning with the people who have agreed to join us. They all have deep interest in music and popular culture and politics—they have an activist spirit and a deep sense of history and a sense of calling as teachers—those things that Sterling Brown so well exemplified.

Paula Giddings is best known for her book *When and Where I Enter*, and it was an important book on the history of African-American women because it called attention to the activism of the black women's club movement around the turn of the century, and made clear how middle-class activism contributed to the social struggles that continued right down through the civil rights movement. She brought that important group of black women activists to the attention of our generation of students and historians. It was an important contribution.

She has worked as a journalist and as an editor at Random House, and she's currently a professor of African-American Studies at Duke University.

Sterling Stuckey is an historian, maybe best known for his book *Slave Culture*. He is someone who also has deep involvements with music. I just discovered he has a weekly jazz show out in California. Those of you who know *The Collected Poems of Sterling Brown* know that he wrote an introduction to that volume. His work is very concerned with cultural inheritances of Africans in this country that allowed them to survive the dehumanization of slavery. *Slave Culture* explains the place of the ring shout ritual and how that gets carried over into the black church. It shows how black people were able to find a space in which they could heal themselves and express their spirituality and carry on, confronting the challenges of a racist America. Professor Stuckey teaches at the University of California, Riverside.

Wahneema Lubiano has not only the Howard connection, but also Williams connections. She was one of the first Gaius Bolin scholars. I should say that it's a little unusual for institutions like Williams to be honoring someone like Sterling Brown, but it's not so unusual for Williams because we do have the Gaius Bolin Fellowship which annually brings a pair of minority graduate students to work on their dissertations and to do a little teaching at the college. We were the first ones to offer that kind of fellowship. Many people have copied our model since then. Wahneema was one of the first recipients, so she spent a year at Williams. We also have a lectureship named for Sterling Brown's doubles tennis partner—Allison Davis—a very fine part of our intellectual life at the college.

But anyway, back to Wahneema. She has taught at the University of Texas and at Princeton. She is now in the Literature Program and African-American Studies at Duke. Professor Lubiano's work is well known for her skill at bringing a combination of Marxist, feminist, and poststructuralist theories to bear in the analysis of African-American popular culture, especially films like *Do the Right Thing* and *Deep Cover*. She is the author of two forthcoming books. I will just mention a book that she edited which appeared last winter, called *The House That Race Built*. It is a collection of essays based on talks given at a Race Matters Conference at Princeton two years ago: certainly the most exciting intellectual event that I ever attended. It commemorated the occasion of Cornel West leaving Princeton and going to Harvard. I'm not sure whether he did the right thing or not, but it was a wonderful conference. And the papers from that are collected in that volume, which I encourage you to sample if you have not. We'll have time for some questions at the end of the session. I'd like to stop talking now, and we'll hear from Paula Giddings.

PAULA GIDDINGS: Good morning. It's wonderful to be here with you and I want to greet the Williams alumni and family and friends, as well as the other guests here on this very, very auspicious occasion. I really appreciate the opportunity to be a part of this symposium and celebration of Sterling Brown's work and life.

I have had a wonderful time these last few weeks revisiting and rethinking my encounters with Sterling Brown: first as a student at Howard University between 1965 and 1969, and then as an editor of Howard University Press between 1971 and 1973.

In many ways, Sterling Brown was a major inspiration for my wanting to become a serious writer at the time—a serious poet—in a period when I took myself *very, very* seriously. I entered college in a period when there was a great push to integrate black students in predominantly white universities. In fact, if I remember correctly, this was a major focus of the United Negro College Fund at that time. But despite their recommendations, and despite the caveats of a domineering New York University-educated grandfather, whose opinion usually held sway in the educational matters of the family, I was set on Howard University. I had to be there. I had to be in that firmament where scholars like Sterling Brown resided. And I felt this especially acutely as a black woman who was interested in writing and being involved in black cultural life.

When I arrived at Howard in the Fall of 1965, I was not disappointed. The first freshman assembly, and the only one that I remember vividly, featured Robert Hayden reading his poetry. When Hayden strode across the stage, head full of wild curls, a red-lined black cape draped fashionably about his shoulders, and read through coke glass thick glasses, "Runagate, Runagate," I knew I was in the right place. I had found my people.

Of course this was also the Howard where Owen Dodson was in the Theater Department directing plays of Baldwin and Baraka, the latter of whom scandalized the place when he stood up after a play of his and carefully informed the audience of every four-letter word that had been excised from it.

And Howard was also the place where Jean Marie Miller and Arthur P. Davis introduced me to Negro literature (as it was called then) and confirmed my determination to lead a writer's life. We read Sterling Brown in Arthur's class, of course, and I came to appreciate the reasons why James Weldon Johnson, in his introduction to Sterling's *Southern Road*, had placed him on the same rung as Jean Toomer, Langston Hughes, Claude McKay and Countee Cullen. Arthur told us about his collaboration with Sterling Brown and Ulysses Lee for the canonical text the three of them co-edited together, *The Negro Caravan*.

It was during one of Dr. Davis's classes when I first laid eyes on Sterling, who was peering in at us through a small rectangular window of the closed classroom door. His presence had been announced by a muffled gasp from the students, as he had a baseball cap on—turned backwards—a baseball bat in hand, and was making faces at us. When Arthur Davis saw him he smiled wanly, waving him away with feigned exasperation, then shaking his head with some amusement. From this first encounter I would expend a great deal of energy during my remaining years at Howard, trying to solve this puzzle of Sterling Brown, a puzzle that I intuitively knew (and it was intuitive—I didn't intellectualize any of this) had to be understood if I were to complete my artistic mission at Howard. I never had him as a professor. I'm not even sure he was teaching in these years, but I tried to understand the whispered narratives about him, because his presence was always there at Howard. I tried to understand the contradictions in the fact that he, as he was fond of saying, was born on Howard's campus, but curiously was an organic part of the campus while also being apart from it—or at least from its pretensions. In my adolescence I wanted to make sense of this distinguished light-skinned, straight-haired scholar, educated in elite schools, who was rarely seen at functions where other light-skinned, straight-haired scholars from elite schools gathered. Here was a Williams and Harvard graduate who cast his lot with the blues and folk language and experience. Here was a man who cast his lot at Howard University despite offers from other prestigious colleges and universities at the time. He was a literary man who denied the reality of the most compelling aesthetic movement in black literature: the Harlem Renaissance. Sterling was the son of a distinguished minister who had no difficulty spouting what was considered profanity, or mocking the idea of Howard being the capstone of Negro education, which it thought of itself as. I remember his presence at another Dr. Davis class where we were watching a 16mm film, when the film machine broke down. And this, of course, caused quite a delay because no one had the slightest idea how to fix it. Suddenly Sterling blurted out, "If just one of you niggers had gone to Tuskegee, we wouldn't have this problem." [*Laughter*] Like you, people started to laugh at the remark, but the laughter was cut short because Sterling's face was absolutely serious—deadpan. And in fact I think some of us began to wonder if indeed one of us should have gone to Tuskegee.

Many tried to explain Sterling's unconventional behavior by noting what appeared to be his emotional instability. Little was mentioned about the disappointments in his own career. Little was mentioned about the treatment of the administration and other professors toward him at Howard, the place that he was somehow bound to. Little was mentioned about the jealousy many professors had of the love and loyalty Sterling's students had for him. Instead, discussions of Professor Brown usually ended with a lowered voice, and meaningful glances which reminded that he had spent time, after all, at St. Elizabeth's. I remember trying to process the fact, and one of the most vivid memories I have is of my friend, the poet Gaston Neal, taking me to the grounds of the psychiatric hospital to point out the window of the room where Sterling had stayed. I remember wondering what he saw when he peered out of it.

To my great loss I let Sterling Brown slip out of my consciousness when I discovered that his iconoclastic nature did not embrace what we younger people thought the very essence of iconoclasm: the black arts movement. I was most excited by the black poetry movement of the mid to late 1960s, that had been given recent institutional recognition by John O. Killen's writers' workshop at Fisk University in Nashville, Tennessee. Brown, however, had no interest in a movement that attempted to separate blacks from the skin of mainstream American culture, a position that so many of us crudely interpreted as unmodern and even worse, reactionary.

I left Howard with poems published in black poetry anthologies, racially righteous criticism in the John Johnson publication *Black World* as a flaming, if superficial cultural nationalist.

After editing a poetry anthology at Random House, where I worked after graduation, and copyediting Baraka books as well as learning a broader social history of American letters through the Random House files, I returned as an editor at Howard University Press, thinking I was quite prepared for anything. When Sterling Brown saw me on the campus, no doubt earnestly going about some editorial task, he was never able to call my name. He would call me "the young lady who runs Howard University Press." I still did not know what quite to make of him, or that comment. I did know that he and Arthur Davis had had some recent tension, and I had recently edited Arthur's book *From the Dark Tower* for Howard Press, so I was a little wary. But I did begin to understand that in some way his approval or validation of what I was doing and hoped to be was important. I think this feeling became clear when I began to get a real idea of his relationship to African-American culture and language. I still hadn't the means to intellectualize that relationship. I had not, as John Edgar Tidwell observes, perceived how Sterling Brown's relationship to the folk and to the folk language and culture, were so profoundly different from that of the romantic Europeanized view of Alain Locke, or Benjamin Brawley's disdainful ideas about it. I didn't understand how Sterling had been able to locate himself in such a way that he dealt with the cultural issues without the double consciousness that so many of us have. He did not see folk culture and language from without but, despite his training, from within. As a result of his worldview, he was able to suffuse folk expression with the power and meaning as none had before him. I still didn't know the significance of his appointment as editor of Negro Affairs for the Federal Writers' Project, between October 1937 and April 1938, when he created a model for humanizing the representation of black subjects, and gave distinct instructions on how to accurately capture the folk idiom. One did this by privileging blacks themselves as their own interpreters, and putting their lives and thus the organic life force of the language at the center of that representation. I certainly didn't understand how his paradigm—insisted upon with great personal and professional cost, by the way—was a model for the study of blacks in all the humanities which would inform the entire Black Studies Movement. And certainly I didn't know how Sterling had even gotten that appointment at the Federal Writers' Project. What had prompted it was a letter from John P. Davis, then Executive Secretary of the Joint Committee on National Recovery, who had written: "You will perhaps remember that in a previous book of photographs published through the Civil Works Administration, there appeared the picture of a group of Negro workers in baseball uniforms. Under this picture there appeared the insulting caption, 'They have substituted baseball for crap shooting.' I am certain," said John Davis, "that such an unfortunate incident gives me good reason to suggest that positive action be taken on your part to confer with Negro authorities on the matter of materials to be included in the *American Guide*." That "action" resulted in the appointment of Sterling Brown, and I couldn't help thinking hauntingly of my first seeing him in that baseball uniform.

I think I began to know something of Sterling when I found myself one late afternoon with others from Howard University Press in that sacred inner sanctum of his: the basement of his house, where he would listen to and share his jazz and blues record collection. He played a lot of 78s, I recall, and it was probably the first time I had heard Bessie Smith and Ma Rainey and a lot of other people I had even vaguer knowledge of. There was no reason to be wary of Sterling's humor here. In that basement his laughter was in sync to the rhythms of music and language we all shared. Every record would lighten his face and his laugh. His features would soften and he would slap, I remember, his knee in appreciation to a particularly important part of the music.

When I looked at him and I looked at his relationship to that music in those moments in the basement, all those razor edges began to soften and they seemed to melt into what it meant to be an African-American, brought up on Howard's campus, schooled at Williams and Harvard, educated on his own southern road where the experiences were rich and where the fidelity to them were profoundly isolating.

If I were a better storyteller, I would end this narrative here. It was such a wonderful moment with Sterling, and I used to wish that indeed that was the last indelible image I had of him. But it wasn't. The last image was much more harrowing. It was on a dreary winter day, and I on one of my earnest missions went to his house to deliver by hand a book contract for a forthcoming collection of his writings to be published by Howard University Press. I was feeling particularly good that day. Not only was I anticipating working with my new-found blues buddy, but I had just published my first article of criticism for Random House in a publication called *Amistad II*. In any case, Sterling Stuckey, by the way, had written an important piece on the Amistad Mutiny, which is another story in and of itself. I had written about a writer of the black poetry movement by the name of Don L. Lee, now Haki Madhubuti. It had just been published and I remember going to Sterling's door, knocking on it, and his opening the door and kind of squinting at me. His face looked very different than I'd seen it just a few weeks before listening to the records, and suddenly he started screaming at me: screaming to the point that his face turned red. He said, "I saw that article that you just published. How dare you write about some of these johnny-come-latelies, when there's so many of us who need to be written about and are being forgotten. How dare you! What do *you* know? What authority do you have to write such a thing, to do such a thing, to make such choices? Get away from me!" he screamed. He cursed at me. "Get away from me!" And slammed the door in my face. It was the only time in my adult life that someone's invectives had reduced me to tears. He had hit me right where it hurt, not only personally, but I felt that I had been cast out of this kind of magical sphere that I thought that I had at least made the most tentative steps in becoming a part of.

Eventually though I recovered—with some help from Sterling Brown himself, who some weeks later I saw standing in line for a play at the Howard Theater. I was standing in back of him when he saw me; he turned around and said to me with a big smile on his face, "How is the young lady who runs Howard University Press?" as if nothing had happened. His wife, I remember, looked at me very sympathetically, understanding everything in that wise black woman way.

But if he had forgotten or dismissed the previous episode, I never did. And now I'm glad it happened. It was a way in which it sharpened some of my ideas and thoughts about things and about legacies and about the need, when writing about anything in the present, to acknowledge the past, if the present is to mean anything.

I also understood about having to engage; that if you aspire to inhabit those sacred realms, dues have to be paid by engagement, not just observation, not just by being smart, but by engagement, and at great cost. That is what creates the art. This is what Sterling Brown, of course, did. And I belatedly pay homage to his example and honor the price he paid for it and will always appreciate Williams for its recognition today of his greatness. Thank you. [*Applause*]

STERLING STUCKEY: After hearing Paula Giddings, I whispered in her ear, "I hope I'm not next," yet here I am.

Sterling was a fine student of American history. The fact that this event is being held in the Charles Sumner Museum, formerly a high school, a public school, resonates with his deep engagement with history and with his appreciation of the abolitionist movement. It is certainly an honor to help celebrate the inauguration of this chair named after Sterling A. Brown, and I am grateful for having been invited.

With a voice as natural as the seasons, Sterling had a way of instructing that left lasting impressions. There was a time in 1964 when I referred to something as "very unique" and Sterling pointed out that such was not possible. When I registered surprise, he explained that if something is "unique" there is nothing else like it; hence, no need for "very" unique. Decades later, when he was suffering from leukemia and living with his sister Helen, next door to the 1222 Kearney NE address, where he and his wife Daisy had lived, I went to visit him and found him gaunt, with long white hair almost reaching his shoulders. He was not in a talkative mood, so I did not stay, but returned a few months later to see him at the Tacoma Park rest home. As I crossed the threshold of his room, I heard him saying, "Oh here he comes, Mr. Very Unique." [*Laughter and applause*]

He taught to the end, the ironic smile no less playful. For all his vanity—and Sterling was certainly vain—there was a lack of pretension that endeared him to workers no less than to intellectuals and artists. My father, who was not an educated man, was perfectly at ease around him. On his numerous visits to our home, there was also a certain ease between him and my mother, the poet Elma Stuckey, some of whose poetry he promised would be in the revised edition of *The Negro Caravan*, in the section with the poetry of Anne Spencer, to whom Part One of *Southern Road* is dedicated.

Sterling was generous with money, his time, and his books. Forty-one years after the appearance of *Southern Road*, he gave me a copy, inscribing it, *"Butterbeans fo' Clara, Sugar Corn for Grace. . . . / And fo' de little feller* [Sterling himself] / *Running space."* Those lines are from "After Winter." There followed these lines: "For a good friend, Dr. Sterling Stuckey, from Helen D. Brown (Sterling's youngest sister), and Sterling A. Brown, June 26, 1973." I wondered then if Helen wanted him to give me that copy of *Southern Road*, for it was one of his last.

I tried to suggest something of the complexity of his character when wondering how a "Williams College Phi Beta Kappa, a Harvard man, a college professor, and an eminent writer, could have a voice with so much of earth and sky and sunlight and dark clouds about it, an instrument Blues-tinged." That was in the introduction to the Beacon Press reprint of *Southern Road*. Two years before the reprint appeared, he looked at the cover of the November 1970 edition of *Negro Digest* on which there were photos of Claude McKay, Langston Hughes, Countee Cullen, Arna Bontemps, and Sterling himself, under the heading "The Harlem Renaissance Revisited," and remarked, "I'm the only one left."

As a guest in his home he insisted that I sleep in the basement, not in the guest room. It was the only time I knew Sterling to be right in a dispute with Daisy. He understood that I would be happier in the basement than in the guest room that she had set aside for me. The attraction there was the light of morning that illuminated vertical stacks of jazz and blues recordings. I imagined having heard them all the way I sometimes imagined having read every book in his library that extended to shelves in closets and to the floor of his living room. Though he had read more than his distinguished colleagues at Howard—"They knew this to be the case," he once said—there was nothing of the pedant about him.

Sometimes following a party, when the guests were gone, I'd play records on an old victrola, that he kept in the basement. No matter how interesting the people invited to Sterling's parties, for me his parties were music parties, the only ones I had known up to that time or since. His guests might include a Broadway singer, a psychiatrist, lawyer Timothy Jenkins, critic Stephen Henderson, poet Samuel Allen, critics Arthur P. Davis and Ulysses Lee, relatives Jack and Betty Dennis, and other friends. One was brought within Sterling's inner circle at those parties, which is how I met Sam Allen and Arthur P. Davis. Though I did not know it at the time, he had brought Arthur to Howard. Sterling was no easy man to get along with but Arthur never said a word against him, even when conversation turned to the abortive, and surely for those working on the project with Sterling, difficult attempt to bring out a revised edition of *Negro Caravan,* which for learning and genuineness remains unsurpassed as an anthology of black literature. In any case, Arthur never forgot how he arrived at Howard and never said a word against Sterling.

Most of Sterling's parties were interracial but black music—he was appalled by the thought of capitalizing the word—was heard, or as he put it Negro music. I recall asking him to play a recording that I liked that had already been played— "Make me a Pallet," one of the many blues and jazz records heard beneath the conversation. Sterling seemed perturbed but played the record. I never did that again. [*Laughter*]

At those parties, each record was selected to precede or to follow another, all constituting a discreet whole. Sterling was a master at playing music, the best I ever heard, so good that I wanted to take notes on artists being played and the order in which they were heard. But one does not long concentrate that way when consuming bourbon in such company, and I wanted to hear Sterling when he talked. Whether through vanity, sheer brilliance or a combination of the two, Sterling was the center of conversation. It is some consolation to know that much of what we listened to can be found in his invaluable record collection, which I assume has been preserved.

The parties given for Sterling in Chicago were poetry parties with people half his age or younger, members of Chicago's Amistad Society, present. Characteristically, a party would follow a Brown public address at which he had drawn a line from some folk source to enthrall his audience. As in his "Slim Greer" poem, in which the South's sensitivity about sexual relations between white women and black men finds singular expression, Sterling drew on lines of folklore to get something of the same effect, in one lecture calling attention to a slave set free by a master who kept his promise. As the freedman walked away, the white man assured him, "Ole Massuh loves you and would gladly accept you back if you was to return." As the man continued to walk, Ole Massuh called out: "The children love you." As the man continued to walk, Old Massuh called out, "And Missus, she likes you."

Sometimes at our improvised parties Sterling, holding a glass of "Wild Turkey," his favorite drink, would recite lines from his "Kentucky Blues":

> I'm Kentucky born,
> Kentucky bred,
> Gonna brag about Kentucky
> Till I'm dead.

. . . .

Ain't got no woman,
Nor no Man O' War,
But dis nigger git
What he's hankering for—

De red licker's good,
An' it ain't too high,
Gonna brag about Kentucky
Till I die . . .

At times, Sterling offered suggestions about what one should read. He referred me to E. C. L. Adams's collections of tales, *Nigger to Nigger* and *Congaree Sketches*, both listed in the bibliography of *Negro Caravan*. These splendid collections appeared at a time when members of the Harlem Renaissance might have been stirred by their riches. This rebirth of genius in South Carolina Sterling thought of lasting worth, an indication of a renaissance a thousand miles from Harlem. Unaware of the degree to which African values pervade the tales, he attributed some qualities tied to those values to Adams's influence when Adams could not possibly have understood such complexities. Still, his insistence on the importance of those volumes helped lead to the discovery of African forms in slavery that revolutionized the study of blacks in America. Students of slavery and folklore owe Sterling a heavy debt.

He knew there were stops in dialect beyond humor and pathos. He knew that dialect had as many stops as the spirituals and the blues, as folklore itself since folklore was conceived in the language of dialect. Sterling used Negro dialect in his poetry out of respect for the creative intelligence of the folk the way Paul Robeson, the greatest sculptor of sound, used it in singing the spirituals and work songs of slaves. While Ralph Ellison may have been ashamed of the southern Negro, Sterling was among those who were not.

In "The Blues as Folk Poetry," Sterling writes:

But at their most genuine, they're accurate, imaginative transcripts
of folk experience with flashes of excellent poetry. They show a
warm-hearted folk filled with a naive wonder at life, yet sophisticated
about human relationships, imaginative here as in their fables and
spirituals, living a life close to the earth. With their imagination, they
combine two great loves: the love of words and the love of life. Poetry
results.

With the blues figuring prominently in his poetry, one understands his anguish when Nate Huggins, in a book on the Harlem Renaissance, gave short shrift to him as a poet of the blues; indeed, to him as a poet, arguing that Sterling did not expect his poetry to be taken seriously. I never saw Sterling so agitated in the twenty-five years I had known him. The consummate artist-scholar opposing stereotyping, he had been accused of it. The charge was damaging in part because a lot of people reading Huggins did not know Sterling's poetry or his landmark essay, "Negro Character as Seen by White Authors," the finest article on the subject of distorting the character of blacks.

Sterling's treatment of the blues in "Memphis Blues" is as ingenious as any known:

> Memphis go
> By Flood or Flame;
> Nigger won't worry
> All de same—
> Memphis go
> Memphis come back,
> Ain' no skin
> Off de nigger's back.
> All dese cities
> Ashes, rust. . . .
> De win' sing sperrichals
> Through deir dus'.

Victory in his poetry is endurance, the struggle being eternal, as Ella Baker put it, until the battle is won. It is a position that draws inspiration from the spirituals and the blues, an offering of hope geared to the limitations and strengths of the oppressed. Yet Sterling taught and inspired some of the nation's leading activists—among them, Mike Thelwell, Charlie Cobb, and Courtland Cox.

I have before me—at least I had before me at the time I was writing this paragraph—a photograph of a young and slender Sterling wearing a hat with a wide brim, peering out from behind eyeglasses, flanked on either side by black men in overalls with straps around the neck. His presence is unobtrusive, almost serene. Such settings and friendships informed his attacks on those who had forgotten their roots. In this regard, I once heard him remark, and Jack Dennis will recall this, that "Harvard has ruined more Negroes than bad whiskey." [Laughter] But Sterling was not unique in holding such views, which accounts in part for his respect for Allison Davis. Though at the head of his class in everything at Williams, Allison refused to ignore the hard lives black people were living in the 1920s during the "Harlem Renaissance," a literary movement that Allison rejected as well. Part 2 of Southern Road is dedicated to him.

Sterling's intelligence leaped before one like headlights, and one could be exhausted following the light. For intellect that could wear one down, there was one other person like him in my personal experience, and that was Earl B. Dickerson, who moved north from Mississippi, where his mother was taking in washing, to attend the University of Chicago Law School. Sixty years later, while signing checks and looking up from his desk at Supreme Liberty Life Insurance Company, he remarked, "There was no one brighter than I in those classes at Chicago." Even in his nineties, Dickerson had flashing quickness that required unflagging alertness to follow him as he rubbed his hands, sometimes smiling.

Because Sterling did not feel the need to show off his learning, the emphasis at Howard on who held a doctorate was cutting, especially since he was the most learned in that constellation of academics. A scholar who, despite brilliant graduate work at Harvard, had not taken the doctorate, his genius was not sufficient to please those in control of Howard until Vassar or another institution of standing among whites beckoned. That was a source of pain that affected him in ways that we still do not fully comprehend. But the larger fault was with American society, for Sterling was easily the equal of David Reisman or Robert Redfield, distinguished scholars without doctorates at Harvard and Chicago.

One longs for Sterling's satiric genius to be applied to current literary criticism, so much of which sags with horrendous jargon. Indeed, one quakes at the thought of his reaction to references to paragraphs being "unpacked," to a subject being "interrogated." One can easily imagine Sterling referring students to warehouses, police stations and to who knows what else. We may be sure that he would have a satiric antidote to the poison in the language of much criticism today.

One recalls Daisy in her rose garden and is reminded that she helped make possible much of what was best in Sterling as a person and scholar. This he acknowledged in the most lasting way available to him, in his poetry:

> We have learned tonight
> That there are havens from all desperate seas,
> And every ruthless war rounds into peace.
> It seems to me that love can be that peace.

Sterling sang beneath the stars, at times his voice the sound of winter. But rhythms of renewal and rebirth were always his greatest strengths as poet and man. [*Applause*]

WAHNEEMA LUBIANO: I'm really delighted to be here today, just like everyone else is. And I have some selfish reasons. There are three connections, real and imagined, that come together for me here. I was a worker at Howard, and I was educated at Howard; I did spend a year, as David said, at Williams College, recovering from my Stanford graduate education; and I really wish I'd gone to Dunbar. [*Laughter*]

There are so many varieties of work that one might undertake at this moment given Sterling Brown's incredible array of talents: as poet, as essayist, as literary historian, as folklorist, but I'm going to direct my attention to talking about Sterling Brown as a founding[1] literary theorist and the important relationship of his work to the field of knowledge organized under the rubric of African-American literary studies. (This talk only skims the surface of a longer work-in-progress on Sterling Brown.) And this seems fitting work for me, because it was at the very beginning of my own labor in the field, before I scarcely knew what a contribution to a field of knowledge really was, that I came in contact with Sterling Brown. I was, as I said, an undergraduate at Howard, sitting quite literally, as we say in the trade, at the foot of a giant whose dimensions I have only begun to grasp thanks to the teaching of a few of my professors then in the English Department and in Black Studies at Howard. If my own work means anything at all in this field, then many of its conditions of possibility were bulldozed into place in a mind barely aware of its own awakenings until maybe 20 years after coming through Howard and passing by Sterling Brown. I remember that as I look back at those moments in that dusty and crowded little study at the top of Founder's Library on Howard's campus. So, today I'm trying to pay at least part of my debt to Sterling Brown by thinking about his work in my field.

I referred a few seconds ago to Sterling Brown as a founding literary theorist. Why do I do so? Founding figures and founding moments have, at least it seems to me, four important functions[2] in the production of knowledge. The work of identifying such a figure and such work establishes particular conceptual emergences. It establishes the centrality of specific theoretical understandings and analyses. It establishes the centrality of particular methods for a field of study, and finally it seems to me, looking at the work of founding figures and founding moments, locates and encourages particular institutionalization of those concepts, those theories, and those methods. How might we consider Sterling Brown as a figure with his particular body of work within this framework? Well, we could begin with organizational schema set out by various thinkers over the past century. Thinkers as varied as Max Weber, Erving Goffman, Thomas Kuhn, Pierre Bourdieu, and Michel Foucault have produced accounts of the generation of core ideas articulated by particular figures or groups of thinkers that circulate in engagement with and against conventional ideas or patterns of thought by means including but not limited to the apparatuses of institutions and sites of powerful influences. These core ideas can come to be seen as ascendant or emerging, or, as I think is the case with Sterling Brown's work, a combination of such factors along with his own charisma, the sweep of his travels, and his presence in a variety of artistic and intellectual genres producing a faster, a more thoroughgoing circulation than is recognized even in the velocity and power of the moment of his ideas. But I pay some attention to that velocity, that power, in this moment. In other words, Sterling Brown's work produces an intersection of his many roads into the field of cultural production as artist, as folklorist, as theorist, as historian, as anthologist, and finally as a figure moving through, connecting with, and commenting on a rapidly emerging and multiply-sited literary and intellectual scene. This is all language to describe the different ways that he, in fact, made a field.

He secured a place for himself that had a profound effect on the body of knowledge that we refer to as African-American literature and its studies. And we can trace an account of his centrality by looking at a number of things. We can look at his artistic output—and critics too numerous to cite here, with incredibly important work, have given interesting attention to his poetry and its importance. They've looked at the way it remade and enlarged the possibilities of black language play; the way it pushed the boundaries of art and its meanings; the way that it changed a whole world of thinking when considered as a domain of more than middle-class thinking and endeavor. We know that Sterling Brown wrote blues poetry; we know that he represented folk art; we know that he reminded some and taught others for the first time about what resulted when everyday life and the possibilities of artistic form found each other in the understanding of cultural movers and shakers like himself. Or, as John S. Wright put it in an article in *The Black American Literature Forum* (Spring 1989), "Brown treated the products of folk imagination as self-conscious wisdom. Tragic, comic, ironic, shrewd, emotionally elastic, an attitudinally complex capable of supporting a variety of stances toward life." Or, if we think about this in Sterling Brown's own words, (and this is taken from *Negro Poetry and Drama*), "Negro folk songs, from the earliest dawn to the most recent moment, are available to anyone seeking to know the American Negro. And dialect or the speech of the people is capable of expressing whatever the people are, and that includes the complexity of what the people think about themselves." But it isn't just that Sterling Brown saw and treated folk imagination with respect; he made others see it and do the same thing against a powerful convention, most insistently articulated by James Weldon Johnson, but dominant among certain critical circles that most folk forms had limited artistic use and virtually no self-consciousness. It wasn't just what his poems did as art, however, that makes me want to attend to them and their circulation; after all, I said at the beginning that I'm interested today in talking about Sterling Brown as a founding figure in terms of theoretical circulation and institutional work. No, I'm also interested in what conceptual schema moved through his poems and emerged in the areas of his work. Kim Benston's work in *Callaloo* (Feb.–May 1982) addresses this. He writes: "Whereas Renaissance poets, especially Langston Hughes, saw the past as a repository of finished structures to be imitated in the poet's representation of an intensified but static moment, Brown sought to make the past available as a hypothetical, hence prophetic version, of the present." In other words, for Benston, Brown's poems inscribed the past not as a nostalgic afterthought but as a process engendering unlimited visions, not as a feeble gesture toward an unrealizable idea but as a dynamic process. And it is that dynamic, the process of the work of his in poetry, that I want to use for thinking through Sterling Brown's importance in the domain of black American literary theorizing. What Kim Benston is arguing about in regard to Sterling Brown's work demonstrates some of what I mean by establishing particular conceptual emergences. In other words, what Sterling did in his poetry, what he articulated in his criticism, was a new emergence against a really hardbound conceptual framework. By attending to Brown as a founding figure we can also see his importance along the axis of three other functions: his theoretical understandings, his methods, and the form of his particular institutional work. What my study requires is a thorough accounting of his work and its specific positioning as it modified the work of others, an effort that I don't have time to undertake here. But I would like to at least sketch out what such a study might include.

The poet Samuel Allen has written of Brown: "The body of Brown's work examines with unblinking stare the historic oppression of black humanity in this century" (*The Massachusetts Review* [Autumn 1983]). When I'm talking about Sterling Brown's work in terms of its relation to convention in this century and at the end of the last century, I want to return to a theme that he used himself to describe his work: that is, his insistence on the importance of attention to historic oppression—his attention to historical materialism and realism. The importance of those ideas as they defined and determined his method of reading and evaluation, and his anthology work, are crucial to considering how Brown influenced work in black American literary studies—especially his determination (along with that of Ulysses Lee and Arthur Davis) as it is on display in *The Negro Caravan*.

I read it through again, for perhaps the fifteenth time, for this occasion because I wanted to think about what it meant to call Sterling Brown an historical materialist and to think about what that means for his folklore, his poetry and his critical work. He talks to himself through this tremendous undertaking about the use of difference, about his fear of what difference meant in the hands of reactionaries. On the other hand, in order to write what he called "the truth about Negro writing," he insisted that we [Negroes] had to write against the "top down" representation that made anxiety its watchword and skewed what could be represented. [*Cornel West hands Lubiano a glass of water.*] Oh, thank you, Cornel. It's not bourbon, but this is great. [*Laughter*]

He begins chapter one by setting out what would be his recurring theme as he does the work of evaluating, as he does the work of trying to account for what it is that literature *does*—*not* just what it is. He talks about material conditions. And in context, he's talking about Herman Melville—the usefulness of material conditions that are reflected in what Melville knew about Negro seamen. And at the end of this chapter—with its extended response to Melville—and every chapter thereafter he puts together discussion questions. What's really compelling about those questions is how deeply embedded in his theorizing (beginning with Melville) is his sense that representation in fiction is representation in life. (I'll come back to that later.) In other words, Sterling was as serious as a heart attack in this work because these matters are serious. He was talking about the way in which literature produces not a simple-minded reflection of the world, but the way it helps make the world, especially on the grounds of a social-economic-political-cultural war in the United States, a race war.

He goes on through his chapters asking questions, providing commentary, about great American writers in general, about Negro representation in those writings, and about what black writers were doing *with* those traditions, *against* those traditions, *modifying* those traditions. He produces summary after summary where he describes the possibilities of realism, the subverting of realism, the work that realism in literature might do in order to subvert the work that real life is doing. He's sympathetic to the way in which realism is growing over a period of time—from the beginning of the century to the middle of the century. He attends to the way realism itself is providing a stage—a ground on which black writers make their own characterizations of Negroes a weapon in the war of the "real," on which some sympathetic, some progressive, white writers are remaking their own characterizations of Negroes. But he is also talking about the way in which realism itself has to break ground for a different kind of realism, a later realism. In short, I'm trying to sketch here really briefly what it means for someone to handle the socially real and to handle realism and literature at the same time without separating the two, but also without confusing the two. He continues, in later chapters of the book, to talk about the changes in the Negro as a result of urban movement and to encompass in his marking of the changes what this means for representational change. And he talks with increasing causticness about the desire of the Negro middle class to be seen in the terms of the white middle class. This caustic response was not for him the direction in which important attention to realism needed to go, but it is a way that he understood the possibility of having a transformative effect on those people who were thinking about literature, those people who were writing literature, and those people—like himself—who were producing evaluations of literature.

He ends with an explicit statement of the importance of what he (with others) called proletarian realism. This speaks of the importance of Negro novelists' treatment of the tragic in Negro experience because he was reminding his audience once again that literature doesn't just reflect the world, it helps make the work, but it helps tremendously, if you're making the world, to know something about the world. He continues in the anthology to address what I am describing here, the importance of defining and determining methods of reading and evaluation, and the importance of institutionalization. Make no mistake about it, *The Negro Caravan* was the work of someone who understood what institutional work does. Institutional work makes a "real" in terms that intellectuals, that scholars, pay attention to and that sooner or later (by whatever complicated process of dissemination is current) the rest of the world pays attention. "What was the purpose?" he asks in the preface. "It is to present a body of artistically valid writings by American Negro authors, to present a truthful mosaic of Negro character and experience in America, to collect in one volume certain key literary works that have greatly influenced the thinking of American Negroes and" ("and, I cannot emphasize this enough," he tells us) "to a lesser degree that of America as a whole." One of the most important of his aims was the need for comprehensiveness: a more accurate and revealing story of the Negro writer than has ever been told before. And why does one do this? Why does one think that this ambition might be fulfilled in, and by, an anthology? That the argument, the ambition, is remembered, is circulated; in order that it might change our conceptual fields. And, indeed, it does change the contours, the language, of our conceptual fields. Because language, institutionalized in anthologies, while seemingly born anew in our moments, never makes a complete break from its moorings. It makes change by remapping what is already available.

He talked, in his introduction, about the work that he and the other editors wanted this anthology to undertake against stereotypes: the work of revealing the Negro "himself in folk expressions and spirituals and satires, work songs and contemporary blues and the work of providing an account of themes of struggle: struggle against slavery, struggle for rights and responsibilities of democracy." This was his mantra.

And finally his—their—undertaking was to think Negro writing influenced by any number of things that now we take for granted but which we weren't quite taking for granted in the moment that the three put together this anthology: the way in which Negro writing is influenced by Puritan didacticism, by sentimental humanitarianism, by local color, by regionalism, by realism, by naturalism, and by experimentalism. In other words, in his work he did more than declare against the dangers of a category called "Negro literature" while extolling its excellences. He reminded us of how we could think about (and also how *little* people had been thinking about) Negro literature in that moment. And if he had to walk on the ground of preexisting convention and at the same time push that convention around in unfamiliar ways to do so, then it is all the more important for *us* to consider when *we* are thinking in a moment of new emergences of how unfamiliar they are. They are unfamiliar and it's that unfamiliarity that is doing much of the work.

He talked about literature by Negroes as a literature-in-process in a way similar to the argument Kim Benston develops to do justice to Sterling Brown's poetry as an interaction with the past that was dynamic (*Callaloo* [Feb.–May 1982]). And Sterling talked about Negro literature as important, of course, because of existing masterpieces, but also such literature illuminates the means by which people could *remake* social reality. Sterling Brown's attention to the socially real was moving within the currents of a larger circulation. Realism was the convention of the moment and it was the convention that he was both moving within and transforming. But he didn't lose sight of formal evaluation. When he said "masterpieces," he wasn't referring to social documents. His attentiveness to the socially real, in other words, came to be magnified, but it also came to be magnified within the terms of artistic production. That complex attentiveness came to be its own convention, unfortunately, after awhile, articulated as it was by numerous others with clumsier mouths. It was reduced to cliché. It became commonplace. On the other hand, that commonplace, that cliché, that conventionality, also provoked new emergences. Talking about those new emergences is work for another day.

But what I'd like to leave us with is this: the perception of an artist and an intellectual speaking with, and back to, his modernist moment. Modernism is vexed and fecund at the same time. In particular, modernism instantiates an intense look. over the shoulder at the past and a sense of telos—that there's something we could be approaching; that there's something we could be making; that there's an end in sight that will mean we've moved somewhere. Modernism also insists, as I've been saying again and again through his words and about his words, that art isn't just a reflection of reality, it is constitutive of reality. It *makes* the real. In his own way, Sterling Brown, like others who were part of the New Negro Renaissance that I know he also rejected in many ways, was engaged in the possibility of remaking the world of Negroes and the larger world with Negro art. He did soon what Ernesto Laclau calls "the necessary ground of inscription" (*Totalitarianism and Moral Indignation*). Sterling's work insisted on what Laclau argues is a historical necessity; that at all times it is necessary to take the ground of what has become available to you and to do some work on that ground, with that ground, and, if necessary against that ground.

So, when I think about Sterling Brown, I think about what was available to him, the language of realism, as well as those conventions against which he contended. Paramount among them was the limited understanding of others around what one might do with the folk. This is what constituted the grist for his intellectual mill. But it also constituted the means by which he made use of the apparatuses available to him, including his influences, including his friendships, including his inclusion in the very circles that he criticized, but most importantly for those of us who work in the field today, is what comes down to us in written form, and that is the construction of a particular field in a particular way. But what might be as important as what his work said and did explicitly, is what it said and did implicitly. And that is what I want to leave us with today. His work tells us that it is possible to work from a middle-class position, a position produced by the forces of history, without self-pitying hand-wringing over the distance between that position and the majority of black people. In other words, Sterling Brown didn't have to romanticize either his class alienation or fantasize his way into a dream of untroubled Negro authenticity, imagining himself *as* one of the folk in order to articulate a project for middle-class black intellectuals trying to *do* something in the service of undoing black race and class oppression. He told us that history is big but there's work to do because of where we are as much as because of who we are.

One of my last meetings with him was early in the Spring of 1978. I was earnestly trying to think about what I was going to do with my future, and I had been encouraged to apply to graduate school and think about being a professor. So, I trooped up to his office, full of self-importance and self-pity, and told him that I thought grad school was what I wanted to do. His response to what I was asking him—and he knew I was asking whether or not I should do this—was to say "Well, do you have anything better to do?" And, you know, my little feelings were hurt. I mean really hurt. And I thought to myself that he wasn't taking me very seriously. Still, I knew Sterling well enough to know that I better laugh; if you didn't laugh at Sterling's cracks, you got punished.

Still, I went off to graduate school and I became, after all, a professor.

In preparing this talk and thinking about Sterling Brown and his work in a field, and thinking about him as a founding figure, and thinking about what black intellectual production is and does as it circulates, I came to realize that he was not just laughing at me; he was asking a serious question: "Is there anything else better?" And as I thought about him, about his work, and about my own contributions to the larger work of black literary studies or black studies generally, I decided there wasn't anything better we could have done. Thank you. [Applause]

DAVID L. SMITH: I'd like to thank all the panelists for their excellent and very provocative presentations and very different presentations. We'd be happy to take questions from the audience.

QUESTION: Was Brown anxious about being defined as black? And do you see the distance between black intellectuals and common folk as a continuing problem in African-American Studies?

LUBIANO: When I was writing this talk about Sterling Brown, I was thinking about things that I had written before, arguments that I had with my graduate students who tended to despair at the distance between being in graduate school and being one of the "folk"; between being middle class and being one of the "folk"; about being in positions where they had access to some circulatory power. And I got really tired of hearing those arguments because I hear them as a kind of self-indulgent agonizing over something that's finally a product of history, and I don't think you ought to agonize over history. You have to figure out what to do with it. So, I think that "founding figures" thinking works as a way not only to understand what a project is, how one becomes part of a project, but also how one thinks about the very distances that make people agonize. What is the difference between Sterling Brown producing blues poetry, producing an anthology that tells us what to read, and what we ought to think about reading, and its distance from people producing poetry on the ground? Well, thinking about that difference and distance could produce an intellectual project that might have importance you don't understand in the moment of your thinking, but more than that, it can get you to pull yourself together and do some work. Does that make sense?

GIDDINGS: It also brings to mind something I also remember Toni Morrison saying when she was asked by the *New York Times* if she minded being called a Black woman writer rather than an American writer. And Toni Morrison said, "No, because by being a Black woman writer my world is larger, not smaller." Sterling Brown had that. That was the model of a philosophic stance that he had. That his world was so large it didn't depend on the authenticity of one or the other or some binary oppositional idea of bad and good and authentic and inauthentic. But he embraced the entire world, sometimes to his great detriment. I think it's tremendous pressure and tension to hold all of that together. But he did it and he showed us the way to do that.

STUCKEY: I think it's true that almost all American Negroes, as Sterling called them, are but a step or two away from being either slaves, or free Negroes— "slaves without masters." It is important that he had the sort of optic on our peasant ancestors that he had, acute awareness that a creative minority within their ranks was mainly responsible for our art forms and spirituality. In giving us jazz, the spirituals, blues, folk tales, and more, they have been the impelling source of the artistic genius of our people. They universalized their own subjectivity as jazz and the blues became world phenomena. By focusing on the specifics of the forms, Sterling deepened our sense of how certain of their qualities fostered such reach. But even he underestimated the power of slave folklore because, much like Adams, he did not grasp the African dimension of that body of work. This is not a criticism of Sterling as much as a commentary on the continuing limitations of scholarship on folklore.

QUESTION: Could you comment on Professor Stuckey's comments about jargon? And I'm just curious to hear any of the panel reflect on perhaps the essential nature of generational conflicts.

LUBIANO: I'd like to take a stab at it since I've had that brick thrown in my direction any number of times. What I couldn't take time to develop here was the relationship between new articulations, including new vocabularies, new complicated ways of thinking about something that are not necessarily more complicated than older ways but differently complicated. And the ways in which those different complexities along with different vocabularies sometimes carelessly used, and sometimes very well used but carelessly read, end up being mushed together in a sort of blanket condemnation. Now, I spend a lot of recreational time reading accounts of American literature and its emergence over the twentieth century. When I read accounts of literature itself as an intellectual project, I continually find the same kinds of quarrels being engaged, the same kind of brickbats being thrown. You know, "Who are these people? What are they saying? Why don't they use the language that we've always used?" Which is not to attack those who use the language that came before or to defend those who don't do anything with the new language but spew it across the page. But it seems to me that there's a reason to think about founding moments as a way to consider what is being changed, what is being challenged, what's being returned to. I was an undergraduate at Howard in Afro-American Studies and English, so, when I got to graduate school and I discovered the theories of post-structuralists, I really was fascinated by how much these theories reminded me of the theories of the black aesthetic critics. I wasn't put off by what people called the "jargon," because I was fascinated by the convergences and the divergences, but I was also spending a lot of time reading that material and that language. Nowadays I spend a lot of time explaining that material. In my graduate courses I'm going back to the black aesthetic critics in order to talk about them as precursors of certain arguments about the contingency value of language. If I'm talking to junior high school kids, and I do sometimes, the teachers in the room will interrupt to ask, "Yeah, but what about deconstruction?" Then I talk about that also, but I do so keeping in mind that I am talking to junior high school kids and their teachers as opposed as to another scholar who does the same kind of thing that I do. Success and clarity depend upon how hard you're willing to work to think about what you do and what its relationship might be to what other people are doing. And I don't mean to suggest that somehow I occupy some pure space where I don't throw some brickbats of my own, I do."

GIDDINGS: Of course you're right in that historically there are always the tensions between generations and it's interesting to think about them and what they mean in particular periods. The Black arts movement was very aggressive in trying to undermine the older generation. There was this need to not only critique the older generation, but to almost erase them as a prerequisite for realizing new notions of Blackness. I think people like Sterling Brown felt not just angry but betrayed. It made the break a terrible one and one that was very emotional.

STUCKEY: Sterling's rebukes could be terrifying, and on such occasions one felt the generation gap as at no other time. When he struck fear, silence filled the chasm. He had spoken!

But once I accompanied him to Allison Davis' apartment near the University of Chicago. The two were talking, I was reading and suddenly the conversation ended. Then Allison got up, went to the front door and opened it, and I followed Sterling out the door. Neither of us ever said a word about what had happened.

In general one felt at home around him, very much so. Typically when you are around a much older person you feel a certain distance. In the case of Sterling there was so much encouragement and so much to learn from him that one did not sense distance of the kind referred to. There were rare forms of communion when he related to the young, as when he read "Kentucky Blues," holding a glass of Wild Turkey. No young man and no other old man could have pulled it off. It is true that he was in his briar patch, surrounded by admirers, but it is equally true that few artists experienced as dry a spell of inattention, of even abuse, as Sterling. In any event, those of us in Chicago struck one helluva bargain with this poet/raconteur/dramatist. On our side, among the males, one aspired to his style of voicing the blues. It was a fair exchange.

I recall him speaking favorably of Baraka's ability. And Baraka respected him. I remember—is Roy Lewis here?—Roy taking Baraka to visit Sterling when Sterling was spiraling downward, just before I saw him with hair nearly at his shoulders, and gaunt. There were moments of tension and resonances between Sterling and the young, but he was continually reaching out to bring you closer.

QUESTION: I'd like to go back a moment to what we were talking about—the issue of the generation gap or the pattern of disruption that went on. I can recall a conversation with James Butcher. We were busy about our sit-ins and our agitation about black drama and other things like that, and Butcher took me aside because I was an older student and he thought I was wiser and he said to me, "All this that you're talking about, we did this in the 1920s." And I thought I had the perfect answer for him. . . . And I said, "Well if you had done it correctly, we wouldn't have." [*Laughter*] I think what we're talking about is really a heritage issue and that is probably what Sterling Brown was kind of struggling with. He wasn't even dead yet but already he saw evidence of being forgotten. And I think basically what he's saying is you can't be here, you can't go forward, without taking me with you. You may have a different idea about it, a different thought, but you really do have to bring me along.

LUBIANO: This reminds me of something that I learned from Cornel, because I tend to be a brute in arguments, and Cornel tends to be able to talk to people as opposed to wanting to shoot them. I learned from him that it is possible to engage across these chasms not necessarily to have happy reconciliation be the outcome, but so that the engagement itself is part of the process. It's something that I wished I'd had confidence enough to do a lot earlier in my career. I wish that when I was an undergraduate, or a graduate student, or an assistant professor, that I knew how to have a discussion across chasms, to be able to talk about these things as opposed either to being hurt by their existence or intimidated away from having a discussion.

STUCKEY: It wasn't simply that Sterling was greatly concerned and disturbed that people of his generation were being forgotten. He was concerned that Melville's *Benito Cereno* was not being read. He was concerned that the tales collected by E. C. L. Adams were not being investigated by scholars or serving as inspiration to black artists. He looked at the sweep of history, at the long process. It was not just the Black Arts Movement and matters of that sort that concerned him. He wanted young people to know and respect a whole line of thinkers from the past.

SMITH: Yes, but I would add that it's not just young people in the 1960s who were rebels and Sterling represented a kind of attachment to tradition in a pure sense. He was a rebel in his generation. He had those sharp frictions.

By writing blues poems and presenting himself the way he did he was radically in contradiction to his own forebears. And so it's not so much a question of whether you are in agreement. I listened to Wahneema's story. It's about having a clear sense of purpose, understanding that if you have talent, if you have something to give, that you have a kind of responsibility to have a larger vision of your place in history and your relationship to a larger culture, and you have to act on that, not simply to act on a self-indulgent sense of "how I feel," you know "am I more gratified personally if I don't feel tension about my place in society." He was putting that aside and saying "understand how history is made and the role you have to play in it." I think that's really the issue and you don't know, you can't predict how that's going to place you relative to the people around you. The main thing is that larger sense of mission.

QUESTION: My question is what role if any do you discern for Williams, what effect on Sterling Brown, either adverse or positive, did Williams have on the intellectual history that we're talking about this morning?

STUCKEY: I never heard Sterling comment on the negative effects of Williams—on himself—on Rayford Logan, on Allison Davis, on any other blacks who studied there. I did hear mention of some really terrible stories about Amherst. [Laughter]

They are stories that I'm not at liberty to repeat in public. But, seriously, I never heard anything said that was negative about blacks at Williams. I suggest that you might find unflattering stories about Williams and blacks in the recent biography of Rayford Logan that Chapel Hill brought out about three years ago. Some of Rayford's experiences are recounted, and I think the environment in which he moved was very similar to the one known by Allison and Sterling.

SMITH: I would just first like to point out to the audience that the questioner [Gordon Davis] is of the family of John Davis and Allison Davis and has a deep feeling for that experience that he's asking us about, having graduated from Williams at a time when there still were not many Black people at Williams. It was not as much different from the 1920s as we might like it to have been or as it was a few years later. I would just add one point about the Harvard-Williams distinction. I think the sort of Harvard style is a very particular thing that Sterling doubtless was pointing to. You know the degree to which even now there is a set of affectations that are associated with Harvard. A kind of style. I think there's not as clearly a Williams style. But there is a particular snobbishness about Harvard that would certainly have been anathema to Sterling Brown, who was so committed to maintaining that link to ordinary folk.

STUCKEY: John Dennis (Jack) is seated out there. I don't know whether Jack would care to comment on whether Sterling ever talked about the negative effects of his experience at Williams.

JOHN DENNIS: Well, Sterling always talked with fondness about his experience at Williams. He talked about his friends, and all the guys—Allison and the others that were close buddies. And when he got down to the point of rather negative things that were there, he treated them rather humorously and brushed over them and laughed at them. And he said, "You can't really believe that those brothers would do that, can you?" It was that kind of dismissal of what had happened. Even though I knew he had felt some chagrin about it in his earlier days, but as he grew older all of this was a big laugh and a big farce to him, so that he would make jokes about it. And he would make jokes about individuals who were involved in the administration. So he would brush it off. But I must say this slight anecdote about Sterling:

Sterling got into some trouble at Williams. He broke some rules that were pretty bad. And he was about to be expelled. So one of the administrators called him in and told him he was going to have to go and Sterling had a perfect tactic. He was going to play this to the hilt. He wanted to talk to whoever was the head of that particular organization. And he announced there was abuse on the part of them white people. He said this was completely racist; there was no way they could throw him out. And the man said, "Sterling I don't think you really mean that, do you?" He didn't mean it but he played it to the hilt again, and said, "I certainly mean it." Anything to him was better than getting expelled and having his minister father find out what he had done.

GIDDINGS: There is a published transcript available—it was an occasion of Sterling Brown speaking at Williams for some anniversary.

STUCKEY: "Didn't He Ramble."

GIDDINGS: Yes, exactly. And he talks . . . it's in a book of collected essays.

LUBIANO: *Chant of Saints*, for one thing and then an essay collection on Sterling Brown's work.

QUESTION: In that collection of essays he delivered the speech at Williams in 1973 and Professor Giddings is absolutely correct. He titled it, "Oh, Didn't He Ramble." But in response to what Gordon has indicated, he also referred to himself as "One of Mrs. Hocken's boys." He did that because at Williams the determination was made at that point that blacks were not allowed to live on campus. As a result they lived with a Mrs. Hocken. Ralph Winfield Scott, Carter Marshall, and Henry Brown. And in response to that our leader said he came to Williams for an education. He wanted Williams to give him an education and they would look out for their own happiness. That was sort of interesting because at that time Allison Davis, Phi Beta Kappa, Sterling Allen Brown, Phi Beta Kappa, Rayford Logan, Phi Beta Kappa. Separate but unique in a rather interesting intellectual environment. Gordon Davis is absolutely correct. Because of that kind of quasi-isolated environment that our leader referred to as a form of benign neglect, as the sun set in a kind of accepting, lasting manner, nevertheless out of that came a sort of steeled determination to be identified with the folk that made it happen. But Sterling Brown was keenly aware of who he was and where he came from.

SMITH: I would point out that collection of essays was published a few months ago. It's edited by Mark Sanders who is himself a former Bolin Fellow at Williams, coincidentally.

GIDDINGS: Cornel, you have a question.

CORNEL WEST: First I want to say this is unbelievable. This panel is unbelievable. I'm trying to catch myself in terms of there's so much coming at me. But my question is this: that when you look at the present situation and the largest generation gap in the black community that we've ever had, the story that Paula tells me is one that hit me very hard because it's difficult to have a deep sense of history and heritage, and how do you transmit that heritage to a younger generation and not then also accent how do you go about doing that? You see it's one thing to acknowledge Sterling Brown as a genius, who he was, and he was a genius. But at the same time he's crushing one of the most talented critics and poets of the younger generation, that raises deep questions, very deep questions. What's going on here? In terms of this bitterness, that becomes so self-pitying that you can't empathize with a younger group who themselves are having these troubles. Now just Sterling Brown at his best produced a whole generation of folk. There's no doubt about it. But there is something about the older generation like ourselves, we thought we'd be the young folk these days. When I'm talking about Sterling I'm talking about us as well. That in being unable to deal with our bitterness we can lash out in that way. And that's not a trivial thing if we're talking about sustaining intellectual tradition linked to the freedom struggle. For a younger generation who feels they have to reinvent the wheel every time again because a break has taken place, and it's partly because of certain cruelty that's been directed in their way when they're too young and rough and fresh to understand all the hell he's gone through. I'm surprised Paula bounced back! [*Laughter*]

That raises issues for us today as Black intellectuals. We see this younger generation of how we could come up with better strategies because none of us has the genius of Sterling that we aspire to.

LUBIANO: One of the things that I do in my own teaching is to remind my students, especially my graduate students, that I'm doing the best I can with my training and the available resources, but also with the very particular individual history that I carry with me. So, we can turn into an object of discussion my relationship with these materials in order to talk about just those cross currents that you're describing, not in order for us to give me some special attention because somewhere along the line somebody put a hand up in front of my nose, but because in a way what we're talking about writ small are the larger historical forces and are the meat of our engagements with each other. What happens between John Hope Franklin and Du Bois when they meet is not just a matter of Du Bois and John Hope Franklin, but it's a matter of the historical and intellectual dynamics that are coming together when the two look at each other. It is not just overweening pride on one hand and younger intimitability

SYMPOSIUM ON STERLING BROWN 339

on the other hand. It's the arguments that are going on. And those arguments mean something. What I have tried to do in my teaching is to talk about where our current interests have a genealogy and how it is worth exploring that genealogy even if we simply want to do the work of distinguishing ourselves from our respective intellectual histories. I mean, I want to do that, but I want to do more than simply distinguish myself. Otherwise I wouldn't spend so much time recycling other generations and older founding moments. I talk about Sterling Brown as a founding figure, not to enshrine him as a "figure" but to get people to think about what it means for those moments to be undertaken; what it means even to talk about generational progression or generational succession in intellectual work.

STUCKEY: Many of us were victims of Sterling's crushing criticism. At times his criticism could come, it seemed, for no reason at all, certainly for no good reason. But the next moment things would be fine—sublime, actually. It is well to recall that while he might have been critical of this or that writer, he was an unfailing supporter of others, of Mike Thelwell, for example. At the same time that he may have been critical of particular cultural movements, he was the one professor at Howard who openly supported the Student Nonviolent Coordinating Committee. He was the advisor to the SNCC chapter at Howard. As for the generation gap, Sterling was no respecter of age. It scarcely mattered to him whether you were eighteen or eighty, or even older. [*Laughter*]

I remember being at a Howard commencement with him when Rayford Logan appeared in his Harvard gown—they had not spoken in years—and asked, "Sterling, will you march with me?" It was a plea for peace, but Sterling waved him away. In Sterling's case, it was not a matter of how old you were, necessarily.

LUBIANO: Oh yeah.

GIDDINGS: I think the question Cornel raises is a very important one. And I think it makes us all sensitive too—because of the history of those fissures— to the younger generation today. We have to maintain those bridges, despite our dislike for much of contemporary popular culture because every generation has its own meaning. And it's our job to understand it. And that's one of the things that people on either side did not do, I think, in the 1960s. In terms of Sterling's behavior, it's not a matter of excusing it but understanding that the same things that made Sterling the genius that he was—that artistic energy—had two sides. And if you're going to accept one part of it, sometimes you have to accept the other part of it as well. And I think I'm much angrier in retrospect at people around him who didn't support, who didn't nurture that genius. And I think that's a lesson as well: we have to support people like him even, or perhaps especially, if they have difficult personalities. We have to learn how to protect people. And certainly institutions do. What Sterling Brown went through at Howard was awful and tragic. In the end Sterling actually helped me because it made me think. I felt with Sterling that, whatever he was doing, there was a truth in it. And I trusted him. One reason why it was so impactful was because you always sensed there was a truth in all of his actions and in all of his works. And you tried to figure out where it came from and what it meant. And that process was a painful process but a very, very important one. Most of us who felt his wrath believed we gained more than we lost.

PRESIDENT HARRY C. PAYNE, introducing keynote speaker Cornel West: I have the great pleasure of introducing arguably the most powerful intellectual voice of Black America, Cornel West, and how appropriate it is for this evening if part of the magic of Sterling Brown was to join the highest of high culture to the deepest and most universal of common roots in his thought and in his writing. So too, that's true of Cornel West. Cornel West was born in Tulsa, Oklahoma, on June 2, 1953. His father was a civilian Air Force administrator. His mother was an elementary school teacher who would later become a principal. The West family moved a great deal and finally settled in a middle-class neighborhood in Sacramento, California. It was there that young Cornel West began what would become a life-long habit of protest by refusing to salute the flag because of the second-class status of African Americans in this country. As a boy West was greatly impressed by the Baptist church. His grandfather had been a preacher. West had been deeply touched by stories of parishioners who only two generations from slavery told stories of blacks maintaining their religious faith during the most trying of times. West was equally attracted to the commitment of the Black Panthers, whose office was near his boyhood church. It was from the Panthers that West began to understand the importance of community-based political action. But, and this is ironic, it was a biography of Teddy Roosevelt that West borrowed from the neighborhood book mobile that would steer his academic future. He felt an affinity to Teddy Roosevelt. Both were asthmatics. He read how Roosevelt had overcome his asthma, went to Harvard and became a great speaker. So at eight years of age Cornel West decided that he, too, would go to Harvard. And so he did, graduating from Harvard, magna cum laude in 1973, in only three years. He went on to Princeton where he received his Master's and his Ph.D. in 1980. He's taught at a number of colleges and universities in the U.S. and abroad, including Williams College where he was Henry Luce Professor of Religion in 1982. At Princeton he was Professor of Religion and Director of the Afro-American Studies Department. He currently serves as Professor of Afro-American Studies and Philosophy of Religion at Harvard University. At the center of his vision is the idea of a politics of meaning. The goal of a politics of meaning is to change the bottom line in American society so that the measure of our institutions is not wealth and power but the degree to which they extend our capacities to sustain loving and caring relationships and to be ethically, spiritually and ecologically sensitive. His many books include: *Prophesy Deliverance!: An Afro-American Revolutionary Christianity; Post-Analytic Philosophy; The Ethical Dimensions of Marxist Thought;*

Prophetic Thought in Modern Times; the truly extraordinary and powerful book, *Race Matters; Keeping Faith: Philosophy and Race in America;* and with Michael Lerner, *Jews and Blacks: Let the Healing Begin.* As Sterling Brown might say, "Great Gawd but he is a man." Cornel West. [*Applause*]

CORNEL WEST: Well, I thank you so very much. At first I'd like to thank my friend and brother and the Captain of the mighty ship of Williams College, President Hank Payne, and also his lovely wife Deborah. I know it's always a family affair when you're in a leadership position. Second, I would like to thank one of the best friends that I have in the world. He's a brother of great integrity. I respect him deeply and love him dearly and I'm talking about David Smith. Let's give him a big hand. [*Applause*]

Anybody who knows anything about Brother David knows that he and Vivian are inseparable, as Natalie Cole would say. I'd like to thank Sister Paula for the vision, the energy, determination to bring us together. Let us not be deceived. This is a unique moment, not just for Williams College, not just for institutions of higher learning, but for the culture. This is a dark moment in American life for people of African-American descent. That's in part what Philadelphia was about today. The black sisters are hungry and thirsty for hope, not the garden variety version of hope, but something that's real and concrete and embodied and has something to do with the passion and vision that pulls out the best in each and every one of us and leaves back the ego. And what we've seen today, the spirit of Sterling A. Brown, is still alive. I can hear the laughter in the back. He would like that too. Let them laugh. Let them laugh, brother. But in bringing us together, and in people of African descent in Williams recognizing the grand insight of T. S. Eliot in his essay of 1919 "Tradition and the Individual Talent" where he says, "Tradition is not something you inherit, if you want it you must obtain it with great labor." And if you are to make the tradition at Williams yours, you've got to earn it. You've got to fight for it and not because it's Williams, it's fetishizing some institution, but because the best of Williams has been a force for good in America past and present. And the question becomes how do we fuse what we are and what we can do with the best of Williams College and leave the worst behind. It's true for Harvard too. Oh, that's a task, I should say.

Ezra Pound writes in the 81st Canto, "What thou lovest well is thy heritage." We know Sterling Brown's sense of who he was and our sense of who we are leads us to conclude that we are and do what we are and do because somebody loved us and cared for us and sacrificed for us. Williams College is not doing this just for Williams and not just for the present, but the hope that we can keep alive a flickering candle in the future for those who come after. I must say in all honesty I feel deeply inadequate to reflect on Sterling Brown. I first read his poetry when I was 19 years old and I had always believed that great art aspires to the condition of music. I got that from Schopenhauer. And especially in the black tradition where music has played such a unique role in soothing the wounds and bruises and caressing the deep scars. And I was looking for an analog in our literature to the genius of a Louis Armstrong and a Duke Ellington and a Sarah Vaughan. Well, I went back and looked at the literary tradition. I said, my God, for every one literary classic we have twenty-five musical classics. What's going on here? It's not just the fact that for over 244 years it was against the law for people of African descent to read under conditions of American slavery. That's one cause, but we have to be more complex than that. It was also because so many of our literary figures were so obsessed with recognition from the mainstream that they would rather emulate and imitate what's going on in the mainstream than dig deep in the wells of foremothers and forefathers who had some questions to raise, not just about America but about the human condition. Sterling Brown spoke so deep to my soul because when I read *Southern Road* I could actually feel what I felt when I listened to Marvin Gaye. And that's a whole lot. That's a whole lot. I said we have a highbrow intellectual who believes that nothing human is alien to him but who is humble enough to recognize that there's a sense of the tragic and majestic and problematic shot through the lives of what Sly Stone calls "everyday people"—James Cleveland calls "ordinary people." I began to see that there was something quite distinctive going on in the pioneering work of Sterling Brown, and let us not forget that he wrote some of his best poems in his twenties. He was born in 1901. *Southern Road* was published in 1932. Most of those poems had been published six or seven years prior. This is a level of intellectual precocity that's rare. It's true that Melville published *Moby Dick* at 32 and the great Faulkner published *The Sound and the Fury* at 32. F. Scott Fitzgerald published his grandest texts in his late twenties—twenty-nine. But even still, Sterling Brown had to cut up against a literary tradition, and specifically a black literary tradition, that was obsessed with bombarding, obsessed with responding to the stereotypical bombardment of black people. It's primitivistic—exotic objects and to fight that battle meant that he could not do one fundamental thing that black people in America had such a difficult time doing which is to simply take black humanity for granted. Don't attempt to make an argument for it. Don't feel as if you've got to make a case for it. But just take it for granted. Just assume it and then move on from there, no energy spent in a quest for recognition and acknowledgement to show how smart you really are because the hype is you're not too smart in white supremacist America past and present. Or that you can compete because the claim is that you can't compete. Just take it for granted. That's nonsense. That's so absurd. Let me go on and do my human thing like the black musicians have done. Just take the humanity for granted. Sterling Brown was the first major figure going far beyond the great Paul Laurence Dunbar. The only comparable figure would be Jean Toomer and he disappeared quickly into a sea of whiteness. He decided he wasn't black one day. Literary genius in his own right but the burden was too heavy. And of course we know the burden for Sterling. He decided to choose the kind of old Negro that he was—to use his language in that wonderful speech of September 22, 1973 that he gave at Williams. That was a choice that he made.

So in my brief analysis tonight of Sterling Brown I want to begin, not with Black America, not with America, not even with Athens. I want to begin with Jerusalem. Sterling Brown was a cosmopolitan intellectual who had a sense of calling, not just a career. He had a sense of vocation, not just a profession. That for him being an intellectual was an act of piety, not in a religious sense but in the sense that he ascribed profound significance to the very act of intellection. That's intellectual. That's different than just being intelligent. We all read Richard Hofstader's great text of 1963, *Anti-Intellectualism in America*. That wonderful second chapter, "The Unpopularity of the Intellect in America." And suggests that Americans have always put tremendous premium on intelligence because that's the manipulative faculty, it's practical. It helps you get by. But when it comes to intellect and the act of intellection Americans get a little frightened because fundamental assumptions and presuppositions are being called into question. Deep critical and constructive and creative thinking is going on, not just how you can manipulate your situation such that you conform to what's in place already. And this is true with every color. But Sterling Brown was first and foremost a highbrow, cosmopolitan intellectual, which meant that he understood himself as part of world history. We saw this at work this morning in such high quality presentations, I must say. It was unbelievable. David Smith, Sterling Stuckey, Wahneema Lubiano, Paula Giddings, it was just high quality. And what we saw was the expansion of their horizons so that any attempt to confine Sterling Brown to one institution or another institution or one culture is too parochial and provincial.

That's why I begin with Jerusalem because, see, my thesis is this: that Sterling Brown was the first major intellectual in America to discern, detect, depict and defend a democratic mode of the tragicomic, which is to say that for the first time there's a tragicomic understanding of the world under democratic conditions created by victims of American democracy. Let me say that again. He's the first to examine the complex dynamics of a tragicomic conception of being human under conditions of modern democracy created in the doings and sufferings of victims of American democracy. You will recall that was Malcolm X's scientific definition of a nigger: a victim of American democracy. And let us never forget that democracy is democratic energy from below. Very rare in human history, very rare. In most societies, the elite's at the top, consolidated, unified, coercing labor, not allowing possibility of opposition and dissent and thinking they will live forever. That's one of the problems I have with my Afrocentric brothers and sisters. They trot out the wonders of Egypt to me. And the unbelievable, and it's true, incredible pyramids, but the question is who built them and did they want to build them? What were the conditions under which they were built? And did those who built them, did they have the right to be buried in them or were they reserved only for the pharaoh's household? Sterling Brown begins in Jerusalem—not just because of his father who was born a slave in east Tennessee, a Christian minister, Fisk University, Oberlin College Seminary, head of Lincoln Temple Congregational Church, but because he comes out of a particular culture of people of African descent who had creatively appropriated stories and narratives linked to Jerusalem called Christianity. We can't understand the distinctive form of the tragicomic without understanding the Black church as this crucible that would dish out such profound products in the United States that would affect not just all Americans but now affects the world given the Americanization of the world. Sterling Brown is a world-class intellectual in terms of his connections. Now what is it about Jerusalem? We know something extraordinary happened in 1250 B.C. For the first time that we know in human history, disenfranchised peasants came together—didn't just talk about it, didn't just project a vision—but they organized and mobilized and viewed themselves in covenant with a God who fundamentally identified with oppressed people and drew a fundamental distinction between history and nature, no longer had polytheistic reflections linked to the functions of nature, but a Yahweh who was identified with a historic people in order to do what? To believe that prevailing historical circumstances could be changed and transformed by means of collective struggle and collective agency and collective insurgency. That is a fissure in the history of the human adventure. This marks the emergence of the Hebrew bible. And they began to reflect and say, "My God! We have different conceptions of justice and mercy and power and humility because we have a covenant." But still a choice, an intentional deliberate choice that says democratic energies from below will now bubble up and the elites in Canaan are in trouble.

That's very important. That's 1250 B.C. For over two hundred years you had this project. And of course the monarchy sets in, a divided monarchy sets in exile, and post-exile and so forth. But this is crucial. Why? Because further down the line there will be a people of African-American descent that will find in these stories—the narratives of Hebrew Bible—and the New Testament in order to understand in their linking of these stories to their enslavement in the most enlightened, free, democratic experiment in the modern world called America. The hypocrisies already begin to surface because both propositions are true. This is our challenge. Both are true. The freest, most enlightened, most democratic project in the world but rooted in white supremacist subjugation. How do we keep track of both? You all recall what F. Scott Fitzgerald said, "The test of a first-rate mind is the ability to hold two opposing ideas in the mind at the same time and still retain the ability to function." That's a difficult thing. But we can't keep track of Sterling if we don't understand the legacy of Jerusalem, if we don't understand the conception of justice and mercy and struggle among the least of these. You all recall that fascinating first chapter in Erich Auerbach's great classic of 1946 entitled *Mimesis* where he begins the juxtaposition of Homer and the Old

Testament. He says, "What is it about Homer that differs from the Old Testament?" It's a fascinating text. Odysseus, the man of sorrow, does move us in so many ways, but in Homer there're only two members of the lower classes who emerge. The sister who finds a thigh in Book 19 of the *Odyssey* and the other servant and they have no life of their own, no individuality whatsoever. Auerbach goes on to say that in this Old Testament, in these stories of the Hebrew Bible we see that everyday people can aspire to the heights of existential elevation and find themselves falling into the depths of existential humiliation. We can begin with David. These are ordinary people. They go up and they go down. We can listen to the wisdom of so-called lower-class home boys like Amos, "Let justice roll down like waters and righteousness like a mighty stream." That's Anacostia kind of language in 1997, that's on the other side of town. That's not Beltway talk. That Old Testament allows everyday, ordinary people that have something to say about not just themselves and their interests but about quality and of course this is so very important in any serious discussion about diversity.

We're here for diversity at Williams, not because we want Williams to be more diverse; because diversity and quality go hand-in-hand when done in the right way. That's what we're talking about. You listen to Josiah or Amos, not because they are underclass or lower class, but because they have something to say. You can listen to the upper-class brothers and sisters if they have something to say. But Jerusalem is very important. And, of course, for Sterling Brown, that Jesus of the New Testament, that particular Jew who flows out of reform energies of Judaism, was very important. Brown was shaped by this particular figure of the artisan class, whose father was a carpenter, whose mother was rooted in the same Judaic tradition but at the same time wondering whether something unique was happening that would transgress against the law—that would bring together disciples from various classes who would come to Jerusalem and do what? Weep. That fundamental prayer that so many Black children have been taught. If you can't say nothing else at the dinner table just say, "Jesus wept. He wept." We'll see when we get to Athens that Socrates never weeps. He never laughs. He argues interestingly but he never weeps, he never laughs. That's different. Why did Jesus weep? Because he loved. Why did he love? Because he thought his love could make a difference in changing the world, that his blood could have an impact. Part of that same tradition. This democratic sensibility believes that everyday people ought to have a right to decency and dignity, a belief that prevailing conditions, no matter how dark, can be changed by means of serious struggle, engagement, and also an attempt to keep track of the contradictions and intentions that shot through our very hearts and souls, hence a humbling aspect. Jerusalem. Sterling Brown. Jerusalem. Black culture. Jerusalem. American culture. Very important. But Athens meant much to Sterling Brown too.

Something did happen in 508 B.C. Cleisthenes engages in the first major democratic reform that we know of that moves an allegiance of persons from family to the deme. Which means what? Which means that we have to break the links between clan and family and tribe and attempt to convince persons to engage in an ascent of allegiance and identity to something bigger than just their family and their tribe and their clan. It's called deme, it's called a democratic entity. And Cleisthenes in 508 does it because of what? Because of energy from below, organizing peasants from below, trying to expand their possibilities, the beginning of a very precarious experiment in democracy called Athenian democracy.

But again, a distinctive moment in the human adventure in terms of democratic energies from below doesn't last too long historically speaking. Alexander the Great, expansionism, Macedonian domination, you all know the story. Sterling Brown learned what from Athens? The unexamined life is not worth living. Know thyself. To plunge within the depths of the abyss of one's own soul requires as much courage or more than that of a soldier on the battlefield. An unexamined life is not worth living, and an examined life is painful. Courage has a distinct virtue. People have criticized Jesus for not asking enough intellectual questions. People criticized Socrates for not learning how to dance or laugh. Nietzsche argues he wants a Socrates who dances, as many Christians have argued they want a Jesus who laughs as well as weeps.

We're on the way to Sterling Brown and the blues. Black America believes in a weeping Jesus and a loving Jesus. It has intellectuals like Sterling rooted in self-examination, in self-exploration and in self-experimentation, digging deep to know thyself and all of the terrifying and horrifying effects that follow from such inquiry: We are going to get a sense of the comic. We are going to get an African people who put a certain premium on body, a passionate physicality that flows from the legacy of Western African cultures, and for the first time we get a major wedding of the spirituality of genuine loving and caring associated with Jesus, and the spirituality of genuine questioning and seeking associated with the legacy of Socrates combined with a deep sense of the comic. Laughing at it, laughing at one's self, knowing that you're dealing with something so absurd that's coming your way called "white supremacy." Hearing fellow citizens talk about how free the nation is but you're enslaved. You've got to look at this and say, this is absurd. It's crazy. It's ridiculous. Have a laugh, John. Tell a joke. Sing a song, Sally. It could be that we're crazy.

De Tocqueville can come as a young French aristocrat and all he sees is equality. Alexis, where have you been hanging out brother? Come over to the plantation of 1825. Come on brother. We know that Alexis is more complex than that. He said, "Well what I really meant was that much of the population were in a different situation than the old world. I was making a nuanced comparative judgment and I really didn't include Black people." Which is the legacy of so much of American scholarship, to make a general claim, "America's the nation of voluntary immigrants." What about Black people? "Well, of course, everybody but them." Everybody but them? Race is constitutive of American life, it's not additive. It's integral to American life. It's not peripheral. How can you make claims about "everybody but them"? Most of "them" been here longer than the ones you're making claims about. It's typical.

The sense of the comic does what? It keeps these people keeping on. The tragicomic. The tragicomic in this sense, W. H. Auden said, "the Christians can generate a tragedy of possibility, the Greeks a tragedy of necessity." But tragedy is about heroic energies against the grain with very little chance of victory, fighting anyway because of the kind of person you want to be or the kind of people you want to be. Integrity. Dignity. Respect. Regardless of consequences. You just act a certain way because that's the way you want to be in the world. Such courage to be is very much Sterling Brown: unpretentious, down to earth, upsetting some folk, affirming other folk, surprising everybody, the courage to be, not going to play a role or wear a mask. And my God, in the American academy you try to make it without wearing a mask or playing a role, you're going to need some supernatural support or something because you're cutting radically against the grain.

This blues sensibility occurs nowhere else in human history, but it cannot be understood without Jerusalem, the deep Christian influence coming out of the Black church, and at the same time the willingness to be deeply suspicious of every form of authority. This dark side of modernity keeps track of the suffering, the social misery, the pain, the grief, the tears, the sadness, and the sorrow which are concealed by a discourse of American innocence and American freedom. The blues emerging. Remember that famous couplet which Sterling Brown says for him is the most powerful couplet in American literature: "Don't know what my mother wants to stay her, for. This old world ain't been no friend to her." But she stays anyway. Why does she stay? Evidence doesn't look good. World's stacked against her. She stays because of the love that she had for those who came after, even if that love as we know—as in Toni Morrison's Beloved—can take the form of killing your children so the children don't have to go through the hell you went through. It's still love. Beloved. It is a profound love ethic for a people to love themselves despite the hatred coming their way, being so despised that their very ontological approach to the world to be is to be loved. That's the only resource that you have in the face of economic and political foreclosure. That's what the blues in part is about. But as we know the blues goes far beyond Christian perspective. That's what makes a tragicomic. That's what makes a tragicomic. He says all we can do is to create ourselves and make ourselves against a fragmented backdrop with no cosmic undergirding at all. That's tragicomic. It reminds me of Chekhov or Beckett. Self-creation, self-making against antecedent fragments and ruins with no guarantee of victory because there is no ultimate moral order to affirm. You're out there on your own doing what? Still trying to love your way through darkness and thunder.

It's a frightening prospect. In many ways it's a dominant prospect in this darkest of centuries. Beckett is the great poet, playwright, artist of the tragicomic. Chekhov is even deeper, but in a fascinating way they both have blues sensibilities because it's not a function of skin pigmentation. It's a function of how do you perceive the weight of darkness in the human condition and how do you attempt to garner and muster resources to respond to it. One of the reasons why the blues itself in the days of Sterling Brown was so unpopular is because it tried to convince many Black folk that their worldviews rest on pudding. That's unsettling. Even the great Du Bois himself—I believe that Billie Holiday would have scared him to death. She's too free, too much courage to be herself. Bessie Smith probably scared him to death, and Du Bois is the best that we have in terms of intellectual work. But he wasn't free enough.

Sterling Brown understood the great insight of Anton Chekhov, which is how do we squeeze the slave inside of us to become free spirits? And that takes, as I mentioned before, more courage than that of a soldier on the battlefield. One of the reasons why the Black musicians set the standard that Sterling Brown articulated is because Black musicians can be viewed at their best as the freest Americans and especially the freest Black folk. So even if you don't have enough courage to dig deep at least you can listen to their products. And say, well, it's so nice to be free, that's too much for me. And of course the irony is that all of this freedom is flowing under conditions of structural and institutional unfreedom. So that even White brothers and sisters who think they're free come running back to the unfree folk who produced these free products. It's true. I mean the major pastime of America of the 1830s was minstrels. Twenty, thirty, forty thousand White brothers and sisters all coming together to do what? Watch White brothers put on Black faces. What's going on? Then they felt free. I said, what's that? You're not enslaved. What's going on? Why you got to put on black? If you woke up Black the next day and didn't have a choice, then you'd be upset.

Well we know we don't have time to go into these complexities, but we're talking about something real here. Sterling Brown was the first major intellectual child of Jerusalem, the legacy of Jerusalem, child of the legacy of Athens, child of the legacy of American Democratic culture, even given its contradictions and then rooted in the doings and sufferings of Africans aspiring for American status. American-born but not treated like an American. And one wonders whether in fact it was a sheer act of providence that Sterling Brown would end up at Williams College. One just doesn't expect Williams to be on the cutting edge in regard to black people and black freedom. It's a wonderful place. It's a lovely place. It's got a rich history and heritage, but my God, how is it that you end up with the leading black intellectual who takes seriously the dignity, the irreducible dignity of everyday people, at Williams. And yet Sterling says lots about Williams. He said, "I learned how to read closely when I sat under George Dutton." George Dutton himself was transgressive. He'd like that. He wrote on the modern novel. And he'd slip in a little Tolstoy and Dostoevsky and Flaubert on the side, and Sterling liked that. And that was cutting against the grain at that time. There was no American Studies, no appreciation of American literature. Melville had been lost for fifty years—the greatest literary artist ever produced in this civilization. The John Coltrane of American literature—Herman Melville. Been lost. George Dutton made a difference, he said.

He also learned from Bliss Perry, a significant figure. A Harvard professor who spent time at Williams. One of the early scholars of American literature. And he opened him up to who? One of the freest individuals of the nineteenth century called Walt Whitman—"Song of the Open Road."

What do we do with Sterling now? Because the irony is that even given the cosmopolitan sensibility that he had, even given the major constraints in his life especially the rejection of *No Hiding Place* in 1937, that we were talking about, that had such devastating impact on him. . . . You think in 1937, 1938, he published three books at the same time. Isn't that something? *Negro in American Fiction, Negro Poetry and Drama,* and *The Negro in Washington.* At 31 years old he already published *Southern Road.* He was on his way. And then BOOM! Here comes America—business as usual. Even someone who goes away and ends up in Harvard can be stopped. He's got to wrestle with those obstacles and those impediments. And yet he did keep on going. Oftentimes when I read Sterling Brown the tears come to my eyes. That Robert Frost poem that he loved so much:

> It is late at night and still I am losing.
> But still I am steady and unaccusing.

That's Robert Frost at 70 years old. But the poem spoke so deeply to Sterling Brown. There's no doubt that Sterling Brown said I have got to be able to look defeat in the face and somehow keep keeping on. That's why I'm a blues intellectual. Because that question has been asked before in America, land of liberty, by a people of African descent. How do you keep keeping on? Buffers, communities, love connections, supports, or, as the old folk used to say, just "stepping out on nothing and landing on something." The fiduciary dimension of the human condition called faith. What do we do with him now in a moment which increasing faithlessness, trustlessness, hopelessness, especially among a significant number of young Black, Brown, Red, Yellow and increasingly among Whites. We've had a very, very tragic series of suicides in South Boston. I'm sure many of you have heard about that. Irish brothers and sisters killing themselves. The suicide rate among young Black folk increased 300 percent in the last 16 years. There was a blues sensibility that led to Black people having the lowest rate of suicide of any group, and you'd think that given the situation they would have a much higher rate. Something was going on. It's no longer the case. Even among the Black professional class. Even among the

Black professional class the deep existential torment in those corporate spaces is still at work. You know, the golden cuffs, big title, big name, no power. But you went to Williams, oh yeah!

Do these people really respect me even given the material toys that I have? Because I come from a people who have been so dishonored that it never matters just having some material toy. I want to know if I'm respected for who I am. You got White backlash. We were concerned only about diversity in the first place and things changed now so we have fewer Black faces. No, no. Williams says something different. Our understanding of the Williams tradition views Sterling Brown as constitutive of that tradition. He's not tacked on. And all of the Sterling Browns—male, female—they're not tacked on; they're part of it, moving toward the core of it. Not because of their pigmentation but because they have a deep commitment to the best of it. And we won't know, but there will be some Black Williams folk who have a commitment to the worst of it too. You've got to fight them comradely, with civility, but you've got to fight them. You'll find many White brothers and sisters, Brown brothers and sisters, committed to the best of it. Form your lines. Thank God you've got leadership committed to the best of it. We don't know where that's going to be all the time. We don't know what happens after Brother Hank [i.e., President Harry C. Payne]. I don't know.

The legacy of Sterling Brown has to do with the cosmopolitan perspective that focuses on suffering and believes in democratic sensibilities and the life of the mind. For what? For the play of the mind and for the transformation of prevailing realities. Can we keep the legacy of Sterling Brown alive? I believe that we can. It's not a guarantee. It depends on how much love you have in your heart, how much courage you have, how broad your vision is, how organized you are, and how disunited the forces that you're fighting are. It's a historical question, but most fundamentally it's an existential question in terms of who we really think we are and what kind of people we want to be. And in the end Sterling Brown, I think, is saying to us that there is some possibility, even if you think that you're losing, that there's a species of winning that has little to do with being able to push back what you think needs to be pushed back. It has to do with the integrity of your soul. It has to do with the quality of your commitment. And in the end the larger consequences may flow. Thank you all so very much.

NOTES

1. My take on "founding" texts/moments/figures is informed by and modifies Cedric Robinson's work ("David Walker and the Precepts of Black Studies," lecture presented in the Literature Program's speakers series, Duke University, October 22, 1997) on "founding texts." He has described the function of such texts in relation to historical authority and their work of establishing antiquity within existing disciplines and/or for resulting disciplines. Their significance

is even greater for establishing conceptual, discursive, and theoretical canons that transmit structures for epistemological, ethical, and methodological patrols which mark off special knowledge. I am less interested than Robinson in establishing antiquity within or for resulting disciplines, but I build on such texts/moments/figures' relation to fields of knowledge in more general conceptual terms.

2. My delineation of functions departs from Robinson's delineation of functions insofar as I am less interested in canon formation and methodological boundary formation as such, and more interested in the thematic conventions interrupted and established by remarking on and (re)making such figures' work—often within the terms of newer vocabularies.

"Steady and Unaccusing": An Interview with Sterling A. Brown

John Edgar Tidwell and John S. Wright

Since the early 1980s a series of symposia, public and academic awards, and other recognitions have testified to continuing popular and scholarly interest in Sterling A. Brown, poet, literary critic, teacher, anthologist, and raconteur. The Collected Poems of Sterling A. Brown, *for example, received the Lenore Marshall Poetry Prize for 1980 from* Saturday Review. *The Modern Language Association, at its December 1981 meeting, paid tribute to Brown's many years of distinguished service as a man of letters. A* Black World *special issue (September 1970) and Michael Harper and Robert Stepto's* Chant of Saints: A Gathering of Afro-American Literature, Art, and Scholarship *(1979) became the first two of many anthologies, critical studies, and journal special issues dedicated to him, for his enduring poetic innovations and his pioneering cultural criticism. At Howard University, on February 14, 1997, a symposium assessed the extent to which Brown's thinking reflected and influenced African-American and American views on culture and literature. His sensitive creative work and astute analyses are captured in four published collections of poetry, six critical studies and anthologies, and over forty essays and speeches, together with the regular book review column he wrote in the early issues of* Opportunity: A Journal of Negro Life. *The following interview—conducted August 2, 1980, but unpublished until now—was one he hoped personally to extend and revise. Nevertheless it offers in retrospect, we think, more testimony that Sterling A. Brown is a presence who remains, in the words from one of his favorite poems, "steady and unaccusing."*

STERLING A. BROWN: Are these rhetorical questions to which you already know the answers? Are you examining me?

JOHN S. WRIGHT: We know you're too much the rhetorician for us to do that.

BROWN: Both of you are all right in my book. Question me, question me, prosecuting attorney!!

JOHN EDGAR TIDWELL: We're interested in a wide range of things, but, first of all, we might start with the Associates in Negro Folk Education who published, among others, two of your studies and two by Alain Locke. We know very little about the genesis of the organization, its participants, and its plan of operation.

BROWN: Bob Martin should help you on that because he was really helping Locke a great deal, sending out the books and things like that. Locke, as you could imagine, was not too good at that and should not have had to be. Locke, as I understand it, got this money from the Carnegie Foundation as part of an Adult Education Project, and he had Howard University people do the books. None of us were experts in adult education, but we knew something of the purposes. Now, for instance, I had to add questions at the end of chapters so they could really be taught. The books were done as booklets. People have attacked them as criticism because I couldn't include long analyses of novels, when what I wanted to do was discuss the treatment of the Negro character in American literature. The first thing I did was *Negro Poetry and Drama.* Now I had done enough work to do more than one book on each of those, but I had to [limit] them to 125 pages. That's what we had to do. When it came to the *Negro in American Fiction,* I just said, "I'm not going to do it," and I added to it. That's a longer and a better book. Locke objected to that and said the [costs would] go up and I'd have to pay for it, but I didn't pay it. So I never got paid. They still owe me about $300. We were making about $300 per volume. No royalty on it. Just flat. Now, Locke did one on the Negro in music and the Negro in art, in both of which Locke would have been at that moment the authority. . . . [But] Locke could not handle the blues. Locke and I contributed to *Folk-Say* in Norman, Oklahoma. He and I did an article together on movies, "Folk Values in a New Medium," and then I did something on the blues. . . . Now Locke would read carefully what was essential. Locke did not like blues. Locke had—and this is anecdotal, so it may be wrong—but Locke had one blues that Langston Hughes gave him—"Ticket Agent, Ease Your Window Down," the only damn blues [he owned]. When the people behind Locke's place on R Street would be out there singing blues, Locke would pull his window down and put on Tchaikovsky. I don't blame him; that's the way he was trained. He knew the hell out of Tchaikovsky. He knew the blues were important, and he knew jazz was important. What you have, then, is a man intellectually aware [but] emotionally attuned to something else. But he would never do what Howard [University] did—disdain jazz in favor of classical music. He loved the classics and tried to understand the importance of jazz. But his hope for jazz unfortunately was the kind of nonsense that Paul Whiteman was doing. Maybe, Locke said, jazz will one day rise to the semi-symphonic level. This is crap.

WRIGHT: My next question follows pretty much directly what you were just saying. Clearly you share with Alain Locke a driving interest in folk art, folk values.

BROWN: No, I didn't share it; I taught him. He taught me a lot, but I knew the folk stuff and he didn't.

WRIGHT: But my question is, what really are the crucial differences between your position on the role of folk tradition in American life and Locke's? What criticism do you have—you offered one partly already here—of Locke's view of folk tradition?

BROWN: Locke's was not condescending, but Locke's position was [that] folk tradition is a minor thing; the major thing is classical art. I think they are both arts. They are oranges and apples. Now there can be very bad folk material. Today [give them] any kind of blues singer, and the white folks go crazy. To me there are good blues singers and bad blues singers. There are good blues lines and good blues standards and bad ones. I would say the difference is that I believe in the validity, the power, the beauty of folk culture at its best. Now, I don't blame Locke for this. How in the hell could Locke have gotten away [from] upperclass Philadelphia, Harvard? More niggers have been ruined by Harvard than by bad gin! Ralph Bunche and I had a thesis that every nigger that went to Harvard was crazy, starting with Bunche and with Brown. So, Locke had a lot against him, but he overcame it. . . . Now, this is going to be in the next *Caravan,* this whole stress of assimilation and the stress of genuine integration, which means an integer, a whole man. Phillis Wheatley is not part of what I think is the most important tradition in our poetry, because she wrote [about the] life of New England, Puritanism, the patriotic, the neo-classic, the pseudo-classic; she wrote very well in that form. But that's all what she wanted to be, and she wanted to be praised for it. So, for a long time that's what we praised people about. But, to me, our tradition starts with "Before I'll be a slave, let me be buried in my grave." Or, from a blues song: "Trouble, trouble, seen it all my days." Now, there are two traditions. Countee [Cullen] could not escape from race, but he wanted to do it in classical terms. He spoke of our problems as though he was Sisyphus. You know, pushing that rock up that hill. He was apt, but he was praised for that. I don't think you should be praised for how many classical references you have. I think you ought to be praised for the content of poetry. So, what you have is a large number of people [like] Jessie Fauset, a brilliant teacher, who wanted to write about our people who knew which fork to use, have the right car, the right family background. Now that is a kind of natural propaganda to write, and, so, I expect that. And I called a number of them the "NAACP School of Fiction." Now it had to be said, but that's not the chief purpose of literature. I mean she *praises* our middle class, which deserves the *blame* that Frazier gives it in *Black Bourgeoisie.* Both of them have to be taken, of course, together. The Black bourgeoisie is a stereotype, a caricature. I can get people to prove both sides. And the best thing—I'm doing this on Frazier in a group of essays—the best answer to E. Franklin Frazier's *Black Bourgeoisie* is Frazier's own *Negro Family in the United States.* You look at the chapter on Black Puritans. It's not scornful, but it describes a Puritan ethic. Which you gentlemen illustrate. [*Laughter*] I mean, you all are not into conspicuous display; you go for your summer down [to Atlanta University] and work like hell. That's a good ethic.

WRIGHT: Mortification of the flesh.

BROWN: With all them roaches. Zora Neale Hurston sitting over there [*pointing*], keeping us entranced. She was a better "liar" than I am, a wonderful liar! Just had us in stitches. She gets up to leave. Being of the folk, she had a cigarette holder from here to yonder with a cigarette in it [*gestures*] and a long ash and stands at the door and tells us goodbye and flicks them damn ashes right down on [my wife] Daisy's rug. Daisy took care of the house. Daisy looked at her flick those ashes, and Zora took her damn big foot and rubbed them into the damn rug and said "good for the roaches." She knew damn well we didn't have no roaches. Daisy could have killed her. Up until that Daisy had open admiration for anybody who could out-lie her husband. Now when Zora dropped them damn ashes over there . . . well, the Puritan ethic [said] no . . . But in *The New Negro Caravan* we're going to illustrate these two trends.

WRIGHT: Let's go back to the blues again. You spent a lot of time studying the blues, obviously, and beyond studying them, transforming them into poetry of your own. What do you think that your essays on the blues and the blues tradition did to alter the prevailing interpretations?

BROWN: They did some, but not much, because I was published in places like *Phylon.* I've got a big bibliography but people don't know about it because they didn't read *Opportunity.* Now those who read it were influenced. Ellison came to Howard—he talked about the blues—and the kids said, "Well, why don't we hear anything like that around here at Howard?" Ellison said, "You got Sterling Brown here." And Larry Neal—I didn't know this—Larry Neal says that this influenced him. I did "The Blues as Folk Poetry," an essay in 1930 in *Folk-Say,* and I did an enlarged one in *Phylon.* They have received attention from people in folklore—from English teachers and people in folklore—and they're going to be brought out by Howard in my essays, *To a Different Drummer.* So, I would say that as literary essays go they've had a modicum of influence.

WRIGHT: Ellison does refer to you explicitly as being one of the living presences that he drew on during his own career. How do you relate your view of the blues to Ellison's?

BROWN: I don't know his too well to comment on. I respect what Ellison says. I think that Ellison does cover up with profundity. I think what I've done frequently is give a capsule, and a guy has put it in a glass of water and got a little bit more. I think I have a quality of terseness. I think they enlarged it. But what I've seen of his I would have to [say], "I'm glad you can interpret me!" He's got an audience I never had.

TIDWELL: How would you define your audience?

BROWN: My audience has been the classroom. I have reached more critics and writers and intelligent kids, more than anybody else, more than Locke. Right behind up there [*pointing*]. All those books up there are signed by critics, writers, and novelists. I just heard from Ossie Davis; he and Ruby Dee called me the other day; they're going to do something and sign me up on that. Tom Sowell, who somebody nominated for the National Academy of Education today. A right-wing economist, a green guy right out of the Marines, he dedicated his book *Black Education: Myths and Tragedies* (1972) to me and other people because I made him study. I was at Yale, and Charlie Davis introduced me and said, "How is it that a man can have a book dedicated to him by Tom Sowell and another book by Don Lee?" I said, "Because I ain't got no principles." [*Laughter*] But the real reason is that I listened—though I'm not doing it now. I listened understandingly, and I listened [patiently]. I don't agree with them; I don't agree with Tom Sowell publicly, but I agree with a lot of the things he says on education. And Don Lee, my Don Lee . . . I ain't going back to Africa, but I'm going to be there before Don Lee, because, while he's in London trying on a new dashiki, I'm going to be standing on the shores waiting for him. I told Hoyt Fuller that down in Atlanta. I said while you're in Paris sipping on a bottle of Courvoisier I'm going to be down there on the sands of Accra. But I ain't going to be there. . . . I don't let you be too serious, but I'm teaching you. I'm teaching like Mark Twain, with anecdotes.

TIDWELL: In several of your essays, you express the concern for the lack of an adequate reading audience to support Black writers, and several of your works seem to function to educate the readership.

BROWN: That is true. I've heard from any number of people who tell me they're glad my book is out, but they ain't never said they're going to buy it. "Can I get it at the library?" is what they say.

TIDWELL: The works you have written seem to function to educate the readership. Would you comment on this purpose, beginning with your *Outline for the Study of the Poetry of American Negroes*?

BROWN: That is one of the first things I did. In *Opportunity* I wrote an essay called "Our Literary Audience" and attacked [Black] middle-class, upper-class standards. Then, the first book I did was for James Weldon Johnson's *Book of American Negro Poetry* because he couldn't do it. I called it *Outline for the Study of the Poetry of American Negroes* because I was teaching that. I wrote an essay called "The Negro Author and his Publisher." Not original, but I hadn't had too much experience with book publishing. There are grave problems right now for publishing because the 1960s had this wave of so-called "Black books." Now if a woman writes a book about Black machoism, she'll get fair attention. A woman like [Ntozake] Shange gets attention. But serious plays that people are doing don't get the attention that Shange gets . . . by not committing suicide and all that. So, we don't have publishers. One of the worthiest was Associated Publishers. A solid thing. But their solidity kept them from having too big an audience. A very valuable thing. But Carter Woodson, of course, had no imagination. Woodson was a [factualist], and he found facts that were of tremendous value. He was a pioneer, [but with] no sense of literature, no sense of poetry, [and] no sense of music. A book from Woodson was [like a recital from] Maude Cuney Hare. And Maude Cuney Hare was a concert pianist, a vocalist, and whatnot. She could deal with the great people of the earth but [getting] closer to the folk would [require a more] sensitive reading. Don't touch the blues [he said]. I mean Benjamin Brawley on jazz and the blues, you know, the genteel Brawley. He doesn't discuss jazz; says it raises questions of musical taste. Something like that. Now the next historians like John Hope Franklin and Benjamin Quarles had no sense of the importance of literature and the arts. Quarles said, "Sterling, should an Irish historian, a historian of Ireland, have to read Joyce's *Ulysses*?" I said, "He better damn sight read it, and he better read criticism." Because I think Joyce is one of the monuments, before he committed suicide with *Finnegan's Wake*, before he had his wake for Finnegan. *Ulysses* is an important—though I think a very much overrated—book. But an important book. I did a 250-page book at Harvard on the treatment of the Irish in English drama.

WRIGHT: What led you into that originally?

BROWN: An interest in minorities. I saw these parallels. I had a course in English drama. I was always conscious of what was happening to our characters in American literature, but never in a scholarly way until I saw what they did with the Irish. Then I saw what they were doing to the Jews. And then the [whole damn cause]. Then the sociological criticism in America. How do you deal with the working class? Well, I was a stereotype, and I became an expert on stereotypes. Now I think that that essay has influenced more teachers than the one on the blues. Because, you see, a lot of English teachers don't want to deal with no damn blues either. You know that, don't you? And they don't want to do but so much with the spirituals. I wrote in my article in *Opportunity* something about the woman who changed "Swing Low Sweet Chariot" to "Descend, welcome vehicle. . . ." So, you see I didn't wait until today [to throw off] humility; I've been mean all my life. [*Laughter*]

TIDWELL: Would you comment further on the Harvard book?

BROWN: That was a thesis in a course. You know you didn't have an MA thesis at Harvard. You just did [four course theses]. I wrote that at Harvard. I'll tell you where I started on us—under Charles S. Johnson. Imagine this lineup at Fisk in 1928–29. Horace Mann Bond in education, political science, history; Charles S. Johnson in sociology; and me in literature. John Work was around there, who could [offer] something in music. But by and large, [it was my exposure to] *The Negro in American Civilization*. Johnson wrote that book for a course I taught there. And so then I came to Howard.

TIDWELL: What about Du Bois? Was he ever considered a potential writer in the Bronze Booklet series?

BROWN: No. I don't know how Du Bois and Locke got along, but I'm afraid not too well. Du Bois did not suffer fools gladly; Du Bois did not have any friends among his peers. It's interesting the comments that [James Weldon] Johnson makes in *Along This Way* on Du Bois. I was on the board of the NAACP, and, when I went in the office, [they] said what you got to know that's constant in this office is that everybody hates everybody else. Now I don't think that Joel Spingarn hated; I just think he was superior to everyone. I know Arthur [Spingarn] didn't. Arthur was a gentleman. But . . . Du Bois left no mantle. Du Bois was close to Allison Davis, respected him highly; for a time liked me, liked me in Atlanta. Close to Abram Harris, very close, until Abe reviewed his book, *Black Reconstruction,* I think for the *Nation,* and spoke of the Marxism as being illegitimate, which it was. The book is a tremendous book, but the Marxism is wishful talk, and the guy that did that for him [was] Sam Dawson, at Howard University. [Sam] did the Marxism, and then Du Bois took it and put it in his book. At the end of his life, Du Bois's mantle was on a good friend of mine, Alphaeus Hunton. And Hunton went to Africa with him. And Hunton died in Africa, recently, my age. Alphaeus Hunton. He was a good man; go to his papers on the last years of Du Bois. Du Bois's ending was tragic. But Du Bois was a tremendous man. Du Bois was my intellectual father. Now Du Bois was my intellectual father more than Locke. Locke and I differed. When we came to *God's Trombones,* which Locke didn't like too much, he put in some sentences about Africa and I took them out. You don't have to go to Africa to explain *God's Trombones.* I ain't never seen any trombones in Africa unless Louis Armstrong left some over there at this time. I mean, these guys, when they come by me on Africa, see, they got to go way back. 'Cause my father was teaching religion at Howard; and my Sunday School teacher was an African, and he was the priestliest Victorian I ever heard. And he'd say, "You never sit like this [*gestures*]; you pull in your diaphragm." He was a great big tall Black man, and I was scared to death of him. Not because he was no damn savage; I didn't see no Congo cutting through no black; I saw the Cannes River or Cambridge. [*Laughter*] You all ought to take a course with me!

WRIGHT: About the *Negro Caravan,* little has been said of the division of editorial labor and the kinds of critical issues that you, [Arthur P.] Davis, and [Ulysses] Lee may have had in planning the anthology. Can you shed any light on that, since it is the best example of its kind?

BROWN: No quarrel. I did most of the work. I think they would agree on that. Ulysses did that wonderful thing at the end [The Chronology]. I was to do the selections about the novel, Ulysses was to do short stories, and Arthur was to do the drama. I was to do the "folk stuff." I think Arthur was to do the poetry. But that broke down. I did most of the work. . . . Arthur was at [Virginia]

Union. Ulysses was available. The rewriting I had to do with the editor Stanley Burnshaw. We had overwritten or run out of [space], and I went up to New York, stayed up all night, counting spaces in the lines. . . . The collaboration [on the *Caravan*] was good. There were no differences of opinion.

WRIGHT: I've come across some of the reviews of *The Caravan*. How did you feel it was perceived by the critics?

BROWN: I've got a lot of those. My wife was a very good person in that respect. I have a gang of wonderful reviews. There were only two antagonistic reviews that I knew about. One of them was by Lorenzo [Dow] Turner. He said it should not have been arranged by types. And his book *Readings of Negro Authors* is arranged by type. Then we had a bad review in *The New Masses* because we didn't have any communists in there.

WRIGHT: That may be an issue that's come full circle historically. Right now, we've got at least a couple of streams of criticism, in contention. One of them is the sociologically oriented criticism, the Black aestheticians of Addison Gayle and the Black neo-Marxians of whom [Amiri] Baraka is probably the best known. That school on one side, and on the other side the varieties of formalistic, textually oriented criticism that Steve Henderson, Bob Stepto, Skip Gates, and some of the others represent. So, in terms of your own grounding in critical realism, how do you read the current critical debates?

BROWN: I have thought about that, and I have a feeling that there is too much fragmentation. I think that the good critic has got to make use of all of these devices. Now with Michael [Harper] and Stepto and Skip, when they say the work is not to be considered sociologically, they are going to do my poetry injustice because there is a great deal of relationship with sociology. Frazier called me his favorite literary sociologist. Now, if you dismiss sociology from consideration and just go to structure—that I think is vulgar. If you dismiss structure, you're not looking at it as poetry. You're just looking at it as message, and that's not good. So, I don't see why we can't have a critic broad enough to depart from these narrow categories that somebody else, by the way, set up. I'm concerned, for instance, [about] all of these long drawn out analyses of a novel. . . . I'm very interested in what is said and how it is said, and often they don't tell me what is said. They will get two novels, and one of them says lies and one of them says truth; and they give the same analysis to each. I don't think they should. I think they're neglecting the importance to me of a book. Again what it says and then how it is said: they go together. They go together because what is said poorly is not really said. I mean, you can have a lousy novel with the most beautiful message, and it's a lousy novel. And I think that our critics lack this breadth of approach, and I think, again, we're back to this "crabs in a barrel." We're back to this divisiveness. I'm right, and you're not right. I don't think the critics should be bothered about the other critics. You ought to be bothered by the work you criticize. I think criticism is judgment, but I think it's not to be two judgments. Now, the trouble with [Addison] Gayle, it seems to me, is that if you come across with "Black is beautiful," then you're good. If you come across with Black men aren't always beautiful [you're bad]. In a way a novel propagates some idea. Propaganda does not defeat a novel—bad propaganda defeats a novel. . . . I think that [in writing] protest—I mean I've talked about this in my criticism—you can't have good fiction with villains and victims. You got to have fiction with *people,* and that's awfully hard. I have been taken to task [because they say] I attack the stereotype of Negroes but I allow the stereotypes of whites. But . . . I got a poem about a no-good cracker, and it's called "Mr. Danny," and I wanted to show an s.o.b., but I would not say that that is the total picture of whites. When they jump on Ralph Ellison, I don't think they should. I think *Invisible Man* is a very important novel. I do not agree with its metaphor anymore than with *The Waste Land*'s. I got an essay, if you young men keep me living till Christmas, that I'll give you, called "Not so Invisible, Not so Strange, Not so Outside"; and I take up three flawed novels: [one is] *Invisible Man. Invisible Man* comes at the time when we were getting visible as hell. Now you see the Negro is not invisible; the Negro is misinterpreted; it's not that you can't see him. You do see him; that's the trouble. White folks see him too much I think. Now. If I look at you and do not read your proper character, which is the way most people look at other people, that don't mean you're invisible. We are not invisible. Now Ralph likes that idea, but we are not invisible. We are misinterpreted. When this Negro—this is *Candide,* this is Voltaire's *Candide*—when you get a nigger that ain't right bright and you put him through all these experiences and at the end he said, "I got to hide," I can't take it. . . . That's the reason I can't do too much with *Song of Solomon.* I am not surrealistic. I must not have no damn imagination. I can't see no nigger. But what I've got against *Invisible Man* is, if this boy is bright, like Ralph Waldo Ellison, he ain't going to take no damn white trustee of Tuskegee to no whore house. Now, one of the best things in the novel is that Bledsoe business; that's realism and beautifully done. What he's got is good snapshots: the Communist Party, the Rastafarians. He never has—and this I miss—he has so little of the people. He's got one old lady there, but no relationships to Harlem. It's like television. You get a nigger on television and they ain't got no culturing. The boy is to me a combination of [things, partly] a smart-alecky guy messing up on purpose. . . . When Ralph handles the people he's got to show you incest. Ain't no question there's going to be incest. But of all the "folk stuff," he has that; so he has selected episodes for [a kind of] *Candide.* I've said it's one of the most complex, one of the best novels to show complex problems of our lives. I agree with that, but I would say that in his carrying it out he is not convincing. The same thing with J. Saunders Redding's *Stranger and Alone.* And there I think you get a whole lot . . . of a subjective thing. Again, *The Outsider* is not one of Dick's [Richard Wright's] best things, I think; but you see Dick has this feeling. Dick felt that if Sartre would pat him on the back, you know, that's something.

Sartre, to me, ain't worth a "fartre." Now, I mean, he is a bright Frenchman but he can't tell me nothing about nothing over here and I ain't going to tell him nothing about Paris. . . . Then you get another one named Genet. He comes over here, and Negroes go running around [him] to be [changed] into Blacks. Ain't nothing Genet and Sartre can tell me about the brothers; but they got "great insight," so Dick goes over there, and he swallows all that stuff. [But] I'm being very negative. Dick had a great power, and Dick is a very important figure in American letters. But Dick was not the spokesman, was not the intellectual leader; and he wanted to be. But when you get Dick talking to [Kwame] Nkrumah, Dick is giving the old party line, plus the national one. Dick and Jean Toomer were much alike. They were always looking for something to give them the answer. And then, when they didn't get the answer they'd go to something else. They wanted a Messiah; they wanted a father. Karl Marx can't tell you; Mao can't tell you; Amiri Baraka's the same way. I don't need no father.

TIDWELL: [How would you sum up your own career and outlook?]

BROWN: Fundamentally, I'm a teacher. I took teaching seriously. I got the papers back to the people. I read them. Sometimes I was called the "red ink man." I wrote more on the side than they wrote. And they kept it. You ought to let Ossie Davis tell you about that. And the same thing with Sowell. The same thing Michael Winston tells me; you know, he brings his stuff to me. I was a teacher. And next I think I was an interpreter; I was a critic, a literary historian. [But] I'm going to fool these guys. I'm gonna take a short story and write about sixty-five pages on it. I've been a family man, close ties, had a beautiful wife, wonderful woman, raised an adopted son—he has four kids—and had a lot of other interests; read everything, not doing that now, because of my eyes, but I'm listening a lot. I'm very aware of politics, and I'm racially obsessed with everything. Well, you know, Rayford [Logan] surprised me. Rayford said I—and Rayford is not modest—Rayford said that I was the cultural spokesman after Du Bois. This is high praise, and biased because, you know, we are both M Street [Dunbar High School], Williams [College], and Harvard. I would say Du Bois and Locke. I would say that I'm important. I've said things—this is not conceit, this is not arrogance—I've said things now that strike a chord that others didn't say. I don't know any poem like "Strong Men" in the 1920s. Langston was saying, "I, too, sing America. I am the darker brother," and so on. They will welcome me later on and say how beautiful I am. They will welcome me at the table. I don't want to be welcome at the table, ain't bothered about the table. I want to be respected. . . . Well, there was that trend; they will see how beautiful I am, and I'll be invited in. It's 1980, and we are *not* invited in; we are no longer completely cut out, but we're not invited in. With me, that does not cause one gray hair. I not only am not invited in, I ain't inviting them out here. If they've paid their dues, they can come. . . . [Look at] Robert Frost's "In Divés' Dive": "It is late at night and still I am losing, / But still I am steady and unaccusing. / As long as the Declaration guards / My right to be equal in number of cards, / It is nothing to me who runs the Dive. / Let's have a look at another five." The word *still* means "continually," "ever"; it's the Elizabethan "still." "Late at night": I'm eighty years old, and still just as always I'm losing. "But still I am steady and unaccusing." I ain't blaming you, ain't blaming me. I ain't blaming my papa, ain't blaming my mama. I'm unaccusing as long as the Declaration, capital "D," of Independence guards, *"G-U-A-R-D-S,"* my right to be equal in the number of cards. You got five; he got five; *he* got five. "It does not matter to me who runs the Dive." He's wrong there, of course. But "Let's have a look at another five." The only time I ever talked to Frost, I mentioned that poem; he says I'm the only person who ever remembered that poem, and he loved it. He asked me, "Are you a poker player?" I said, "No, but I'm a loser."

Br'er Sterling and the Blues: An Interview with Michael S. Harper

Graham Lock, with a preface by Michael S. Harper

Negro writers are not numerous; their audience, with few exceptions, is small; the subject matter they know best is often controversial; and almost all of them make their livings from jobs other than writing.

—Introduction to *The Negro Caravan* (1941),
Sterling A. Brown, Arthur P. Davis, and Ulysses Lee, editors

Preface

Sterling Brown inscribed my copy of *The Negro Caravan* "For Michael, one of my very best fellow-poets, readers, and friends, from Sterling. Be seeing you soon, son. See you soon, June, 1975." We were in Providence, Rhode Island; he had received an honorary Doctor of Letters degree at Brown University's commencement. I had met him in the fall of 1972 in New York City, where he was honored as Dean of African American Letters by the Black Academy. The novelist Ernest J. Gaines and I were seated at one of the head tables, Gaines for his novel *The Autobiography of Miss Jane Pittman*, and me for my second volume of poetry, *History Is Your Own Heartbeat*. I was told by insiders that the judges were Jay Saunders Redding and John A. Williams. At our table Professor Brown chortled to Gaines and me, "you've never heard of me." We professed otherwise and promised to visit him at his home in Washington, D.C., the following winter, January 1973. We visited Brown at his house on Kearny Street NE after several sessions at a Creative Writing Conference at the Library of Congress. Gaines and I arrived by cab, and Brown held court for several hours. The family residence, where his sister lived, was next door. We signed and exchanged books, and I invited him to visit Brown's campus in the spring to lecture on his favorite subject, "Images and Reality in American Literature." I also asked him to read his poems, from *Southern Road* (1932) and from *No Hiding Place*, his second book, which had been rejected for being "too political" after he'd been awarded a Guggenheim Fellowship in 1937. Brown's editing as "chief editor for Negro Affairs" for the Federal Writers Project was legendary; without his monitoring of the State and City Guides in the project, the bulk of stereotypes legion in the country, on race, gender, and minorities, would have been worse than they were. His essays on folklore and stereotyping were seminal among insiders, but he was marginalized among his colleagues. It was no accident that Arthur P. Davis taught at Virginia Union and Ulysses Lee at Lincoln. *The Negro Caravan* was a landmark compiled by pioneers, though the term "Negro" is of course an anachronism in the twenty-first century: what people of color call themselves, how the world responds, is now a global subject, like the elements, a world of fundamentals and the fossil fuels of cultural, historical, anthropological, theoretical, exegetical debate.

I had heard a recording of a lecture he gave at the University of California, Berkeley, on local radio in 1964, while I was caught in traffic commuting from the east bay to San Francisco. The sound of Brown's voice was so distinctive I called the radio station to try to secure a copy of his talk for the campus library. Later, a former student who was a technician at KPFA/Pacifica, secured a copy; a decade later, I gave Brown a copy of his talk, on reel-to-reel tape, for his gift as honorand. Often he would provide gifts of his own from his copious library: *The Reader's Companion to World Literature*, edited by Hornstein, Percy, and Brown; *Negro Poetry and Drama; The Negro in American Fiction; A Treasury of Mississippi River Folklore*, edited by B. A. Botkin. Brown was known as a "red-ink teacher" in all his classes; he added more red ink in the margins than students wrote in the body of their papers; he was legendary as a teacher across the curriculum. He held seminars with students, past and present, in his Kearny Street NE residence. His wife, Daisy Turnbull Brown, was his stablemate and the "Rose Anne" of his poetry, particularly the "Vestiges" section of his *Collected Poems*, which I selected for the National Poetry Series in 1979. I was to present a copy to Gunnar Myrdal in Stockholm in 1980 at Myrdal's home in Sweden. Brown had introduced Myrdal to a large portion of the Black Intelligentsia at Howard University, where he taught; he was Myrdal's guide into Harlem, and across the South as well, as Myrdal prepared to write his monumental *An American Dilemma*. Brown introduced Myrdal to Ralph J. Bunche, his colleague at Howard, later a Nobel laureate for his work on the Palestinian question (see "Call Boy" in *Collected Poems*).

In the new world of anthologies, on- and off-line, one begins one's reading on Negro Affairs in the New World with *The Negro Caravan*. A reading of Sterling Brown's poems is another matter entirely: as Brown himself claimed, "I learned the Arts and Sciences at Williams and Harvard; I learned the Humanities at Lynchburg, Virginia."

—Michael S Harper

Interview with Michael S. Harper, by Graham Lock, at Yaddo, June 2003

I met Michael S. Harper in Saratoga Springs in June 2003. I had hoped to elicit a little information about Sterling Brown's attitudes to blues and jazz, and the music's influence on his poetry, for a research project on which I was then engaged. [1] *In the event, I was treated to a richly detailed and wide-ranging discourse that encompassed many facets of the life and work of "Br'er Sterling,"* [2] *as seen from the uniquely authoritative viewpoint of a close associate and fellow poet. Later, Professor Harper kindly provided the above preface.*

—Graham Lock

GRAHAM LOCK: I'd like to talk to you about Sterling Brown and the influence of jazz and blues in his work. I know you edited his *Collected Poems*.

MICHAEL S. HARPER: I also selected his poems for the National Poetry Series. He hadn't written any since the 1940s but so many of his poems were so pioneering that he was an influence in many, many areas. I'm glad I did it and I'm glad I did the book, because the poems were brought back and made more available. There's a kind of reclamation that certain people just deserve.

It was a very important thing for Sterling's career, for his life, because you know he died in '89 and he was already retired when we made the decision to do the book. But I've never had a regret, not one. The poems stand up, after all these years. I had a little resistance from a couple of people; they said, well, the guy is old. I said, that's not the point. If we were talking about Keats . . . you know, Keats is not "old," Milton . . . these people are not "old," they're classic.

The first time Sterling came to Brown University he gave this talk called "Images and Reality" and I had the good sense to realize—this was a two-day visit—I asked him, would he mind reading some poems if I could get him a room. He was so pleased to be asked to read, and I had a tape recorder—this was a really raggedy tape recorder, back in 1973—and I had a tape that was an hour long in both directions. Sterling read for an hour and 15 minutes, with a break in between. It was the most incredible reading I've ever heard. With his comments. The first twenty minutes were all about his education, why he loved Frost, E. A. Robinson, Sandburg, and then he read his poems in his marvelous voice.[3] When he paused and asked if he could have a glass of water and would I turn the tape over, the students didn't move. The whole place was just . . . whew! He read in a room called the Crystal Room, with no microphone. It had a capacity of 100 and there were almost 200 people in there. It was then I realized I had to get those poems back into print. I just said to myself, those poems have got to be out there.

LOCK: The idea of our research project is to look at the influence of jazz and blues on other African American art forms, and our starting point is that it does have a special and central role in the culture. Would you agree with that?

HARPER: Absolutely.

LOCK: And that there are certain historical reasons for this, to do with slavery and the fact that music was basically the only form of expression allowed?

HARPER: Yes, all of that. And, of course, Sterling Brown did remarkable pioneering work, not only his essays, many of them on the blues, but *Southern Road, The Negro Caravan,* his work with the Gunnar Myrdal study, with the Federal Writers' Project, all of that was extremely important.[4] And his collaborations with people like Ben Botkin, the whole slave narrative project, *Lay My Burden Down,* he was involved in that, he was involved in *Folk-Say.*

Sterling was going to do what he called *The New Negro Caravan* and he wanted he and I to be editors. He talked about this all through the '80s. He wanted to upgrade his notion of what the first *Caravan* had achieved. Of course, the impact of music was very important. I don't know what Sterling would have done, for example, with hip hop; but it would certainly have been interesting, given some of his characterizations, given his famous prototype of the heroic figure who was semi-literate or illiterate, Big Boy Davis, the blues singer in "When de Saints Go Ma'ching Home," who was an actual man.[5] As Sterling used to say, "I learned the Arts and Sciences at Williams and Harvard; I learned the Humanities at Lynchburg, Virginia." Which is to say that when he went to Lynchburg, Carter Woodson, who was one of his high school teachers, told him, you need to go and be immersed in your people. And Sterling had such extraordinary gifts as a scholar and a poet that even James Weldon Johnson said, in his introduction to *Southern Road,* that of all the poets, it was Sterling who best captured the genuine black folk idiom.

Sterling never characterized his efforts at folk speech in his poems as "dialect poetry," he would never call it that. He would say, "I am writing these poems in the folk idiom." The reason why Sterling said that is because he felt the values of Black American speech . . . it was so penetrating, so laconic and so resonant that to be in that speech community was to be given this information. What Sterling had was the ability to arrange it, because he studied—among other people—Shakespeare, Milton, Chaucer; he had what we call a classical education, Greek and Latin. So he could see the value of what his people had done; one could say a semiliterate or illiterate people, but you don't have to be literate to have a tradition. All of those great ballads that you know and grew up with, many of them anonymous, were crafted over generations by people who couldn't read and write. So it's not an anomaly for you to have a resonant past, which is captured by people who don't have a written tradition.

Sterling was always involved in a battle over this because of American racism, because of the New Critics, the Agrarians—people who took it upon themselves to create a mythology, which had absolutely nothing to do with the facts, but which they felt comfortable in doing because they were trying to create a mythology of their own. So that a Jean Toomer or a Sterling Brown or a Langston Hughes were not in the pantheon, as they envisioned it. And, of course, Sterling had a tremendous grievance with some of these people. He was always at war with the New Critics, in particular Robert Penn Warren—he would say, "I wonder what Robert Penn Warren knows about segregation, having never been segregated in his entire life, yet he edited a book on it." You know the reference that Robert Penn Warren makes, "Nigger, your breed ain't metaphysical"; and Sterling replied, "Cracker, your kind ain't exegetical." With Sterling, the Agrarians were dangerous people because they had no appreciation of what slavery had done, and how much courage it took to survive at all. And, of course, his grandmother was a slave.

He had a sense of why it is that people need to read more widely than their own discipline. For example, Robert Bone, the guy who wrote the book about the Negro in American fiction, in the 1950s, told me a story about getting on a train and going down from New York to have a seminar with Sterling in African American literature. This would have been in the early '50s. There were just the two of them, and Sterling taught him the history of Black American jokes, what we used to call Negro jokes. He knew more about folklore than anybody. When Arna Bontemps and Langston Hughes published their quote unquote comprehensive anthology of African American folklore, they borrowed most of their stuff from Sterling. He used to say, "they never asked me permission to reprint my articles as their own!" But he had a sense of humor about this.

Sterling was just a comprehensive person. You know his comment about the Harlem Renaissance? He never called it the Harlem Renaissance; he always called it the New Negro movement. He would say the Harlem Renaissance was just a publishing vehicle, and most of the great writers from the Black American tradition were from somewhere else; they were all over the country. Sterling had a bias for Howard University because so many of his colleagues were important figures. He was in a group, all the intellectuals . . . you've got to understand this is in the context of segregation. I mean, the trolleys and the streetcars and the buses and the movie theatres were all segregated; Sterling would work in the Library of Congress and he couldn't go into the cafeteria. So there were alternative options and they had this group called the Gourmets, who would get together and talk: people like Ralph Bunche and Abe Harris, the economist, Arthur P. Davis, the historian Raymond Logan, Thurgood Marshall, who was the best dirty joke teller in the world, even better than Sterling. They would get together and talk about "the problem," which meant, you know, segregation, racism in America. I remember a couple of times Sterling got together the remaining people, and they would sit and talk, to give me a sense of what intellectual life was on the Howard University campus.

LOCK: Can I ask you about the '60s? The idea of music as central to African American culture seems to have been especially emphasized by the Black Arts movement in the 1960s . . .

HARPER: You're asking a political question.

LOCK: I am?

HARPER: It happens to be a very worthwhile one, an important thing to talk about. You know Ralph Ellison's famous review of Amiri Baraka's *Blues People*?[6] So we have what I would say is a rift between the Black Arts people and their elders. Robert Hayden's anthology *Kaleidoscope* gathers together the efforts of previous generations: I don't know too many people from the Black Arts movement who paid any attention to this. Sterling Brown's *The Negro Caravan*, which came out in 1941, was comprehensive. How many people mastered what was put together by three extraordinary critics: Arthur P. Davis, Sterling Brown, and Ulysses Lee?

But it was not only the Black Arts movement. Many conservative teachers and critics did not like Sterling's capacity for encouragement and innovation.

LOCK: Was he sympathetic to the New Music of the '60s?

HARPER: Oh sure. But it's interesting: Sterling had an enormous impact on a great many people he taught, but not many poets. The only poet he had an influence on, whom he taught, was Lucille Clifton and that was in the 1950s. I asked her, when we were at Emory together (it was Lincoln's birthday), to tell the students what it was like to be in Sterling's class. Lucille said the first thing was that I was too dark, on the Howard campus, to be allowed to speak, and the only person who spoke to me by name was Sterling Brown. It's amazing! This would've been in the early 1950s. She had some wonderful things to say about Sterling, about how egalitarian he was; but he was not Howard University, he was Sterling Brown.

The '60s were very hard on him because they called him Pollyanna. He'd written these wonderful poems in the 1930s and people had discovered them but they were not poets, they were opportunists. I don't mean that in a negative sense. I'm glad they found his poems; but at the same time he was on the downturn of his career, and he lost many battles on the Howard campus, which is very conservative. Sterling was not. They would refer to Sterling's class in Negro Literature as Nigger Lit; they did not want him to teach that class. He started this in the 1930s, so you would think a black institution would support him, but it was Sterling's commitment.

LOCK: What did they want him to teach?

HARPER: He taught everything. He taught eighteenth-century drama, he taught Milton, he taught Shakespeare, he taught the Romantics, he ran the

Howard Theater . . . you name it. Sterling was a virtuoso. And he was a real mentor. Mentoring is very important, and Sterling taught many, many students and made the difference to them being able to take on the segregated school system in Washington, D.C. He trained a lot of those teachers, so his energies went there. But he was writing essays and doing all kinds of things. He was doing the jobs of two or three people. But I think, had his second book not been rejected, it would have been a different story.

LOCK: I'm curious about the school system in Washington. There's a story in Duke Ellington's autobiography about when he was growing up in Washington—apparently there was a move to desegregate the schools and it was the black community who opposed it because they thought their children's education would suffer.

HARPER: Well, not only that. They had so many black teachers who could only get jobs as caretakers. It's a very contradictory story in this country about race and class and education. Because there's always something to be lost. Sterling used to say this over and over: "an integer is a whole number." Meaning, integration is not assimilation. An integer is a whole number. He was against segregation, because he knew what it meant.[7] But if Sterling wanted to have a dinner party, even into the '6os, he would call up Harrison's, which was a black-owned restaurant, and have his friends gather there. He wouldn't go downtown to a white restaurant. He had spent his whole life supporting black institutions. There's nobody black that I know who doesn't have ambivalence when, say, he can't use the Library of Congress cafeteria when he's down there working on papers. I mean, these wounds go very deep. Sterling, for many years, would not read his poems at the Library of Congress. He finally did read there. William Meredith finally got him to read.

So it's a complex question, the whole business about class and color. And Sterling did not believe in reducing complexity. He told me a wonderful story about when he first saw his wife, before they were married, he said, "I was playing tennis and this woman walked up the street dragging two little kids with her, who happened to be her sister's children." And he said, "For the first time in my life, I double faulted." [Laughs.] That was his comment. Daisy was a wonderful woman—her eyes were bluer than yours. They got married and they spent their honeymoon with the Bibbys: this is the famous poem "Sister Lou," it's all about Amherst, Virginia, a farm called "Coolwell"; that's where they spent their honeymoon. Daisy . . . Sterling called her Rose Anne, so when you see that section of poems dedicated to Rose Anne, the "Vestiges" section in the Collected Poems, that's Daisy.

LOCK: Why did he call her Rose Anne?

HARPER: That was his nom de plume for her. And most of those poems in the "Vestiges" section are poems that he wrote in tutelage to the tradition. And you notice that they're very formal: Petrarchan sonnets, Shakespearean sonnets . . . Sterling was indicating his poetic fluency, his craft. I'm sure that he was reading *A Shropshire Lad* to his wife on their honeymoon, because A.E. Housman was his favorite English poet. The "Vestiges" section is all about that. He loved Housman. He loved Robert Frost too; loved Shakespeare; loved Milton. Sterling thought I was semiliterate, I didn't have as good an education as he did. He would say things like, you don't understand the pause, meaning the caesura; you're a modern poet but you don't understand the pause. Meaning Milton.

LOCK: Didn't he say he understood the caesura because he was a preacher's son?

HARPER: Yeah, exactly, he was a preacher's son. Sterling proofread Du Bois's *Black Reconstruction in America* because Du Bois used to lecture at his father's church. When he spent time in Washington, he would stay with the family, and he gave *Black Reconstruction* to Sterling and said, you're the only person I trust in the talented tenth to proofread this. And he gave Sterling a bottle of crème de menthe as a present. [*Laughs.*] Sterling told me he'd just let it crystallize; crème de menthe wasn't his drink. [*Laughs.*] That's a true story.

Sterling said that Du Bois didn't know very much about Marxism; he knew a great deal of history, but his Marxism was weak. Sterling was never a member of the Communist Party but he was a leftist and he certainly had all kinds of heat brought on him by the House Un-American Activities Committee and all the rest of it.[8] I'm sure they tried to intimidate Bunche . . . in fact, Sterling introduced Bunche to Gunnar Myrdal.

Here's a story for you. I met Myrdal in Sweden in 1980. I had been in Copenhagen at a seminar on Black American literature; I was one of the keynote speakers, and from there I flew to Stockholm. When I got off the plane, I was met by a diplomat, who said, is there anything you would like to do today? I said, I would like to meet Gunnar Myrdal, and he laughed. He said, everybody wants to meet him. I said, do you have a notepad? When you call Gunnar Myrdal, this is what I want you to say: "I bring greetings from Sterling Brown." Period! The guy I was talking to didn't even know who Sterling Brown was. This was nine o'clock in the morning. I get deposited at the Hotel Diplomat. About eleven o'clock I get a call: Mr. Myrdal will see you at his residence at two o'clock this afternoon, and a car will be there to pick you up at one. Now, what had happened? [*Laughs.*] You know! I don't know what happened, but I knew that was the thing to say to him. Myrdal lived in the old section of Stockholm, not far from the monument of St. George slaying the dragon. So I get in the car at one o'clock and the guy says to me, would you like to hear anything on the radio? I said, sure, just put on some jazz music. The first tune that came up is "Dear Old Stockholm," which is a tune Miles Davis wrote, based on a Swedish folk song. It was a magical moment!

We get to Myrdal's house and he had an elevator: you go in the first floor, get on the elevator and go up to the second floor. So I get out and I say to him, before I forget, I want to give you a copy of the book I've selected for the National Poetry Society, Sterling Brown's *Collected Poems*. Myrdal stands there stunned. He says the greatest problem with Sterling is he never published his own books. He says this to me; so I'm looking at him. I said, well, he certainly has one now, his *Collected Poems*.

This trip was also the first time I met Maya Angelou; we were supposed to do a reading together in Stockholm. She was teaching at Winston Salem, and later she invited Sterling and myself to come to Winston Salem and read in her church. He and I spent two or three days down there: we read in her church and were guests in her house. And she and Sterling clashed, because Sterling . . . he'd read almost all of her books and he had a critique of them. I said to him, Prof, you don't have to tell her what you think. In her own house! [*Laughs.*] Sterling just couldn't resist, he would have to say something, oh God! [*Laughs.*] So the two of them clashed. It was a momentous meeting.

LOCK: Can I ask you about Sterling's poems? There are several that are either about or influenced by the blues and the spirituals, yet he doesn't seem to write very much about jazz. The only poem I know where he features jazz is "Cabaret" and he portrays it in a negative light there.[9] But in his essays, he appears to like jazz as much as anything else.

HARPER: Oh, Sterling had an incredible record collection. I'll tell you the story of "Cabaret" because it's very important. In fact, it's one of the poems that he read that first time at Brown. The reason why the poem is cast in the way it is, is because he was at a black and tan in Chicago in 1927, and Fletcher Henderson's was the band. And because of the impact of Tin Pan Alley on the blues, and music *period*, he decided he would have to, in legitimate fashion, critique the phoniness—this was during Prohibition. So remember it's Fletcher Henderson's band and he's talking about where these people, who are the entertainers, the dancers, really come from, right? Then, all of a sudden, the poem shifts into the levee, the 1927 Mississippi flood, and those black people chained to the levee. And, of course, Bessie Smith, "My heart cries out for muddy water."[10] Now Sterling didn't talk about it like this; he just read the poem. But it's a poem that has at least three levels to it; it's a very complicated poem, with various voicings. I think what he was after, certainly at the time, was an assault on Tin Pan Alley music as a substitute for the real blues, and the pressure that was put on theatrical people—what he'd call his people—to bastardize something that was really sacred to him.

If you look at the essays he did, you notice that he wrote a wonderful essay on Jelly Roll Morton, which was in *Black World*.[11] Sterling's favorite people were mostly piano players: he loved Willie "The Lion" Smith, he loved James P. Johnson, he loved the guy who played for the Mafia . . . Earl Hines. He knew all of that music. He had the record collection. He had the first blues ever recorded in the United States, 1920, "Crazy Blues" by Mamie Smith. He said he bought it when he was a student at Williams College, so he was a student of the blues way back. And so many of those poems are written with a blues consciousness to them. And, more than anything, when you look at his ballads—

> Look at old Scrappy puttin' on dog,
>   Puttin' on dog, puttin' on dog,
> Look at old Scrappy puttin' on dog,
>   Todle-oh-in' with his Jane"[12]

—the theme of people being pushed too far and the kind of style that couldn't be suppressed. The way in which his characters in the Slim Greer cycle were able to do impossible things: well, they were all based on people he knew. When he was tellin' those damn stories about the woman who . . . where Slim goes and plays the piano and all of a sudden he loses his sense of things and the cracker says to him, "No white man could play like that."[13] Sterling was just full of that kind of stuff. He loved to attack the conventions, the conventions of race. And, of course, the famous poem about all of the people laughing in the phone booth in Atlanta:

> Down in Atlanta,
>   De white folks got laws
> For to keep all de niggers
>   From laughin' outdoors.[14]

And they're all trying to get in the telephone booth to laugh! These kind of things. And the famous poem called "Slim in Hell," which was based on Orpheus and Eurydice: you know, Slim goes to Hell, which turns out to be Dixie. Sterling said to me one day, he said, every one of those places that I mention in the poem, there was a race riot. Race riot in Waco, race riot in Rome, race riot in Vicksburg, every one of those place names. So Sterling had an extremely well-developed social conscience. And enormous courage.

LOCK: I was just puzzled that he had all these poems on blues and ballads and didn't write very much about jazz. Whereas Langston Hughes does include jazz and he also concentrates more on urban blues, while Sterling Brown seems to refer more to folk and rural blues.

HARPER: Oh, I think that's true. Sterling was very much immersed in that. But he wrote those wonderful poems, you know, "They don't come by ones, they don't come by twos, but they come by tens."[15]

LOCK: Some critics have seen this aspect of his work as implicitly anti-modernist. The fact that he's looking at the rural rather than the urban, that he's into folk and blues—and using those forms—rather than commercial jazz. Do you think that's a fair comment?

HARPER: Well, I think it's contrary to what I know about Sterling. I know he'd read "The Waste Land" in 1922. He was just out of Williams and into Harvard when he was reading *The Dial* and *The Double Dealer* and all of those damn poems. He knew Pound and he knew him early. But he would choose a Frost over an Eliot. It wasn't so much that he didn't appreciate what Eliot was doing, but he felt . . . I'm not sure Sterling ever said this, probably I intuited it . . . he didn't feel that Eliot had made the proper choice by becoming an Anglican and leaving the country. Here he was, born on the Mississippi River in St Louis. Why was it good enough for Twain but not good enough for him? Because Sterling was very much an Americanist. He believed in American literature. I mean, he was studying American literature when it was a new literature.

I think Sterling was so prescient on the arteries of blues and jazz and where they came from. He knew a tremendous amount about New Orleans, he knew a lot about Kansas City, and he learned this stuff early and he was writing about it early. I think that had Sterling been left alone . . . There are a couple of things I'll say. I think it was probably a bad thing for him to stay at Howard—because he could have left, he had opportunities—I think as a poet he would have prospered had he gotten out of the provincialism of Washington, D.C. into a more urban setting, which could have been New York. And I think the turning down of his second book of poems, *No Hiding Place*, was a devastating blow. He was not content to sit on the achievement of his first book. *Southern Road* had some wonderful poems in it, some incredible poems, but a lot of the more famous poems, as I think about it, were in his second book; ones that he loved, which were . . . I guess they were political. He loved "Remembering Nat Turner," for example, which was his work on the Federal Writers Project. In fact, that poem was written for Roscoe Lewis, who was the guy who wrote the book *The Negro in Virginia*. In Sterling's copy, it says "To Dutch" (which was his nickname), "his book," meaning without Sterling there would have been no *Negro in Virginia*.

Like Myrdal said, Sterling never finished his own books because he was helping other people finish theirs. He was helping Bunche, he was helping Du Bois, he was helping Roscoe Lewis, he was helping Zora Neale Hurston. And I think he suffered for it. But Sterling just knew everybody. I mean, he certainly had a relationship with Richard Wright. He knew Jean Toomer. Toomer would periodically write to him, asking for assurance or whatever in some of his experimentations and . . . you know, Sterling's premise was always that Toomer never passed for white.

LOCK: Oh, I thought he did.

HARPER: Sterling's thesis was that Toomer never said that he *wasn't* black, he just allowed people to think whatever . . . He didn't hang out in Harlem, he was hanging out in the Village when he was in New York. His poetic models, his literary models, were not the same people that the Renaissance writers had. But a book like *Cane*, can you say that's not a black book? I mean, *Cane* is certainly a black book.

LOCK: But when James Weldon Johnson wanted to include an extract from *Cane* in a collection of Negro writing, didn't Toomer refuse permission because he didn't want to be classified as Negro?

HARPER: Yes, well, I would say that that again is an anomaly. But I'm telling you what Sterling said, what Sterling's estimate of Toomer was, and he didn't feel that Toomer ever passed for white. The point is Sterling was talking about artistic freedom and people who were casting a paintbrush too easily when Toomer was interested in other things, including Gurdjieff, all that mystical business. Sterling was not willing to concede that a person who had written that important and that profound a book, if only the one, that he could ever be disconnected from his people.

So the whole color and class question . . . Sterling and my mother got into a terrific argument about Dunbar High School.[16] Sterling could be very imperious with his friends and associates, and my mother stopped him one day. She said, Sterling, my son—meaning me—has what you don't have, noblesse oblige. Would you have had your poems in a book without my son? Sterling didn't say anything. He had been talking about the black bourgeoisie, various talented tenth families that he had been raised by and educated by. My mother told him, you know, my father went to M Street High (which later became Dunbar) and he was an outsider—meaning my grandfather, her father, who was a Canadian. He was Arthur Schomburg's best friend and they were both outcasts. Part of it was to do with color, part of it had to do with the fact that they were outsiders; one a black Puerto Rican, one a black Canadian. So you have a split in the black community, along intellectual lines. My mother said to Sterling, in my own family we have a deep crisis over color. The light ones were all ready to pass for white; the black ones had the best education and the money and the devotion to their people.

Sterling shut up. He was so formidable that he was not used to being confronted, certainly not by a woman, a black woman at that, and a person who had more pedigree than he had, or an equal pedigree, and could talk about things that are kind of sacred. Because my mother's father's father—my great grandfather—was one of the presiding elders at Frederick Douglass's funeral. He was an A.M.E. bishop and a founding member of the American Negro Academy, along with Du Bois and the rest.

I'm telling you some complex stories. When I write my memoirs, I'll have to write an essay about Sterling and include some of this, because Sterling was right about a great many things but he was the youngest of six children. He had five older sisters and they used to tease him. "What are you doing writing about unrequited love? You don't know anything about that." They were all schoolteachers and they were all over him. He was very close to his family. So for him to be the youngest of six, and his father's favorite, and the one that his parents put all of their hopes on—he carried the hopes and dreams of the whole family.

NOTES

1. The other part of this interview, in which Michael Harper talks about the influence of jazz and blues on his own poetry, appears as Graham Lock, "Phraseology: An Interview with Michael S. Harper," in *Thriving on a Riff: Jazz and Blues*

Influences in African American Literature and Film, eds. Graham Lock and David Murray (New York: Oxford University Press, 2009): 80–105.

2. See Michael S. Harper, "Br'er Sterling and the Rocker," in Michael S. Harper, *Songlines in Michaeltree: New and Collected Poems* (Urbana: University of Illinois Press, 2000), 115.

3. Sterling Brown can be heard reading his poems on the CD *The Poetry of Sterling A. Brown* (Smithsonian/Folkways SF47002, 1995); the recordings were made in various locations between 1946 and 1973.

4. Several of Brown's essays on the blues are reprinted in Sterling A. Brown, *A Son's Return: Selected Essays of Sterling A. Brown*, ed. Mark A. Sanders (Boston: Northeastern University Press, 1996). He gives a seven-minute talk entitled "What Are the Blues?" on the CD *Freedom* by the Golden Gate Quartet and Josh White (1940; Bridge 9114, 2002). *Southern Road*, Brown's first book of poems, was originally published in 1932; it is reprinted in Sterling A. Brown, *The Collected Poems of Sterling A. Brown*, ed. Michael S. Harper (1980; repr., Evanston, IL: TriQuarterly Books/Northwestern University Press, 1996). *The Negro Caravan* (1941), a landmark collection of material on African American culture and life, was co-edited by Brown, Arthur P. Davis, and Ulysses Lee. (repr., New York: Arno Press, 1969).

5. Brown, "When de Saints Go Ma'ching Home," *Collected Poems*, 26–30.

6. The review of *Blues People* (which was published under Baraka's original name, LeRoi Jones) first appeared *The New York Review* on 6 February 1964. It has since been reprinted in various Ellison collections, including *Shadow and Act, The Collected Essays* and, most recently, *Living with Music: Ralph Ellison's Jazz Writings*, ed. Robert G. O'Meally (New York: Random House, 2001), 121–32. Ellison's review was highly critical of Baraka's understanding of the blues. It included what became a famous signifying parry when, complaining about the sociopolitical burden the book tried to place on the music, Ellison remarked that Baraka's thesis was enough to give even the blues the blues.

7. The quotation comes from a speech Sterling Brown gave at Williams College in 1973, reprinted in *A Son's Return*, 16–17. I think the passage is worth quoting in full:

I am an integrationist, though that is an ugly word, because I know what segregation really was. And by integration, I do not mean assimilation. I believe what the word means--an integer is a whole number. I want to be in the best American traditions. I want to be accepted as a whole man. My standards are not white. My standards are not black. My standards are human. I love the blues. I love jazz, and I'm not going to give them up. I love Negro folk speech and I think it is rich and wonderful. It is not *dis* and *dat* and a split verb. But it is "Been down so long that down don't worry me," or it is what spirituals had in one of the finest couplets in American literature: "I don't know what my mother wants to stay here for. This old world ain't been no friend to her."

8. In a 1978 interview, Brown recalled being questioned by an FBI official as to whether he was a Communist. He replied: "Listen son, any Negro who has been to the seventh grade and is against lynching is a Communist. I have been to the eighth grade and am against a hell of a lot more than lynching." Quoted in Joanne

V. Gabbin, *Sterling A. Brown: Building the Black Aesthetic Tradition* (1985; repr., Charlottesville: University Press of Virginia, 1994), 51.

9. Brown, "Cabaret," *Collected Poems*, 111–13.
10. "Muddy Water," recorded by Bessie Smith in 1927, is a sentimental Tin Pan Alley song, the lyrics of which Brown threads through "Cabaret" in telling counterpoint to his descriptions of the appalling conditions African Americans were forced to endure in the wake of the 1927 Mississippi flood. For a detailed account of the poem's complexities and different levels, see Mark A. Sanders, *Afro-Modernist Aesthetics and the Poetry of Sterling A. Brown* (Athens: University of Georgia Press, 1999), 77–81.
11. Brown, "Portrait of a Jazz Giant: 'Jelly Roll' Morton," *Black World*, February 1974, 28–48.
12. Brown, "Puttin' on Dog," *Collected Poems*, 239. He reads this poem on the Smithsonian CD.
13. Brown, "Slim Greer," *Collected Poems*, 78.
14. Brown, "Slim in Atlanta," *Collected Poems*, 81.
15. Brown, "Old Lem," *Collected Poems*, 180. He reads this poem too on the Smithsonian CD.
16. Dunbar High School, in Washington, D.C., was probably the most prestigious all-black high school in the country, famed for the academic excellence of its teachers. Both Sterling Brown and Jean Toomer were students there, although at different times, Brown being the younger by some six and a half years.

Clarifying Philosophy: Sterling A. Brown and the Nonviolent Action Group

John Edgar Tidwell

The origins of the Nonviolent Action Group, known by its acronym, NAG, now seem shrouded in the mysteries of historical anonymity. Such a fate is undeserved for an organization that, through its association with the Student Nonviolent Coordinating Committee (SNCC), played a significant role in funneling black student insurgency into the Civil Rights Movement of the early 1960s. Even today, those who recall their own participation in the movement are hard pressed to state unequivocally names of founding NAG members, the organization's actual birth date, its longevity, its precise site of origin, and the specific activities it engaged in. Despite such apocrypha, NAG once lived and thrived. In our postmodern world, where truth is not absolute but relative, an importance for NAG emerges from the collective memory of four individuals who gathered on a June afternoon in 2005 to relive their student experiences nurtured in the political activism of that era.

Timothy Jenkins, Charlie Cobb, Jean Wheeler Smith-Young, and Courtland Cox joined me at the home of Timothy and Lauretta Jenkins in Washington, D.C., to revisit experiences they had as undergraduates and NAG members at Howard University in the early 1960s. As the collective interview demonstrates, theirs was not merely a fond recollection of the past or a roseate ambling down memory lane. That day, mind and memory worked in tandem to retrace and reveal a special context, a crucible, if you will, shaping and defining their intellectual and political development.

The one constant binding the testaments of these participants was the crucial role played by Sterling A. Brown as their unofficial advisor. Brown's long association with the Howard faculty began with his appointment in 1929. His immense loyalty to the institution was superseded only by a profound commitment to his students. When asked to sum up his life and career, he described himself as "minor poet" but "a major teacher." His legacy, he felt, would be most easily discerned in his students. Brown had developed a reputation for walking to the beat of a different drummer. His preoccupation with teaching unconventional subjects, like blues and jazz, in unconventional places, like dormitory sitting rooms, earned him the status of "outsider" among those who felt it their bounden duty to uphold a bourgeois idea of Howard. With this reputation, it seemed quite natural for Brown to gravitate toward the members of NAG, whose enthusiasm for social reform outpaced the gradualism favored by the university. The most immediate result of this alliance, in the words of one member, was that Brown forced them to clarify their philosophy. Enthusiasm without the discipline that comes from a studied knowledge of one's historical and cultural past was doomed to dissipation. From Brown's informal tutelage, often accomplished through vigorous discussion and even contentious debate, the students came to understand the nexus of past and present, with a view toward developing a more promising future.

The individual experiences recounted here demonstrate the power of cultural memory to preserve and perpetuate the history of racial struggle. Intellectually, the NAG members came to understand his aesthetic focus on recording the lives, language, and lore of black people. As they matured and developed their own worldviews, they continually returned to Brown's teaching. For they saw in his example a transformative power, an ability to convert prosaic fact into myth. That is to say, he was especially artful in capturing the strengths and weaknesses of the people he so loved. Through an innovative poetry and an equally expressive prose, he revealed the extraordinary in the lives of ordinary people. It was this power that enabled the members of NAG to appreciate the steadfastness, the determination, and the will to succeed of a people who continued, in the words of his poem, to get stronger in spite of overwhelming odds.

Collectively, the narrative impulse toward mythmaking becomes the legacy bequeathed to the next generation. It is a guide for helping people make sense of the world in which they live. One generation speaks to and through a succeeding one as a means of ensuring the continuity of tradition. Brown, the teacher, instilled the importance of intelligent engagement in his students, who, later in life, found themselves becoming the people they admired in their youth. As if speaking in one voice, the participants came away with a feeling that the substance of their learning needed to be shared with the next generation of young people. More than feeling, it became their *responsibility* to impart the wit and wisdom they gained from their elders.

While history, formally constituted in published records and extant documents, has failed to preserve the coalition of Brown and NAG, the narrative persists. It inheres in the lives of those who experienced it. It also resides in what novelist Toni Morrison, a student of Brown's, aptly named "rememory" in her novel *Beloved:* "If a house burns down, it's gone, but the place—the picture of it—stays, and not just in my rememory, but out there, in the world." The spirit of Brown survives in the NAG members. To keep his essence alive, they too will ensure, as this interview attests, that the "picture" of him will be out there, "in the world."

JOHN EDGAR TIDWELL: I came to Sterling rather late in his life and didn't have the advantage of having studied under him or much protracted experience with him. To augment my knowledge, I have conducted intensive investigations into correspondence, records, documents, and published sources and have depended on knowledgeable people like you to give me their personal insights. I have come to know how highly regarded he was as a teacher, which opened up an area I continue to explore: that is, the nature of his relationship to the younger generation coming after him. This issue, for me, is inextricably tied to his reputation at Howard University for being a bit of a pariah because he was interested in ideas and topics that seemed to go against the bourgeois, institutional grain at Howard, such as when he talked about the blues, spirituals, and jazz.

CHARLIE COBB: He did go against the grain at Howard.

TIMOTHY JENKINS: He didn't seem to go against the grain.

COBB: The grain at Howard. [*Laughter*] They didn't like Sterling the folklorist; they didn't like any of his poetry. My mother had Sterling as a student. She was at Howard in the 1930s, and they didn't like the poems like "Slim Greer" and "Old Lem" and all of his poetry that's rooted in his interest essentially in rural black life. It's a great irony about Sterling: he's a guy who grew up in middle-, upper-middle-class Washington, developed a literary career separate from the teaching career around rural Southern black life, which as far as Howard University was concerned, according to my mother and my brief experience with that university, was beyond the pale. [*Laughter*] The whole point of the people, not just those who ran Howard, but that whole black bourgeoisie, to use Frazier's phrase, was that you were supposed to be escaping from that; you were supposed to be moving upward. It's the same hostility. That's why they're hostile to the blues, and jazz was just seen as another piece of that "riff raff–type music." Sterling came here romanticizing this is what they always said, and they didn't like that. Sterling used to talk about that too.

TIDWELL: Ironically, Reverend Sterling Nelson Brown started the Extension and Correspondence Division at the School of Religion because a woman somewhere in the South wrote and asked him: "Do you have any advice, or can you give me some readings that I can suggest to my husband, because he's having such a hard time in his ministry?" Reverend Brown responded with a lot of suggestions that he eventually worked into the beginnings of his correspondence course. Then he went throughout the South lecturing and extending the school in that way. So, he himself became involved with the folk in just the opposite way. When Sterling talks about going to Virginia Seminary College . . .

JENKINS: Opposite of what?

TIDWELL: When Sterling was sent to Virginia Seminary and College, his father hoped that he would hear "the call" to preach because he wanted Sterling to accept the family mantle and succeed him in the ministry. Sterling was the only son, and Rev. Brown desperately wanted Sterling to succeed him. In my mind, sending him to Seminary was the not so subtle subtext for getting Sterling to follow in his footsteps. Sterling, as you know, heard *a* call, but not *the* call at Seminary. [*Laughter*] He responded to the secular world, not the sacred one his father intended. He heard Calvin "Big Boy" Davis, and he heard Mrs. Bibby, and a whole host of other characters who immersed him into the tradition of black folk life, language, and lore.

JEAN WHEELER SMITH-YOUNG: That's what he found?

TIDWELL: That's what he heard.

SMITH-YOUNG: But that's what happened when I went South, too. I'm from Detroit, and when I went South it was like a whole world opened up to me. I had never heard that language; I had never heard that music. It was so beautiful. And the first time I ever heard a line hymn in a little tiny church, I said, "What is this?" It was just amazing; I never, ever got over that. But it was a moment of expanding; it's the same kind of thing.

COBB: But if you think of the Howard bureaucracy listening to something like "Can't never tell how far a frog's gonna jump when you see him sitting on his big broad rump" or "what a monkey's thinking about the working of his jaw." [*Laughter*] This is not proper English to start with, let alone talking about "big broad rump" and all of that. This was the same. My mother would say this, and it seemed the same to me by the time I made my way down. It didn't seem to have changed very much in that regard.

SMITH-YOUNG: Well, I've got a theory. This is just a theory, you can tell me if it's correct. It seems to me that the teachers that gravitated to us, that helped NAG were the ones, as I recall, that were outsiders. I remember Chancellor . . .

COBB/JENKINS: Williams.

SMITH-YOUNG: Chancellor Williams, he was like a total outsider. In fact, one time I went to see him. I had just gotten interested in NAG, and I was trying to sort out what I was doing here on Howard's campus. He was rather grouchy and didn't want to talk very much, so he hands me a book called *Man Alone* and says, "Read this!" That's who he was; he was a man alone. He was one of our advisers. There were others who were maybe more in but acted like they were not quite in this circle, like Sterling Brown. A lot of these guys who found us attractive and wanted to help us were in a sense outsiders.

COBB: They were.

TIDWELL: I'm not sure if you know this or not, but Sterling had ambivalent feelings about Williams College and Harvard. He felt alienated. That was one of the most important admissions that I've seen by Sterling in talking about his relationship with those schools.

JENKINS: I think Sterling also in the later periods was alienated from Harvard because he was alienated from his colleagues who graduated from Harvard, who were not alienated. People like Frank Snowden and William Banner, Rayford Logan. Those faculty people had a different orientation to Harvard as the gold standard. Both Snowden and Banner, he used to always remark, went around Howard's campus with their little Harvard bags over their shoulders. He would always disparage them by talking about "Hahvard," with that broad "a." [*Laughter*] What he also didn't appreciate—and I don't know this to be the case with Rayford—was that Banner and Snowden had had integrated educational experiences back to high school, so the degree to which they were comfortable at Harvard was likely to be a little different than Sterling's early education and exposure.

TIDWELL: We all know that Sterling was a very complicated person. A couple of summers ago when I was at Harvard, I had a chance to meet Cleveland Sellers, who wrote *The River of No Return: The Autobiography of a Black Militant and the Life and Death of SNCC*. I said to him: "I just found out that you were involved in NAG! Maybe you could give me some information about it." His reply further astounded me: "Sterling Brown was our unofficial adviser, and what was most important about Sterling was that he made us *clarify our philosophy!*" That, for me, was another profound statement. It offered further evidence that Sterling did take the time to interact with the younger people, not only to promote them, but to teach them. As you know, he would invite different people over, and they would go down into his basement, listen to the music, and talk art and politics. I am really curious about what they learned from Sterling, what they actually took away from these sessions. Ideologically, what did they learn from him? What did he help them clarify?

SMITH-YOUNG: I have two things to say about him. One is that—and this is important from my point of view as a psychiatrist—what I valued so much about him was that he was always around, always available. You could just sort of sidle up to him, or he would kind of sidle up to you. He'd just be there. And it was very important that he would come to informal meetings. We'd just be standing around together, and all of the sudden there's Sterling Brown, sort of checking on us and making sure we're thinking good thoughts . . . thinking correctly. But the relationship with him as a person of the upper generation, and as a representative of the university, and as a learned man, and there he was taking time for our small, untested group. This meant a lot. This legitimized, for me, our role in the university. Actually, I've often thought in general that in SNCC and NAG, we were just lucky to have survived. There were so many ways that we could have been wiped out in about two weeks, and yet we didn't get wiped out. It was because of people like Sterling, who were part of this structure, part of the place, the university. He was in support of us so that we were about to survive. We were standing around one day, on the steps of Founders Library, and I don't even know who was with us. It was about ten of us from NAG; I don't think there was anything formal about it, just standing at the library. And Sterling sort of appeared. It seems to me he appeared on my right side, and he said, "What are y'all doing?" And we kind of didn't answer much. And he says, "Come on. I'm gonna give you some culture." And he took this whole group of people—I remember it to be 10 people—to see *The Three Penny Opera* at the Arena Stage. I don't know where he got the tickets; I don't know where he got the money. But he just took all of us. I had never seen a large theatre. And I didn't know much about literature, because I think it was maybe my second year of college. It was such a lesson. This play was about protest, or at least it was about protest and dissent and another way to think about the reality that you find around you. I hadn't known that either. I had joined NAG more because it was compelling at the time, but I didn't have any historical perspective. And when he took us to see the play, it gave me my first historical perspective on movement kinds of activities. So that's my story about Sterling. [*Laughs*]

TIDWELL: I'm sure all of you have read Stokely Carmichael's autobiography, *Ready for Revolution*. Even Stokely Carmichael began talking about the ways in which Sterling made them see things in a larger perspective. It's almost as if they were locked into a political focus but never able see beyond all of that. But under Sterling's guidance, they began to see cultural issues more broadly, and then understand the depth and breadth of the history of African Americans and culture.

COBB: Not just broadly, though. Sterling also pointed you where you really didn't have the instincts to look, and that was really at the grassroots. You see that in his writing. Sterling was basically saying—whether you're talking to him on U Street, whether you're talking to him at his basement on Kearny Street, or at the Highlander Center—what we constantly got from Sterling, and what we really didn't get from the other Howard University professors in my recollection, was that we ought to pay attention to these other voices, these street voices, these rural voices. It's more than just broader. He had a language that the other professors didn't have, and that language connected you to people you weren't sent to Howard University to connect to. [*Agreement, laughter*] I remember my first night at Howard. My parents made me stay at Drew Hall, the dormitory. Now I've got relatives all over Washington, D.C. My mother's from here, my aunts and uncles, and all that, but I'm staying at Drew Hall. The very first night, the head of the dorm takes us to the roof, and he waves over the streets of northwest Washington. I can almost see one of my aunt and uncles' houses. The first thing out of his mouth was, "These streets are dangerous to

Howard men." [*Laughter*] He gives us this lecture about it, and I'm waiting for the guy to get done so I can walk up these streets to get some food from one of my aunts. He ends this sort of discussion about this saying that "one of your duties as Howard men is if you're out there and see unescorted Howard women, you are to escort them back to the dorms."

JENKINS: Who was this?

COBB: This is Mr. Saunders. [*Agreement, laughter*] I remember this. I remember just being astounded by this lecture. But I bring this all up to say we weren't sent to Howard to know anything about those streets that Mr. Saunders said were hostile to Howard, let alone these rural people like Slim and Old Lem that Sterling Brown wrote about. So Sterling was the only professor that I can think of on that whole campus—although there were other professors that had a great deal to offer intellectually—he's the only professor I can remember that pointed us in this direction. He said listen to these voices, the numbers runners out here. And he knew them all up and down U Street, all these shady people. And listen to these voices, these rural voices, with knives in their back pockets and whiskey in their side pockets.

JENKINS: I was at Howard just a ways beforehand, because I graduated in 1960. We had a thing called the Little Forum, which was an ad hoc collection of students and faculty who used to have discussions on a monthly basis. We would meet in the dormitory lounges and the professors would provide us with cookies, snacks, or something like that, maybe some coffee. We would take a book, and there would be a presentation of a faculty member and a student. Then we would launch into a discussion running from 7 o'clock to perhaps 11. Sterling was a member of that group, but there was a cluster of people. There was Harold Lewis, a historian . . .

SMITH-YOUNG: Harold Lewis, yes.

JENKINS: . . . Sam Dorsey, McAllister in Philosophy, Sylvia Eden in Classics, Virginia Callahan in Classics, Dotty in History or Political Science.

TIDWELL: Gene Holmes?

JENKINS: Gene Holmes was not part of that, but I do want to make a mention about him at a later point. What they did was step off their platform as professors, and we had peer discussions on those issues. I remember one of the books we did was C. Wright Mills's *Power Elite*. I still remember that discussion. These were meetings where you could take a professor to task and say, "That didn't make any sense," and "How could you think that," and "Did you read the third page?" [*Laughter*] It was a great empowering experience. They encouraged us to come back at them and defend our positions. Gene Holmes, that you mentioned, is the other exception that I would put in the class with Sterling in terms of folk wisdom and folk respect. I remember he was a big aficionado of jazz and the blues, and on one occasion, more than one occasion, actually, he had Willie "The Lion" Smith come and teach his course. [*Laughter*] He said that Willie "The Lion" Smith, in his view, represented more philosophy than most Ph.D.'s had in terms of understanding. "The Lion" represented for us that kind of street-level, gut-bucket contact. Eugene Holmes was connected with numbers runners and people like that, just like Sterling. In fact, one of Sterling's anecdotes was about this guy who was the numbers runner in the neighborhood of Howard, and he said that Gene Holmes had the highest tab. [*Laughter*]

COURTLAND COX: The older I get, the more I appreciate Sterling Brown, because I think, at this point, we are almost where Sterling was when we were students. I think a lot of the stuff that has been said about what he was able to do suggests he functioned at a lot of levels. I mean he helped give us perspective. In 1960s, we were trying to not only be students but create a different frame of reference. He would come to the dormitory. We lived in Slowe Hall, and he would bring his records. He would do maybe blues once, and then he would do jazz. He would sit and talk about the particular artist and give us their history and give us their sense. What was important for those of us who were trying to not only be students but create a different environment in the society was that it gave us the kind of institutional knowledge that was helpful as we fought the cultural war that existed outside, which tried to tell us we added up to zero. That was one. I think the second thing is that he used to take us over to his house and talk about Du Bois and others, and make these people live; it gave us a sense of continuity, a sense of history, gave us a sense that we were part of a tradition, that we were not isolated, that we were not new. At this point in my life, as we talk to younger people, that's basically what we can offer them: a sense of continuity, a sense of tradition, a sense of belonging to a long line.

SMITH-YOUNG: Strong men keep coming on. [*Agreement*]

COX: I think that's kind of what we can do. Now I think that, and as Tim said, there were probably a number of professors who were connected but probably, as Du Bois said, had to live double lives; they lived in two worlds. I remember Emmett Dorsey, who was a professor in Political Science. One of the things he would do in class is he would rail about how racism is architectonic to the Constitution of the United States, [*Laughter*] and he would go into the three-fifths clause and say, "How can you be three-fifths?" I remember we started Project Awareness. We were not only SNCC; we represented an energy. We were NAG, we were Project Awareness, we were the editors of the newspaper, we were the student council, we were everywhere. We were a small group of people who brought a lot of energy and change, and a lot of professors gravitated toward that. We brought Malcolm X in 1961 to speak at Howard to debate on the question of separation versus integration.

COBB: That's the Bayard Rustin and Malcolm X debate?

COX: Yes, the Rustin and Malcolm X debate. And, you know, a lot of the professors did not want their students to be there. A lot of professors thought this was the end of the world at Howard University. But Emmett Dorsey said, "What? There's no issue here. I'll moderate the debate." Not only that, at the dinner we had before these debates, he was the one that was hardest on this country. Malcolm said, "Professor, I need to let you speak tonight." [*Laughter*] If we think about it, we were fairly fortunate. I mean, we represented energy; they saw us as somebody who could carry on a tradition. Somebody who would help change the dynamic, and they needed to invest in us. And I now begin to see that because as I get to be as old as Tim, [*Laughter*] I feel the need to invest because in that way there's continuity. So I do appreciate Sterling. There were a lot of specific stories we could tell about him, but all of them were geared to investing and providing continuity. And showing us, as Jean said, taking us to see the play to give us perspective for us to understand. Youth has energy; what it lacks is perspective. Age has perspective, but what it lacks is energy. [*Laughter, agreement*] That, I think, is the value. And I begin to understand him more and more at this point in my life.

SMITH-YOUNG: I was thinking about those smoke-filled basement rooms, listening to Sterling read his poetry or other people reciting poetry, but listening to him and to . . . Who was the West Indian? C.L.R. James?

COX: C.L.R. James.

SMITH-YOUNG: I remember sitting in these places. I didn't understand what in the world C.L.R. James was talking about. [*Laughter*] The point I want to make here is that I am not a feminist, but this is a gender issue. When I was at Howard, the only things for girls to be were prom queens or something. The only thing to be if you wanted to be important was to be the queen of the . . .

COX: You could be homecoming queen.

SMITH-YOUNG: . . . right, or of the sorority or the fraternity or something. But when I was with NAG and with Sterling, I was important as an individual. When I was in the smoke-filled room listening to his poetry, I was as vital as everybody else in there. And that was not an easy thing to accomplish at Howard. [*Laughs*]

COX: They were two different people. Sterling was a person who was very personable, liked to tell stories and so forth. C.L.R. would come into the room, take his watch off, and he would say, "I am going to speak for precisely one hour." [*Laughter*] And at the end of the hour, he was finished. I mean, he came from a British tradition. He would lecture you on the question of cricket.

COBB: Cricket and Trotsky. [*Laughter*]

COX: That's right. I'm just saying that we came through at a time when we were very fortunate. But we were very fortunate for them too. I mean, while we didn't understand it, we were very fortunate for them also because they could have had no one to pass anything on to, and we could have had nobody to give us anything.

JENKINS: I have, on numerous occasions when I've gone up to Howard to speak after graduating, tried to impress upon the students who are still there as undergrads that really there are two Howards. There is a Howard University that is credential bestowing, so that you can integrate into the larger economy and society of America. Some of the ladies are there to marry husbands, so they can integrate that way. Others are there to get their credentials and their professional degree, so they can get their jobs. And that is part of the Howard tradition. There's another part of Howard, side by side, cheek to jowl, that's very different. It's about anger, social change, self-development, and anti-establishment. The traditional Howard that is producing people as replicas of the middle class is clearly the majority segment of the kingdom, but there has always been the dissident element. And that tradition has been in all of its professional schools as well as the undergraduate school, and the faculty represented that kind of schism. You had the dissidents who were always catching hell from the establishment. They were not getting the promotions, they weren't getting the offices with the view, they were not getting parking spaces. Everything that you can imagine that the bureaucracy could impose upon them in a hostile way, they were suffering. And similarly, there were the students who did not get the respect; they did not have the letters of recommendation that the establishment side of the university offered. They had this kind of very rigid Frazier notion of the black bourgeoisie regenerating itself. A lot of the people at Howard prided themselves that their father or somebody else had gone to Howard, and they were set in that. They had dress codes, they had some money, they had a clear expectation that they were going to medical or dental school or to law school, and that was it. All they were going to get was a job and go into Foreign Service or something like that. Their whole ideal was parallel to America's ideal. The dissidents did not accept America as the ideal at all. When you listen to Sterling, he says, "I do not accept America's values as my values, white America's values as my values." So what we had there was the vantage point of being seen as people who weren't accepting the values of white America. They weren't accepting the values of white America, and so we had a natural affinity for each other.

SMITH-YOUNG: Right. And they loved us. We loved them, but we were kids. You could see their eyes shining; you could see Sterling's eyes shining.

COX: I see that today. It's interesting. I belong to a golf club called the Pro-Duffers. After I joined it, I found out that the Pro-Duffers were started by Mordecai Johnson and some other people. Basically, all the institutional groups that you talk about belong to this. They like to play golf, but that is the institutional group. You have the Boulé, the same group. They're the same people. Guardsmen: they're the same group and the same people. Links, they're the same group and the same people.

JENKINS: Jack and Jill.

SMITH-YOUNG: You mean over the years, over generations?

COX: I mean, the same people who belong to the Boulé belong to the Guardsmen. A lot of people who belong to the Guardsmen belong to the Pro-Duffers. I mean, if you go around in that circle, you will see the same people all the time. [Laughter] They're the ones who have made it.

JENKINS: What do you mean by "made it?"

COX: I mean financially. Made it financially. But if you talk to them about anything serious, they don't have a clue. If you gave them a clue, it would break the bank. [*Laughter*]

JENKINS: That's why I pressed you when you said "made it." None of those people are cutting edge in their professions . . .

COX: No. They're not.

JENKINS: . . . or in the broader society. They are people who stay below the horizon and basically take care of themselves and their families.

COX: That's it. That's it. They're not out there. They are not people who are moving. They're not movers. And even within the institutions, the Boulé, the Pro-Duffers, and so forth have little or no organizational skills. I'm telling you. Sometimes I look at these guys and I wonder.

TIDWELL: Given all you've said, somebody please tell me this. Before you met Sterling, how did NAG come together? What was it that brought you and the students together to form this organization?

COX: Let's see. As students of the Nonviolent Action Group, we were basically doing a lot of public accommodations things. You know, there was this place out there, the amusement park . . .

COBB: Glen Echo.

COX: Glen Echo. We were demonstrating there. We were demonstrating in sympathy at Woolworth's for the people who were trying to integrate a lot of stuff in the South. A lot of that was the impetus. In this town, when we came to Washington in 1960, black people couldn't drive buses. There were very few black policemen who could even ride in police cars. This town was a segregated town. The *Washington Post* had ads, black and white ads, they had black people and white people. Clifton Terrace was all white. You couldn't go in a clothing store and try on clothes. There were no blacks on the Redskins. I remember demonstrating at the new RFK stadium because they didn't have any black people there. I think the major impetus was in sympathy with what was going on in the South. But all around us we had a lot of things to do, and so therefore those were the driving forces. On campus, I remember we had this big demonstration when they were constructing a building. I forgot what building it was, and there were no black tradesmen. And then again back to Tim's point about the two Howards. In order to get numbers, NAG had to make an alliance with the sororities and fraternities. Karen House, who is now . . .

SMITH-YOUNG: One of the vice presidents.

COX: OK. She was the one who helped us get the AKAs [Alpha Kappa Alphas] to demonstrate. In the early days, we went down in our finest to demonstrate. So the genesis of NAG was in sympathy with the South, but also in dealing with a lot of the stuff that existed in this environment.

COBB: But there were also broader things, because I came to Howard in '61. The way I first heard of NAG was through Bill Mahoney and Jan Trix. I met them when I was going through the administration building, and Bill and Jan were squatted on the steps of the administration building holding signs protesting ROTC.

cox: Oh yeah, we were opposed to ROTC too.

cobb: They were protesting because ROTC was mandatory then. I didn't even know what ROTC was, so I stopped and said, "What's ROTC?" And I got this whole little thing from them. That's how I heard of NAG. And then Ivanhoe [Donaldson] told me once, years later, that he came to Washington as part of a protest against the House Un-American Activities Committee.

cox: HUAA.

cobb: And then he met Howard students that were backing the sit-ins. I don't know if they had the name NAG then or not. Stokely was also down there. Nobody knew each other then. Stokely didn't know Ivanhoe; they didn't meet then. So, there was this group of Howard students, these black faces, protesting HUAA in this sea of white people. These were the Howard students who would ultimately be a part of Howard's civil rights movement, so there's something broader going on here.

cox: Well, even that dynamic reflected itself in SNCC, because the people from Howard were the very political and dynamic ones; the people from Fisk and so forth were much more religious and philosophical.

smith-young: Well, my memory is that we had this excitement around Project Awareness and in bringing Malcolm to the campus and so on, and, as I remember, we kind of morphed into NAG. I don't remember there was a day when we stopped being one group and started being NAG. What I remember is that it didn't have a name; in fact, our group didn't have a name to me until Stokely came over and gave me a ticket to go south around 1963. I had said, "Oh, I think I'd like to do what you guys are doing," and then I went south and I met Tim down at Cornelia. Remember the retreat?

jenkins: In Georgia.

smith-young: In Georgia. But somehow in this seething cauldron of intellectual and I'll call it social activity, I said, "Oh, I think I'd like to do that too." Then about three days later, Stokely comes over and gives me this bus ticket south. That's how I went south the first time. But the actual name of NAG came to me later, that that's who we were.

cobb: I had left Howard and then came back for something. I had gone to Mississippi at the end of that first year. I didn't meet Sterling until I had already left Howard and then I was back on campus for another reason. It might have been Michael Thelwell who pointed me to Sterling Brown.

cox: I think that NAG was a group of people who were interested. A lot of it really started, I think, in the sympathy peace.

tidwell: When you say "the sympathy peace" ...?

cox: To the South.

tidwell: Do you mean sympathetic to SNCC?

COX: No, sympathetic to the activities.

SMITH-YOUNG: The direct action.

COX: I mean the freedom rides and so forth. Because, you know, Dion [Diamond] was in jail, who was a Howard student. He was in jail for criminal anarchy. Stokely had gone south, Hank Thomas had been there, so there were a number of people who were involved in the South. We not only knew people who were in the South, but we also had seen what was going on. A lot of us grew up with Emmett Till. At that point we had been bombarded by discussions of Emmett Till, the stuff in Birmingham and Montgomery. The stuff in the South was a driver; we were now involved in, as Tim talked about, moving against what we saw as the restrictions of the American society, whether it was HUAC or whatnot. Remember. We were just coming out of the period of McCarthyism. Even when we went south later, in 1963, a lady leveled the charge that "The Communists are coming." And, you know, one lady said to me one day, "I'm so glad you Communists are here." [*Laughter*] So you had all the stuff. Whether we're talking about Project Awareness, whether we're talking about the issue of HUAC, which was, you know, the anti-Communist discussion, or whether we were talking about newspapers, we were just all over.

TIDWELL: About the name NAG itself, does anybody know who actually assigned it to the group or to the activity?

COX: No, but we were nonviolent everything at that point. We were the Student Nonviolent Coordinating Committee; we wanted to identify with the young people. Now the Nonviolent Action Group was a chapter of SNCC because in the early days SNCC had campus chapters. We were the NAG group. And I was the representative from the NAG group, along with some others who were there before me. My sense is that we were a group of chapters before we became a group of organizers. And people of the organizers always felt frustrated because the executive committee was composed of these students who really didn't understand what it was to be an organizer.

JENKINS: There's another antecedent and parallel nexus that needs to be appreciated. In my last year—I graduated in 1960—we had created the Awareness Committee. In fact, it was called the ABC's: the Awareness Committee, the Boosters Committee, and the Culture Committee. Awareness was to deal with politics, Boosters was to support athletics, and Culture was to deal with all of the aesthetic life. It was also during that period of the '60s when I was Student Body President of the Liberal Arts that the sit-ins occurred. The Liberal Arts Student Council had a big battle with the administration because we wanted to send money that had been collected in the student fees to support the students down in Raleigh. And they said, "You can't do that; that's for campus activity." And we said, "It is campus activity, and as long as we have the power to sign the check, it's done." Well, that was the beginning of a nexus between Howard and the student movement then. We also sent delegates to the subsequent conferences. I don't think we attended the Raleigh conference as an organization, but we certainly attended everything after that. And then the year that I had spent between undergrad and graduate school, I was National Affairs Vice President of the National Student Association. During that period, I again constantly made linkages to Howard and the movement. In fact, the training session that we organized for the SNCC leaders, I had a whole roster of Howard professors come in, including Rayford Logan and others, to lecture the students on the history and the connection so that they saw nonviolent action against the 1940s of the CORE movement, and the time when Ralph Bunche and Franklin Frazier and those people were demonstrating to integrate the cafeterias at the Capitol, get jobs at the Capitol, ride on the streetcars, and so forth. Those were the things that I think also are silent reinforcements of this connection on Howard to the militant stuff because, again, this dissident side of Howard has always been there.

COBB: Although I never pursued it with him, I think Sterling had at least a little bit of difficulty with decisions we made either to drop out of school for the movement or not go on to graduate school . . .

SMITH-YOUNG: He thought it was a mistake.

COBB: . . . and that he never quite reconciled in his head his admiration on one hand for SNCC and CORE and the young people and his feeling—this Du Boisian kind of feeling—that you had some obligation in terms of the race to further your education and actually be prepared to take advantage of these opportunities.

JENKINS: Well, what that is is he was basically an intellectual. He believed that the world was moved by the mind, and we were taking a step that was not relying on the mind. Our claim was "Where is your body?" which is definitely an anti-intellectual posture, that the mind wasn't going to do it. This had to be at a different level. He was estranged from that kind of a notion, as we would expect of his generation and his family and everything else that he was. But he also had some other issues. He always would emphasize, "I am an old Negro." [*Laughter*] He was opposed to that "black" stuff. A lot of those things that were part of the rhetoric he didn't buy.

COX: I know. But the other thing is that was personally troubling was that he didn't have a Ph.D. He always had grief about it. While he understood more than most of those guys, they would say, "Well, where are your credentials?" That always gave him a lot of grief.

JENKINS: I dispute that, Courtland. I dispute that. I think that that might have been a phenomenon in his early career. I think just the opposite. I think he converted that to a point of distinction and arrogance that he didn't have a Ph.D.

SMITH-YOUNG: And he knew as much as those guys.

JENKINS: Because he was so erudite and could cite all these books and things and everything from memory, they would always call him Dr. Brown.

And he would make a real point of it. Anybody who was embarrassed by this would not draw the whole thing to a close to focus on that fact. He'd say, "I do *not* have a Ph.D." And I think what he was saying was that when you have as much knowledge as I have, and you know as much as about how things are organized, you do not need a paper credential to establish it. There are lots of Ph.D.'s out there; there is only one Sterling Brown. I heard that loud and clear many times in his career. And in fact, when we got him the honorary degree from Howard, he snickered. He said the only reason he'd accept it was because we were giving one to Duke Ellington at the same time. [*Laughter*]

COBB: I don't know. I think there were two kinds of frustration. Then again, I'm speaking as someone from the periphery, of just a year at Howard and a little bit through the family. I think there was frustration. Whether it's linked to having the Ph.D. or not, I mean, there's a certain kind of frustration I picked up. I'm remembering this: the lengthiest conversation/interaction with Sterling I had was at Highlander Center where he came down to talk to a whole group of us about writing. He spent the whole weekend and told us all of these stories of his life. Somewhere along the way, my sense was that, there's a kind of frustration, if that's the right word . . .

COX: Or resentment.

COBB: . . . or resentment that Howard didn't recognize what he was about. I mean, he was kind of shoved aside. He had this little office. And he really got no acknowledgment. That whole set of people: Leo Hansberry the same, and Chancellor Williams.

SMITH-YOUNG: Bitter.

COBB: Yes. There was that. And the reason I link it to him not having the Ph.D. is that I remember feeling pressure from him that I was supposed to get my credentials, whatever my commitment was. I felt that it was somehow linked, if not to him not having his Ph.D., it was linked to his bitterness/resentment at his lack of recognition by his own people at Howard. Which is a little bit different from some professors who are black who had a different kind of resentment. There was another set of these guys who resented teaching—Sterling wasn't in this group—at a black university. They felt they should have been at Harvard and weren't there.

JENKINS: Well, yes. Many people were at Howard against their will.

TIDWELL: Certainly Sterling could have left. He was a visiting professor at Vassar in each of the fall semesters in 1945 and 1946. He taught summer school at Minnesota in 1946. After they saw what he was able to do, both schools wanted him to stay.

COX: And then the New School.

TIDWELL: The New School for Social Research.

COX: In New York.

TIDWELL: The interest in Sterling expressed by white schools started earlier than that. When James Weldon Johnson died in 1938, an effort was made to replace him at New York University. Alain Locke had gone up and tried to combine the NYU job with a then-open position at the Schomburg. Elmer Carter, the editor of *Opportunity Magazine* and very close associate of Sterling, because Sterling was writing his column, said, "Would you be interested in taking both of these positions and coming up? This way, we'll get a chance to see you more often–at least we think we would." So Sterling had several excellent opportunities to leave Howard. But whatever was enticing out there, he found a greater enticement to return home.

JENKINS: I think it's a lovers' quarrel. I think it's an attraction and repulsion. He was engaged in a fight at Howard that ultimately, I think, he relished because basically it was them against us, and he was in some respects what Roosevelt was called: a class traitor. He represented all those things. His father was a minister of a prominent church, a Congregationalist church, and on the faculty of the School of Divinity. And in that circle of right-bright, damn-near-white Washington and owning property and all that kind of stuff. And here is Sterling, going down there collecting stuff on blues and jazz and folklore. [*Laughter*]

SMITH-YOUNG: A class traitor.

JENKINS: And associating with these people on Beale Street. I mean, what has come of your son?

TIDWELL: How much of that was just rebelliousness against his father or against the family?

COX: It may have started as that, I don't know.

JENKINS: Well, I take him as his word when he said that when he went down there and had his first teaching experiences and saw how much those illiterate people who were older than him—some were his own age, but mostly old men—how much they knew. And yet their tools were just so inadequate. He came to have a deep respect for the difference between credentials, packaging, and substance. Once he made that distinction, he saw how phony the rest of the people were who had these degrees, cars, houses, titles, you name it, and didn't stand for anything; who couldn't think, had no motivation for it, had no compassion, had no political will, had no courage. And he opted out of that. I don't think that's rebellion.

COX: Other than that, they were good people. [*Laughter*] I think Tim's analysis is also pretty decent because I think for a lot of us our background was not that restricted. Once you'd gone South and you saw what life was really about, going back to that foolishness was like a waste of time.

SMITH-YOUNG: One thing I would say about him is that he was such a classy man. He had an aura of personal strength and stature. I actually never really knew his wife. I just saw her all the time, and I was so impressed. I mean, how did he pull this lady? How did he make this happen? There was a synergy between them that I understood had something to do with a strong love and with how good she was. But also he had a kind of strength that he needed to keep that. And even when he wasn't doing well emotionally, he still had that. In the middle of one of his emotional crises, he still had this aura of inner strength. But she was right there, supporting him. You have to be somebody to evoke that kind of caring for you.

TIDWELL: Do you recall any particular experiences that you had with Daisy that would help me to understand Sterling even more so, just like the one you just related?

SMITH-YOUNG: She was devoted. She was always at his side.

COX: She seemed to be mainly in the background. When we went to her house, she would deal with us in terms of hospitality and so forth, but she never came into the room. He would always refer to her, she would always be part of his discussion, but she was never sitting down with us in that sense. And I guess as Jean was talking about when he was having issues with his health in later life, she was always there supporting him. I thought I saw more at that time than before, when he was not in that condition.

COBB: I saw Daisy as the consummate Southern woman, Southern gentle lady. Really a very fine upperclass kind of Southern character. Kept a meticulous house, everything was in order. She was there, a quiet kind of presence. What I also saw was a moderating force on Sterling because I had seen her at times kind of pull him aside or sort of make gestures to suggest that, "That's enough." [*Laughter*] Kind of an unspoken way: "Not that again."

[TIDWELL: Given all of these wonderful remembrances, how would you sum up the inheritance Sterling bequeathed to you?]

JENKINS: One of the things that I guess is most difficult to put into words is the gift he gave to me of the sense of dignity that was a leveler between people of status and non-status.

SMITH-YOUNG: I think that's what I was trying to say.

JENKINS: Once he had made the judgment that substance counted, then irrespective whether you came in rags, broken English, poor family background, criminal record, the test was substance or non-substance. And that's a tremendous gift because when we went South, we were confronted by all these people who were raggedy, criminal records for reasons out of their hands, poor education, no property, but who had ideas, courage, conviction, energy, commitment, faith. We could see that these are the real people. It's not the people who are doctors, lawyers, teachers, preachers, who are living in these manicured houses and are scared to open their mouths. It's almost like the gift of X-ray vision so that you can walk into a room and not be misled by the clothes these people have on. You look right through and see who really counts in a room. That's why we could see a Fannie Lou Hamer for what she was—a powerful politician. Forget the fact she had a limp, was overweight, had heart trouble, broken English, all those things. You knew that she had the makings of a senator. But for these things, she would have been.

cox: You know, we were strong men. [*Laughter*] Oh man, I mean, that period was also very dynamic, but we were also engaged in a lot of foolishness. [*Laughter*] I mean, God, we were engaged in foolishness.

TIDWELL: But you must have been committed too because look where you are now.

cox: I guess I've been very lucky. I look at all the stuff I did at this point, and the ability to analyze, as Tim said, separate the wheat from the chaff and go to the things that are important. I've been very fortunate because basically I've defined my life's work. Where I have been, I've defined what I do. I mean, I get paid for it, but I define what I do. And that's because in a lot of instances, people will not stop you if you know the important thing is to establish the frame of reference and you go about doing it. Because they don't know what else to do, so they sit there and say, "Oh, OK." You know, "It seems like you're doing all right." I'm just saying that I do think that period of mentoring that we got from people like Sterling has stayed with us. What really occurred to me is that we were becoming the people we admired. I recognized our responsibility to these young people. I just hope that, at some point, we can at least try to be faithful to some of the stuff that they helped us with. Because we have a responsibility to carry on.

NOTE

I wish to express my deepest appreciation to Timothy and Lauretta Jenkins for opening their home up and providing a most welcoming place for this interview. To each of the participants, I want to express my gratitude for their generous sharing of ideas and inspiration about this important moment in the history of Sterling A. Brown, Howard University, and the modern day Civil Rights Movement. For her meticulous transcription of this collective interview, I am once again endebted to Andrea Craig Gruenbaum.

A Conversation with John H. Bracey, Esther Terry, and Mike Thelwell

Steven C. Tracy

When I first arrived at the W.E.B. Du Bois Department of Afro-American Studies at the University of Massachusetts Amherst over a dozen years ago for a job interview, one of the first things I noticed was a large portrait of Sterling A. Brown in the office of department head Esther Terry. It sat on a table, propped up against the wall, directly across from Professor Terry's desk, a reminder, perhaps, both that Brown was watching the proceedings with an expert and exacting eye and that he was there as a resource and for support in case (read: when) the road got rocky. Professor Terry always spoke in glowing terms about the experiences she and her husband had had with Professor Brown—those memories resided on hallowed ground. She smiled spontaneously when his name arose, with the pride of someone whose mentor was a hero of epic expansiveness, albeit unsung in the literary mainstream at the time.

As time passed, it became clear that "Prof," as Mike Thelwell called him, had been instrumental in establishing the department that Professors Terry, Thelwell, and Bracey helped elevate to PhD-granting status in 1996 through their outstanding teaching, scholarship, and, especially—and you know this if you know the inner workings of academia—administrative shit, grit, and mother wit. I'm sure part of that came from Brown and the knowledge of literature and folklore he imparted to these people whom he sent very deliberately to Sidney Kaplan for further education. Then they decided to make community in a place that had become so suffused with Brown's intellectual and passionate spirit and energy that it fairly buck-dances down the halls of New Africa House Master Juba style, with a scrappy twinkle and muscular dynamism. That rooted energy and spirit keep coming on, advising "Don't you get weary," and reminding, until, with renewed strength in the old folk verities, the reply "Guess we'll give it one more try" allows Brown's portrait to lean contentedly back against the wall again, until the next time.

The love and admiration of Professors Bracey, Terry, and Thelwell come through in their words about Brown here. Each has a unique perspective on the way Brown moved through the world and affected those around him. Nonetheless, this is not a sainted portrait of the man—there seems to have been more than enough of the trickster devil in him to keep that portrait from being painted, and thankfully so. As the folklore shows, in a bedeviled world, sometimes you need a "devil" to set it right.

Thanks, Sterling, for that.

STEVE TRACY: I want to get a sense of where you all first came upon Sterling Brown, where you first encountered him—it may be in print, as a family acquaintance, or a teacher or something like that. Give me a sense of how you first became aware of Sterling Brown in your lives, including what state or city you were in or anything that you think will be relevant in placing where you were and who you were in relation to that first interaction with Brown. Shall we start with you, John?

JOHN H. BRACEY: Sterling Brown was part of that remarkable group of faculty and intellectuals that were gathered in and around Howard University and Dunbar High School in Washington, D.C., as I was growing up in Washington, D.C., in the late 1940s and early 1950s. He was one of those people my sister and I would bump into at my mother's office. Her office was in Douglass Hall and she taught in the School of Education at Howard and served on the editorial board of the *Journal of Negro Education*. There were always these gatherings in her office, since it was on the second floor near the elevator, 202. We would run there from my school on the way home, to check in before we went to the playground. Sterling Brown would be one of those people, along with E. Franklin Frazier, Emmett Dorsey, Bob Martin, or people like that who were just a regular part of the grown-ups around us as we were growing up. Just as a physical thing, I encountered a group of black scholars and thinkers and grown-ups who were part of the work in which I was coming of age. My mother always gave me autographed copies of all the books from these people, including copies of Frazier's *Black Bourgeoisie* and the *Negro in the United States*. From day one, I think, or from the time I was old enough to read, I had an autographed copy of *The Negro Caravan* and somewhere I had an old copy of *Southern Road*—I don't know whatever happened to that. But he was just part of that ambience and part of that environment if you grew up in Washington, D.C., in Northwest in or near Howard's campus or in or near Dunbar High School—Northwest LeDroit

Park area. The other context was the veneration given poetry during that time. The leading black high school was named after a poet and they had choices; they could name it after Bruce, Banneker, and so forth. The leading black high school in the country, we thought, the Dunbar High School, was named after a poet, so we were in an environment that was saturated with poets and we learned the language of black poetry as part of our street language. So I grew up using Washington, D.C., poet language. If we were showing off, somebody would call you "Sporting Beasley." If we got into a fight on the playground we'd say, "They don't come by ones, they don't come by twos, but they'd better come by tens." You know, sellin' them woof tickets, and that kind of thing. On my father's side, since they were railroad people, I always liked "Break of Day." I always heard in my head "man in full, babe, man in full." I must have been 8, 9, 10 years old when I first met Sterling Brown. But that's how I came to see him: as a person in a group of very talented and committed people. Like all the people, he was friendly and warm; he paid attention to us. He'd correct our papers if we were doing homework or a school paper. He'd reach over and put the comma in the right place. He was part of that Howard group.

TRACY: So he wasn't just an academic; he was a part of the broader community in a sense.

BRACEY: Well, we never saw those people just as academics anyway. If you're growing up it's hard to see people who are scholars as just scholars, because in fact they also live on your street, or near your playground. In Sterling Brown's case, his father had been the pastor at Lincoln Temple Congregational Church, which was one of the leading black Congregational churches in D.C. It had a long history of activism. My family went to People's Congregational Church. And that particular group, United Church of Christ— it's the Puritans or the American Missionary Association people—were always doing political stuff. So you'd bump into them at meetings, rallies, etc. If there was some complaint about something or other, they'd be talking about it; they'd be aware of it. They were "race people" in the old fashioned sense and so you never saw them just over here or over there. They'd come into your school. When I was at Mott Elementary School, people like Sterling Brown would come and read, Willie "The Lion" Smith would come and play the piano, Harry T. Burleigh would come and talk about classical music, etc. Somebody out of the music department at Howard would come and sing German lieder. We got all this stuff. We went to plays on Howard's campus—Owen Dodson's plays—in which all of the faculty showed up. We had a cultural ambience that we grew up in that he was a part of. We all lived in the world where the Howard Theater was only two blocks from Howard University. The idea that there was a Howard up on the hill and the rest of the people were down here is a very weak metaphor. Because you walk two blocks down the hill, and you're on U Street. There you got the Lincoln Republic, the Booker T. Theater, the Casbah, and the Howard Theater, where all the street folk hung out. We lived in both of those worlds.

That's where we went to see Motown, James Brown, Little Miss Cornshucks, and all that business. And vaudeville was black vaudeville. The difference between Sterling and the other people was that Sterling was more attuned to that, I think, than some others. Like today, if you talk with academics who know hip-hop, some like it. But Sterling knew the blues and all that street culture and liked it, as opposed to those people that knew it and said, "Okay, they do that, but that's not what we do." Sterling says, "What they do is not so bad." So you could joke with him about having come back from the Howard Theater or wearing your pants like high-waters, like James Brown. And he would know he could start that conversation with you. If you were trying to do some silly dance steps, he'd say: "Who do you think you are, Jackie Wilson or somebody?" He was into the popular culture thing in a very big way and would help us get into that without feeling that we were violating some norm. He just legitimized that interest—it's like, "That's okay, because I'm in that too. It's okay to be in the honors track at your school and also be at the Howard Theater lined up there waiting for the James Brown Revue to show up. That's all right." And I think he did function in that role. It wasn't always a formal thing; it was just the way he interacted with people.

TRACY: Sterling Stuckey says that few people related so well to younger people as Sterling Brown did, and that's your experience as he read in the schools, and saw people on the streets and things like that.

BRACEY: Or just the way he talked to you. He would be telling stories—he was always a great story-teller—and there were at least three or four cases where my sister and I would run into the office and he'd turn and stop in the office and say, "Uh oh, here come the young ones—I have to finish this one later." It was literally ten or twelve years later in 1968 when he came to Northwestern and came to my house for dinner where we sat around drinking coffee. And I had to ask him: "Mr. Brown, what were those stories you were telling when my sister and I would run into my mother's office, and you would stop and say, 'I have to finish this one later'?" And then he told a couple and I said, "Okay, now I understand why you had to hold off on those." It was the midnight show at the Howard Theater is what it was. There was a whole difference—there was the regular show and then there's the midnight show. If you don't think there's a difference, turn 18 and go to the midnight show and see Moms Mabley and Redd Foxx when there was no holds barred, when the Midnighters come out there without their underwear on and stuff. Sterling knew the world of gandy dancers, the guys on the corner playing the dozens, talking about your momma, Shine—he could go on Shine for hours. And the signifying monkey. He could do that. That was what was so funny about that, because he'd start in on one of those and we would bust out laughing, saying, "How did you know that stuff, we thought that was our stuff," and he'd say, "Oh no, this came long before you." No, no, he was different, very comfortable in that sense.

TRACY: He knew the material but he also knew the people who generated the material too. So he didn't separate himself from . . .

BRACEY: No, he wasn't studying people like bugs, like people do with hip-hop. They'll get somebody and stick 'em and analyze them. He liked the music and he liked the stories. When he was at my house he must have stayed up to two o'clock in the morning. We had him some Southern Comfort, I think.

MIKE THELWELL: Wild Turkey.

BRACEY: He sat there drinking and he complained about the Evanston water, because you got to have the right kind of water with your bourbon. I told him, "It's the only water that comes out of the tap." And he just talked and talked and talked, and he'd get on a whole string of Signifying Monkey stanzas I had never heard, and just go on and on. He was not showing off; he was just comfortable. And the more we laughed, and the more we thought of something, and we said, "Well, what about this," and he'd go off on another trip. And we'd say, "Well, who was Sporting Beasley anyway?" And he'd go tell us that story about a guy he met who dressed in a certain way. He wasn't being analytical or antiseptic about it. This was a world that despite his upbringing—coming up in the black middle class that came out of the Congregational church where his father was a minister for one of the elite black churches in D.C.—he, like the other ministers, thought that their job was to be like everybody else. That you may know something different from somebody else but that wouldn't make you better than other people. You treated everybody as an equal. He didn't have any class prejudices; he didn't have any prejudices about status or whatnot. He'd talk to the janitors. 'Cause at Howard some people would go off on the janitors because they didn't do what they were supposed to do sometimes. Or the telephone operators who were at Howard. If they didn't like you, they wouldn't put your phone calls through. And I don't know anybody at any level of Howard who would say something bad about Professor Brown. He was a good citizen in that sense.

TRACY: Did his colleagues respond well to his getting along with everybody? Was there an attitude about him with regard to the interactions he had with people of various socioeconomic levels?

BRACEY: That whole group all had their own particular quirks. Frazier's thing was wearing a beret and talking in French half of the time just to annoy people. But that was just Frazier. Nobody said, "Why don't you stop doing it?" But it was just like, "Here he goes again!" Everybody made fun of Mordecai Johnson even though he's the best president that Howard ever had. But people talked about him like he was some fool. Like, "What did he do this time?" Well, he went and got money every year for the school is what he did. And made the school from a mid-level bad college into a school with professional schools. He was a great college president. But to hear people talk about him, you'd have thought how did this guy get out the door in the morning, or make it down the street without falling down. Everybody had their little quirks. John

Lovell working on his spirituals for like fifty years and that was always a joke. Every time you saw John Lovell, people would ask: "How were his spirituals coming?" You would think he was working on one per year. The book was about 600 pages when it finally came out. Everybody had those kind of quirks. Margaret Just Butcher, as everybody knew, if you didn't do the homework in her class, [just] mention the Civil Rights Movement and she'd take off. She'd just go into a tirade and talk the whole period so you didn't have to do any homework. Eeverybody knew that, but nobody thought that made her a bad person or anything. He just was himself—Sterling Brown. That's just who he was. He was who he was; Frazier was who he was. When Howard Thurman was there, Thurman was a complete mystic. You never knew what he was talking about. But nobody thought that made him a bad person or anything.

TRACY: Well, how about you, Mike. What was your introduction to Sterling Brown? Had you read him before you met him?

THELWELL: I enrolled as a freshman at Howard in 1959. And as John said, Sterling, "Prof" we'd call him, was part of the ambience of the place. I first met him in an oral tradition before I ever saw him. People would talk about who the good professors were, and they talked about who this great poet was. They talked about this figure, this guy Sterling Brown, with great affection, great reverence, and sometimes great irreverence because he was a very irreverent guy. My first meeting with him: I don't know when that was, but we encountered each other on campus. He'd come up and talk to students. And something impelled me to go take a course with him. His poems I was introduced to because people would recite them and he would talk about them. Maybe I went somewhere and I heard him reading some poems on campus. I don't remember exactly how that all shook out, but I ended up in a class of his which wasn't about black culture at all or black literature; it was one of those introductory courses to literature. The English Department at that time was what we used to call colonized intellectuals. I don't think I really studied any black writers in the English Department except maybe Ellison, who would sneak in because of *Invisible Man*. All of the texts that were used were classic conventional whitefolks texts. In this introduction to literature—it wasn't Western literature and it wasn't European literature—it was literature because that was literature and beyond that there was no other and the usual suspects were there. I remember one of the short stories was "The Cask of Amontillado," which I think is by Poe, and another short story I remember from that course was "Matteo Falcone." I forget who the author of that was [Prosper Mérimée]. And on and on and on, the classic white male writers and a few token white women like Katherine Anne Porter. I mean this was 1959–60 . . .

BRACEY: Faulkner's "The Bear" was in there. They had an anthology.

THELWELL: . . . that kind of anthology, very limited, very smug considering itself universal. And there was Professor Brown teaching. I had a distinct impression that this was simply a concession to the attitudes and the biases of the English Department, the colonial attitudes of the literature department. I remember studying in that literature department *The Education of Henry Adams,* and wondering what the hell it got to do with black people. It was classic American in that sense, classic American establishment. My sense was that Professor Sterling Brown was bored with the material but very conscientious, so he talked about the stories with a vacant look in his eye. But the context, the structure, the characters, the theme of the story—he talked about how stories were constructed according to that order. The kind of lecture you could get from any white professor. It was little more pointed than that. You had a sense that his heart wasn't in it but that "this is what instruction and literature are and I'm going to give it to you and I'm going to give it to you in a classic sense." He was very thorough talking about those stories. It never occurred to me, since I was only a freshman, to ask him why weren't we talking about black authors or anything else. There might be an occasional reference to them; there might be an occasional expression on his face, but I know at the end of the class after we have gone through a requisite number of stories he brought in Willie "The Lion" Smith. And "The Lion" started to talk about Stripe John, singing jazz and blues, and Sterling Brown just lit up and came alive. I concluded afterwards that that was the absolute misuse of an invaluable resource and national treasure by a very backward English Department, Literature Department. The kind of course he was offering was a reflection of a certain ongoing tension and a debate between them.

TRACY: And why was Willie "The Lion" Smith there?

THELWELL: It had nothing to do with the subject. [*Laughs*] This was the last class of the semester . . .

TRACY: Unless it did have something to do with the subject, just by his presence.

THELWELL: Professor Brown was saying let's talk about something real, something you can relate to, and he lit up and came alive. But Willie "The Lion" was impeccably dressed and somehow a piano was gotten because he was playing the hell out of a piano in Douglass Hall. It's like he's saying, I've done my duty according to what is obligatory, so now let us talk about something real.

BRACEY: I think his sister lived in Washington, D.C.

THELWELL: Whose sister?

BRACEY: Willie "The Lion" Smith, 'cause I think he came to the elementary school because I think his sister taught at Mott Elementary School. 'Cause when he came to play for us he came out on the stage and said, "I got a choice; they told me take off my hat or stop smokin' the cigar."

THELWELL: That derby . . .

BRACEY: Yeah, yeah, a derby hat and he smoked a cigar. So he comes out on the stage at Mott and says, "They told me I got to give up my hat or give up my cigar, and I figured you're all too young to smoke but you're going to wear a hat. This is a nice hat so I thought I'd wear the hat." And he had his cigar sittin' in the ashtray the whole time and just looked at it from time to time, and he'd laugh. He'd play ragtime. He could rag anything. Like we'd say "Mary Had a Little Lamb Rag" and he'd play "Mary Had a Little Lamb," right. That's part of the ambience in D.C. That part of D.C. is like the university town where all of the resources of Howard's campus were readily available back and forth, up and down, 'cause of segregated schools. It was not unusual to have people like that pop up somewhere. We'd see him at assemblies like at Mott or at Banneker. We would have a special assembly with a special guest, and somebody would come out and do a ballet. Or it might be Dorothy Maynor who would come and sing opera for us. You know it was a whole range, like Dorothy or Roland Hayes or Willie "The Lion" Smith. Nobody thought that was unusual much at all, really 'cause Sterling got 'em into Howard's campus.

TRACY: The material I've read said that he was kind of tolerated for his inclusion of those kinds of things in the classroom, and his connection with those kinds of things in the broader community. Like you said earlier, people just say, "Well, that's Sterling." Was he particularly honored for those things the way we would honor him today?

BRACEY: No, it's even worse, just giving the attention was . . . Like Warner Lawson was the head of the choir. He had this beautiful concert, gospel choir.

THELWELL: It was quite a music department; he had control of Crampton Auditorium.

BRACEY: I will never forget they used have this Easter sunrise service. We'd get up and go back to the library. It's like 3 or 4 o'clock in the morning, and we'd sit down. We were as cold as hell. Then the sun comes up and they'd sing *The Messiah* and all this stuff. They were singing some spirituals and the choir started to sway a little bit. He stopped 'em and said, "You're not down in some holy roller church on Georgia Avenue. We will begin again." And he'd apologize to the audience. We thought they were getting ready to get into it, but he said, "Just stop." And he said, "I apologize" and he turned around; he chastised 'em and says, "If you want to do that, go down on Georgia Avenue."

THELWELL: He was head of Crampton Auditorium; he was in charge of the programming for it. He announced that as long as he was dean, no jazz would [be] played in Crampton Auditorium. . . . He'd bring those German lieder and he'd bring those god damn operas and all that stuff that nobody was interested in. Not even Duke Ellington. No jazz was to be played in Crampton Auditorium.

BRACEY: And the spirituals had to be in the concert tradition, not the spirituals.

THELWELL: So he became, to us the students, one of the lost, like a walking mockery, and we'd tease him. Sterling Brown, on the other side, became a hero for us as a representative of black culture. But that was the ambience of the place, at least of the establishment of the place. An enforced assimilationist mediocrity in terms of what actually passed as English courses. We could see that Professor Brown was very impatient with it, but he taught that book, that anthology, of essentially white American and European authors very rigorously. He taught it with great insight and he taught it with great conscientiousness, but we didn't have to be very sensitive to feel a real distance from it. I got to know him in other ways outside the classes, and it was clear also—I had determined this after looking at it—that he had established a modus vivendi for it. Where he had said, "Okay, you know what? Those imbeciles in there are what we called three-named Negroes, Mike, Let me tell you something; you can't trust no three-named Negro." [*Laughs*] He would concede them space in Douglass Hall during the day but then he'd say, "Come on by my office. Us going to drink some liquor and us going to tell some lies." A group of us would go by his office and then [experience] his amazing skills as a raconteur and as a reservoir of black culture. Because he knew everybody. I mean when he talked about Duke Ellington, it was as friend Duke. When he'd talk about Leadbelly, it was as friend Leadbelly. That's why Leadbelly said, "It's a bourgeois town, the only decent man is Sterling Brown." When he'd talk about "okay, I'm going to get my bookie," or "I'm going to get my bootlegger" and so on, he knew all these people: that's my barber and that's my taxi driver, who would come for him. He really moved among the people of the street people—14th Street, U Street people—as well as with the Howard bourgeoisie. There were some elements of the bourgeoisie who tolerated him. The more progressive, the more insightful ones, like John's mother, recognized him as a magnificent defender of black culture for one thing, really recognized him as a magnificent poet in the oral tradition and new world tradition. But as a man and his popularity, everything that John said about his popularity, there were janitors and other people who loved Prof. Brown because he was very easy-going, very easy, and a thorough-going Democrat. When he treated those people with respect, it was like out of the Southern tradition; it wasn't fake, it wasn't forced, and he treated everybody with respect. He would even give the imbeciles in the English Department a certain measure of respect. But for simple people, for poor folk, for people who would normally be patronized, Professor Brown was particularly good at making them feel human, making them feel respected. Now we, of course, idealized him as a kind of cultural rebel. We'd get into, as the relationship developed, much more involved political discussions where there would be real differences between us. But Professor Brown affected, in rare ways, the education of whole host of people in that school beyond anything that took place in the classroom. I think some of Toni Morrison's cultural orientation comes simply from sitting at the feet of Sterling Brown and from the influence of Sterling. Some of LeRoi Jones, the same thing, though they are very different politically. Eleanor Traylor is clearly one of Sterling's children. And to a very real extent, I am certainly one of Sterling's children. I remember when I was working with Carmichael on his book and I was writing "The Professor and the Activists." Carmichael would say, "Are you writing something?" and I would say, "Yeah, I'm writing a book; I'm writing a piece on Sterling Brown." Carmichael, who was at the time suffering from the cancer that would kill him, was lying down in the back of the car. He sat upright, bolt upright, at the name of Sterling Brown. He said, "I always will be eternally gratefully to that man"—I can almost quote him verbatim—"for first teaching me how to appreciate and love my culture." And he said it very passionately and forthrightly, and I understood exactly what he was talking about, because here's another guy, Ed Brown, who Prof. used to call "Cuz Brown" just because the name was Brown. Now Brown was one of the guys who had been kicked out of Southern University for sittin' in. So he arrived at Howard in something that looked like ballet shoes. Didn't have no clothes, and didn't have no money. Sterling Brown asked him over to his house to clean up the yard and to do certain things. He didn't have to do much of anything. But in turn he would give him a sum of money so Ed Brown could survive. That's H. Rap Brown's older brother. Ed Brown was part of us. Sterling Brown always referred to him as "Cuz" Brown, and Ed would refer back to him as "Cuz" Brown because of the Brown. Now the reason I talked about him is because he came from Louisiana and had been exposed to rural culture, the musical culture, the oral traditions—it's not an accident that his brother was called "Rap." I used to ask Ed to perform songs, to perform sermons, to perform snippets of sermons, still do even today when I see him, because he was such a brilliant exponent of the oral tradition, of the musical traditions of the Southern folk. But to him that was what people did. He just knew how to do it because people around him, such as his grandparents and the minister, used to do that and were brilliant at doing it. But going back to what Stokely said, "Sterling Brown first taught me how to really love and appreciate, and understand my culture." Ed Brown had the same experience because what he was practicing, what he knew was part of his repertoire. He never understood it in a structural and analytical way. He got that from Sterling Brown.

ESTHER TERRY: Well, I met Sterling Brown first through his work. I grew up in North Carolina in the heart of apartheid and went from first grade to twelfth grade in a black school. It was one of the schools started by Julius Rosenwald, the Rosenwald schools. And there was a sense of the people who helped to start that school that they wanted their children to be educated above all things. Now they had to work out a way that the education could come simultaneous with getting the crops picked because many of them were sharecroppers as were my parents. So they had to work out a way. But they paid very close attention to the schools. We would have PTA sessions where families would come to know what their children were doing, what their children were studying, and to be a part of it with the teachers. Sterling Brown's poetry was always a wonderful way to tie people together. I recognized very early that Sterling Brown's poetry, probably more than any other poet, some of Langston Hughes maybe, but Sterling Brown's poetry reached out and included all of those farmers, all of those people who did whatever. They weren't educated people, they weren't the teachers themselves, but they were people who felt good when I read "Ma Rainey." They had an experience with that. Sterling Brown was the person, I think, of all the poets whose poetry we would learn. We would show off because the teachers would want and the parents would [want] us to do something to let them see what we had read . . .

THELWELL: To perform . . .

TERRY: . . . and perform—to be up in front, to let them know what we were doing and they liked that very much. Sterling Brown I think was always a hit. And here's the thing that cracked me up or just always amazed me: my father and people like that would call him Mr. Brown; they would say, "You know, I remember that." Sterling's poetry described an incident or reminded them of a time in their lives or a position or a party they all had: "I remember one time," and you would always think that they were there but they weren't. There was the vitality and the inclusiveness of Sterling that made them feel good. They found themselves in Sterling's poetry in ways that [he] was one of us, so I met him first through his poetry. Then I went off after I graduated from high school to Bennett College, to the sit-ins. People talked about the fact that we could go into Woolworth and buy everything there was in the store, but we couldn't sit down to have a cherry coke or something. It was set up to make people feel less than themselves and less than their work, and to make people angry. The sit-ins were bound to happen or something of that sort. It couldn't have been a better program. But Sterling, somebody read Sterling. I don't know why we did it, on reflection. We celebrated something called Negro History Month. Negro History Month was the month that was just very special if you got an award because we got the biggest crowd of people coming to the Negro History Month programs. And Sterling Brown's poetry was always, always, a part of the winning anything that happened during Negro History Month. Well, because I had read Sterling and knew about Sterling, I went off to Bennett. In the midst of all of what was happening around the tensions that led to the sit-ins and that whole historical moment, Sterling Brown became very important to me to read, because I think he helped to shape the kind of person that I wanted to be as a professor. Here we were talking about what is happening here; we're being ignored; our culture was being devalued; we were being devalued and there was ole Sterling, who, you know, picked up a book. We knew we were reading somebody pretty special. Sterling Brown and James Baldwin were the two most important writers that I read all the time. Of course you read other people too. But they were the ones who pointed me, I think, and shaped me in a way about who I was and how important it was that I continue to be who I was. Well, I left Bennett and went off to teach for a moment at St. Augustus College at Raleigh. I went off to University of North Carolina–Chapel Hill and got a masters and did not want to stay there for a doctorate. I just didn't want to do that. So I wrote him, and this was my introduction to Sterling Brown the man and not the poet, to ask his advice. I actually wrote him to ask about the possibility of my coming to get a PhD, to study with him in the graduate school there and if he would direct my dissertation if I came. He wrote me back, and that was another thing, he wrote me back. He literally sat down and wrote me a very nice letter congratulating me on wanting to go to school, asking me questions that made me think about why I did. Then he said to me that he was very sorry to inform me but he was no longer going to be teaching in a graduate program. I never could understand what all of that meant. But he was no longer going to be teaching in a graduate school. John, was he fired from there? Did you know what happened now?

BRACEY: That was part of the, what's his name—the guy that came after Mordecai—Nabrit, that was his name. When the movement for Civil Rights began to develop, there were several schools, basically AMA schools—Tougaloo, Fisk, Howard—that despite what the leadership might have said or not said supported in fact activist students on their campus. And in Washington, D.C., this meant that the Davis Committee which oversaw the District of Columbia and gave money to Howard, said if you want your money then you sit on these people. Part of the conflict were those faculty. This happened all across the South. People like Felton Clark just fired everybody; Chuck [Charles] Hamilton got fired from Tuskegee and Drake got fired from Dillard. What happened at Howard was they tried to squash the influence or reduce the influence of those faculty who were the most visible supporters of what was going on around them. It's like Frazier; they forgot to invite Frazier to faculty [meetings]. It was always a kind of joke that Frazier would get a notice in his box about a faculty meeting next Tuesday and they had it the last Friday. Sterling Brown was one of those people who was seen as too close to the students. It's not that he had the politics because I'm not sure he did, but he thought they had a right to have politics and that they couldn't fire him because somebody had to teach those eight o'clock classes in the morning. He taught at eight o'clock in the morning. So they took away his right to do the specialty stuff that he liked. They stuck him with those eight o'clock classes . . .

TERRY: They were undergraduate courses for the most part.

BRACEY: If you notice, he taught like five classes per semester, and they started at eight o'clock in the morning and he'd be on campus all day every day. They did the same thing with Frazier. They gave him this huge sociology intro class, with nobody to help him do it. That was the institution's way of trying to attempt to discipline what they thought were faculty who were not behaving in the proper manner, you know, showing the proper subservience. Sterling Brown got caught up in that. At one point they even accused him of being insane and had him confined to Saint Elizabeth . . .

THELWELL: What year was that?

BRACEY: That was when they had the student takeover, in 1966 maybe.

THELWELL: Oh, after I left.

BRACEY: When the students demanded a black university, Sterling Brown opposed the idea. He said that if anybody tried to make Howard into something crazy, he and the ghost of E. Franklin Frazier would meet them at the gate. But on the other hand, he thought they had a right to state their position. And that was enough for them to think, well, he's obviously lost his mind. They literally declared him to be mentally incapable of functioning.

TERRY: Well, he wrote me back and said that he wasn't able to teach me, but that I should come . . .

BRACEY: What year was this?

TERRY: It was in 1963 or 1964. And he said I should come here too, if I wanted to go on to graduate school. I should come here to UMass and study with Sid Kaplan.

THELWELL: He wasn't sending anybody to UMass, he was sending them to Sid Kaplan.

TERRY: Yes, yes he did. He said, "Go to UMass and study with Sidney Kaplan," that's what he did, that's exactly what he said. I wrote him back to say "Why?"—because I really understood that he was putting me off. And I just said, "UMass? I don't know anything about UMass." So I said, "Well, you know, Professor Brown. . . ." He didn't say Harvard, or some bigger school; he said UMass. And nobody knew anything about UMass. I asked people about UMass and nobody knew. . . .

THELWELL: UMass barely existed.

TERRY: . . . So I didn't understand why he was suggesting that I come here. And he wrote back a letter that I wish had not been destroyed in the fire that destroyed my parents' home, that said, "Young lady, you do not study with a university, you study with a professor and you would be fortunate indeed to study with Sidney Kaplan." He went on about how important Sidney was, and how Sidney knew materials. Of course, I ended up here studying with Sidney Kaplan and I met my husband, who had in fact gone to Howard just as Mike and John had. Professor Brown and he, of course, had had their own wonderful relationship and experience. Mike came, I think, and John, were you here? It was the UMass Press or the *Massachusetts Review* that finally invited Sterling here, and that was the first time that I met him.

THELWELL: In my own case, I studied with Prof. Brown and showed him a story that I had written and we talked about it in class. And we had the relationships that he had with the activist students, which I describe in the essay "The Professor and the Activist." So I was close to him. But I didn't consult him about going to school. But a process very similar to the one Esther went through occurred in my case because one day I'm sittin' in the MFDP [Mississippi Freedom Democratic Party] Office and, providentially, a letter appears on the letterhead of the University of Massachusetts, of which I had not heard. When I was editor of the student newspaper, we exchanged newspapers with Boston College, Howard University, and Brandeis, but the University of Massachusetts was not on the radar. I didn't play any sports. I'd never heard of a University of Massachusetts. What the hell is that? But this letter appeared from

Sidney Kaplan and saying that under recommendation of Sterling Brown he was writing to offer me a fellowship at the university. The last thing I was thinking about was going to graduate school, so I threw it out. So about two weeks later, a couple agents of the FBI came in to ask what the fuck I was doing and pointed out to me, which I knew very well, that I was a foreign student. They made it very clear that they would escort me to the plane and ship me out of the country if I was not back in school by September. This was in the summer so this was in July. And when they left everybody ran in there and said, "What happened?" I said, "They are going to deport me unless I'm back in school."

TERRY: Oh, what happened to that letter from Sterling? [*laughter*]

THELWELL: I said, "Oh shit, we threw it out." And my associate John Gavick says, "Yeah, but I pulled it out of the wastebasket." But it was Sterling Brown who got me here in the same way that he got you here, Esther.

TERRY: And my husband Eugene and Bernie Bell. Sterling Brown became the person to just send all the black folk he knew who wanted to go on to school to Sidney Kaplan, to pass the mantle from himself in that way to Sidney Kaplan. When he came, he came one or two times here to visit us. He always came by our house, and he would always have his drink and tell his tales. He was very, very fond of my husband Eugene, of course. Gene had grown up in the North and had not gone South until he went to Howard. He had gone to all-white schools where he and his cousin were the only two black kids in the school. He had always been in the North. Sterling used to always ask him, "Terry, when did you learn you were black?" and they would have stories about that. Then Mr. Brown would ask my husband that in ways that were not insulting at all, but it was a recognition that he too was very fair, and people could pass you if you didn't know him. You could think that he was someone who was a white person. So they would share memories and incidents about people having mistaken them to be somebody that they weren't. And he had a few wonderful and unrepeatable stories about passing and people who pass and why he wouldn't pass. About why he wouldn't jump from a wonderful wholesome world into whatever he had. He would say a few things about that. Every time he left our house, Professor Brown knew we didn't have any money; he knew we had scraped up every penny extra that we could find to get him his Wild Turkey, 'cause it certainly cost more than what anything my husband was drinking at the time or could afford, and he knew that. He would always come past us and say "Here's fifty dollars for a war bond for the baby." And I know Professor Brown knew that we did not take that money and buy no war bond. He knew that but he always used to say "Now here's fifty dollars, Terry, for the war bond." And one time we were particularly stressed out financially and he said, "I want to give both of you one this time. You put your war bond in for the baby, and you put your war bond in for the baby." So that day he left we had one hundred dollars, and we had had a wonderful conversation with him. He was an incredible man. I met him through his poetry, learned by my experience with his poetry how he resonated, how he could manage to make black farmers and sharecroppers and people in North Carolina feel good about themselves. I just loved that. And then I met the man; there was nothing like it in anything that I have ever imagined about this wonderful and incredible human being.

THELWELL: I want to pick up on that. Academics write a lot of bullshit, and less than accurate, less than perceptive, less than helpful criticism. What made Sterling Brown the unique figure he was in African American and American culture, what made him the powerful figure he was, and what made him as beloved as he was by the masses of black people? Listen. Once I went back to Howard and they were having a big conference. I forget what it was, but the movie showing against the wall was that long interview movie [the] Ethiopian brother [Haile Gerima] had made on Sterling. As I walked into the room there was Sterling with a creased face, a little bit older than you. He was talking in a voice, unmistakable. And what was he saying? Obviously I had to figure out the question from the answer, but the question was his relationship to the Harlem Renaissance. And Sterling was growling and he says, "Look, when the resident niggers was up there drinking Carl Van Vechten's bad wine, I was down in Virginia teaching the folk. I was where the people farmed and so and so." As we were coming over here, you played a tape where he was talking about the blues and he was talking again about the traditional relationship. The tradition he was talking about was the Tin Pan Alley blues and the George Gershwin blues as in fact a kind of commercial exploitation, falsification and artificialization of black culture. What Sterling represented, the reason why black people loved him and what made his poetry to this very day unique only a few black poets have done it. He was one of those who went against the distortion of educated sensibilities that was the accomplishment of the minstrel tradition, blackface tradition, which forced educated or caused educated black people to move away from their authentic indigenous tradition, their so-called folk speech, the rural tradition, and try to write educated stuff. Sterling Brown understood the power and the beauty of the oral tradition, and also the dignity. That's what Carmichael was talking about. He managed to create and to approximate a literary language: that is to say a written language, which had all the sensibility, all the poetry, all of the oral tradition of the so-called black dialect. So he was working in a literary form. He created a literary poetic language, in which to express not just the dialect, yes, the language, yes, but what that language is based on and what that language implies. What that language carries is a posture, a political posture, a political sensibility, a cultural posture which expresses, to coin a phrase, the *Souls of Black Folk*. And that is what those farmers recognized. The other person who tried to do it but not with the same literary skill was the *Their Eyes Were Watching God* lady. She didn't have the literary skills. She understood the same poetry, understood the same force, understood the same vitality and integrity of that tradition, and she tried to work it. There have been other authors along the line who have done so, but for the most part that colonialist impulse and imperialist impulse tried to move black people away from it. That was the experience Sterling Brown was trying. The point is, he wasn't a visiting poet appropriating a language and a vocabulary and a sensibility. It also expresses real feeling. That's what you saw in the man. He was an expression of that. When we would go to his office to drink liquor and tell some lies, he would play blues for us. He'd play the best blues from the expensive collection he had in his office.

TRACY: What was his best blues?

THELWELL: I ain't going to give you a playlist right now, but particular tapes. Somebody singing Ma Rainey. Now listen to this, listen to that; they were all one gathered classic treasured moment. He'd play Leadbelly and he'd play the whole tradition and he'd talk to us about it. He'd talk to us not in a lecture kind of way but where this was played, what was going and what it represented in the oral tradition. Then, he would tell persons' stories; he'd tell very funny stories about W.E.B. Du Bois, which were funny stories that humanized Du Bois. They were very respectful of Du Bois, but they were as funny as hell. He had a story about Mordecai Johnson. And yeah, there's the questioning about his attitude and about religion. We never discussed religion with Sterling Brown, but we did discuss the black church. There's a certain grunt that the bishop has, and there's a certain grunt that the pastor has. He was a raconteur. And he'd talk about pastoral counseling to one of the big-legged sisters, and the pastor or counselor would have to run without his pants because the husband came home. He'd tell all of those kinds of bawdy irreverent stories, but they were never racist; they were never pejorative, they were never condescending, and there was an abiding love for black people that radiated out of the way he related to that material. That's what he attempted to do; that's what he did very successfully and skillfully in his poetry.

TRACY: I like that; when you talk about religion, there's that notion, he says, "She has found faith sufficient for her grief." Frequently he seems to try to locate some center of support that people need, and the institutions that can arise to fulfill those needs, to take care of those needs for people. He identifies that as being part of the church even as, in other places in his poems, he talks about the preacher getting women and wanting to make some money—that "I'm gonna be a preacher" sort of thing.

TERRY: He wouldn't destroy the church. He was close to the church.

BRACEY: His father was a preacher. That's the split between the congregations. His father split off from a Methodist church when he came over to Lincoln Temple. There was a big kind of cultural and political and doctrinal dispute that kind of wracks black [culture], like that at the end of Reconstruction. Saying "What are you going to do, what is the purpose of this institution?" And Sterling's father was one of those people who came over to the AME churches, the Congregational churches. That's the tradition out of which I see him, and that's the tradition he grew up in. I always saw him as the heir to Paul

Laurence Dunbar. Dunbar was the person before him. The feeling always was that if Dunbar had lived and had made a direct connection they would have been friends. That would have been the direct line if it had come that way. Because the person whom you've quoted as much as Sterling or more than Sterling was Dunbar. Our lives were saturated with Paul Laurence Dunbar. I mean, if we didn't know ten Dunbar poems we were considered blithering idiots. Part of the struggle at Howard was in fact to get all of that stuff out of us that we learned at the lower grades. If we came out of, like I got out of Mott School, all we recited was black poetry until the white people showed up. We did Shakespeare, but we thought Shakespeare was black because of the language. It never occurred to us that a white man could write that good. He certainly didn't sound white. All the great people we knew who did Shakespeare, whether it was Robeson or anybody else at Howard, the drama students, it sounded like a black way of speaking. Just like the King James Bible. We were convinced that whoever translated the King James version had a brother sittin' right next to him making sure that the rhythm was right. That's the language we were part of, and Dunbar was the one who's the repository of that, after slavery. And then it disappears for a bit there. Langston Hughes can't do it because Langston Hughes is an urban poet, and Langston Hughes doesn't talk about the world that I used to hang around and why I went to my grandparents' house in Florida for the summers. His poems aren't about that world. He can talk about the city, getting on the train and going to Baltimore, Countee Cullen and that kind of stuff. But Hughes doesn't have a rural poem. Sterling Brown talks about the world that I lived in growing up, sitting on my grandmother's front porch while we're watching the guys come in from the turpentine camps or bringing in the loads of sugarcane off the truck and so forth. Just listen to that language, the language and the churches he's making fun of—like my grandmother's AME Zion Church down in Florida where they'd have these month-long revivals. I was a kid and we'd go around imitating all of these preachers and banging on the table and hollering and stuff. And Sterling Brown was one of the few people who picked that up. Dunbar did it. Dunbar had "An Ante-Bellum Sermon." Brown goes and picks up that tradition and brings it back to the new generation. So you don't have to leave that alone; it didn't die back here. There's somebody that picks that up again and it's okay, and brought it back again. And it's very unique because people still don't quite have that. There's not a lot of black poets that do that, have the comfort level with that. When you get to the Black Arts Movement, people can do rhythm and blues and so forth, but for the Jim Crow generation—the generation that runs from 1896 to 1954—here's the poet that handles the whole range, up and down and sideways.

TRACY: We were talking about Dunbar and the question of whether Sterling Brown would see himself as an heir or in the tradition of Paul Laurence Dunbar.

THELWELL: He wouldn't act out very much and call himself "the heir" of Paul Laurence Dunbar or the son of Paul Laurence Dunbar. He certainly respected Dunbar and certainly quoted him a lot. He recognized him as a kindred spirit. He recognized him as a literary and cultural ally, as two poets, two figures who shared the same appreciation and sensitivity towards traditional black culture and who worked in it and were exponents of it in literary form. He would see himself [and Dunbar] as allies. That's what I think had happened.

TRACY: But it's interesting that Dunbar, after all, wasn't born in the South and has been vilified by some people for his dialect, his dialect poetry, and the ambience he creates in dialect.

THELWELL: Look. The rise of blackface minstrelsy and the appropriation of elements of black culture and its use to ridicule, parody, humiliate, and dehumanize the creators of the culture is an expression of the evil and the sickness of white people. But it had an effect in the black community that has to be recognized. In the nineties, educated black folks started to shy away from it simply because their culture was being parodied. People talk about blackface as the first entrance of black culture into the national culture and into the popular culture; that is bullshit. What it did was it got people embarrassed about themselves. So when you say some attacked Dunbar for his use of dialect, his use of dialect was not as sophisticated as Sterling Brown's was because he captured the poetry of dialect, the resonance of dialect, without actually knowing so and so. The effect of this parodying of black culture caused black people to turn against themselves, and that is why they were attacking Dunbar. That's what I was talking about.

TRACY: So Brown was able to understand that, contextualize it in that way, and embrace, then, the value of Dunbar's work in a broader context.

THELWELL: I guess you could say that.

BRACEY: You have to be clear as to who is devaluing Dunbar. There are more high schools named after Dunbar than any other black figure. Dunbar isn't lost to black people, and there are some white people who say they don't like Dunbar. But that didn't stop him from being taught in elementary schools. It didn't stop me from knowing and having to memorize the poetry, and it didn't stop people from venerating him in every black context I've ever been in. I haven't met any black people other than people in the past thirty years maybe who thought there was something wrong with Paul Laurence Dunbar because he used these two different forms. And I like the forms. I have never had much trouble with Dunbar's poetry at all [and neither] did a whole lot of other black people. Otherwise they wouldn't be naming the schools after him because this is their choice. This is not white people naming schools for black people. They are black people in Jim Crow environments picking their cultural figures. Dunbar is absolutely far and away the most popular cultural poet.

TRACY: Well, I think some of the problem had to do with what seemed to some critics a kind of acceptance of certain elements of plantation tradition, the happy darkies on the plantation, and those kinds of things, which are reflected in some of the poetry.

BRACEY: Dunbar's dead by 1906. The poetry of the Renaissance is urban poetry; this is a response to migrations; this is a response to people who are now in cities who have a totally different sensibility, and they are very actively rejecting a kind of paradigm. It's like the New Negro and the whole point of being the New Negro is that you're not the Old Negro anymore. I think Dunbar in a lot of people's minds represented the highest level of expression of the "Old Negro" sensibility. But we're not doing that anymore. We are doing Claude McKay, "If We Must Die," rather than the kind of ambiguity in "An Ante-Bellum Sermon," where Dunbar has to dissemble a little bit. I think that's what you see among people who consider themselves young and sophisticated and hip to the latest black poetic expressions. That's why Sterling Brown is so different, because Sterling Brown sits right in the middle of all this and he says, "Harlem, there's Negroes that live in places other than Harlem. What's this Harlem thing?" He says the same thing that he says to Mike, when we talk about the Harlem Renaissance. He said, "Only a fool would live in Harlem—have you ever seen [what] these people live in?" and "Name me one poet that was actually born in Harlem that wrote anything worth reading," I guess other than Countee Cullen. But he thought this was a complete kind of hype, like some white people made up this whole thing and took a lot of poetry and didn't have a lot of respect for it really and made this to be black culture and left behind his people, which is to say, the people . . .

THELWELL: Precisely. It was the same process that you were recalling in the blues you were talking about. A certain merchandising, a certain appropriation, and a privileging of certain black writers, many of whom catered to the exotic, primitive expectations of the white avant garde. I mean the Carl Van Vechtens of this world. It's a constant debate; it's a constant tension in black culture. What happens to the culture and the point where it enters into the discourse of white people and starts to be conditioned by their expectations?

BRACEY: And who gets paid. See. Dunbar got paid by black people for the most part. I mean Booker T. brought him down to Tuskegee and supported him as best he could, and he got invited to read in black genres, black environments, black schools, and black churches and whatnot. It's not clear that the Harlem Renaissance audience is that same kind of audience. It really is a vernacular audience that consists of lodges, Elks clubs, and the Men's Day, and the Black and Negro History Week performances. If you were an artist you could live in that world. The black artists that I met who never had much popularity at all outside black communities and who did like black concert music, like Dorothy Maynor and people like that, were primarily in black environments. They may have [given] one concert in Paris which gave them the goal [in] a few days to come back and sing opera to the youth for the next twenty years, but they also sang spirituals. So even like Marian Anderson or Leontyne Price, they could take it all the way through *Tristan and Isolde* and then in the same CD drop in "Nobody Knows the Trouble I've Seen" because they don't want to let you know that they are somebody different. Again, like Leontyne Price when she signed a contract with the Met saying she's going to get a million dollars a year plus car fare. That was a hint: "I know where I came from and what black women have been fighting for many years as maids." White people don't pay your car fare. So she says, "Okay, I'll take a million dollars, but who is going to pay my car bill to get here?" And when she did that that was a clear sign: "Okay, I can do this, but I know who I am." What you get in Sterling Brown's poetry are the artistic expressions that there's an experience that hasn't gone away. It should not be left behind; it should not be jettisoned because a new experience has been added on to it—an urban experience to migration experience. This [is] just as valuable; it's just as beautiful. He was pretty unique. There's not a lot of people writing in this kind of genre. All about the same kind of people. And they were also not giving you the characters and human beings that Brown writes about because his poems are people poems; they are not conditions poems. Like "Break of Day" about Big Jess getting killed because he's a fireman on the Alabama railroad. It's about a person but it's talking about class conflict and racial conflict on the railroad system, which was very big in those days. He didn't write an essay about it but he captures it.

THELWELL: That is what I meant about the sensibility thing, because it proceeds outward from the people and there's a sense of community in the poetry so that these are not stock black characters; these are not minstrel types; these are complex human beings with their quirks, with their expectations, and with enormous, enormous humanity and dignity. That is the value of his poems, and they are all unique, individual. That's why Carmichael could say, "When I went to Mississippi I was in Sterling Brown territory." And the Fanny Lou Hamers were Sterling Brown's people in all [their] complexity. It's entirely different from when black people's realities and experience get projected into the commercial media whether that be of literature or of music or anything else.

BRACEY: Or Bigger Thomas in a tenement building.

THELWELL: What is going to be useful. Sterling was a great raconteur who would tell us all of these stories.

BRACEY: This [is] always my favorite because it's about a black father—he didn't say it's a black father. He starts talking with the voice of a black father who is either a sharecropper or has his own little place. In those terms, he says as much about the sharecropper or a tenant farmer as a hundred Department of Labor reports on the conditions of crops and so forth. This is a man who wants to do something. He has a vision of how the world will work and despite the fact that he's stuck down here with ten acres he's got to struggle through. These are modest goals but they are very specific, very precise kinds of goals. So it's not a dissertation on racism in the plantation system, but it illuminates it in a way that a dissertation couldn't. And he has tons of poems like that.

TRACY: It serves as a metaphor for generational relationships in a way that is immediately understandable to everybody.

THELWELL: But you also have to understand that this brother controls ten acres. Ten acres in terms of survival can be very productive, and you ain't poor, and you see the variety of what he produces. The other course is in standard English.

BRACEY: Yeah, except for the speaking of it.

THELWELL: Before I forget, when you're talking about Sterling Brown being fired, he had a formula in describing himself. I can't remember but it went something like this, "This is the only Negro in the history of Howard University that had been fired, re-hired, re-tired, re-fired, and hired again . . .," something like that. [*Laughter*] It described [his] complex relationship to the university. There's one aspect of Prof. Brown that really needed an audience, but I think he might have been bipolar because I had to come down on him at certain times. The taxi driver would be looking out for him to bring him home to Miss Daisy, and that's when he wanted to invite us to his office to "drink some liquor and tell some lies." Very little liquor got drunk, you know; everybody would take a glass and sip it ceremoniously. And then, he'd launch into all of these stories, these tales, which were very educational because they were about the elders. He'd tell us about the true history of Howard University—that was hilariously funny. [Robert O'Meally], after graduating from some Ivy League school, went to teach at Howard to be close to Sterling. Sterling was in that mood when he needed an audience. What was happening, he'd have an ongoing party. He'd sit there in his house drinking that may go on for two days, and he would just tell stories, play music, tell stories, play music, and get more energized as he went along. So Bob O'Meally had a speaking engagement some place. It was about six o'clock in the morning. Sterling Brown calls up, "tell Bob O'Meally to come over. We're drinking some liquor and telling some lies," and O'Meally's wife would say, "Well, he just come home from traveling and he's asleep." The wives would never really approve of going out with Sterling, so they would go on to tell folks that he was asleep. So Bob said he woke up about 10 o'clock and said, "Oh shit, I got to call Brown." So he called up Prof. and somebody answers the phone, and hears the professor's voice clearly saying "Who's that?" and the guy who answered the phone said, "Bob O'Meally," and then he said he hears Brown's voice clear as day, "Tell the nigger I'm asleep." [*Laughter*] He said that he invited him to speak at some school where he was teaching, and during the dinner prior to the speech, prior to the reading, somebody asked a question about Howard University—which [appeared] to Prof. to be condescending and pejorative. This was at the university. So he told off this academic, whoever he was, and then he gets up to read. He reads a poem and is very enthusiastic. He goes into a story, and he says, "I ain't sayin' a word until I get paid." And there's a hush—this is a small private, Ivy League school. A hush descends on the gathering, and Brown stands up there and says, "I'm not saying another damn word until I get paid. If this was Howard University, three Negroes would take a check to the back, get the money and bring it back up here, man . . ." And O'Meally is horrified. Professor Brown says, "Well, get me some water, but I ain't saying another word until I *get my money.*" And they bring him a glass down. Glub, glub, glub, glub—he drinks it down. And O'Meally finally inveigles him to proceed to the end of the thing, but he's still in high dudgeon. So O'Meally takes him over to the black students entering campus, and says, "I know what to do." So he gets him a big glass of Wild Turkey and sends the two prettiest girls to ask him questions. But the prettiest of the girls was going out with a black quarterback on the football team. So he walked in and sees his girl on Sterling's arm. The young jock walks in the door and says, "Who's that old white man over there?"— [He] took Prof. Brown [for] a white man. Professor was on his feet and ready to go to war with this young man. He was going to beat his ass because the guy called him a white man and O'Meally has to cool the whole situation out. He was, you know, irreverent and he was rambunctious when he wanted to be, and he was unpredictable. One time, he revived that institution—I don't know if you remember this, John, the Howard Players where the faculty would put on skits and plays. Well, the whole time I was there it had fallen into disuse. So one year Professor revives it and he gets all of these faculty members. Remember that tall guy they use to call "Watutsi" who went to become head of a black school in the South?

BRACEY: Elias Blake.

THELWELL: What he did was he made parody of *Gunsmoke* which was very clear. And that historian who was very close to NAG who found[ed] that reading circle—kind of light skin—he played Matt Dillon, and he looked like him in a cowboy hat. You know, that reading program that Stokely and all of them were in, where they would select a book and read it. Then there was a very charming plump lady who was maybe head of the Classics Department.

BRACEY: That's probably Margaret Just Butcher, because she taught Greek and Latin.

THELWELL: Could have been. She played Miss Kitty. All these dignified people. Sterling Brown, I forget who he was playing—the raconteur, right? And Elias Blake, who was called "Watutsi," was playing the sidekick, the fool. So it was hilarious, it was funny. And Brown wrote the text, and there were sounds and such. It was hilarious, certainly, and a great hit at Howard University. But Prof. wasn't satisfied. He says, "This is so good we got to take it downtown." He goes and rents the theater. And some of the faculty said, "Shit, its one thing to do it up here at Howard, but we ain't goin' downtown amongst the white folks and play the fool." But several of them hung tough and decided to take the show downtown. So we in NAG got drafted, those of us who were closest to him. We got drafted to be the technical people. I was sent to run the lights. I've never seen a lighting system in my life before and we're supposed to get the props. I remember at one point he said to me, "Thelwell, I want a coffin." Where am I going to get a coffin from and [he] don't give me a penny? By the time we went down to rehearsal, I hadn't gotten the coffin, but I hadn't forgotten. So all of us now are running technical things for this production. We rented this theater downtown. It's a little theater downtown, and luckily the audience wasn't big. But there was an audience. The first thing is Ed Brown was supposed to get props. He didn't know that for a whiskey bottle you [poured] tea in there. So Ed brought this big bottle of bourbon which was 90 proof; it wasn't freaking tea, right? So the first thing is Elias Blake's wife is across in cowboy boots, and he—he poured it into the cup and whiskey flies all over the stage and the guy is choking and the audience is applauding like the guy is acting [*Laughter*] . . . And I'm upstairs and I'm cracking up. So the lights are supposed to go down and I'm upstairs cracking up so hard I couldn't dim the lights on Sterling, who was sitting at the table—I forget who he was playing—[he] yells "Lights, god damn it," "Lights, dim the lights!" It just went from bad to friggin' worse, as everybody upstairs got drunk from this bottle of whiskey. [*Laughter*] The funny thing was it was one of the most amazing performances, I guarantee, ever to play at Howard University—well in Washington, D.C., with Howard University faculty. At the end, the folks are supposed to gather and have a talk about what happened and what didn't happen, and that itself was hilarious. [At] the same theater there was an actor production of *Brecht on Brecht*, and Prof. Brown decided that it had a lot of black actors in the production and it was going very well so we went and we saw it. Roscoe Lee Browne was in it, I remember, and Prof. was so impressed with this that he said, "Howard University has to see this." The next thing you know he's sitting with the director of [the] theater writing a check. He's held over the production for a whole week which means he's responsible for ninety tickets for a seven-day performance. So we ran back to Tom Kahn, who was treasurer of the student government, and we found out from the theater how much it would cost to hold over this production. So we got the student government to write the check—totally illegal. We gave it to them and they tore up Prof. Brown's check. Then they gave us these rolls of tickets and we then walked over to campus:"Hey, would you like to see a play, would you like to go to theater, we're giving out tickets to the students." And that's the kind of stuff that we would do just impulsively. We headed over and we were walking around campus giving free tickets to the theater to try to fill up the theater. He wasn't a choirboy; let's put it that way.

BRACEY: The other thing that was fascinating, given his background and skin color and all, is that he joined Omega Psi Phi fraternity and not the Alphas or the Kappas and I think that is fairly significant.

TRACY: Can you differentiate between them?

BRACEY: Well, when I was growing up the Kappas were like, "light, bright, damn near white," and were like the pretty boys, I mean, completely kind of doofuses. They had no brains but they had all the women because they were cute, and they had light skin.

THELWELL: And were probably more affluent, where some of their fathers were doctors, etc.

BRACEY: Yeah, everybody in that circle was not working class. The Alphas were the intellectual heavyweights; you're talking about Charles Wesley, Du Bois, Martin Luther King— they were Alphas. The Omegas were always like the working class, like the guys that you had to have a fraternity for, people who wanted to be in a fraternity but they weren't . . .

THELWELL: And their stomps and steps were very African.

BRACEY: Yeah, they were street; that's why they called them the "Q dogs." One of the first fights I ever got in when I was a little kid was breaking up an Omega frat show because they had dog collars on people and I thought this was just horrible. They were going around at sundown at Howard, and I came from elementary school and just busted right in there, saying "You are human beings; take these collars off; this is crazy." They had to go get my mother out of class to come rescue me. She tried to explain it was a ritual, and I said, "Ritual or not, you shouldn't be wearing dog collars." They were always in some sort of trouble. If anybody was on probation for violation of university policy it would likely be them. Today it's the fraternity of choice for most black athletes: Michael Jordan, Shaquille O'Neal, these people are all Omegas. Jesse Jackson is an Omega and he's a quarterback for North Carolina A&T. They branded themselves with the "Q." Sterling Brown clearly paid enough attention either to his athletic side or to his street side to join them and not join the ones that clearly he could have gotten in to. Given his father's background, he would easily qualify to be in the Kappas, and intellectually he could have been an Alpha given the schools he went to and so forth. But he joined a fraternity that was noted more for athletes than for people who were intellectuals. I think that was interesting because Brown did consider himself an athlete.

TRACY: Can you talk about that a little bit? I mean, how was Brown an athlete?

BRACEY: He played tennis. He was very much into tennis. There's the whole thing about the mind/body that we have today that didn't exist among this class of people when I was growing up. A lot of the greatest athletes in the black community during this period were also the smartest people.

THELWELL: A lot of the stories Brown would tell us about Williams, that all the black guys there were either track men or football players. So a lot of the stories are really jock stories; I mean, he's very much into that.

BRACEY: Yeah, that whole tradition, like Charles Drew was a football player, Montague Cobb was a football player, and John West who set up the radio station was a football player. And even today the head surgeon at Howard [University] Hospital, John Syphax, led Howard's basketball team in scoring for four years. He's the best basketball player I've ever seen. You know, he's better than Elgin Baylor but he wanted to be a surgeon because his father was a surgeon and his grandfather was a surgeon. And so there's a expectation that just because you had a brain didn't mean you couldn't play a sport. You went to the same playground as everyone else. There wasn't a class segregation. When you played ball at Banneker, if you played pick-up football or pick-up basketball, everybody played. If you went on a tennis court, you picked a time like anybody else. Nobody said, "Well, I'm Sterling Brown and I get it at nine o'clock"; they said, "No no, you get in line behind these other people and if you win you get your side of the court." So he grew up in that kind of world where clearly that was important enough to him that when he chose an affiliation he chose an affiliation that's more identified as that than as what you would expect given his skin color and class. I don't think anybody has ever talked to him about this topic, or that he's written about it. It certainly was a part of his identity, very much so. I think he played tennis almost his whole life.

THELWELL: A skin color sufficiently evident that this young athlete could walk into the black culture [center], "What is an old white man doing in a black house?" He didn't know if he was upset that he was old or because they called him white; professor was ready to get down.

BRACEY: But he was in that, and he was fairly active and never outgrew it in a sense. He had this very deep set of institutional networks that were part of the way of the Washington, D.C., community operated. And there was another little group that I'm still not sure about because my violin teacher was a part of it, Louie Jones. He taught violin at Howard for many years, but he was also in Langston Hughes's *The Big Sea* as Louie Jones the jazz drummer in Paris. Well, Louie got this scholarship to go study at the Sorbonne, and as soon as he got there he put his violin in the cabinet and got these drums and went to the brick tops in somewhere and tried to make a living playing drums until his family found out and brought him back. Well, this whole group of people at Howard had this dichotomy. So Louie had taught classical violin; that's what I studied. He was a beautiful violinist, but give him five minutes off and he'd go sit it in with a jazz combo somewhere. So he and Sterling Brown were part of that little group that read at Brown's house. They all got together and it's a little club they had where they'd talk about books, and talk about music, and culture, and drink and eat. And Louie was a part of that group and they all have this kind of black cultural orientation that "I can do this but I can also do this." I think Sterling kind of embodied that. I think that Mike just said this: that he's right about him being bored with the English classes. He was not bored with Shakespeare or with the language of the King James Bible because that language is the language that black people spoke; it was the language of black ministers.

THELWELL: He was bored with the curriculum, and his teaching was very, very rigorous and very good.

TRACY: Were there contemporary writers, for example, that he was more excited about than, say, some of the writers he was teaching in the course that you took? Say like a Sandburg or E. A. Robinson, Vachel Lindsay, or people like that—all of whom he has said in print that he admired a great deal.

BRACEY: I think he liked those '30s people, like Dreiser, you know, realists.

THELWELL: Discussions that I particularly remember, I was—what was that Southern group called?

BRACEY: Oh, the Fugitives.

THELWELL: And he had real running feuds with many of those Fugitives because of what they said about black people. He got off on those, I mean, that's when we saw him best. When we would sit in his house talking, we saw him best as a defender of black people and black culture. If he talked about white writers he admired—and he did, but I can't remember.

TRACY: Frost maybe.

THELWELL: He may have talked about a Frost poem or Steinbeck in his poetic expressions.

TRACY: So he liked more politically aware or obviously committed writers?

THELWELL: That wasn't the issue. The issue is the realism in his representation of people, the representation of people who don't usually get represented in literature. Representation of real folk, if you will, that kind of stuff.

BRACEY: Yeah, working-class people.

TRACY: One of the things that I wanted to talk about a little bit was Brown as a teacher, and we've touched on this a little bit already, but to come back to some more of that. You said that he brought people into classes or came into classes. Was he very dramatic in his presentational materials either as a teacher or a poet, I mean as you saw him?

BRACEY: You got the wrong person for teaching because I've never taken a class with him. I knew him when I was a little kid growing up and so forth, and at Northwestern he did a reading. I've seen him read before. He reads, I wouldn't say dramatic. You know it's kind of funny because in fact he's not . . .

TRACY: He's a preacher's son so you might expect a certain amount of . . .

BRACEY: He was ironic, I guess—you know, most of poems aren't really dramatic poems. He doesn't have dramatic poems. He has poems that, you know, Gwendolyn Brooks has the same kind of poems. It sounds like it's kind of lurking along and then it zips you some kind of way and you realize that this guy just described some horrible event in this very straightforward language. Before you knew it, you're in it. And I think he read that way. He didn't read to build up towards something—the language conveyed the buildup, but he's reading it on a fairly even keel. He didn't have a lot of histrionics.

TRACY: He captures the rhythms in reading like "Puttin' on Dog" or something like that, and sometimes he reads in a nasal tone when his white folks are talking.

BRACEY: But in fact he was nowhere near the dramatic presentations you got coming out of the Black Arts Movement where people would sing and stamp their feet. The rhythms were in the language. If the poem is set up rhythmically, then if you read it then you don't have to add to it; it's there, in the thing itself. He's not saying I'm going to make this sound like a blues. He reads it and it's a blues and when he reads it you understand its blues rhythm. So you didn't have to announce it so that you know it's about to come—you listen to it and you get into the rhythm, and the rhythm is through his speech and not him having to emphasize that by making gestures and so forth. But I think that's the beauty of his language because his language is. And it's hard to do; people think that's easy to do, but it's . . . He and Gwendolyn Brooks are the only people I know that can actually do that.

THELWELL: It's unpretentious and it doesn't call attention to itself with verbal pyrotechnics, and get into the integrity of the rhythms and the textures of black speech and by extension of black thought.

BRACEY: He and Gwendolyn Brooks are the only people that can sit there with that look—they are perfectly still almost, and they read something and it's like beatin' you all upside the head right in the poem itself; but they never raise their voice; there's no ups or downs but there's just this kind of ironic flow, flow, flow. And you realize that some horrible thing has been described to you or some momentous occasion has been laid there in front of you with the words themselves.

THELWELL: Do you remember when Achebe was here and he read that eulogy for Christopher Okebo, and he read it in Ibo and how nobody understood a word of Ibo, but the rhythms and the music of it, do you remember that? He did that in Jamaica the other day; that's why it springs into my head. There is something which no language can describe, no critical language can describe. That happens with a Sterling Brown poem and that Achebe poem in Ibo; the tonality and the language and the rhythms are very, very close, but there's no language in the discourse to describe it.

BRACEY: It's a type of expression, but it's an expression that the language itself contains the rhythm without having to add on to it. My experience a lot of time during the Black Arts years was—I played conga drums, and you'd have to play behind a poet and in fact you were giving the thing rhythm because if they had read it without you playing behind it there was nothing happening. But anything else with Sterling Brown would have been superfluous; he doesn't need a guitar player to let you know that this is the blues—I can hear; like I got it you don't have to tell me. And the lines are like that. The "Sporting Beasley" or "When de Saints Go Ma'chin' Home," or even "The Ballad of Joe Meek" starts off with this ironic thing: "You cain't never tell how far a frog will jump, when you jes' see him planted on his big broad rump." And then it goes to this thing, and this nice little quiet guy is all of a sudden wreaks havoc all over the place. He ends up this whole thing: "So you cain't never tell how fas' a dog can run when you see him a-sleeping, in the sun." And then he stops. That's tremendous use of language, beautiful use of language, without him having to say this guy just killed a whole bunch of white people because that's what happens in the poem. I mean Joe Meek gets pissed, had enough is enough, and shoots up a whole bunch of white people, but he ends up with that's that. He ends up with "so you cain't never tell how fas' a dog can run when you see him a-sleeping, in the sun." He can do that, and Gwendolyn Brooks can do that, but not a lot of people can do that. That is a very, very important skill, a very novelistic skill.

THELWELL: But it's also the African tradition of proverbs and indirection, which he expressed with the terms "hittin' a straight lick with a crooked stick"—but not coming up and saying something directly but finding in fact an appropriate metaphor for saying it. That is a distinctive outtake of the linguistic resources and traditions of black people coming straight out of Africa, which exists equally to the same degree in Jamaica and the English-speaking Caribbean and the French-speaking Caribbean. It is essentially a linguistic tradition not unique to but particular to African-descended people.

TRACY: We talked a good bit about poems that make use of rhythms from the African American folk tradition, but Brown also wrote poems that were not in that folk tradition, too. And one of the beautiful things about it is even in those standard English poems the language flows so nicely, so naturally that it seems like—why I was thinking about Frost earlier, the blank verse of Frost. You have this very natural language that emerges from that. So whatever rhythms he was trying to use, he seemed to be able to speak very directly, and straightforwardly and unpretentiously, and communicate the honesty of the human being who is talking in the poem. In a speech at Williams College in 1973—I'm going to read this quote—Brown said this: "I'm an integrationist. Though that is an ugly word because I know what segregation really was, and by integration I do not mean assimilation. I believe what the word means, an integer is a whole number. I want to be in the best American traditions. I want to be accepted as a whole man. My standards are not white, my standards are not black, my standards are human."

THELWELL: That's an unfortunate version of that quote. The reason I say that is because the last part could be misunderstood. He used to use that argument with us, so I understand it very well. He says that "I'm an integrationist, integer, wholeness." What he was saying, first of all, is I'm not an assimilationist. I'm not advocating that black people go play white. He was saying, and what he would always have said, is the integer is complete, it is whole, and they have to accept all black people—all of us, not a part of us. And we have to look and see what is whole and wholesome about them. He was always talking about what should move into discourse, into encounters, into relationship with white people, is not a fraction of what black people represent, but all of it. And by that he was talking about the folk tradition; he's talking about street people. Black people's culture has that integrity as a whole, and that's what he was talking about. That's the argument he used to make with us.

BRACEY: But he's also talking about accepting black people as individuals, being accepted [in] all their complexity without trying to label them. That's what he embodied and that's the contradiction that runs through this generation now, the kind of black middle class that I very much grew up a part of. All of that stuff is there, and it never occurred to me that learning how to play the violin meant I wanted to be white—I mean it just never entered my head. My violin teacher was a black man, and I played in an all-black orchestra until I got to high school. I never thought this way; it was music some people liked so I learned how to play it. I didn't think that I would walk out on the stage and all of a sudden people would see me as a white person. There's a black person who plays the violin; a black person plays in the orchestra. I didn't think that Roland Hayes was white because he could sing German lieder and opera. This is a black man that sings opera. Paul Robeson for that matter. So I think part of the argument is is that he's very much anti-ideological in terms of defining who people are and what they are. You know, like you're this, you're that. That's what he really got annoyed about with the Black Arts stuff, and what he got annoyed [with] about the Harlem Renaissance. Somebody said, "This is who black people are," and he said, "No, no, no I'm not that, like I'm not that." Arna Bontemps said the same thing. I raised that question with him about the same time I raised it with Sterling Brown because Bontemps was in Harlem, working in Harlem for a couple of years. He must have had a great time being right there at the Renaissance and going to all of these clubs and stuff. He said, "I wouldn't go to anyplace like that. I didn't pay any attention to that stuff at all." It's like, how did a guy live at Harlem just ignore all of that? "I had my wife and kids at home, so why would I be out going to all these clubs and all these filthy people, and going to some parties with some drunk white people. Like what does that have to do with black people? I'm from Fisk. I don't need to go to Harlem to find out about being black."

THELWELL: The white stereotypical view of black people . . .

BRACEY: Yeah, "the Dark Towers" stuff. That salon stuff. The salon was in fact there. That was a whole different ambience than what you had at Harlem, where, in fact, decadence was the norm of the day, and the buffet parties, and the house parties, and all of that stuff. There really was; he was right about that. Van Vechten put everybody over the edge. But Georgia Douglas Johnson wasn't like that. I mean her salon really was, like, "I want the best of the artists out of this community, and then you come and you present yourself to people who understand and love this music, this culture, this art, and we will give you an experience that will benefit you as well as benefit us." And so it was always one of those status things in cultured D.C. to be invited. If you were a poet and if you weren't invited to read at Georgia Douglas Johnson's, it's like, "Go back and work on your stuff because when it gets good enough somebody will let her know and then you'll get a little card in the mail saying that Mrs. Georgia Douglas Johnson requests your presence at two o'clock on Sunday afternoon to read some of your work. Food will be served, proper attire." But it wasn't about decadence; it wasn't about pandering to people. It was about bringing people in, monitoring and evaluating an entire group of cultures.

THELWELL: On whose terms?

BRACEY: On her terms.

THELWELL: That's what I'm talking about—if the folks are going to present to white folks what they expected to see about black people. We show you black culture on our terms and this is what we mean by it.

BRACEY: It would be Sterling there or Anne Spencer, and Miss Daniels. Walter Daniels was a dean at Howard. They lived up the street from me, and she wrote poetry. Her whole thing was writing and publishing these books of poetry, which she'd always have us read. She was always trying to write something good enough that Georgia Douglas Johnson would like. I mean, that seemed to bother her. She'd read something and say Mrs. Johnson doesn't think this is good enough.

THELWELL: But Sterling also had a sense of humor when he started having differences with the Black Arts Movement. There was this woman who taught at Princeton or someplace, and she had Native American blood. She was after our time, but she was a student of Sterling and happened to mention that she had Native American blood. Sterling said what tribe, and she said "Black Feet." Sterling said, "Hey, hey I don't play that shit, 'Negro Foot,' you are 'Negro Foot.'"

BRACEY: He thought that the craziest thing that had happened during the period—black consciousness—he says, "This damn nigger obsession with hair. Every time we have a new way of looking at the world we got to talk about our hair," and "Any other people in the history of human beings spend so much time talking about their damn hair?" This is after he had gone about halfway through a bottle of Wild Turkey. That's what struck him ironic about a demand to assert one's blackness. You know, why is this manifested in hair? You either got hair or you don't, and the hell with it.

THELWELL: That's because Prof. couldn't raise an Afro anyway.

BRACEY: If you grew up in that part of the world, you got "blow hair" contests and you got people talking about good hair, bad hair. I mean a lot of his fights are the same fights that Frazier had. It's the internal stance that came out of the middle class. Like I grew up in that world, and I know about "brown bag" parties, and "blow hair" and all this business. I got put out of the Hi Fi club because I invited my friends from the playground to the dance. They weren't acceptable because they were either too dark or they weren't the right kind of people—these are the guys I played ball with. That was real. It's the same way that life was at Howard. I made a whole bunch of money 'cause the freshman queen was light-skinned. Remember Joyce Brown who everybody loved? Joyce Brown was the finest sister in the world. People would get up early in the morning to sit in Clark Hall to watch Joyce Brown walk across campus. She was dark brown skin and came out of Atlanta. She carried four trunks of clothes. She never wore the same outfit twice the whole year. Everybody in the whole world, out of the freshman class . . .

THELWELL: Is she the one who was in the Honors Program with us.

BRACEY: Yeah, yeah, yeah, and everyone would rush in there to see where she would sit.

THELWELL: She's in Virginia.

BRACEY: I thought that she was further south than that. Well, she was dark-skinned, so of course she's obviously the freshman queen. "I'll bet money," I said, "there is no way in the world Howard University is going to put her picture in the *Afro*." They said, "What are you talking about?" And I said, "She's too dark," and they said, "Nonsense, and put your money up." They found some light-skinned kid out of New York who nobody knows to this day; I don't even remember her name, who won homecoming, freshman queen. That was Howard in 1959. That stuff is real. A friend of the treasurer, Jim Clark, whose family I grew up with, Ann, brought her boyfriend back from Oakland. He was playing football with the Colts, matter of fact—we used to get free tickets to Colts games. Ralph Brooks was dark-skinned, so nobody invited him anywhere. This is not something off somewhere. This is the world that Sterling Brown was trying to negotiate as a light-skinned black person—that you automatically assume would have those attitudes. He's light-skinned and his wife is light-skinned, and so if you look at them in that community, you would drop stuff on him. That's why him being an Omega I think is significant, because that's not where he's supposed to be; he's supposed to be over here. Why is [he] over there? Why is he on U Street when he should be somewhere else? And I think a lot of him working his way through the integrity of people as human beings is trying to work past the external racism; but the internalized sets of values—they stifled black people's ability to function as human beings. I think that's where he was going with that. I think integration as an integer, which is a whole unit. You as a person are yourself, whatever that might be, whatever skin color you have, whatever values you have, whatever you like, whatever you don't like. If you are going to take me, you have to take all of this. You can't just take the black side of Sterling Brown; you have to take this part of Sterling Brown and take this other part of Sterling Brown. I think he thought any ideological stuff just blocked that. He was very much opposed to any kind of dogmatism. The world was too interesting to put people into boxes. Why don't you just go with the flow of things and stop labeling everything? He hated this labeling thing.

VII

"ON THIS I STAND":
A BIBLIOGRAPHY

An Annotated Bibliography of the Works of Sterling A. Brown

Robert G. O'Meally

Sterling A. Brown is a distinguished writer whose poems, short stories, reviews, and scholarly works have appeared for nearly more than fifty years. His poetry reflects the innovative impulse of contemporary verse as well as the toughness, humor, and protest of black American folklore. His reportorial narratives and sketches of the Southern scene are alive with black talk, and they convey vividly the terror and the irony of "living Jim Crow" during the 1940s. Brown has studied the role of blacks in American folklore, literature, and music since the New Negro Renaissance period. His work also has provided perspective to *New* New Negroes, including Black Aesthetic writers of the 1960s and 1970s.

This annotated bibliography, arranged according to subject and date of publication, is designed to assist readers in locating Brown's works, many of which are uncollected or out of print. For assisting me in tracking down materials, I am indebted to Cornelia Stokes and Ahmos Zu-Bolton at Founder's Library, Howard University. For help in revising this work for 1998, many thanks go to John Edgar Tidwell. Special thanks go, forever, to Sterling A. Brown, teacher, hero, friend.

POEMS

Poems included in Southern Road, but published previously:

"For a Certain Youngster." *The Oracle,* 3.1 (March, 1925), p. 33. An experiment using the Italian sonnet form.

"Vignette: from Virginia Woods." *The Oracle*, 5.1 (1926), p. 14. Later revised for the planned volume *No Hiding Place*; included in *The Collected Poems* as "Coolwell Vignette (From Virginia Woods)."

"Challenge," "Odyssey of Big Boy," "Return," "Salutamus," "To a Certain Lady, in Her Garden." *Caroling Dusk*. Ed. Countee Cullen. New York: Harper and Brothers, 1927, pp. 130–39.

"Foreclosure." *Ebony and Topaz: A Collectanea*. Ed. Charles S. Johnson. New York: Opportunity, 1927, p. 36.

"Old Man Buzzard." *The Carolina Magazine*, 58 (May, 1927), p. 25–26.

"When de Saints Go Ma'ching Home." *Opportunity, Journal of Negro Life*, 5 (July, 1927), p. 48. (Hereafter, *Opportunity, Journal of Negro Life* will be cited as *Opportunity*.) This poem won the *Opportunity* poetry prize for 1927.

"Thoughts of Death." *Opportunity*, 6 (August 1928), p. 242.

"Long Gone." *Anthology of Negro American Literature*. Ed. V. F. Calverton. New York: Modern Library, 1929, pp. 209–10.

"Riverbank Blues." *Opportunity*, 7 (May, 1929), p. 148.

"Effie." *Opportunity*, 7 (October, 1929), p. 304.

"Dark of the Moon," "Ma Rainey," "Southern Road." *Folk-Say, a Regional Miscellany*, 2. Ed. Benjamin A. Botkin. Norman, Oklahoma: University of Oklahoma Press, 1930, pp. 275–79.

"Kentucky Blues." *Palms*, 7.2 (March, 1930), p. 115.

"Memphis Blues," "Slim Greer," "Strong Men." *The Book of American Negro Poetry*. Ed. James Weldon Johnson. New York: Harcourt, Brace, 1931, pp. 252–54, 258–60.

"Convict," "New St. Louis Blues," "Old King Cotton," "Pardners," "Revelations," "Slow Coon" (later published as "Slim Lands a Job"), "Tin Roof Blues." *Folk-Say, a Regional Miscellany*, 3. Ed. Benjamin A. Botkin. Norman, Oklahoma: Oklahoma Folklore Society, 1931, pp. 113–23.

Southern Road. New York: Harcourt, Brace, 1932.

Brown's first book of poems.

Poems not in Southern Road

"After the Storm." *The Crisis, a Record of the Darker Races*, 34 (April, 1927), p. 48. (Hereafter *The Crisis, a Record of the Darker Races* will be cited as *The Crisis*.)

"A Bad, Bad Man," "Call Boy," "Long Track Blues," "Puttin' on Dog," "Rent Day Blues," "Slim in Hell." *Folk-Say*, 4. Ed. Benjamin A. Botkin. Norman, Oklahoma: Oklahoma Folklore Society, 1932, pp. 249–56.

"He Was a Man." *Opportunity*, 10 (June, 1932), p. 179.

"Let Us Suppose." *Opportunity*, 13 (September, 1935), p. 281.

"Southern Cop," "Transfer." *Partisan Review*, 3 (October, 1936), p. 220–21.

"Master and Man." *New Republic*, (November 18, 1936), p. 66.

"All Are Gay." *American Stuff*. New York: Viking Press, 1937, pp. 79–81.

"Break of Day." *New Republic*, (May 11, 1938), p. 10.

"The Young Ones." *Poetry*, 3 (July, 1938), pp. 189–90.

"Glory, Glory." *Esquire*, 10 (August, 1938), p. 78.

"Colloquy (Black Worker and White Worker)," "Conjured," "Old Lem." *This Genera-tion*. Ed. George Anderson and Edna L. Walton. New York: Scott, Foresman, 1939, pp. 645–46.

"Sharecropper." *Get Organized*. Ed. Alan Calmer. New York: International Press, 1939, pp. 24–25.

"Bitter Fruit of the Tree." *The Nation*, 149 (August 26, 1939), p. 223. "Remembering Nat Turner." *The Crisis*, 46 (February, 1939), p. 48.

"An Old Woman Remembers," "The Ballad of Joe Meek." *Freedomways*, 3 (Summer, 1963), pp. 405–11. These poems, according to a headnote, were "written over a score of years ago."

"Arkansas Chant," "Crossing," "Memo: For Race Orators," "Slim Hears 'The Call.'" *Les Poètes Nègres des États-Unis*. Jean Wagner. Paris: Librairie Istra, 1963, pp. 592–600.

"Crispus Attucks McCoy." *Ik Ben de Nieuwe Neger*. Ed. Rosie Pool. Den Haag: B. Dak-ker, 1965, p. 49.

The Last Ride of Wild Bill and Eleven Narrative Poems. Detroit: Broadside Press, 1975.

Collection of ballads, including previously unpublished poems, "The Last Ride of Wild Bill" and "Slim Hears 'The Call'"; "Sam Smiley" from *Southern Road* appears here as "Sam Yancy."

The Collected Poems of Sterling A. Brown. New York: Harper & Row, 1980.

Brown's complete published poems, except for "After the Storm."

SHORT STORIES, SKETCHES, REPORTAGE

"Out of Their Mouths." *Survey Graphic*, 21 (November, 1942), pp. 480–83. Anecdotes, conversations, statements by black and white Americans on race relations. Assembled as part of a planned book tentatively entitled *A Negro Looks at the South*.

"Words on a Bus." *South Today*, 7 (Spring, 1943), pp. 26–28. Narrative about a black man who flirts with a black woman on a segregated bus.

"Farewell to Basin Street." *The Record Changer*, 3 (December, 1944), pp. 7–9, 51. Sketch in which a first-person narrator recalls a trip to New Orleans, which he found more of a monument to the past than a thriving jazz center.

"The Muted South." *Phylon, the Atlanta University Review of Race and Culture*, 6 (Win-ter, 1945), p. 22–34. (Hereafter *Phylon, the Atlanta University Review of Race and Culture* will be cited as *Phylon*.) Five sketches of the South dealing with racism and the war as well as black American life styles and folk art forms.

"Georgia Sketches." *Phylon*, 6 (Summer, 1945), p. 225–31. Two sketches of Atlanta: one dealing with two blacks' attempt to visit Joel Chandler Harris's home, the other consisting of recollections of public jazz dances.

"Georgia Nymphs." *Phylon*, 6 (Autumn, 1945), pp. 362–67. Sketch about two black men who happen upon sun bathing white women; the men leave town with cau-tion and haste.

"And/Or." *Phylon*, 7 (Fall, 1946), pp. 269–72. Narrative reportage focusing upon a black collegian's struggles to vote in segregated Alabama.

BOOKS OF CRITICISM

Outline for the Study of the Poetry of American Negroes. New York: Harcourt, Brace, 1931.
Supplement to James Weldon Johnson's anthology, *The Book of American Negro Poetry*; includes topics for papers, study questions, definitions of poetic forms and elements, and an essay on contemporary American verse.

The Negro in American Fiction. Washington: Associates in Negro Folk Education, 1937.
Critical essays on the portrayal of blacks in American fiction.

Negro Poetry and Drama. Washington: Associates in Negro Folk Education, 1937. Critical history of black American poetry and drama.

The Negro Caravan. Ed. Sterling A. Brown, Arthur P. Davis, and Ulysses Lee. New
York: Dryden Press, 1941. Anthology of Afro-American writing from its folk foundations to 1940; includes critical and historical interchapters by the editors.

The Reader's Companion to World Literature. Ed. Lillian H. Hornstein and G.D. Percy.
New York: New American Library, 1956. Dictionary of international writers and their major works; Brown contributed entries on Matthew Arnold, Charles Baudelaire, Emily Brontë, Robert Burns, Emily Dickinson, Ralph Waldo Emerson, Benjamin Franklin, Robert Frost, Heinrich Heine, A.E. Housman, Thomas Jefferson, Abraham Lincoln, Henry Wadsworth Longfellow, Herman Melville, *Moby Dick,* Edgar Allan Poe, Henry Thoreau, Mark Twain, and Walt Whitman.

ESSAYS ON AMERICAN LITERATURE AND THE ROLE OF BLACKS
IN AMERICAN WRITING

"Sterling A. Brown." *Caroling Dusk.* Ed. Countee Cullen. New York: Harper & Brothers, 1927, pp. 129–30. Brown wrote his own biographical headnote for this anthology.

"Negro Literature—Is it True? Complete?" *The Durham Fact-Finding Conference,* Durham, North Carolina: Fact-Finding Conference, 1929, pp. 26–28. Statement in defense of realism in the portrayal of blacks in literature.

"Our Literary Audience." *Opportunity,* 8 (February, 1930), pp. 42–46, 61. Criticism of readers who are put off by realistic portraiture of Negroes in literature.

"James Weldon Johnson." *The Book of American Negro Poetry.* Ed. James Weldon Johnson. New York: Harcourt, Brace, 1931, pp. 114–17. Biographical headnote preceding the selection of Johnson's poetry.

"A Literary Parallel." *Opportunity,* 10 (May, 1932), pp. 152–53. Discussion of stereotypes in fiction and drama: English, Irish, and American.

"In Memoriam: Charles W. Chesnutt." *Opportunity,* 10 (December, 1932), p. 387. Eulogy of Chesnutt and evaluation of his stories and novels.

"Negro Character as Seen by White Authors." *The Journal of Negro Education,* 2 (April, 1933), pp. 179–203. Discussion of black stereotypes in American literature of the nineteenth and twentieth centuries; a few true portraits, "realizations," also noted.

"Albery Allson Whitman." *Dictionary of American Biography.* Vol. 10. New York: Charles Scribner's Sons, 1936, pp. 138–39. Entry for the black poet.

"Problems of the Negro Writer." *Official Proceedings, National Negro Congress.* Washington: National Negro Congress Publications, 1937, pp. 82–83. Transcript of a speech advocating techniques and perspectives of realism in black writing.

"The Negro in American Literature." *James Weldon Johnson, a Biographical Sketch.*
    Nashville: Fisk University, 1938, pp. 20–28. Transcript of a speech surveying black
    literature; the contributions of Johnson are highlighted.
"The American Race Problem as Reflected in American Literature." *The Journal of
    Negro Education,* 8 (July, 1939), pp. 275–90. Study of racial attitudes expressed in
    American writing of the nineteenth and twentieth centuries.
"The Negro Author and His Publisher." *The Quarterly Review of Higher Education
    among Negroes,* 9 (July, 1941), pp. 140–46. Discussion of the problems black writ-
    ers face getting published, stressing their responsibility to practice their craft
    without excuse or compromise.
"Negro in the American Theatre." *Oxford Companion to the Theatre.* Ed. Phyllis Hart-
    noll. London: Oxford Press, 1950, pp. 672–79. Essay surveying the contributions
    of Afro-American actors and playwrights to American theatre from the colonial
    period to 1947.
"In the American Grain." *Vassar Alumnae Magazine,* 36 (February, 1951), pp. 5–9. Essay
    tracing realism in American literature, from Emerson to Faulkner.
"James Weldon Johnson." *Dictionary of American Biography.* Vol. 2, Part 2, Supple-
    ment 2. New York: Charles Scribner's Sons, 1953, pp. 345–47.
"Seventy-five Years of the Negro in Literature," *Jackson College Bulletin,* 2 (September,
    1953), pp. 26–30. Transcribed address at Jackson College, outlining American
    writers' uses and abuses of black folklore.
"The New Negro in Literature (1925–1955)." *The New Negro Thirty Years Afterward.*
    Washington: Howard University Press, 1955. Transcript of a speech surveying
    American literature (1925–1955) by and about blacks.
"A Century of Negro Portraiture in American Literature." *The Massachusetts Review,* 7
    (Winter, 1966), pp. 73–96. Essay on the treatment of racial themes and black char-
    acters in post–Civil War literature.
"The Federal Theatre." *Anthology of the American Negro in the Theatre: A Critical Ap-
    proach.* Ed. Lindsay Patterson. New York: Publishers Co. (under the auspices of
    the Association for the Study of Negro Life and History), 1967, pp. 101–107. Essay
    (culled from Brown's work in 1940 for Carnegie/Myrdal) on the impact of the
    Federal Theatre, established by the W.P.A. in 1935, on black playwrights, actors,
    and spectators.
"The Negro Actor Attempts Legitimate." *Anthology of the American Negro in the The-
    atre: A Critical Approach.* Ed. Lindsay Patterson. New York: Publishers Co. (under
    the auspices of the Association for the Study of Negro Life and History), 1967,
    pp. 123–25. Essay (culled from Brown's work in 1940 for Carnegie/Myrdal) briefly
    surveying black efforts of the early nineteenth century through the 1930s as Amer-
    ican actors beyond minstrelsy and other such U.S. vernacular traveling shows.
"Arna Bontemps, Co-Worker, Comrade," *Black World,* 22 (September, 1973), pp. 11,
    91–97. Eulogy of Bontemps and appraisal of his writings.

ESSAYS AND COMMENTARIES ON BLACK FOLKLORE AND MUSIC

"Roland Hayes," *Opportunity,* 3 (June, 1925), pp. 173–74. Brown's first published writ-
    ing, an award-winning sketch of the renowned tenor.

"The Blues as Folk Poetry." *Folk-Say, 2.* Ed. Benjamin A. Botkin. Norman, Oklahoma: University of Oklahoma Press, 1930, pp. 324–39. Discussion of the forms and meanings of blues songs.

"The Folk Roots," Vanguard LP–VSD-47/48. Liner notes. Copyright 1973. Excerpt from a speech on the blues given at the "Spirituals to Swing" concert at Carnegie Hall, December 24, 1939.

"Blues, Ballads and Social Songs." *Seventy-five Years of Freedom.* Washington: Library of Congress Press, December 18, 1940, pp. 17–25. Discussion of the meaning and "mood" of Afro-American folk music.

"The Negro in American Culture." Unpublished memoranda, Carnegie/Myrdal study of blacks in America, 1940. Survey of the contributions of blacks to American theatre, music, and sports.

"Stray Notes on Jazz (Part 2)." *Vassar Brew,* 27 (June, 1946), pp. 15–19. Discussion of the influence of recording companies on jazz. (Part 1 seems not to exist.)

"The Approach of the Creative Artist." *Journal of American Folklore,* 59 (October, 1946), pp. 506–7. Transcript of Brown's 1942 speech on folklore, "living-people-lore," as important to artists, folklorists, and historians. [The publication of the speech was delayed by the war.]

"Negro Folk Expression." *Phylon,* 11 (Autumn, 1950), pp. 318–27. Analysis of the origins and meanings of Afro-American jokes and tales.

"Athletics and the Arts." *Integration of the Negro into American Society.* Ed. E. Franklin Frazier. Washington: Howard University Press, 1951, pp. 117–47. Discussion of the struggles for integration by blacks in literature, art, music, dance, and sports.

"The Blues." *Phylon,* 8 (Autumn, 1952), pp. 286–92. Paper read at the "Post-Tanglewood Round Table on Jazz," Lenox, Massachusetts, August, 1952; deals with the underlying themes and the poetry of the blues.

"Negro Folk Expression: Spirituals, Seculars, Ballads and Work Songs." *Phylon,* 14 (Winter, 1953), pp. 45–61. Essay on the history, meanings, and poetic elements of Afro-American folk songs.

"Negro Producers of Ragtime." *The Afro-American in Music and Art.* Cornwell Heights, PA: The Publishers Agency (under the auspices of the Association for the Study of Negro Life and History), 1967, 1978, pp. 49–50. Essay (culled from Brown's work in 1940 for Carnegie -Myrdal Study) briefly noting black composers of ragtime songs and piano pieces.

"Portrait of a Jazz Giant: 'Jelly Roll' Morton (1885?–1941)." *Black World,* 23 (February, 1974), pp. 28–49. Essay on Morton's importance as composer, pianist, and singer.

REVIEWS AND NOTES ON BOOKS, MOVIES, PLAYS

"Two African Heroines." *Opportunity,* 4 (January, 1926), pp. 24–26. Review of David Garnett's novel *The Sailor's Return* and Louis Charbonneau's novel *Mambu, et Son Amour.*

"The New Secession—A Review." *Opportunity,* 5 (May, 1927), pp. 147–48. Review of Julia Peterkin's novel *Black April.*

"Our Book Shelf." *Opportunity,* 6 (March, 1928), pp. 91–92. Review of *Dwellers in the Jungle,* a novel by Gordon Casserly.

"Fabulist and Felossofer." *Opportunity*, 6 (July, 1928), pp. 211–12. Review of *Ol' Man Adam an' His Chillun*, a novel by Roark Bradford.

"Mamba's Daughters." *Opportunity*, 7 (May, 1929), pp. 161–62. A review of DuBose Heyward's novel *Mamba's Daughters*.

"Black Ulysses at War." *Opportunity*, 7 (December, 1929), pp. 383–84. Review of *Wings on My Feet*, a novel by Howard Odum.

"Unhistoric History." *Journal of Negro History*, 15 (April, 1930), pp. 134–61. Essay on historical fiction and biography focusing on *Quiet Cities* and *Swords and Roses*, novels by Joseph Hergesheimer; *Stonewall Jackson* and *Jefferson Davis*, biographies by Allen Tate; *John Brown*, a biography by Robert P. Warren; *Abraham Lincoln*, a biography by Raymond Holden; and *The Tragic Era*, a novel by Claude Bowers.

"Not Without Laughter." *Opportunity*, 8 (September, 1930), pp. 279–80. Review of *Not Without Laughter*, a novel by Langston Hughes.

"Black Genesis." *Opportunity*, 8 (October, 1930), pp. 311–12. Review of *Black Genesis*, a collection of stories by Samuel G. Stoney and Gertrude M. Shelby.

"Chronicle and Comment." *Opportunity*, 8 (December, 1930), p. 375. Notes on literary and scholarly works by Abram Harris, Carter Woodson, George Schuyler, and Randolph Edmonds.

"Folk Values in a New Medium." Co-author, Alain Locke. *Folk-Say*, 2. Ed. Benjamin A. Botkin. Norman, Oklahoma: University of Oklahoma Press, 1930, pp. 340–45. Review of two movies, "Hearts in Dixie" and "Hallelujah."

"The Literary Scene." *Opportunity*, 9 (January, 1931), p. 20. Notes on *Folk-Say 2*, an annual collection of folklore materials, edited by Benjamin A. Botkin; *Short History of Julia*, a novel by Isa Glen; *Po' Buckra*, a novel by Samuel G. Stoney and Gertrude M. Shelby; *Gulf Stream*, a novel by Marie Stanley; *Strike!*, a novel by Mary Vorse; and essays and poems by Carl Carmer.

"The Literary Scene." *Opportunity*, 9 (February, 1931), pp. 53–54. Notes on *The Black Worker*, a study of the relation of blacks to the American labor movement, by Abram Harris and Sterling Spero, and *Black No More*, a novel by George Schuyler.

"The Literary Scene, Chronicle and Commentary." *Opportunity*, 9 (March, 1931), p. 87. Notes on many books, including the scholarly works *Race Psychology* by Thomas R. Garth and *The Negro Wage Earner* by Lorenzo Greene; a novel *Jungle Ways* by William Seabrook; and a collection of short stories, *Golden Tales from the South*, edited by May Becker.

"A Romantic Defense." *Opportunity*, 9 (April, 1931), p. 118. Review of *I'll Take My Stand*, a collection of essays by twelve Southerners.

"An American Epoch." *Opportunity*, 9 (June, 1931), p. 187. Review of Howard Odum's novel *An American Epoch: Southern Portraiture in the National Picture*.

"Our Bookshelf." *Opportunity*, 9 (June, 1931), p. 199. Review of Arna Bontemps' novel *God Sends Sunday*.

"As to 'Jungle Ways.'" *Opportunity*, 9 (July, 1931), pp. 219–21. Review of John Seabrook's novel *Jungle Ways*.

"Caroling Softly Souls of Slavery." *Opportunity*, 9 (August, 1931), pp. 241–52. Commentary on Louis C. Hughes's autobiography *Thirty Years a Slave*.

"Concerning Negro Drama." *Opportunity,* 9 (September, 1931), pp. 284–88. Comments on *The Green Pastures, The Emperor Jones,* and other plays of black life by white playwrights.

"Poor Whites." *Opportunity,* 9 (October, 1931), pp. 317, 320. Review of Erskine Caldwell's collection of stories *American Earth;* John Fort's novel *God in the Straw Pen;* and George Millburn's novel *Oklahoma Town.*

"The Point of View." *Opportunity,* 9 (November, 1931), pp. 347–50. Discussion of "point of view" in literature with reference to Elizabethan drama, American minstrelsy, black folklore, and the fiction of William Faulkner, Roark Bradford, and DuBose Heyward.

"Pride and Pathos." *Opportunity,* 9 (December, 1931), pp. 381–84. Review of *The Carolina Low Country,* a collection of essays by Members of the Society for the Preservation of the Spirituals.

"Never No Steel Driving Man." *Opportunity,* 9 (December, 1931), p. 382. Review of *John Henry,* a novel by Roark Bradford.

"Truth Will Out." *Opportunity,* 10 (January, 1932), pp. 23–24. Review of Frederic Bancroft's *Slave Trading in the Old South,* a history.

"Never No More." *Opportunity,* 10 (February, 1932), pp. 55–56. Review of James Millen's play, *Never No More.*

"Weep Some More My Lady." *Opportunity,* 10 (March, 1932), p. 87. Comments on Louis Untermeyer's presentation of black folklore in his anthology, *American Poetry: From the Beginning to Whitman.*

"Joel Chandler Harris." *Opportunity,* 10 (April, 1932), pp. 119–20. Review of *Joel Chandler Harris: Editor and Essayist,* a collection of Harris's essays, edited by Julia Collier Harris.

"More Odds." *Opportunity,* 10 (June, 1932), pp. 188–89. Review of Edwin Embree's *Brown America,* a social history of blacks in America.

"Local Color or Interpretation," *Opportunity,* 10 (July, 1932), p. 233. Review of Julia Peterkin's novel *Bright Skin.*

"A Poet and His Prose." *Opportunity,* 10 (August, 1932), p. 256. Commentary on Claude McKay's novels and stories.

"Signs of Promise." *Opportunity,* 10 (September, 1932), p. 287. Comments on *University of Michigan Plays,* an anthology edited by Kenneth T. Rowe.

"Amber Satyr." *Opportunity,* 10 (November, 1932), p. 352. Review of Roy Flannagan's novel *Amber Satyr.*

"A New Trend." *Opportunity,* 11 (February, 1933), p. 56. Comments on *Inchin' Along,* a novel by Welbourne Kelley, as well as *Free Born* and *Georgia Nigger,* novels by John L. Spivak.

"Alas the Poor Mulatto." *Opportunity,* 11 (March, 1933), p. 91. Review of *Dark Lustre,* a novel by Geoffrey Barnes.

"Time for a New Deal." *Opportunity,* 11 (April, 1933), pp. 122, 126. Review of *The Southern Oligarchy,* a study of the politics and economics of the American South by William Scaggs.

"Smartness Goes Traveling." *Opportunity,* 11 (May, 1933), p. 158. Review of Evelyn Waugh's narrative of travels in Africa, *They Were Still Dancing,* and his novel *Black Mischief.*

"John Brown: God's Angry Man." *Opportunity*, 11 (June, 1933), pp. 186–87. Review of
   God's Angry Man, a biography of John Brown by Leonard Ehrlick.

"Banana Bottom." *Opportunity*, 11 (July, 1933), pp. 217, 222. Review of Claude McKay's
   novel *Banana Bottom*.

"From the Southwest." *Opportunity*, 11 (October, 1933), p. 313. Review of *Negrito*, a novel
   by J. Mason Brewer, and *Tone the Bell Easy*, a journal of folklore studies, edited by
   J. Frank Dobie.

"Kingdom Coming." *Opportunity*, 11 (December, 1933), pp. 382–83. Review of Roark
   Bradford's novel *Kingdom Coming*.

"Arcadia, South Carolina." *Opportunity*, 12 (February, 1934), pp. 59–60. Review of *Roll,
   Jordan, Roll*, a narrative history and pictorial essay on black Americans, by Doris
   Ulmann and Julia Peterkin.

"Satire of Imperialism." *Opportunity*, 12 (March, 1934), pp. 89–90. Review of Winifred
   Holtby's novel *Mandos, Mandos!*

"Six Plays for a Negro Theatre." *Opportunity*, 12 (September, 1934), pp. 280–81. Review
   of *Six Plays for a Negro Theatre*, a collection of Randolph Edmond's plays.

"The Atlanta Summer Theatre." *Opportunity*, 12 (October, 1934), pp. 308–9. Commentary on Atlanta University's five dramatic productions, summer, 1934.

"Stars Fell on Alabama." *Opportunity*, 12 (October, 1934), pp. 312–13. Review of Carl
   Carmer's novel *Stars Fell on Alabama*.

"Mississippi—Old Style." *Opportunity*, 12 (December, 1934), pp. 377–78. Review of *So
   Red the Rose*, a novel by Stark Young.

"Mississippi, Alabama: New Style." *Opportunity*, 13 (February, 1935), pp. 55–56.
   Commentary on Southern novels by Thomas Wolfe, William March, and
   T. S. Stribling.

"The Negro in Fiction and Drama." *The Christian Register*, 114 (February 14, 1935),
   pp. 111–12. Review of fiction by Stark Young, William March, T. S. Stribling, Zora
   Neale Hurston, and Langston Hughes.

"Imitation of Life: Once a Pancake." Opportunity, 13 (March, 1935), pp. 87–88. Review
   of *Imitation of Life*, a novel by Fannie Hurst.

"Mr. Sterling Brown." *Opportunity*, 13 (April, 1935), pp. 121–22. Reply to Fannie Hurst's
   objections to the review of *Imitation of Life*.

"Correspondence." *Opportunity*, 13 (May, 1935), p. 153. Response to a letter to the editor
   about "Imitation of Life: Once a Pancake" and *Southern Road*.

"Come Day, Go Day." *Opportunity*, 13 (September, 1935), pp. 279–80. Review of Roark
   Bradford's collection of short stories *Let the Band Play Dixie*, and Richard Coleman's novel *Don't You Weep, Don't You Moan*.

"Realism in the South." *Opportunity*, 13 (October, 1935), pp. 311–12. Review of *Kneel to the
   Rising Sun*, a collection of short stories by Erskine Caldwell, and *Deep Dark River*,
   a novel by Robert Rylee.

"Southern Cross Sections." *Opportunity*, 13 (December, 1935), pp. 380–85. Review of *Si-
   esta*, a novel by Barry Fleming, and *South*, a novel by Frederick Wright.

"Shadow of the Plantation." *Journal of Negro History*, 21 (January, 1936), pp. 70–73. Review of Charles S. Johnson's sociological study, *Shadow of the Plantation*.

"Old Time Tales." *New Masses*, 25 (February, 1936), pp. 24–25. Review of Zora Neale
   Hurston's *Mules and Men*.

"The First Negro Writers." *The New Republic,* (May 6, 1936), pp. 376–77. Review of
    Benjamin Brawley's anthology *Early Negro Writers.*
"Two Negro Poets." *Opportunity,* 14 (July, 1936), pp. 216–20. Review of *Black Thunder,*
    a historical novel by Arna Bontemps, and *Black Man's Verse,* a collection of poems
    by Frank Marshall Davis.
"Book Reviews." *Opportunity,* 15 (September, 1937), pp. 280–81. Review of *The Negro
    Genius,* essays on black artists and intellectuals, by Benjamin Brawley.
"Biography." *Opportunity,* 15 (September, 1937), pp. 216–17. Appraisal of Benjamin
    Brawley's *Paul Laurence Dunbar, Poet of His People,* a biography.
"'Luck is a Fortune.'" *The Nation,* 145 (October 16, 1937), pp. 409–10. Review of Zora
    Neale Hurston's novel *Their Eyes Were Watching God.*
"Prize Winning Stories." *Opportunity,* 16 (April, 1938), pp. 120–21. Review of *Uncle
    Tom's Children,* Richard Wright's collection of short stories.
"From the Inside." *The Nation,* 166 (April 16, 1938), p. 448. Review of *Uncle Tom's Chil-
    dren,* Richard Wright's collection of short stories.
"South on the Move." *Opportunity,* 16 (December, 1938), pp. 366–69. Review of *A
    Southerner Discovers the South,* a travel book by Jonathan Daniels, and *Forty Acres
    and Steel Mules,* an economist's portrait of the South by Herman Clarence Nixon.
Review of *American Folk Plays* and of *Out of the South. The North Georgia Review,* 5.1
    (Spring 1940): pp. 27–29. Review of *American Folk Plays,* edited by Frederick H.
    Koch, and of *Out of the South,* by Paul Green.
"Insight, Courage, and Craftsmanship." *Opportunity,* 18 (June, 1940), pp. 185–86. Re-
    view of Richard Wright's novel *Native Son.*
"Foreword." *Place: America,* a play by Thomas Richardson. New York: NAACP Press,
    1940, pp. 4–5. Introductory note recommending this play.
"Let My People Go." *Phylon,* 2 (1941), pp. 307–309. Review of *Let My People Go,* Henri-
    etta Buckmaster's history of the Underground Railroad.
"Three Ways of Looking at the South." *Journal of Negro Education,* 14 (Winter, 1945),
    pp. 68–72. Review of William Percy's autobiography *Lanterns on the Levee;* Anne
    Walker's study of Tuskegee Institute and town, *Tuskegee and the Black Belt;* and Ira
    De A. Reid's discussion of tenant farmers, *Sharecroppers All.*
"By the Rivers of Babylon." *The Nation,* 2 (May, 1946), pp. 574–75. Review of *Lay My
    Burden Down: A Folk History of Slavery,* edited by Benjamin A. Botkin.

ON RECORD, TAPE, FILM

"Readings by Sterling Brown and Langston Hughes." Folkways LP-FP90. Copyright
    1952. Recitation by Brown of "Break of Day," "Old King Cotton," "Old Lem," "Put-
    tin' on Dog," "Sharecropper," "Slim in Hell."
"Anthology of Negro Poets, Edited by Arna Bontemps." Folkways LP-FL 9791. Copy-
    right 1966. Recitation by Brown of "Long Gone" and "Ma Rainey."
"Sixteen Poems of Sterling A. Brown." Folkways LP-FL 9794. Copyright 1978. Recita-
    tion by Brown of poems published in *Southern Road* and in periodicals; also, "Clo-
    teel," "Parish Doctor," and "Uncle Joe" are presented here for the first time.
"Sterling Brown." Interview by Steven Jones. On file at the Institute for Arts and Hu-
    manities and the Afro-American Resource Center, Howard University, May 4, 14,

1978. Tape-recorded interview at Brown's home concerning the poet's early years in Washington, D.C.

"Sterling Brown Lectures." On file at the Institute for Arts and Humanities and the Afro-American Resource Center, Howard University, September 19 and October 10, 17, 31, 1973.

"Sterling Brown." Interview by Dyalsingh Sadhi. On file at the Institute for Arts and Humanities and the Afro-American Resource Center, Howard University, January 10, 1974. Videotaped interview at Howard University concerning Brown's years at Lincoln University.

"Sterling Brown Poetry Recital." On file at the Institute for Arts and Humanities and the Afro-American Resource Center, Howard University, May 17, 1974. Speech by Brown at the M. L. King Library, Washington, D.C., about the influences on his poetry; a reading of 17 published poems.

"After Winter." 16mm. film by Haile Gerima, 1985. Portrait of the poet-scholar-teacher using stills and moving pictures.

"The Poetry of Sterling A. Brown." Smithsonian Folkways CD-SF47002, 1995. Complete Folkways recordings on compact disk, 1946–1973. Notes by Dr. Joanne V. Gabbin.

MISCELLANEOUS

"The Negro in Washington." *Washington: City and Capital*. Federal Writers' Project. Washington: Government Printing Office, 1937. An essay by Brown dealing with the political and cultural history of black Washingtonians.

The Negro in Virginia. Writers' Project. New York: Hastings House, 1940. A collectively written book on the history and folklore of blacks in Virginia. As Federal Writers' Project Editor for Negro Affairs (1936–1940) Brown helped edit virtually every Project essay dealing with black life; he consulted most extensively on *The Negro in Virginia*.

"Poetry Corner." Mary Strong. *Scholastic*, 36 (April 29, 1940), pp. 25, 27. Strong's discussion of Brown's life and poetry includes lengthy statements by the poet himself.

"Saving the Cargo (Sidelights on the Underground Railroad)." *The Negro History Bulletin*, 4 (April, 1941), pp. 151–54. Historical essay on the trials of Underground Railroad conductors and riders.

"Count Us In." *What the Negro Wants*. Ed. Rayford Logan. Chapel Hill: University of North Carolina Press, 1944, pp. 308–44. Essay on segregation and prejudice, with focus on the black serviceman. Reprinted in his posthumously-published *A Negro Looks at the South* (New York: Oxford University Press, 2007): 317–44.

"The Contributions of the American Negro." *One America*. Ed. Frances Brown and Joseph Roucek. New York: Prentice-Hall, 1945, pp. 588–615. Essay surveying the Negro's contributions to American political and cultural history.

"Black, White, and Blue." *The Best of Negro Humor*. Ed. John H. Johnson and Ben Burns. Chicago: Negro Digest Publishing Co., 1945, p. 20.

"Point of View." *A Treasury of Southern Folklore*. Ed. B. A. Botkin. New York: Crown Publishers, 1949, p. 59. Joke.

"Ralph Bunche—Statesman." *The Reporter,* 1 (December 6, 1949), pp. 3–6. Biographical sketch.

"Efficiency." *A Treasury of American Anecdotes: Sly, Salty, Shaggy Stories of Heroes and Hellions, Beguilers and Buffoons, Spellbinders and Scapegoats, Gagsters and Gossips, From the Grassroots and Sidewalks of America.* Ed. B. A. Botkin. New York: Random House, 1957, pp. 48–49. (Listed by Botkin as deriving from "Negro Jokes," unpublished mimeographed sheets by Sterling Brown, n.d.) Joke.

"King of the Jungle." *A Treasury of American Anecdotes: Sly, Salty, Shaggy Stories of Heroes and Hellions, Beguilers and Buffoons, Spellbinders and Scapegoats, Gagsters and Gossips, From the Grassroots and Sidewalks of America.* Ed. B. A. Botkin. New York: Random House, 1957, pp. 270–72. (Listed as recorded and transcribed by B.A. Botkin in Washington, D.C., January 13, 1949.) Joke.

"Negro, American." Sterling A. Brown, John Hope Franklin, and Rayford Logan. *Encyclopedia Britannica,* 16. Chicago: William Benton, 1968, pp. 188–201. Essay on the role of blacks in American life, from slavery through the mid–1960s.

"The Teacher . . . Sterling Brown, The Mentor of Thousands . . . Talks About Art, Black and White." Sterling A. Brown and Hollie West. *The Washington Post,* 113.346 (November 16, 1969), pp. F1–F3. Interview dealing with black folklore, music, and the relation of blacks and whites.

"Appendixes." *The American Slave: From Sunup to Sundown.* Ed. George Rawick. Westport, CT: Greenwood, 1972, pp. 172–78. Outlining certain WPA procedures for interviewing ex-slaves, these official memoranda (1937) were influenced by the Project's Editor for Negro Affairs, Sterling A. Brown.

"Ralph Bunche at Howard University." *The Crisis,* 79.1 (January, 1972), p. 34. Tribute emphasizing Bunche's Howard years.

"My Dear Dr. Du Bois." *The Correspondence of W.E.B. Du Bois,* vol. 1. Ed. Herbert Aptheker. Amherst: University of Massachusetts Press, 1973, p. 346. A letter (March 28, 1927) from Brown inquiring about the publication of "After the Storm," and requesting entry blanks for the poetry contest held by *The Crisis.*

"Sterling Brown, a Living Legend." Genevieve Ekaete. *New Directions,* 1 (Winter, 1974), pp. 4–11. Tribute by Ekaete, containing statements by Brown on culture and politics.

"A Son's Return: 'Oh Didn't He Ramble.'" *Berkshire Review,* 10 (Summer, 1974), pp. 9–30. Reprinted in *Chant of Saints: A Gathering of Afro-American Literature, Art, and Scholarship.* Ed. Michael S. Harper and Robert B. Stepto. Champaign: University of Illinois Press, 1979, pp. 3–22. Transcript of a talk in which Brown recalls his student years at Williams College.

"Blacks in Brookland." *The Washington Star* (April 18, 1979), A-17. Letter to the Editor defending Brown's neighborhood in Washington, D.C., as something more than a "ghetto."

"My Dear Dr. Du Bois." *The Correspondence of W.E.B. Du Bois,* vol. 2. Ed. Herbert Aptheker. Amherst: University of Massachusetts Press, 1976, pp. 22–23. A letter (Jan. 29, 1935) from Brown evaluating the manuscript of *Black Reconstruction,* as requested by Du Bois.

VIII

"A GEOGRAPHY OF POETRY AND SONG": A DISCOGRAPHY

"Fear Did Not Catch His Tongue and Throttle His Breath": A Discography of Recordings by and Related to Sterling A. Brown

Steven C. Tracy

All of the commercially released recordings in this discography stem from sessions recorded by Moe Asch and Folkways Records in the 1940s, and from a ceremony honoring Brown at the Ira Aldridge Theater at Howard University in 1963. These have been reissued on a variety of sources, but are all collected together on *The Poetry of Sterling A. Brown*. Other recordings not commercially released that feature Brown's voice, as well as commercially released recordings by others of Brown's poetry and Michael Harper's recording of his poem "Br'er Sterling and the Rocker," should be of interest to Brown scholars and students. Though performers do not seem to have taken to recording Brown's poems the way they did to the works of Langston Hughes, this situation may well be remedied as Brown's fame grows. His poems certainly lend themselves to performance.

COMMERCIALLY RELEASED RECORDINGS BY STERLING BROWN

Anthology of Negro Poets. Ed. Arna Bontemps. Folkways LP FL 9791, 1966. Includes "Long Gone" and "Ma Rainey."

An Anthology of Negro Poetry for Young People. Compiled and Read by Arna Bontemps. Smithsonian-Folkways FC 7114. Includes "After Winter."

The Audio Compact Disc to Accompany Call and Response. Ed. Robert Cataliotti. Boston: Houghton Mifflin, 1998. Includes the Folkways recording of Brown reading "Ma Rainey."

Every Tone a Testimony. Smithsonian Folkways CD 47003. Includes the Folkways recording of Brown reading "Ma Rainey."

Freedom: The Golden Gate Quartet/Josh White at the Library of Congress 1940. Bridge CD 9114, 2002. Includes "What are the Blues?" and "The Social Song," about eight minutes and thirty-seven seconds of commentary by Brown, plus introductions to "Poor Lazarus," "John Henry," "Silicosis Blues," and "Trouble."

From Spirituals to Swing. Vanguard 3 CD set 169/71-2. "Spoken Introduction."

The Norton Anthology of African American Literature, 2nd ed. Ed. Henry Louis Gates et al. New York: W. W. Norton, 2004. Accompanying compact disc includes the Folkways recording of Brown reading "Strong Men."

Our Souls Have Grown Deep Like the Rivers. Rhino CD 78012. Includes the Folkways recordings of Brown reading "Ma Rainey" and Strong Men."

The Poetry of Sterling A. Brown: The Complete Folkways Readings, 1946-1973. Smithsonian Folkways CD 47002. This CD recording collects the Brown recordings on the following LPs, plus "Ma Rainey" and "Long Gone." See the selection of poems listed there.

Sixteen Poems of Sterling A. Brown. Folkways LP FL 9794, 1973. Brown recites "The Long Track Blues," "Sporting Beasley," "Sam Smiley," "After Winter," "Conjured," Children's Children," "Puttin' On Dog," "Uncle Joe," "Parish Doctor," "Cloteel," "Old Lem," "Break of Day," "Transfer," "Remembering Nat Turner," "Ballad of Joe Meek," "Strong Men."

Sterling Brown and Langston Hughes. Folkways LP FP 90, 1952; rpt. FL 9790, 1967. Brown recites "Break of Day," "Old King Cotton," "Old Lem," "Puttin' on Dog," "Sharecropper," and "Slim in Hell." NB: "Break of Day," "Puttin' On Dog," and "Old Lem" are on both LPs.

Strong Men. Recorded by Kamau Kenyatta. Omni Arts Records # OA 00001 (1982). With jacket notes titled "Portraits in African-American Modality," by Kofi Natambu.

NONCOMMERCIAL AUDIO AND VIDEO

"After Winter." 16 mm film by Haile Gerima, 1985.

"Sterling Brown." Videotaped interview conducted by Dyalsingh Sadhi. January 10, 1974. Currently held at the Institute for Arts and Humanities and the Afro-American Resource Center, Howard University.

"Sterling Brown." Interview by Steven Jones. May 4, 14, 1978. Currently held at the Institute for Arts and Humanities and the Afro-American Resource Center, Howard University.

"Sterling Brown Lectures." Taped September 19, October 10, 17, 31, 1973. Currently held at the Institute for Arts and Humanities and the Afro-American Resource Center, Howard University.

"Sterling Brown Poetry Recital." May 17, 1974. Currently held at the Institute for Arts and Humanities and the Afro-American Resource Center, Howard University.

Yusef Jones, in his notes to the Folkways CD *The Poetry of Sterling A. Brown*, reports that there exist eight reel-to-reel tapes of Brown reading works written by other American poets, recorded April 1, 1963.

RECORDINGS OF BROWN'S POEMS BY OTHERS

Rhapsodies in Black: Music and Words from the Harlem Renaissance. Rhino CD R2 79874. Includes recitations of "Long Gone" by Darius Rucker and "Odyssey of Big Boy" by Chuck D.

RECORDINGS OF POEMS TREATING BROWN

Michael Harper. *Use Trouble*. Modo Records. Includes Harper reading "Br'er Sterling and the Rocker."

——. *Selected Poems*. Includes Harper reading "Br'er Sterling and the Rocker."

Vernacular Recordings Relevant to the Study of Sterling A. Brown's *Southern Road*

Steven C. Tracy

The following list of commercial and field recordings, made primarily in the 1920s and 1930s, is intended to indicate the strong connections that a large number of Sterling A. Brown's poems have to material in the African American vernacular tradition. After individual poems are listed recordings of African American vernacular materials that have reference to the style, subject matter, characters, attitudes, or language of that particular poem. The listings refer to the most currently available, or most recently available, CDs, LPs, 78 RPM records, or DVDs. The listings are not meant to suggest that Brown was familiar with that particular recording, though in some cases (such as "Back Water Blues") he most likely was, and in other cases he was certainly familiar with the performers ("Big Boy" Davis and Ma Rainey, for example). Indeed, in some cases the recordings were made after the publication of *Southern Road*, though nobody would suggest that Brown's poems were the source of the material recorded later. Rather, they suggest sources in the vernacular tradition with which Brown, in his extensive contact with that tradition, could have been familiar in one incarnation or another. The listings are also not meant to suggest that these are the only relevant recordings. Rather, they are meant to help supply a context for discussion both in the classroom and in print of Brown's poetry as it draws on, modifies, or extends the tradition. Using such materials also frequently makes for a much livelier and enjoyable class for both students and instructors.

The reference to record label following the artist's name is most frequently to the exhaustive series of recordings produced by Document Records in Austria, which has made available on CD almost the complete recordings of African American vernacular music up to 1945—and in some cases beyond 1945. If no CD/LP title is listed, the CD is indexed under the artist's name as a volume of his or her complete recorded works. Titles of CDs and LPs indicate the title of the CD or LP on which the song is included. Some of these recordings may be available on other labels with slightly better sound or prettier packages, but the comprehensive and scholarly presentation of materials by Document Records make the label the most logical source for completists and scholars. These will likely stay in print longer than major label reissues. Still, some other releases of the recorded material are sometimes indicated.

Entry example: "Song Title": Artist (sometimes the artist name is the CD title, and thus will be italicized). *CD or LP name.* Label and number. All Document CDs referenced under the artist's name are in the series with the title *Complete Recorded Works in Chronological Order,* except where noted.

"ODYSSEY OF BIG BOY"

"Kassie Jones Pts. 1 and 2." *Furry Lewis (1927–1929).* Document 5004.
"Stack O' Lee." Mississippi John Hurt. *The Greatest Songsters.* Document 5003. (See also *Avalon Blues: The Complete 1928 OKeh Recordings.* Sony 64986.)
"Stack O' Lee Blues": *Ma Rainey Vol. 3.* Document 5583. (See also *The Essential Ma Rainey.* Classic Blues CBL-200020.)
"John Henry." "Big Boy" (Davis?). *Too Late Too Late Vol. 10.* Document 5601.
"Blues." "Big Boy" (Davis?). *Field Recordings Vol. 1.* Document 5575.
"Monkey Man Blues." *Sara Martin Vol. 1.* Document 5395.
"Chocolate to the Bone." *Barbecue Bob Vol. 1.* Document 5046.
"Jazzbo Brown from Memphis Town." Bessie Smith. *The Complete Recordings Vol. 3.* Columbia C2K 47474.

"LONG GONE"

"Kentucky Blues." Little Hat Jones. *Texas Blues (1927–1935).* Document 5161.
"Long John." Washington ("Lightnin'"). *Field Recordings Vol. 6.* Document 5580.
"Freight Train Blues." *Trixie Smith Vol. 2.* Document 5333.

"WHEN DE SAINTS GO MA'CHIN' HOME"

"Blues" and "John Henry." "Big Boy" (Davis?). Document 5575 and 5601 (as above).
"When the Saints Come Marching Home." Bo Weavil Jackson. *Backwoods Blues (1926–1935).* Document 5036.
"When the Saints Go Marching Home." *Memphis Minnie Vol. 1.* Document BDCD 6008.

"SCOTTY HAS HIS SAY"

"New Orleans Goofer Dust Blues." Thelma LaVizzo. *Richard M. Jones and the Blues Singers*. Document 5390.

"Black Cat Hoot Owl Blues." *Ma Rainey (1928)*. Document 5156. (See also *The Essential Ma Rainey*. Classic Blues CBL-200020.)

"Big Fat Mama Blues." *Charlie Spand (1929–1931)*. Document 5108.

"Shootin' Star Blues." *Lizzie Miles Vol. 2 (1923–1928)*. Document 5459.

"Cake Walkin' Babies From Home": Eva Taylor—Classics 810.

"Ma Rainey's Black Bottom." *Ma Rainey Vol. 4 (1926–1927)*. Document 5584. (See also *The Essential Ma Rainey*. Classic Blues CBL-200020.)

"VIRGINIA PORTRAIT"

"Bye and Bye We're Going to See the King." *Arizona Dranes (1926–1929)*. Document 5186.

"Bye and Bye When the Morning Comes." *Rev. Edward W. Clayborn (1928–1928)*. Document 5155.

"We Will Understand It Better Bye and Bye." *Alphabetical Four*. Document 5374.

"FRANKIE AND JOHNNY"

"Frankie and Johnny Pts. 1 and 2." Nick Nichols. *Whistlin' Alex Moore (1929–1951)*. Document 5178.

"Frankie." Mississippi John Hurt. *The Greatest Songsters (1927–1929)*. Document 5003. (See also *Avalon Blues: The Complete 1928 OKeh Recordings*. Sony 64986.)

"KENTUCKY BLUES"

"Pony Blues." *Charley Patton Vol. 1 (1929)*. Document 5009. (See also Charley Patton, *Screamin' and Hollerin' the Blues*. Revenant 212.)

"My Man o' War." *Lizzie Miles Vol. 3 (1928–1939)*. Document 5460.

"MISTER SAMUEL AND SAM"

"Monkey Man Blues." *Sara Martin Vol. 1 (1922–1923)*. Document 5395.

"Black Gal Swing." *Son Bonds and Charlie Pickett (1934–1951)*. Wolf 003.

"SOUTHERN ROAD"

"Spike Driver Blues." Mississippi John Hurt. *The Greatest* Songsters. Document 5003. (See also *Avalon Blues: The Complete 1928 OKeh Recordings*. Sony 64986). (See also "Spike Driver Blues" on *Pete Seeger's Rainbow Quest*. Shanachie DVD 607.)

"Old Alabama." Convicts. *Negro Prison Blues and Songs*. Legacy International 326.

"Down In the Chain Gang." Unknown. *Nobody Knows My Name*. Heritage LP 304.

"Chain Gang Blues." Unknown. *Cap'n You're So Mean*. Rounder LP 4013.

"Chain Gang Blues." *Ma Rainey Vol. 3*. Document 5583.

"You Don't Know My Mind." Unknown. *Cap'n, You're So Mean*. Rounder 4013.

"Cold Iron Shackles." Unknown. *Negro Songs of Protest*. Rounder LP 4004.

"Black Name Moan." *Bessie Tucker (1928–1929)*. Document 5070.

"Section Gang Blues." *Texas Alexander Vol. 1 (1927–1928)*. Document 2001.

"STRONG MEN"

"Keep A Inching Along." *Fisk University Jubilee/Singers Vol. 3 (1924–1940)*. Document 5535.

"Bye and Bye We're Going to See the King." *Arizona Dranes (1926–1929)*. Document 5186.

"Bye and Bye When the Morning Comes." *Rev. Edward W. Clayborn (1926–1928)*. Document 5155.

"We Will Understand It Better Bye and Bye." *Alphabetical Four*. Document 5374.

"Walk Together Children." *Bronzemen (Radio Transcriptions 1939)*. Document 5501.

"This Ol' Hammer." Unknown. *Cap'n, You're So Mean*. Rounder 4013.

"EPIGRAPH TO PART TWO"

"Lonesome Day Blues." *Blind Willie McTell Vol. 2 (1931–1933)*. Document 5007. (See also Blind Willie McTell. *Statesboro Blues*. BMG Heritage 82876551572).

"MEMPHIS BLUES"

"Memphis Blues." *Esther Bigeou (1921–1923)*. Document 5489.

"What You Going to Do When the World's on Fire?" *Norfolk Jazz and Jubilee Quartet Vol. 2 (1923–1925)*. Document 5382.

"What You Gonna Do When the World's On Fire." *Birmingham Jubilee Singers Vol. 2*. Document 5346.

"What Yer Going to Do When the Rent Comes Round?" Pete Hampton. EB 6857 (cylinder).

"MA RAINEY"

Ma Rainey's recordings: Document 5581/5582/5583/5584/5156. (See also *The Essential Ma Rainey*. Classic Blues CBL-200020.)

"Back Water Blues." *Bessie Smith*. Columbia C2K 47474.

"Little and Low." *Roosevelt Sykes Vol. 5 (1937–1939)*. Document 5120.

"OLD KING COTTON"

"Cotton Seed Blues." *Tampa Red Vol. 4 (1930–1931)*. Document 5076.

"Mississippi Bo Weevil Blues." Charley Patton Vol. 1 (1929). Document 5009. (See also Charley Patton, *Screamin' and Hollerin' the Blues*. Revenant 212.)

"CHILDREN OF THE MISSISSIPPI"

"When the Levee Breaks." *Memphis Minnie and Kansas Joe Vol. 1 (1929–30)*. Document 5028. (See also Memphis Minnie, *Me and My Chauffeur*. Proper 129.)

"High Water Everywhere Pts. 1 and 2." *Charley Patton Vol. 2 (1929)*. Document 5010.
(See also Charley Patton, *Screamin' and Hollerin' the Blues*. Revenant 212.)

"Tallahatchie River Blues." Mattie Delaney. *Mississippi Blues Vol. I (1928–1937)*.
Document 5157.

"Back Water Blues." Bessie Smith. *The Complete Recordings Vol. 3*. Columbia C2K
47474.

"Southern Flood Blues." *Big Bill Broonzy Vol. 5 (1936–1937)*. Document 5127.

"NEW ST. LOUIS BLUES"

"The St. Louis Blues." *Bessie Smith. The Complete Recordings Vol. 2*. Columbia C2K
47471. (See also "St. Louis Blues" on *At the Jazz Band Ball*. Yazoo DVD 514).

"Hard Times Ain't Gone Nowhere." *Lonnie Johnson Vol. 1 (1937–1940)*.
Document 6024.

"Frost Texas Tornado Blues." *Texas Alexander Vol. 3 (1930–1950)*. Document 2003.

"Mean Old Twister." *Kokomo Arnold Vol. 4 (1937–1938)*. Document 5040.

"Mean Twister." *Lucille Bogan Vol. 2 (1930–1933)*. Document 6037.

"Texas Tornado Blues." Big Bill Broonzy. *Too Late, Too Late Vol. 7 (1927–1955)*.
Document 5525.

"St. Louis Cyclone Blues." *Elzadie Robinson Vol. 1 (1926–1928)*. Document 5248.

"Cooling Board Blues." *Blind Willie McTell Vol. 3 (1933–1935)*. Document 5008.

"The Market Street Blues." *Clara Smith Vol. 3 (1925)*. Document 5366.

"Market Street Rag." *Kid Price Moore (1936–1938)*. Document 5180.

"Tornado Groan." *Luella Miller (1926–1928)*. Document 5183.

"CHECKERS"

"Stack O' Lee." Mississippi John Hurt. *The Greatest Songsters (1927–1929)*. Document
5003. (See also *Avalon Blues: The Complete 1928 OKeh Recordings*. Sony 64986.)

Stack O' Lee Blues." *Ma Rainey Vol. 3 (1925–1926)*. Document 5583.

"Big Boy Pete." Don and Dewey. Ace 358.

"'Flicted Arm Pete." Unknown. *Get Your Ass in the Water and Swim Like Me*. Rounder
LP 2014.

"Reachin' Pete." Memphis Minnie. *Too Late, Too Late Blues Vol. 1 (1926–1944)*.
Document 5150. (See also Memphis Minnie, *Me and My Chauffeur*. Proper 129.)

"MOSE"

"Black and Evil Blues." Alice Moore. *St. Louis Bessie and Alice Moore Vol. 1 (1927–1929)*.
Document 5290.

"Chocolate to the Bone." *Barbecue Bob Vol. 1 (1927–1928)*. Document 5046.

"SLIM GREER" POEMS

Various Artists. *Get Your Ass in the Water and Swim Like Me*. Rounder CD 2013.

The Johnny Otis Show. *Cold Shot/Snatch and the Poontangs*. Ace 855.

"SLIM LANDS A JOB"

"Big Boy Pete." *Don and Dewey.* Ace 358.
"Reachin' Pete." Memphis Minnie. *Too Late, Too Late Blues Vol. 1 (1926–1944).*
      Document 5150. (See also *Me and My Chauffeur.* Proper 129.)

"SLIM IN ATLANTA"

"Negro Got No Justice." Unknown. *Negro Songs of Protest.* Rounder LP 4004.

"SLIM HEARS 'THE CALL'"

"Hard Times." Peg Leg Sam. *The Last Medicine Show.* Flyright LP 517/518.
"Preachers Blues." *Kansas Joe and Memphis Minnie Vol. 2 (1930–1931).* Document 5029.
      (See also *Me and My Chauffeur.* Proper 129.)

"SLIM IN HELL"

"The St. Louis Blues." Bessie Smith. *The Complete Recordings Vol. 2.* Columbia C2K
      47471. (See also "St. Louis Blues" on *At the Jazz Band Ball.* Yazoo DVD 514.)
"Me and the Devil Blues." Robert Johnson. *The Complete Recordings.* Columbia C2K
      46222.
"Devil Blues." *Sylvester Weaver Vol. 2 (1927).* Document 5113.

"NEW STEPS"

"Climbing High Mountains, Tryin' to Get Home." *Blind Willie McTell (1940).*
      Document 6001.

"CONVICT"

"Down in the Chain Gang." Unknown. *Nobody Knows My Name.* Heritage LP 304.
"Chain Gang Blues." Unknown. *Cap'n, You're So Mean.* Rounder LP 4013.
"Chain Gang Blues." *Ma Rainey Vol. 3 (1925–1926).* Document 5583.
"Black Name Moan." *Bessie Tucker (1928–1929).* Document 5070.
"Section Gang Blues." *Texas Alexander Vol. 1 (1927–1928).* Document 2001.

"STRANGE LEGACIES"

"John Henry." *Furry Lewis (1927–1929).* Document 5004.
"My Own Story of the Big Fight Part 1." Jack Johnson. *Lost Sounds: Blacks and the Birth
      of the Recording Industry.* Archeophone 1005.
"Tiger Rag." Jack Johnson's Jazz Band. *Times Ain't Like They Used to Be.* Yazoo DVD 512.

"REVELATIONS"

"You Got to Walk That Lonesome Valley." *Rev. F.W. McGee Vol. 1 (1927–1929).*
      Document 6031.

"RIVERBANK BLUES"

"Mississippi River Blues." *Big Bill Broonzy Vol. 2 (1932–1934)*. Document 5051.
"Rock and Gravel Blues." Peg Leg Howell. *Peg Leg Howell and Eddie Anthony.*
     Document 2004.

"TIN ROOF BLUES"

"Tin Roof Blues." *Edna Hicks Vol. 1 (1923)*. Document 5428.
"Tin Roof Blues." King Oliver. *Dippermouth Blues: His Twenty-Five Greatest Hits*. ASV 5218.

"CHILLEN GET SHOES"

"Silver Slippers." Shands Superior Jubilee Singers. Vocalion 1265/NA (78 RPM).
"Golden Slippers." *The Tuskegee Institute Singers/Quartet (1914–1927)*. Document
     5549.
"Bye and Bye We're Going to See the King." *Arizona Dranes (1926–1929)*. Document
     5186.
"Bye and Bye When the Morning Comes." *Rev. Edward W. Clayborn (1926–1928)*.
     Document 5155.
"We Will Understand It Better Bye and Bye." *Alphabetical Four*. Document 5374.

"FUNERAL"

"Goin' to Virginia." *Ralph Willis Vol. 1 (1944–1951)*. Document 5256.

"SPORTING BEASLEY"

"Mysterious Coon." Alec Johnson. *Mississippi String Bands & Associates (1928–1931)*.
     Document 6013.
"Sporty Joe." Nora Lee King. *Sonny Boy Williams (1940–1947)*. Document 5521.
"Signifyin' Monkey Pt. 2." The Johnny Otis Show. *Cold Shot/Snatch and the Poontangs.*
     Ace 855.

"CABARET"

"Muddy Water (A Mississippi Moan)." Bessie Smith. *The Complete Recordings Vol. 3*
     Columbia C2K 47474.
"When the Levee Breaks." *Memphis Minnie and Kansas Joe Vol. 1 (1929–30)*. Document
     5028. (See also Memphis Minnie, *Me and My Chauffeur*. Proper 129.)
"High Water Everywhere Pts. 1 and 2." *Charley Patton Vol. 2 (1929)*. Document 5010.
     (See also Charley Patton, *Screamin' and Hollerin' the Blues*. Revenant 212.)
"Tallahatchie River Blues." Mattie Delaney. *Mississippi Blues Vol. I (1928–1937)*.
     Document 5157.
"Back Water Blues." Bessie Smith. *The Complete Recordings Vol. 3*. Columbia C2K
     47474.
"Southern Flood Blues." *Big Bill Broonzy Vol. 5 (1936–1937)*. Document 5127.

Index

Achebe, Chinua, 423
Adams, E. C. L., 160, 231, 323, 333, 335, 403
Aesopian, 13, 26, 27, 158
African American folklore, 4, 13–14, 369
Afro–Modern moment, 15
Afro-modernism, 180, 184
"After the Storm" (Brown), 106–107
"After Winter" (Brown), 65, 248, 277, 321
"Against That Day" (Brown), 195
"Alexander's Ragtime Band," 287
"All Are Gay" (Brown), 284
Allen, Samuel, 321, 328
Along This Way (James Weldon Johnson), xix, 359
America's Coming of Age (Brooks), 83
American Dilemma: The Negro Problem and Modern Democracy, An (Myrdal), xiv, 10, 15, 154, 187, 209, 211–12, 215–16, 219–23, 280, 366
American Negro Academy, 5, 376
American Negro Folk Songs (Newman White), 160
"American Race Problem as Reflected in American Literature, The" (Brown), 100
ametaphysicality, 180

Amistad II, 319
anaphora, 51, 53, 130
Anderson, Marian, ix, xiv, xvii, 15, 98, 193, 234, 415
Angelou, Maya, 373
Anglo-American poets, 61
"Ante-Bellum Sermon, An" (Dunbar), 413, 415
Aptheker, Herbert, 261
Aran Islander, 62
Arnold, Matthew, vii, 215, 219, 222, 296, 299
Asch, Moe, 294
Associated Publishers, 358
Athletics and the Arts, 215, 221
Auden, W. H., 173, 347
Autobiography of a Black Militant and the Life and Death of SNCC, The (Cleveland Sellers), 383
Autobiography of an Ex-Colored Man, The (James Weldon Johnson), 292
Autobiography of Miss Jane Pittman, The (Gaines), 275, 365
autoethnography, 187, 189

"Bad, Bad Man, A" (Brown), 139, 190
bad badman, 141

Badman, x, xiv, 139, 143, 146, 200, 206–207
bad nigger, 140
Baker, Ella, 324
Baker, Houston, 85, 92, 132–34, 168, 175, 186, 194, 206
Bakhtinian, 101
Baldwin, James, 261, 316, 407
ballad, 8, 32–34, 62, 63, 65, 74, 76, 79, 89, 105, 112, 118, 120, 123, 143, 146, 160–61, 181–82, 202, 234, 249, 277–78, 305
ballade, 8, 105
Banana Bottom (McKay), 303
Banjo (McKay), 303
Banneker, Benjamin, 399, 404, 421
Banner, William, 383
Baraka, Amiri (LeRoi Jones), xvii, 3, 16, 66, 289, 292, 294, 298, 316, 318, 336, 360, 362, 370, 377, 405
"Bear, The" (Faulkner), 402
Be-Bop, 46–47
Beethoven, 165, 290, 299
Bell, Bernard, 256, 410
Benito Cereno (Melville), 335
Bennett, Lerone, Jr., 169, 407
Berea College, 5
Berlin, Irving, 246, 287–88
Bibby, Mrs., 8, 217, 248, 279, 281–82, 382
Bible Mastery (Sterling N. Brown), 278
Big Sea, The (Langston Hughes), 421
"Birches" (Frost), 62
"Bitter Fruit of the Tree" (Brown), 63
Black Arts Movement, xviii, xx–xxi, 9, 99, 335, 370, 413, 422–23, 425–26
Black Bourgeoisie, The (Frazier), 260
black cultural critique, 185
black dialect, 8, 62, 411
Black expressive culture, 31
black modernity, 15, 180
Black No More (Schuyler), 304
Black Reconstruction in America (Du Bois), 279, 372
Black and Tan Club, 43
Black Thunder (Bontemps), 299, 304
black vernacular structures, 59

Black World, 11, 318, 353, 373, 378
blackface minstrelsy, 5, 414
Blake, Elias, 267–68, 418–19
Bloodline (Gaines), 275
Blue Monday Blues (Gershwin), 169
blues, xxi, 5, 8, 10, 13, 15–17, 31–43, 48–51, 53–57, 61, 63–65, 70, 74–75, 85, 98, 101–103, 112, 132–34, 142–43, 147, 151, 158, 161, 163–65, 167–75, 182, 199, 201–202, 232–33, 239, 241–44, 246, 262, 266, 271, 273, 287–90, 292–95, 297–98, 305–306, 314, 317, 319, 321–24, 327, 330, 332–33, 335–36, 346–49, 354–56, 358, 367–68, 373–77, 380–81, 385–86, 394, 400, 403, 411–13, 415, 422–23
"Blues, The" (Brown), 165, 168, 173, 175, 201–202, 206
"Blues as Folk Poetry, The" (Brown), 165, 168, 170, 173, 175, 201–202, 206, 323, 356
blues suite, 39
blues-ballad, 63
Boas, Franz, 161, 188
Bok, Sissela, 219, 221
Bond, Horace Mann, 358
Bontemps, Arna, 79, 174–76, 299, 304, 321, 369, 425
boogie-woogie, 165
Book of American Negro Poetry, The (James Weldon Johnson), xix, 16, 22, 79, 135, 184
Book of American Negro Spirituals (James Weldon Johnson), 160, 176
Botkin, Benjamin A., 11, 171
Boyd, Walter (alias Huddie Ledbetter), 157. *See also* Leadbelly
Boyle, Virginia, 159
Bradford, Roark, 234–35
Braithwaite, William Stanley, 60
Brawley, Benjamin, 318, 358
"Break of Day" (Brown), 148, 399, 416
Brecht on Brecht, 268, 419
Brewer, J. Mason, 160
Brooks, Gwendolyn, 74, 283, 422–24
Brooks, Van Wyck, xviii, 83, 92, 427
Broonzy, Big Bill, 46, 51, 56

Broun, Heywood, 60–61

Brown Allen, Adelaide, 6–7

Brown, Clara (sister), 65, 201, 248, 277, 321

Brown, Ed, 261, 264, 406, 419

Brown, Edna (sister), 277

Brown, Elsie (sister), 160, 277

Brown, Grace (sister), ix, 65, 248, 277, 321

Brown, H. Rap, 262, 406

Brown, Helen (sister), 277, 320–21

Brown, Henry, 337

Brown, Sterling Nelson, 6, 18, 99, 105, 248, 278–79, 381

Brown, William Wells, 159

Browne, Roscoe Lee, 268, 419

Bunche, Ralph, 212, 260, 279, 299, 355, 366, 369, 372, 375, 392

Burke, Kenneth, 232, 248

Burleigh, Harry T., 399

Burns, Robert, xx, 6, 234, 305

Burnshaw, Stanley, 85, 87–88, 93, 360

Butcher, 299, 335, 402, 418

Butcher, James, 335

Butcher, Margaret, 299

"Cabaret" (Brown), 16, 43, 48, 129, 189, 194, 203, 244–47, 373, 378

"Call Boy" (Brown), 279, 366

Candide (Voltaire), 361

Cane (Toomer), 29, 134, 229, 280, 303–305, 375

Carmer, Carl, 144, 148

Carmichael, Stokely, xx, 261, 264, 269, 270, 384, 405, 411, 416

Carnegie Corporation, 210, 213

Carnegie-Myrdal Study, 4, 15, 222

"Casey Jones," 22

Castle of Perseverance, The, 49

Cat on a Hot Tin Roof (Tennessee Williams), 267

Catherine Carmier (Gaines), 275

Cavalcade of the Negro, The (Illinois Writers Project), 300

Césaire, Aimé, 66

Challenge, 107, 134, 195

Chant of Saints (Harper and Stepto), 337

Characteristics of the American Negro (Klineberg), 215

"Characteristics of Negro Expression" (Hurston), 170, 176

Chaucer, Geoffrey, 17, 234, 368

Chesnutt, Charles, 159, 234

"Children's Children" (Brown), 27, 43, 194, 203–205, 245

"Chillen Get Shoes" (Brown), 194

Christian Workers Training School, 6

Civil Rights Movement, xx, 379, 396, 402

Clark, Walter Van Tilburg, xvii, 248, 262, 284, 408, 426–27

Clarke, Kenneth, 66

"Clean, Well-Lighted Place, A" (Hemingway), 47

Clifton, Lucille, 370, 389

"Cloteel" (Brown), l, 63

Cobb, Charlie, 324, 379

Cobb, Montague, 420

Cobb, Ty, 250

Cold Blue Moon (Odum), 160

Coleman, Ornette, 275, 289, 298

Coleridge-Taylor, Samuel, 126–27, 159

Collected Poems (Brown), ix, xiii, xxi, 3, 9, 13, 59, 79, 92–93, 113, 117–18, 123–24, 126–30, 134, 141, 148, 156, 176, 184, 192, 194, 206, 274, 279, 315, 353, 366–67, 371–73, 377–78

Collected Works (Langston Hughes), xxi, 3

"Colored Man in Heaven" (folktale), 153

"Comic Spirit in Shakespeare and Moliere, The" (Brown), 7

communal intersubjectivity, 113–15, 119–20, 122, 124–25, 128–30, 132

Conference on the Character and State of Studies in Folklore, 163

Congaree Sketches (E. C. L. Adams), 160, 323

Conjure Woman, The (Chesnutt), 159

Conn, Butch, 264

Conrad, Joseph, 263

Constitution, 85, 155, 386

"Contributions of the American Negro" (Brown), 215, 222

"Convict" (Brown), 172

Coulette, Henri, 275

"Count Us In" (Brown), 215–16, 219, 221–22

Cox, Courtland, 154–56, 264, 324, 379

Crane, Hart, 168

"Crazy Blues" (Mamie Smith), 373

Crimson & Black, The, 277

Crisis, The, 106, 107

critical realism, 103, 277

cultural anthropologists, 15, 131, 185–86

Cunard, Nancy, ix, 166, 173, 175–76

Cuney, Waring, 174, 302–303, 358

Custis, George Washington Parke, 301

D.C. Board of Education, 60

dadaist, 47

Daniels, Jonathan, 10, 218

Daniels, Sporting Beasley, 236, 247, 254

"Dark of the Moon" (Brown), 24, 113–14, 117–20

Davis, Allison, 315, 324, 334, 336–37, 359

Davis, Arthur P., xx, 93, 104, 148, 176, 192, 206, 209, 215, 260, 316, 321–22, 365–66, 369–70, 377

Davis, Calvin "Big Boy," 8, 37–38, 69, 78, 100, 180, 182–84, 236, 242, 248, 253, 278, 304, 368, 382

Davis, Charlie, 357

Davis, John P., 318

Davis, Miles, 298, 372

Davis, Ossie, 66, 290, 357, 362

Dawson, Sam, 359

"Dear Old Stockholm" (Miles Davis), 372

"Death of the Hired Man" (Frost), 62

deconstruction, 112, 334

Dee, Ruby, 47, 245–47, 357

Dennis, Connie (Daisy Brown's niece), 276

Dennis, Jack and Betty, 321

Department of Extension Work and Correspondence Study, 7

DeSylva, Buddy, 169

Dett, R. Nathaniel, 170

Dial, The, 135, 184, 374

dialect, 4, 13, 22, 24–25, 28, 55, 59–62, 101, 111, 115, 158–60, 170, 195, 204, 229, 243, 323, 327, 368, 411, 414

Diamond, Dion, 261, 391

Diggs, Duke, 150

Divés and Lazarus, 89, 93

Dixon, Thomas, 229

Dodson, Owen, 260, 316, 399

Dorsey, Emmett, 299, 386, 398

Dorsey, Sam, 385

Dorsey, Thomas, 36

Dorson, Richard, 155, 159, 161, 166

Double Dealer, The, 374

Douglass, Frederick, 60, 240, 276, 398, 403, 405, 425–26

Dove, Rita, 283

Dowson, Ernest, 81

Dr. Faustus (Marlowe), 49

Dreiser, Theodore, 421

Drew, Charles, 384, 420

"Dry Spell Blues" (Son House), 39

Du Bois, W. E. B., viii, xvii, xxi, 7, 17, 66, 78, 90, 97–98, 107, 158, 166, 179, 187, 192, 219, 222, 265, 278–79, 292, 298, 303, 338, 348, 359, 362, 372, 375–76, 386, 392, 397, 412, 420

Duke, Zelma Watson, 299

Dunbar High School, 7, 17, 60, 312–13, 362, 376, 378, 398–99

Dunbar, Paul Laurence, 6–7, 13, 17, 25, 28, 60, 74, 76–77, 79, 82, 150, 245, 277, 305, 311–13, 325, 342, 362, 376, 378, 398, 399, 413–15

Dutton, George, 277, 305, 348–49

Editor of Negro Affairs, 4, 9

"Education of the Poet, The" (Brown), 281

Edwards, G. Franklin, 260

"Effie" (Brown), 194

Eliotic, 16

Ellington, Edward Kennedy "Duke," xix, 57, 93, 150, 266, 299, 315, 342, 350, 371, 393, 404–405

Ellison, Fanny, 240

Ellison, Ralph, xvii, xviii–xix, xxi, 3, 14, 62, 97, 139–40, 148, 154, 156, 182, 184, 209–10, 212, 215–16, 219–20, 222–23, 244, 246, 266, 275, 289, 293, 298, 300, 302, 323, 356, 361, 370, 377, 402

Emanuel, James, 173

Emerson, Ralph Waldo, 60, 234

emic approach, 187

English Folksongs from the Southern Appalachians (Sharp), 160

etic ethnography, 187, 213

Everyman, 49

Extension and Correspondence Division at the School of Religion, 381

fabliaux, 234

fakelore, 141, 161

Fauset, Arthur Huff, 170–71

Fauset, Jessie, 170, 176, 303, 355

Federal Writers Project, 4, 299, 366, 368, 375

Finnegan's Wake (Joyce), 358

Fire and the Flint, The (Walter White), 303

First World, 11

Fisher, Rudolph, 136, 303

Fisk Jubilee Singers, The, 170

Fisk University, 6, 8, 105, 219, 278, 300, 317, 344

folk balladry, 24, 132

Folk Beliefs of the Southern Negro (Puckett), 160

Folk Culture on St. Helena Island (Guy B. Johnson), 160

folk epic, 22, 32, 82

folk idiom, 3, 14, 29, 39, 132, 174, 243, 278, 305, 318, 368

folk-life, 23, 29, 158, 171

"Folk Values in a New Medium" (Brown), 354

Folklore of the Sea Islands (Parsons), 160

folklorist, 9, 11, 163, 219–20, 271, 325–26, 381

folk-portraiture, 29

folk-say, 11

Folk-Say: A Regional Miscellany, 33–34, 175–76

Folkways Records, 38, 56, 66, 294, 377

"For a Certain Youngster" (Brown), 106–107

"Foreclosure" (Brown), 197

Forrest, Leon, 62

Foster, Stephen, 169, 202

"Frankie and Johnny" (Brown), 123

Franklin, John Hope, 293, 338, 358

Frazier, E. Franklin, 209, 221, 231, 236, 260, 299, 355–56, 360, 388, 392, 398, 401–402, 408–409, 426

free indirect discourse, 111, 131

free verse, 63, 114–15, 127–29, 134, 195

"Freight Train Blues" (Thomas Dorsey), 36

"From the Dark Tower" (Cullen), 318

"Frost at Midnight" (Coleridge), 126

Frost, Elinor, 86

Frost, Robert, x, xiii, xix, 3, 8, 31–32, 65, 81–82, 84–88, 91–93, 126–27, 227, 243, 245, 253, 277, 283, 305, 349, 362–63, 367, 372, 374, 422, 424

Fugitives, 422

Fuller, Hoyt, 11, 357

Further Range, A (Frost), 85–88, 93

Gabbin, Joanne, 18, 63, 66, 83, 93, 132, 134–35, 156, 167, 176, 187, 192, 194, 206, 222, 378

Gaines, Ernest, 248, 274–75, 284, 365–66

Garvey, Marcus, 292

Gaskell, Elizabeth, 88, 93

Gavick, John, 410

Gayle, Addison, 360–61

Gellert, Lawrence, 172–73, 175–76

Genet, Jean, 362

George White's Scandals, 169

"Georgie Grimes" (Brown), 37, 62

Gerima, Haile, 411

Gershwin, George, 169, 176, 411

Gillespie, Dizzy, 46

Gillie, 248

Gingertown (McKay), 303

God Sends Sunday (Bontemps), 235, 303

God's Trombones (James Weldon Johnson), xviii, 76, 183, 296, 359

Goethe, Johann, 49
gospel music, 50
Grant, Miki, 269
Graves Prize, 7
Great Depression, 161
Green Pastures (Connelly), 59, 229
Green, Paul, 34, 59, 86, 229–30
Guggenheim Fellowship, 108, 366
Guillen, Nicolas, 66

Hallelujah, 298
Hamer, Fannie Lou, 267, 395
Hamsun, Knut, 234
Handy, W. C., 171, 289
Hardy, Thomas, 62, 81, 233–34, 276, 305
Hare, Maude Cuney, 358
Harlem Renaissance, xviii–xx, 14, 16, 57,
   61, 78, 93, 134–35, 175–76, 206–207,
   240, 256, 297, 299, 302–303, 317, 321,
   323–24, 369, 411, 415, 425
"Harlem Street Walkers" (Brown), 194
Harper, Michael S., vii–ix, xv, xviii, xx,
   2–3, 9, 13–14, 16–17, 62, 66, 74, 79, 93,
   95, 134–35, 148, 156, 176, 192, 206–207,
   221–22, 240, 248, 273, 279, 298, 353,
   360, 365, 367, 376–77
Harris, Abram ("Abe"), 299, 359, 369
Harris, Joel Chandler, 60, 159, 170, 291
Harvard University, xvii, xxi, 7, 93, 105,
   135, 148, 150, 155, 176, 192, 340
Hawthorne, Nathaniel, 263
Hayden, Robert, xviii, 283, 316, 370
Hayes, Roland, 101, 104, 292, 404, 425
Hearts of Dixie (film), 298
Hegel, 60
Heine, 62, 276
Hemingway, Ernest, 263
Henderson, Fletcher, 373
Henderson, Stephen, ix, xiii, xviii, 11, 13,
   31, 56, 63, 71, 73, 79, 132, 135, 169, 176,
   187, 194, 206, 321, 360
Herskovits, Melville J., 215
Higginson, Thomas Wentworth, 90
High Modernism, 102
Hilltop, 255, 261
Hines, Earl, 373

History Is Your Own Heartbeat (Harper),
   365
Hofstader, Richard, 343
Holiday, Billie, 266, 348
Holmes, Eugene, x, 17, 260, 302, 311–12,
   385–86
Home to Harlem (McKay), 256, 303
Hooker, John Lee, 293
Horne, Frank, 303
House, Son, 39
Household Training Department, 6
Housman, A. E., 62, 81, 205, 276, 372
Houston, Charles Hamilton, 265
"How to Tell a Story" (Twain), 151
Howard Theater, 212, 320, 371, 399–400
Howard University, xviii, xx, 6–7, 12, 16,
   56, 192, 209, 221, 255, 269, 279, 297,
   300, 316–20, 353–54, 359, 366, 369,
   370, 379, 381, 384, 386–87, 396, 398,
   399, 409, 417–19, 427
Howard University's School of Religion, 7
Howells, William Dean, 13, 60
Howling Wolf, 293
Huggins, Nathan I., 55–57, 303, 323–24
Hughes, Langston, xxi, 3–4, 8, 13, 21, 24,
   27, 29, 33, 46, 55, 60–61, 74, 82, 93,
   136, 150, 158, 173–76, 216, 230, 234, 245,
   266, 289, 292–93, 297–98, 302–303,
   305, 314, 316, 321, 327, 354, 369, 374,
   406, 413, 421
Hume, David, 60
Hunter, Alberta, 294
Hunton, Alphaeus, 359
Hurston, Zora Neale, xix, 14, 17, 60, 62,
   78, 111, 131, 139, 148, 158, 160, 170, 176,
   234, 282, 296–99, 356, 375
Hyman, Stanley Edgar, 161, 237
hymn, 8, 105, 382

"I Got a Home in That Rock" (spiritual),
   89
I'll Take My Stand (Fugitives), 62
iambic pentameter, 107–108, 114–15,
   119–20, 124, 126, 128–29
"If We Must Die" (McKay), 415
"Image and Reality" (Brown), 367

improvisation, 36, 56, 71, 75, 97, 268
"In Divés' Dive" (Frost), 62
individuated subjectivity, 113–14, 119–20, 122–23, 128, 132
influence, 81–84, 92
Institute for the Arts and Humanities, xviii, 222
intersubjectivity, 120, 128
intertextuality, 83–84
Invisible Man (Ellison), xix, 3, 66, 209, 244, 246, 361, 402
Irish Revival, 16, 240
Isherwood, Christopher, 275
"It's a Bourgeois Town" (Leadbelly), 262
Ivanhoe (Scott), 232, 390

Jackson Bruce, viii, 140, 148, 153, 161, 166, 175–76, 211, 213, 222–23, 399, 420
Jackson, Mahalia, 292
James, Henry, 228
jazz, 5, 10, 17, 29, 49, 51, 56, 164, 169, 246–47, 261, 263, 271, 288–89, 297–98, 315, 319, 321–22, 333, 354–55, 358, 367–68, 372–77, 380–81, 385–86, 394, 403–404, 421
Jazz Age, 9, 158, 161, 246
Jefferson, Blind Lemon, 51
Jefferson, Thomas, 60, 169, 276, 279
Jenkins, Timothy, 321, 379, 396
Jim Crow, 85, 146, 154–55, 243, 258–59, 413–14
"Jingles and Croons," 60
John Henry, 5, 38, 121–22, 133, 139–42, 145, 147–48, 180–82, 234, 242, 287, 306, 308
"John Henry" (folk ballad), 22, 38, 133, 180–82, 250, 305
"Johnny Thomas" (Brown), 24
Johnson, Blind Willie, 49
Johnson, Charles S., 215, 219, 278, 358
Johnson, Fenton, 27
Johnson, Georgia Douglas, 195, 425–26
Johnson, Guy, 57, 141, 160, 294, 301
Johnson, Jack, 5, 140, 147, 236
Johnson, James P., 373
Johnson, James Weldon, ix, xiii, xviii, 5, 13, 16, 21, 28, 35–36, 50, 60–61, 76, 79, 82–83, 90, 93, 111, 135, 150, 158, 160, 170–71, 176, 179, 183, 231, 234, 241–43, 279, 292, 296, 298, 303–304, 316, 327, 357, 368, 375, 393
Johnson, John, 318
Johnson, Lonnie, 289, 292
Johnson, Mordecai, 265, 388, 401, 412
Johnson, Robert, 40
Jolson, Al, 169
Jones, C. C., Jr., 159
Jones, Casey, xviii, 65, 140–42, 180–81, 184
Jones, Junebug Jabbo, 260
Jones, Lois Mailou, 260
Jones, Louie, 421
Jones, Tom, 288
Joplin, Janis, 288
Joplin, Scott, 299
Journal of Negro Education, 148, 192, 398
Joyce, James, 240, 358, 426
"Just Like a Tree" (spiritual), 275, 284

Kafka, Franz, 263
Kahn, Tom, 264, 269, 419
Kaleidoscope, 370
Kant, Immanuel, 60
Kaplan, Sidney, 397, 409–10
Karenga, Maulana Ron, 16, 289–90, 298
Keats, John, 126–27, 367
"Kentucky Blues" (Brown), 32, 322, 334
Kern, Jerome, 287–88
Killens, John O., 51
King, Martin Luther, Dr., 11
Kipling, Rudyard, 81, 263
Kittredge, George Lyman, 89, 150, 277, 305
Klineberg, Otto, 215
Kneel to the Rising Sun (Erskine Caldwell), 233
Krehbiel, Henry, 160, 166
Ku Klux Klan, 5, 9
Kunitz, Stanley, 283

Lady Gregory, 229, 240
"Lady of the Lake" (Scott), 65

Lady Windemere's Fan (Oscar Wilde), 231

Lafitte, Jean, 46

Larsen, Nella, 303

Last Ride of Wild Bill, The and Eleven Narrative Poems (Brown), 9, 62, 65, 143, 148, 192

Lawson, Warner, 404

Lay My Burden Down (Botkin), 368

Leadbelly, 46, 157–58, 164–65, 262, 266, 291, 294, 405, 412. *See also* Boyd, Walter

Lee, Ulysses, 93, 104, 148, 165, 176, 206, 215, 302, 316, 321, 328, 359, 365–66, 370, 377

"Left All Alone Blues" (Kern), 287

Lenore Marshall Prize for Poetry, 9

Lester, Julius, 288

Lewis, Furry, 39, 52, 56

Lewis, Harold, 260, 267, 301–302, 385

Lewis, Roscoe E., 10, 279

lie, 32, 50, 96–98, 133, 146, 149, 150–51, 154–55, 183, 236, 356

"Lift Every Voice" (James Weldon Johnson), xviii, 5

Lincoln Temple Congregational Church, 60, 344, 399

Lincoln University, 8, 95, 105, 150, 156

Lindsay, Vachel, 8, 14, 62, 82, 421

literary historian, 9, 87, 325, 362

"Literary Parallel, A," 202, 206, 236

Little Rock High School, 11

Little Theatre Movements, 230

living-people-lore, 4, 11

local color, 204, 206

Locke, Alain, ix, xiii, xix, 9, 13, 17, 23, 60–62, 90, 158, 160, 170, 173–74, 176, 219, 222, 265, 296–99, 318, 354–55, 357, 359, 362, 394

Logan, Rayford W., 5, 206, 216, 221–22, 260, 264, 299, 336–37, 339, 362, 369, 383, 392

Lomax, Alan, 79, 148, 157, 160, 163, 166

Lomax, John A., 171

"Long Gone" (Brown), 22, 37, 79, 304, 306, 308

"Long Gone John" (folk song), 22

"Long Track Blues" (Brown), 34, 38, 64, 174

Longfellow, Henry Wadsworth, 6

Louis, Joe, 141, 145

Lovell, John, 90–91, 93, 159, 166, 209, 402

"Low Down" (Brown), 38

Lowell, Amy, 14, 62

Lyrical Ballads (Wordsworth), 62

Madhubuti, Haki (Don L. Lee), 319, 357

Mahoney, Bill, 261, 389

Malcolm X, xvii, 261, 290, 343, 386

Maltese Falcon, 263

Man Alone (Josephson), 382

Mann, Thomas, 263

Mansfield, Katherine, 305

Mao Zedong, 362

"Market Street Woman" (Brown), 38

Marshall, Carter, xxi, 267, 337, 353, 369

Martin, Bob, 354, 398, 420

Marx, Karl, 362

Mary Barton (Gaskell), 88, 93

mascon, 50–51

Masters, Edgar Lee, 8, 31, 62, 82, 127, 305

"Maumee Ruth" (Brown), 24–25, 62

Maynor, Dorothy, 404, 415

McCarthyist, 174

McKay, Claude, 21, 27–28, 115, 158, 195, 236, 300, 302–303, 316, 321, 415

"Mean Old Frisco" (blues song), 34

"Mecca," 117–19, 194

Meek, Joe, 37, 144, 146, 148, 184, 236, 284, 423

Melville, Herman, 215, 234, 328, 342, 349

"Memphis Blues" (Brown), 22, 24, 35, 38, 48, 51–52, 55, 62, 175, 197, 288, 324

Mencken, H. L., 303

"Mending Wall" (Frost), 62

Meredith, William, 283, 371

MFDP [Mississippi Freedom Democratic Party], 409

"Mill Mountain" (Brown), 62, 126–28, 130, 195, 312–13

Miller, Dean Kelly, 7, 265, 279, 301

Miller, Jean Marie, viii, 316

Milton, John, 305, 367–68, 370, 372

"Miniver Cheevy" (Robinson), 62

minstrel traditions, 22

"Mississippi Flood Song," 202

"Mister Samuel and Sam" (Brown), 22

Moby Dick (Melville), 342

modernists, 13, 280

Montage of a Dream Deferred (Langston Hughes), 46

Moon, Henry Lee, 300

moral badman, 141–42, 145

Morrison, Toni, 62, 69, 227, 333, 347, 381, 405

Morton, Jelly Roll, 289, 373, 378

Mott Elementary School, 399, 403

"Muddy Water Blues" (Bessie Smith), 43–44

Muddy Waters, xxi, 293

Mules and Men (Hurston), 160, 297

Münchausen, Baron, 234

Murphy, Everett, 36

Murray, Albert, 39, 56–57, 142, 148, 209, 222, 377

music critic, 9, 160

My Southern Home (William Wells Brown), 159

Myrdal, Gunnar, xiv, 10–11, 15, 17, 154, 187, 209–22, 280, 366, 368, 372, 375

Myth of the Negro Past, The (Herskovits), 215

myth of Orpheus and Eurydice, 153

NAACP School of Fiction, 355

nada, 47

national club movement, 5

National Conference of Colored Women, 5

National Poetry Series, 206, 274, 366–67

Native Son (Richard Wright), 232, 289, 302

Neal, Gaston, 317

Neal, Larry, 356

Negro in American Civilization, The (Charles S. Johnson), 219, 222, 358

"Negro in American Culture, The" (Brown), 10, 212, 215, 222

Negro in American Fiction, The (Brown), 4, 9, 79, 162, 206, 241, 295–96, 299, 366

"Negro Author and His Publisher, The" (Brown), 215, 222, 236

Negro Caravan, The (Brown, et al.), 4, 11, 17, 89, 90–91, 93, 97, 104, 148, 163, 165, 169, 176, 181, 206, 215, 292, 302, 304, 316, 321–23, 328–29, 359, 365–68, 370, 377–98

"Negro Character as Seen by White Authors" (Brown), 9, 140, 188, 192, 236, 324

Negro Character in American Literature, The (Nelson), 9

Negro dialect, 13, 25, 170, 323

Negro Family in the United States (Frazier), 356

"Negro Folk Expression" (Brown), 165, 173–74, 201, 206

Negro Folk Rhymes (Talley), 160, 166, 294

Negro Folk Songs as Sung by Leadbelly, 160, 166

Negro folk-expression, 29

Negro in Music, The (Brown), 214–15, 299

Negro in Poetry and Drama, The (Brown), 4

Negro and His Songs, The (Odum and Johnson), 57, 160–61

Negro in Virginia, The (Lewis), 10, 163, 279, 301, 375

"Negro in Washington, The" (Brown), 10, 100, 237

Negro Looks at the South, A (Brown), xx–xxi, 4, 10–11, 215, 218–22

Negro Poetry and Drama (Brown), 9, 79, 162, 171, 176, 204, 206, 296, 299, 327, 349, 354, 366

Negro Sermons (James Weldon Johnson), 28

"Negro Wants First-Class Citizenship, The" (Logan), 216

"Negro Wants Full Equality, The" (Wilkins), 216

Negro Workaday Songs (Odum), 160

Nelson, John Herbert, xvii, 7, 9, 211, 222, 291

New American Poetry, 8, 150

New Criticism, 102

New Deal, 87–88

New Negro, The, ix, xi, xiii–xiv, xix, 13–14, 23, 156–58, 166, 170, 176, 207, 222, 298–99, 303, 356, 368

New School for Social Research, The, 393

"New St. Louis Blues" (Brown), 38–39, 172, 174, 197

New York *Times Book Review,* 61

Nigger to Nigger (E. C. L. Adams), 160, 323

No Hiding Place (Brown), 9, 62, 106, 349, 366, 375

"Nobody Knows the Trouble I've Seen" (spiritual), 416

Nonviolent Action Group (NAG), xv, 11, 17, 261, 270, 379, 389, 391

Not Without Laughter (Langston Hughes), 237, 303

Notes on the State of Virginia (Jefferson), 169

Oberlin College, 5, 6, 344

Odum, Howard, 57, 160–61, 210, 222, 301

"Odyssey of Big Boy" (Brown), 15, 22, 37–38, 65, 79, 107, 120, 122, 128, 141, 180, 182, 184, 248, 278, 287, 304, 306, 308–309

"Oh, Didn't He Ramble" (folk song), 100, 337

Okebo, Christopher, 423

"Old Lem" (Brown), 92, 148, 189, 248, 378, 381

"Old Man Buzzard" (Brown), 62

Old Negro, 66, 158, 415

O'Neill, Eugene, 230

Oliver, Paul, 40, 56, 288–89

Omega Psi Phi, 108, 419

On the Trail of Negro Folk-Songs (Scarborough), 148, 160

Oracle, The, 106, 108

Ottley, Roi, 300, 302

"Our Literary Audience" (Brown), 168, 170, 176, 194, 206, 228, 236–37, 357

"Out, Out—" (Frost), 62

Outline for the Study of the Poetry of American Negroes (Brown), 4, 135, 236, 357

Outsider, The (Wright), 361

Owen, Chandler, 260, 303, 316, 399

Ox-Bow Incident, The (Clark), 284

Page, Thomas Nelson, 60, 229, 291

Parks, Rosa, xxi, 11

Parsons, Elsie, 160

Passing (Larsen), 303

Patterns of Negro Segregation (Charles S. Johnson), 215

Patterson, Raymond, 173

Penny Savings Bank, 6

Perry, Bliss, 349

Peterkin, Julia, 234

Petrarchan sonnets, 371

Phylon, 162, 164–66, 175–76, 206, 293, 356

Pickens, William, 179

Pinckney, Darryl, 279

plantation tradition, 60, 79, 158, 291, 414

Plessy decision, 11

Plumpp, Sterling, 173

"Pondy Woods" (Warren), 59, 163, 184, 241

Pope, Alexander, 123

Porgy and Bess (Gershwin), 169

Porter, Dorothy, 260, 402

postmodern, 15, 131, 185, 186, 190, 192, 379

postmodern ethnographer, 15, 131, 185–86

Poston, Ted, 300

Powell, Adam Clayton, 292

Powys John Cowper, 234

Preacher, 150

Presley, Elvis, 288

Price, Leontyne, 415–16

primitivism, 9, 158, 183

Project's guidebook series, 10

Prosser, Gabriel, 140

Puckett, Newbell Niles, 160

"Puttin' on Dog" (Brown), 142, 148, 254, 378, 422

Quicksand (Larsen), 303

Rabelais, 234

ragtime, 5, 180, 287–88, 404

Railroad Bill, 140–44, 306

Rainbow Round My Shoulder (Odum), 160

Rainey, Ma, 31, 38, 41–43, 45, 65, 70, 79, 99, 131, 168, 174–75, 183, 189, 198–99, 201, 236, 248, 266, 279, 289, 292, 319, 406, 412

Randolph, Phillip, 303

Reader's Companion to World Literature, The (Brown, et al.), 366

Ready for Revolution (Thelwell), xx, 384

realists, 13, 230, 233, 421

Reconstruction, 5–6, 9, 136, 159, 162, 359, 372, 412

"Red Cross Store Blues" (Leadbelly), 46

Reddick, Lawrence, 162

Redding, J. Saunders, 361, 365

regionalist, 61

"Remembering Nat Turner" (Brown), 148, 243, 247, 279, 295, 301, 375

"Remembrances" (Brown), 106

"Rent Day Blues" (Brown), 33, 174

"Return" (Brown), 195

"Richard Cory" (Robinson), 62

Riley, James Whitcomb, 60

"Riverbank Blues" (Brown), 32–33

"Road So Rocky" (Brown), 127

Robert Frost: Himself (Burnshaw), 85, 93

Robeson, Paul, 266, 292, 323, 413, 425

Robinson, Edwin Arlington, 8, 14, 31–32, 62, 82, 127, 243, 245, 305, 351, 367, 421

Rogers, J. A., 169, 220, 222

Roosevelt, Franklin Delano, 87, 182, 340, 394

Rosenwald Fellowship, 215, 218

Roughing It (Twain), 154

Rourke, Constance, 234

Ruffin, Susie, 267

"Ruminations of Luke Johnson" (Brown), 26, 118

"Runagate, Runagate" (Hayden), 316

Rustin, Bayard, 261, 386

Saint Elizabeth's Hospital, 408

"Salutamus" (Brown), 107, 195

Sam Smiley, 65, 92, 122–23

"Sam Smiley" (Brown), 24, 62, 65, 118–19, 122–24

Sandburg, Carl, 3, 8, 14, 31–32, 62, 65, 82, 126, 130, 141, 243, 305, 367, 421

Sartre, Jean Paul, 361–62

Scarborough, Dorothy, 148, 160

Schomburg, Arthur, xxi, 222, 376, 394

"Schoolhouse Blues" (Berlin), 287

Schuyler, George, 304

Scott, Ralph Winfield, 275, 299, 337, 342, 344

"Scotty Has His Say" (Brown), 124

Second Book of American Negro Spirituals (James Weldon Johnson), 160

Second World War, 161

Sellers, Cleveland, 264, 383

Senghor, Leopold, 14, 66

Sertima, Ivan van, 169

Shakespearean sonnets, 371

Shakespearian, 89

Shamrock and the Rose, The (Owen Davis), 241

Sharp, Cecil, 160

Shine, 34, 46, 148, 400

Shropshire Lad, A (Housman), 372

signifier, 111–12, 114–15, 118, 120, 123, 128–31, 134, 179

Signifying Monkey stanzas, 401

Sister Lou, 77, 127–28, 132, 134, 190, 248, 281–82, 313, 371

Slave Songs of the United States (William Frances Allen, et al.), 159

Slim Greer, x, xiv, 8, 14, 22, 79, 90, 92–93, 124, 132, 149, 150–51, 153–55, 189, 217, 279

"Slim Greer" (Brown), 22, 24, 63, 79, 90, 92–93, 151, 156, 322, 378, 381

"Slim Hears 'The Call'" (Brown), 153

"Slim in Hell" (Brown), 63, 124, 152–54, 190, 374

Smith, Bessie, 35, 41, 54, 65, 124–26, 199, 201, 289, 291–92, 319, 348, 373, 378

Smith, Clara, 201

Smith, Mamie, 201, 373
Smith, Willie, 263, 373, 385, 399,
    403–404
SNCC, xx, 11, 261, 339, 379, 383, 386,
    390–92
Snowden, Frank, 260, 383
Social Darwinism, 161
social realist, 15, 169
Social Settlement Center, 6
Some Current Folk-Songs of the Negro
    (Will H. Thomas), 171, 176
"Sometimes I Feel Like a Motherless
    Child" (spiritual), 251
sonata form, 49
Song of Roland, The, 150
Song of Solomon (Morrison), 361
"Song of the Open Road" (Whitman), 349
sonnet, 8, 63, 106–107, 134, 173, 195
"Son's Return, A" (Brown), xx, 85, 92, 107
Souls of Black Folk, The (Du Bois), 166,
    187, 219, 222, 248, 279, 292
Sound and the Fury, The (Faulkner), 342
Southern Agrarians, 62
"Southern Cop" (Brown), 62
Southerner Discovers the South, A
    (Daniels), 10, 218
Sowell, Tom, 357, 362
Spencer, Anne, viii, 183, 195, 303, 321, 426
Spicer, Eloise, 273
Spivey, Victoria, 201, 294
Spoon River, 62
"Sporting Beasley" (Brown), 22, 189, 194,
    248, 254, 399, 423
Stagolee, 22, 308
Steed, Hal, 217
Steinbeck, John, 422
Steptoe, E. W., 267
"Strange Legacies" (Brown), viii, 5, 13, 62,
    139, 147–48, 253
Stranger and Alone (Redding), 361
"Strong Men" (Brown) 128–29, 131–32,
    147–48, 183, 189, 191, 193, 195, 254, 278,
    281, 298, 362
Stuckey, Sterling, x, 17, 41, 304, 311, 314–15,
    319, 321, 343, 400
Styron, William, 295

subjectivity, 112, 122, 128
Sutton, Dolores, 269
Swarthmore College, 96
Sweets, Nathaniel, 150, 155
"Swing Low Sweet Chariot" (spiritual),
    358
Synge, 16, 229, 240, 242–44

tall tales, 8, 267, 294
Talley, Thomas, 160–61, 166, 294
Taylor, Cecil, is, 18, 298
Tchaikovsky, 354
"Telling Fortunes" (Brown), 62, 195
"That Evening Sun" (Faulkner), 233
"That's Why Darkies Were Born"
    (Broadway song), 169, 202
the dozens, 55, 400
Thomas, Hank, 261, 391
Thomas, Will H., 171
Thompson, Stith, 86, 93, 164
"Thoughts of Death" (Brown), 195
three-fifths compromise, 85
Three Negro Classics, 166, 293
Three Penny Opera (Brecht), 269
Thurman, Howard, 304, 402
"Ticket Agent, Let Your Window Down"
    (blues song), 297
Tilbury Town, 62, 305
Till, Emmett, 11, 54, 199, 322, 391
Tin Pan Alley, 43, 45, 54, 169, 202, 287,
    290, 373, 378, 411
"Tin Roof Blues" (Brown), 35, 38, 194–95,
    304
"To a Certain Lady, in Her Garden"
    (Brown), 77, 107, 195
"To an Old Man Twiddlin' Thumbs"
    (Harper), 2, 253, 275
"To Midnight Nan at Leroy's" (Langston
    Hughes), 61
Toomer, Jean, 21, 27–29, 62, 158, 183, 280,
    303, 316, 342, 362, 369, 375–76, 378
"Tornado Blues" (Brown), 38–39, 64, 197
Turnbow, Hartman, 267
Turner, Darwin, 14, 103–104
Turner, Lorenzo Dow, 360
Turner, Nat, 140, 145, 191, 295

Tuskegee, 317, 361, 408, 415

Twain, Mark, xx, 33, 151, 154, 156, 234, 243–44, 357, 375

Twenty-Four Negro Melodies (Coleridge-Taylor), 159

Ulysses (Joyce), 93, 104, 148, 165, 176, 206, 215, 302, 316, 321, 328, 358–60, 365–66, 370, 377

"Uncle Joe" (Brown), 244, 279

Uncle Remus, 59, 159, 291

Uncle Tom's Children (Stowe), 231, 289, 302

Untermeyer, Louis, 61, 134, 150

Up From Slavery (Washington), 292

Van Doren, Dorothy, 59, 60

Van Vechten, Carl, 256, 297–98, 302–303, 411, 415, 425

Vaughan, Sarah, 342

vernacular discourse, 115

vernacular speech, 8, 150

"Vestiges" (Brown), 31–32, 83, 106, 126, 133–34, 194–95, 205, 275, 304, 366, 371–72

Victorian poetry, 105

villanelle, 8, 105

"Virginia Portrait" (Brown), 13, 18, 77, 281

Virginia Seminary and College, 8, 276, 305, 382

Wagner, Jean, 54–55, 57, 93, 153, 156, 295

Walker, Alice, 62

Walker, David, 169, 350

Walker, Margaret, 300, 302

Waller, Fats, 266

Walls of Jericho, The (Fisher), 303

Warren, Robert Penn, xvii, 59, 96, 163, 179, 184, 241, 281, 297, 369

Washington Star, 280

Washington, 6, 10–11, 18, 46, 66, 79, 97–98, 105, 142, 165–166, 192, 221, 235, 237, 241, 248, 262, 267, 274, 276, 280–281, 287, 301, 303, 305–306, 308, 311–12, 314, 349, 365, 371–72, 375, 378–79, 381, 384, 389–90, 394, 398–99, 403, 408, 419, 421

Washington, Booker T., 60, 141, 158–59

Washington: City and Capital, 10, 237

Waste Land, The (Eliot), 40, 244–45, 247, 361, 374

"Water-Boy" (folk song), 230

"Weary Blues, The" (Langston Hughes), 33, 174, 305

"Weep Some More My Lady" (Brown), 176, 202, 206

Wesley, Charles, 420

What the Negro Wants (Brown), 216, 221–22

Wheatley, Phillis, 355

"When I Was One and Twenty" (Housman), 62

"When Smoke Stood Up From Ludlow" (Housman), 62

White, Josh, 174–76, 377

White, Newman, 90, 160, 163, 166

White, Walter, 303

Whiteman, Paul, 354

Whitman, Walt, xviii, 33, 62, 236, 245, 349

Whittier, John Greenleaf, 60

Wild Negro Bill, 65

Wilkins, Roy, 216

Williams College, xx, 7, 17, 60, 85, 105, 150, 243, 277, 305, 311–15, 317, 319–21, 324–25, 336, 340–41, 345, 348–50, 353, 362, 367, 373–74, 377, 382–83, 420, 424

Williams, Chancellor, 260, 382, 393

Williams, Eric, 260, 299

Williams, John A., 365

Williams, Poodle, 307

Williams, Robert, 248

Williams, William Carlos, 14, 61, 135

Williams, Wirt, 275

Wings on My Feet (Odum), 160

Winston, Michael, 362, 373

With Aesop Along the Black Border (Ambrose Gonzalez), 160

Woodson, Carter G., 7–8, 105, 169, 179, 358, 368

work songs, 8, 147, 157, 167, 262, 323, 330

Work, John, 279, 358

Working Women's Clubs, 6
Worrying the Line, xiv, 111–12, 120, 128–30
WPA, 101, 187, 299–300, 302
Wright, Richard, viii, xi, xiv–xv, xix, xxi,
    11, 14, 17, 66, 93, 98, 100, 157, 165, 184,
    194, 207, 223, 229, 231–32, 266, 275,
288–89, 292–93, 297, 300, 302, 327,
    353, 361, 375, 385

Yeats, William Butler, 16, 141, 229, 239–41,
    243–44
Yoknapatawpha, 62